Bernice E. Cullinan

NEW YORK UNIVERSITY

in collaboration with

Mary K. Karrer

WORTHINGTON, OHIO, CITY SCHOOLS

and

Arlene M. Pillar

C. W. POST CENTER / LONG ISLAND UNIVERSITY

Literature
and the
Child

For Sandra Brown,
Beautiful wife, mother, daughter-in-law,
teacher, gourmet cook, and
friend. It is a pleasure to
get to know you.
Bee Cullinan
July, 1985

Literature and the Child

HARCOURT BRACE JOVANOVICH, PUBLISHERS

San Diego   New York   Chicago   Atlanta   Washington, D.C.
London   Sydney   Toronto

Cover Art by Anna Kopczynski

Illustrations on pp. 268, 404, 473–75, and 477 by Anna Kopczynski
Illustrations in color section by Walter Crane from *The Baby's Own Aesop,* courtesy The Humanities Research Center, The University of Texas at Austin.
Illustration in color section by Arthur Rackham from *Peter Pan in Kensington Gardens* by J. M. Barrie. Copyright © 1906 by Charles Scribner's Sons; Copyright renewed. Reprinted with permission of Charles Scribner's Sons.

PHOTO CREDITS FOR PROFILES
PP. 53, 60   Culver Pictures; 88   Photograph by Thomas Wommack; 99   Photograph by Antony Di Gesu; 128   Photograph © by Candid Lang; 219   Photograph courtesy of Robert Kraus, Windmill Books, Inc.; 230   Photograph by Jessie Zellner; 292   Photograph by Martha Swope; 350   Photograph by Bruce Curtis; 352   Photograph by Johan Elbers; 366   Photograph by Janet Fletcher; 513   Photograph by Deborah Hall

Requests for permission to make copies of any part of the work should be mailed to:
Permissions, Harcourt Brace Jovanovich, Inc., 757 Third Avenue, New York, N. Y. 10017.

ISBN: 0-15-551110-6

Library of Congress Catalog Card Number: 80–85329
Printed in the United States of America

Acknowledgments appear on pages 556–62, which constitute a continuation of the copyright page.

preface

The riches of our literary heritage can be as fulfilling for children as for adults. This book is about that heritage and for those who would help pass it on to generations to come. It grew from our conviction that without a teacher, parent, or librarian to share the joys of good books, children are unlikely to discover them on their own. In consonance with this view, we discuss outstanding books of yesterday and today, and offer ways they can be introduced to readers through creative interaction. We also outline a comprehensive activity-based literature program appropriate to children at the nursery, elementary, and junior high school levels. The approach of *Literature and the Child* is child-centered and is based in Piagetian developmental principles, language learning research, and reader response theory.

The text has three major parts—"The Child," "The Books," and "The Child and the Books." In the first, the child is seen as dynamically interacting with the environment—of which books are a critical part—to create knowledge. The historical view of childhood as reflected in children's books is also examined, and the interaction of child and books in terms of language learning is described for each developmental stage.

Part two devotes a chapter to each of seven major genres. Pictures books are examined from the view of the young child in an expanding world, with a focus on the child's personal and social concerns; folklore, with its recurring themes and patterned stories, is studied through archetypes; and fantasy and science fiction are examined via their imaginative themes of the known and unknown, seen and unseen. Poetry, the heart of all literary experience, is discussed mainly in terms of the pure pleasure it can give, but, because we believe that poetry is central to children's apprehension of the music and rhythm of language, we include some in each chapter. Contemporary realism—a mirror of life and window on it—is considered mainly from the standpoint of the interpersonal preoccupations of adolescence. Historical fiction and biography are viewed in relation to the curriculum, with teaching units provided for particular periods, from the prehistoric to the contemporary. Similar units for classroom use are offered for informational books.

Each of these chapters includes features to help extend the literary experience—the "Teaching Idea" and the "Activity: Teacher to Student." Each Teaching Idea offers information useful to the teacher in engaging the students' interest in the books under discussion. Activities, addressed directly to students, consist of suggestions and guidelines for activities that can generate insights about themselves and the interrelatedness of their world and of literature. Taken together, Activities and Teaching Ideas offer many alternatives for making teaching and learning memorable. Criteria for evaluating books are given at the end of each genre chapter.

Part three addresses contemporary concerns about children's literature. A chapter on "Literature and Children with Special Needs," which looks into books that portray handicapped children and gifted children, emphasizes, for both child and teacher, the uniqueness of the individual in balance with a common humanity. A chapter each provides practical ideas for using books in the classroom and developing a literature curriculum. The former includes a language arts-based literature program involving the creative arts, while the latter includes a basic list of books worthy of study. Controversy in the creation and use of children's books—on such issues as racism, sexism, and realism—is explored in the context of specific books, and ways of dealing with related issues such as censorship are suggested. Because knowing something of the people who create them can make books come alive, we have included two dozen profiles—brief biographical vignettes—of favorite authors and illustrators.

This text, although primarily about literature as it can be used with children in the classroom, embraces a wide range of books and includes ample annotated lists of recommended books at the ends of most chapters. In these lists, as throughout the text, books are identified as to appropriateness to an age group with a parenthetical symbol: (N), Nursery; (P), Primary; (I), Intermediate; (A), Advanced. In some cases, we have identified book-based recordings, filmstrips, and films that can enhance appreciation of the books.

The appendixes provided were selected on the basis of their potential usefulness in planning comprehensive units of study. To deal with the problem of the sexist pronoun, while avoiding the awkward constructions this sometimes compels, we have used the feminine and masculine forms at random throughout.

We are convinced that children learn to read by reading and that they learn to love to read from adults who convey their enthusiasm for good books. It is our hope, then, that *Literature and the Child* will foster a love and enthusiasm for children's literature that our readers will convey in turn to their students. Children deserve the rarest kind of best; we hope this book helps you give it to them.

Although we can never fully express our gratitude to all those who had a hand in the evolution and consummation of this book, we make an effort to that end by thanking the following. First, Margaret Anzul, librarian and teacher, whose good taste and constructive insights brought a depth of understanding that was crucial to our approach to the project. Her special love of fantasy and her convictions about sharing it with children are reflected in the text. Another friend, S. Lee Galda, shared our enthusiasm for the concept of language development through literature and critical analysis of texts; she helped shape the final form of Chapters Three and Ten. Alvina Treut Burrows, dear friend and colleague, read and critiqued many chapters with perceptive and loving attention. Charlotte S. Huck, friend and mentor, is responsible for our early introduction to and lasting love for literature; her continuing concern was a source of strength.

The children's librarians at Port Washington Public Library—Corinne Camarata, Carey Jacobs, Nancy Curtin, Margaret Ripton, and (Mrs.) Elizabeth Wood—were invariable in the grace and patience with which they answered questions, suggested books, and tracked down sources. The staff at the Children's Book Council—John Donovan, Paula Quint, Christine Stawicki, and Peter Dews—encouraged us with an enthusiasm they bring to any project that promotes good books and reading. Our students and colleagues at New York University, Worthington Hills School, and C. W. Post College read books, tried out projects, and showed us the magic that happens when students and creative teachers share good books. John Mayher, Gordon Pradl, and M. Trika Smith-Burke from the Language and Reading Commission at New York University gave constructive criticism of Chapters One and Three, with emphasis on the child development basis of the text. Valuable suggestions were made by Gwendolyn Kerr, Pat Parker, Christine San Jose, and Ruth Stein, who reviewed the manuscript in its early stages.

At Harcourt Brace Jovanovich, William J. Wisneski had the vision to encourage this enterprise and the patience to see it to completion. Editor Philip Ressner, a children's book author in his own right, showed his skill and his love for the subject by setting standards worth the striving. Marguerite L. Egan, copy editor; Anna Kopczynski, designer; Yvonne Steiner Gerin, art editor; and Robert Karpen, production manager, were dedicated in their several roles.

Finally we thank our families and friends—Paul Cullinan and Jim Ellinger; Janie, Jim, and Kali Brooke Ream; Richard, Russell, Meredith, and Matthew Pillar; Scott and Angela Jaggar; and Hal, Joan, and David Kindy—for their patience and understanding when time taken in preparation of the book infringed upon our time with them.

BEC, MKK, AMP

NOTE In the text, the notation in parentheses that follows the titles of books indicates the level for which each book is most appropriate, as follows: (N), Nursery; (P), Primary; (I), Intermediate; (A), Advanced.

contents

The Books

The Child and The Books

13 A Literature Curriculum, 487

14 Issues in the World of Children's Books, 509

Appendixes

The Child

one

N. M. BODECKER

HELLO BOOK!

Hello book!
What are you up to?
Keeping yourself to yourself,
shut in between your covers,
a prisoner high on a shelf.
Come on book!
What is your story?
Haven't you ever been read?
Did you think
*   I would just pass by you,*
And pick me a comic instead?
No way book!
I'm your reader.
I open you up. Set you free.
Listen, I know a secret!
Will you share
*   your secrets with me?*[1]

―――――――――

The Study of Literature for Children

What children read is formative in their lives; it behooves us to know their books. Thousands of such books are published each year in America, and few can read them all, let alone catch up on the forty thousand already in print. Therefore, we need to develop guidelines for choosing the best. Whether or not children benefit from the best inevitably depends upon the adults in their lives who know them and know their books.

Children surrounded by adults who read become avid readers themselves: in this as in so many other areas, children do as we do—not as we say or tell them to do. Readers are made in childhood; the models we provide and the books we select influence children in lasting ways. If you are one of the lucky ones who, as a child, could climb onto a lap and share a book with someone special or read late into the night under the covers, then you know firsthand the enriching role that books can play. Equipped with knowledge of and love for books and children, you can lead children to the joys and unforgettable experiences of literature.

Many times, teaching reading and teaching literature are considered separate entities in school curricula, despite their interdependence. Often, the reading program is directed toward teaching decoding and practical skills while the literature program is aimed at reading appreciation and reading as an art. Research indicates, however, that we lead children into reading most successfully when the two programs are merged. All reading is concept development, and learning to read better and the reading of literature for appreciation compose one organic process; separations are artificial and detrimental.

The ultimate goals of a reading teacher and of a literature teacher are the same: both want students to read a wide variety of literary and expository material for many purposes, one of which is recognition of the idea that the process of reading can be a source of enjoyment as well as knowledge. Too often, the stress on reading as information-getting or, worse yet, as decoding rather than meaning-making, outweighs reading as a pleasurable activity, so that children think of reading as saying words aloud or as a means of acquiring facts. Little

Reading for pleasure, the most important kind. (Photograph at right by Hugh Rogers/Monkmeyer Press Photo Service; photograph below by Sam Falk/Monkmeyer Press Photo Service.)

is gained by teaching students the mechanical skills of reading and, in the process, teaching them to hate reading. Students who pass through school with high scholastic standing but never read an unassigned book represent hidden failures of education. Though 94 percent of the nation is literate, only 55 percent read from a book within the last year. Avoidance of reading signals a lack of value for reading or an active dislike of it. Voluntary or freely elected reading indicates that the process is valued and enjoyed. When reading and literature programs are successful, enthusiasm for reading parallels and enhances the skills of reading.

Louise Rosenblatt, in *The Reader, The Text, The Poem,* defines two types of reading—efferent and aesthetic. Efferent reading is done for the practical purpose of taking something away from the text—something we need to know, learn, remember for practical purposes—much like your reading of this textbook. Aesthetic reading is done for the joy of the experience—a total engagement with the text for the sheer pleasure therein.[2] In

(Photograph at left by Mimi Forsyth/Monkmeyer Press Photo Service; photograph below © Bettye Lane.)

much teaching of literature, we ask students to read efferently—to recall characters, events, and metaphors—instead of encouraging aesthetic reading—giving oneself over to the literary experience—and allowing the reader the right to determine what to make of it.

When children make independent choices about how to spend their time, they turn to reading if it is a source of pleasure. The degree to which enjoyment effectively motivates reading depends largely on the strength of the pleasurable experiences associated with books. Children who have satisfying experiences with books continue to turn to them. One purpose of this text is to acquaint you with books that show children that reading is worth the effort. Our selection is guided by C. S. Lewis's precepts that "no book is really worth reading at the age of ten which is not equally (and often far more) worth reading at the age of fifty" and that the only imaginative works we ought to outgrow are those it would have been better not to have read at all.[3]

The age-old phenomenon of sibling rivalry unmistakably expressed. (Text and art excerpts from *I'll Fix Anthony,* written by Judith Viorst, illustrated by Arnold Lobel. Text copyright © 1969 by Judith Viorst. Pictures copyright ©1969 by Arnold Lobel. By permission of Harper & Row, Publishers, Inc.)

The definition of literature, as all instances in which language is used imaginatively, is usually qualified implicitly to include the characteristics of permanence and excellence. Although children's books, like adult books, vary greatly in quality, the imaginative expression of human experience that is part of the mainstream of universal literature appears in literature for children as well. As Myles McDowell observes, a good children's book makes a complex experience available to its readers, whereas a good adult book draws attention to the inescapable complexity of experience.[4]

Literature for children differs from other literature not only in this way but in keeping with the social, emotional, and cognitive developmental levels of its readers. Guidelines for content, characterization, structure, point of view, theme, and style of a book appropriate for a particular child differ according to the developmental and conceptual levels of the child who happens to be reading it. Thus, we cannot just say, "This is a good book," but must ask ourselves, "Good for whom?" For example, Judith Viorst's *I'll Fix Anthony* (P) always evokes a lively and empathetic response from readers in the primary grades because sibling rivalry is a near-universal experience. The nature of the response varies, however, according to the developmental level of the reader and of the place he or she holds in the sibling lineup. Recently, two brothers, about twenty months apart in age, read *I'll Fix Anthony* on the same day. The seven-year-old commented with a chuckle, "What he doesn't know is that Anthony will *always* be bigger than he is!" The five-year-old at first said nothing, but later in the day was overheard chanting to himself, "When I'm six we'll have a skipping contest and I'll skip faster. Then we'll have a jumping contest and I'll jump higher. When I'm six I'll be able to tell time. . . ." It was clear that his identification with the book was very strong and that he was vicariously enjoying a triumph over the "Anthony" in his life, with almost total recall of the story. Both responses to the story were equally valid, each child responding from his own vantage point. The developmental level of the reader is a major factor in the equation when selecting a good book. Through knowing books and children, we can be right more often in the books we select.

LITERATURE IN RELATION TO THE READER'S DEVELOPMENT

Literature for children as well as for adults speaks of the mysteries of the human condition, although, in books for children, treatment of these themes is adjusted according to the age-related interests and capacities of the audience. As with music, art, drama, and dance as creative expression, prose and verse for children sift experience and interpret life. And, although we may tire of them, the books that do this, and that children ask for time and time again, are always breathtakingly new for each new generation.

Current theorists reject the examination of a literary piece without consideration of the process involved in responding to the text. A literary experience is not created solely by a text, but by a reader interacting with that text. Renowned critic Wolfgang Iser states that a literary work is more than the text, for the text takes on life only when it is "realized," and, furthermore, that realization is influenced by the individual disposition of the reader, who is in turn acted upon by different patterns of the text.[5] The convergence of text and reader brings a literary work into existence; it cannot be identified totally with the reality of the text *or* with the individual disposition of the reader. The literary experience, then, shaped by interaction of reader and text, becomes a "virtual" experience—one that the reader could have had himself. Readers add to their stock of experiences through the many possible lives they lead in the books they read; books *are* experiences.

A text may be realized in several different ways, depending on the singular cast of mind of the reader. A literary text must, by definition, contain "gaps" that allow readers to fill in for themselves, to make inferences, build metaphors, and create characters. In filling these gaps, a reader, creating meaning from a text, makes choices. These choices invest the text with a more personal meaning, but also exclude all those choices not made. Thus, no reader can ever exhaust the full potential of any text. There is, therefore, no one "correct" reading for a text, but merely readings that are more or less complete, both in terms of encompassing the information presented explicitly in the text and in making use of those gaps in the text that allow the reader to create a personal meaning.

The importance of interaction between reader and text can be seen in the following account of a discussion by a group of sixth-grade students who had just finished reading Ursula Le Guin's *A Wizard of Earthsea* (I-A) and had previously read several books in the "Chronicles of Narnia" series (I-A), by C. S. Lewis, and two of Madeleine L'Engle's space fantasies, *A Wrinkle in Time* (I-A) and *A Wind in the Door* (I-A).

MICHELLE: I liked Narnia best—it was so magicky.

JON-PAUL: Well, I liked it a lot, but not the best. For me, *A Wrinkle in Time* was best—"It," you know, the Naked Brain, and the shadowed planets, and all that.

TEACHER: There was a shadow in *A Wizard of Earthsea,* and the "black thing" caused shadowed or dark planets in *A Wrinkle in Time*. Somehow, the bad thing, the evil in several of the books we read, seems to be pictured in some way by blackness or shadows.

SARAH: Except for Narnia, and there it wasn't a black witch but a white witch. The evil spell was snow and winter.

HEDY: That's because nothing could grow or be alive then. Aslan brought the Spring.

SARAH: But still whatever it appeared like, there was a battle against the forces of evil.

TEACHER: What about *A Wizard of Earthsea?*

JON-PAUL: Well, like we read, the shadow that was following Ged was really the evil in himself, but he didn't recognize it until the end. I don't really understand that very well, but I understand it some.

TEACHER: In *A Wind in the Door* you could be "x-ed" if you weren't trying to be your real self. Again, the picture the author gives us to imagine in our own minds is rather similar: If you are "x-ed," what has happened to you?

JON-PAUL: You become annihilated. You don't exist any more. If you were a planet, where you used to be there was just a black hole of nothingness in the universe.

SARAH: And for Ged, if he didn't recognize that there *was* a bad side to his own nature, it could destroy him. He would be "x-ed" by his shadow, and he wouldn't be living any more, but just the power of evil could live in his body.

TEACHER: We talked a lot when we were reading the books by Madeleine L'Engle about the *theme* of her books—that the central idea was the battle between good and evil in the universe. What would you say is the theme of the other fantasies?

HEDY: Well, in Narnia it was sort of the same because Aslan was good and the White Witch was evil.

SARAH: I see it! I see it! I just finished reading Susan Cooper's *The Dark Is Rising,* and it's the same theme in that book, too. It's the light against the dark. It's good against evil. *They're all about the same thing!*[6]

The other children sat in silence, mulling over this idea. They understood Sarah in a way. Certainly, they understood momentarily the words she was saying, though possibly they would soon forget them. They clearly would need time to read and reflect more before they could understand deeply this aspect of what literature is. Try as Sarah might to explain to them the meaning of her personal insights, in so doing she will invalidate the experience. Sarah's life has been changed and mere explanation will not affect her classmates. She can report how the literary works affect her, but her classmates will not know the new reality Sarah has discovered until they themselves similarly discover it. Each reader derives his own meaning from a work through direct participation; another's explanation remains a hazy outline until the images become clear firsthand.

Sarah had taken one of those rare steps to a new level of understanding. From now on, every book she reads cannot only be a delightful world in itself, but can relate in some way to other books. She is on that threshold where every human experience she reads about, and thus enters into vicariously, will begin to relate somehow to all human experience, and where human experience

transmuted into literature begins to relate to all other literature. Northrop Frye explains it this way:

All themes and characters and stories you encounter in literature belong to one big interlocking family. . . . You keep associating your literary experiences together: you're always being reminded of some other story you read or movie you saw or character that impressed you. For most of us, most of the time, this goes on unconsciously, but the fact that it does go on suggests that perhaps in literature you don't just read one novel or poem after another, but that there's a real subject to be studied, as there is in science, and that the more you read, the more you learn about literature as a whole.[7]

When children compare a particular work with others similar to it in some way, even at the elementary-school level, they begin to develop an understanding of the unity of literature.

Reading, then, is an active process of meaning-making in which the reader's imagination is engaged with a text created by an author. Stories that spell out every last detail leave little room for the reader to participate. At the other extreme, stories that are very abstract and complex may not allow the reader access to them. In the first case, the reader becomes bored; in the second, there is never any engagement with the text. Boredom and overstrain form the boundaries within which a reader will continue to read. For these reasons, we not only search for good books, but must also continually ask, good for whom? A focus on literature must include a focus on the reader. This text, then, explores books in relation to the developing child.

Since a literary experience is evoked only when a reader creates meaning from the words on the page, we cannot select literature solely on the basis of literary merit and apart from a consideration of the reader who will experience it. When we consider books for children, the child as meaning maker is ever present as the other half of the equation.

The sweep of development from birth to adolescence is large, and the breadth of literature appropriate to each developmental level is tremendous. Choosing literary experiences that are meaningful requires a knowledge of child development as well as a knowledge of books. In this text, concepts of general developmental stages in the child's construction of reality, derived from the work of Jean Piaget and others, inform the guidelines used for selecting literature. Each book referred to will be designated N, P, I, or A, the letters corresponding to school and age levels as follows:

N (Nursery), birth to age 4—nursery school
P (Primary), ages 5 to 9—Grades K–3
I (Intermediate), ages 10 to 12—Grades 4–6
A (Advanced), ages 13 to 15—Grades 7–9

Developmental stages are *not* applied rigidly since we know each child is a unique being who develops in an individual way. Further, no stage is discrete, but rather overlaps and is incorporated into the next in an ever-spiraling sequence of development. Children at every stage draw upon the ways they learned at all prior stages and use their growing fund of knowledge to learn new things. Earlier stages are never left behind. In situations that are strange or unfamiliar, children regress to less mature thought in working their way toward understanding. Examples that follow are drawn from the behavior of actual children, while the general characteristics for various stages are described in terms of some hypothetical "typical" child.

Cognitive Development

The child is an active, dynamic being who interacts with the environment to create knowledge. We cannot pour knowledge into the child as we would liquid into an empty vessel, but can create situations in which the child makes meanings without help. Developmentalists such as Piaget portray the human organism as an open system in a steady state, which means that it must engage in exchanges with the environment to learn and at the same time regulate itself to maintain a manageable condition (called homeostasis). The child comes to an understanding of the world through single-handed efforts of reaching out and assimilating new information. When the new information contradicts what is known, the child accommodates or changes cognitive structures. Thus, through discoveries made primarily by direct ex-

perience, the child organizes unique ways of viewing the world; books can offer some of this experience.

The material that follows is arranged according to several developmental stages postulated by Piaget—sensorimotor, preoperational, concrete operations, and formal operations. (Piaget is exceedingly cautious about how to construe the term *stages*, acknowledging that there is considerable overlap.)

SENSORIMOTOR STAGE Although children in the sensorimotor stage may not be of classroom age, teachers should know that during this stage (approximately birth to age two), children learn through their senses and motor movements. They feel, grasp, taste, touch, smell, see, and hear people and objects in their environment. Books appropriate for them during this stage parallel experiences they have in real life. Tactile, visual, kinesthetic, and auditory experiences made available by specific books provide opportunities for children to learn through all modalities. At the same time, children are developing language, which is learned *only* in context and because of the needs it serves. A child learns language to tell people what he wants, to relate to others, to say, "Hey, this is me!" Books for this stage provide infinite opportunities to stimulate language by engaging child and adult in talk about things meaningful to both.

Children continue to learn through sensorimotor modalities throughout later stages and, in fact, accumulate the cognitive developmental learnings associated with each stage as they acquire later ones. "We make ourselves as we go" aptly describes the growing process, and although the baggage we acquire throughout our childhood may become heavy, it is necessary because it is filled with our own experiences.

PREOPERATIONAL STAGE The broad stage of preoperational learning (approximately two to seven years) is best divided into smaller units. Two- to four-year-olds carry with them many of the ways of sensorimotor learning, but because they are acquiring language, they make great strides in organizing knowledge about their world. The developmentally later phase, four to seven years, is marked by tremendous growth in language with all its attendant accomplishments.

Children in the preoperational stage continue to learn primarily through interaction with the real world around them. They continue learning through their senses by exploring their environment physically, and gradually refine and expand sensorimotor learning as they acquire greater control. At this stage, children still learn more effectively through direct experiences than through verbal or pictorial illustrations. For example, a two-year-old looking at a picture of a cup and hearing the phrase "this is a cup" lifted the book to look underneath for the bottom of the cup. His past experiences with cups led him to expect a bottom and sides instead of flatness. Children at this age are just beginning to learn that a picture of a cup and the word *cup* are not the thing itself. Abstractions are less desirable than representational stories or illustrations for such children. Stories about themselves and their immediate world seem to fascinate them, although the nonsense rhymes and verses of Mother Goose enchant as well.

Several crucial learnings related to language and literature occur during the preoperational stage. At the beginning of the stage, children cannot distinguish between reality and fantasy; they believe what they see and read (or have read to them) and do not consider the possibility of fantasy. Giants and fairies exist, Cinderella is a real person, and Jack actually climbed the beanstalk that grew to the sky. Responses of five-year-olds to the book *The Dragon in the Clock Box* (P), by M. Jean Craig, are very different from those of seven-year-olds. At the end of the story the dragon flies away. When asked, "Where do you think he went?" five-year-olds say believingly, "to a castle," whereas seven-year-olds say disparagingly, "No place. Dragons aren't real." Seven-year-olds, whose thinking generally continues to be characteristically preoperational, begin to make distinctions between make-believe and real, a mark of the concrete operational stage into which they are moving. Animism, the attribution of life or con-

sciousness to inanimate objects, still has a tenacious hold on children's thinking in the preoperational stage. They believe that the clouds in the sky are alive, and they respond enthusiastically to Virginia Lee Burton's *Mike Mulligan and His Steam Shovel* (P) because they know that Mary Anne, the steam shovel, has feelings like theirs.

In any group, however, there are likely to be children of different developmental stages and some who are wavering between stages. One group of kindergarten children heard Edna Miller's *Mousekin's Golden House* (P) read aloud, and commented about Mousekin living inside a discarded Halloween pumpkin through the cold winter. As winter came, the pumpkin shriveled and the cut openings gradually closed. One child said, "Pumpkin was the mice's friend. He doesn't want him to get cold so he closed his eyes." Another child asked, "If the pumpkin closes his eyes because the air is cold, will he open them again when it gets warm?" But another budding scientist chimed in, "No, once it gets all dried up and shrivels up, it won't change back again."

In the same discussion, the children talked about the way Mousekin carried grass, feathers, thistledown, and milkweed to make a bed inside the pumpkin. One child said, "He just got in at the top and he slided down into his bed." Another realist claimed, "Yes, but if you throw away your pumpkin, it gets soft and falls apart. What if Mousekin was in it when it got mushy?" Such responses to a fanciful story reveal different levels of understanding and sometimes lead to spirited discussions.

Most children in the preoperational stage do not conserve; that is, if they see equal amounts of liquid in two similar containers, they do not recognize that equal amounts of a liquid are the same after they have been poured into two dissimilar containers—one tall and narrow, for example, the other wide and low. A parallel for literature is that they would not be likely to recognize that several chapters, read to them one each day, were, in fact, one long story. Stories that can be completed in one sitting work best at this stage. Cumulative stories, which repeat each incident in the telling of

Children in the animistic stage find it easy to believe that a steam shovel can feel joy and sadness.
(From *Mike Mulligan and His Steam Shovel,* by Virginia Lee Burton, published by Houghton Mifflin Company. Copyright 1939 and © renewed 1967 by Virginia Lee Demetrios. Reprinted by permission.)

the next, such as *One Fine Day* (P), by Nonny Ho-grogian, and *Why Mosquitoes Buzz in People's Ears* (P), by Verna Aardema, are structured in a way pleasing to children of this age. In *One Fine Day,* from the time the fox begs: "Dear Cow, please give me some milk so I can give it to the old woman so she will sew my tail in place," to the end of the story, children know that each request will be repeated as a new one is added. Similarly, in *Why Mosquitoes Buzz in People's Ears,* the chain reaction set off by the mosquito's tall tale leads to predictable disaster in the jungle. Children chime in with the storyteller when the animals go "mek, mek," "wasawusu, wasawusu," or "krik, krik" through the jungle.

CONCRETE-OPERATIONS STAGE During the con-crete-operations stage (about seven to eleven years), children can formulate a concept and can deal with generalizations. They are able to classify, and they become more systematic in the way they organize their storehouse of knowledge about their world. During this stage, children become predic-tors; they observe that wood can float and, thereby, can come to predict that other materials may float. If they have had rich experiences with stories, they develop expectations about endings, and can often predict them.

The concrete-operations stage is a period in which children do not move freely in the world of the *possible,* where hypothetical reasoning reigns. They do not tolerate much ambiguity, often re-shaping what they perceive in order to make it fit their apprehension of the world. During the early phase, many children ascribe reality to the fantasy they read. Later, they distinguish between stories that could happen and stories that are make-believe, and also begin to exhibit a decided prefer-ence for realistic stories: books about a person "just like me."

Only in rare cases do children at this stage in-terpret language beyond the literal, text meaning. Some fourth-grade students, asked if the symbolic bridge in Katherine Paterson's *Bridge to Terabithia* (I) could mean anything other than the rope or planks used to cross the gully, said flatly, "No." Teachers who discuss alternate possibilities, how-ever, influence children's ability to perceive sym-

Although some intermediate-grade children, who are in the concrete-operations stage, may be able to grasp the symbolic meaning of Terabithia and of the rope bridge by which it is reached, younger children, in the preoperational stage, will not be able to.
(An illustration by Donna Diamond from *Bridge to Terabithia,* by Katherine Paterson. Copyright © 1977 by Katherine Paterson. By permission of Thomas Y. Crowell, Publishers.)

bolic meanings. It may be that we also *teach* children to be literal by the very nature of the questions we ask. The progressive decrease in children's use of figurative language from grades three to five may indicate the results of teaching rather than children's developmental patterns. It is no coincidence that most basal readers contain literal prose and that teachers are instructed to ask literal questions continually in the accompanying teacher's manual. These children are also comfortable with pat endings and predictable stories that end the way they expect them to. It is a period in which they devour series books, such as Nancy Drew, because they know that, in them, everything will come out all right.

Children in the concrete-operations stage do not easily accept the idea that one thing can substitute for another. If their hearts are set on a candy bar, it is hard to convince them that a piece of fruit will taste better. Their firm expectations for clear resolutions apply to the stories they read, and in order for a story to be satisfying, it must resolve the central character's problems definitively and not offer a substitute reward. In a group discussing Katherine Paterson's *The Great Gilly Hopkins* (I), younger children were distressed with the ending, in which Gilly realistically stays with her maternal grandmother despite her great love for another. They wanted her to return to her foster mother, Maime Trotter, who epitomizes the understanding, all-forgiving mother figure in their idealized fantasies. Older children understood the role that Gilly might play in bringing love into her natural grandmother's life. They knew that Gilly could never be the same person she had been, hardened by her life in several bad foster homes, for now, having learned how to love from Maime Trotter, she could accept her grandmother as a surrogate for Maime.

FORMAL-OPERATIONS STAGE When children reach the formal-operations stage (around age eleven), they can reason logically, deal with abstractions, consider alternate ways of viewing a situation, and tolerate ambiguity. The type and quantity of literature appropriate for them compound dramatically. Early adolescence brings dramatic changes: the onset of puberty, the search for personal identity, and the striving for independence, among other things. The entire period is rife with events that shape the adult the child will become.

Joan Lipsitz characterizes the early adolescent as one who is "growing up forgotten," and draws implications from adolescents' behavior for their literature.[8] Still somewhat egocentric, some early adolescents create a personal fable in which they tell themselves that they are all alone, no one understands them, and they must face the cruel world unaided. Others adopt a view of themselves described as "playing to an imaginary audience," in which they believe that everyone is watching them at all times. Because of the imagined audience, the pre-teen takes great care to dress and behave like everyone else so he or she will not be singled out or noticed as being different in any way. Early adolescents are saying, "I am the center of my world. Everyone is looking at me." They search for books that validate experience as they see it and for characters who face developmental tasks comparable to their own. Paul Zindel's zany characters, Lorraine and John, in *The Pigman* (A), validate experience as adolescents see it. Early adolescents face a great deal of ambiguity in their personal lives, and they find books with predictable, pat endings very comforting. Cognitively, they can cope with conflicts in literature that are not resolved, but they do prefer happy endings because they are emotionally satisfying.

LATE ADOLESCENCE TO ADULTHOOD Although this book does not include later adolescent and adult responses to literature, the parallels between children as readers and the readers they become need to be mentioned. For one thing, adults, like children, seek a wide range in the types of material they read. Some adults read only the newspaper, but others shift back and forth from best sellers and detective stories to Shakespeare and D. H. Lawrence. Probably few adults read at the peak of their reading ability very often; junk reading is interspersed with books of high literary quality. This fact in itself is one reason teachers and librarians need not be concerned about children who,

though they consume series books, comic books, and riddle and joke books, also read books of greater literary merit.

Adult reading tastes and habits are formed in childhood and adolescence. If children are to become adults with a richer and deeper sense of literary values, they need to be exposed to works of quality along the way. Books need not be all high-quality texts, so long as some are included. Teachers may urge, or at least introduce, works of quality so that children have the chance to discover the joys of all kinds of literature. Children helped to develop insights into books they read can carry these insights, as meaningful experiences and expectations, into their adult lives.

The child as meaning-maker is our guide to the kind of literature that is appropriate at every developmental stage. Children should not, in the name of literary quality, be forced to try to cope with concepts that are too difficult for them. Not only is it all right to let children stay at the level where they are, but there really is not much you can do about it. Children will move toward higher-level material in their own good time in a properly nourishing environment. The teacher's job is to keep many alternatives available for pupils and to entice them with books of quality. Children do develop at their own rate, and if we let them know the pleasure of reading at every stage, they will become reading adults.

The chart on pages 14–15 describes characteristics of literature appropriate to children according to their developmental level and suggests books.

Language Development

Studies of child language development provide a broad base for inferences about appropriate literary experiences.[9] Although many others are possible, three principles guide our discussion of language and literature. First, language develops naturally in an adequate environment; that is, children learn language when they hear it spoken. Stories told or read to children give them opportunities to hear words in use and, in the process, to support, expand, and stimulate their own experi-

GUIDE TO STORY SELECTION ACCORDING TO DEVELOPMENTAL STAGE

Age Characteristics	Story Characteristics	Suggested Books
Infants and Toddlers (Approximately Birth to Age 2)		
Explores through senses	Provides tactile, auditory, and visual experiences	*Pat the Bunny*
Learns by hands-on approach	Invites participation	*The Haunted House*
		This Little Piggy
Learns language as label	Patterned language	*Eye Winker, Tom Tinker, Chin Chopper*
	Brief rhythmic song games	*Mother Goose*
	Objects associated with words	*Things to See*
Nursery and Early Childhood (Approximately Age 2 to 5)		
Builds concepts through direct experiences	Deals with simple concepts	*Shapes and Things*
Learns word and thing are different	Identifies objects	*ABC*
Sees self as center of world	Focuses on child	*Umbrella*
		A Baby Sister for Frances
Learns language rapidly	Repetitive and rhythmic language	*Millions of Cats*
		Lullaby
Begins to develop sense of story	Simple plots	*The Baby*
	Structured plots	*The Three Little Pigs*
Sees events as discrete	Cumulative plot structure	*This Is the House That Jack Built*
		One Fine Day
Early Primary (Approximately Age 5 to 7)		
Expresses normal fears	Reassuring themes	*Goodnight Moon*
Develops self-identity	Deals with importance of self	*Dandelion*
Has rich imaginative life	Presents fantasy believably	*Come Away from the Water, Shirley*
Has developed sense of story	Clear plot sequence	*Squawk to the Moon, Little Goose*
	Predictable plots	*The Three Bears*
	Surprise endings	*Just Like Everyone Else*
Has eye-for-an-eye morality	Shows justice prevailing	*I'll Fix Anthony*
		Sam, Bangs and Moonshine
Develops powers of observation	Gives attention to details	*Brian Wildsmith's Puzzles*
Primary (Approximately Age 7 to 9)		
Recognizes differing points of view	Clear identification of point of view	*Nothing Ever Happens on My Block*
Develops independence in reading	Some easy-to-read vocabulary	*Mouse Tales*
		Little Bear
Prefers realism and law-and-order rules	Realistic settings and events	*Betsy's Play School*
		Ramona and Her Mother
Recognizes existence of multiplicity of meaning	Multiple layers of meaning	*Frederick*
		Once a Mouse
		Charlotte's Web

Age Characteristics	Story Characteristics	Suggested Books
Primary (Approximately Age 7 to 9)		
Begins to manipulate ideas and actions mentally	Characters with whom to identify	*Stevie*
"Conserves," remembers, organizes knowledge	Episodic (longer stories with chapters)	*Me and the Terrible Two*
Intermediate (Approximately Age 9 to 12)		
Begins to recognize symbolic meaning and figurative language	Multiple layers of meaning	*The Magic of the Glits*
	Figurative language	*Tuck Everlasting*
Sees humor in language	Play with idiosyncrasies of language	*Ballpoint Bananas and Other Jokes for Kids*
Has bizarre sense of humor	Silliness and nonsense	*How to Eat Fried Worms*
Sees relationships between events and feelings	Identifiable character motivation	*The Borrowers*
Strengthens independence in reading	Episodic, simple narratives	*Tales of a Fourth-Grade Nothing*
Plays team games	Action-filled suspense and sports	*The Baseball Trick*
Likes adventure and suspense	Intrigue and mystery	*Alvin's Swap Shop*
Concerned with self	Deals with personal and social concerns	*Are You There, God? It's Me, Margaret.*
Intermediate-Advanced (Approximately Age 11 to 13)		
Considers alternative realities	Represents alternatives to real world	*Mrs. Frisby and the Rats of NIMH*
		A Wrinkle in Time
		The White Mountains
Becomes aware of mortality	Confronts death and other painful issues	*Bridge to Terabithia*
		Beat the Turtle Drum
Understands figurative language	Interesting language use	*The Phantom Tollbooth*
		Words by Heart
Understands complexity	Complex plot structure	*Unleaving*
Becomes aware of social injustice	Confronts issues of prejudice	*Roll of Thunder, Hear My Cry*
Generalizes from past experience	Reflects historical conflicts	*My Brother Sam Is Dead*
Develops compassion	Presents emotional and social conflict	*The Man Without a Face*
		All Together Now
Advanced (Approximately Age 13 and Beyond)		
Accepts responsibility for behavior	Deals realistically with issues	*The Pigman*
Appreciates subtle humor	Understated humor	*Bagthorpes Unlimited*
Recognizes moral conflicts	Presents moral issues	*The Chocolate War*
Seeks role models and heroes	Biographic material and heroic characters	*The Helen Keller Story*
Accepts alternate realities	Offers imaginative fantasy and science fiction	*A Wizard of Earthsea*
		Z for Zachariah

ments with language. As children listen to language they gradually assimilate meanings and eventually express meanings through their own sounds. Language development is a natural process of generalizing and discriminating finer meanings and sounds. As children learn, books can help at every stage to fulfill their need to make sense of language and of the world.

We also know that, in language development, comprehension generally exceeds production. Though they may not be using sentences in their own speech production, children understand sentences and draw meaning from the contexts in which they are heard. For example, when asked, "Where's your teddy bear?" a child can pick up the toy or point to it long before he or she can say the words. Similarly, the six-year-old who responds to a question with "I know it in my head but I can't say it," understands more than he can say. Through experience, children assimilate meaning and associate words as labels that they use to express meaning. Books, which provide experience beyond the immediate environment, contribute to the meaning base of language. Through books we learn to comprehend many more words than we actually use; books expand vocabulary by providing new words in a context that helps children understand them.

Finally, language learning never ends. As students mature, language skills increase and awareness grows in direct proportion to experiences. Older students come to recognize that written material and society affect each other and that language is used for a variety of purposes. Along the way they come to understand the persuasive uses of language, the figurative uses of language, the existence of different points of view, and the influence of literature. From wide exposure to many uses of language, then, students recognize the need to evaluate what they read and hear. The young child who interprets Simon and Garfunkel's "I Am a Rock" literally—who thinks of the singer as having been turned magically into stone—becomes the adolescent who understands the figurative use referring to character and a psychological state. Young children interpret metaphoric language through physical resemblances between things; later they may recognize conceptual or psychological links.

As their metaphoric competence increases, children can be helped by books to extend their ability to comprehend the subtleties and ambiguities of language.

Social Development

Although discussed separately for its implications in selecting literary experiences for children, social development cannot be considered apart from a child's cognitive and language development: all are intricately intertwined. Again, a developmental perspective is used to outline roughly the sequence of socialization. The ability to take another's perspective, an essential part of the socialization process, is used as the basis of defining and identifying the stages of social development.[10]

Children between the ages of three and six years are interested primarily in themselves and their immediate desires. They can differentiate self from others but do not distinguish between the social perspective (thoughts and feelings) of self and that of others: they believe others see the same thing they see and feel the same way they feel. Even though they label others' overt feelings—for example, to say that a child who is crying is sad—they do not see the cause-and-effect relation between reasons and social actions. They would not be likely to infer character motivation to explain behavior. For example, they would probably not interpret Max's fantasy trip in *Where the Wild Things Are* (P), by Maurice Sendak, as an escapist reaction to Max's mother's scolding. Although Sendak's book is certainly appropriate for this age, discussions of character motivation in relation to it are likely to fall flat.

The stage of social role taking, called social-informational, usually appears between ages six and eight and is one in which a child is aware that another may have a different perspective. Children know that a person's perspective is based upon that person's feelings and reasoning and that this may or may not be similar to one's own. Despite the awareness of another perspective, the child tends to focus on only one rather than coordinating viewpoints or dealing with more than one at the same time. Books that tell a story from only one point of view are appropriate for children at this age. Beverly Cleary's *Ramona and Her Father* (P-I) fittingly maintains Ramona's point of view instead of counterpointing with her father's as Ramona tries to get him to stop smoking.

Between the ages of eight and ten, self-reflective role taking is characteristic. Children are aware that each individual can recognize the other's perspective, and this awareness influences their views of one another. The ability to put oneself in another's place is developed, enabling the child to judge the other's intentions, purposes, and actions. In addition to the tremendous impact this ability has upon social behavior, it also holds tacit implications for children's literary experiences.

Children now identify closely with a character and take on the role of one or another person they are reading about. For these children there are very few dry eyes at the end of E. B. White's *Charlotte's Web* (P-I); they have become involved with the characters and want Charlotte to live.

Approximately between the ages of ten and twelve years, mutual role taking becomes possible. Preadolescents realize that both they and others can view each other mutually and simultaneously as having unique points of view. A child can step outside of a two-person relationship and view the interaction from a third-person perspective. In literary terms, the child is achieving distancing and recognizes that regardless of the empathy he or she feels for the character in a book, it is only a character in a book. These readers are certainly deeply affected by the traumatic situations read about, but

Most children enjoy Max's fantasy, while some readers probe its symbolic meanings. All appreciate its art.
(An illustration from *Where the Wild Things Are,* written and illustrated by Maurice Sendak. Copyright © 1963 by Maurice Sendak. By permission of Harper & Row, Publishers, Inc.)

LITERATURE IN RELATION TO THE READER'S DEVELOPMENT

the screen of fiction helps them to experience vicariously events that they could not cope with directly in real life. For example, as they read Mollie Hunter's *The Third Eye* (I-A), they may recognize the Earl of Ballinford's act of sacrifice and courage and Mollie Hunter's theme that courage needs witness. The fact that they rehearse such courageous behavior through identification with Jinty may strengthen their resolve to behave nobly in the future.

Finally, between the ages of twelve and fifteen, students can reflect upon and truly understand the motivations underlying actions. This stage, called social and conventional role taking, enables a person to realize mutual perspective-taking although it does not always lead to complete understanding. Social conventions are seen as necessary because they are understood by all members of the group (the generalized other), regardless of their position, role, or experience. Readers of Robert Cormier's gripping novel *I Am the Cheese* (A) can alternate, with Adam Farmer, between a bicycle trip and an analyst's couch. They can recognize the violation of trust as Adam fights against overwhelming orga-

nizational odds in a plausible, albeit shocking, story. They also may recognize, in Harper Lee's *To Kill a Mockingbird* (A), the conflict that rages because of different points of view.

Teachers aware of the progression of cognitive, linguistic, and social development are able to provide children with books that are compatible with their age-related capacities. The next several chapters describe books suitable to readers in each of the developmental stages. The art of providing an array of suitable books for a child at any developmental level depends on understanding developmental theory and how development influences response to literature. One such influence can be made clear by examining children's concepts of story.

Developing a Sense of Story

Read Steven Kellogg's *Can I Keep Him?* (P), a tightly structured story with a repetitive phrase, to a group of five-year-olds; by the time you reach the third page, they will be "reading" it with you. Hearing only the first three pages, children can recognize the story structure and predict what is

Telling stories is a primary human activity; children tell stories to make sense of their world.
(Photograph © Rosemary Ranck.)

In *Albert's Story*, Albert knows what happened but isn't yet able to tell his story in sequence.
(From *Albert's Story*, by Claudia Long, illustrated by Judy Glasser. Used by permission of Delacorte Press.)

ALBERT'S STORY

by Claudia Long • pictures by Judy Glasser

coming next. They are not memorizing the text—as so many very young children do who "read and reread" their favorite story (even when it is held upside down)—but know intuitively how the story works. Children acquire such intuition by hearing many stories and developing expectations about them; this is called developing a sense of story.

Albert's Story (P), by Claudia Long, illustrates a child's efforts to grasp the structure of a story, and while the theme may not seem funny to children who are grappling with the same problem, it will seem hilarious to those who already have. Albert announces that he will tell a story, but begins "He put the thing on his back," which is the ending. Gradually his older sister pulls the story out of him piece by piece and then retells it in a logical sequence. But when Albert runs to tell it to his mother, he again puts the last sentence first. Albert is so taken with the ending and anticipates it so well that he can't be bothered with details and sequence. In time, this, too, will come.

In addition to developing an understanding of the sequential structure of stories, children also learn to use the content of stories to organize what they encounter of the world. Their vision of reality is shaped by the stories they tell themselves. Telling ourselves stories is a primary human activity, engaged in by adults as well as children. Each of us selectively perceives the world from a unique vantage point, and we "tell ourselves stories" about what we perceive. Children who are sent to bed in a dark room may fear the monsters that lie hidden there, and no amount of logical reassurance convinces them that the stories they have told themselves about the presence of monsters are unfounded. In the same way, stories function in adult life to shape perceptions; if we go to a class unprepared, we rehearse continually the script to be played out when the instructor calls on us to reveal our ignorance about the topic of discussion. Philosophical treatises debate what reality actually is, but there is a consensus that one's own reality is what one perceives it to be; it is largely shaped by what we select to perceive and by the stories we "tell ourselves." We believe these stories, for most often we appear as the central characters and we shape our stories to reflect our fears and needs.

James Britton describes "storying" as serving an assimilative function through which we balance out inner needs with external realities.[11] Children's make-believe play and the stories they tell (often based on the stories they read) are among the activities in which they improvise freely upon events in the actual world, and, in doing so, they enable themselves to return and meet the demands of real life more adequately. Britton sees play and imaginative storytelling as areas of free activity that lie between the world of shared and verifiable experience and the world of inner necessity. The essential purpose of this kind of play is to relate inner needs to the demands of the external world. Children who hear or read stories of witches and fairy godmothers (symbols that may embody and work upon the hate and love that are part of a close, dependent relationship) adapt or use—in their own stories—these symbols to accommodate their own needs. In doing so, they work toward a more harmonious relationship between external demands and their inner needs. Through such fantasies we organize our inner needs and selectively perceive external reality so that we can make sense of our world.

Research into the stories children tell shows that their sense of story grows as they mature. Arthur Applebee found that children's stories change from disconnected strings, to sequential orderings, and eventually contain distinct "story markers."[12] One such marker is evident when young children signal that they are telling a story by giving a title. Another appears when they begin their stories with a formal opening, such as "once upon a time," and end with a closing phrase like "they lived happily ever after." Most children use recognizable opening and closing story frames by the time they are five years old. Many children at this age also use the past tense when they tell a story, and some lower their speaking tone into a dramatic "story voice." The fact that these story markers appear regularly in children's oral language indicates the extent to which literature has been assimilated and dramatically illustrates the potential power of literature to affect language as well as cognitive and affective development.

The stories children enjoy change as they mature intellectually and accumulate experience. Applebee identified the patterns evident in children's stories and found predictable characteristics at each level of thinking from preoperational, through concrete operational, to formal operational thought as defined by Piaget and discussed above. When asked about a story, young children usually respond with a retelling of the narrative, telling the story in whole or in part. They have great difficulty in summarizing a story. Asked what a story is about, they will often respond with a short list of the characters:

Lisa knows stories are about "Cinderella, Humpty Dumpty, and Jack and Jill." Stephen, a bit older, thinks the three little pigs or the little red hen more appropriate. And Ernest answers in the same vein [when asked]: "If you were feeling sad, what kind of story would you like?" "Bears, The Three Bears." "Why?" "Because that makes me happy." "What is it about?" "Three Bears, and Goldilocks, and her mother."[13]

Yet when Ernest is asked to *tell about* the three bears, he gives a detailed, accurate retelling of the story, and even imitates the deep-, middle-, and high-toned voices of the characters. Even though he gives the list of characters as the response to the question "What is the story about?" there is no question that he knows the story in its entirety.

As children mature further and their cognitive development becomes classifiable as concrete operational, their original stories and retellings tend to include summaries and categories of behavior as well as lists of characters. When asked to "tell about" *Bridge to Terabithia* (I), by Katherine Paterson, a ten-year-old responded: "It's about a boy who likes to run but Leslie beats him. Then Jesse and Leslie become good friends and build Terabithia. Then Leslie dies and Jesse takes his sister there." This ability to summarize reflects the concrete operations of serial ordering and classification, operations that a simple retelling does not require.

As children move toward the formal operational mode of thinking, their comprehension of a story is revealed through analogy. For example, Xan equated story with gossip: "Reading something is like the same as hearing from somebody, 'Oh, did you hear what happened?' or something like that." They may recognize a character's motives, as when they understand that Mafatu is driven by his need to overcome his fear of the sea in Armstrong Sperry's *Call It Courage* (I). Their generalizations about a work entail a consideration of its theme and point of view. They can deal with the ambiguity of two things being true at the same time, even where they are contradictory. They recognize that the point of view from which we view events affects our perception of them. For example, they can recognize that the story in Richard Peck's *Father Figure* (A) would be told much differently were it told from the father's point of view rather than from the adolescent's. Many students interpret the theme of Peck's story as the need for better communication between people who love each other, whereas others may see it as a story of a boy growing up and becoming less self-centered. Students at the formal-operations level of thinking can also compare books that develop a similar theme. This reflects the ability to consider several rather than just one reality and to engage in critical judgments in the light of these possibilities.

Fostering Creative Interaction

Teachers who are aware of the changing nature of a child's concept of story can provide experiences with literature that both build upon and expand that concept by suggesting books that clarify and reconcile the complexities of the world and also stretch their minds. Children seem to have innate taste. Although they generally like well-crafted books, which build suspense, avoid anticlimaxes, and have memorable themes, they also enjoy "formula" stories. They generally enjoy fantasy in the early grades, realistic books and mysteries in the middle grades, and both realism and fantasy in junior high and high school. Teachers do make a difference, however, and the books you share with children can be influential in fostering new interests, shifting focuses, and developing latent tastes. Usually popular are stories full of action, with characters approximately the same age as, or a little older than, the readers. Biographies, informational books, and realistic animal books become increasingly popular from the upper elementary grades on. However, these general interests are just that—general. It is important to have a variety of books on hand, and while Nancy Drew mysteries shouldn't be discouraged, other, more complex stories should be encouraged.

Along with providing for a variety of reading experiences, teachers should also provide for variety in responses. Children need time to respond and reflect upon any learning experience, and this is especially true for literature. Response and reflection can take many forms. The response may be through art, drama, or oral or written language activities related to a book. Reflection may occur in silence or discussion. Sometimes the perfect follow-up sprouts naturally; other times teachers need to sow the seeds.

Flexible teachers with a good stock of possibilities are prepared to give children choices. Books are meaningful events in children's lives; when they are the center of classroom activities that free children's spontaneity, they lead to more reading. With options, children spin off on their own, stretching their imaginations to limits beyond ours. The spark from a freely developed project may ignite many imaginative fires.

Teachers who want to foster creative interactions with stories must allow readers to respond to the text in a way that makes the text meaningful to them. One child may be fascinated by the ghostly legend of the sea in Natalie Babbitt's *The Eyes of the Amaryllis* (I), another by the character of the grandmother, another by the problem the granddaughter has in dividing her loyalty between her father and her grandmother. Children should be allowed to explore their own responses as well as to share the responses of others, and to discuss all responses in the light of the text itself. A teacher who wants to hear only one kind of response to a story will soon have children who read "for the teacher" rather than for themselves, for they learn to give us what they see we value; if we applaud the narrowly focussed, one right answer, that is what we will be given. A teacher who encourages each child to work out a personal response, to share that response with others, and to return to the text for verification will soon have students

NATALIE BABBITT
Tuck Everlasting
A NOVEL

prehension of a text, and the ability to view the story in another light may increase both understanding and enjoyment. Natalie Babbitt's *Tuck Everlasting* (I) might be construed as a philosophical question about the worth of eternal life, a character study of Winnie Foster, or a thematic statement about choices made in life. All three interpretations are plausible. Singly, each represents a limited evocation of the possibilities of the text; together they enable a more comprehensive response.

It should be evident at this point that our responses to stories inevitably will *not* be the same as the responses of our students. Rather than impose our own reading and interpretation of a text upon our students, we should make an effort to listen to their responses. Our job is to provide a rich supply of literature and give students many occasions to talk about what they read—but not to decide beforehand how they should respond to it. We can nurture the gift of imagination by letting students know that many interpretations are possible.

In this same vein, the teacher's response is crucial. The teacher who gushes about how lovely, touching, and sensitive a book is may find students turning away in disgust. Similarly, adopting an affected, overly dramatic stage voice when reading poetry or prose turns students away from what we want them to know and enjoy. Sincere enthusiasm and genuine enjoyment, however, are likely to be contagious.

THE MULTIDIMENSIONAL VIEW OF LITERATURE

There are many valid extraliterary reasons for using children's books in schools. For example, teachers can help foster concept development by incorporating in their teaching plans books that explore specific concepts, or they can enhance understanding of a historical period by including historical fiction and biography with factual books of history. Knowing books leads you to see endless possibilities for their use.

who read for pleasure, immersing themselves in the stories and becoming critically aware.

Another way of encouraging fully developed and individual responses to literature is to teach children to be critically flexible. A story can be viewed from many different perspectives. Sometimes one perspective doesn't allow for full com-

Insofar as it embraces proponents of many differing points of view and interest, the field of literature and its critics are analogous to the storied blind men of Hindostan, each of whom identified a different part of an elephant as the whole creature. The problem for the beginning student of children's literature lies in identifying differing points of view and interests while developing a personal philosophy.

Literature means many things to many people; each unique perspective, however, is equally valid. We dare not believe that our view of literature is the only view, lest, like the blind men of Hindostan, each of us be partly in the right but all of us in the wrong. The proper perspective seems to vary according to the purpose; our purpose is to develop flexibility in students so that they have access to many different views.[14] In addition to describing the role of good books in the curriculum, this text presents a multidimensional approach to learning about children's literature, with the child always the dominant element in any formulation.

When we teach literature we relate this one book to all others we know and to our lives as well. We may emphasize parts of a story that might remind a reader of an ancient Greek myth, or we may focus on a character who reflects ourselves or a character met in another book. Through personal response and relating books to life, children become aware of the eternal stream of literature and of life and are encouraged to develop a sense of wonder, a pondering of other ways of seeing, thinking, feeling, and being. Opening up a book to children in this way may lead beyond understanding that single piece of literature to an illumination of their lives in relation to the world and a broader spectrum of humanity.

The teacher who is able to approach a piece of literature in a variety of ways encourages students to respond with versatility. We can look at stories for theme, archetype, or element; as a mirror or window on life; or in a developmentally expanding frame. We teach children to be flexible by being flexible in our own approach to literature, for they follow our actions more than our words. When we play with possibilities affably, we foster children's ability to respond to books in fulfilling ways.

The following multidimensional view of Ursula Le Guin's *A Wizard of Earthsea* (I-A) can be exemplary; it takes many turns. The book tells the story of Ged, who, when his village is attacked by marauding warriors, discovers that he has magical powers. He devotes his life to perfecting his skill, but, plagued by overwhelming pride, sometimes flaunts his powers before he fully masters them. When Jasper, a fellow student of magic, challenges him, Ged attempts to show greater skill than he possesses and, in the process, calls forth a spirit from the land of the dead. This nameless shadow beast roams Ged's world and haunts him endlessly. His struggle to evade the shadow and his inevitable confrontation with it are told in a compelling style.

If we look at the story for archetypes and themes, we see reflections of ancient mythology and biblical literature:

On the day the boy was thirteen years old, a day in the early splendour of autumn while still the bright leaves are on the trees, Ogion returned to the village from his rovings over Gont Mountain, and the ceremony of Passage was held. The witch took from the boy his name Duny, the name his mother had given him as a baby. Nameless and naked he walked into the cold springs of the Ar where it rises among rocks under the high cliffs. As he entered the water clouds crossed the sun's face and great shadows slid and mingled over the water of the pool about him. He crossed to the far bank, shuddering with cold but walking slow and erect as he should through that icy, living water. As he came to the bank Ogion, waiting, reached out his hand and clasping the boy's arm whispered to him his true name: Ged. Thus was he given his name by one very wise in the uses of power.[15]

The ritual described suggests religious ceremonies of passage such as the Jewish bar mitzvah at the thirteenth birthday, or confirmation in Christian rites, or perhaps baptism. The idea of naming and the value of one's name is used in a way to convey the power of naming in the biblical sense.[16] Ged makes frequent references to the importance of his name: he says, "By my name, I will do it" and "Unless I can learn the word that masters it: its name." The power of Ged's name glows again near the end of the story:

In silence, man and shadow met face to face, and stopped. Aloud and clearly, breaking that old silence, Ged spoke the shadow's name, and in the same moment the shadow spoke without lips or tongue, saying the same word: "Ged." And the two voices were one voice.[17]

Ged's friend, Vetch, watches the struggle between man and his shadow and fears that the evil thing might take Ged's form. He remains silent as he wonders what will come.

Now when he saw his friend and heard him speak, his doubt vanished. And he began to see the truth, that Ged had neither lost nor won but, naming the shadow of his death with his own name, had made himself whole: a man: who, knowing his whole true self, cannot be used or possessed by any power other than himself, and whose life therefore is lived for life's sake and never in the service of ruin, or pain, or hatred, or the dark. In the *Creation of Ea* which is the oldest song, it is said, "Only in silence the word, only in dark the light, only in dying life: bright the hawk's flight on the empty sky."[18]

Traces of mythology and biblical stories emanate from Le Guin's powerful story. Ged is the seventh son of a seventh son, a place that bears significance in biblical and mythical terms. His journey emerges from the struggle between good and evil within him and echoes the biblical Jacob's struggle with the devil. The promise of eternal life after death rings through theology and through this story.

From a psychological point of view, the shadow that haunts Ged is symbolic of the unconscious or of the dark underside of a person's being. Jungian or Freudian psychoanalysts would interpret the shadow in many ways.

At first it was shapeless, but as it drew nearer it took on the look of a man. An old man it seemed, grey and grim, coming towards Ged; but even as Ged saw his father the smith in that figure, he saw that it was not an old man but a young one. It was Jasper: Jasper's insolent handsome young face, and silver-clasped grey cloak, and stiff stride. . . . It brightened, and in its light the look of Jasper fell from the figure that approached, and it became

Pechvarry. But Pechvarry's face was all bloated and pallid like the face of a drowned man, and he reached out his hand strangely as if beckoning. . . . Then the thing that faced him changed utterly, spreading out to either side as if it opened enormous thin wings, and it writhed, and swelled, and shrank again. Ged saw in it for an instant, Skiorh's white face, and then a pair of clouded, staring eyes, and then suddenly a fearful face he did not know, man or monster.[19]

Each of the people the shadow represents is one that Ged wrongs or one for whom he has been less than he could be. Ged needs to return to himself— to what Jung calls the inferior side of oneself or the shadow—and to see his behavior in a clear light. It is the shadow Ged tries to flee and only when he faces it does he become whole.[20] The shadow as an image of guilt becomes evident, as do other literary symbols, the more widely and thoughtfully one reads. There is a strong possibility, however, that such esoteric symbolism may elude many. Still this does not deny the validity of using psychological insights to discuss the book with readers who can grasp the additional layers of meaning.

Looking at *A Wizard of Earthsea* sociologically, teachers can help mature readers see Ged as a prototype of the adolescent who wavers between adult capabilities and childish needs. For some readers, the theme is about the misuse of power that learning bestows. Ged struggles with power: flaunts it to impress Jasper, misuses it, and finally accepts responsibility for it. In another sense, the story shows the need for balance and equilibrium in life and the effect that one person can have on the entire world.

A structural look at the story for motifs or recurring images would focus on the play between light and dark. The nameless evil shadow that haunts Ged lunges at him from darkness repeatedly. Light, sunshine, and brightness of day force the shadow to recede. Transparent whiteness, greyness, fog, and mist that obscures vision convey strong visual images. The ship that carries Ged to the island of Roke, *Shadow*, forebodes danger.

We see from this multidimensional discussion of Ursula Le Guin's novel that many interpretations are possible. Whether a teacher chooses to pursue one type of exploration is determined by the literary background of the students and the goals of instruction. It might seem unlikely that high fantasy, in which a boy learns to be a magician in a fanciful world of islands and strange creatures, would appeal to modern readers. However, teachers aware of this compelling story about a strong character with whom children identify and its tension- and conflict-laden plot, can help them discover the story's relevance for their lives. *The Tombs of Atuan* (I-A) and *The Farthest Shore* (I-A) are sequels to *A Wizard of Earthsea*.

If you are aware of numerous possibilities for viewing books, your choice of alternatives can expand children's thinking. Some books lend themselves to one view more readily than others. Some children, responding in a characteristic mode, may choose only one view; others, more flexible in response, consider many dimensions. An informed teacher can open many windows for viewing books.

TYPES OF LITERATURE

Until they have read widely and discussed what they read, children are generally unaware that there are different types of books or that stories can be categorized. Indeed, it is not important to pigeonhole books for children because each book is an experience unlike any other. However, literary forms provide a frame of reference for exploring books and studying the field, and help simplify the task of presenting literature in meaningful and varied ways. With approximately forty thousand children's books in print, the student of children's literature would be overwhelmed were the books to be treated as an amorphous mass. Further, knowledge of literary types and of different ways to explore them makes the informed use of books possible.

Classification schemes for children's books are fraught with problems. Formal literary divisions are inadequate because format sometimes takes precedence over content and tone, as in the case of the picture book. Divisions by content or mode are problematic, too; for example, books grouped as "animal stories" may have fantasy, realistic, and factual books among them. At best, boundaries within any system are indistinct.

Literature can also be divided into poetry and prose, or fiction and nonfiction. It can be divided along the lines of genre; as contemporary or traditional; as short story, novel, or drama; or as tragedy, romance, comedy.

Various distinguishing features help categorize the various forms. For example, whatever has no known author is designated "folklore"; stories focussing on events that could happen today are works of "contemporary realism"; stories that could have happened in the past, "historical"; those that could not happen in the real world, "fantasy"; and those that might happen in the future are designated "science fiction." Children discover the distinctions gradually as they read widely and have books read to them.

Picture Books

The classification of picture books is based on format: picture books tell a story through a unique combination of text and illustration in that meaning conveyed in the text is extended by the illustrations. The content may be realistic, fanciful, or factual but the format of text and illustration combined defines it as a picture book. An example is Robert McCloskey's popular *Make Way for Ducklings* (P).

As children become increasingly aware of an aesthetic world, picture books come to be appreciated for their art. Children are sensitive to color, sound, and pattern. As they create their own pictures, they become aware of pictures others create. Books that draw attention to the aesthetic world are in keeping with the ever-expanding interests of the child.

Picture books are also appreciated for the stories they tell. Young children are egocentric, fascinated with themselves and their own needs, interests, and concerns. Because young children have their primary experiences in and are dependent upon the home and family, books that help them explore their personal world are uniquely suited to their needs and interests.

As children mature, they begin to expand beyond their personal world of self, home, and family into a broader social world. They perceive friends, school, and neighborhood as integral parts of their lives and relationships. They expand their interests beyond the familiar and immediate to show an interest in other children and adults. Books that deal with the child's social world are congruent with developmental interests. Thus, art, story, and children's interests are three avenues by which to explore picture books.

Features characteristic of picture books are as follows:

Appeal to all ages
Fusion of words and pictures
Numerous illustrations
Brief and uncomplicated plot
Broad spectrum of subject matter and form

Folklore

Folklore has no single identifiable author; the stories came to us through the generations by word of mouth before they were ever written down. As people told the stories to one another, they were changed and molded to suit the teller's style or fancy. Folklore is a broad category encompassing many types. For example, the Mother Goose nursery rhymes, which delight the ear of the young child even before the meaning of the words is known, are a part of folklore. Folk and fairy tales, which mirror the language and values of a culture, constitute another major category of folk literature. Fables, too, those simply told and highly condensed morality tales that often use animal characters to embody human virtues and vices, belong to the folklore tradition.

In addition, classical mythology, which reverberates with symbolic meaning, makes up a large portion of folk literature. Some of the great myths explain the origin of the earth, the phenomena of nature, and the relation between humans and their gods according to the beliefs of the people who created them. Legends are exaggerated hero tales grown hardly recognizable through retellings that embellished the initial grain of truth. The American version of hero tales, called tall tales, exaggerates the strength, the size, and the riches of America. Our Paul Bunyan, John Henry, and Pecos Bill epitomize American values in the same manner as Robin Hood and King Arthur epitomize those of the English.

Recurring themes, motifs, and patterns involving characters, images, incidents, and conventional story shapes are archetypes evident in traditional literature. The struggle between light and dark, a lost child or superhuman character, an image of eternal spring, the transformation of a frog into a prince, or the repetitive cycle of a story pattern are examples of archetypes.

Features characteristic of the major forms of folklore are as follows:

Folk Tales

Simple repetitive plots
Stereotyped characters symbolizing good or evil
Obvious themes illuminating human values
Repeated use of the numbers three and seven (characters and incidents)
Repetitive and rhythmic language

Fables

Single-incident plots
Animal characters symbolizing human traits
Explicitly stated morals
Didactic language

Myths

Explanations of the origins and cycles of the universe
Gods and mortals as characters
Symbolic language

Tall Tales

Regional settings and dialect
Heroic themes
Earthy wit and humor
Exaggerated size and deeds

Fantasy and Science Fiction

Fantasy is distinguished by the imaginary nature of places and events: surreal worlds in which animals talk, inanimate objects have feelings, time is manipulated, or humans accomplish superhuman feats. Plot, character, and incident make believable whatever the fantasy maker says is so within the framework he sets. E. B. White's *Charlotte's Web* (P-I) is a well-known fantasy. Fantasy can embrace themes of eternal or universal truths that reflect human concerns.

Children can learn about fantasy through noticing the devices used to create it—miniature people, as in Mary Norton's *The Borrowers* (I), time warp, as in Margaret Anderson's *To Nowhere and Back* (I), or talking animals, as in Kenneth Grahame's *The Wind in the Willows* (I).

Among the features characteristic of fantasy are:

Imaginary worlds made believable
Characters who possess supernatural qualities
Themes often dealing with the struggle between good and evil
Language sometimes used symbolically

Science fiction employs imaginative extrapolation of fact and theory: stories project what could happen in another time through logical extension of established theories and scientific principles. Science fiction describes worlds that are not only plausible, but possible, and considers the impact of science on life. Early science fiction writers extrapolated primarily from technology, but the genre now attracts writers who use sociology and anthropology. Science fiction themes often question the effect of progress upon the quality of life and examine the values of contemporary society. John Christopher's *The White Mountains* (I-A) is a popular piece of science fiction.

Science fiction readers are intrigued with the consideration of alternative futures. Science fiction writers themselves say they are not attempting to predict the future; instead, they consider many po-

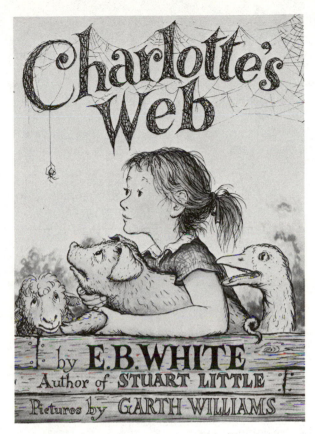

The unlikely friendship of a spider and a pig is woven into a surpassing fantasy.
(From *Charlotte's Web*, by E. B. White, illustrated by Garth Williams. Harper & Row, 1952.)

tential futures. They also say that while science fiction readers do not know what the future holds, they won't be surprised when it gets here.

The characteristic features of science fiction include:

Alternate views of the future
Extrapolation from facts and theories
Consideration of impact of technology on life

Poetry and Verse

Poetry is the shorthand of beauty. Poetry, as Emerson suggested long ago, says the most important

28

things in the simplest way. Poetry is distilled language that captures the essence of an idea or experience and encompasses the universe in its vision.

Much poetry is metrical, rhythmic, and rhymed, appealing to the ear as well as to the mind and the emotions. Taking many forms, the best poetry and verse—from nonsense rhymes and limericks through lyrical and narrative poetry—always shapes a taken-for-granted ordinary into thoughts extraordinary.

Some fine examples of poetry and verse for children are David McCord's *A Star in the Pail* (P), Aileen Fisher's *Listen, Rabbit!* (P-I), Karla Kuskin's discussion of the ideas that grow into poems in *Near the Window Tree* (I), and Myra Cohn Livingston's *The Way Things Are* (I).

Sometimes mystifying, often difficult, poetry can enrich life and fire the imagination. Poetry engages the heart for reasons that reason may never know.

Children love poetry: it echoes their language and their conception of the world. If young children are discovering turtles, for example, they should hear Vachel Lindsay's

There was a little turtle.
He lived in a box.
He swam in a puddle.
He climbed on the rocks.[21]

Or, if city traffic is part of their lives, they should hear Rowena Bastin Bennett's "Motor Cars," in which she says:

From a city window, 'way up high
I like to watch the cars go by.
They look like burnished beetles, black,
That leave a little muddy track
Behind them as they slowly crawl.[22]

Older students, occupied with plans for their future, should hear Louise Driscoll's "Hold Fast Your Dreams," which says:

Within your heart
Keep one still, secret spot
Where dreams may go

And sheltered so
May thrive and grow—
Where doubt and fear are not[23]

Whatever the occasion, poetry infuses greater meaning and imparts a sense of joy in the process.

Among the distinctive features of poetry are:

Condensed language calling attention to itself
Extensive use of figurative language
Clearly discernible particular forms
Considerable dependence on manipulation of sounds and structures

Contemporary Realism

Fiction set in modern times, with events that could occur, is called contemporary realism. Although plot, character, and incident are created and manipulated according to an author's design, all remains within the realm of the possible. Sue Ellen Bridgers' *Home Before Dark* (I) is a typical work of contemporary realism.

Children with a strong desire for realistic books are sometimes looking for clues about what life might hold for them. Reading about children a few years older than they serves as a rehearsal for anticipated experiences. Books often provide a mirror for the reader; they also become a window through which to view other lives.

Numerous studies show that a country's social and political philosophies are evident in its children's books. Obviously, the social concerns that impinge upon authors are reflected in their work and show in the problems and conflicts they write about. In the past, the problems were often solved when virtue was rewarded, justice triumphed, and good overcame evil. More recently, this is not the case. Contemporary realism is frequently open-ended; the problem is not resolved and the central character accepts a less-than-perfect world.

Among the distinguishing characteristics of contemporary realism are:

An illusion of reality, a believable slice of life
Characters who represent the full range of humanity

Real-world settings
Themes dealing with basic truths of human
  nature
Language similar to natural spoken language

Historical Fiction and Biography

Historical fiction is categorized by the time of the setting and the believability of events: the stories are set in the historical past with events that could possibly have occurred. An author creates plot, character, and incident and casts them into an authentic historical setting that is true to the facts of history. Esther Forbes's *Johnny Tremain* (I-A) is a well-known historical novel.

Biography tells the story of a person's life in part or in its entirety. It bears the imprint of the author; although the story of a person's life provides the basic facts, the writer interprets, selects, and organizes elements to create an aesthetic work. Carl Sandburg's extensive biography, *Abe Lincoln Grows Up* (A), is an outstanding example.

Children who read about the past through biography and historical fiction gain a richer and more immediate understanding of life than through a book of historical facts. Many children learn more about life on the frontier through Laura Ingalls Wilder's "Little House" series (P-I) than through their school textbooks.

Teachers can enrich the school curriculum by including books of historical fiction and biography with textbooks. Many different books about a historical time can give readers rich insights about life and provide them the unique opportunity of evaluating divergent reports of the same event.

Features that characterize historical fiction are:

An illusion of reality set in the past
Believable characters
Real-world settings in the historical past
Themes dealing with basic conflicts of
  humans
Language reflecting the historical period and
  people

Distinguishing features of biography include:

A plot structured around a person's life
Themes often dealing with a struggle for success
Emphasis on the strength and moral fiber of the
  subject

Informational Books

Factual books aimed at explaining a subject are called informational books. They present information in a variety of formats: in picture books and photographic essays, as reproductions of original documents, as how-to-do-it manuals, or as direct expository texts. Informational books outnumber fiction in most children's libraries, yet little critical attention is given to them. History, science, mathematics, arts and crafts, and social sciences are but a few of the topics included in nonfiction. Anne and Harlow Rockwell's *The Toolbox* (N) presents clear illustrations of the objects found therein. Victor Scheffer's *The Seeing Eye* (I) visualizes the forms, textures, and colors of nature. Edwin Tunis presents a panorama of *Colonial Living* (I-A) with intricate detail in text and illustration.

Organizing a unit in the science and social studies curricula requires that teachers locate numerous books on a topic. Selecting the books involves attending to the recency, adequacy, accuracy, and authenticity of the information in them. Further, the qualifications of the author are assessed when such information is available.

Characteristic features of informational books are:

Concentration on facts and concepts
Logical presentation of information
Expository language

Books and Children with Special Needs

Books reflect the diversity of our world and its people, some of whom are children with special needs.

Books play a primary role in acquainting able-bodied children with handicapped children. Literature, educating the heart as it educates the mind, is unequaled for portraying disabled children in a fully human light. Furthermore, if books speak to us early enough in a positive, nonthreatening way, they can blunt the formation of stereotypes before they are set.

Some educators hold that giving a child in a wheelchair a book about a child in a wheelchair narrows the focus only to the disability, to the neglect of the child as a whole person—one with feelings and interests common to all children. However, reading about a role model who copes successfully with a disability can help disabled children see themselves positively; it affirms a healthy self-image.

It goes without saying that a well-rounded curriculum for children with special needs is not limited; rather, it encompasses *all* books.

A Literature Curriculum

A literature curriculum for children who will live in the twenty-first century, who may travel in space to worlds beyond our own, needs to stress the place of difference and multiplicity in life. Conformity leads to conventional and ordinary thinking while originality promises creative change. The rapidly changing world demands imaginative flexibility if we are not to suffer from future shock.

Through literature, imagination grows to become a natural and necessary part of the way we construct our world and deal with reality. Books are essential for grappling with the world in which we live and for envisioning possibilities for the world of tomorrow. Incorporating the very best books into a developmental program assures that children will touch hearts with the finest: "What the heart knows today the head will understand tomorrow."[24] And once they climb to the pinnacles of literature, children are not satisfied with anything less.

Issues in Children's Books

The most exciting feature of the field of children's literature is that it is ever changing. Each new publications list brings new talents and fresh surprises from our old talents, and each shift in social and political climates brings demands for changes in children's books. Revisionists demand that certain books of the past be discarded or rewritten to reflect contemporary ideas; others disagree. But such controversy and debate indicate that people care deeply; an absence of issues would forbode a dead area.

Welcome, then, to the world of children's books—it's a good place to be. You cannot give beauty to children without the scent of roses clinging to your hands.

Notes

1. N. M. Bodecker, "Hello Book," from a bookmark for Children's Book Week (New York: Children's Book Council, 1978).
2. Louise Rosenblatt, *The Reader, The Text, The Poem* (Carbondale, Ill.: Southern Illinois Univ. Press, 1978), p. 24.
3. C. S. Lewis, "On Stories," in *Essays Presented to Charles Williams* (London: Oxford Univ. Press, 1947), p. 100.
4. Myles McDowell, "Fiction for Children and Adults: Some Essential Differences," *Children's Literature in Education,* No. 10 (March 1973), p. 51.
5. Wolfgang Iser, "The Reading Process: A Phenomenological Approach," in *The Implied Reader* (Baltimore: Johns Hopkins Univ. Press, 1974), pp. 274–94. For further explication of the transaction between the reader and the text, see Wolfgang Iser, *The Act of Reading: A Theory of Aesthetic Response* (Baltimore: Johns Hopkins Univ. Press, 1978);

Louise Rosenblatt, *Literature as Exploration,* 3rd ed. (1938; rpt. New York: Noble and Noble, 1976); Louise Rosenblatt, *The Reader, The Text, The Poem;* and Norman Holland, *Five Readers Reading* (New Haven: Yale Univ. Press, 1975).

6. Margaret Anzul, Madison Elementary School, Madison, N.J., 1978.
7. Northrop Frye, *The Educated Imagination* (Bloomington, Ind.: Indiana Univ. Press, 1970), pp. 48–49.
8. Joan Lipsitz, Children's Book Council Meeting, New York City, 15 March 1979.
9. For a detailed discussion of language and development of a sense of story, see James Britton, *Language and Learning* (Harmondsworth, England: Penguin Books, 1970) and Arthur Applebee, *The Child's Concept of Story* (Chicago: Univ. of Chicago Press, 1978).
10. William Damon, *The Social World of the Child* (San Francisco: Jossey-Bass, 1977).
11. Britton, *Language and Learning,* p. 11.
12. Applebee, *The Child's Concept of Story,* p. 36–37.
13. Arthur Applebee, "Where Does Cinderella Live?" in *The Cool Web: The Pattern of Children's Reading,* ed. Margaret Meek, Aidan Warlow, and Griselda Barton (New York: Atheneum, 1978), p. 55.
14. Robert D. Robinson, "The Three Little Pigs: From Six Directions," *Elementary English* (now *Language Arts*), 45, No. 3 (March 1968), 354–59, 366.
15. Ursula Le Guin, *A Wizard of Earthsea* (1968; New York: Puffin-Viking Penguin, 1971), p. 25.
16. The archetypal patterns are discussed at length in Eleanor Cameron, "High Fantasy: Wizard of Earthsea," *Horn Book Magazine,* 47, No. 2 (April 1971), pp. 129–38.
17. Le Guin, *A Wizard of Earthsea,* pp. 197–98.
18. Ibid., pp. 199–200.
19. Ibid., p. 197.
20. Ursula Le Guin discusses her own interpretation of *A Wizard of Earthsea* in "Child and Shadow," *The Quarterly Journal of the Library of Congress,* 32, No. 2 (April 1975), 139–48.
21. Vachel Lindsay, "The Little Turtle," in *The Arbuthnot Anthology of Children's Literature,* 4th ed., ed. Zena Sutherland et al. (New York: Lothrop, Lee & Shepard, 1976), p. 42.
22. Rowena Bastin Bennett, "Motor Cars," in *The Arbuthnot Anthology of Children's Literature,* 4th ed., p. 55.
23. Louise Driscoll, "Hold Fast Your Dreams" in *Time for Poetry,* 3rd ed., comp. May Hill Arbuthnot and Shelton Root (Chicago: Scott, Foresman, 1967), p. 192.
24. James Stephens, *The Crock of Gold,* as quoted in Myra Cohn Livingston, "Children's Literature: In Chaos, a Creative Weapon," in *Using Literature and Poetry Affectively,* ed. Jon E. Shapiro (Newark, Del: International Reading Association, 1979), p. 52.

Professional References

Applebee, Arthur. *The Child's Concept of Story.* Univ. of Chicago Press, 1978.

Britton, James. *Language and Learning.* Penguin Books, 1970.

Cameron, Eleanor. "High Fantasy: Wizard of Earthsea." *Horn Book Magazine,* 47, No. 2 (April 1971), 129–38.

Damon, William. *The Social World of the Child.* Jossey-Bass, 1977.

Frye, Northrop. *The Educated Imagination.* Indiana Univ. Press, 1970.

Holland, Norman. *Five Readers Reading.* Yale Univ. Press, 1975.

Iser, Wolfgang. *The Act of Reading: A Theory of Aesthetic Response.* Johns Hopkins Univ. Press, 1978.

_____. *The Implied Reader.* Johns Hopkins Univ. Press, 1974.

Le Guin, Ursula. "Child and Shadow." *The Quarterly Journal of the Library of Congress,* 32, No. 2 (April 1975), 139–48.

32

Lewis, C. S. *Essays Presented to Charles Williams.* Oxford Univ. Press, 1947.

Lipsitz, Joan. Children's Book Council Meeting, New York City. 15 March 1979.

McDowell, Myles. "Fiction for Children and Adults: Some Essential Differences." *Children's Literature in Education,* No. 10 (March 1973), pp. 50–63.

Meek, Margaret, Aidan Warlow, and Griselda Barton, eds. *The Cool Web: The Pattern of Children's Reading.* Atheneum, 1978.

Robinson, Robert D. "The Three Little Pigs: From Six Directions." *Elementary English,* 45, No. 3 (March 1968), 354–59, 366.

Rosenblatt, Louise. *Literature as Exploration.* 3rd ed. 1938; rpt. Noble and Noble, 1976.

————. *The Reader, The Text, The Poem.* Southern Illinois Univ. Press, 1978.

Shapiro, Jon E., ed. *Using Literature and Poetry Affectively.* International Reading Association, 1979.

Children's Books Cited in Chapter

Aardema, Verna. *Why Mosquitoes Buzz in People's Ears: A West African Tale.* Illus. Leo and Diane Dillon. Dial, 1975.

Adler, Carole S. *The Magic of the Glits.* Macmillan, 1979.

Anderson, Margaret J. *To Nowhere and Back.* Knopf, 1975.

Arbuthnot, May Hill, and Shelton L. Root, Jr., eds. *Time for Poetry.* 3rd ed. Illus. Arthur Paul. Scott, Foresman, 1968.

Babbitt, Natalie. *The Eyes of the Amaryllis.* Farrar, Straus & Giroux, 1977.

————. *Tuck Everlasting.* Farrar, Straus & Giroux, 1975.

Blume, Judy. *Are You There, God? It's Me, Margaret.* Bradbury, 1970.

————. *Tales of a Fourth-Grade Nothing.* Illus. Roy Doty. Dutton, 1972.

Bodecker, N. M. "Hello Book," from a bookmark for Children's Book Week. Children's Book Council, Inc., 1978.

Bridgers, Sue Ellen. *All Together Now.* Knopf, 1979.

————. *Home Before Dark.* Illus. Charles Robinson. Knopf, 1976.

Brown, Marcia. *Once a Mouse.* Scribner's, 1961.

Brown, Margaret Wise. *Goodnight Moon.* Illus. Clement Hurd. Harper & Row, 1947.

Burningham, John. *ABC.* Bobbs-Merrill, 1967.

————. *The Baby.* Crowell, 1975.

————. *Come Away from the Water, Shirley.* Crowell, 1977.

Burton, Virginia Lee. *Mike Mulligan and His Steam Shovel.* Houghton Mifflin, 1939.

Christopher, John. *The White Mountains.* Macmillan, 1967.

Cleary, Beverly. *Ramona and Her Father.* Illus. Alan Tiegreen. Morrow, 1977.

————. *Ramona and Her Mother.* Illus. Alan Tiegreen. Morrow, 1979.

Collier, James Lincoln, and Christopher Collier. *My Brother Sam Is Dead.* Four Winds-Scholastic, 1974.

Conford, Ellen. *Me and the Terrible Two.* Illus. Charles Carroll. Little, Brown, 1974.

Corbett, Scott. *The Baseball Trick.* Illus. Paul Galdone. Little, Brown, 1965.

Cormier, Robert. *The Chocolate War.* Pantheon, 1974.

————. *I Am the Cheese.* Pantheon, 1977.

Craig, M. Jean. *The Dragon in the Clockbox.* Illus. Kelly Oechsli. Norton, 1962.

Cresswell, Helen. *Bagthorpes Unlimited.* Macmillan, 1978.

Dalgliesh, Alice. *The Courage of Sarah Noble.* Illus. Leonard Weisgard. Scribner's, 1954.

Fisher, Aileen. *Listen, Rabbit.* Illus. Symeon Shimin. Crowell, 1964.

Forbes, Esther. *Johnny Tremain.* Illus. Lynd Ward. Houghton Mifflin, 1946.

Freeman, Don. *Dandelion.* Viking, 1964.

Gág, Wanda. *Millions of Cats.* Coward, McCann & Geoghegan, 1928.

Galdone, Paul. *The Three Bears.* Scholastic, 1973.

————. *The Three Little Pigs.* Seabury, 1970.

————. *The House That Jack Built.* McGraw-Hill, 1961.

Glazer, Tom. *Eye Winker, Tom Tinker, Chin Chopper: A Collection of Musical Finger Plays.* Doubleday, 1973.

Grahame, Kenneth. *The Wind in the Willows.* Illus. Ernest H. Shepard. Scribner's 1933.

Greene, Constance C. *Beat the Turtle Drum.* Illus. Donna Diamond. Viking, 1976.

Haywood, Carolyn. *Betsy's Play School.* Illus. James Griffin. Morrow, 1977.

Hicks, Clifford B. *Alvin's Swap Shop.* Illus. Bill Sokol. Holt, Rinehart & Winston, 1976.

Hoban, Russell. *A Baby Sister for Frances.* Illus. Lillian Hoban. Harper & Row, 1964.

Hoban, Tana. *Shapes and Things.* Macmillan, 1970.

Hogrogian, Nonny. *One Fine Day.* Macmillan, 1971.

Holland, Isabelle. *The Man Without a Face.* Lippincott, 1972.

Hunter, Mollie. *The Third Eye.* Harper & Row, 1979.

Juster, Norton. *The Phantom Tollbooth.* Random House, 1961.

Keller, Charles. *Ballpoint Bananas and Other Jokes.* Illus. David Barrios. Prentice-Hall, 1976.

Kellogg, Steven. *Can I Keep Him?* Dial, 1971.

Kunhardt, Dorothy. *Pat the Bunny.* Golden Press-Western, 1962 (1940).

Kuskin, Karla. *Just Like Everyone Else.* Harper & Row, 1959.

————. *Near the Window Tree.* Harper & Row, 1975.

Lee, Harper. *To Kill a Mockingbird.* Lippincott, 1960.

Le Guin, Ursula. *The Farthest Shore.* Illus. Gail Garraty. Atheneum, 1972.

————. *The Tombs of Atuan.* Illus. Gail Garraty. Atheneum, 1971.

————. *A Wizard of Earthsea.* Illus. Ruth Robbins. Parnassus, 1968.

L'Engle, Madeleine. *A Wind in the Door*. Farrar, Straus & Giroux, 1973.

————. *A Wrinkle in Time*. Farrar, Straus & Giroux, 1962.

Lewis, C. S. The Chronicles of Narnia. 7 bks. Macmillan, 1970.

Lionni, Leo. *Frederick*. Pantheon, 1967.

Livingston, Myra Cohn. *The Way Things Are: And Other Poems*. Illus. Jenni Oliver. Atheneum, 1974.

Lobel, Arnold. *Mouse Tales*. Harper & Row, 1972.

Long, Claudia. *Albert's Story*. Illus. Judy Glasser. Delacorte, 1978.

McCloskey, Robert. *Make Way for Ducklings*. Viking, 1941.

McCord, David. *The Star in the Pail*. Illus. Marc Simont. Little, Brown, 1975.

Matthiesen, Thomas. *Things to See: A Child's World of Familiar Objects*. Platt & Munk, 1966.

Miller, Edna. *Mousekin's Golden House*. Prentice-Hall, 1964.

Minarik, Else. *Little Bear*. Illus. Maurice Sendak. Harper & Row, 1957.

Ness, Evaline. *Sam, Bangs and Moonshine*. Holt, Rinehart & Winston, 1966.

Norton, Mary. *The Borrowers*. Illus. Beth and Joe Krush. Harcourt Brace Jovanovich, 1953.

O'Brien, Robert. *Mrs. Frisby and the Rats of NIMH*. Illus. Zena Bernstein. Atheneum, 1971.

————. *Z for Zachariah*. Atheneum, 1975.

Paterson, Katherine. *Bridge to Terabithia*. Illus. Donna Diamond. Crowell, 1977.

————. *The Great Gilly Hopkins*. Crowell, 1978.

Peare, Catherine O. *The Helen Keller Story*. Crowell, 1959.

Peck, Richard. *Father Figure*. Viking, 1978.

Pienkowski, Jan. *The Haunted House*. Dutton, 1979.

Preston, Edna Mitchell. *Squawk to the Moon, Little Goose*. Illus. Barbara Cooney. Viking, 1974.

Rackham, Arthur, illus. *Mother Goose Nursery Rhymes*. Viking, 1975.

Raskin, Ellen. *Nothing Ever Happens on My Block*. Atheneum, 1966.

Rockwell, Anne and Harlow. *The Toolbox*. Macmillan, 1971.

Rockwell, Thomas. *How to Eat Fried Worms*. Illus. Emily McCully. Watts, 1973.

Sandburg, Carl. *Abe Lincoln Grows Up*. Illus. James Daugherty. Harcourt Brace Jovanovich, 1974 (1931).

Scheffer, Victor B. *The Seeing Eye*. Scribner's, 1971.

Sebestyen, Ouida. *Words by Heart*. Little, Brown, 1979.

Sendak, Maurice. *Where the Wild Things Are*. Harper & Row, 1963.

Sperry, Armstrong. *Call It Courage*. Macmillan, 1940.

Steptoe, John. *Stevie*. Harper & Row, 1969.

Sutherland, Zena, et al., eds. *The Arbuthnot Anthology of Children's Literature*. 4th ed. Lothrop, Lee & Shepard, 1976.

Swados, Elizabeth. *Lullaby*. Illus. Faith Hubley. Harper & Row, 1980.

Taylor, Mildred. *Roll of Thunder, Hear My Cry*. Illus. Jerry Pinkney. Dial, 1976.

Tunis, Edwin. *Colonial Living*. Crowell, 1976.

Viorst, Judith. *I'll Fix Anthony*. Illus. Arnold Lobel. Harper & Row, 1969.

Walsh, Jill Paton. *Unleaving*. Farrar, Straus & Giroux, 1976.

White, E. B. *Charlotte's Web*. Illus. Garth Williams. Harper & Row, 1952.

Wilder, Laura Ingalls. Little House Books. 9 vols. Harper & Row, 1973.

Wildsmith, Brian. *Brian Wildsmith's Puzzles*. Oxford Univ. Press, 1970.

Yashima, Taro. *Umbrella*. Viking, 1958.

Zindel, Paul. *The Pigman*. Harper & Row, 1968.

two

RALPH HODGSON   From *TIME, YOU OLD GIPSY MAN*

Time, you old gipsy man,
Will you not stay,
Put up your caravan
Just for one day?[1]

A Historical View of Children and Books

A few hours spent in the children's section at a local bookstore or public library can bring home some of the considerable changes that have occurred in children's books since you were a child. More striking is the vast transformation that has taken place since the first children's books were published, nearly four hundred years ago.

What can account for these tremendous changes? Primary among several factors is the way adults regard children. It followed from the early view of the child as a miniature adult that there was no need for a special literature for children, who were given ABC's and rhymed couplets to memorize until they could master simple Bible verses and other adult literature of the times.

Only when children came to be seen as developmentally distinct from adults, with unique perceptions of the world and with different needs and abilities, was there a demand for books that children could call their own.

We live in a society that recognizes childhood as a distinct and very special phase of life. Much time and effort are devoted to the education of children. Childhood and adolescence extend over a longer period than in any other culture, and most people have very definite ideas about what is suitable for children, both for their work and for their play.

In some ancient and primal societies there was a definite age—usually betokened by a ceremony, a rite of passage—at which the child passed into adulthood. From our perspective it seems that this point of demarcation often occurred quite early. In other societies, where children were regarded as miniature adults, little distinction was made between occupations and recreations for children and those for adults, and no special learning materials were provided for children. Still other societies viewed children as happy, unthinking creatures, not deserving of special consideration. Finally, children came to be viewed as seeking, learning individuals, and materials created especially for them developed rapidly.

Our society depends, and knows that it depends, on the success of the educational system. We have a formal plan of education, a concept of what it means to be educated, and an awareness of its importance. Further, this is a time of scientific child study. The disciplines of psychoanalysis and psychology devote considerable attention to the problems of childhood; and their findings are transmitted to parents and teachers by the mass media and professional or popular literature. Recent emphasis upon the primacy of reading in cognitive development has provided the impetus for a continuing expansion of the realm of children's books.

The prevailing perception of childhood is itself a part of the social, ethical, philosophic, and aesthetic forces of the given time, all of which also leave their mark on children's books. Books do not exist in a vacuum; they are shaped by the world around them. Henry Steele Commager states it succinctly:

. . . we have in literature not only a continuous record of childhood, but a continuous record of society as a whole, and—what is more important—of the ideals and standards that society wishes to inculcate into each new generation.[2]

In early colonial days, when religion was a prime motivator, books for children were of a religious nature. Later, as our young nation attempted to promote the merits of our democracy, children's books tended to focus on the glories of the nation. Gillian Avery points out that authors are surprisingly likely to dance to the tune of their age:

The heroes of the children's story show the qualities that the elders of any given time have considered desirable, attractive, or interesting in the young. Sometimes they have wanted the obedient, diligent, miniature adult, sometimes the evangelical child, or perhaps they have had a penchant for sprightly mischief, or sought to inculcate self-knowledge and independence. The surprise lies not in the swings of fashion in the pattern child, but in the unanimity of opinion at any given time about his qualities.[3]

This should not be surprising, however, since authors write from the world in which they live—the world they know. How else could we account for the rash of books about national heroes during wars, or the increase in books about blacks during the Civil Rights movement, or those about liberated females since the rise of the women's movement? Although some authors may write about whatever is currently fashionable, lasting trends represent generally accepted customs of conduct and right living. By depicting characters and circumstances that mirror society, authors leave for posterity pictures of the prevailing social codes that allow us to look into the world of their times.

Thus, in evaluating children's books of the past, we must be careful to remember the social climate in which they were written, and dare not assess them with today's values and standards; rather, they must be examined in terms of the social milieu in which they grew. In light of the current feelings concerning racial equality, we can look at earlier literature for children and see that black characters were stereotyped and narrowly depicted. Similarly, female characters in children's books published prior to 1970 seldom have the broad range of roles characteristic of females today.

Although we need to weigh these considerations when sharing books with children, they are not appropriate as a basis for studying the history of children's literature. Literary judgments of books of the past cannot be made in the context of current social knowledge and attitudes. It is important not to read twentieth-century preoccupations into seventeenth-, eighteenth-, and nineteenth-century literature.

THE COLONIAL PERIOD

Religious and Moral Instruction

To have a clear perspective on American children's literature of the colonial period it is necessary to recall the literary and social conditions in Europe at that time. The Gutenberg Bible, the first book to be printed with movable type, appeared only about 150 years before the Pilgrims settled in New England in 1620. At that time bookmaking was still a slow and costly process, and the Bible and other religious books were the chief products of the printer's craft. The English novel was not to appear for more than a hundred years, and would not be a well-developed genre until the 1800s. Prior to the 1800s books for pleasure reading, as we know it, were nonexistent; the earliest books were meant to inform. Further, there were few distinctions between books for children and books for adults.

During the 1600s people experienced literature largely as an oral tradition—through folk tales and fables, ballads, epics, romances, and the performances of wandering players and minstrels. Games and sports appear to have been more widely participated in than they are now. Slight distinction was made between forms of recreation appropriate for adults and those for children. Books were scarce and relatively expensive, and so were available primarily to a small, wealthy class of which few early colonists were members. In addition, living conditions were harsh for the general population, with everyone, including children, working long hours. During the dark winter months, even light to read by was a luxury.

The values held by the colonists reflected their desire to be obedient to the will of God and to cast off the wages of original sin in order to redeem the soul. These values were transmitted to children primarily through direct instruction by adults. The few books that were available for colonial children were, therefore, moralistic, didactic, and riddled with sanctions. Through books of catechism and lists of duties, children were instructed to live deeply spiritual lives, to obey their parents, to prepare for death, and to avoid incurring the wrath of God. Having been born in sin they could be saved only by cleansing themselves through piety.

John Cotton's *Milk for Babes, Drawn out of the Breasts of Both Testaments, Chiefly for the Spiritual Nourishment of Boston Babes in either England, but may be of like use for any Children* (1646) was a catechism for children. Explicit questions such as "How did God make you?" were to be memorized with the answer "I was conceived in sin and born in iniquity." James Janeway's *A Token for Children. Being An Exact Account of the Conversion, Holy and Exemplary Lives, and Joyful Deaths of several Young Children* (1672) was popular both in

THE COLONIAL PERIOD

	1636	*Youth's Behavior*
	1646	*Milk for Babes* (John Cotton)
● 1650		
	1657	*Orbis sensualium pictus* (John Amos Comenius)
	1665	*All the Principal Nations of the World* (Henry Winstanly)
	1672	*A Token for Children* (James Janeway)
● 1675		
	1678	*Pilgrim's Progress* (John Bunyan)
	1683–90	*The New England Primer* (Benjamin Harris)
● 1700		
	1702	*A Token for the Children of New England* (Cotton Mather)
	1715	*Divine & Moral Songs for Children* (Isaac Watts)
● 1725		
	1740	Chapbooks
	1744	*A Little Pretty Pocketbook* (John Newbery)
● 1750		
	1765	*The Renowned History of Little Goody Two Shoes* (Oliver Goldsmith)
	1769	Battledores
	1783	*Webster's Blue-Backed Speller* (Noah Webster)

England and in the colonies. Cotton Mather's American edition of the same book, *A Token for the Children of New England, or Some Examples of Children in Whom the Fear of God was Remarkably Budding Before they Died,* was first published in Boston in 1702. The preface of the 1749 edition reads:

You may now hear (my dear Lambs) what other good Children have done, and remember how they wept and prayed by themselves; how earnestly they cried out for an Interest in the Lord Jesus Christ. . . . Do you do as these Children did? Did you ever see your miserable state by Nature? Did you ever get by yourself and weep for sin?[4]

The Puritans regarded human nature as inherently sinful. According to their doctrine, children were born naturally depraved; religion led to salvation, and children were taught to read in order to read the Bible. The average life expectancy was not long, and the mortality rate among infants and children was very high. The Puritans are criticized for their grim concentration on deathbed scenes, but indeed, sickness and death were an ever-present part of their lives.

The funeral elegy was a popular form of literature for children. It gloomily detailed the death of a young person who had given wise counsel from

[107]

A

TOKEN

FOR THE

CHILDREN

OF

NEW-ENGLAND.

IF the Children of New-England should not with an Early Piety, set themselves to Know and Serve the Lord JESUS CHRIST, the GOD of their Fathers, they will be condemned, not only by the Examples of pious Children in other Parts of the World, the publish'd and printed Accounts whereof have been brought over hither; but there have been Exemplary Children in the Midst of New-England itself, that will rise up against them for their Condemnation. It would be a very profitable Thing to our Children, and

[108]

highly acceptable to all the godly Parents of the Children, if, in Imitation of the excellent JANE-WAY's Token for Children, there were made a true Collection of notable Things, exemplified in the Lives and Deaths of many among us, whose Childhood hath been signalized for what is virtuous and laudable.

In the Church-History of New-England is to be found the Lives of many eminent Persons, among whose Eminencies, not the least was, Their fearing of the Lord from their Youth, and their being loved by the Lord when they were Children.

But among the many other Instances, of a Childhood and Youth delivered from Vanity by serious Religion, which New-England has afforded, these few have particularly been preserved.

Cotton Mather's foreword to the New England edition of Janeway's *A Token for the Children of New England,* which presented stories of pious children held up as models to the reader.
(From *Yankee Doodle's Literary Sampler of Prose, Poetry & Pictures.* Selected from the Rare Book Collections of the Library of Congress and introduced by Virginia Haviland and Margaret N. Coughlan. Crowell, 1974.)

dying lips, as in Benjamin Colman's *A Devout Contemplation On the Meaning of Divine Providence, in the Early Death of Pious and Lovely Children. Preached upon the Sudden and Lamented Death of Mrs. Elizabeth Wainwright. Who Departed this Life, April the 8th, 1714. Having just compleated the Fourteenth Year of Her Age.* The first of many of its kind to come, this book contained an address to the mournful relatives of the deceased, an address to the children of the town, and the sermon at her funeral. Similar in kind was *A Legacy for Children, being Some of the Last Expressions, and Dying Sayings, of Hannah Hill, Junr. Of the City of Philadelphia, in the Province of*

Pennsilvania in America, Aged Eleven Years and near Three Months, published in 1717. The preface to this sentimental account of the death of a young Quaker states that it was published at the "ardent desire of the deceased." Hannah took several days to die and used the time to give moral advice to her family and friends. Children were taught to be in constant preparation for death and warned that it could come at any moment.

The simple text of horn books was mounted on a wooden paddle covered with a sheet of hammered cow's horn—hence the name.
(Facsimile of a horn book reproduced by The Horn Book, Inc., Boston, Mass.)

Books from this period affirm the Puritan ethic and the role of religious guidance in children's lives. The concern for children's souls and the search for salvation appear only grim and dreary to us today, but the images of fire and brimstone rife in these books were frighteningly real for Puritan children.

In contrast to this threatening picture is the work of Isaac Watts. Somewhat more subtle in his moralizing, Watts states in the preface to *Divine and Moral Songs for Children,* published in England in 1715, that his work is intended to "give the minds of children a relish for virtue and religion." Some of Watts's hymns are still sung today, notably "Joy to the World," "O God, Our Help in Ages Past," and "Hush, My Dear, Lie Still and Slumber."

Generally, damnation lay everywhere for the American child 300 years ago; preachers warned of the lurking danger of a sin-filled life, while death was a constant companion. Children who were trying to get to heaven faced the twin threats of impending death and a fall from grace. They and their elders feared Satan, who actively sought their souls. Working for salvation was a full-time job mirrored in books, social organizations, and daily life.

Hornbooks, first used around 1550, were small wooden paddles. Lesson sheets were attached to the paddles and covered with a sheet of transparent horn—made from hammered cow's horns—and fastened with small strips of brass. They were used to teach the alphabet (in upper and lower case) and often contained a list of syllables and vowels, the Lord's Prayer, or short verses. "In Adam's fall we sinned all" began one such alphabet verse. These instructional materials were aimed at combining the learning of skills with religious salvation—the ultimate goal.

Secular Tales: Chapbooks and Battledores

Chapbooks, crudely printed little books that were sold for a few cents by peddlers, or chapmen, contained badly retold stories. Despite their poor quality, the wide circulation of chapbooks created a readership for later books published for children.

Battledores, made of heavy, folded cardboard, offered alphabets, simple pictures, and religious precepts. Reverse side is shown opposite, on facing page. (Facsimile of a battledore reproduced by The Horn Book, Inc., Boston, Mass., from an original in the Boston Public Library.)

A dame school in session. Lessons consisted largely of recitation of Bible verses and syllabaries.
(Historical Pictures Service, Inc., Chicago, Ill.)

Perhaps even more important, they preserved many fairy tales and nursery rhymes for later and better reproduction.

The earnest spiritual leaders of the Puritans were dismayed by the sale of chapbooks. Cotton Mather decried the "foolish Songs and Ballads, which the Hawkers and Peddlars carry into all parts of the Countrey." He urged the publication of "Compositions full of Piety, and such as may have a Tendency to advance Truth and Goodness."[5]

Battledores, of folded cardboard, contained some of the same material found on hornbooks. The cover was embellished with crude woodcuts of animals, while the inside was filled with alphabets, numerals, and simple reading lessons. They were intended "to instruct and amuse" and contained only vague religious references. Battledores were prevalent in the mid-1700s, and their popularity continued well into the 1800s.

Books for Formal Education

Typical colonial schools were "dame schools," conducted in private homes, with children attending to their lessons while the teacher carried on her household duties. The curriculum included reading, writing, spelling, arithmetic, prayers, hymns, and catechism read from hornbooks, the Bible, and a few other books.

The New England Primer has often been called the most important book for children in the eighteenth century because it provided religious education in language children could understand. First published in London as *The Protestant Tutor* or *The Royal Primer,* its author, Benjamin Harris, was sent to the pillory in 1681 for printing the book, which was one of the first to depart from traditional religious catechism. Harris came to Boston in 1683, where he reissued the book as *The New*

ABCDEFGHIJKLM
NOPQRSTUV
WXYZ

◆

Aa Ee Jj Nn Rr Ww
Bb Ff KkOo Ss Xx
Cc Gg Ll Pp Tt Yy
Dd Hh MmQq Uu Zz

◆

abcdefghijklmn
opqrstuvwxyz

◆

ff fi ffi fl ffl æ œ

TRAIN up a child in the way he
should go, and when he is old, he
will not depart from it. PROV. xxii. 6.

[A facsimile of an original Battledore owned by the Boston Public Library.]
[Published by The Horn Book, Inc., Boston.]

ELKE.

OPOSSUM.

ADAM.

LESSON 1.					
at	et	it	ot	ut	
ax	ex	ix	ox	ux	
LESSON 2.					
ba	be	bi	bo	bu	by
ca	ce	ci	co	cu	cy
da	de	di	do	du	dy
LESSON 3.					
fa	fe	fi	fo	fu	fy
ga	ge	gi	go	gu	gy
la	le	li	lo	lu	ly
LESSON 4.					
na	ne	ni	no	nu	ny
pa	pe	pi	po	pu	py
ra	re	ri	ro	ru	ry
LESSON 5.					
sa	se	si	so	su	sy
ta	te	ti	to	tu	ty
za	ze	zi	zo	zu	zy

Below is a page from one version of *The New England Primer*, showing a portion of the alphabet with biblical and other rhymes as mnemonic devices. (The Rare Book Division, The New York Public Library.)

England Primer. Pictures in the *Primer* were crude woodcuts, but they held children's attention with their gruesomely detailed accounts of burnings and other punishments.

There were numerous editions of the *Primer* and, although the subject matter varied, all editions had certain features in common, including the alphabet in couplets of admonitory sentences, the catechism, and various hymns and prayers. A. S. W. Rosenbach says that "a woodcut of the burning of John Rogers, retained from *The Protestant Tutor*, the violently anti-Catholic forerunner of *The New England Primer*, was rarely omitted, and was usually accompanied by the verses of Advice to his Children."[6] Children were expected to learn it "up and down, backwards and forwards" until they had memorized it word for word.

George Fox, founder of the Society of Friends in England, wrote a primer called *Instructions for Right-Spelling and Plain Directions for Reading and Writing True English. With several delightful things very Useful and Necessary, both for Young and Old, to Read and Learn.* The first American edition of this text appeared in 1702 and the second was printed by Benjamin Franklin in 1737. This book contained sections designated "The Marks of a true Christian; the Catechism; the Names which the children of God are call'd by;

G   As runs the Glass, Our Life doth pass.

H   My Book and Heart Must never part.

I   JOB feels the Rod,— Yet bleſſes GOD.

K   Proud Korah's troop Was ſwallowed up

L   LOT fled to *Zoar*, Saw fiery Shower On *Sodom* pour.

M   MOSES was he Who *Israel's* Hoſt Led thro' the Sea.

Proverbs, tables of Numeration, Multiplication, etc.; A ready Way to reckon what one's daily Expenditure comes unto in a whole year; and Proper Names in Scripture, with their signification in English, and other useful information.''

MANNERS AND MORALS Major sections of the books the colonists gave their children were filled with directives for manners and morals. Any child who followed all these today would be considered priggish indeed. Typical of some of the rules for table manners are the following:

Grease not thy fingers or napkin more than necessity requires. Lean not they elbow on the table, or on the back of the chair. Stuff not thy mouth so as to fill thy cheeks, be content with smaller mouthfuls. Smell not of thy meat nor put it to thy nose, turn it not the other side upward to view it upon thy plate. Gnaw not bones at the table but clean them with thy knife (unless they be very small ones) and hold them not with a whole hand, but with two fingers.[7]

The authors of these behavior manuals tried to anticipate all situations where guidance might be required. One such compendium of rules included:

I. Twenty Mixt Precepts. II. One Hundred and Sixty Three Rules for Childrens Behaviour. III. Good Advice for the Ordering of their Lives; With a Baptismal Covenant. IV. Eight wholesome Cautions. V. A short, plain, & Scriptural Catechism. VI. Principles of the Christian Religion. VII. Eleven short Exhortations. VIII. Good Thoughts for Children, a compendious Body of Divinity; An Alphabet of useful Copies; and Cyprian's Twelve Absurdities.[8]

Treatises on manners and morals, popular since the beginnings of Western civilization, were circulated in manuscript form even before printed books were available. Codes of behavior differed for girls and boys; separate sets of instructions were written. *School of Good Manners,* written for boys in 1685, contains the following directives:

When in Company, If thou canst not avoid Yawning, shut thy mouth with thine hand or handkerchief before it, turning thy face aside. Spit not in the Room, but in the Corner, and rub it with thy Foot, or rather go out and do it abroad. If thy Superior be relating a Story, say not I have heard it before, but attend to it as if it were to thee altogether new; Seem not to question the Truth of it; If he tell it not right, snigger not, nor endeavor to help him out or add to his Relation.[9]

Children's behavior and manners were of great importance to the prim and unbending writers of the colonial period. It was recommended that children live well in order to die well, so nearly every book intended for other purposes also included instructions on proper behavior, with large doses of humility and correct manners. The didactic nature of books for children during this period established a trend that was to influence children's literature for years to come.

EMERGENCE OF CHILD-CENTERED EDUCATION

Throughout the seventeenth and eighteenth centuries, while the American colonists were wresting a living from an untamed country and winning their political independence, there were some in Europe whose thoughts were moving away from the stern Puritan morality and toward a child-centered system of education. The forerunners were Comenius, Locke, and Rousseau.

John Amos Comenius, a Moravian educational reformer and theologian, believed in a uniform system of education for all children and wrote a compendium of the information he believed every child should know. His *Orbis sensualium pictus* (*Illustrated World of the Senses*) appeared in 1657 and is particularly noteworthy because it was the first textbook in which pictures were as important as the text.

A stronger and more lasting influence came from John Locke, the English philosopher whose *Some Thoughts Concerning Education* (c. 1693) set forth the view that when an infant comes into the world his mind is a ''tabula rasa''—a ''blank slate''—upon which we can write what we choose. Accordingly, the impressions made upon the child are most important. Locke's precept,

"The light of reason is the candle of the Lord," caused him to view self-control and self-discipline as the ultimate goals of all education. He believed that children should be treated as rational creatures, that their curiosity was an expression of an appetite for knowledge. His view of childhood as a time of special significance, as well as his stress on human reason rather than religious precepts, had widespread influence throughout the eighteenth century.

Locke's work held many implications for early childhood training. Fire-and-brimstone preachers interpreted his philosophy (however mistakenly) to say that children should be brought up with strict discipline and that they should learn to bury their desires and endure privation even from the cradle. People had believed children had demonic natures, and Locke held out the promise of change through the careful use of rewards and punishments. He believed the strongest of these incentives to be esteem and disgrace.

Fifty years later, French philosopher Jean Jacques Rousseau startled the world with a view of the inner-directed nature of child growth. Here, too, were implications for the education of the child. In *Émile* (1762) Rousseau set forth the idea that the child is born with an innate sense of right and wrong that is only warped and distorted by the efforts of parents and teachers. Left to follow his natural impulses, the child, like the "noble savage," would develop and grow into an adulthood superior to that imposed by civilization.

Rousseau brightened the view of childhood by denying the idea of original sin and by deeming childhood important in its own right. His cry against the established educational practices led to a revision in thinking about how children learn. Still debated today is one of the primary principles of his theory of natural education: "Do not teach but let the child instruct himself through experience." He held that we should allow a child to follow his natural inclinations and take our lead from the child's questions. Another maxim, "Nature wants children to be children before they are men," embodied an affirmation of the importance of childhood and countered the "miniature adult"

notion prevalent at the time. He sowed the seeds for the ensuing "developmental" stance that was to lead to the scientific study of children.

Locke and Rousseau, alike in their positions that childhood is a special time, differed dramatically in their views of how the child learns. Locke's emphasis on the importance of training, discipline, and reason foretold the assertions of modern behavioral psychologists, who believe that the child's behavior is molded primarily by rewards and punishments the environment affords. Rousseau's views, on the other hand, prefigured those of developmental psychologists, who assert that the child's growth is primarily the result of the development of innate abilities.

THE NATIONAL PERIOD

At the beginning of the nineteenth century, the "good godly" books of the Puritans were still widespread and characters were noble, virtuous, and strongly religious. Reproving tones were used to describe "rough house and knock about" characters; the exemplary child was never guilty of rudeness or improper thoughts. Child characters were continually admonished to exercise moral judgment, and whenever they strayed from the path of righteousness, were ultimately punished.

Moral Instruction in the Guise of Entertainment

The child portrayed in books was polite, diligent, dutiful, and prudent. The young were expected to be well-informed and, to that end, to seek information doggedly. Questions by children, such as "Pray Papa, what is a camel?" would trigger a flow of factual information from the all-knowing adult. Parents, teachers, and ministers were unquestioned as ultimate sources of information and as translators of God's prescriptions for behavior.

Fairy tales and other imaginative literature were held in disfavor through most of the early 1800s. Belief in magical powers and the idea of receiving anything through means other than hard work and persistence were frowned upon. Few people wanted their children to waste time on frivolous stories, and it was widely believed that fairy tales were dangerous and corrupting influences on the child.

In spite of this earnest regard for instilling in children the fundamentals of moral and righteous living, there emerged early in the nineteenth century a belief that these same ideas could be made more palatable by presenting them in the guise of entertainment. Children had already taken for their own several books that had been written for adults, but in the early 1800s there began to appear a new type of book: stories expressly for enjoyment by children.

BOOKS FROM EUROPE Many of the books read by American children were first published in Europe, then brought to the New World. A few of these, in addition to the textbooks and books of religious and moral instruction, were epics and ballads, as well as narrative accounts of explorations and stories of adventure. Several books (in particular *Pilgrim's Progress, Robinson Crusoe, Gulliver's Travels,* and *The Swiss Family Robinson*), although not for children, were widely read by them. Despite the somber, moralistic tone of some of these,

children no doubt relished them for their departure from the rigid lessons of their textbooks.

In 1678, John Bunyan, who spent much of his life in jail for preaching against the accepted religious beliefs of his day, wrote *Pilgrim's Progress,* one of the epics. The story, of a Christian who travels from the land of destruction to the New Jerusalem, contains long theological dialogues but was enjoyed by children, who undoubtedly skipped the theology and savored the adventure.

In 1719, Daniel Defoe wrote for adults *The Wonderful Life, and surprizing adventures of the renowned hero, Robinson Crusoe: Who Lived Twenty-eight Years on an Uninhabited Island, Which he afterwards colonised,* but it, too, was soon adopted by children. *Robinson Crusoe* contains many of the elements that we look for in today's children's literature. For example, a hero, cast away on a remote island, is pitted against seemingly insurmountable odds and, through bravery, hard work, and the faith and trust of a valued friend, survives.

Jonathan Swift's *Gulliver's Travels,* written in 1726, combines fantasy and adventure in a story originally penned as a scathing social satire. Gulliver's voyage to the land of the Lilliputians, Brobdingnagians, and others interests children today.

Johann David Wyss used Defoe's survival theme in his *Swiss Family Robinson,* which was published in Switzerland in 1812. This story of a shipwrecked family is filled with pious and pedantic overtones, but the adventure and excitement also emerge to hold young readers' attentions even today.

These forerunners of the modern adventure story provided the basis for many stories that followed. It was not until the middle of the nineteenth century that educational thought caught up with Defoe, and people began to believe that children were not harmed by reading books that entertained as well as informed. True, these stories, too, were filled with righteous morality, but adventure was acceptable if the hero worked hard to reach his goal.

In addition to those adult books that children adopted from mainstream literature, other stories written specifically for young people became popular and many undoubtedly made their way to America. Although the stern work ethic that still prevailed well into the 1800s condemned such frivolity, many children did have access to fairy tales and other books published abroad including Charles Perrault's *Histoires ou contes du temps passé avec moralités* (*Stories or Tales of Times Past with Morals*) and *Contes de ma Mère l'Oye* (*Tales of Mother Goose*), which included Sleeping Beauty, Little Red Riding Hood, Blue Beard, Puss in Boots, Cinderella, and Tom Thumb.

In 1744, a London businessman, John Newbery, undertook a venture that was to affect children not only in England but in the United States and Canada as well. Newbery was an English merchant who perhaps saw in the popularity of Perrault's tales a potential market. He opened The Bible and The Sun, a London shop where he offered for sale, along with a variety of medicines, the first book that, though intended for instruction, was specifically designed to entertain children. *A Little Pretty Pocket-Book: Intended for the Instruction and Amusement of Little Master Tommy and Pretty Miss Polly* was a new attempt to teach children the use of the alphabet by way of diversion, and included rhymed directions and morals, games, fables, proverbs, rules of behavior, poems, and a rhyming alphabet. This publication and Newbery's bookshop earned him a place in children's literature matched by no other. In 1765 he published *The Renowned History of Little Goody Two Shoes.* Attributed to Oliver Goldsmith, the bittersweet story tells of Margery Meanwell, an orphan who is taken in by a virtuous clergyman and his wife. When they buy her new shoes she is so overcome with gratitude that she cries out, "Two shoes, Madam, see my two shoes"—and thus her name. ("Goody," an archaic, polite term for a woman of humble social standing, was often used as a title preceding a surname.) Margery, forced to leave the house of the clergyman, persists in learning to read and goes from house to house teaching other children. Her virtue and goodness spill forth from the pages, and even today "Little Goody Two Shoes" connotes a saintly, pious, albeit saccharine child.

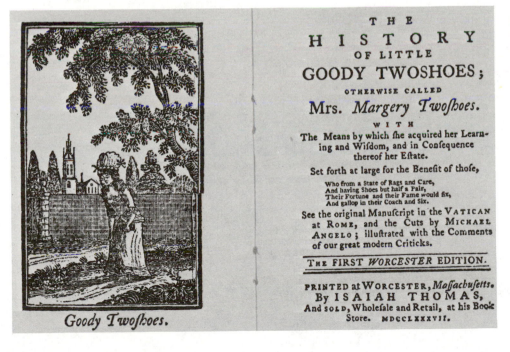

Title page from *The History of Little Goody Twoshoes,* attributed to Oliver Goldsmith. After much privation Goody Twoshoes acquired "learning and wisdom," which she passed on to others. (The Rare Book Division, The New York Public Library.)

With a market for children's books clearly established soon after Newbery's first efforts, there appeared a deluge of writers who capitalized on the opportunity to set forth their views on the instruction of children. A notable group of English women, who purported to know everything about raising children, used "Mrs." in front of their names as if to authenticate themselves as wives and mothers. The foremost figures, Mrs. Trimmer, Mrs. Barbauld, Mrs. Sherwood, and Mrs. Edgeworth, were stern sanctimonious matrons who filled their books with reproving tones and ominous threats of damnation for children who strayed from the righteous path. Oddly, these writers mistakenly believed that they were applying the principles of Locke and Rousseau by cloaking their lessons on moral and proper living in the guise of a story. Their assumption was that children would reject the errant characters, who were always soundly trounced, and thus learn the rules for decorous behavior.

In book after book children were put into situations that tested their characters and demanded strong moral convictions to make the correct decisions. Predictably, those who rose to the occasion remained properly virtuous, while those who failed accepted their punishments with remorseful penitence. Mrs. Maria Edgeworth's *Moral Tales* and *Early Lessons,* both written in 1801, contained stories of saintly children who were expected to act with adult consciousness and practicality. In one, Rosamond, a young girl of about seven, walking in London with her mother, stops to admire a purple jar in a chemist's window. She begs for the jar and her mother gives her a choice between buying the jar or new soles for her shoes. Rosamond opts for the jar and agrees to make do with her worn shoes for another month. When Rosamond empties the jar to refill it with fresh water for flowers, she finds that it is only plain glass that had been filled with colored water. Rosamond nobly endures her folly by limping around in her thin shoes and foregoes an outing with her father, who will not be seen with so slovenly looking a lass.

Among the many books produced by this venerable group was Mrs. Trimmer's *Fabulous Histories* (1786), famous for its fable "The History of the Robins." Since Locke approved of Aesop, Mrs. Trimmer used the fable form freely to teach children about the sins of selfishness, disobedience, and intolerance. She abhorred fairy tales and Mother Goose verses, believing that they would "fill the minds of children with confused notions of wonderful and supernatural events."[10] Likewise, she thought *Robinson Crusoe* would lead to "an early taste for a rambling life and a desire for adventures."[11]

Most of these didactic tales portray children as avid collectors of knowledge and truth. Among the all-knowing adults there was often a tutor whose sole purpose was to train the children in the ways of righteous and moral living. In Thomas Day's *The History of Sandford and Merton,* published in 1783, a wise teacher lectures endlessly to his young charges, Tommy Merton, the spoiled son of a rich man, and Harry Sandford, who is the son of a poor farmer and is held up as a model for Tommy. The tutor perseveres in his efforts to turn the stubborn and ignorant Tommy into a righteous and intelligent boy like Harry.

Harry Sandford in customary productive pursuits. His good example was held up to spoiled Tommy Merton in Thomas Day's *The History of Sandford and Merton.* Day tried to embody the ideas of Rousseau in these didactic stories.

PARLEY'S TALES

Peter Parley.   page 5:

THE
TALES
OF
PETER PARLEY.

—

HERE I am. My name is Peter
Parley. I am an old man. I am
very grey and lame. But I have
seen a great many things, and had
a great many adventures in my time,
and I love to talk about them. I
love to tell stories to children, and
very often they come to my house,
and they get around me, and I tell

Opening of *The Tales of Peter Parley About America,* stories of travel and adventure with a wise mentor that also offered lessons on geography and manners. There were more than one hundred titles in the series.
(From *Yankee Doodle's Literary Sampler of Prose, Poetry & Pictures.* Selected from the Rare Book Collections of the Library of Congress and introduced by Virginia Haviland and Margaret N. Coughlan. Crowell, 1974.)

BOOKS ORIGINATED IN AMERICA In America, while religious leaders continued to influence many writers who instructed the young in ways to lead proper and virtuous lives, other books were produced that were intended to imbue a feeling of patriotism. After the Revolutionary War, Americans, struggling to become a united nation, were eager to show that they were no longer a part of England. In trying to develop a sense of pride in their country, authors extolled the virtues of the new land to such an extent that many books were tainted with provincialism, and their case was often overstated; Americans were more fortunate than others, and people across the sea were to be pitied because they were strange and different.

Adventures of travel on the American frontier and courageous stories of daring battles with the Indians became a part of the reading material for young people. Most of these books retained the didacticism of the earlier "teach and preach" books but added lessons on history and geography as well as recitations on the new American "work hard and make good" ethic.

The American Sunday school movement grew along the same lines as those laid down by Mrs. Trimmer and her contemporaries. Between 1825 and 1850, Samuel and Charles Goodrich, brothers who believed in the power of books to guide children along the right path, collaborated with other writers, including Nathaniel Hawthorne, to produce the Peter Parley books. These books combined history, geography, and science with themes of truth and moral conduct. The Peter Parley character was a venerable older gentleman who answered—in *Tales of Peter Parley About America* (1827) and in more than one hundred titles that followed—the many questions children put to him. Although some were designed as textbooks, most were what were then called "toy books," which were books intended for out-of-school hours. They were simple, well illustrated, clearly

Frontispiece of Jacob Abbott's *Rollo in Paris* (of the series *Rollo's Tour in Europe*). The stories were essentially travelogues with advice on proper deportment. (The New York Public Library.)

printed, and inexpensive. Despite the wide approval for the information and codes of conduct in the books, the slight story frames were often criticized as contrivances that made children imaginative and indolent.[12] Nevertheless, the Peter Parley books were the first of a new kind of literature for children—series books.

The 1800s saw a deluge of series books, which children eagerly devoured as an alternative to their textbooks. Jacob Abbott wrote a series of books about a young boy who gratefully and eagerly learns all that he can about his world while remaining ever mindful of his supposedly superior American heritage. The series, *Rollo's Tour in Europe,* reads much like a travelogue, with wise Uncle George serving as guide and mentor to young Rollo. Endless descriptions of the geography and history of each place they visit are interspersed with frequent injunctions about responsibility, thriftiness, manners, and morals. Abbott, mindful of ways of encouraging sales, would conclude each book with a device aimed at provoking interest in the next. *Rollo in Paris* (1854), for example, concluded with Rollo's receiving an invitation to Switzerland (and an implied new adventure—in the next book). Rollo eventually returns to America, joyous and proud of his country, "with the satisfied consciousness of hailing from a land superior to those inhabited by foreigners."[13] The democratic form of government was still budding, and authors felt obliged to tell readers they were very lucky to live in America.

Books for General Instruction

The New England Primer continued to be a popular textbook for children during the first half of the 1800s. It was revised several times, with additions and deletions reflecting the changing American values. Three successive editions show the shifting attitudes toward the English crown in these couplets for the letter *K*:

(pre-1776)
Our King the good
No man of Blood
. . . .

(1780)
The king should be good
No man of blood

. . . .

(1782)
Kings should be good
Not men of Blood

In later editions (1784, 1786) the king is omitted altogether and a new verse substituted.[14]

During the period immediately following the American Revolution there was a great increase in the production of new textbooks for the young nation's children, the intent being to develop a purely American education. Books were marked by practicality, Noah Webster pointing the way with his spelling book—"a book from which American children could really learn how to spell." After various changes of title it was eventually known as *The Elementary Spelling Book,* or, more popularly, as "The Blue-Backed Speller" and was to sell more than eighty million copies during the nineteenth century.

A concern that children learn through understanding resulted in the publication of reading textbooks that were whole-word based instead of alphabet based, so that understanding word concepts, rather than reading by spelling and rote memorization, was the basis of acquiring information. Arithmetic books gradually began to concentrate on practical problems, often dealing with agricultural and industrial concerns of the new nation. The pride Americans felt in their new country, evident in the provincialism of content and topics, which often dealt with only "American" spelling, "American" mathematics, and American history, was mirrored in such titles as: *The American Primer* (1779) and *The American Accountant: Being a Plain, Practical and Systematic Compendium of Federal Arithmetic* (1797). The famous *History of the United States of America* (1822) was one of the abovementioned Peter Parley books by Charles Goodrich.

The textbook was the primary tool of education in early nineteenth-century America. Because school attendance was sporadic, at best, and children most often learned their lessons at home, the textbook was the one constant in a pupil's educational experience. Even where schools existed, teachers changed frequently and families were continually on the move to new territories. Difficulties in reaching distant schools, especially in bad weather, and the need for children to help their families with the daily chores of survival often precluded school attendance. Yet students always knew where they were in their studies: they had completed the Primer, or were halfway through Webster; textbooks marked pupils' progress. In addition, the method of study was always the same: students memorized the lessons and then recited them to the teacher or parent.

The United States was sixty years old before the first system of public education was established —in Massachusetts, under the leadership of Horace Mann. As the young country expanded westward, organized public education was slow to follow, so that decades would pass before all children had access to schools.

McGuffey's *Eclectic Readers,* first appearing in 1834, were considered a landmark. These were a series of books of increasing difficulty and were filled with good stories by many authors as well as a wide range of information. They provided a national literature and a national curriculum for a people who sought stability, a common culture, and continuity in their rapidly changing lives.

In the early nineteenth century the work of a Swiss educator, Johann Heinrich Pestalozzi, had an immediate and far-reaching reform influence on American education. This influence was extended throughout the century by such organizations as the American Institute of Instruction. New textbooks appeared that were based on the concept that the child learns best through his own ability to observe and understand. The first of these, *First Lessons in Arithmetic* (1821) by William Coburn, used teaching devices such as asking the child, "How many thumbs do you have on your right hand? How many on your left hand? How many on both together?"

50   Another innovation brought about by the spread of Pestalozzian theory was the use of what was known as the inductive method, which was based on a progression of learning from simple facts to ones more complex, with questions to lead the student to an understanding of rules and definitions. Today we accept these as common-sense approaches that also have a basis in research. Only by contrasting these innovative textbooks with those that had preceded them, in which children learned to read by memorizing meaningless syllables and learned to spell long lists of difficult and seldom-used words, is the child-centered approach seen in its true significance.

Escape in Fantasy

Children had little time for childhood in mid-nineteenth-century America. The social conditions of the time dictated that many young people work, often in truly horrible circumstances. The industrial revolution brought with it the necessity for a plentiful supply of cheap labor, and so women, children, and immigrants were enticed to the cities to lives that were filled with unremitting drudgery. Ruth Holland describes those lives in *Mill Child: The Story of Child Labor in America:*

> Twelve hours a day, six days a week, the children fed the endless, ravening hunger of the machines. Machines which were never tired, never sleepy, never sick. Nothing could stop the swift shuttles as they hurled themselves across the looms. And the children raced to keep up. Anyone who couldn't keep up was out. Out of a job. If the machines went faster, hands went faster. And eyes. The mechanical mouths were not choosy about what they ate. They would just as soon munch on a strand of hair as a silk thread from the bobbins.
> Little girls must not bend too closely over their work. A lock of hair could easily get caught in the whirring wheels. It took just a moment for the machine to pull the hair and a piece of scalp from a child's head. It was not an uncommon accident.[15]

Out of the thinking of a society that tolerated such conditions—and, indeed, often took pride in justifying them—grew a literature that served both as a fantasy escape from the harsh workaday world and a justification of the work ethic.

Around this time, two books that heralded changes to come were published in England. In 1806, Charles and Mary Lamb offered children *Tales from Shakespeare,* which was immediately successful and remains in circulation today. Two years later Charles Lamb produced *The Adventures of Ulysses,* which has been called a classic in its own right. Other rich and imaginative literary works were published as the century began: Washington Irving's *The Sketch Book of Geoffrey Crayon* (1819–20), which included "The Legend of Sleepy Hollow" and "Rip Van Winkle"—two stories set in the Catskill region—helped build an American treasury of legends.

CLOSE OF THE CENTURY: A MOVE TOWARD REALISM

The desire to instruct children in the work ethic was nowhere more evident than in the series Horatio Alger began in 1868. The humble characters, who reaped generous rewards for hard work and conscientiousness, epitomized the virtues of the day and had so strong an impact that the name of Horatio Alger still invokes this ethic. Alger was a prolific author, turning out more than one hundred stories in which the male characters acquire power and wealth through fortitude, dauntless courage, and the exercise of impeccable morality. The stories were dramatic—snatching a baby from a burning building or a damsel from the heels of a runaway horse were all in a day's work for the Alger hero—and children read them avidly. Alger broke literary tradition—for example, by setting *Ragged Dick* (1868) in a New York slum rather than in the customary rural surroundings. Subtitled "Street Life in New York with the Boot Blacks," it, like all the other books in the series, traces a poor boy's achievement of wealth and respectability.

Mass-produced series books that appeared during the middle of the nineteenth century set a trend that continues today. *Rollo Learning to Talk* (1834) by Jacob Abbott, *Boys of '76* (1876) by Charles C. Coffin, and *The Young Buglers* (1880) by George Henty signaled a torrent of such books to follow.

(*Left*) Walter Crane's illustrations for "The Fox and the Crane," "The Crow and the Pitcher," and "The Eagle and the Crow" reflect the essentially decorative character of his work, in which the text is often a prominent graphic element. ("The Fox and the Crane," "The Crow and the Pitcher," and "The Eagle and the Crow" by Walter Crane from *The Baby's Own Aesop* by Walter Crane. 1886. Frederick Warne & Co., Ltd., London & New York.)

(*Above*) A strong line, careful composition, and skillful draftsmanship mark all of Randolph Caldecott's illustrations, here of the traditional nursery rhyme "Four and Twenty Blackbirds." ("Sing a Song for Sixpence" by Randolph Caldecott from *Picture Book No. 2* by Randolph Caldecott. 1880. Frederick Warne & Co., Ltd., London & New York. Prints Division, The New York Public Library.)

Ring-a-ring-a-roses,
A pocket full of posies;
Hush! hush! hush! hush!
We're all tumbled down.

(*Above left*) Beatrix Potter's felicitous use of water color captures human emotions and character in representations of woodland and domestic animals. (Reproduced from *The Tale of Peter Rabbit* by Beatrix Potter by the permission of her publishers. Copyright © 1902 Frederick Warne & Co., Ltd., London & New York.)

(*Left*) Kate Greenaway's work set new styles in illustration and, by the end of the nineteenth century, in fashion, when parents began dressing their daughters in clothes designed along the lines of Greenaway's quaint styles. ("Ring-a-ring-a roses" by Kate Greenaway from *Mother Goose* by Kate Greenaway. 1881. Frederick Warne & Co., Ltd., London & New York.)

(*Above*) In a work of typical delicacy and exquisite detail by Arthur Rackham, fragile and lovely fairies tread gossamer webs in a threatening world. In addition to these insubstantial creatures, Rackham's gnomes, gnarled trees, and limpid pools inspired the work of many later artists. ("The Faeries Are Exquisite Dancers" by Arthur Rackham from *Peter Pan in Kensington Gardens* by J. M. Barrie. New York, 1906. Charles Scribner's Sons. Prints Divisions, The New York Public Library.)

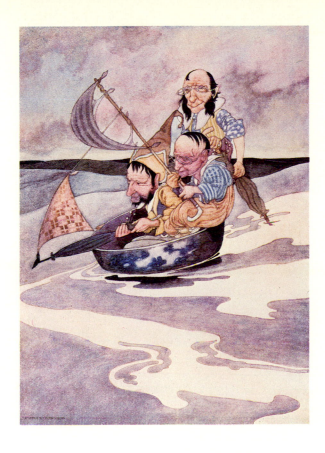

(*Above*) "Three Men in a Tub" negotiate the sea in one of Charles Robinson's imaginative illustrations, which capture the whimsy and nonsense of the Mother Goose rhymes. ("The Wise Men of Gotham" by Charles Robinson from *The Big Book of Nursery Rhymes* by Walter Jerrold. London, 190?. The Donnell Central Children's Room, The New York Public Library.)

(*Above right*) Ludwig Bemelmans used the stylized figures of the twelve little girls in his "Madeline" books as design elements. Here, clustered around Miss Clavel, their identical circular hats, boxy capes, and straight-line legs form a strongly symmetrical composition. (Reprinted by permission of Viking Penguin Inc. from *Madeline and the Bad Hat* by Ludwig Bemelmans. Copyright © 1957 by Ludwig Bemelmans.)

(*Right*) In this illustration from *Where Does the Butterfly Go When It Rains?* Leonard Weisgard departs from his representational style in strong saturated colors to create a delicate composition in a restrained palette. (Reprinted from *Where Does the Butterfly Go When It Rains?*. Copyright © 1961 by May Garelick, illustrations copyright © 1961 by Leonard Weisgard. A Young Scott Book, by permission of Addison-Wesley Publishing Company, Inc.)

(*Above*) Maurice Sendak cooks up a playful cityscape composed of kitchen objects in this scene from *In the Night Kitchen*. (Illustration from *In the Night Kitchen* written and illustrated by Maurice Sendak. Copyright © 1970 Maurice Sendak. By permission of Harper & Row, Publishers, Inc.) (*Right*) Using rich, muted colors and drawing on a period folk style, Janina Domanska portrays King Krakus, Polish folk hero, contending with a dragon. Her work is reminiscent of Walter Crane's in its exploitation of the whole picture space. (Illustration from *King Krakus and the Dragon* by Janina Domanska. Copyright © 1979 by Janina Domanska. Reproduced by permission of Greenwillow Books, A Division of William Morrow & Company, Inc.)

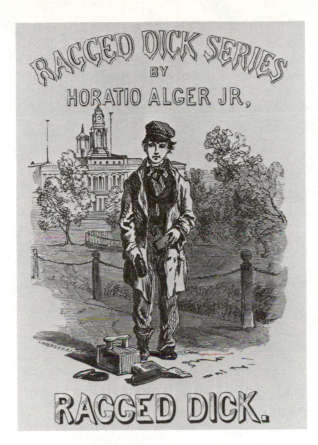

Cover of *Ragged Dick,* one of many formula stories by Horatio Alger, Jr., with the theme that hard work and exemplary behavior will be rewarded with success.
(The New York Public Library.)

girls devoured these stories and eagerly followed Elsie throughout her lifetime. (Unlike many children's series book characters, Elsie grew old—somewhat more quickly than her audience—leaving the secure world of childhood and quickly passing through the traditional roles of girlhood, wifehood, motherhood, and, to continue the tears, widowhood.)

Elsie Dinsmore's sentimental righteousness made the stories enormously popular throughout the last half of the 1800s. In a typical episode Elsie's father asks her to sing for his friends during a Sunday afternoon tea. Although Elsie shows unremitting respect toward her father, her strict piety will not allow her to sing on the Sabbath:

Elsie sat with her little hands folded in her lap, the tears streaming down from her downcast eyes over her pale cheeks. She was trembling, but though there was no stubbornness in her countenance, the expression meek and humble, she made no movement toward obeying her father's order.[16]

Elsie remains sitting, unable to bring herself to sing, until she faints, whereupon her forgiving father carries her gently to her room. Elsie Dinsmore is one link in the chain of tearful, saintly girls that includes Little Goody Two Shoes, Rosamond (of *The Purple Jar*), and the somewhat more believable *Sara Crewe,* written by Frances Hodgson Burnett in 1888.

Gradually a new type of literature appeared in which characters were more human. Priggishness gave way to devilment as boys—but not yet girls—were portrayed more realistically. Thomas Bailey Aldrich's semiautobiographical *The Story of a Bad Boy* (1870) acknowledges tricks, pranks, and mischievous behavior in a "boys will be boys" spirit:

It was a custom observed from time immemorial for the towns-boys to have a bonfire on the Square on the midnight before the Fourth. I did n't ask the Captain's leave to attend this ceremony, for I had a general idea that he would n't give it. If the Captain, I reasoned, does n't forbid me, I break no orders by going. Now this was a specious line of argument, and the mishaps that befell me in consequence of adopting it were richly deserved.[17]

However, the "Immortal Four"—Martha Farquharson [Finley], Horatio Alger, Jr., William Taylor Adams (who wrote under the name Oliver Optic), and Charles Austin Fosdick (who wrote under the name Harry Castlemon)—win the prize for productivity, in which it was quantity, not quality, that counted.

While books for boys, filled with thrills of travel and adventure, urged them to strive and succeed, those for girls urged their readers to practice the tamer virtues of kindness, sympathy, and piety.

Martha Farquharson [Finley] epitomized melodrama in the Elsie Dinsmore stories, wherein tears and prayers were called forth regularly. Young

This book began an era of "bad boy literature" that peaked in Mark Twain's *The Adventures of Huckleberry Finn* fourteen years later, but continues even now.

The last half of the nineteenth century brought a surge of inexpensive, aesthetically poor, mass-produced books written according to a formula and printed on spongy, poor quality paper. These series books—unlike those, such as The Peter Parley books, of the early part of the century—had no literary distinction or originality to recommend them. Children, however, devoured them with the same uncritical enthusiasm of readers of today's series books. The so-called Immortal Four were responsible for this bumper crop of fast-moving adventures. Finley, Alger, Adams, and Fosdick all used a variety of pseudonyms under which they ground out hundreds of books. This wave of fast-paced, cheap, and extremely popular books provoked objections that recall Mrs. Trimmer's distaste for *Robinson Crusoe,* but as entertainment they gained much popularity with children.

Building on the success of Horatio Alger and the Elsie Dinsmore stories, other writers produced quantities of fast-moving adventure stories. To turn the growing demand to account, Edward Stratemeyer, an enterprising writer, developed a scheme that was to turn into a vast syndicate responsible for the mass publication of millions of tawdry juvenile books—some available even today. With this development, children no longer had to read books under an adult's Sunday supervision and with clean hands; inexpensive production had made books dispensable.

After working for pulp magazines, Stratemeyer wrote *Under Dewey at Manilla* shortly after the Spanish-American War. He enjoyed writing war stories and began several series with America's wars as background. As Stratemeyer's syndicate grew, he limited his participation to outlining the stories and hiring hack writers to do the actual writing, producing in this way the Colonial Boys series, the Mexican War series, and the Pan American series. He continued with other series—including those of the Rover Boys, the Motor Boys, Tom Swift, and the Bobbsey Twins—using the pseudonyms Arthur Winfield, Clarence Young, Victor Appleton, and Laura Lee Hope, respectively. Stratemeyer produced sixty-eight different series under forty-six pseudonyms. At his death in 1935, his daughter, Harriet Stratemeyer Adams, took over the massive operation, which is still producing books.

Harriet Stratemeyer Adams continued the family tradition by writing—under the pen name Carolyn Keene—Nancy Drew stories—more than eighty of them! The Nancy Drew series and the Hardy Boys series, another Stratemeyer creation, are the best-selling of all series books and have been translated into Spanish, French, German, Italian, Danish, Finnish, Norwegian, Swedish, and Icelandic. Despite bitter criticism from literary critics, Stratemeyer's books, like Enid Blyton's cozy stories of children in rural England, continue to sell amazingly well.

Girls were given an alternative to the melodrama of Elsie Dinsmore when Louisa May Alcott wrote *Little Women* in 1868. Although considered too worldly by fundamentalist leaders, *Little Women* has been called the century's most signifi-

Louisa May Alcott grew up in what she described as "genteel poverty." Her father was Bronson Alcott, a visionary whose educational and social views were well in advance of his times, and their neighbors were outstanding minds of the day—Emerson, Thoreau, Hawthorne. Rich in books and ideas, Louisa's life and writings reflect many of the time's popular literary and social movements. Magazine stories and cheap novels in the gothic style inspired by Mary Shelley's *Frankenstein* were great popular favorites, and Louisa began her life's work of rescuing her beloved family from chronic poverty by scribbling these potboilers for the ever-hungry publishers.

She was deeply affected by—and involved in—the social issues of her day, emancipation of the slaves being the greatest of these. Louisa spent several months as a nurse during the Civil War caring for wounded soldiers in an army hospital, where conditions were deplorable. With her own health impaired, Louisa returned home from this exhausting experience to produce her first serious book, *Hospital Sketches* (c. 1866). Its instant popularity was an inspiration to continue writing serious fiction. Her astute publisher, Thomas Niles, encouraged her to do "something for girls." *Little Women* (1868) was the result. In its pages and in those of the several novels and dozens of short stories that followed, readers can glimpse much of popular culture of the times.

Louisa herself was an avid reader, and through Jo (in *Little Women*) we see the influence of *Pilgrim's Progress* and the work of Charles Dickens. We also hear the story of Rosamond (of *The Purple Jar*) retold and find occasional references to the very popular novels of "dear Miss Yonge," one of Alcott's predecessors in writing the American family story.

A succession of novels followed *Little Women: An Old-Fashioned Girl* (1869), *Little Men* (1871), *Work* (1873), *Eight Cousins* (1874), *Rose in Bloom* (1876), *Under the Lilacs* (1877), *Jack and Jill* (1879), and *Jo's Boys* (1886); all of these are still widely read. Alcott's short stories have also been reissued: *Glimpses of Louisa* appeared in 1968 to celebrate her centenary, as did *An Old-Fashioned Thanksgiving*, which was reissued in picture-book format.

Interested readers can find additional information in such sources as "Louisa May Alcott and the American Family Story" in *A Critical History of Children's Literature,* by Cornelia Meigs et al.; *Bronson Alcott: His Life and Philosophy,* by F. B. Sanborn and W. T. A. Harris; and Meigs's *Invincible Louisa.*

LOUISA MAY ALCOTT

cant piece of fiction. Alcott's subsequent work focused on the homespun virtues of the wholesome American family.

Girls also found pleasure in a series of family stories by Margaret Sidney (pseudonym of Harriet M. Lothrop). *The Five Little Peppers and How They Grew* (1880) begins a series—filled with touching sentimentality—about a widowed mother and her brave struggles to raise her children. Embedded in the idyllic family life portrayed is the idea that generosity, humility, and proper manners earn rewards, whereas the contrary warrant atonement.

The turn of the century brought a new surge of stories for children. Although moral overtones were not forgotten, most books now contained humor, adventure, and spirit—and enough connection with rough-and-tumble to provide a firm ground for the even more true-to-life stories that were to follow.

Dora V. Smith describes *The Children's Catalog* of 1909 as being

filled with stories of vigorous battles on land and sea, in which American boys took on Indians, foreign invaders, phantom vessels, grizzlies, or their brothers on one side or other of the Mason-Dixon line.[18]

Boys were reading George Grinnell's *Jack among the Indians* (1900), Henry H. Clark's *Joe Bentley, Naval Cadet* (1899), Everett T. Tomlinson's *Boy Soldiers of 1812* (1895), and George Henty's *Under Drake's Flag* (1883) and *With Kitchener in the Soudan* (1903). Girls' stories retained their emphasis on the quieter virtues of home and family. Among the favorites were Kate Douglas Wiggin's *Rebecca of Sunnybrook Farm* (1903), Lucy M. Montgomery's *Anne of Green Gables* (1908), and Frances Hodgson Burnett's three books, *Little Lord Fauntleroy* (1886), *Sara Crewe* (1888), and *The Secret Garden* (1911). One story, *Pollyanna* (1912), by Eleanor Porter became so well-loved that the character's name still symbolizes an ever-joyful optimistic disposition.

As interest in other peoples grew and provincialism waned, authors began to write about children in lands beyond the American shores. Mary Mapes Dodge wrote *Hans Brinker; or, The Silver Skates* (1865), which, though ostensibly to teach American children about life in far-off Holland, was enjoyed most for its exciting story. The drama of the skating race and the picture of the poor family combine to offer a tale of courage and adventure more lasting than the pallid geography lesson. Similarly, Johanna Spyri wrote *Heidi* (1884) to give a glimpse of life in Switzerland, but children loved it for its portrayal of a young girl's relationship with her grandfather.

There is a tendency to regard the books of yesteryear as "quaint" and to laugh at the simple virtues and life styles pictured in them. Perhaps we should, rather, applaud those writers of the past without whom our vision of former days would be so much poorer. Moreover, those books from the recent and distant past that have become classics help us to recognize the universal—as opposed to simple timeliness—in children's books.

CHILDREN'S LITERATURE ESTABLISHED

The Beginnings of Fantasy

Once upon a time, before there was fantasy as we know it, there was folklore. From what began as the oral tradition of folklore and then was invested with the convoluted morals and manners of the seventeenth and eighteenth centuries, there finally emerged a literature with the sole purpose of delighting the fancy. But not until the middle of the nineteenth century, with the publication of *Alice in Wonderland* (1865), by Lewis Carroll, did children have fantasy they could call their own.

Fairy tales came in and out of favor through the two hundred years of American history. Told to children and adults long before writing was invented, the ethereal tales, tough as shoe leather in their ability to survive, reappear time and again. Puritan children, their minds filled with Biblical stories, heard few of them. Even though the tales had, by their time, been written down, Victorian children, too, heard few of them, for morality and the seriousness of life were the keynotes of their time, and fairy tales were considered frivolous.

Surviving in oral form and in underground chapbooks sold by peddlers, fairy tales burst forth sporadically into the legitimate marketplace. In *Contes de ma Mère l'Oye* (1697), Charles Perrault wrote down the tales told in the French court, but more than thirty years passed before his collection was translated into English (1729), and another fifty years before there was an American edition (1785). Although the Grimm Brothers' *Household Tales* (*Kinder- und Hausmärchen*, 1812) was translated into English in 1823 (by Edgar Taylor), children rarely saw the stories again because of the conservatism of educational thought of the time.

Hans Christian Andersen is credited with the literary fairy tale, which first appeared in his *Fairy Tales* (1835), translated into English by Mary Howitt in 1846. Andersen adapted basic folk tale themes, adding his own fanciful elaborations, including a strong measure of pathos and melancholy. His work shows clear connections between folklore and fantasy.

Despite repeated attempts by well-intentioned adults to subvert them, fanciful stories survived and eventually blossomed in full glory near the end of the 1800s. In 1863 Charles Kingsley, a clergyman and scientist, wrote one of the earliest fanciful tales—*The Water Babies*, which was grounded in science and laced with the stern moral lessons of his day. In the story (written for Kingsley's son), Tom, a chimney sweep, is carried off into a world under the water, where he becomes a Water Baby. The not so subtle lessons evident in the names of characters—such as stern Mrs. Bedonebyasyoudid, loving Mrs. Doasyouwouldbedoneby, and powerful Mother Carey —show that, even though fantasy had emerged, it did so still laden with the moral lessons of its predecessor forms. The story reflects Kingsley's view that redemption can be attained through love and compassion as well as punishment, and the mixture of fact and fancy attempts a reconciliation of the seemingly conflicting views of science and faith. Through this period fantasy continued to be burdened with heavy moral lessons; it was as if children needed to be given a dose of goodness with every taste of imagination.

THE BEGINNINGS OF FANTASY	
1484	*Aesop's Fables* (printed by Caxton)
1697	Perrault's *Contes de ma Mère l'Oye*
● 1725	
1726	*Gulliver's Travels* (Jonathan Swift)
1729	English translation, *Tales of Mother Goose*
● 1775	
1785	First American edition, *Tales of Mother Goose*
● 1800	
1808	*The Adventures of Ulysses* (Charles and Mary Lamb)
1812	*Kinder- und Hausmärchen* (Jakob and Wilhelm Grimm)
1819	"Rip Van Winkle," "Legend of Sleepy Hollow" in *The Sketch Book* (Washington Irving)
1823	Grimms' *Popular Stories* translated
● 1825	
1835	*Fairy Tales* (H. C. Andersen)
● 1850	
1856	*Heroes* (Charles Kingsley)
1863	*The Water Babies* (Charles Kingsley)
1864	*Journey to the Center of the Earth* (Jules Verne)
1865	*Alice in Wonderland* (Lewis Carroll)
1867	*Ting-a-Ling* (Frank Stockton)
1871	*At the Back of the North Wind* (George Macdonald)
● 1875	
1881	*Uncle Remus* stories (Joel Chandler Harris)
1883	*The Merry Adventures of Robin Hood* (Howard Pyle)
1889	*The Blue Fairy Book* (Andrew Lang)
1891	*Pinocchio* (C. Collodi)
1894	*The Jungle Book* (Rudyard Kipling)
1899	*The Story of the Treasure Seekers* (E. Nesbit)
● 1900	
1900	*The Wizard of Oz* (L. Frank Baum)
1902	*The Tale of Peter Rabbit* (Beatrix Potter)
1904	*Peter Pan* (James M. Barrie)
1906	*The Fairy Ring* (Kate Douglas Wiggin)
1908	*The Wind in the Willows* (Kenneth Grahame)
1911	*Peter and Wendy* (James M. Barrie)
1920	*The Story of Dr. Dolittle* (Hugh Lofting)
● 1925	
1926	*Winnie-the-Pooh* (A. A. Milne)
1934	*Mary Poppins* (Pamela Travers)

Although *Gulliver's Travels* (1726) and *The Water Babies* (1863) preceded them, *Alice's Adventures in Wonderland* (1865) and *Through the Looking Glass* (1871), by Charles Dodgson (pseudonym, Lewis Carroll), are recognized as the first significant works of fantasy for children. Dodgson, cleric and mathematics professor who wrote under the name of Lewis Carroll to avoid identification with his books, often told stories to the three Liddell girls, daughters of a minister friend at Christ Church, Oxford. On an afternoon boat ride, his favorite, Alice, asked for a story with nonsense. The story she heard became the world-famous one after he wrote it for her the following Christmas.

The curious, complicated kind of nonsense Alice Liddell loved intrigues readers, who become curioser and curioser along with Alice, who, when she saw a white rabbit with pink eyes check his pocket watch, muttering "I shall be too late,"

ran across the field after it and was just in time to see him pop down a large rabbit hole under the hedge. In another moment down went Alice after it never once considering how in the world she was to get out again.[19]

Thus begins the story of memorable madness read by generations of children and adults alike. The story is filled with subtleties that poke fun at English social customs of the time; the satiric meaning often eludes modern readers, but the cleverness of the story holds them.

George Macdonald, a personal friend of Charles Dodgson, read *Alice* to his own children while it was still in manuscript form. Macdonald's writing moved toward more symbolic, religious allegorical fantasy—a forerunner of C. S. Lewis's "Narnia" series to come later. In *At the Back of the North Wind* (1871), Macdonald presents a story of allegorical search and wearisome trials before joy, a theme that reverberates throughout literature. One night little Diamond, a child with divine powers, who was named after old Diamond, a horse above whose stall he sleeps, hears a voice from a knothole his mother had stuffed with paper: "What do you mean, little boy—closing up my window?"[20] In this way Diamond meets the North Wind, who is to take him on magical journeys through sea storms and great cathedrals. He walks on ice to the Back of the North Wind, where he feels the disturbing awareness that, although nothing went wrong there, neither was anything quite right.

Diamond's family becomes poor and they take up the hansom cab business in London, but fortunately they are able to buy old Diamond to pull the cab. When his father is ill, Diamond takes over. Many times during his busy life the North Wind comes to him in different guises—as an old woman, a beautiful young woman, or a terrible one—but each time he recognizes her. Later, Diamond is taken into a household as a page and is given the religious instruction whose basis he had known intuitively. Through all he longs to be with the North Wind, and, at last, the weary child finds his way there—through death—to eternal happiness.

American children received their first fantasy from English writers. One of these was E. Nesbit, who delighted children with the series *The Story of the Treasure Seekers* (1899), which featured the six mischievous Bastable children, who had an unmistakable propensity for getting into trouble. The mixture of realism and fantasy in their chaotic adventures laid the foundations for many stories to come, notable among them P. L. Travers's *Mary Poppins* (1934).

A classic story-play by J. M. Barrie, *Peter Pan* (1904), loved by adults and children everywhere, takes us to Never-Never Land to meet Peter Pan, a boy who refuses to grow up, and Tinker Bell, a fairy who loses her shadow. Wendy, John, and Michael—proper children with proper parents—are taken by Peter Pan to Never-Never Land, where they encounter a ticking crocodile, lost boys, redskins, and Captain Hook and his pirates. The children begin to forget their parents in the time-held-still place, but a story Wendy tells convinces her brothers and the lost boys that they should return to reality in order to continue the serious business of growing up. A tense moment in the play occurs when Tinker Bell seems certain to die. Only one thing will save her—the belief, by children, in fairies. And, when Peter Pan asks the audience, "Do you believe in fairies," the usually tremendous roar of "Yes. Yes. We do!" assures Tinker Bell's life for yet another generation.

The truth in fantasy is so strong that it continues to permeate our culture in the form of film—*Pinocchio, The Wizard of Oz, Mary Poppins;* opera—*Cinderella (La Cenerentola);* ballet—*The Sleeping Beauty;* Broadway shows—*Peter Pan;* and continual interpretations and retellings by talented illustrators and storytellers—*Thumbelina* as retold by Amy Erhlich and illustrated by Susan Jeffers.

Fantasy is durable and universal for it tran-

Scene from the film *The Wizard of Oz,* adapted from the book by L. Frank Baum. (Culver Pictures / Copyright © 1974 Metro-Goldwyn-Mayer, Inc.)

scends time and place across the generations. Timeless in its appeal, it rises from the depths of folklore, deeply ingraining itself in human lives, forever feeding the imagination.

Poetry

In the day of literature for children, poetry is just a-dawning. And, although great poetry is written much less often than prose, what does exist would seem capable of enduring through the ages. Taste and fashion in poetry change less rapidly than in the case of prose stories, particularly realistic ones. Outstanding poetry from days gone by comes alive for each succeeding generation. Poetry's history, which meshes with that of all literature, is indistinguishable at times from the history of adult poetry,

for children often appropriate works that were intended for adults.

Three hundred years ago young children had poetic forms and lilting songs to delight the ear in the verses of Mother Goose, and a great deal of doggerel and sentimental stanzas existed as well. Riddles and traditional rhymes were also plentiful, but of actual poetry written for children there was little until the middle of the nineteenth century.

In children's poetry, as in all other literary forms, there were the rare exceptions of truly great works that became pieces of lasting attraction. William Blake, who lived near the edge of London in relentless poverty from birth to the end of his days, was one of the first to capture the spirit of childhood in verse. Barely noticed in his lifetime, his *Songs of Innocence* (1789) was eventually recognized as the masterpiece it truly was. Although not written for children, the poems in *Songs of Innocence* had, in their portrayal of the human mind before the restraints of reason and maturity set in, a childlike quality. In the introduction, Blake says:

Piping down the valleys wild,
Piping songs of pleasant glee,
On a cloud I saw a child,
And he laughing said to me:
"Pipe a song about a Lamb!"[21]

The answer to the child's request, "Little Lamb, who made thee?" is one poem, among many others in the collection, that achieved prominence. Blake's poems, which show the child as refreshingly curious and responding intuitively to unfathomable beauty, are a benchmark for all subsequent poetry of this kind.

Ann and Jane Taylor, daughters of a British engraver, began writing verses when they were very young. Ann, the elder, won a puzzle contest sponsored by publishers Harvey and Darton, and began

to contribute to their magazine; Jane soon followed her sister's lead. When Ann was twenty-two and Jane twenty-one, *Original Poems for Infant Minds by Several Young Persons* (1804) was published. (Adelaide O'Keefe and their seventeen-year-old brother Isaac also contributed to the volume.) Among their memorable verses, brightened with childlike spirit despite an intent to teach a lesson, and read and memorized avidly by children through centuries to follow, are "Twinkle, Twinkle, Little Star," by Jane Taylor, and "Welcome, welcome little stranger, to this busy world of care," by Ann Taylor. Their poems were rare exceptions among the somber lessons of their time that were taught in biblical verses and hymns, most of which, sentimental and sermonlike, are now forgotten.

Many early stories and poems became so commonly known and so widespread it is difficult to remember they are not from Mother Goose or folklore: "Mary Had a Little Lamb" (1830), for example, by Sarah Josepha Hale; "Cradle Hymn" (1715), by Isaac Watts, which began, "Hush thee, my dear, lie still and slumber"; "The Three Bears" (1834–37) by Robert Southey; and "'Will you walk into my parlor!' said the Spider to the Fly" in *Fireside Verses* (1799–1888) by Mary Howitt.

Most nineteenth-century poets still had a strong desire to teach a lesson, but some went beyond the moralistic verses. Some of the early English poets were able to portray life from the perspective of children and to sing the pleasures of childhood as children saw them. Among these—some of whom continued the tradition begun by William Blake and added to the poetic tradition we draw upon today—were Edward Lear, *A Book of Nonsense* (1846); Robert Louis Stevenson, *A Child's Garden of Verses* (1885); A. A. Milne, *When We Were Very Young* (1924) and *Now We Are Six* (1927); William Roscoe, *The Butterfly's Ball* (1806); William Allingham, *In Fairyland* (1870), in which "The Fairies" begins, "Up the airy mountain, Down the rushy glen"; and William Brighty Rands, "Wonderful World," which begins "Great, wide, beautiful, wonderful World, With the wonderful water round you curled."

An American, Clement Moore, produced a work, *A Visit from St. Nicholas* (1823), that would keep the magic of Christmas in our hearts. Written for his children, it appeared (anonymously) in the *Troy* (N.Y.) *Sentinel* on December 23, 1823; it was one of the rarities in its complete freedom from the didacticism so prevalent at the time. Children's delight in the visions his words called forth caused them to take it for their own and, as an owner's right, to rename it "The Night Before Christmas," which it shall forever remain. Moore's call

To the top of the porch, to the top of the wall!
Now, dash away, dash away, dash away all![22]

might have been signaling the beginning of the boundless visions future poets would paint.

Illustration

It may be true, as some educators claim, that the pictures children see in their minds are better than any an illustrator can make. Still there is no doubt that book illustration has developed into a fine art through the establishment of publishing specifically for children. Illustrations can carry great importance because the art in children's books may be the only art they ever see; certainly it is the first they see and has a lasting impact upon the development of a taste for beauty.

Illustrated books can be considered to have begun with the artless (and often anonymous) woodcuts of children's eighteenth-century catechism pages. Among the earliest outstanding work is that by George Cruikshank (1792–1878). In Cruikshank's day, the artist was limited because the final say was always the engraver's. Despite the restrictions, his delicate artistry showed a feeling for the magic of the folk tale and the ephemeral qualities of the fairies so prevalent in children's stories and poems. Cruikshank illustrated *Grimm's Fairy Tales* (1823) in a luxuriant style that extended the fancy of the tenacious tales; his interpretations were so enchanting they were republished in Germany with the original text. Cruikshank came into his own with fairy art, and *George Cruikshank's*

The white rabbit, by John Tenniel for Lewis Carroll's *Alice's Adventures in Wonderland* and *Through the Looking Glass.* Carroll and Tenniel conferred frequently during the preparation of the drawings.

Fairy Library (1853–54), published in four volumes, contains some of his most memorable work.

At first artists merely lightened the text with decoration or with incidental illustrations that filled gaps in the page or emphasized crucial moments in the story. Because of technical limitations they seldom achieved a perfect match between their picture images and the author's literary images.

Full-fledged illustrations—by Walter Crane, John Tenniel, Kate Greenaway, and Randolph Caldecott—soon followed. Walter Crane, the son of a portrait painter, abhorred the cheap, crudely illustrated books for children of his day. Apprenticed to a wood engraver, he would wander at lunch time to the offices of *Punch,* a popular magazine of high quality. Despite the venture's high financial risk, publisher Frederick Warne brought out Walter Crane's first nursery picture books—*Sing a Song of Sixpence, The House that Jack Built, Dame Trot and Her Comical Cat,* and *The History of Cock*

Profile

O ring the bells! O ring the bells!
  We bid you, sirs, good morning;
  Give thanks, we pray,—our flowers are gay.
  And fair for your adorning.

Under the Window

KATE GREENAWAY

Kate Greenaway has few peers when it comes to conveying the beauty of children and the world in rose-colored images.

Born in London on March 17, 1846, the daughter of Elizabeth Jones and John Greenaway, Kate was devoted to her father, a prominent wood-engraver and draftsman, and delighted in those times when her father brought his wood blocks home to complete an engraving job. His work was a source of inspiration to her.

When Kate Greenaway was two years old she went to live on an aunt's farm in Nottinghamshire, where she learned first-hand a love for nature—hedgerows, apple blossoms, and especially the lovely flowers in gardens surrounding her home. She described standing under an apple tree and looking at the sky through the white blossoms as going into another country. Most of her early education was conducted at home, where she took French lessons and music instruction. Recognizing their daughter's artistic gift, the Greenaways enrolled Kate in art classes, where she won her first prize at the age of twelve.

Starting in 1871, at the age of twenty-five, Kate Greenaway produced a number of "toy books" and other illustrated collections. In 1878, Edmund Evans, friend of Kate's father, published

Robin and Jenny Wren—in 1865–66, launching Crane's productive career.

John Tenniel left his artistic mark on Lewis Carroll's *Alice's Adventures in Wonderland* (1865) and *Through the Looking Glass* (1871). His mark is so substantial that we find it difficult to think of Alice except in the ways Tenniel envisioned her. Tenniel had worked on *Punch* and was recommended by George Macdonald, noted fantasy writer, as an illustrator for Carroll's books.

Kate Greenaway, born in London in 1846, is noted for renditions of prim, well-groomed children surrounded by the bouquets and garden scenes from her childhood; her name identifies a line of quaint Victorian-style children's dresses today. *Under the Window* (1878), which was her first picture book, was followed by a long and distinguished line of books marked with her unique style and charm. The Greenaway Medal, the English counterpart of our Caldecott Medal for distinguished illustration, is named in her honor.

Randolph Caldecott, like Kate Greenaway, born in 1846, was interested in art very early but was not encouraged to pursue it. He worked in a bank for ten years, but, in 1872, decided to return to the work he loved so much. His work appeared in several magazines both in England and the United States, but the turning point in his career was *The Diverting History of John Gilpin* (1878), a picture book that immortalized him in the field of

her first important work, *Under the Window,* a collection of about fifty drawings with quaint verses. It was in this book that Kate developed the fresh, highly original style that was to become her hallmark. Evans was chided for printing a large first edition of 20,000 copies, but the book sold out before he had time to reprint another edition. Within the next few years more than 70,000 copies were sold. *Under the Window* and many other Greenaway titles continue to be reprinted.

The Birthday Book for Children, published in 1880, is special even today. In addition to 350 miniature black-and-white illustrations and twelve in color, there are month-by-month verses and space to record birth dates.

Kate Greenaway's watercolor drawings and portraits are marked by children attired in charmingly adapted eighteenth-century smocks and frocks, bonnets and breeches, ribbons and aprons. The term "Greenaway costumes" was quickly attached to the designs she fashioned and remains a distinctive label to this day. Characterized by elegance, delicacy, and grace, children from Greenaway's brush reflect her vision of childhood as a time of happy innocence. This has widespread appeal, whether in the scores of Christmas and Valentine cards she created or the numerous books of verse she illustrated. During the years of Britain's industrial revolution, Kate hewed to the Pre-Raphaelite injunction to venerate the simple and poetic in nature.

For the unique impression of childhood her illustrations have left on the minds and hearts of readers, Kate Greenaway's name has a place in children's literature not easily matched.

children's literature around the world, and that was followed by sixteen others. A scene from *John Gilpin* is shown on the Caldecott Medal.

Gradually, illustrations became more integral to the text than the early decorative panels, and the storyteller's word conjoined with the illustrator's line to produce books of lasting impression. No longer were artists a bridge between wonderland and reality; rather, they were interpreters and partners in the storytelling itself. With the spread of literacy in the nineteenth century, the distribution of books expanded, and publishers sought more than a frontispiece or sporadic illustration. In the 1860s Edmund Evans, who joined with Walter Crane in criticizing the poor quality of art in children's books, introduced the use of color, and, in the 1880s, the development of photoengraving processes finally freed the artist from the tyranny of the hand-engraved (and distorting) translation of his art. Illustrations in children's books were well along in their evolution into distinct style and design.

In the early 1900s Arthur Rackham and Beatrix Potter, unique in their own ways, gave form to fictitious characters who became memorable because of the rare talent they reflect.

Picture books as we know them today emerged around the turn of the century, when many of today's classic illustrations were published. Some of these were W. W. Denslow's pictures in *The*

Wizard of Oz (1900), Charles Robinson's for *Lilliput Lyrics* (1899), and Leslie Brooke's in *The Golden Goose Book* (1905). These earn them a place beside Cruikshank, Crane, Tenniel, Potter, Rackham, Greenaway, and Caldecott as outstanding illustrators of early children's books.

The golden age of the picture book (1950 to 1980) attracted many skilled artists to the field of children's books. Leonard Weisgard, Janina Domanska, and Maurice Sendak are among those whose work typifies the changing styles of the period. Comparing an early Weisgard (*The Little Island*) with a later one (*Where Does the Butterfly Go When It Rains?*) will give some idea of the range of the changing art styles as well as the growth of an artist. Comparison of Janina Domanska's earlier and later work also reveals the strength in her developing style and the changing fashions in art. With strong black line drawings and bold use of vivid color, Domanska's work echoes peasant art of the old world and speaks of the regal and mysterious land of its origins.

The best of today's illustrators show remarkable ability to tap and share their own childhood. Some modern artists use old methods, sometimes called revivalist techniques; others spark the reader's imagination with stark black-and-white photographs or the full array of color and technique made possible by today's technology. Maurice Sendak credits artists of the past with in-fluencing the growth of his own singular style, particularly evident in *Where the Wild Things Are* (1963), *In the Night Kitchen* (1970), and *Outside Over There* (1981). For all illustrators, the cultural legacy that is art's is glimpsed in countless proof-sheets.

During the period of the Second World War, many talented European artists came to work and live in America. Ingri and Edgar Parin d'Aulaire (*Abraham Lincoln,* 1939), Ludwig Bemelmans (*Madeline,* 1939), and Roger Duvoisin (*White Snow, Bright Snow,* by Alvin Tresselt, 1947) are a few of these. For many years during this period the lack of quality paper and other resources hindered the production of beautiful books.

The Last Two Decades

Sputnik's 1957 flight, taken as evidence of Soviet educational superiority, resulted in increased funding for the nation's schools and libraries, and a consequent increase in the number of books published (although great preference was given to science and mathematics over literature of imagination). However, only a few brilliant books resulted, amply demonstrating that masterpieces are seldom produced on order. Children's picture books blossomed fully in the 1970s with a seemingly endless bounty, and continue to grow in visual surprise through the 1980s.

Magazines

Many of the early magazines for children were Sunday school periodicals filled with religious writings, sayings, and anecdotes. There was *The Encourager* (Methodist), *The Children's Magazine* (Episcopal), *The Juvenile Instructor* (Mormon), and *Catholic Youth Magazine.* Even secular ones such as *Frank Leslie's Chatterbox* (1879–86) advertised that it intended to "improve the mind, diffuse knowledge," and provide good, healthy, and interesting literature for the young. Each sketch promised to convey a moral or some useful information in only the purest tone and language. Despite an avowed "immense circulation," the magazine lasted only seven years.

ILLUSTRATORS

1823	*German Popular Stories* (George Cruikshank)
● 1850	
1860	Color printing
1867	*Sing a Song of Sixpence* (Walter Crane)
1872	*Alice In Wonderland* (John Tenniel)
● 1875	
1878	*Under the Window* (Kate Greenaway)
1878	*The Diverting History of John Gilpin* (Randolph Caldecott)
1880	Photoengraving process developed
1885	*A Child's Garden of Verses* (Jesse Willcox Smith)
● 1900	
1902	*The Tale of Peter Rabbit* (Beatrix Potter)
1906	*Peter Pan in Kensington Gardens* (Arthur Rackham)
● 1925	
1939	*Madeline* (Ludwig Bemelmans)
1939	*Abraham Lincoln* (Ingri and Edgar d'Aulaire)
1947	*White Snow, Bright Snow* (Roger Duvoisin)

Some prestigious children's magazines had excellent writers contributing to them. Notable among them was Frank Stockton, a frequent contributor to and later associate editor of *St. Nicholas,* which ended seventy years of publication in 1943. Another editor of *St. Nicholas,* Mary Mapes Dodge, best known for her *Hans Brinker; or, The Silver Skates,* actively sought established writers and artists to contribute to the magazine. The creative leadership of these two accounted for the primary position the magazine maintained for three quarters of a century and the standards of excellence it set for the entire children's publishing world. Work by Arthur Rackham, Frances Hodgson Burnett, Howard Pyle, Rudyard Kipling, and Laura E. Richards also often graced its pages. Dodge intended to make the periodical a child's pleasure ground with no sermonizing, no spinning out of facts, and no rattling of dry bones; under her

guidance, the intention was achieved. Many of the short stories were reprinted as books, and anthologies of its articles were published; some of the serialized novels remain classics today. Frances Hodgson Burnett's *Sara Crewe* (1888), Frank Stockton's *America's Birthday Party* (1876), Susan Coolidge's *What Katy Did* (1872), Louisa May Alcott's *Jo's Boys* (1873), *An Old-Fashioned Girl* (1870), and *Eight Cousins* (1875), Rudyard Kipling's *The Jungle Book* (1894), and Lucretia P. Hale's *The Peterkin Papers* (1880), first appeared in the pages of *St. Nicholas*.

The Youth's Companion (1827–1929) survived longer than any other magazine in America; in 1929 it merged with *The American Boy,* which ceased publication in 1941. From the beginning, editorial policy demanded that its content remain seemly; parents could give the weekly magazine to their children without fear of introducing them

A cover from *St. Nicholas* magazine, in which many authors who subsequently became noted in the field of children's books were first published.
(From *Yankee Doodle's Literary Sampler of Prose, Poetry & Pictures*. Selected from the Rare Book Collections of the Library of Congress and introduced by Virginia Haviland and Margaret N. Coughlan. Crowell, 1974.)

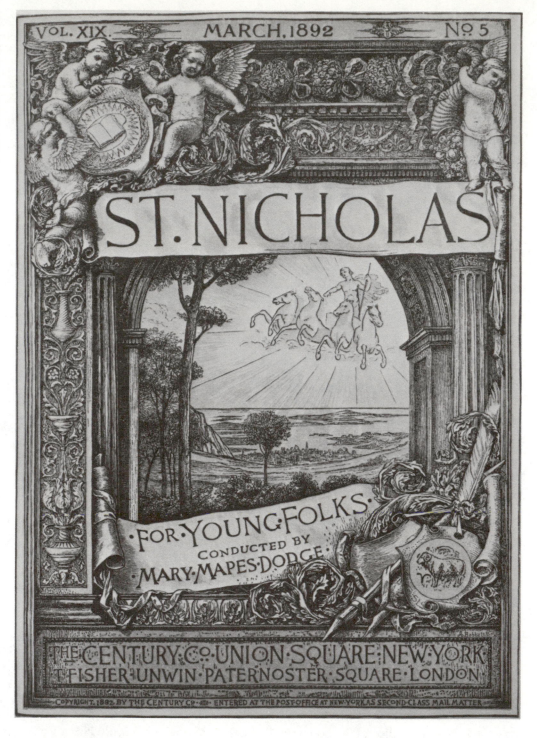

VOL. XIX. MARCH, 1892 № 5

ST. NICHOLAS

·FOR·YOUNG·FOLKS·
CONDUCTED BY
·MARY·MAPES·DODGE·

THE·CENTURY·C⁰·UNION·SQUARE·NEW·YORK·
T·FISHER·UNWIN·PATERNOSTER·SQUARE·LONDON·
COPYRIGHT, 1892, BY THE CENTURY C⁰. ENTERED AT THE POST OFFICE AT NEW YORK AS SECOND-CLASS MAIL MATTER.

to any untoward subject. In addition to the enticement of a distinguished list of contributors—Sarah Orne Jewett, Jack London, Theodore Roosevelt, Henry Wadsworth Longfellow, Alfred Lord Tennyson, James M. Barrie, H. G. Wells, and Oliver Wendell Holmes, among others—the editors offered various premiums to its readers.

The pioneer children's magazine (the first published in America), *The Juvenile Miscellany (1826–34)* was edited by Lydia Maria Child and became an immediate success. Lydia Maria Francis (later Mrs. Child) was a former teacher who wanted children to learn to read with material they could enjoy, but found very little that answered this requirement. *The Juvenile Miscellany* filled the void, but, when Lydia Maria Child spoke out with a tongue of flame against slavery, sales dropped so drastically that the magazine stopped publication in 1834. Sarah Josepha Hale's "Mary Had a Little Lamb" first appeared in this magazine.

Children's magazines have always been an important part of children's reading material; the fresh surprise of each issue brings a special plea-

MAGAZINES	
1826–1834	*Juvenile Miscellany*
1827–1929	*The Youth's Companion*
● 1850	
1865–1873	*Our Young Folks*
1867–1870	*Riverside Magazine for Young People*
1873–1943	*St. Nicholas*
● 1875	
1875–1893	*Wide Awake*
1879–1895	*Harper's Young People*
1879–1886	*Frank Leslie's Chatterbox*
● 1900	
1911 to present	*Boy's Life*
1917–1979	*American Girl*

sure. Some of the most popular magazines today center on nature and the environment with *Ranger Rick's Nature Magazine, National Geographic World,* and *The Curious Naturalist* exemplifying the best. *Cricket Magazine* is the best of the ones that include literature; established authors often write for this high-quality journal. *Cobblestone,* a magazine that focuses on American history, also promises a bright future for magazine readers.

Notes

1. Ralph Hodgson, "Time, You Old Gipsy Man," in *Come Hither: A Collection of Rhymes and Poems for the Young of All Ages,* ed. Walter De La Mare (New York: Knopf, 1966), pp. 434–35.
2. Henry Steele Commager, in Cornelia Meigs et al., *A Critical History of Children's Literature* (New York: Macmillan, 1969), pp. xvi–xvii.
3. Gillian Avery, "Fashions in Children's Fiction," *Children's Literature in Education,* 12 (Sept. 1973), p. 10.
4. A. S. W. Rosenbach, *Early American Children's Books* (1933; rpt. Millwood, N.Y.: Kraus Reprint Co., 1966), p. 19.
5. Cotton Mather's diary.
6. Rosenbach, *Early American Children's Books,* p. 19.
7. Ibid., p. xxxix.
8. Ibid., p. 21.
9. Ibid., p. 22.
10. Cornelia Meigs et al., *A Critical History of Children's Literature,* p. 79.
11. Ibid., p. 78.
12. For a full discussion, see Henry J. Perkinson, "American Textbooks and Educational Change" in National Institute of Education, *Early American Textbooks 1775–1900* (Washington, D.C.: Alvina Treut Burrows Institute, 1978).

13. Alice Jordan, *From Rollo to Tom Sawyer, and Other Papers* (Boston: Horn Book, 1948), p. 76.
14. Rosenbach, *Early American Children's Books,* pp. 42–43.
15. Ruth Holland, *Mill Child: The Story of Child Labor in America* (New York: Macmillan, 1970), pp. 16–17.
16. Martha Farquharson [Finley], *Elsie Dinsmore,* cited in Virginia Haviland and Margaret N. Coughlan, comps., *Yankee Doodle Sampler of Prose, Poetry and Pictures* (New York: Crowell, 1974), p. 233.
17. Thomas Bailey Aldrich, *The Story of a Bad Boy* (1870), cited in Haviland and Coughlan, *Yankee Doodle Sampler,* pp. 346–47.
18. Dora V. Smith, *Fifty Years of Children's Books* (Urbana, Ill.: National Council of Teachers of English, 1963), p. 3.
19. Lewis Carroll, *The Annotated Alice: Alice's Adventures in Wonderland and Through the Looking Glass,* ed. Martin Gardner, illus. John Tenniel (New York: Macmillan, 1960), pp. 25–26.
20. George Macdonald, *At the Back of the North Wind* (London, 1871; rpt. New York: Macmillan, 1964), p. 4.
21. William Blake, *Works* (London: Oxford Univ. Press, 1925), p. 65.
22. Clement Clarke Moore, *A Visit from St. Nicholas,* illus. T. C. Boyd (1823; rpt. New York: Simon and Schuster, 1971), unpaged.

Professional References

Avery, Gillian. "Fashions in Children's Fiction." *Children's Literature in Education,* No. 12 (Sept. 1973), pp. 10–19.

Haviland, Virginia, and Margaret N. Coughlan, eds. *Yankee Doodle Sampler of Prose, Poetry and Pictures.* Crowell, 1974.

Jordon, Alice M. *From Rollo to Tom Sawyer, and Other Papers.* Illus. Nora S. Unwin. Horn Book, 1948.

Locke, John. *Some Thoughts Concerning Education.* c. 1690.

Meigs, Cornelia, et al. *A Critical History of Children's Literature: A Survey of Children's Books in English.* Illus. Vera Bock. Macmillan, 1969.

National Institute of Education. *Early American Textbooks 1775 –1900.* Alvina Treut Burrows Institute, 1978.

Rosenbach, Abraham S. W. *Early American Children's Books.* Kraus Reprint Co., 1966 (1933).

Rousseau, John Jacques. *Emile.* 1762.

Sanborn, F. B., and W. T. A. Harris. *Bronson Alcott: His Life and Philosophy.* 2 vols. Ticknor Bros., 1893.

Smith, Dora V. *Fifty Years of Children's Books.* National Council of Teachers of English, 1963.

Children's Books Cited in Chapter

Abbot, Jacob. *Rollo in Paris.* 1854.
_____. *Rollo in Rome.* 1858.
_____. *Rollo Learning to Talk.* 1834.
_____. *Rollo's Tour in Europe.* 1858.

Adams, William T. *Oliver Optic* series. 1854–1894.

Aesop. *Aesop's Fables.* Ed. Anne Terry White. Random House, 1964.

Alcott, Louisa May. *Eight Cousins.* Golden Press-Western, 1977 (1874).
_____. *Glimpses of Louisa: A Centennial Sampling of the Best Short Stories by Louisa May Alcott.* Little, Brown, 1968.
_____. *Hospital Sketches.* 1866.
_____. *Jack and Jill.* Grosset & Dunlap, 1971 (1879).
_____. *Jo's Boys.* Grosset & Dunlap, 1971 (1886).
_____. *Little Men.* Macmillan, 1963 (1871).
_____. *Little Women.* Macmillan, 1962 (1868).
_____. *An Old Fashioned Girl.* Grosset & Dunlap, 1971 (1869).
_____. *An Old Fashioned Thanksgiving.* Illus. Holly Johnson. Lippincott, 1974 (c. 1870).
_____. *Rose in Bloom.* Grosset & Dunlap, 1971 (1876).
_____. *Under the Lilacs.* Grosset & Dunlap, 1971 (1877).
_____. *Work.* 1873.

Aldis, Dorothy. *All Together: A Child's Treasury of Verse.* Putnam's, 1952 (1925).

Aldrich, Thomas Bailey. *The Story of a Bad Boy.* Garland, 1976 (1870).

Alger, Horatio. *Ragged Dick.* 1868.

Allingham, William. *In Fairyland.* 1870.

The American Accountant: Being a Plain, Practical and Systematic Compendium of Federal Arithmetic. 1797.

American Boy magazine. 1929–41.

American Girl magazine. 1917–79.

The American Primer. 1779.

Andersen, Hans Christian. *Fairy Tales.* Illus. Lawrence B. Smith. Macmillan, 1963 (1835).

_____. *Thumbelina.* Retold by Amy Erhlich. Illus. Susan Jeffers. Dial, 1979 (1836).

Appleton, Victor. *Tom Swift* series. Grosset & Dunlap, 1977 (1910).

Barbauld, Mrs. Anna. *An Easy Introduction to the Knowledge of Nature.* 1782.

_____. *Easy Lessons for Children.* 1760.

_____, and Dr. Aiken. *Evenings at Home.* 1786.

Barrie, James M. *Peter and Wendy.* 1911.

_____. *Peter Pan.* Ed. Eleanor Graham. Illus. Nora S. Unwin. Scribner's 1950 (1904).

_____. *Peter Pan in Kensington Gardens.* Illus. Arthur Rackham. 1906.

Baum, L. Frank. *The Wizard of Oz.* Macmillan, 1970 (1900).

Bemelmans, Ludwig. *Madeline.* Viking, 1939.

Benét, Rosemary and Stephen Vincent. *A Book of Americans.* Illus. Charles Child. Holt, Rinehart & Winston, 1952 (1933).

Blake, William. *Songs of Innocence.* Illus. Ellen Raskin. Doubleday, 1966 (1789).

_____. *Works.* Oxford Univ. Press, 1925.

Boy's Life magazine. 1911 to present.

Brooke, Leslie, illus. *The Golden Goose and Other Favorites.* Warne, 1977 (1905).

_____. *Johnny Crow's Garden.* Watts, 1967 (1903).

Browning, Robert. *The Pied Piper of Hamelin.* Illus. Kate Greenaway. Coward, McCann & Geoghegan, 1971 (1888).

Bunyan, John. *Pilgrim's Progress.* Dodd, Mead, 1979 (1678).

Burnett, Frances Hodgson. *Little Lord Fauntleroy.* Garland, 1976 (1886).

_____. *Sara Crewe,* rev. as *The Little Princess.* Lippincott, 1963 (1888).

_____. *The Secret Garden.* Illus. Tasha Tudor. Lippincott, 1962 (1911).

Caldecott, Randolph. *The Diverting History of John Gilpin,* available as *Randolph Caldecott's John Gilpin and Other Stories.* Warne, 1978 (1878).

Carroll, Lewis. *Alice's Adventures in Wonderland & Through the Looking Glass.* Illus. John Tenniel. Macmillan, 1963 (1865 & 1872).

_____. *The Annotated Alice: Alice's Adventures in Wonderland & Through the Looking Glass.* Ed. Martin Gardner. New American Library. 1960.

Child, Lydia Maria. *The New England Boy's Song about Thanksgiving Day or Over the River and Through the Woods.* Illus. Brinton Turkle. Coward, McCann & Goeghegan, 1974 (1845).

Clark, Henry H. *Joe Bentley, Naval Cadet.* 1899.

Coburn, William. *First Lessons in Arithmetic.* 1821.

Coffin, Charles C. *Boys of '76.* 1876.

Collodi, C. *The Adventures of Pinocchio.* Illus. Naiad Einsel. Macmillan, 1963 (1891).

Colman, Benjamin. *A Devout Contemplation On the Meaning of Divine Providence, in the Early Death of Pious and Lovely Children. Preached upon the Sudden and Lamented Death of Mrs. Elizabeth Wainwright. Who Departed this Life, April the 8th, 1714. Having just compleated the Fourteenth Year of Her Age.* 1714.

Comenius, John Amos. *Orbis sensualium pictus.* 1657.

Coolidge, Susan. *What Katy Did.* J. M. Dent, 1977 (1872).

Cooper, James Fenimore. *The Last of the Mohicans.* Illus. N. C. Wyeth. Scribner's, 1919 (1826).

Cotton, John. *Milk for Babes, Drawn out of the Breasts of Both Testaments, Chiefly for the Spiritual Nourishment of Boston Babes in either England, but may be of like use for any Children.* 1646.

Crane, Walter, illus. *Dame Trot and Her Comical Cat.* c. 1865.

_____. *The History of Cock Robin and Jenny Wren.* c. 1866.

_____. *The House That Jack Built.* c. 1865.

_____. *Sing a Song of Sixpence.* 1867.

Cruikshank, George, illus. *George Cruikshank's Fairy Library.* 4 vols. 1853–54.

_____. *German Popular Stories.* 1823.

_____. *Grimm's Fairy Tales.* Green Tiger, 1977 (1820).

D'Aulaire, Ingri and Edgar Parin. *Abraham Lincoln.* Doubleday, 1957 (1939).

Day, Thomas. *The History of Sandford and Merton.* Garland, 1977 (1783).

Defoe, Daniel. *Robinson Crusoe.* Illus. N. C. Wyeth. Scribner's, 1920 (1719).

De La Mare, Walter. *Come Hither.* Illus. Warren Chappell. Knopf, 1957.

_____. *Peacock Pie.* Illus. Barbara Cooney. Knopf, 1961 (1913).

Dickens, Charles. *A Christmas Carol.* Illus. Arthur Rackham. Lippincott, 1952 (1843).

Dodge, Mary Mapes. *Hans Brinker; or, The Silver Skates.* Illus. Hilda Van Stockum. Collins-World, 1975 (1865).

Edgeworth, Maria. *Early Lessons.* 1801.

_____. *Moral Tales.* 1801.

_____. *Parent's Assistant.* 1796.

Field, Rachel. *The Pointed People.* 1924.

_____. *Taxis and Toadstools.* 1926.

Finley, Martha. *Elsie Dinsmore.* Garland (1867).

First Lessons in Arithmetic. 1821.

Fox, George. *Instructions for Right-Spelling and Plain Directions for Reading and Writing True English. With several delightful things very Useful and Necessary, both for Young and Old, to Read and Learn.* 1702.

Frank Leslie's Chatterbox magazine. 1879–86.

Garelick, May. *Where Does the Butterfly Go When It Rains?* Illus. Leonard Weisgard. Addison-Wesley, 1961.

Goldsmith, Oliver. *The Renowned History of Little Goody Two Shoes.* Illus. Alice Woodward. Macmillan, 1924 (1765).

Goodrich, Samuel G. *Peter Parley's History of the United States of America.* 1822.

68

Goodrich, Samuel and Charles. *Tales of Peter Parley About America*. Garland, 1976 (1827).

Grahame, Kenneth. *The Wind in the Willows*. Illus. Ernest H. Shepard. Scribner's, 1908.

Greenaway, Kate. *The Birthday Book for Children*. Warne, 1880.

————. *Under the Window*. Warne 1878.

Grimm Brothers. *Kinder-und Hausmärchen*. Trans. Lucy Crane. Illus. Walter Crane. McGraw-Hill, 1966 (1812).

Grinnell, George. *Jack among the Indians*. 1900.

Hale, Lucretia. *The Peterkin Papers*. Houghton Mifflin, 1960 (1880).

Hale, Sarah Josepha. *Mary's Lamb*. 1834.

Harper's Young People magazine. 1875–93.

Harris, Benjamin. *The New England Primer*. 1683.

————. *The Protestant Tutor*. Garland, c. 1681.

Harris, Joel Chandler. *Uncle Remus Stories*. Schocken, 1966 (1881).

Henty, George. *Under Drake's Flag*. 1883.

————. *With Kitchener in the Soudan*. 1903.

————. *The Young Buglers*. 1880.

Holland, Ruth. *Mill Child: The Story of Child Labor in America*. Macmillan, 1970.

Hope, Laura Lee. *Bobbsey Twins* series. 1904–to present.

Howitt, Mary. *Fireside Verses*. c. 1871.

Irving, Washington. *The Sketch-Book of Geoffrey Crayon* (*Rip Van Winkle & The Legend of Sleepy Hollow*). Illus. David Levine. New American Library 1819–20.

Janeway, James. *A Token for Children: Being An Exact Account of the Conversion, Holy and Exemplary Lives, and Joyful Deaths of several young Children*. Garland, 1976 (1672).

Johnson, R. Brimley, ed. *Lilliput Lyrics*. Illus. Charles Robinson. 1899.

Juvenile Miscellany magazine. 1826–34.

Keene, Carolyn. *Nancy Drew* series. c. 1890 to present.

Kingsley, Charles. *Heroes*. Illus. Vera Bock. Macmillan, 1954 (1856).

————. *The Water Babies*. Illus. Harold Jones. Watts, 1961 (1863).

Kipling, Rudyard. *The Jungle Book*. Illus. Robert Shore. Macmillan, 1964 (1894).

————. *Rudyard Kipling's Verse: Definitive Edition*. Doubleday, n.d.

Lamb, Charles. *The Adventures of Ulysses*. 1808.

Lamb, Charles and Mary. *Tales from Shakespeare*. Illus. Richard M. Powers. Macmillan, 1963 (1806).

Lang, Andrew. *The Blue Fairy Book*. Ed. Brian Alderson. Illus. John Lawrence. Viking, 1978 (1889).

Larcom, Lucy. *Childhood Songs*. Illus. Winslow Homer. 1875.

Lear, Edward. *A Book of Nonsense*. Garland, 1976 (1846).

A Legacy for Children, being Some of the Last Expressions, and Dying Sayings, of Hannah Hill, Junr. Of the City of Philadel-phia, in the Province of Pennsilvania, in America, Aged Eleven Years and near Three Months. 1717.

Lofting, Hugh. *The Story of Dr. Dolittle*. Lippincott, 1967 (1920).

MacDonald, Golden. *The Little Island*. Illus. Leonard Weisgard. Doubleday, 1971 (1946).

Macdonald, George. *At the Back of the North Wind*. Illus. Ernest H. Shepard. Macmillan, 1964 (1871).

McGuffey, William H. *McGuffey's Eclectic Readers*. Gordon, 1973 (1834).

Mather, Cotton. *A Token for the Children of New England, or Some Examples of Children in Whom the Fear of God was Remarkably Budding Before They Died*. 1702.

Meigs, Cornelia. *Invincible Louisa*. Little, Brown, 1968.

Milne, A. A. *Now We Are Six*. Illus. Ernest H. Shepard. Dutton, 1927.

————. *When We Were Very Young*. Illus. Ernest H. Shepard. Dutton, 1924.

————. *Winnie the Pooh*. Illus. Ernest H. Shepard. Dutton, 1926.

Montgomery, Lucy M. *Anne of Green Gables*. Bantam, 1976 (1908).

Moore, Clement Clarke. *A Visit from St. Nicholas*. Illus. T. C. Boyd. Simon and Schuster, 1971 (1823).

Nesbit, Edith. *The Story of the Treasure Seekers*. Illus. Ceal Leslie. Penguin, 1959 (1899).

Newbery, John. *A Little Pretty Pocket Book: Intended for the Instruction and Amusement of Little Master Tommy and Pretty Miss Polly*. Harcourt Brace Jovanovich, 1967 (1744).

Our Young Folks magazine. 1865–73.

Perrault, Charles. *Contes de ma Mère l'Oye* (*Tales of Mother Goose*). 1697.

————. *Histoires ou contes du temps passé avec moralities* (*Stories or Tales of Long Ago with Morals*). 1697.

Porter, Eleanor. *Pollyanna*. 1912.

Potter, Beatrix. *The Tale of Peter Rabbit*. Warne, 1902.

Pyle, Howard. *The Merry Adventures of Robin Hood of Great Renown in Nottinghamshire*. Scribner's, 1946 (1883).

Richards, Laura E. *Sketches and Scraps*. 1881.

Riley, James Whitcomb. *Rhymes of Childhood*. Core Collection, 1976 (1891).

Riverside Magazine for Young People magazine. 1867–70.

Roscoe, William. *The Butterfly's Ball*. 1807.

Rossetti, Christina. *Sing-Song*. Illus. Marguerite Davis. Macmillan, 1924 (1872).

St. Nicholas magazine. 1873–1943.

Sandburg, Carl. *Early Moon*. Illus. James Daugherty. Harcourt Brace Jovanovich, 1930.

School of Good Manners. 1685.

Sendak, Maurice. *In the Night Kitchen*. Harper & Row, 1970.

————. *Outside Over There*. Harper & Row, 1981.

————. *Where the Wild Things Are*. Harper & Row, 1963.

Sewell, Anna. *Black Beauty*. Illus. John Groth. Macmillan, 1962 (1877).

Sherwood, Mrs. Mary Martha. *The History of the Fairchild Family,* Part I. 1818.

Sidney, Margaret. *The Five Little Peppers and How They Grew.* Lothrop, 1976 (1880).

Spyri, Johanna. *Heidi.* Illus. Greta Elgaard. Macmillan, 1962 (1884).

Stevenson, Burton, ed. *The Home Book of Verse.* 1915.

Stevenson, Robert Louis. *A Child's Garden of Verses.* Illus. Jesse Willcox Smith. Scribner's, 1905 (1885).

————. *Treasure Island.* Illus. N. C. Wyeth. Scribner's, 1911 (1883).

Stockton, Frank. *America's Birthday Party.* 1876.

————. *Ting-a-Ling.* 1867.

Stratemeyer, Edward. *Under Dewey at Manilla.* 1898.

Swift, Jonathan. *Gulliver's Travels.* Illus. Arthur Rackham. Dutton, 1952 (1726).

Taylor, Ann and Jane. *Original Poems for Infant Minds.* Garland, 1977 (1804).

Thayer, Ernest L. *Casey at the Bat.* Illus. Wallace Tripp. Coward, McCann & Geoghegan, 1978 (1888).

Tomlinson, Everett T. *Boy Soldiers of 1812.* 1895.

Travers, Pamela L. *Mary Poppins.* Illus. Mary Shepard. Harcourt Brace Jovanovich, 1972 (1934).

Tresselt, Alvin. *White Snow, Bright Snow.* Illus. Roger Duvoisin. Lothrop, Lee & Shepard, 1947.

Trimmer, Mrs. Sarah. *Fabulous Histories.* Garland, 1976 (1786).

Twain, Mark. *The Adventures of Huckleberry Finn.* Harper & Row (1884).

————. *The Adventures of Tom Sawyer.* Harper & Row (1876).

Verne, Jules. *Journey to the Center of the Earth.* Dodd, Mead, 1979 (1864).

Watts, Isaac. *Divine and Moral Songs for Children.* 1715.

Webster, Noah. *The Elementary Spelling Book (Webster's Blue-Backed Speller).* 1783.

Wide Awake magazine. 1875–93.

Wiggin, Kate Douglas. *Rebecca of Sunnybrook Farm.* Illus. Lawrence B. Smith. Macmillan, 1962 (1903).

————, and Nora Archibald Smith. *The Fairy Ring.* 1906.

Winfield, Arthur. *Rover Boys* series. 1899.

Winstanly, Henry. *All the Principal Nations of the World.* 1665.

Wyss, Johann. *The Swiss Family Robinson.* Illus. Lynd Ward. Grosset and Dunlap, 1949 (1812).

Yonge, Charlotte. *The Daisy Chain.* Garland, 1977 (1856).

Young, Clarence. *Motor Boys* series. 1899.

Youth's Behavior. 1636.

The Youth's Companion magazine. 1827–1929.

three

DAVID McCORD   From *BOOKS*

*Just begin when you're young:
when a book in your eye
seems as tall as the sky;
when words, words in their flight
are as birds in your sight;
when it thrills you to find
you are using your mind,
and inside it is what
someone else hasn't got.*

*You! Begin when you're young,
when the tip of your tongue
is still limber. Books reach
with the splendor of speech.
Who can say things well said
is well read.*[1]

Expanding Language through Literature

It is when they are young that children learn language most rapidly. During this critical period books can have a vital role in providing a stimulating environment that contributes to language growth.

Language development is natural in an environment well-supplied with language in use. Even where this is not the case, language is so central to the need to communicate that it breaks through formidable barriers. Most children gradually learn language as label; for Helen Keller, blind and deaf from infancy, the realization that everything has a name came in one profound moment, best described in her own words:

Some one was drawing water and my teacher placed my hand under the spout. As the cool stream gushed over one hand she spelled into the other the word water, first slowly, then rapidly. I stood still, my whole attention fixed upon the motions of her fingers. Suddenly I felt a misty consciousness as of something forgotten—a thrill of returning thought; and somehow the mystery of language was revealed to me. I knew then that "w–a–t–e–r" meant the wonderful cool something that was flowing over my hand. That living word awakened my soul, gave it light, hope, joy, set it free![2]

Language comprehension generally exceeds production: children understand more than they can say. As children hear stories and poems read aloud, they build a linguistic storehouse of story patterns and language possibilities. It is clear that what goes in one ear does not come out the other, but instead contributes toward a framework of meanings, patterns, and sounds. As the meanings, patterns, and sounds of language become internalized, the child draws upon the schema to generate language of his own (as well as to anticipate what comes next in a story). The language children encounter—in their experiences with books as elsewhere—affects their concept development at every level. It shapes their perception of reality, and although language itself is based on what they perceive, their concept of reality, in turn, is affected by the language they learn.

Books are an unequaled resource for expanding children's language. After hearing Beatrix Potter's *The Tale of Peter Rabbit* (N-P), one little boy was heard muttering to himself, "I implore you to exert yourself. I implore you to exert yourself." Another time, enchanted with the words "otherwise not," from a story, he mimicked them incessantly.[3] Books enlarge children's environments and extend opportunities for meaningful language learning.

As children learn to deal with the subtleties of language, they begin to see that their views may differ from those of others. They soon find, for example, that some words whose meanings they know may have other meanings for adults. In Beverly Cleary's *Ramona the Pest* (P-I), Ramona is excited about her first day at kindergarten. When her teacher leads her by the hand to one of the tables and chairs and says, "Sit here for the present," Ramona is doubly excited:

A present! thought Ramona, and knew at once she was going to like Miss Binney. . . . Nobody had told her she was going to get a present the very first day. What kind of present could it be, she wondered, trying to remember if Beezus had ever been given a present by her teacher.[4]

Ramona stays glued to her chair all day. When her teacher finally explains what she meant, Ramona is chagrined:

"Oh." Ramona was so disappointed she had nothing to say. Words were so puzzling. *Present* should mean a present just as *attack* should mean to stick tacks in people.[5]

We could say Ramona misunderstood the teacher; on the other hand, we could say the teacher did not understand Ramona.

As Ramona, like other children, interacts with a widening circle of adults and children, she gradually develops a larger repertoire of meanings from which she draws. The developmental view of children as language learners has parallels in the books written for them. For example, many books for children who are learning language as label have pictures for them to label.

As they learn language, children develop a sense of its pattern and sound and a sense of story as well. At later stages, as they develop further mastery, all literature spreads before them like the treasures that "Open sesame!" commands from Sinbad's cave. Increasingly sophisticated meanings become comprehensible. Puns, plays on words, metaphoric and symbolic uses, stylistic devices, and ironic relationships come to make sense, and a recognition of satire and parody emerges. As the growth in language mushrooms, literature can help expand meaning further. Books help in the steps along the way as children develop independence in language and reading.

DEVELOPING LANGUAGE: BOOKS FOR BEGINNERS

Books can broaden experiences with language from infancy through childhood, adolescence, and adulthood. The language we hear and read affects the language we use in speaking and writing. Physical, intellectual, and interpersonal needs determine the types of books suitable at each level. Parents who sing Mother Goose rhymes to the infant in the cradle are off to the right start, and can soon follow this with sturdy cloth or cardboard books to establish very early the idea that books are a source of pleasure.

Books for the youngest child are called participation books, for they are ones that invite the child to participate in touching, pointing, looking, and playing with the materials in the book. They provide opportunities for endless rehearsal of language as label. Alphabet books and counting books, generally the next appropriate materials, contain realistic pictures of commonplace objects for identification and counting; those for the later, nursery school years may contain simple stories. Concept books contribute to the continuing process of developing vocabulary by presenting numerous examples of colors, shapes, time, relational terms, and other basic concepts. These books encourage children to expand their language, to convey meaning, and to develop concepts.

Participation Books

Language learning is rooted in perception, and many books discussed in this section provide concrete visual and tactile materials for children to explore—textures to touch, flaps to lift, "flowers" to smell, and pieces to manipulate. Toddlers, notoriously heavy-handed as they develop control over hand and finger muscles, may treat books roughly. Fortunately, there are many books made from heavy fabric, cardboard, or plastic that are nearly indestructible as well as being suitable for a toddler's developmental level. Two- to four-year-old children acquire language rapidly and enjoy pointing to pictures and identifying known objects. The best way to share a book is to have the child in the adult's lap, with the book held directly in front of the child to focus attention on the pages. Learning occurs while the adult and child are turning the pages, enjoying the experience together, and treating the book as a valued object.

Dorothy Kunhardt's *Pat the Bunny* (N) qualifies as a classic because it has appealed to young children since 1940, which augurs well for its future. The book shows Paul and Judy doing many things and develops the idea that the child can do lots of things, too. Judy feels Daddy's scratchy face, and the toddler can feel Daddy's scratchy face—a bit of sandpaper—in the picture. There is also a place to stick a finger into Mommy's ring, a piece of cloth to raise and lower in a peek-a-boo game, and scented-paper "flowers" to smell—all intended to engage the child in play and conversation.

Now YOU feel Daddy's scratchy face.

Word and experience here combine when the child hears "scratchy" and feels the rough coating that has been applied to "Daddy's" face.
(From *Pat the Bunny* by Dorothy Kunhardt. Copyright 1940, renewed 1968 by Western Publishing Company, Inc. Used by permission of the publisher.)

Alphabet Books

Alphabet books serve many useful purposes, only one of which is related to learning the alphabet.

Teaching Idea

SHARE A BOOK (N)   You can hardly introduce books too early as long as making use of them is a pleasurable experience for you and the child. Select a book with well-defined illustrations, preferably of objects familiar from the child's environment. Clear, representational pictures are better than complicated or abstract designs for this age group. Talk to the child about the pictures as you turn the pages, and, as much as possible, relate what is in the pictures to things that are in the child's real world.

B is for bicycle, but the borders conceal as well a bean, bee, bell, bird, and button.
(Illustrations from *Anno's Alphabet: An Adventure in Imagination* by Mitsumasa Anno. Copyright © 1974 by Fukuinkan-Shoten. By permission of Thomas Y. Crowell, Publishers.)

Two- to four-year-old children will point to and "label" objects on the page, five-year-olds may say the letter names and words that start with each letter, and six-year-olds may read the letters, words, or story to confirm their knowledge of letter and sound correspondences. However they are used, alphabet books help to develop children's awareness of print. Young children learn that talk can be represented by print and that there is an agreed-upon way to represent language in writing. They learn that the text on a page is fixed and that, no matter how often it is read, it always says the same thing. They also learn that words and letters have a unique configuration or representation. Alphabet books play a useful part in language learning in addition to the pleasurable hours they provide a child.

Outstanding illustrators use the alphabet as a structural frame to display their skills, to tell a story, to play with letter sounds and words, to collect nonsense verse, and to delight the imagina-

tion. No one need settle for a mediocre alphabet book, because there are magnificent ones available. One of the best, *Anno's Alphabet* (P), by Mitsumasa Anno, is appropriately subtitled *An Adventure in Imagination,* and the aptness becomes evident when you open the book. An apparently wood-carved question mark, a tree, an axe, a vise, a saw, and a wood carver's tool foreshadow what is to come. Each wood-carved letter is represented by one large object, but there are many related ones hidden in the borders of the page. The book becomes a treasure hunt and a genuine adventure in imagination as children try to find the objects and guess the relationships of all the things Anno has put into his alphabet.

Alice and Martin Provensen use an alphabet rhyme from the "Shaker Manifesto" of 1882 as the basis for *A Peaceable Kingdom* (N-P). With a subtitle, *The Shaker Abecedarius,* the tone is set for the rollicking verses for the letters of the alphabet. "Alligator, Beetle, Porcupine, Whale / Bobolink, Panther, Dragonfly, Snail'' represents only the beginning of a procession of animals illustrated in delicate watercolor and pen-and-ink drawings. Shaker objects, motifs, people, and religious verses are interspersed among the animals in this truly beautiful alphabet book.

Thomas Matthiesen's *ABC: An Alphabet Book* (N-P) has clear color photographs of familiar objects and is appropriate for very young children, as is C. B. Falls's *The ABC Book* (N-P). For this age group it is important that the relationship between the letter and the object whose name starts with that letter be very clear. For example, one child, seeing a nest with eggs in it for the letter N said, ''Oh, N is for eggs.''

In *Jambo Means Hello* (P), Tom and Muriel Feelings show that an alphabet book can be much more than just a representation of letters. Their book gives Swahili words and concepts for the letters and develops a sense of the majesty and dignity of the people who created the Swahili language. The magnificent illustrations extend the meanings of the words and convey the warmth and sense of community felt among these African people.

Leonard Baskin drew the pictures, but the words for *Hosie's Alphabet* (N-P) were made up by Hosie, Tobias, and Lisa Baskin. Hosie was only three years old when he asked his father to draw the alphabet for him, and the whole family contributed to the delicious-sounding word list. A ''bumptious baboon,'' a ''carrion crow,'' and an ''imperious eagle spangled and splendid'' are among the array of exotic animals. It does not matter whether children know what a ''ghastly garrulous gargoyle'' is or what ''primordial protozoa'' are; the fun comes from saying such delectable words and looking at the fantastic illustrations.

Counting Books

Counting books contribute to children's cognitive structuring by reinforcing their grasp of number and seriation. Like alphabet books, counting books are used for much more than learning to count.

An alphabet book that uses transliterated Swahili terms: ''baba means father'' in Swahili. Customs of East African life are depicted in detailed double-spread paintings for each letter.
(Excerpted from the book *Jambo Means Hello: Swahili Alphabet Book* by Tom and Muriel Feelings. Illustrated by Tom Feelings. Illustrations copyright © 1974 by Tom Feelings. Used by permission of The Dial Press.)

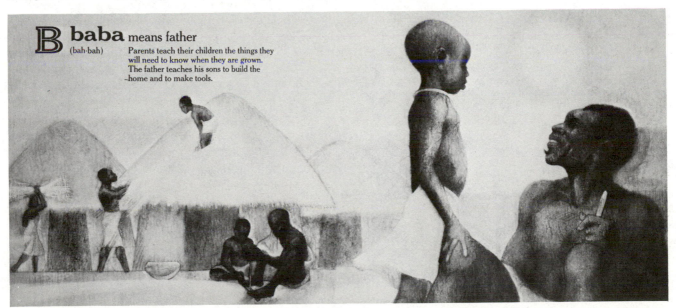

Teaching Idea

AN ALPHABET SCRAPBOOK (N-P) Nursery school and primary-grade children can find pictures in magazines for their own alphabet books. As new letters are introduced, children can collect pictures of objects whose names start with those letters and paste them in a scrapbook. In this activity, children's receptive competence is called upon as they are asked to recognize words and pictures rather than produce them.

They may also help children learn to add or subtract, or just to enjoy the visual portrayal of numerical concepts. Children delight in pointing to the objects displayed and checking to see if the illustrator presented the exact number of items for each numeral. The best illustrations for young children avoid distracting clutter so that the objects can be identified and counted without confusion. With such books children rehearse counting until it is learned by heart.

Books for very young children often make counting a game or invite the child to participate, the way Eric Carle does in *The Very Hungry Caterpillar* (N-P). The hungry caterpillar eats holes right through the pages, and the holes lure children to stick tiny fingers through them as they count. The caterpillar changes into a huge brilliant butterfly

The voracious caterpillar leaves holes in the page large enough for children's fingers as they count them up. (Reprinted from *The Very Hungry Caterpillar* by Eric Carle, 1969, with the permission of Philomel Books, A Division of the Putnam Publishing Group.)

that opens its wings across the entire spread of the final pages.

Mitsumasa Anno creates a visually appealing work for older children who recognize the sets or clusters of objects to be counted in *Anno's Counting Book* (P-I). Anno starts with the concept of zero and gradually adds people and objects to the same scene until he reaches twelve. The page for zero contains nothing but a barren, snow-covered landscape, but, one at a time, page by page, houses, people, boats, and trees appear on the scene, while the seasons change. Cubes shown in stacks at the sides of the pages represent the number to be found in each category—for example, three people, three houses, three boats, and three trees.

In a companion to their above-mentioned alphabet book, Tom and Muriel Feelings give the Swahili words for numbers in *Moja Means One* (P). Artful illustrations with a soft chalklike texture extend one's awareness of customs of the African people.

Concept Books

Concept books contribute to expanding language by providing materials that lead to refining and elaborating concepts the child is building. The books contain illustrations of basic shapes, colors, size relationships, and positions (such as over and under). In some cases they tell a simple story that develops a concept such as time, or an emotion. Often the books present an abstraction, such as a shape, color, size, or sound, and then give many examples of it, from which the child draws a generalization about the meaning.

COUNTING IN THE CLASSROOM (N) Children enjoy exploring counting books and, within a short period, are reciting the numbers as they go. Read to small groups or to individual children so that each can check to see if the illustrator has the correct number of objects for each numeral. (A few have made mistakes!)

ONE WAS JOHNNY (N-P) Show the animated 16-mm. film "One Was Johnny" or "Really Rosie" (both available from Weston Woods) based on "Nutshell Library" characters (Maurice Sendak, Harper & Row, 1962). You might begin by talking about Johnny's feelings as the parade of characters interrupts his reading. Johnny shows his displeasure by standing on a chair and threatening to eat them all if they are not gone by the time he has counted backwards from ten. Children will quickly learn the song by Carole King and will sing along on replays of the film or rereadings of the book.

Activity: Teacher to Student

MAKE A BOOK (P) Staple together several pieces of plain paper or make holes in them and tie with a ribbon to form a book. Write down numbers and tell a story about each one. Draw pictures that show the number of things in your story. Or you might draw pictures to go along with a counting song like "This Old Man" or rope-skipping counting songs.

Tana Hoban's work is exemplary of the kind. She views the world through a photographer's eye, and, in *Look Again* (P-I), invites the reader to do just that. A plain white page with a small opening becomes a frame that reveals only a small part of a larger photograph to come. The invitation to predict what is coming is clear, although no words are used. On the first page children might see a network of filaments and speculate that the item is a spiderweb or a milkweed. On the next page they discover a huge dandelion puff enlarged to fill the whole page and, on the next, a child blowing away the dandelion filaments as she holds the flower in her hand. The changing per-spectives involve the child in imaginative guessing and show the many dimensions of a dandelion. The book develops the idea of careful observation and how perspective changes perception.

Donald Crews's *Truck* (N) has several levels of potential interest. The subtle story line is insignificant to the very young child, who will go through the book repeatedly pointing to the signs along the road that the truck travels and naming the vehicles, whereas older ones will read the road signs and try to figure out the origin, route, and destination of the huge truckload of tricycles. Children alert to the signs in their environment will turn to the book again and again to confirm the words they recognize and to demonstrate to themselves the growing repertoire of words they can read.

In Arnold Lobel's *The Great Blueness and Other Predicaments* (P), a wizard in a colorless world creates a pot of color with which he paints everything in sight. Because the people are not satisfied with this monochrome world, he devises another color, but again applies it to everything, again to everyone's dissatisfaction. The message, that many colors are necessary to make a balanced world, is an important one.

Books that develop concepts of the months of the year or the cycle of holidays are a natural follow-up to the counting books described earlier.

Maurice Sendak's lilting rhyme in *Chicken Soup with Rice* (N-P) takes the reader through the months of the year with activities appropriate for each month, but nonsensically relates every activity to eating chicken soup.

Tasha Tudor presents holiday traditions for each month in *A Time to Keep* (P). The exquisite watercolor paintings catalogue bygone activities in response to a child's question, "Granny, what was it like when Mummy was like me?" Traditional values and activities, including making Yorkshire pudding, apple pie, and ice cream in January, syrup in March, and cider in October, are portrayed throughout the book.

Teaching Idea

EXPANDING LANGUAGE CONCEPTS: OPPOSITES (N-P) Books provide opportunities to reinforce concept development and to build new concepts by showing examples of what something is, is not, and does, or what its attributes are. While sharing these books with children, adults are modeling language, expanding upon the words used in the books, and making progressively finer distinctions. Children may imitate these words and eventually assimilate them into their own language system.

Building the concept of opposites through repeated examples is done in many books, such as Peter Spier's *Fast-Slow, High-Low* (N-P, Doubleday, 1972), a treasure house of humor and detail, and Joan Hanson's *Antonyms: Hot and Cold and Other Words That Are Different as Day and Night* (P, Lerner Publications, 1972). Children above the primary grades will find comparable ideas in Richard Wilbur's *Opposites* (P-I, Harcourt Brace Jovanovich, 1973), which adds a touch of humor.

Activity: Teacher to Student

WORD SEARCH (P) Make up a list of opposites and write them in pairs in a book you have made. (Make the book out of sheets of paper held together with a piece of cord or ribbon pulled through a hole in the corner of the sheets, or staple the sheets together along the edge.) Draw pictures that show the meanings of the words. Choose a partner; then one can act out a word, and the other can act out the opposite.

Vivid colors and strong shapes make things easy to recognize. (Illustration from *Truck* by Donald Crews. Copyright © 1980. Reproduced by permission of Greenwillow Books, A Division of William Morrow & Company, Inc.)

Beginning readers like word games that allow them to confirm their growing vocabularies. (HBJ photograph by Richard C. Polister.)

80

The beginning illustration in *Frog, Where Are You?* can be the beginning of a valuable composition experience for children.
(Excerpted from the book *Frog, Where Are You?* by Mercer Mayer. Copyright © 1969 by Mercer Mayer. Used by permission of The Dial Press.)

DEVELOPING A SENSE OF STORY

Children learn intuitively that language and stories are sometimes used in direct ways, other times in deliberate literary ways that have many possible interpretations. They also learn that stories follow a special pattern and have a form. Experience with books enlarges the understanding of language and story by expanding vicarious experience and by providing examples of language used in countless ways.

The characteristics of wordless books, literary folk tales, and plays make them uniquely suited for use with children who are developing a sense of story. Wordless books, with the story revealed through illustrations alone, stimulate and extend children's storytelling. Literary folk tales, written by contemporary authors who shape the stories on the time-proven frame of the ancient folk tale, strengthen the child's concept of story patterns. These stories expand the child's perception of the substance of literature, while plays, told almost entirely through dialogue, reveal in stark relief the elements of fundamental story forms. Each type of book makes its own contribution to the child's developing sense of story.

Wordless Books

Wordless books first appeared in the 1960s and are now plentiful. They are used at many levels: very young children who do not yet read can tell the stories through the pictures, while beginning readers "read" them since they do not tax decoding skills, intermediate-grade students use them as models for story writing, and junior-high-school students use them to delineate the elements of fiction.

Mercer Mayer has created some of the best wordless books. One of them, *Frog Where Are You?* (N-P), deals with the problems a boy faces because of the behavior of his impetuous frog friend. *Frog Goes to Dinner* (N-P) is a favorite because of the slapstick comedy and uninhibited behavior of the frog. The irrepressible frog hides in the boy's pocket when the family goes to dinner at a fancy restaurant and creates havoc by jumping into a salad, a glass of champagne, and a saxophone. The family is disgruntled when they are evicted from the restaurant, but the reader shares the smirks of delight observed on the boy's face *and* the frog's face when they are sent to their room.

Pat Hutchins, John Goodall, and Paula Winter are other masters of the wordless book form. In *Changes, Changes* (N-P), Hutchins creates a world, characters, and a story from a pile of building blocks. The magic of the story has been caught on film (Weston Woods), and children recreate it endlessly in block corners, roller movies, murals, taped retellings with sound effects, and written stories. (Goodall and Winter are discussed in Recommended Reading at the end of the chapter.)

Complex wordless books require mature readers in the upper elementary grades to detect the subtleties. *Thirteen* (I), by Remy Charlip and Jerry Joyner, is an intricate group of thirteen stories told in a collage of thirteen drawings on each page, one drawing from each of the stories. Readers' expressions change from quizzical to superior when they unlock the secret of how the stories are told.

Literary Folk Tales

A sense of story grows as children experience a wide range of works and acquire familiarity with recognized forms. Archetypal story forms, dis-

cussed in Chapter 5, are basic to a literary education and reflect the human desire for story across the ages. Literary folk tales are written by contemporary authors who consciously use traditional folk tale conventions to tell their story. The cyclical plots, stereotypic characters, and rhythm, repetition, and refrain of the folklore style accommodate the child's developing sense of story and account for the durability of the old tales. Stories modeled on the classic folktale form add diversity to the stock of stories and yet are comfortable, like new words to a familiar tune. The clarity of their structure aids comprehension.

The pattern of the cumulative tale is especially suitable for young children, since each scene is repeated and brought into the next as the story

Teaching Idea

STORY SEQUENCE (P-I) Wordless books can be used to reinforce the concept of story sequence. Buy two paperback copies of the same title and cut the books apart. Mount each page (making sure that you have each front and back) on construction paper and laminate them. Children can then put the story in sequence by arranging the pages in order. Sequencing can also be practiced with Ruth Krauss's *The Backward Day* (P, Harper & Row, 1959), in which a small child reverses the order of his daily routine. Although this is not a wordless book, children gain the same storytelling experience when they draw individual pictures of each event and then arrange drawings in either the logical order of a normal day, or in the (more fun) mixed-up pattern of the book.

Activities: Teacher to Student

TAPE-RECORDED STORYTELLING (P-I) Choose a wordless book and tell its story into a tape recorder. Mercer Mayer's series, which starts with *A Boy, a Dog, and a Frog* (Dial, 1967), is especially fun. After you have made the recording, you can share your story and the book with other children.

DRAMATIZATION (P-I) Choose a partner and, together, dramatize a story by taking the roles of different characters. If there are parts where there is no character talking, choose another partner who will be the narrator and tell those parts.

builds. The chain that is created latches each event to the next and recaptures all that has occurred before in a repetitive refrain. John Burningham plays off the cumulative form in *Mr. Gumpy's Outing* (N-P) and *Mr. Gumpy's Motorcar* (N-P), in which children and animals pile into Mr. Gumpy's boat for an outing and into his motor car for a ride. On the outing, because they do exactly what Mr. Gumpy tells them *not* to do, they end up spilling into the water. In the motor car, they run amok when rain turns the dirt road into a quagmire of mud.

Adelaide Holl tells a story akin to "Chicken Little" in *The Rain Puddle* (P). Barnyard animals see their own reflections in a huge rain puddle and fear that one of their kind has fallen in. When the sun dries up the puddle, Mrs. Hen, the originator of the rumor, explains simply, "The animals have all climbed out safely." The time-proven formula of the cumulative tale serves well today; original stories children tell show that they adopt this formula for their own. Part of the appeal lies in the predictability of the episodes and the use of a refrain, which enables listeners to recall the tale and become participants by retelling it.

A delightful story of poetic justice in which the bad guy loses and the good guy wins is found in Pat Hutchins's *Rosie's Walk*, (N-P), (also available as a film). Rosie the hen leads a charmed life; every time the predatory fox tries to grab her, some terrible misfortune befalls him and she saunters merrily on her way. The twinkle in her eye suggests that she arranges all of the accidents. The film (Weston Woods) combines music and animation to extend the pleasure of the humorous story. A similar tale in which the heritage of the folk tale is artfully reflected is *How the Rooster Saved the Day* (P), written by Arnold Lobel. A robber, who uses the night to cloak his deeds, plans to do away with the rooster because he interferes by summoning the day. The rooster cleverly outwits the robber, and the sun rises, forcing the robber to flee. Anita Lobel fills the illustrations with sunshine and sophisticated humor in this first collaborative effort by the Lobels.

Plays

Young children engage in dramatic play spontaneously when left to themselves: we hear them shouting from the top of the jungle gym, "I'm Spi-

Teaching Idea

PRESENTING LITERARY FOLK TALES TO EXPAND LANGUAGE (P) Children expand their language when they actively participate in using it in meaningful contexts. If you recall your childhood reading, you may find that particular words or phrases are associated with pleasant literary experiences. We know that children are attracted to new words and, once they use them in their speech, make them their own. For this reason, giving children opportunities to tell and retell stories with flannel board cutouts enhances language development. (See Chapter 12 for a discussion of flannel board stories.)

Choose a favorite story that has only a few characters. *Squawk to the Moon Little Goose,* by Edna Mitchell Preston, illustrated by Barbara Cooney (P, Viking, 1974), any of Rudyard Kipling's *Just-So Stories,* and *Mr. Gumpy's Motor Car,* by John Burningham (N-P, Crowell, 1976), are especially good because the stories are fun, easy to remember, and accumulate events and characters one at a time.

Water Rat gives mole his first ride in a boat.
(From *The River Bank* from *The Wind In The Willows* by Kenneth Grahame, illustrated by Adrienne Adams. Copyright © 1977 by Adrienne Adams. Reprinted by permission of Charles Scribner's Sons.)

derman,'' or one telling another, ''I'll be the doctor and you be sick.'' Imaginative play is natural and should be encouraged throughout childhood. Elementary-school children respond enthusiastically to drama experiences that focus on a specific theme or story as well as to spontaneous and creative improvisation. The fundamental urge to play-act or express oneself dramatically leads to wholesome educational experiences.

Think of the fun of playing the role of the pompous Toad in Kenneth Grahame's *The Wind in the Willows* (I), which is adapted to play form in *Toad of Toad Hall* (I) by A. A. Milne. In one of Toad's exploits he masquerades as a washerwoman and, when his deceit is uncovered, he rages:

TOAD: You common, low, fat, barge-woman, don't you dare to talk to your betters like that. Washerwoman, in-

84 deed! I would have you know that I am the Toad, the Terror of the Countryside, the Scourge of Barge-women! Keep your stupid little barge! I prefer—riding! (He unfastens the towrope, jumps on the horse's back and gallops off.) The Toad! The Toad![6]

Plays, stories told completely in dialogue, are unlike narrative stories in that they rely very little on description of characters and scenes. Plays contain the essential elements of story and are discussed here because of the similarities between their form and the stories children tell. Arousing anticipation of what happens next is a universal requirement for any good story and absolutely essential for a play. Scheherazade, the Sultan's bride in The Arabian Nights, escapes death by telling seemingly endless suspense stories to the Sultan, who, since he's eager to hear their outcomes, lets her live. Although the stakes are seldom that high, the necessity for a strong plot is great. The structure of the plot in a traditional play is very clear: there is a distinct beginning, a middle, and an end. Plot segments are clearly divided into acts or scenes and the climax is unquestionably clear; for when the conflict is resolved, the play is over. Thus, story structure is clearly evident in play form.

Narrative sequence undergirds a play; it builds a coherent plot and gradually unfolds the theme.[7] As students read or dramatize plays, the pivotal

Teaching Idea

PLAYING WITH PADDINGTON (P-I)   Children who know Paddington Bear will respond enthusiastically to Alfred Bradley's and Michael Bond's *Paddington on Stage* (P-I, Houghton Mifflin, 1977), which contains seven short plays adapted from Bond's stories about the lovable, accident-prone English bear. In the brief scenes, Paddington arrives at Paddington Station (the source of his name), visits a laundromat, goes to the dentist, wins a painting contest, and celebrates his birthday. Through their roles in dramatizing these episodes students learn to empathize with Paddington, adopting his perspective and beginning to feel what it is like to be someone else. Students who engage in creative dramatics often learn to get inside a character and originate speech and behavior consistent with it.

Activity: Teacher to Student

PADDINGTON ON STAGE (P-I)   A good way to start preparing for a play is to elect a leader and form committees to take care of scripts, casting, props, scenery, sound effects, programs, and invitations, or other things you may need. Each committee needs a chairperson to keep things running smoothly and to report back to the group.

If you decide to dramatize ''Paddington and the Old Master,'' for example, you will need to cast characters such as the bear himself, Mr. Brown, Mrs. Brown, Mr. Gruber, and Mrs. Bird. Props needed include paints, paint brushes, an easel, and a smock. Instead of memorizing the lines, have a reader's theater. Here, each player *reads* the character's part. This kind of play permits actors to take turns acting the different parts and gives them a chance to read with dramatic expression.

role of narrative structure becomes apparent; it is the essence of story and provides cohesiveness and complexity in the plot. In this case, the shape of story becomes another of the mental schemas of aspects of the world that students forge as they select from and organize their direct experiences. Plays and play acting accommodate a developing sense of story.

Features of plays such as direct dialogue, brevity of plot, and limited numbers of characters make them easy to read, while the lack of description and narration requires the reader to fill in details. The immediacy of drama contributes to its appeal to children. Even where enthusiasm for reading long, complicated novels is lacking, there is often a spirited zest for reading plays.

A play for children, *Maurice Sendak's Really Rosie* (P-I), contains the characters and props from the Nutshell Library: Johnny, Pierre, Alligator, Chicken Soup, Jennie, Buttermilk, Kathy, and Rosie—director, producer, and star of her block. Sendak's bouncy lyrics, scenario, and unparalleled illustrations are extended through the music written by Carole King. The script and musical arrangements give Sendak fans rousing material for their own productions.

Richard George, a sixth-grade teacher, adapts a story to play form in *Roald Dahl's Charlie and the*

Teaching Idea

PLAYING WITH POETRY (P)   Many poems can be dramatized. Appropriate ones will (1) have a narrative that contains action that can be visualized, with a story line that is interesting and fun; (2) contain dialogue for individual speaking parts; and (3) have a refrain, descriptive lines, or a chorus for small groups of children to speak. See Chapter 7 for narrative poems that work especially well. Try " 'Quack!' Said the Billy Goat," by Charles Causley, in *An Arkful of Animals,* selected by William Cole, illustrated by Lynn Munsinger (P, Houghton Mifflin, 1978), for some fun and nonsense about animals.

Activity: Teacher to Student

MAY I BRING A FRIEND? (P)   After reading the story poem *May I Bring a Friend?* (Atheneum, 1964), by Beatrice Schenk De Regniers, decide who will play the part of the boy narrator, the King, the Queen, the giraffe, monkeys, and other animals. You will also need about six people to speak as a chorus.

There are some simple costumes and props you can make to turn this story poem into a play. They include two crowns, an invitation, and some cups of tea. Here, use Beni Montresor's fine illustrations, which resemble stage settings, as a guide for scenery. A good way to portray the animals, such as the giraffe, the hippopotamus, and the lions, is to make face masks on paper plates. These are held up (on a stick) in front of the face as the character speaks. You don't need to memorize the parts; simply paste them to the back of the masks and read them aloud. Once your production is complete, share it with other groups.

Masks—here made of paper plates—help even shy children take on a role from a story.
(HBJ photograph by Richard C. Polister.)

Chocolate Factory: A Play (I). (Dahl's introduction to the play notes his approval of the adaptation.) Interested students and teachers can rewrite other stories into play form.

Paul Zindel won the Pulitzer Prize for *The Effect of Gamma Rays on Man-in-the-Moon Marigolds* (A), a play that appeals to mature readers for its sensitive portrayal of the relationship between an alcoholic mother and her gifted daughter.

DEVELOPING INDEPENDENCE IN LANGUAGE AND READING

Children learning to read are engaged in an exhilarating experience; it is an adventure that never ends, for we continue to learn to read throughout life. Mark Twain's *Huckleberry Finn,* read when one is an adult, carries a very different meaning from when we read it at twelve. One reason for this is that we use our experience to create meaning from the printed page, and so read differently as we gain more experiences on which to draw. Learning to read is not something that happens once; it is a lifetime job.

For children learning to read, the easy-to-read books, transitional books, and books for language play discussed in this section contain intangible assets, the greatest of which is the joy the book brings to the reader. When interesting books are provided, children struggling to learn to read find out that reading is worth the effort. The meager meaning that a child finds in "The cat sat on a mat" does not encourage him to read more. Books discussed here can convince children that reading leads to laughter and tears and other sorts of worthwhile meaning; children who discover that what they find in print is truly worth the effort will read. In *The Uses of Enchantment,* Bruno Bettleheim, speaking of fairy tales, but in a comment applicable to other types of literature as well, says:

The acquisition of skills, including the ability to read, becomes devalued when what one has learned to read adds nothing of importance to one's life. . . . The idea that learning to read may enable one later to enrich one's life is experienced as an empty promise when the stories the child listens to, or is reading at the moment, are vacuous.[8]

The wealth of fine books that exists insures that children can be surprised by joy at every stage in the process of learning to read. Learning to read with good literature translates to a promise fulfilled.

Books discussed in the first part of this section are called easy-to-read books because they are written with a limited vocabulary, which young children can begin to comprehend unassisted. We should not overwhelm beginning readers by throwing the entire English language at them at once, and so restrictions are set on the words used —but the stories themselves are good stories. Many easy-to-read books have strong characterization, worthy themes, and tight plots. The sentences are generally simple, without a lot of embedded clauses, and the language is often direct dialogue. The lines are printed so that sentence breaks occur according to natural phrasing, with meaningful chunks of language grouped together. This plus a limited number of different words and interesting stories insures a happy introduction to reading.

Children who are read to from an early age build expectations about stories and about the kind of language that comes from books. They go to books with enthusiasm, anticipating good stories and pleasant experiences. The bumper sticker stating "Kids Who Read Were Read To" proclaims a well-documented fact. Moreover, children who watch their own words being put onto paper learn intuitively the relation between print and sound. This means of teaching, called the language experience approach, provides a meaningful foundation for reading, especially when accompanied by a strong reading-aloud program based on good literature.[9] Mary Anne Hall, Sylvia Ashton-Warner, Roger Landrum, and many others have used this approach, which has as its basis the writing down by the teacher of the child's own familiar words, which, in turn, become the material used for reading instruction. The method assumes that a child will know what he says, will see what he has said when it is written, and will then be able to read his own words with meaning. Literature experiences that are shared and recorded in homemade books or on large charts for reference provide a strong base for beginning reading since the words used are integral to students' listening and speaking vocabularies. When children begin to read books written by others as well as those they write themselves, easy-to-read books are received with pleasure.

The second part of this section discusses books that provide a bridge between easy-to-read books and the unlimited wealth of independent reading material discussed elsewhere in this book. These so-called transitional books are appropriate for children who have mastered basic reading skills and are ready to read longer, more complex books. The concluding section describes books that play with language, building upon its idiosyncrasies and stretching its meanings. Simple jokes, riddles, and puns lead the child toward understanding more subtle and complex meanings embedded in figurative language. Language learning never ends; language-play books also feed the imagination of the language learner.

Easy-to-Read Books

Books that beginning readers can read on their own combine the controlled vocabulary of the basal reader with creative storytelling; their authors try to tell a good story using a limited number of words. Some early books written with such vocabularies were stilted and bland, but gradually authors mastered the form so that we now have many excellent easy-to-read books that tell good stories in a natural way. Children learn to read only through materials that make sense to them; many books of this type are genuinely sensible— not meaningless bits of language.

Else Minarik was one of the first to create good stories within the constraints of a restricted vocabulary. *Little Bear* (P), *Father Bear Comes Home* (P), *Little Bear's Friend* (P), *Little Bear's Visit* (P), and *A Kiss for Little Bear* (P) reveal the lovable, childlike nature of Little Bear. In one story, Little Bear wears his new space helmet on an imaginary trip to the moon. When he arrives he finds a house just like his own, a table just like his at home, and a Mother Bear just like his mother. This Mother Bear on the moon invites him for lunch because her own Little Bear has gone to Earth that day. The two continue the fantasy play until Little Bear wants to be reassured that she is really his Mother Bear and that he is in his very own home. Minarik's stories present exciting plots with plenty of action, and develop clear, vivid themes in a natural language style. Maurice Sendak's visual interpretation makes Little Bear even more appealing.

Arnold Lobel made beginning reading more fun when he created Frog and Toad and, in doing so, loosened the restrictions of the easy-to-read form. His two amphibian friends evoke unrepressed giggles from beginning readers who view Frog and Toad's naiveté with a feeling of superiority. *Frog and Toad Are Friends* (P), a Caldecott Honor Book, and *Frog and Toad Together* (P), a Newbery Honor Book, were recipients of these prestigious awards, which are rarely given to re-

Profile

ARNOLD LOBEL

Frog took the box outside. He shouted in a loud voice, "HEY BIRDS, HERE ARE COOKIES!"

Birds came from everywhere. They picked up all the cookies in their beaks and flew away.

"Now we have no more cookies to eat," said Toad sadly. "Not even one."

"Yes," said Frog, "but we have lots and lots of will power."

"You may keep it all, Frog," said Toad. "I am going home now to bake a cake." *Frog and Toad Together*

Frog and Toad, Arnold Lobel's famous friends, reveal human frailties familiar to us all. Super-organized list makers, compulsive gardeners, voracious cookie eaters, and brave foes of dragons and monsters, Frog and Toad and Lobel become lasting friends of children the very first time they meet.

Frog and Toad's idiosyncracies thrive in their comfortable relationship. Even when Toad, who would rather have cookies than will power, goes home to bake his cake, you know that he will return to share it with friend Frog. Lobel shares his whimsies in what he says is the last of the series: *Days With Frog and Toad*. Arnold Lobel describes his discovery of Frog and Toad:

I remember sitting on the front porch rooting around in my paper bag of life experiences until I hit upon frogs and toads. They look a good deal alike but are still very different. A frog seems to smile, while a toad is clearly a more introverted, slow-moving, worrisome creature (David W. McCullough, "Arnold Lobel and Friends: An Interview," *New York Times Book Review,* 11 Nov. 1979, p. 54).

An easy-to-read book is not easy to write. "Writing," Lobel says, "is very painful for me." He continues:

It is very hard for me to sit in a chair and do nothing until I have something to write down. I have to force myself not to think in visual terms, because I know if I start to think of pictures, I'll cop out on the text. When I think the text is perfect, I take a look at it as the illustrator, and sometimes the illustrator asks for a rewrite. With *Grasshopper on the Road* the illustrator/me got the writer/me to rewrite the whole thing, and then the illustrator had to do a whole new series of drawings" (McCullough, "Arnold Lobel," *New York Times Book Review,* p. 54).

He finds that sticking to an easy-to-read vocabulary is no problem at all, since most of us, he says, including himself, have easy-to-read minds.

Recipient of numerous awards, Arnold Lobel was born in Los Angeles and raised by his grandparents in Schenectady, New York. He was a lonely and rather unhappy child, and the highlight of his day was watching "Kukla, Fran, and Ollie" on television. Lobel met his wife Anita, also an author and illustrator, while attending Pratt Institute; he was directing a school play in which she had the leading role. Their two children are now grown, and the Lobels live in Brooklyn, New York.

Listen, Stanley.
I know you are there.
I know you are in back of the fence.
But I don't care, Stanley.
I don't want to play with you.
I don't want to talk to you.
You stay there, Stanley.
Stay in back of the fence.
I don't care.

And I Mean It, Stanley

CROSBY BONSALL

The rejection is not genuine of course, but is intended to entice Stanley over to play. When Crosby Bonsall does anything, however, she means it! In the world of children's books, she means it most often in the easy-to-read area. Although her career as a writer started almost accidentally, having been a partner in an advertising agency first, Crosby Bonsall is an important writer of books that hook beginning readers. Her first success was a book about a doll named Annie Beansprout, which she had designed.

Crosby Bonsall's illustrations are stories in themselves. If you look carefully at what's happening in the background of the pictures in *And I Mean It, Stanley*, you will see another story happening at the same time as the primary one. She says that many children may miss the subtle parallel story, but she puts it there for the special child to discover. Crosby Bonsall's pioneering success with the easy-to-read genre derives from a background of study in art, sculpture, and design. The subtle touches of humor in her illustrations cause readers to go back to them often, to pore over them, and to savor their whimsy.

Crosby Bonsall and her husband recently moved from rural Pennsylvania to New York City where, she says, one never wants for excitement and energy. People who know her think she creates her own excitement.

In *Frog and Toad Are Friends,* one of many human embarrassments is portrayed when Toad fears—correctly—that others will laugh at the sight of him in a bathing suit. (Illustration from *Frog and Toad Are Friends,* written and illustrated by Arnold Lobel. Copyright © 1970 by Arnold Lobel. By permission of Harper & Row, Publishers, Inc.)

stricted-vocabulary books. Only once before had an easy-to-read book been so recognized—when Minarik's *Little Bear's Visit* was named a Caldecott Honor Book for Sendak's illustrations. Lobel's *Frog and Toad Are Friends* (P), the first book in the series, shows Toad anxious to get under the water so no one can see him in his bathing suit because he feels so silly. Anyone who feels self-conscious will identify with Toad's feelings. The affectionate teasing between Lobel's all-too-human characters continues in *Days with Frog and Toad* (P).

Despite the fact that there are hundreds of easy-to-read books of literary quality, children should also have access to regular picture books that do not restrict vocabulary, control phrase length, or conform to the other constraints of easy-to-read books. In order to see if several well-known picture books—that is, with unrestricted vocabularies—differed greatly from the easy-to-

read books in the number of different words used, Alden J. Moe[10] analyzed seventy-five books. Whereas easy-to-read books use 10 to 250 different words, Moe found only 30 different words in Barbara Emberley's *Drummer Hoff* (N-P), 31 in Pat Hutchins's *Don't Forget the Bacon* (P), 48 in Robert Kraus's *Herman the Helper* (P), and 64 in Martha Alexander's *Blackboard Bear* (P). Moe does not claim that the number of different words is the only factor in readability, but he does show that many standard picture books can be used in beginning reading programs, especially if the teacher initially reads them aloud to the children.

Transitional Books

Children are proud to be able to read alone, and will soon march into a library and ask for a "real" book—"a book with chapters." Seeing older children reading, they think of thick books as a sign of growing up, and that only "little kids" read easy-to-read books; they want to demonstrate that they are beyond that stage. We know that, beyond the child's ego satisfaction, there are other benefits to be gained from reading a broader range of materials. The new words and structures encountered in their leisure reading will help children continue to grow in reading ability and experience.

The child making the transition to unlimited reading needs special consideration beyond readability of the material. The transitional books described in this section have features that offer such help. The format of these books is close in appearance to that of the textbooks the child is reading: print is large and well-spaced, and there is some illustration, though not on every page.

Transitional books have chapters. Although the same characters and plot continue throughout the book, each chapter is a self-contained episode, so that the child can complete it in a reasonable time. Characters and events link the episodes, so that children who are beginning to retain the continuity of a story over a period of several days obtain experience in remembering and building onto story lines. The stories develop one or more characters engaged in a number of interesting episodes and are often laced with humor.

USING NEW WORD POWER (P) Beginning readers are proud of their newly developed skill and take every opportunity to flaunt it. They are enthusiastic about activities that give them a chance to use their new word power and, at the same time, confirm their grasp of what they know. Word games, matching games, parallel stories, and crossword puzzles are enjoyable ways for them to show their word mastery. Harper & Row, Publishers, have several packets of crossword puzzles for primary-grade children with word clues based on their series of I Can Read books. (See Appendix for the address of Harper & Row.)

Activity: Teacher to Student

WORD PUZZLES (P) Do some crossword puzzles and then see if you can make up your own. Use titles and characters from your favorite books. You can also make up matching games with book titles and characters, or twenty-question-type guessing games in which you give clues from books:

1. Little Bear   a. Fixed lunch for an earthling.
2. Mother Bear   b. Was shy in a bathing suit.
3. Frog   c. Wrote a letter to his friend.
4. Toad   d. Made birthday soup.

Studies of reading preference consistently show that humor is a quality that appeals to children of all ages.[11] The type of humor that children respond to changes as they mature, but humor per se remains a constant in their book choices. The International Reading Association and the Children's Book Council co-sponsor a project in which children across the nation evaluate newly published books annually.[12] The resulting lists show that humorous books are among the favorites each year.

Many children have an insatiable appetite for reading at this time; unfortunately, the supply of quality transitional books, including humorous books, is small, and librarians often struggle to find enough books for them.

Some authors who meet the needs of children who are developing independence in reading are Beverly Cleary, Eleanor Clymer, Matt Christopher, Scott Corbett, Natalie Savage Carlson, Rebecca Caudill, Molly Cone, and Elizabeth Coatsworth— all of whose names, curiously, begin with C, a possibly mnemonic fact discovered by my daughter Janie, who spent many happy hours at the public library's C shelf.

Beverly Cleary's work has wide appeal and lasting value. *Henry Huggins* (P-I), the first in a series, introduces the ingenious Henry, who carries his dog home in a box on the bus. The dog is enough of a personality to be featured in a book of his own, *Ribsy* (P-I), in which he continues to lead the way into trouble and fun. We also meet Beezus, Henry's friend, in the earlier books and later follow her and her sister's exploits in *Beezus and Ramona* (P-I). Ramona, another star character, emerges here and merits having several more books with her as the focus: *Ramona the Pest* (P-I),

Ramona and Her Father (P-I), and *Ramona and Her Mother* (P-I).

Ramona and Her Father (P-I) is a Newbery Honor book, a notable fact in that this award is rarely given to books that appeal to the transitional reader. In this story, Ramona, now an impish second-grade student, approaches her world with an enthusiasm and naiveté that endears her to the readers, who laugh at her gullibility, having themselves passed that stage so very recently. In *Ramona and Her Father* (P-I), she assumes much more responsibility for her unemployed father, family finances, and her father's smoking than she can possibly handle, but her undaunted spirit makes the reader cheer her on. Cleary's characters remind you of children who live down the street in many neighborhoods across America; therein lies part of the secret of their universal appeal.

Dudley Pippin (P-I) and *Dudley Pippin's Summer* (P-I), by Philip Ressner, are two books well suited to the transitional reader. Dudley was singled out as a model character in Marlo Thomas's *Free to Be You and Me* (P-I) because he had the courage to cry. Dudley Pippin is not just known for crying, however, but for his imagination, fascination with the way people use words, and interest in friendship in these stories with subtle action and gentle humor.

Scott Corbett writes about a boy named Kirby in one of the many Corbett series. In this group of books, it is not so much character development (as in Beverly Cleary's books) as plot that works repeatedly. An eccentric old woman gives Kirby an amazing chemistry set that works wonders in *The Lemonade Trick* (I), *The Disappearing Dog Trick* (I), *The Hairy Horror Trick* (I), and many other books in the series. Readers striking out for independence find the exaggerated humor and ridiculous situations leading to a variety of disasters hilarious and engaging.

Third- and fourth-grade students with an overriding enthusiasm for sports devour the books of Matt Christopher, the prolific author of over fifty books, each with a central character struggling and training hard to become a good athlete. Christopher inevitably involves his character in a highly tense game that often involves sportsmanship and concludes with a hard-won victory. *Ice Magic* (P-I), *Soccer Halfback* (P-I), and *Football Fugitive* (P-I) are among recent favorites.

Children also like to read biographies of their favorite sports heroes. Sports biographies are usually available in great quantities but, unfortunately, are often of low quality. Because sports superstars (and, hence, books about them) rise rapidly and often descend nearly as rapidly, and because publishers want to keep current with the new stars, books are often commissioned to be written quickly, and so are sometimes hastily and poorly done. Sports biographies are ordinarily available in paperback, so a modest investment provides a collection large enough to meet the changing interests of students.

Mysteries are also a favorite part of the reading fare for children who are gaining some measure of independence in reading. In *Encyclopedia Brown, Boy Detective* (P-I), Donald Sobol has created a character who logically and methodically tracks down clues to solve mysterious events. Sobol's books are especially enjoyable because the reader is invited—since all the facts are given in the text—to participate in solving the cases along with the hero. For those readers who want to check their answers with the young detective's, the solutions are given at the end of the stories. Favorites in this series include *Encyclopedia Brown Takes the Case* (P-I) and *Encyclopedia Brown Tracks Them Down* (P-I).

Two series of mystery stories that need no introduction to children are the Nancy Drew and Hardy Boys stories. Harriet Stratemeyer Adams, using the pseudonym Carolyn Keene, has written all but the first three of the over eighty Nancy Drew mysteries. These widely read books have been translated into a number of languages, reprinted, mass marketed, sold through book clubs, and adapted into a television series. They, like so many of the series books, have little by way of literary quality, but they do appeal to children. Since these books have simple, predictable plots, children can read through them rapidly, and often go through a collecting phase with the books as they do with baseball cards, pennants, and other memorabilia. The collecting and series-reading stage is a normal developmental phase that children should be allowed to pursue. Teachers and librarians, however, do not need to allow children to remain at one level. Most teachers are not opposed to using any type of book to get children into reading, but do try to lead them gradually toward books of more lasting value. This is a process that is achieved gradually, as children learn to trust the teacher's judgment; this, in turn, comes from finding that books recommended are truly interesting and exciting. Thus, as long as series books are only a part of a child's total reading, they can be considered a stepping stone to books of higher literary quality.

Children who have passed through the transitional phase often can recognize for themselves what it is that makes the Nancy Drew and Hardy Boys books so appealing. The books are exciting, full of danger and intrigue, and the hero or heroine comes out the victor. Mature readers can see that therein lies the lack of distinction: as one sixth-grade girl put it, "Nancy Drew always wins." There is a sameness, and eventually a boredom, because the reader knows that these books do not reflect the real world, but do provide escape reading, much as gothic romances do for adults.

In dealing with such popular books of so little literary quality, librarians struggle to decide whether to make them available in schools. As with most things in life, there is no single right answer. If the books serve to get nonreaders into the reading habit and show them the enjoyment of reading, then, of course, they should be used. If, however, children have access to these books outside of school, they should be given heartier fare in school.

Teaching Idea

CHILD-MADE BOOKS (P-I)   As students gain competence in reading, they can put their language skills to use to produce their own materials. Children are literature makers as well as receivers, and they need opportunities to compose their own stories. Writing and reading are reciprocal processes that both draw upon and feed the child's imagination.

Initially, children can dictate their individual stories to a "scribe" or contribute to a group story that the teacher writes on the board or on a chart. Children prefer to write their own stories and should be encouraged to do so from the start, even though their writing skills seldom match their oral expression until fourth or fifth grade. Diaries or journals are excellent ways to encourage children to write every day and often lead to long stories in chapter format. Progress in writing ability becomes apparent over time.

Several books can help teachers guide children's writing of poetry and prose. Kenneth Koch describes the use of children's fantasies in *Wishes, Lies and Dreams: Teaching Children to Write Poetry* (Chelsea House, 1970) and the use of great poetry in *Rose, Where Did You Get That Red?* (Random House, 1974). Howard Greenfeld's *Books: From Writer to Reader* (I, Crown, 1976) describes his research and writing, and follows the publishing process through agents, editors, illustrators, designers, printers, and book promoters to the delivery for sale at a bookstore.

Activities: Teacher to Student

WRITE A BOOK (P-I)   Choose your favorite book character and write a new story about him or her. Perhaps you will choose to write a new episode about Henry Huggins or Ramona. Or you may think of a new adventure for Kirby to have with his chemistry set. When you have finished your story, reread and see if you can improve it; then illustrate and bind it.

A CLASSROOM NEWSPAPER (P-I)   Write articles that feature your favorite book characters in situations in your school. For example, write about Encyclopedia Brown and a cafeteria riot or stolen gym shoes. Interesting articles can also be based on biographies (write to publishers for them) of your favorite authors, and you can make up crossword puzzles about popular book characters. Write editorials about the types of books you like and don't like, and write book advertisements to persuade others to read your favorite books. Your newspaper may also include such features as book reviews, joke and puzzle columns, cartoons, advice columns, or an article about a forthcoming television special.

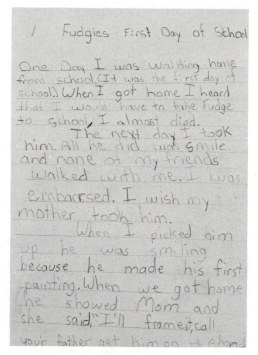

Cover of child-made book that is an extension of Judy Blume's *Tales of a Fourth-Grade Nothing* (Dutton, 1972). Such books often become cherished works, read again and again.

Books for Language Play

Ten-year-old David, eager to administer his version of an "I.Q. Test," quickly writes $\frac{G.I.}{CCCCCCCCCCCCC}$ and asks what it is. When we admit that we do not know, he explains, "It's a G.I. overseas—over Cs, get it?" He then administers several more items, including R/E/A/D/I/N/G (reading between the lines), BLCOUSE (a see-through blouse), and $\frac{O}{B.S., M.A., Ph.D.}$ (three degrees below zero). Although we failed the test, we shared the fun he was having with language.

Kornei Chukovsky describes children's delight with absurdities and their inexhaustible need to introduce nonsense into the world. He demonstrates that children play with ideas the way they play with blocks, marbles, or dolls, and states that no sooner does a child master an idea than he is eager to make it his toy.[13] New ideas and the language in which they are embedded become playthings as soon as they are learned.

Further, children learning to read use their ears to guide their eyes; they "listen" to the sound of language as they read, and they predict what is coming in the text on the basis of how it should sound. They have learned intuitively how language works and have expectations for meaning that come from reading print. Thus, the actual process of reading is a hypothesis-driven activity in which the child has hypotheses—expectations—about what the text says, and samples from the text enough information to check out whether his expectations are confirmed.[14] The hypotheses are based on previous language experiences.

Children quickly recognize the structure of Maurice Sendak's *Pierre* (N-P) and know that Pierre will say "I don't care" to everything his parents suggest. Pierre even gives his familiar response to a lion who wants to eat him. The lion says, "Is that all you have to say? . . . Then, I'll eat you if I may."[15] Children predict that Pierre will remain adamant throughout the clever cautionary tale.

Sendak's story vividly reflects the feelings and expectations of one small boy who responded with Pierre's words to teasing, reading failure, and general insecurities about himself. Brad was a first-grade dropout until he discovered Pierre. He found every opportunity he could to have the story read to him and soon was reading it himself. The easily repeatable phrase "I don't care" gave form to his feelings and, in turn, became the first words he read alone.

Young children experiment with the sounds of language as they are learning it and often accompany their play with "zooms" and "zowies" that are meaningless to others. They begin to notice that words rhyme and can supply the rhyming word in verse when given the opportunity. Soon they are playing with tongue twisters and delight in showing their mastery over phrases like "Rubber baby-buggy bumpers." Jokes, riddles, and puns, which illustrate the whimsy in language, then capture their fancy and soon become the source of much language play. During the elementary-school years, children recognize ambiguities in language; they learn that the same word can mean more than one thing and that some words that sound alike are not, in fact, the same word. They recognize a story that parodies a familiar tale, and they begin to learn that language is elastic and can be stretched, turned, and manipulated to play with meanings. From here it is a natural step to identifying figurative language and more subtle uses of language. Children's knowledge of language and how it works underlies all other learning.

Many books stimulate language exploration by calling attention to odd and distinctive aspects of some words and meanings. Children who are developing power in reading need a great deal of experience with brief, predictable, and humorous texts; it is through easily mastered, fun-giving material that children's decoding skills become automatic, and they learn that reading is a source of pleasure.

Young children like the sounds of language and often use phrases from television and elsewhere even when they do not know what the phrases mean, as in the case of a three-year-old who said, "I'm King Kong—now playing at your neighborhood theater,'' or the two-year-old whose first word was ''Clairol.'' When we read stories aloud to children our aim is not only to give pleasure, but to convey the meaning through the rhythm, pattern, and sound of language. Mother Goose verses embody rhythm and repetition in the language, which helps establish the child's developing sense of these patterns even before meaning is attached to the sounds. Children often accompany their play with words that become not only part of the play, but playthings themselves.[16] Winnie the Pooh sings ''Tiddley pom, tiddley pom'' as he walks in the snow, and the boy in Ruth Krauss's *A Very Special House* (P) says ''dee dee dee oh'' as he verbally accompanies his play.

Books that build on the sound and rhythm of language appeal to young children. ''Caps for sale, Caps for sale. Fifty cents a cap''[17] quickly becomes a chant for play and is heard as echo when you read Esphyr Slobodkina's *Caps for Sale* (N-P). Children also repeat the refrain in *Millions of Cats* (N-P), by Wanda Gág: ''Hundreds of cats, thousands of cats, millions and billions and trillions of cats.''[18] These stories become basic fare in the nursery and primary schools, where children play with the sounds of their language.

As they grow in language power, children play not only with the sounds but with the sense of language. Dennis Nolan's *Big Pig* (N-P) encourages both in that it describes overweight animals with rhyming words, such as a whopper grasshopper, a fat bat, and a thick chick. The book is a natural lead-in to a game of ''stinky pinky'' in which the questioner must define two words that go together and rhyme, such as ''What is a comical rabbit?'' (A funny bunny.) Children given encouragement for language play in the books they read go on to other imaginative uses of language. It is not long until they are breaking the code of Steven Kroll's *Gobbledygook* (P), in which ''Edward clumped out of bed . . . fumbled over his flippers and splashed to the roar.''[19]

Tongue twisters are verbal playthings that give as much fun when they are failed as when they are mastered—maybe even more so. ''She sells sea shells down by the seashore'' and ''The sheik's sixth sheep's sick'' lead to peals of laughter when said in any resemblance to the original. Verse is a natural setting for language that calls attention to itself, and verbal play is often found in verse form. The title for Sara and John Brewton's collection of humorous poems, *My Tang's Tungled and Other*

The refrain, ''Hundreds of cats, thousands of cats, millions and billions and trillions of cats,'' in Wanda Gág's old favorite invites participation by children.
(Reprinted by permission of Coward, McCann & Geoghegan, Inc. from *Millions of Cats* by Wanda Gág. Copyright 1928 by Coward McCann, Inc.; renewed 1956.)

STRETCHING AND TWISTING LANGUAGE (P-I)   The idea of exchanging one part of a word for another is used for comical effect in a retelling of "The Lion and the Mouse." In this backward-language version, adjacent words have the initial consonants switched. First, the unreversed version:

THE LION AND THE MOUSE

Once upon a time a big lion was lying fast asleep in the deep woods when a little mouse came running by. Alas for the wee mouse! She ran right over the mighty beast's nose!

The King of the Forest woke up with a loud roar. He clapped his huge paw on the little mouse and was about to gobble her down. The tiny mouse cried pitifully: "Please don't eat me. Set me free, and some day I may be able to do you a good turn."

The mighty beast smiled at the silly thought, but he set her free. A few days later, the big lion, while hunting in the woods, fell into a trap. He roared with a horrible sound. The little mouse heard him and came running fast. She began to nibble at the stout ropes that bound the huge beast, and in a short time the King of the Forest was free.

So the big lion learned that even the littlest creatures can be true friends in time of need.

And the reversed version:

THE MION AND THE LOUSE

Once upon a time a lig bion was fying last asleep in the weep doods when a mittle louse came bunning ry. Alas for the mee wouse! She ran right over the bighty neast's mose!

The Fing of the Korest woke up with a roud loar. He clapped his puge haw on the mittle louse and was about to dobble her gown. The miny touse pied critifully, "Dease plon't eat me. Fret me see, and some day I bay me able to do you a tood gurn."

The bighty meast smiled at the thilly sought, but he fret her see. A dew fays later, the lig bion, while wunting in the hoods, trell into a fap. He roared with a sorrible hound. The mittle louse heard him and came funning rast. She negan to bibble at the rout stopes that bound the buge heast, and in a tort shime the Fing of the Korest was free.

So the lig bion learned that even the crittlest leatures can be true friends in nime of teed.[20]

Although young children will enjoy hearing such a story read aloud, they probably will not feel comfortable reading it alone until they are firm in their grasp of letter-sound correspondences. Many well-known stories can be profitably retold in fractured language.

Another example of this kind of language play is found in Lewis Carroll's *Jabberwocky* (P-I), which has intrigued linguists and children since its publication in 1872. In the 1977 edition, published by Warne, Jane Breskin Zalben creates beautiful watercolor illustrations that enrich the poem and invite readers to explore the fascinating possibilities of nonsense words.

Ridiculous Situations (I), is found in one of the verses:

> Tongue twisters twist tongues twisted
> Trying to untangle twisted tangles:
> My tang's tungled now.[21]

Virginia Tashjian selected material for two books that quickly become favorites with intermediate-grade students. *Juba This and Juba That* (I) and *With a Deep Sea Smile* (I) are collections of chants, rhymes, riddles, songs, and tongue twisters that bring repeated requests for encores. Tashjian gives instructions for combining action with the verses for increasingly complex routines. Clapping hands, slapping knees, and stamping feet accompany "Juba this and Juba that / Juba killed a yellow cat."

Dr. Seuss writes stories that hinge on the strong rhythm and steady beat of the language. *Yertle the Turtle and Other Stories* (P) is a tribute to his skill with words. On the far-away Island of Sala-ma-Sond, Yertle rules with pompous self-importance, while Seuss plays with sound and nonsense, the trademark of all his books.

Jokes, riddles, and puns are very funny to children during their middle years. Language is used as a verbal plaything to create humor based on meanings children have learned intuitively. One advantage beyond the fun of these materials is that children often pursue poetry along with them, especially such humorous verses as those of Shel Silverstein and William Cole, discussed in Chapter 7.

Riddles and jokes that turn upon the peculiarities of language are continually popular; their appeal lies in the game they make of language. The humor in Ann Bishop's books—which number more than ten—entices primary-grade children. A good example, one of the jokes in *Oh Riddlesticks* (P), is: "What do you get from a sheep that studies karate?" (A lamb chop.) Jane Sarnoff's collections —such as *The Monster Riddle Book* (P-I)—are comparable, but for a slightly older audience. Young children who do not recognize the ambiguity or word play do not see the joke in "How can

you make a slow horse fast?" (Stop feeding it.) But upper-primary and intermediate-grade students find Sarnoff's riddles hilarious. Once children begin to understand the jokes they become voracious collectors of one-liners, frequently boring their audiences before they exhaust their supply of jokes. Adults respond with groans, but the joke teller's enthusiasm is seldom dampened by such discouragement. Bill Adler says that his book *The World's Worst Jokes* (P-I) does contain the worst, but the knock-knock, elephant, and pickle jokes he provides only fortify the ceaseless jokester. The supply of joke and riddle books seems endless, but because of their extreme popularity, a collection is soon frayed by overuse.

Charles Keller's work produces hours of giggles and belly laughs. *Going Bananas* (P-I), *Ballpoint Bananas* (P-I), and *Star Spangled Banana* (P-I) are among the many favorites. *Glory Glory How Peculiar* (P-I) parodies some of our most dignified songs by substituting new words sung to a familiar melody. The title song is sung to the tune of "The Battle Hymn of the Republic" and opens "Glory, glory how peculiar, Teacher hit me with a ruler," and "On Top of Old Smokey" becomes "On top of spaghetti, all covered with sauce." Not until the intermediate grades will students be likely to understand Keller's *Daffynitions* (I), because they are more subtle, as in the daffynition for the word kindred—"a fear of relatives coming." Once students start using puns they make life miserable for those who do not appreciate them. Ennis Rees collected many verbal ambiguities in *Pun Fun* (I), one of which could be referring to boring lectures:

> Some speeches are like the horns of a steer,
> Such as I hope you've seen—
> A little point here, a little point there,
> And a lot of bull between.[22]

Leone Adelson asks readers to consider the possible origins of words in *Dandelions Don't Bite* (I). She gives some theories about the origins of language, tells how words develop, how new words come from old ones or get patched together and grow in use until they are given formal acceptance. Howard Greenfeld shows—in *Summer Is*

There are few to whom the strange and fantastical creations—grinches, gacks, sneetches, ooblecks—of Theodor Seuss Geisel, also known as Dr. Seuss and Theo Le Sieg, do not appeal. Who can help but love the grouchy grinch, who tries to keep Christmas from coming, in *How the Grinch Stole Christmas,* or the kindly Thidwick of *Thidwick the Big Hearted Moose,* whose generosity nearly leads to his demise.

An avowed "doodler," Dr. Seuss often relies on chance to develop a sketch into a character or story. "I was doodling around with some drawings, the way I like to do, and a sketch of an elephant on some transparent paper happened to fall on top of a sketch of a tree. After a short while, it was obvious to me that Horton [the elephant] was sitting in the tree hatching an egg" (Lee Bennett Hopkins, *Books Are by People* [New York: Citation Press, 1969], p. 256). *Horton Hatches the Egg* was the result of that chance.

Dr. Seuss plays with language much as he plays with drawing. His first book, *And To Think That I Saw It On Mulberry Street* was written aboard ship during a long, rainy crossing of the Atlantic. "I amused myself by putting words to the rhythm of the ship's engine" (Hopkins, *Books Are by People,* p. 25). This story, considered by many to be one of his best, was rejected by twenty-nine publishers because it was different from any other children's book then on the market. That uniqueness heralded a new kind of literature for children.

In 1957, after reading an article about the poor quality of the supplementary readers used in schools, Dr. Seuss created a new kind of book, one with controlled vocabulary for children just learning to read. He remarks that he spent over a year on that book—*The Cat in the Hat*—which he had thought he could dash off in two or three weeks. In 1980 Dr. Seuss was honored with the Laura Ingalls Wilder Award, given every five years "to an author or illustrator whose books, published in the United States, have over a period of years made a substantial and lasting contribution to literature for children." There is no doubt that children would concur with this selection.

Dr. Seuss, who currently serves as president and editor-in-chief of the "Beginner Books" series at Random House, is a native of New England who now lives on a mountaintop in La Jolla, California, where he continues to produce those delightful, zany characters.

DR. SEUSS

Icumen In: Our Ever-Changing Language (I)—that even when words are widely accepted, they still change. He cites, for example, the euphemisms we use to avoid saying someone has died: passed away, departed, no longer among the living, lost.

The Phantom Tollbooth (I), by Norton Juster, is an old favorite with children who enjoy language play; the entire story is filled with puns, innuendo, and word play. Despite its age, the book is perennially fresh.

Ambiguity and parody become accessible to children as they become sophisticated about language and literature. They knowingly manipulate the structures and forms; many books encourage them to do so. Ambiguity in language and parodies of literary works are humorous when, of course, the reader understands the joke. A word that has more than one dictionary meaning can be ambiguous out of context and, when this condition is exploited so as to play with the multiple meanings, it becomes a tool of humor. Peggy Parish plays with multiple meanings in all of the *Amelia Bedelia* (P) stories, which primary-grade children appreciate. Children laugh because Amelia Bedelia interprets her instructions literally. They know that the instruction to "draw the drapes" does not mean to draw a picture of the drapes, as Amelia thinks, and that "plant a bulb" does not mean to plant an electric light bulb.

Homonyms include words that sound alike (homophones) but differ in meaning, such as bare/bear, blue/blew, and words that are spelled alike but differ in meaning and pronunciation (homographs), such as wind the clock/the wind is blowing, here is a present for you/let me present it to you, project your voice/do a project. Emily Hanlon's *How a Horse Grew Hoarse on the Site Where He Sighted a Bare Bear* (P) and Bernice K. Hunt's *Your Ant Is a Which* (P) are books that show children the fun that homonyms can create.

A parody is a piece of writing in which familiar work is imitated or mocked, usually in a light-hearted or comic way. Children recognize parodies and see the humor in them *if* they know well the original work that is parodied. Many familiar folk tales are the basis of parodies for children.

Brinton Turkle reverses the characters in the story of "Goldilocks and the Three Bears" in *Deep in the Forest* (N-P). In this droll wordless book, Baby Bear wanders through the forest, finds Goldilocks' home, eats her porridge, rocks in her chair, and bounces on her bed before he falls asleep in it. Of course, Goldilocks and her parents discover him and the damage he has wrought when they return from their walk in the forest. When you observe children exploring this book alone, you can detect the instant they recognize it as a reversal of their beloved story.

Teaching Idea

WHAT'S IN A NAME? (I) Many children are interested in the origin of their family name; some came from occupations, such as Farmer, Smith, Baker, Merchant, Taylor, and Hunter; some were coined from a distant father's name, such as Peterson, Abramson, and Richardson; while others developed from the location of the home, such as Hill, Rivers, and Lakeland. Several books are useful for researching students' names, including Christine Fletcher's *100 Key Names Across the Land* (I, Abingdon, 1973), Susanne Hilton's *Who Do You Think You Are?* (I, Westminster, 1976), Flora Loughead's *Dictionary of Given Names with Origins and Meanings* (I-A, Arthur Clark, 1974), Elsdon Smith's *New Dictionary of American Names* (I-A, Harper & Row, 1973) and *The Story of Our Names* (I, Gale Research, 1970), and Margaret Taylor's *What's Yr Nm?* (I, Harcourt Brace Jovanovich, 1970).

REGIONAL AND SOCIAL DIALECTS (I-A) Sociolinguists underscore the idea that language varies in different social contexts, that no one "standard" form is appropriate in all contexts, and that all language forms are equally valid as a means of communication. As the idea spreads, a trend toward greater variation has become evident in the language found in children's trade books (books of general interest, including all fiction). Your students can explore variations in language by comparing books with visible differences in dialogue and narrative.

Read aloud from the following books and see how the sound of the language differs.

Stevie (P, Harper & Row 1969) by John Steptoe: "I could never go anywhere without my mother sayin, 'Take Stevie with you now.' 'But why I gotta take him everywhere I go?' I'd say."

Jack and the Wonder Beans (P-I, Putnam's, 1977) by James Still: "Way back yonder there was a widow woman and her son Jack and they were poor as Job's turkey."

Wonderful Nice! (P, Lothrop, Lee & Shepard, 1960) by Irma Selz: " 'Lost you are, maybe?' asked the man in black. 'Well, now we'll see about that. I am Jacob Zook and this is my little girl, Katy. Home we go and soon where you live find out. Come on once—rootch over, Katy.' "

Where the Lilies Bloom (I-A, Lippincott, 1969) by Vera and Bill Cleaver:

Sometimes when I look at him I am stirred to an unholy anger. I think, God help me, Roy Luther. I don't want you dead and that's the truth. But since it's going to happen anyhow I wish it could hurry up and be over with for it's pulling us all to pieces and I need to get on with things and try to fix them around so that life will be easier for those of us who are left.

Garden of Broken Glass (I, Delacorte, 1975) by Emily Cheney Neville:

"See that cool leather hat that cat had for five dollars? I goin get me one." Dwayne tipped his head as if the hat were already on it.

"Where you gettin five dollars?" Melvita said.

"Girl, can't you keep yo ole evil mind off money for even one minute?" Dwayne let the grocery cart he was pulling thud to a stop. "Here. They yo groceries. You pull 'em up this big hot hill!"

His Own Where (A, Crowell, 1971) by June Jordan:

"You be different from the dead. All them tombstones tearing up the ground, look like a little city, like a small Manhattan, not exactly. Here is not the same. Here, you be bigger than the buildings, bigger than the little city. You be really different from the rest, the resting other ones."

Questions for discussion might be: What differences do you notice in the language of these books? One represents Pennsylvania Dutch, two represent an Appalachian dialect, and three represent a Black English vernacular. Where do variations occur in word order? What specific words show the flavor of the dialect? Can you hear differences in the intonation when you read them aloud? Which pattern of language is easiest for you to read aloud?

Raymond Briggs builds *Jim and the Beanstalk* (P) around a return visit to the giant years after the "Jack and the Beanstalk" story. Jim climbs the beanstalk and finds the aging giant toothless, nearly blind, and bald. The giant says that he used to enjoy fried boy on a slice of toast but no longer has any teeth. Jim makes three trips down the beanstalk to get a huge pair of false teeth, eye glasses, and a curly red wig to help the giant recapture some of the pleasures of his younger days.

Some very funny stories use children's familiarity with old folk tales to create humor. Mary Rayner uses "The Three Little Pigs" as the vehicle for *Mr. and Mrs. Pig's Evening Out* (P). Children know that there will be trouble when they see the wolf tail hanging out below the baby sitter's long dress, even though Mother Pig does not notice it. Through quick wit, the pigs survive to have another encounter in *Garth Pig and the Ice Cream Lady* (P).

Teaching Idea

PLAY WITH PARODY (P-I) At first, primary-grade children may not feel comfortable with parodies on favorite stories, but when such parodies are presented in a spirit of fun, they quickly catch the humor and join in the laughter. Most intermediate-grade students see the joke immediately and create their own versions of other stories. Ask your students to collect parodies, write their own, or present them in dramatic form.

Activities: Teacher to Student

FAVORITE TALES REVISITED (I) Write a modern version of a folk tale. You might have Cinderella go to a disco on roller skates, Snow White run away to a high-rise apartment, or Jack climb a space-rocket launching pad.

Tell a familiar story from a different point of view; for example, have the wolf tell the story of "Little Red Riding Hood."

UPDATED NURSERY RHYME (I) Discuss the meaning of this modern version of "Sing a Song of Sixpence."

CONTEMPORARY NURSERY RHYME

The Queen was in the parlour,
  Polishing the grate;
The King was in the kitchen
  Washing up a plate;
The maid was in the garden
  Eating bread and honey,
Listening to the neighbours
  Offering her more money.[23]

Choose a nursery rhyme and make some satirical changes in the words (as above) without losing the rhythm of the original. You might make a traditional verse into a modern one by discussing current topics.

Growth in comprehending figurative language continues from early childhood through adulthood, but our knowledge of the process is limited. We do know that social interaction with others who use figurative language encourages children to do the same. Howard Gardner finds that primary-grade children understand simple metaphors based on physical resemblance—for example, "the sun is a ball" and "snowy bushes are popcorn balls," but "the prison guard's heart is stone" requires a different base for comparison to make it comprehensible.[24] Familiarity with the content referred to in figurative language is obviously necessary but not sufficient to understand it. Adult learners of a second-language find metaphoric expressions in the second language difficult to comprehend.

Children's use of figurative language in speaking exhibits an even more erratic pattern than that of comprehension. Kornei Chukovsky[25] and Selma Fraiberg,[26] as well as many parents, give examples of young children's inventive comparisons that delight the adult ear. Chukovsky describes as a linguistic genius the young child who said that a bald man has a "barefoot head," that a mint candy "makes a draft in your mouth," and that the husband of a grasshopper is a "daddyhopper." Howard Gardner and Ellen Winner heard a four-year-old call a streak of skywriting a "scar on the sky."[27]

Linguistic creativity emerges around the age of two and increases until about the age of six, but then the expression of figurative language begins to decrease. The curve of production of metaphor between ages three and nineteen is roughly U-shaped, with high production for ages three to five and seventeen to nineteen, but with lowest production around the age of eight or nine. Thus there is a seeming paradox: young children, who so often interpret adult expressions literally, create very sophisticated figurative comparisons in their own speech, yet, when their comprehension of other people's metaphors improves (around eight or nine) their own use of metaphor practically disappears. During the early stage of concrete operations, when children can reason but need to see objects physically in order to do so (about seven to nine years), they are very literal in their use of language; thus, when they say that "hair is spaghetti" it may represent a literal statement to them and not the use of language in a figurative way. Gardner and Winner note that almost all early metaphors are based on a physical resemblance between elements rather than on conceptual, expressive, or psychological links. When asked how a snowball fight and a battle could be alike, eight-year-olds said, "Because they're both outside," ignoring the idea of an adversary relationship.

There are few studies exploring the development of metaphoric competence. Those in which children were asked to paraphrase, however, indicate that there is little evidence of understanding of metaphor until preadolescence. However, a great deal of what children learn about language and its use cannot be assessed easily. Further, mastery of a language riddled with figurative usage—as ours is —depends upon a child's exposure to numerous examples of it. For these reasons and others, children should be exposed to the beauty of language as it is used by our finest authors.

Katherine Paterson and Natalie Babbitt are two contemporary authors who use words to paint panoramas for the imagination. Their work is replete with examples of language used beautifully. In Natalie Babbitt's *The Eyes of the Amaryllis* (I-A), her descriptions, although simply stated, evoke complex pictures in the mind's eye:

The beaming sea lay far out, at low tide, much as it had the afternoon before, and it sparkled in the early sunshine, flicking tiny, blinding flashes of light into the air. The horizon, impossibly far away, invited her. This was a mermaid morning—a morning for sitting on the rocks and combing your long red hair.[28]

It is easy to close your eyes and know what Jenny is experiencing at this memorable point. Her mermaid morning marks a turning point in the story.

In *Bridge to Terabithia* (I), Katherine Paterson describes Jesse's feelings as "mad as flies in a fruit jar" and bubbling inside him "like a stew on the back of the stove." At another point we are told, "it seemed to him that his life was delicate as a dandelion. One little puff from any direction, and it was blown to bits." After his friend's death, he is described as stranded "like an astronaut wandering about on the moon. Alone."[29] The book also contains large metaphors, such as the meaning of Terabithia and what the bridge represents. The dandelion image can be particularly meaningful for teachers who would want to impart the beauty of language to students. Bearing in mind its delicacy, we should avoid sending children on deliberate hunts for metaphors and similes. Indeed, nothing is more certain to blow a love of language to bits.

CRITERIA FOR SELECTING BOOKS FOR LANGUAGE DEVELOPMENT

Viewing books from the perspective of the child's developing language provides a broad framework for criteria. Most important is to select books that match the conceptual level of the child or that are just slightly above it, to lead them toward expanded language use.

The very early books for the youngest child may be primarily visual and need to be used with an adult guide, who encourages the child to talk. Bright and clear pictures that represent the child's world are best. Gradually, the full story context becomes important as children learn to love a story.

Certainly, books for language development are ones that contain interesting language, but, again, we are guided by the developmental level of the child. Subtle word play is not funny to the very young child, nor are obvious jokes funny to the older one. Choose books that encourage playing with language; however, as children's vocabularies grow and their understanding increases, choose books that promote manipulating language and stretching meanings. Finally, look for books that encourage imaginative play. Children's imaginations grow with free reign and continual feeding; watch for books that feed the fancy.

Notes

1. David McCord, "Books," *One at a Time,* illus. Henry B. Kane (Boston: Little, Brown, 1977), pp. 200–01.
2. Helen Keller, *The Story of My Life* (Garden City, N.Y.: Doubleday, 1905), p. 36.
3. Annis Duff, *Bequest of Wings* (New York: Viking, 1944), pp. 55, 94.
4. Beverly Cleary, *Ramona the Pest,* illus. Louis Darling (New York: Morrow, 1968) p. 17.
5. Ibid., p. 27.
6. A. A. Milne, *Toad of Toad Hall: A Play from Kenneth Grahame's Book* (1929; New York: Scribner's, 1957), p. 130.
7. Events arranged in a time sequence are necessary but not sufficient to develop a plot; a plot emphasizes causality and makes the reader ask why the events occurred. According to E. M. Forster, "The king died and then the queen died" is a story, but "The king died and the queen died of grief" is a plot. In both we must consider the death of the queen but in the first, we say "and then?" but in the second we ask "why?" (E. M. Forster, *Aspects of the Novel* [New York: Harcourt Brace Jovanovich, 1947], p. 130.)
8. Bruno Bettelheim, *The Uses of Enchantment: The Meaning and Importance of Fairy Tales* (New York: Knopf, 1976), p. 4.

9. Mary Anne Hall, *Teaching Reading as a Language Experience* (Columbus, Ohio: Merrill, 1970). The language experience approach is also discussed in Roger Landrum et al., *A Day Dream I Had at Night and Other Stories: Teaching Children How to Make Their Own Readers* (New York: Teachers and Writers Collaborative, 1971); Rosellen Brown et al., *The Whole Word Catalogue,* 4, No. 3 (New York: Teachers and Writers Collaborative, 1972); Sylvia Ashton-Warner, *Teacher* (New York: Simon and Schuster, 1966).

10. Alden J. Moe, "Using Picture Books for Reading Vocabulary Development," in *Using Literature in the Classroom,* ed. John Warren Stewig and Sam L. Sebesta (Urbana, Ill.: National Council of Teachers of English, 1978), pp. 13–19.

11. George W. Norvell, *What Boys and Girls Like to Read* (Silver Burdett, 1958); and Dianne L. Monson, "Children's Responses to Humorous Stories," Diss. Univ. of Minnesota 1966.

12. Since 1974, five regional teams of literature specialists, teachers, and librarians annually field test approximately six hundred books with nearly ten thousand children. Each year the results of that selection process are published in the October issue of *The Reading Teacher* as "Children's Choices" (formerly "Classroom Choices").

13. Kornei Chukovsky, *From Two to Five,* ed. and trans. Miriam Morton (Berkeley: Univ. of California Press, 1963), p. 98.

14. For further information on reading as a hypothesis-driven activity, see Frank Smith, *Comprehension and Learning: A Conceptual Framework for Teachers* (New York: Holt, Rinehart & Winston, 1975); Frank Smith, *Reading Without Nonsense* (New York: Columbia Univ. Press, Teachers College Press, 1979); Kenneth Goodman, *Psycholinguistics and the Teaching of Reading* (Newark, Del.: International Reading Association, 1968).

15. Maurice Sendak, *Pierre* (New York: Harper & Row, 1962), p. 32.

16. For further exploration of children's language play, see David Holbrook, *Children's Games* (Chester Springs, Pa.: Dufour, 1968); and Iona and Peter Opie, *Lore and Language of School Children* (London: Oxford Univ. Press, 1959).

17. Esphyr Slobodkina, *Caps for Sale* (New York: Young Scott, 1947), unpaged.

18. Wanda Gág, *Millions of Cats* (New York: Coward, McCann & Geoghegan, 1928), unpaged.

19. Steven Kroll, *Gobbledygook,* illus. Kelly Oechsli (New York: Holiday House, 1977), pp. 2–3.

20. Norton Mockridge, "The Lion and the Mouse/The Mion and the Louse," in *Sounds of the Storyteller,* ed. Bill Martin, Jr., and Peggy Brogan (New York: Holt, Rinehart & Winston, 1972), pp. 26–27.

21. Sara and John Brewton, eds., *My Tang's Tungled and Other Ridiculous Situations* (New York: Crowell, 1973), p. 1.

22. Ennis Rees, *Pun Fun* (New York: Abelard, 1965), p. 55.

23. Myra Cohn Livingston, ed., *Speak Roughly to Your Little Boy,* illus. Joseph Low (New York: Harcourt Brace Jovanovich, 1971), p. 131.

24. Howard Gardner, et al., "The Development of Figurative Language," in *Children's Language,* Vol. I, ed. Keith E. Nelson (New York: Gardner Press, 1978), pp. 1–38.

25. Chukovsky, *From Two to Five,* pp. 1–18.

26. Selma Fraiberg, *The Magic Years* (New York: Scribner's, 1968), pp. 112–26.

27. Howard Gardner and Ellen Winner, "The Child Is Father to the Metaphor," *Psychology Today,* May 1979, pp. 81–91.

28. Natalie Babbitt, *The Eyes of the Amaryllis* (New York: Farrar, Straus & Guroux, 1977), p. 47.

29. Katherine Paterson, *Bridge to Terabithia,* illus. Donna Diamond (New York: Crowell, 1977), pp. 1, 76, 114.

Professional References

Ashton-Warner, Sylvia. *Teacher*. Simon and Schuster, 1966.

Bettelheim, Bruno. *The Uses of Enchantment: The Meaning and Importance of Fairy Tales*. Knopf, 1976.

Brown, Rosellen, et al. *The Whole Word Catalogue*, 4, No. 3. Teachers and Writers Collaborative, 1972.

Chukovsky, Kornei. *From Two to Five*. Ed. and trans. Miriam Morton. Univ. of California Press, 1963.

Duff, Annis. *Bequest of Wings*. Viking, 1944.

Forster, E. M. *Aspects of the Novel*. Harcourt Brace Jovanovich, 1947.

Fraiberg, Selma. *The Magic Years*. Scribner's, 1968.

Gardner, Howard, and Ellen Winner. "The Child Is Father to the Metaphor." *Psychology Today*. May 1979, pp. 81–91.

Goodman, Kenneth. *Psycholinguistics and the Teaching of Reading*. International Reading Association, 1968.

Hall, Mary Anne. *Teaching Reading as a Language Experience*. Merrill, 1970.

Holbrook, David. *Children's Games*. Dufour, 1968.

Keller, Helen. *The Story of My Life*. Doubleday, 1905.

Landrum, Roger, et al. *A Day Dream I Had at Night and Other Stories: Teaching Children How to Make Their Own Readers*. Teachers and Writers Collaborative, 1971.

McCullough, David W. "Arnold Lobel and Friends. An Interview." *New York Times Book Review*. 11 Nov. 1979, p. 54.

Martin, Bill, Jr., and Peggy Brogan. *Sounds of the Storyteller*. Holt, Rinehart & Winston, 1972.

Monson, Dianne L. "Children's Responses to Humorous Situations." Diss. Univ. of Minnesota 1966.

Nelson, Keith E., ed. *Children's Language*, Vol. I. Gardner Press, 1978.

Norvell, George W. *What Boys and Girls Like to Read*. Silver Burdett, 1958.

Opie, Iona and Peter. *The Lore and Language of School Children*. Oxford Univ. Press, 1959.

Smith, Frank. *Comprehension and Learning: A Conceptual Framework for Teachers*. Holt, Rinehart & Winston, 1975.

_____. *Reading Without Nonsense*. Columbia Univ. Press, Teachers College Press, 1979.

Stewig, John Warren, and Sam L. Sebesta, eds. *Using Literature in the Elementary Classroom*. National Council of Teachers of English, 1978.

Children's Books Cited in Chapter

Adelson, Leone. *Dandelions Don't Bite: The Story of Words*. Illus. Lou Myers. Pantheon, 1972.

Adler, Bill. *World's Worst Riddles and Jokes*. Illus. Ed Malsberg. Grosset and Dunlap, 1976.

Alexander, Martha. *Blackboard Bear*. Dial, 1969.

Anno, Mitsumasa. *Anno's Alphabet: An Adventure in Imagination*. Crowell, 1976.

_____. *Anno's Counting Book*. Crowell, 1977.

Babbitt, Natalie. *The Eyes of the Amaryllis*. Farrar, Straus & Giroux, 1977.

Baskin, Hosie, Tobias Baskin, and Lisa Baskin. *Hosie's Alphabet*. Illus. Leonard Baskin. Viking, 1972.

Bishop, Ann. *Oh Riddlesticks!* Illus. Jerry Warshaw. Whitman, 1976.

Bonsall, Crosby. *And I Mean It, Stanley*. Harper & Row, 1974.

Brewton, Sara, John E. Brewton, and G. Meredith Blackburn. *My Tang's Tungled and Other Ridiculous Situations*. Illus. Graham Booth. Crowell, 1973.

Briggs, Raymond. *Jim and the Beanstalk*. Coward, McCann & Geoghegan, 1970.

Burningham, John. *Mr. Gumpy's Motor Car*. Crowell, 1976.

_____. *Mr. Gumpy's Outing*. Holt, Rinehart & Winston, 1971.

Carle, Eric. *The Very Hungry Caterpillar*. Collins-World, 1969.

Carroll, Lewis. *Jabberwocky*. Illus. Jane Breskin Zalben. Warne, 1977.

Charlip, Remy, and Jerry Joyner. *Thirteen*. Parents, 1975.

Christopher, Matt. *Football Fugitive*. Illus. Larry Johnson. Little, Brown, 1976.

_____. *Ice Magic*. Illus. Byron Goto. Little, Brown, 1973.

_____. *Soccer Halfback*. Illus. Larry Johnson. Little, Brown, 1978.

Cleary, Beverly. *Beezus and Ramona*. Illus. Louis Darling. Morrow, 1955.

_____. *Henry Huggins*. Illus. Louis Darling. Morrow, 1950.

_____. *Ramona and Her Father*. Illus. Alan Tiegreen. Morrow, 1977.

_____. *Ramona and Her Mother*. Illus. Alan Tiegreen. Morrow, 1979.

_____. *Ramona the Pest*. Illus. Louis Darling. Morrow, 1968.

_____. *Ribsy*. Illus. Louis Darling. Morrow, 1964.

Corbett, Scott. *The Disappearing Dog Trick*. Illus. Paul Galdone. Little, Brown, 1963.

_____. *The Hairy Horror Trick*. Illus. Paul Galdone. Little, Brown, 1969.

_____. *The Lemonade Trick*. Illus. Paul Galdone. Little, Brown, 1960.

Crews, Donald. *Truck*. Greenwillow, 1980.

Emberley, Barbara. *Drummer Hoff*. Illus. Ed Emberley. Prentice-Hall, 1967.

Falls, C. B. *The ABC Book*. Doubleday, 1957.

Feelings, Tom and Muriel. *Jambo Means Hello: Swahili Alphabet Book*. Dial, 1974.

_____. *Moja Means One: Swahili Counting Book*. Dial, 1976.

Gág, Wanda. *Millions of Cats*. Coward, McCann & Geoghegan, 1928.

George, Richard. *Roald Dahl's Charlie and the Chocolate Factory: A Play*. Intro. Roald Dahl. Knopf, 1976.

Grahame, Kenneth. *The Wind in the Willows*. Illus. Ernest H. Shepard. Scribner's, 1933.

Greenfeld, Howard. *Summer Is Icumen In: Our Ever-Changing Language*. Crown, 1978.

Hanlon, Emily. *How a Horse Grew Hoarse on the Site Where He Sighted a Bare Bear: A Tale of Homonyms*. Illus. Lorna Tomei. Delacorte, 1976.

Hoban, Tana. *Look Again*. Macmillan, 1971.

Holl, Adelaide. *The Rain Puddle*. Illus. Roger Duvoisin. Lothrop, Lee & Shepard, 1965.

Hopkins, Lee Bennett. *Books Are by People*. Citation Press, 1969.

Hunt, Bernice Kohn. *Your Ant Is a Which*. Illus. Jan Pyk. Harcourt Brace Jovanovich, 1976.

Hutchins, Pat. *Changes, Changes*. Macmillan, 1971.

_____. *Don't Forget the Bacon*. Greenwillow, 1976.

_____. *Rosie's Walk*. Macmillan, 1968.

Juster, Norton. *The Phantom Tollbooth*. Random House, 1961.

Keller, Charles, comp. *Ballpoint Bananas and Other Jokes for Kids*. Illus. David Barrios. Prentice-Hall, 1973.

_____. *Daffynitions*. Illus. F. A. Fitzgerald. Prentice-Hall, 1976.

_____. *Glory, Glory, How Peculiar*. Illus. Lady McCrady. Prentice-Hall, 1976.

_____. *Going Bananas*. Illus. Rodger Wilson. Prentice-Hall, 1975.

_____. *The Star-Spangled Banana and Other Revolutionary Riddles*. Illus. Tomie de Paola. Prentice-Hall, 1974.

Kraus, Robert. *Herman the Helper*. Illus. Jose Aruego and Arienne Dewey. Windmill-Dutton, 1974.

Krauss, Ruth. *A Very Special House*. Illus. Maurice Sendak. Harper & Row, 1953.

Kroll, Steven. *Gobbledygook*. Illus. Kelly Oechsli. Holiday House, 1977.

Kunhardt, Dorothy. *Pat the Bunny*. Golden Press-Western, 1962 (1940).

Lobel, Arnold. *Days with Frog and Toad*. Harper & Row, 1979.

_____. *Frog and Toad All Year*. Harper & Row, 1976.

_____. *Frog and Toad Are Friends*. Harper & Row, 1970.

_____. *Frog and Toad Together*. Harper & Row, 1972.

_____. *The Great Blueness and Other Predicaments*. Harper & Row, 1968.

_____. *How the Rooster Saved the Day*. Illus. Anita Lobel. Greenwillow, 1977.

McCord, David. *One at a Time*. Illus. Henry B. Kane. Little, Brown, 1977.

Matthiesen, Thomas. *ABC: An Alphabet Book*. Platt & Munk, 1966.

Mayer, Mercer. *Frog Goes to Dinner*. Dial, 1974.

_____. *Frog Where Are You?* Dial, 1969.

Milne, A. A. *The House at Pooh Corner*. Illus. Ernest H. Shepard. Dutton, 1928.

_____. *Toad of Toad Hall*. Scribner's, 1957.

Minarik, Else H. *Father Bear Comes Home*. Illus. Maurice Sendak. Harper & Row, 1959.

_____. *A Kiss for Little Bear*. Illus. Maurice Sendak. Harper & Row, 1968.

_____. *Little Bear*. Illus. Maurice Sendak. Harper & Row, 1957.

_____. *Little Bear's Friend*. Illus. Maurice Sendak. Harper & Row, 1960.

_____. *Little Bear's Visit*. Illus. Maurice Sendak. Harper & Row, 1961.

Nolan, Dennis. *Big Pig*. Prentice-Hall, 1976.

Parish, Peggy. *Amelia Bedelia*. Illus. Fritz Siebel. Harper & Row, 1963.

Paterson, Katherine. *Bridge to Terabithia*. Illus. Donna Diamond. Crowell, 1977.

Potter, Beatrix. *The Tale of Peter Rabbit*. Warne, 1902.

Provensen, Alice and Martin. *A Peaceable Kingdom: The Shaker Abecedarius*. Viking, 1978.

Rayner, Mary. *Garth Pig and the Ice-Cream Lady*. Atheneum, 1977.

_____. *Mr. and Mrs. Pig's Evening Out*. Atheneum, 1976.

Rees, Ennis. *Pun Fun*. Illus. Quentin Blake. Abelard-Schuman, 1965.

Ressner, Philip. *Dudley Pippin*. Illus. Arnold Lobel. Harper & Row, 1965.

_____. *Dudley Pippin's Summer*. Illus. Ben Shecter. Harper & Row, 1979.

Sarnoff, Jane, and Reynold Ruffins. *The Monster Riddle Book*. Scribner's, 1975.

Sendak, Maurice. *Chicken Soup with Rice*. Harper & Row, 1962.

_____. *Maurice Sendak's Really Rosie: Starring the Nutshell Kids*. Harper & Row, 1975.

_____. *Pierre*. Harper & Row, 1962.

Seuss, Dr. *And to Think That I Saw It on Mulberry Street*. Vanguard, 1937.

_____. *The Cat in the Hat*. Random House, 1957.

_____. *Horton Hatches the Egg*. Random House, 1940.

_____. *How the Grinch Stole Christmas*. Random House, 1957.

_____. *Thidwick the Big Hearted Moose*. Random House, 1948.

_____. *Yertle the Turtle and Other Stories*. Random House, 1958.

Slobodkina, Esphyr. *Caps for Sale*. Scott, Foresman, 1947.

Sobol, Donald. *Encyclopedia Brown, Boy Detective*. Illus. Leonard Shortall. Nelson, 1963.

_____. *Encyclopedia Brown Takes the Case*. Illus. Leonard Shortall. Nelson, 1973.

_____. *Encyclopedia Brown Tracks Them Down*. Illus. Leonard Shortall. Nelson, 1971.

Tashjian, Virginia. *Juba This and Juba That*. Illus. Victoria De Larrea. Little, Brown, 1969.

_____. *With a Deep Sea Smile: Story Hour Stretchers for Large or Small Groups*. Illus. Rosemary Wells. Little, Brown, 1974.

Thomas, Marlo, et al. *Free to Be You and Me*. McGraw-Hill, 1974.

Tudor, Tasha. *A Time to Keep: The Tasha Tudor Book of Holidays*. Rand McNally, 1977.

Turkle, Brinton. *Deep in the Forest*. Dutton, 1976.

Twain, Mark. *The Adventures of Huckleberry Finn*. Harper & Row, 1884.

Zindel, Paul. *The Effect of Gamma Rays on Man-in-the-Moon Marigolds*. Harper & Row, 1971.

Recommended Reading

Participation Books

John Burningham's books for toddlers tell very simple stories about *The Rabbit, The Snow* (both N, Crowell, 1975), *The Blanket,* and *The Dog* (both N, Crowell, 1976). Gunilla Wolde introduces a charming moppet in a series that includes *This Is Betsy* and *Betsy's Baby Brother* (both N, Random House, 1975), while Rosemary Wells tells about a young rabbit's new experiences in *Max's First Word, Max's Toys, Max's Ride,* and *Max's New Suit* (all N, Dial, 1979).

Angela Banner's Ant and Bee stories have a nice British flavor and use different colors to teach key words. *Ant and Bee and the ABC* (N, Watts, 1967), *Ant and Bee and the Doctor* (N, Watts, 1967), and *One, Two, Three with Ant and Bee* (Watts, 1959) are among the favorites.

Poetry for toddlers with a healthy dose of Mother Goose verses is found in Josette Frank's *Poems to Read to the Very Young* (N-P, Random House, 1961) and *More Poems to Read to the Very Young* (N-P, Random House, 1968), and in Dorothy Aldis's *All Together* (N-P, Putnam's 1952).

May Hill Arbuthnot's *Time for Poetry* (all ages, Scott, Foresman, 1967) includes poems young children ask for repeatedly —among them Vachel Lindsay's "The Little Turtle," Evelyn Beyer's "Jump or Jiggle," A. A. Milne's "Hoppity," Muriel Sipe's "Good Morning," and Jane Taylor's "Twinkle, Twinkle Little Star."

Alphabet Books

Many illustrators use the alphabet to display their artistic skills in books whose titles declare their authorship: *Bruno Munari's ABC* (N-P, Collins-World, 1960), *Celestino Piatti's Animal ABC* (N-P, Atheneum, 1966), *Brian Wildsmith's ABC* (N-P, Watts, 1963), *Helen Oxenbury's ABC of Things* (N-P, Watts, 1972), *John Burningham's ABC* (N-P, Bobbs-Merrill, 1967), and *A for Angel: Beni Montresor's ABC* (N-P, Knopf, 1969).

Robert Crowther combines the alphabet with pop-up cutouts in *The Most Amazing Hide and Seek Alphabet Book* (N-P, Viking, 1978), where each letter has a flap to be pulled or turned to reveal a sprightly animal and its name. Marcia Brown uses pairs of sequential letters to make a phrase in *All Butterflies* (N-P, Scribner's, 1974).

Ed Emberley's ABC (N-P, Little, Brown, 1978) shows how to form letters; for example, a *b*ear watches a *b*eetle place *b*lueberries in the shape of a *B*. Victoria Chess tells a cumulative tale with letters in *Alfred's Alphabet Walk* (N-P, Greenwillow, 1979), as does Jane Yolen in *All the Woodland Early: An ABC Book,* illustrated by Jane Breskin Zalben (P, Collins-World, 1979).

Poems about the alphabet include Phyllis McGinley's "All Around the Town," Wanda Gág's "The ABC Bunny," and Edward Lear's "A Was Once an Apple Pie" in May Hill Arbuthnot's *Time for Poetry* (all ages, Scott, Foresman, 1967), and David McCord's "Alphabet" in his *Take Sky* (P-I, Little, Brown, 1962). Mary Ann Hoberman's *Nuts to You and Nuts to Me* (P, Knopf, 1974) is subtitled *An Alphabet of Poems.*

Counting Books

Many Mother Goose verses include rhymes that increase familiarity with counting, such as "One, two, Buckle my shoe," "1,2,3,4,5! I caught a hare alive," "This Little Pig Went to Market," and "One-ery, two-ery, tickery seven."

Books that provide objects for young children to count and simple pictures on uncluttered pages are Jan Pienkowski's *Numbers* (N-P, Harvey House, 1975) and John Reiss's *Numbers* (N-P, Bradbury, 1971). Tana Hoban's clear photographs invite children to *Count and See* (N-P, Macmillan, 1972) the familiar objects, while Helen Oxenbury's *Numbers of Things* (N-P, Watts, 1968) gives sets of objects for each numeral.

Maurice Sendak capitalizes on children's love of scary things in *Seven Little Monsters* (N-P, Harper & Row, 1977). Jane Yolen's *An Invitation to the Butterfly Ball: A Counting Rhyme,* illustrated by Jane Breskin Zalben (N-P, Parents, 1976), includes a colorful menagerie of assorted creatures. Another book with outstanding illustrations is Nicola Bayley's *One Old Oxford Ox* (P, Atheneum, 1977), which is a delightful play with language as well as a counting book.

Concept Books

Tana Hoban creates outstanding concept books with her skillful photography. Among her many titles are *Shapes and Things* (N-P, Macmillan, 1970), *Circles, Triangles and Squares* (N-P, Macmillan, 1974), *Over, Under, and Through and Other Spatial Concepts* (N-P, Macmillan, 1973), and *Push-Pull, Empty-Full* (N-P, Macmillan, 1972).

The concept of sound presented in a series of books by Margaret Wise Brown include *The Noisy Book,* illustrated by Charles G. Shaw (N-P, Harper & Row, 1947), *The Country Noisy Book,* illustrated by Leonard Weisgard (N-P, Harper & Row, 1940), and *The City Noisy Book,* illustrated by Leonard Weisgard (N-P, Harper & Row, 1939). Two books by Peter Spier also focus on sounds: *Gobble, Growl, Grunt* (N-P, Doubleday, 1971) and *Crash Bang Boom* (N-P, Doubleday, 1972) feature sounds of animals and sounds around us in a fantasia of fine illustrations.

Harlow Rockwell shows young children some of the people and things in their lives. *My Doctor* (N-P, Macmillan, 1973) is a woman who explains the simple medical instruments children may encounter, while *My Dentist* (N-P, Greenwillow, 1975) shows the tools of his profession. *The Supermarket* (N-P, Macmillan, 1979) gives a child's-eye view of that place.

The concept of time, a difficult one for young children, is treated in Charlotte Zolotow's *Over and Over* (P, Harper & Row, 1957), which attempts to convey it by highlighting the significant holidays of the year. Lucille Clifton's *Everett Anderson's Year* (P, Holt, Rinehart & Winston, 1973) is similar as it celebrates the days of the year important to a young black child. Tasha Tudor's *Around the Year* (P, Walck, 1957) is a more subtle overview featuring old fashioned activities for each month.

Many poems focus on colors, often dealing with the mood or feelings they evoke. Mary O'Neill's *Hailstones and Halibut Bones,* illustrated by Leonard Weisgard (P-I, Doubleday, 1961), is subtitled *Adventures in Color* and can be used as a springboard for children's own writing. May Hill Arbuthnot's *Time for Poetry* (all ages, Scott, Foresman, 1967) contains many poems that illustrate simple concepts, including Christina Rossetti's "What Is Pink?" Christopher Morley's "Smells (Junior)," Zhenya Gay's "The World is Full of Wonderful Smells," and Frances Frost's "Sniff." David McCord also presents various concepts in his poems, including "Yellow" and "How Tall?" in *One at a Time,* illustrated by Harry Kane (all ages, Little, Brown, 1977).

Wordless Books

Mercer Mayer's mastery of the wordless book is evidenced in his books *One Frog Too Many,* with Marianna Mayer (P, Dial, 1975), *Hiccup* (P, Dial, 1978), *Achoo* (P, Dial, 1977), and *Oops* (P, Dial, 1977)—all equally funny as they play with the causes and effects of human foibles.

John Goodall's work is characterized by meticulous detail in the illustrations and the clever use of half pages to advance the story lines. Among his many titles are *The Adventures of Paddy Pork* (P, Harcourt Brace Jovanovich, 1968), *Naughty Nancy* (P, Atheneum, 1975), and *The Surprise Picnic* (P, Atheneum, 1976). Goodall shifted from the small format of these books when he began a series to depict his homeland in masterpieces of detail and beauty: *An Edwardian Summer* (all ages, Atheneum, 1976), *An Edwardian Christmas* (all ages, Atheneum, 1978), and *The Story of an English Village* (all ages, Atheneum, 1979).

Many wordless books rely on humor to sustain the story. Paula Winter's *The Bear and the Fly* (P, Crown, 1976) shows how a simple house fly can create havoc when an over-zealous swatter is determined to catch it. Fernando Krahn invents intriguing fantasies in *Little Love Story* (P, Lippincott, 1976), *Who's Seen the Scissors?* (P, Dutton, 1975), and *Sebastian and the Mushroom* (P, Delacorte, 1976).

Literary Folk Tales

Many of the stories of Hans Christian Andersen, father of the literary folk tale, are available in beautifully illustrated editions, among them *Thumbelina,* illustrated by Susan Jeffers (P-I, Dial, 1979), *The Snow Queen,* illustrated by Errol Le Cain (P-I, Viking, 1979), *The Nightingale,* illustrated by Nancy Eckholm Burkert (P-I, Harper & Row, 1965), and *The Princess and the Pea,* illustrated by Paul Galdone (P-I, Seabury, 1978). Rudyard Kipling's stories have also been made into outstanding picture books; noteworthy are *How the Rhinoceros Got His Skin,* illustrated by Leonard Weisgard (P-I, Walker & Co., 1974), and

How the Leopard Got His Spots, illustrated by Leonard Weisgard (P-I, Walker & Co., 1972). The cumulative pattern of the literary folktale is evident in Mirra Ginsburg's adaptation of a Russian story, *Which Is the Best Place?* illustrated by Roger Duvoisin (P, Macmillan, 1976), William Wiesner's *Little Sarah and Her Johnny-Cake* (P, Walck, 1974), and Harve Zemach's *The Judge,* illustrated by Margot Zemach (P, Farrar, Straus & Giroux, 1973). Jay Williams's *The Reward Worth Having,* illustrated by Mercer Mayer (P-I, Four Winds-Scholastic, 1977), follows three young men in search of wealth, power, and love, while Susan Jeffers's *Wild Robin* (P, Dutton, 1976) is the enchanting story of a wayward young boy who is rescued from fairies by his loving sister.

Arnold Lobel's *A Treeful of Pigs* (P, Greenwillow, 1979) is a humorous tale in which a wise wife tricks her lazy husband into doing his share of the work.

Plays

Most plays for children appear in anthologies. Among those that primary children will enjoy dramatizing are Bernice Wells Carlson's *Funny-Bone Dramatics,* illustrated by Charles Cox (P-I, Abingdon, 1974), Sue Alexander's *Small Plays for Special Days* (P, Seabury, 1977), and Alice Childress's "Let's Hear It for the Queen," illustrated by Loring Eutemey (P-I, Coward, McCann & Geoghegan, 1976).

Plays, Inc. publishes a magazine that contains plays, skits, and other material for children to dramatize. They publish many of the plays in anthologies, including *Patriotic and Historical Plays for Young People* (I, Plays, Inc., 1975) and *Children's Plays from Favorite Stories* (I, Plays, Inc., 1970). Virginia Bradley's *Is There an Actor in the House?* (I, Dodd, Mead, 1975) offers tips on staging, casting, designing props and costumes, and rehearsing—in addition to a variety of skits, plays, and improvisations. Ted Hughes's *The Tiger's Bones and Other Plays for Children,* illustrated by Alan E. Cober (I, Viking, 1974), and Carol Korty's *Silly Soup: Ten Zany Plays,* photographs by Jamie Cope (I, Scribner's, 1977), contain humorous material while Gerald G. Glass and Muriel W. Klein's *From Plays Into Reading* (I, Allyn & Bacon, 1969) stresses the importance of drama to the entire reading program.

Lowell Swortzell, a leader in children's and educational theater, writes and collects plays that adolescents enjoy reading or dramatizing. *Here Come the Clowns* (A, Viking, 1978) describes comedians with unique styles from ancient Greek drama to those of the present. *All the World's a Stage* (A, Delacorte, 1972) is a collection of plays for reading or dramatizing. Joan Aiken's *Street: A Play for Children,* illustrated by Arvis Stewart (I-A, Viking, 1978), and *The Mooncusser's Daughters: A Play for Children,* illustrated by Arvis Stewart (I-A, Viking, 1973), are full length plays older children enjoy reading or producing.

Of the few individually bound plays, Ossie Davis's *Escape to Freedom* (I, Viking, 1978), a moving dramatization of Frederich Douglass's formative early years, is bound to intrigue dramatists.

Some of the poems in May Hill Arbuthnot's *Time for Poetry* (all ages, Scott, Foresman, 1967) are particularly suitable for dramatic presentation; these include Robert Louis Stevenson's "Block City," "Marching Song," and "A Good Play," Emma C. Dowd's "Fun in a Garret," and Laura Lee Randall's "Our Circus."

Easy-to-Read Books
There are hundreds of outstanding easy-to-read books so readers need never settle for second best. Lillian Hoban, among those who creates a clearly identifiable character using only a limited vocabulary, writes about Arthur, a young chimpanzee, in *Arthur's Pen Pal* (P, Harper & Row, 1976) and *Arthur's Prize Reader* (P, Harper & Row, 1978). Arnold Lobel's *Mouse Tales* (P, Harper & Row, 1972) and *Mouse Soup* (P, Harper & Row, 1977) produce many giggles, as does Dick Gackenbach's story *Hattie Rabbit* (P, Harper & Row, 1976). Marjorie Weinman Sharmat's *Mooch the Messy*, illustrated by Ben Shecter (P, Harper & Row, 1976), and *Sophie and Gussie*, illustrated by Lillian Hoban (P, Macmillan, 1973), contain child-like adventures in easy-to-read vocabulary. Wilson Gage writes easy stories that follow the traditions of American folklore; both *Squash Pie,* illustrated by Glen Rounds (P, Greenwillow, 1976), and *Down in the Boondocks*, illustrated by Glen Rounds (P, Greenwillow, 1977), contain humor, rhythm, and just enough repetition for beginning readers.

Some poets capture the child's delight in learning to read and in the pleasures of reading throughout life. Eleanor Farjeon knows that a book is the ultimate choice in "Choosing"; Langston Hughes tells about "Aunt Sue's Stories," and Lucia M. and James L. Hymes, Jr. describe "Tombstone Stories." All these poems are found in the fourth edition of *The Arbuthnot Anthology of Children's Literature* (all ages, Lothrop, Lee & Shepard, 1976).

John Ciardi creates a whole collection of poems around reading and books in *You Read to Me, I'll Read to You*, illustrated by Edward Gorey (P-I, Lippincott, 1961), and David McCord spells the charm of "Books" in *One at a Time* (all ages, Little, Brown, 1977).

Transitional Books
For children making the transition from easy-to-read books to longer and more complex chapter books, episodic stories with realistic characters and events are appealing. Two that have held up well over the years are Eleanor Estes's *The Moffats*, illustrated by Louis Slobodkin (P-I, Harcourt Brace Jovanovich, 1968), and *Ginger Pye*, illustrated by Louis Slobodkin (P-I, Harcourt Brace Jovanovich, 1959). Seymour Simon introduces a new character who solves mysteries with science facts in *Einstein Anderson: Science Sleuth* (P-I, Viking, 1980).

Johanna Hurwitz created two characters who appeal to second- and third-graders. *Busybody Nora*, illustrated by Susan Jeschke (P-I, Morrow, 1976), and *New Neighbors for Nora*, illustrated by Susan Jeschke (P-I, Morrow, 1979), are two of her

stories about a busy young girl. *Aldo Applesauce,* illustrated by John Wallner (P-I, Morrow, 1979), has difficulty adjusting to his new school, but both he and his readers learn that adjustment takes time.

In *Follow That Bus!* illustrated by Laurence Hutchins (P-I, Greenwillow, 1977), Pat Hutchins writes a very funny story about how a second-grade class on a field trip gets caught in a series of chases. Other books that appeal to the often bizarre humor of seven- and eight-year-olds are Judy Blume's *Freckle Juice*, illustrated by Sonia O. Lisker (P-I, Four Winds-Scholastic, 1971), Barbara Brooks Wallace's *Hawkins,* illustrated by Gloria Kamen (I, Abingdon, 1977), Thomas Rockwell's *How to Eat Fried Worms*, illustrated by Emily McCully (I, Watts, 1973), and Constance C. Greene's *The Ears of Louis*, illustrated by Nola Langer (I, Viking, 1974).

Robert McCloskey's *Homer Price* (I, Viking, 1943) and *Centerburg Tales* (I, Viking, 1951) have delighted children for many years with their strong humor. Robert Newton Peck's stories about *Soup*, illustrated by Charles Gehm (I, Knopf, 1974), are filled with hilarious adventures in which the characters often get into trouble in a small town.

Poetry for the transitional reader contains many of the same characteristics as stories suitable for them. Humor, mystery, and sports attract poets who write for this age. Always popular are Shel Silverstein's *Where the Sidewalk Ends* (P-I, Harper & Row, 1974), Myra Cohn Livingston's *Listen, Children, Listen* (P-I, Harcourt Brace Jovanovich, 1972) and *What a Wonderful Bird the Frog Are* (I, Harcourt Brace Jovanovich, 1973), and William Cole's anthologies, which include *Oh, Such Foolishness*, illustrated by Tomie de Paola (P-I, Lippincott, 1978), and *Oh, How Silly*, illustrated by Tomi Ungerer (I, Viking, 1970).

Jack Prelutsky weaves a gruesome spell in his poems in *Nightmares: Poems to Trouble Your Sleep*, illustrated by Arnold Lobel (P-I, Greenwillow, 1976), in which a grisly ghoul waits patiently beside a school to feast on girls and boys. Daisy Wallace edited a series of books that contain poems of appeal to children who ask for spooky stories; included are *Monster Poems*, illustrated by Kay Chorao (P-I, Holiday House, 1976), and *Ghost Poems*, illustrated by Tomie de Paola (P-I, Holiday House, 1979).

Books for Language Play
Two books by Ruthven Tremain encourage readers to play with words and to explore and experiment with language: *Fooling Around with Words* (P-I, Greenwillow, 1976) and *Teapot, Switcheroo, and Other Silly Word Games* (P-I, Greenwillow, 1979). Arthur Steckler tells about *101 Words and How They Began*, illustrated by James Flora (P-I, Doubleday, 1979). Fred Gwynne shows the confusion that is caused when children misinterpret homonyms and idiomatic expressions in *The King Who Rained* (P-I, Windmill-Dutton, 1970), *A Chocolate Moose for Dinner* (P-I, Windmill-Dutton, 1976), and *The Six-Hand Horse* (P-I, Windmill-Dutton, 1980). Other books that focus on words and phrases include Bernice Kohn Hunt's *The Whatcha-*

macallit Book, illustrated by Tomie de Paola (P-I, Putnam's, 1976), Charles Funk's *A Hog on Ice: And Other Curious Expressions,* illustrated by Tom Funk (I, Harper & Row, 1948), Ann and Dan Nevins's *From the Horse's Mouth,* illustrated by Dan Nevins (I-A, Prentice-Hall, 1977), and many books by Joan Hanson, including *Similes* (P-I, Lerner, 1976).

There are many books that contain chants, rhymes, tongue twisters, and songs to encourage children to have fun with their language. Among the best are John M. Langstaff's *Shimmy Shimmy Coke-Ca-Pop!* (P-I, Doubleday, 1973), Edith Fowke's compilations, *Sally Go Round the Sun,* illustrated by Carlos Marchiori (P-I, Doubleday, 1970), and *Ring Around the Moon,* illustrated by Judith Gwyn Brown (P-I, Prentice-Hall, 1977), and Duncan Emrich's collections, *The Whim Wham Book,* illustrated by Ib Ohlsson (I, Four Winds-Scholastic, 1975), and *The Nonsense Book of Riddles, Rhymes, Tongue Twisters, Puzzles and Jokes from American Folklore,* illustrated by Ib Ohlsson (I, Four Winds-Scholastic, 1970).

Ideas for expanding language abound in Bernice Wells Carlson's *Listen! And Help Tell the Story,* illustrated by Burmah Burris (P-I, Abingdon, 1965), and in Margaret Taylor Burroughs's *Did You Feed My Cow? . . . Street Games, Chants and Rhymes,* illustrated by Joe E. De Velasco (P-I, Follett, 1969).

There is an abundance of books of jokes and riddles, including Janet and Alan Ahlberg's *The Old Joke Book* (P-I, Viking, 1976) and Jane Sarnoff and Reynold Ruffins's *I Know! A Riddle Book* (P-I, Scribner's, 1976).

Children enjoy working with codes and can find much material in books, including Clifford B. Hicks's *Alvin's Secret Code* (P-I, Holt, Rinehart & Winston, 1963), Walt Babson's *All Kinds of Codes* (I, Four Winds-Scholastic, 1976), Barbara Rinkoff's *The Case of the Stolen Code Book,* illustrated by Leonard Shortall (P-I, Crown, 1971), Jane Sarnoff and Reynold Ruffins's *The Code and Cipher Book* (I, Scribner's, 1975), and Herbert S. Zim's classic *Codes and Secret Writing* (I, Morrow, 1948).

Language play is often embodied in verse and poetry, sometimes in riddles, chants, and limericks. A delightful collection of the latter is John E. and Lorraine A. Brewton's *They've Discovered a Head in the Box for the Bread,* illustrated by Fernando Krahn (I, Crowell, 1978).

The Books

four

WILLIAM CARLOS WILLIAMS

THE RED WHEELBARROW

*so much depends
upon*

*a red wheel
barrow*

*glazed with rain
water*

*beside the white
chickens*[1]

‗

Picture Books

In this chapter we look at books that tell the story through a combination of text and illustration, both elements sharing equally in the telling. Such "picture" books parallel the child's expanding world. Children begin to explore their inner world and move in ever-widening circles to encompass family, then school, friends, and others in their social world, and eventually the world beyond. Their expanding horizons come to include nature, pets, and, in the aesthetic world, art, dance, and literature. In this regard, children are explorers who reach out to people and events in the environment to discover meanings for themselves.

There are picture books that correspond to every developmental stage of childhood. In treating the books in this chapter, our intent is to show the correspondences by using the psychological and developmental characteristics of children as an underlying framework for the chapter. This developmental perspective, then, serves as a guide for selecting the right book at the right time, and is reflected in the structure of the chapter, which begins with the child's inner world and follows through the various stages of expanding interest.

Children learn through a continual process of relating the unfamiliar and the new to what they already know. Concomitantly, children's minds cannot be separated into cognitive and affective "pieces" or domains, for "it is in the child's nature to express and develop innate intellectual capacities, integrating all experience into an intricate view of life that includes hopes and fears, loves and hates, beliefs and expectations, and attitudes toward other people and toward himself."[2]

The child, associating what is learned with the context surrounding it, forms a network or schema of ideas. For example, a child cuddled on an adult's lap while being read to not only learns the content of the story, but associates with reading the pleasures of the moment—the warmth of a loving adult, security, and the shared laughter or joy.

Past feelings coupled with the context of the present come to bear upon the act of learning. This is to say that children—and adults—associate past and present feelings with any supposedly simple, objective fact that is being taught. Teachers use this understanding of learning, drawing upon the prior knowledge children possess and relating the new to the known. In a cumulative fashion, children perceive the world and respond to events in terms of their past experiences and current predilections. When we involve children's interests and provide ways for them to use what they already know, they are empowered to learn.

Books become a part of children's lives and provide a base for them to compare, share, and learn; they offer vicarious experiences for children to draw upon as they encounter new people and events in their expanding world. For example, an only child who hears the story *Great-Grandfather, the Baby, and Me* (P), by Howard Knotts, feels some of the sadness and confusion of the small boy who shares his thoughts about his new baby sister with his great-grandfather. The reader who faces a similar situation will return to this book for comfort.

Children gain confidence through stories when they meet characters who share their feelings. Tomie de Paola's *Oliver Button Is a Sissy* (P) tells about a small boy who is teased because he doesn't like to play football or other rough-and-tumble games. Instead, he likes to jump rope, draw pictures, and play dress-up. Most especially, Oliver likes to dance, and when he enters a talent contest, the other children change their assessment of him to "Oliver Button is a star!" This book shows that conformity need not be the rule; it also expands children's knowledge and understanding of people in their world.

THE ART IN PICTURE BOOKS

The purpose of a picture book, indeed of any book, is to communicate meaning. Picture books are unique in that they use words and pictures in combination to tell a story, the two working closely together, with neither taking precedence. As with the verbal elements of the story, the individual pictures interrelate, creating a visual story that supports and extends the text. The storytelling quality of the art calls up mental images and sparks imaginative powers. Though one might expect that children do not remember their first books and that the quality of the art is irrelevant, early experiences take deep root, and beauty becomes a memorable part of a child's early experience.

Art in children's picture books involves the entire range of media, techniques, and styles used in art anywhere. The medium, the material used in the production of a work, may be watercolors, oils, acrylics, ink, pencil, charcoal, pastels, tissue paper, acetate sheets, or fabric. The technique might be painting, etching, wood and linoleum cuts, air brush, collage, and many other means. Finally, it is the individual artist's style, determined by the use made of the media, that evokes the mood. Since medium, technique, and style are intricately combined to produce the art, they are best discussed in that way.

Many sophisticated processes are involved in the reproduction of color illustrations. The colors of the illustration are separated by inking (or filling in by other means), on a separate acetate sheet for each color, the area occupied by that color in the drawing. Usually, in more complex pictures, in which colors are blended, separation is achieved by photographing the artist's design four times, each time through a different colored filter. The result is four transparencies (like the handmade acetate sheets), each of which shows the areas of one color. Printing plates are made from these transparencies or acetate sheets—again, one for each color. Each plate prints one color, so that the paper must pass through the printing press four times (or once through four rollers) in order to produce a full-color picture.

Leo and Diane Dillon achieve with an air brush a luminescent quality in their Caldecott award-winning illustrations for Verna Aardema's *Why Mosquitoes Buzz in People's Ears* (P-I). Tom Feelings uses wet tissue paper and linseed oil with inks and tempera to obtain the luminous, crackled-texture paintings in *Moja Means One* (P) and *Jambo Means Hello* (P).

Many types of illustration and medium can be models for children in creating their own books. Watercolors and pastels are relatively simple to use. Watercolor, a combination of powdered color, gum arabic, and glycerine, has a transparent look. Pastels, essentially soft, colored chalks, produce an opaque image. Peter Spier uses watercolors to compose meticulously detailed and aesthetically pleasing scenes with a touch of nostalgia. The exuberant pages of *Noah's Ark* (N-P) exemplify his art. Careful attention to the hundreds of small details Spier puts into his work will reward readers with the fullest delight. Adrienne Adams, Margot Zemach, Robert McCloskey, and William Steig are others who use watercolors imaginatively. Strong and vivid use of pastels is found in Nonny Hogrogian's purple heather and green fields in *Always Room for One More* (P), a Scottish folk song adapted by Sorche Nic Leodhas. Pen-and-ink line with crosshatching add distinction to the illustrations. Hogrogian visualizes the story almost as a shadow play rising out of the mist.

Oils and acrylics are oil- or resin-based combinations of color mixed with turpentine and other thinners and vehicles. These paints are usually opaque, with depth and dimension obtained from layering the colors. Few artists use oils for children's book illustration, although Nonny Hogrogian does in *One Fine Day* (N-P). Gouache and tempera or poster color are water-based and usually have a white filler. Gerald McDermott uses gouache and black ink to create vivid, strong, stylized designs in *Arrow to the Sun* (P-I). Blair Lent uses acrylic paints and gray pen-and-ink drawings in Arlene Mosel's *The Funny Little Woman* (P). The underground action in the story as the funny little woman goes into the world of the wicked *oni* appears in color; the change of seasons and the events occurring at her home are shown in gray line drawings that convey the passage of time.

Woodcuts, linoleum cuts, cardboard cuts, and wood engravings all involve cutting the design into the various materials (areas not to be printed are cut away), applying color to the surface, and pressing this against the paper. Where the final composition is multicolored, separate woodcuts are usually made for each color.

Ed Emberley used woodcuts for the pictures in *Drummer Hoff* (N-P), first drawing the pictures on pine boards, then, in conventional woodcut fashion, cutting away all the areas that were not to print. Although he used only the three primary colors, he created the impression of thirteen by using transparent inks printed one over another:

> The drawings in *Drummer Hoff* are woodcuts. They were drawn on pine boards, all the white areas were cut away, ink was rolled on the remaining raised areas, and a set of prints was pulled on rice paper. . . . Although only three inks were employed—red, yellow, and blue—we were able to create the impression of thirteen distinct colors. This effect was accomplished by taking advantage of the fact that the inks with which most picture books are printed tend to be transparent. Therefore, by printing one ink over another, or "overprinting," a third color is made.[3]

Cardboard cutouts, made from laminated cardboard (usually cut with a razor blade), are used to achieve unusual forms. Examples of this relatively uncommon graphic technique are found in Blair Lent's work for *John Tabor's Ride* (P) and Margaret Hodges's *The Wave* (P). Wood engraving, a form of woodcut in which cuts are made across the grain, generally in hardwood, is used for much finer detail. Lynd Ward used wood engraving for *The Biggest Bear* (P).

Stone lithography is an artistic process used infrequently today because of advances made in offset and other types of lithography. Stone lithographers draw on a fine grade of stone with a crayon or greasy compound. (The image is drawn in reverse of the final picture, as in woodcuts and wood engravings.) The stone is rolled with ink that has an affinity for the greasy lines of the drawing. The ink transfers to the paper when the stone is pressed against it. The process is time consuming and difficult. The illustrations for Ingri and Edgar Parin d'Aulaire's *Abraham Lincoln* (P) were stone lithographs in the original 1940 edition; offset lithography, more commercially feasible, was used when the book was republished in 1957.

Photography is questioned as an artistic technique by those who say it is more technical skill than art. The work of Tana Hoban in *Look Again* (P-I), however, shows that it is a combination of the artist's eye and the photographer's skill that produces the true works of art found there.

Collage is a technique of cutting or tearing

Profile

LEO AND DIANE DILLON

Working together for more than twenty years, Leo and Diane Dillon have blended their art so that even they do not know where one's contribution stops and the other's starts. The Dillons first met at the Parsons School of Design when they were assigned adjacent seats and had to share a drawing board. Leo was furious because he had hoped to have the drawing board to himself; furthermore, he had always been the best artist in his class and did not like the competition offered by Diane. They speak of their three years in school together at Parsons as a time of fierce competition with each other. Ultimately they decided to work together and to collaborate on everything, including marriage.

For a while, Leo worked as an art director for a magazine and Diane was the only woman artist in an advertising agency. In the early years of their joint career, the Dillons worked together on movie posters, book jackets, and magazine illustrations. Leo speaks of that time:

It used to be that one of us would do the actual drawing and the other would make comments or draw a change on a tissue overlay. But now one of us can just pass the piece of art to the other, and he or she can erase what's wrong and redraw right on the original. Our egos aren't at stake anymore (Leo Dillon, "Diane Dillon," *Horn Book Magazine,* 53, No. 4 [Aug. 1977], 423).

It amazes many people that two artists can work on the same painting the way the Dillons do. Their successful collaboration earned them the Caldecott Medal for an unprecedented two consecutive years, 1976 and 1977. Discussing their work in the 1976 acceptance speech for *Why Mosquitoes Buzz in People's Ears,* by Verna Aardema, they say:

shapes from paper and fabric and arranging them to portray the characters and scenes in a story. Ezra Jack Keats uses it so effectively that his work is consistently cited as an outstanding example of the technique. In *The Snowy Day* (N-P) his materials were scraps of wrapping paper, grass cloth, wallpaper, newspaper, and cotton.

THE CHILD'S INNER WORLD

In a supportive environment children soon come to know that they are unique and capable of expressing themselves and of making choices. This individuation process begins when children first perceive themselves as distinct beings. Until about the age of four, children perceive others egocentrically; that is, others exist only in relation to themselves. Early in this phase children begin to understand that they are not the only ones who have needs and feelings. Much later they learn that others perceive things differently from them, and they begin to develop a concept of self based upon reflections from others. Many picture books address such developmental characteristics and appeal to children who are in a corresponding stage.

Children in the preschool years, then, are busy learning about themselves—who they are and

. . . the color was done in airbrush with frisket, which is a form of stencil. One area is done and then masked out, or covered, and the next area is done. The black areas are painted in last, then glazed with blue or purple. But as for who does what—sometimes even *we* aren't sure. Each illustration is passed back and forth between us several times before it is completed, and since we both work on every piece of art, the finished painting looks as if one artist has done it. Actually, with this method of working, we create a third artist. Together, we are able to create art we would not be able to do individually (Leo and Diane Dillon, "Caldecott Medal Acceptance," *Horn Book Magazine,* 52, No. 4 [Aug. 1976], 376).

The third artist the Dillons created has rare talent.

The Dillons were at work on *Ashanti to Zulu,* by Margaret Musgrove, when they received the Caldecott Medal for *Mosquitoes.* In order to represent authentically the many African groups dealt with in the book, they did extensive research. They found that Africa is comprised of many peoples and customs and, in order to portray them accurately, needed pictures of, for example, the special blankets of the Sotho and the embroidered clothing of the Hausa. For every group the jewelry and even the style of hair had meaning. A Lozi barge, the last item, was tracked down by one of the editors at Dial Press. Leo Dillon is the first black artist to be named a Caldecott medalist.

Lee, their teenage son, who thinks that he, too, will someday be an artist, speaks of his parents with love:

What I really like about my parents is that I can work with them. I can work with my father on the house, and we can talk a lot of things out without blowing up. I make jewelry, and I really enjoy going to the jewelry district with my mother and talking about jewelry designs with her. And we all have fun teasing back and forth, too (Lee Dillon, "Leo and Diane Dillon," *Horn Book Magazine,* 53, No. 4 [Aug. 1977], 425).

what they can do—and about others, but only as those others affect them. As they perceive people reacting and responding to them, children learn to adjust their actions to elicit the desired responses. A five-year-old in a grocery ran from shelf to shelf snatching up highly-advertised cereals and urging his mother to buy them. When, unpersuaded, she turned into another aisle and disappeared from sight, he looked up in fright and yelled, in egocentric misperception, "Hey, you better watch it! You're going to lose me!"

Early development of the child's self-concept is a direct result of his interaction with his environment. Part of this environment is composed of the kinds of reactions young children receive from others. Given positive reactions and reinforcement, they feel good about themselves. When they see that their actions meet with approval they are encouraged to explore, to express themselves, and to discover their world. Conversely, disapproval and negative feedback may cause children to pull in their boundaries.

Children need to know that their feelings, as well as their actions, are acceptable. Knowing that joy, sadness, fear, and anger are natural helps children learn to accept and control them. In picture books, they find others who are afraid, sad, joyous, or angry and associate the characters' feelings with their own. Dealing with emotions, talking about them, and learning how to live with them are vital to an overall sense of well-being. Felice Holman's poem expresses the feelings of those times a child is given too much overt "understanding" and just wants to be left alone:

LEAVE ME ALONE

Loving care!
Too much to bear.
Leave me alone!

Don't brush my hair,
Don't pat my head,
Don't tuck me in
Tonight in bed,

Don't ask me if I want a sweet,
Don't fix my favorite things to eat,
Don't give me lots of good advice,
And most of all just don't be nice.

But when I've wallowed well in sorrow,
Be nice to me again tomorrow.

FELICE HOLMAN[4]

Self-Concept

Books can mirror the primary experiences that shape children's actions, reactions, and feelings, and help them reflect upon them.

Charlotte Zolotow's *Someone New* (P) illustrates this process dramatically. A young boy feels a sense of unrest when things seem to be changing. He no longer likes the wallpaper he chose for his room, nor does he want to play with his familiar toys. Only gradually does he realize that it is he who is changing. Stories like this play an important role for the child experiencing the conflicts of growing up; they enrich understanding when they relate to one's own life. In addition to providing new experiences, stories also show children that their thoughts, feelings, and reactions are not unusual—that they are like other people and a part of the human race.

In *Titch* (N-P), Pat Hutchins tells about a boy who always gets the smallest toys. His self-worth is boosted when his tiny seed grows into a large plant, symbolizing the fact that Titch, too, will grow. Another child, in Pat Hutchins's *Happy Birthday, Sam* (N-P), can't reach his clothes, the light switch, or the sink until his Grandfather sends him a stool for his birthday. Sam's pleasure is evident as he gets himself ready for his party and floats his new toy boat in the sink.

One of the most important steps in the development of self-concept is the understanding that each of us is important. The advice to "be yourself" is heard often and is a necessary part in the development of children's feelings about themselves. In a world where conformity is pervasive, children need to know that they are valued for their uniqueness, not because they conform to the standards of a group.

Making a life-size facsimile of oneself can heighten self-esteem. (HBJ photograph by Richard C. Polister.)

A LEARNING CENTER ABOUT ME (N-P) Create a learning center in which children discover special things about themselves by engaging in independent or dyadic activities. Some materials for the center could include:

Small hand mirrors and a full-length mirror placed so children can see themselves from any angle

Clay, plasticene, or flour-based play dough to make handprints (with a hole at the top so they can be hung when dry)

A tape recorder to record and listen to their own voices

Materials for making individual books about themselves

A bulletin board for photographs (current and baby pictures)

A flip chart in which each child makes a special "Me" page

Books for this center include the following and others that are discussed in this chapter:

I'm Terrific (P) by Marjorie Weinman Sharmat. Illustrated by Kay Chorao. Holiday House, 1977.
Leo the Late Bloomer (N-P) by Robert Kraus. Illustrated by Jose Aruego. Windmill, 1971.
Look What I Can Do (N-P) by Jose Aruego. Scribner's, 1971.
Me! A Book of Poems (P), edited by Lee Bennett Hopkins. Illustrated by Talivaldis Stubis. Seabury, 1970.
Whistle for Willie (N-P) by Ezra Jack Keats. Viking, 1964.

Activity: Teacher to Student

POETRY ABOUT ME (N-P) Read some poems in the book *All Together,* by Dorothy Aldis, (Putnam's, 1952). Choose one that says something about you and draw a picture about it.

Many books have as their themes the importance of being true to oneself. The title character in Don Freeman's *Dandelion* (P) is a lion who spruces himself up for a party, only to be turned away because his hostess does not recognize him. When a sudden rainstorm ruins his fancy hairstyle and new clothes, Dandelion returns to the party looking himself and is greeted warmly. Children enter into lively discussions about the ways in which people try to impress others. In *"You Look Ridiculous," Said the Rhinoceros to the Hippopotamus* (P), Bernard Waber tells about a sad hippopotamus who longs to look like his friends. True to the title, the hippo imagines what it would be like to have spots like the leopard, a mane like the lion, a shell like the turtle, and many other unlikely attributes—all at the same time. Children enjoy dramatizing these stories of pretense.

Leo Lionni's *Alexander and the Wind-Up Mouse* (P) shows that while we may envy others for lives that seems to be better than ours, given the chance to change, we choose to be ourselves. Alexander, a real mouse, envies Willy, a toy mouse, because he is loved by and kept close to

Teaching Idea

LOOSE-TOOTH CENTER (P) First experiences are important to young children. Even though the event may be one that is universal, for a child it is a brand-new experience. The first loose tooth is an especially significant milestone, symbolizing a step from babyhood to childhood. Books build on the excitement of first experiences and give children the opportunity to compare their experiences with those related in the stories.

Make a "loose-tooth" center that features a large cardboard tooth. Smaller cutout teeth bear the names of each child who has lost a first tooth. In addition, when a child comes to school with a brand new gaping hole in his mouth, attach a piece of yarn to a cardboard tooth that says "I lost one" and allow the child to wear this around his neck for the day. Place the following books in the center as the class reads them, so that the children can go back and look at them on their own:

Albert's Toothache (P) by Barbara Williams. Illustrated by Kay Chorao. Dutton, 1974.
The Bear's Toothache (P) by David McPhail. Little, Brown, 1972.
Little Rabbit's Loose Tooth (P) by Lucy Bate. Illustrated by Diane de Groat. Crown, 1975.
The Mango Tooth (P) by Charlotte Pomerantz. Illustrated by Marilyn Hafner. Greenwillow, 1977.
One Morning in Maine (P) by Robert McCloskey. Viking, 1952.

Activity: Teacher to Student

NOW I AM SIX (P)

THE END

When I was One,
I had just begun.

When I was Two.
I was nearly new.

When I was Three,
I was hardly Me.

When I was Four,
I was not much more.

When I was Five,
I was just alive.

But now I am Six, I'm as clever as clever.
So I think I'll be six now for ever and ever.   A. A. MILNE[5]

This poem talks about how one child felt about being six years old. What can you do now that you couldn't do before? Would you like to "be six now for ever and ever"? Why? Draw a picture of yourself now and a picture of you when you were one and "had just begun." Memorize the poem and surprise your parents by saying it on your sixth birthday.

Annie, a real girl, while everyone chases Alexander away. But when Alexander sees that Willy is to be thrown away with the trash after the new birthday toys arrive, Willy's life does not seem so idyllic. A lizard witch and a magic purple pebble give Alexander a rare choice—and the choice he makes is one children applaud.

Each of these books enables children to see characters trying to be something other than what they really are. Discussing children's reactions to the stories leads to explorations on how they would solve the problems themselves.

During the last decade the roles of men and women in our society have expanded dramatically; children's books reflect the changes. Until recently, the traditional mother, often complete with apron, was portrayed as the keeper of the home—doing the cooking, laundry, cleaning, and caring for the children. The father was shown rushing off to work, briefcase in hand, and returning home only to mow the lawn, service the car, and paint the garage. Children in the family engaged in similarly sex-assigned activities: big brother played baseball while little sister tended to her dolls. This standard idyllic family was seen in advertising, television, and children's books. Deliberate attempts to change the stereotyped image include many so-called bandaid books, which have such strong messages that the stories are overshadowed by the statements. These stories lack realism, characterization, and imagination, and in many cases actually undermine the movement to provide a balanced view of society today. Other books, however, offer a positive picture; they qualify as literature on their own and, at the same time, give the reader something to think about.

Fear

Children develop many fears as a normal part of growing up. Fears can arise from a general insecurity and anxiety about the world; young children's sense of reality is not yet strong enough to sort out

Teaching Idea

MAX (P) Prepare two charts with the headings "Girls can . . . " and "Boys can . . . ." Ask the children to think about jobs, games, and other activities for each chart and to list them on the charts. Try to include chores, games, and after-school activities. Allow the children to give their reasons for each choice, but try to hold off a discussion—or debate.

Read Rachel Isadora's *Max* (P, Macmillan, 1976), a picture story about a boy who stops off at his sister's dance class on the way to baseball practice. Unable to remain a passive observer, Max mimics the dancers' movements and later finds that the leaps, splits, and stretches help improve his performance on the baseball field. His mimicry is so successful that he also becomes a member of the dance class.

Have a discussion about dance and sports. Many boys will probably deny that they would ever go to a dance class. Information about professional athletes who study ballet may not convince them, but at least the children will begin to think about traditional sex roles. Other books useful in this discussion include:

The Girl Who Would Rather Climb Trees (P) by Miriam Schlein. Illustrated by Judith Gwyn Brown. Harcourt Brace Jovanovich, 1975.
Just the Thing for Geraldine (P) by Ellen Conford. Illustrated by John Larrecq. Little, Brown, 1974.
Rafiki (P) by Nola Langner. Viking, 1977.

124   the various phenomena confronting them and they may express uncertainty through fear.

Books can be an element in coming to terms with fears by presenting experiences similar to those of the child, who then compares his actions and feelings with those of the characters in the stories. While bibliotherapy (using books to resolve problems) is a separate issue, books can play a role in lessening fears by helping children learn about their inner world.

Children's fears frequently manifest themselves at night, with monsters and ghosts common focuses. Simply telling a child that there are no monsters is ineffective; the fear is real to the child. Even children who no longer have nighttime fears appreciate *Clyde Monster* (P), by Robert Crowe, which is a marvelous reversal of the traditional monster story. Clyde is an adorable monster creature who is afraid to go to bed because people might be hiding in his cave waiting to get him. His parents tell him that monsters and people made a deal a long time ago: people don't scare monsters and monsters don't scare people. The reassurance convinces Clyde, who goes into his cave—still with just a bit of caution: "But could you leave the rock open just a little?"

Mercer Mayer's *There's a Nightmare in My Closet* (P) shows a small boy overcoming his fear —but not his fantasy—when he comforts a monster who has a nightmare. Mayer's ugly but lovable creature who climbs into bed with the child may reassure the frightened listener that, although the monster is "real," it is nothing to be afraid of.

A toy often serves a useful purpose for a child who is trying to overcome his fears. This alter ego provides companionship, security, and comfort, and can be the vehicle through which a child plays out unconscious fears. Martha Alexander's *I'll Protect You from the Jungle Beasts* (P) illustrates this kind of role substitution. A small pajama-clad boy and his teddy bear are walking through the woods amidst frightening growls and roars. "Oh, yes, Teddy, there are lions and tigers and elephants in this forest—big ones. But don't worry, I'll protect you from the jungle beasts." As they get deeper into the woods—and the possibility that they are lost seems real—the boy continues to comfort his friend who, by now, is gowing in size. Almost imperceptibly Teddy becomes the comforter and carries the boy home to their safe, warm bed. Children who empathize with the boy understand his conversation with, and transfer of feelings to, the teddy bear. They also recognize that the whole experience is a dream, foreshadowed by showing the boy in his pajamas and confirmed on the last page when he awakens in his bed beside his normal-sized teddy bear.

Another boy who needs his teddy bear for protection is found in Bernard Waber's *Ira Sleeps Over* (P). Ira is invited to sleep at his friend Reggie's house, but his sister keeps planting seeds of doubt about the experience. How will Ira feel without his teddy bear? He's never slept without him. Reggie will laugh, not only at the bear, but at his name—Tah Tah. Torn between his sister's taunts and the fear of sleeping without his teddy bear, Ira vacillates between taking him and not taking him. Big sister wins, but when Reggie starts telling ghost stories and sneaks his own teddy bear —Foo Foo—out of his dresser drawer, Ira returns home to get Tah Tah. This very funny story can provoke a lively discussion of "When I *used* to have a teddy bear . . . " in which children readily relate their experiences (past and present).

The bear of all bears, in A. A. Milne's *Winnie the Pooh* (I), is a well-developed character who suffers from being "a bear of very little brain." The author developed the stories around a stuffed bear belonging to his son and added a menagerie of companions in the stories. The joys and troubles that come from being loved by Christopher Robin are the basis for two collections of poetry and two of stories. The stories contain subtle word play and humor that put them beyond the range of most primary children, but many of the poems appeal to the teddy bear set, especially this one:

US TWO

Wherever I am, there's always Pooh,
There's always Pooh and Me.
Whatever I do, he wants to do,
"Where are you going today?" says Pooh:

TEDDY BEAR WEEK (N-P) Bring your favorite stuffed animals to school during Teddy Bear Week, but don't be surprised if they need to go home each night. Read stories to your bears, write letters between them, and tell others of some adventures they've had. Read lots of stories and poems about bears, and compare your bears with the ones in books. Have a bread and honey party to highlight the week. Make a V.I.B. (Very Important Bear) bulletin board featuring book jackets from teddy bear books and your drawings of teddy bears.

"Well that's very odd 'cos I was too.
Let's go together," says Pooh, says he.
"Let's go together," says Pooh.

A. A. MILNE[6]

Children who own teddy bears are certain that they have feelings, too. The teddy bear often reflects their own feelings of need for love, reassurance, and solitude. In Don Freeman's *Corduroy* (N-P), a lonely teddy bear in a department store fears that his lost button will interfere with someone selecting him. He is finally purchased by a small girl who is also looking for a friend. Small children feel a special affection for this bear. When Freeman wrote the sequel *A Pocket for Corduroy* (N-P), one group of kindergarten children insisted on having a party to celebrate the new book.

Liesel Skorpen's teddy bear in *Charles* (P) has feelings of his own: he is purchased and put into a box where he thinks he's certain to be buried. Charles is eventually unwrapped by a little girl who tosses him aside amidst her other toys. His life is miserable because she obviously does not care

for him. One day when she has dressed Charles up and taken him for a ride in her doll carriage, she meets a boy who has a live kitten. The two agree to trade, and Charles begins a new life with a friend who loves him.

BEDTIME While it is not possible to prevent all fears from surfacing—and indeed this is not desirable—a feeling of security allays many nighttime fears. Children are reassurred through pleasurable experiences in previously frightening situations. For example, children who fear the dark learn to be less fearful when they hear pleasant bedtime stories told in the dark.

Many books serve to soothe children and provide them with the sense of security necessary for an overall good feeling about themselves. One such book that has endured is Margaret Wise Brown's *Goodnight Moon* (N). The moon appears in the window as it travels across the sky while the bunny bids each object in the room goodnight.

Teaching Idea

BEDTIME STORIES (I) Intermediate-grade boys and girls who have younger brothers and sisters, or who will soon be babysitting for neighbor children, can collect stories and poems that will make bedtime a pleasant experience for their young charges.

Activity: Teacher to Student

BABYSITTER'S HANDBOOK (I)   Start a collection of poems and stories that you can use when you babysit. Several collections of bedtime poems will be useful:

The Bed Book by Sylvia Plath. Illustrated by Emily Arnold McCully. Harper & Row, 1976.
Go to Bed, edited by Lee Bennett Hopkins. Illustrated by Rosekrans Hoffman. Knopf, 1979.
The Sleepy Time Treasury, edited by Dale Payson and Karen Wyant. Prentice-Hall, 1975.
Songs the Sandman Sings, edited by Gwendolyn Reed. Illustrated by Peggy Skillen. Atheneum, 1969.

Many lullabies are also available in picture book format.

Soothing coziness from bedtime classic Goodnight Moon, *by Margaret Wise Brown.*
(Illustration by Clement Hurd from *Goodnight Moon* by Margaret Wise Brown. © Copyright, 1947, by Harper & Row, Publishers, Inc. Renewed © 1965 by Roberta Brown Rauch and Clement Hurd. By permission of Harper & Row, Publishers, Inc.)

Responsibility

The development of moral reasoning progresses through sequential and qualitatively differentiated stages. As they grow older, children learn to distinguish between good and bad, and between right and wrong. Very young children usually behave out of fear of punishment. Later they do so because they want to please and want to be considered a good boy or girl. Eventually, they will come to act in accordance with the idea of upholding law and order and, ultimately, in accordance with the dictates of conscience.

The beginnings of conscience are sparked when a child feels remorse for his bad behavior. Marjorie Weinman Sharmat's young hero tells a lie in *A Big Fat Enormous Lie* (P) and feels the pangs of guilt creep over him. David McPhail's lively illustrations show an ugly green creature—the lie—lurking behind a tree, and as the pressure mounts, the boy talks to the lie. The book cleverly shows how guilt often manifests itself in real physical discomfort when Lie plops itself on top of the boy: "Is that you sitting on my stomach, Lie? That hurts."

As children internalize concepts of right and wrong, they perceive that their actions affect not only themselves. Whereas the boy who told the "big, fat enormous lie" was the only one who actually suffered, Evaline Ness, in *Sam, Bangs, and Moonshine* (P), shows that one's lie can bring real danger to others. Sam (short for Samantha) lives with her father and her cat, Bangs, on a small island near a large harbor. Her best friend, Thomas, is an innocent younger child who idolizes Sam and believes all her wild tales. Her father's efforts to convince Sam that her fantasies are lies—moonshine, he calls them—only push her deeper into her dream world. She sends Thomas to a nearby island to search for her baby kangaroo—another figment—and, when the tide comes in early, Thomas and Bangs are nearly drowned. "There's good MOONSHINE and bad MOONSHINE, . . . the important thing is to know the difference," her father tells her. Sam finally realizes that she must take responsibility for her actions.

Imagination

Children's imaginative lives are an important part of their early years. Adults can sometimes get a glimpse of that fantasy world by observing the child at play with an imaginary friend or a favorite toy that has been invested with life. The importance of these symbolic beings is attested to by nursery school teachers or custodians who have received frantic requests to unlock a building at night from parents trying to retrieve a left-behind Snoopy.

Children develop a vivid imaginative life by attributing human characteristics to inanimate objects. A child's favorite teddy bear or blanket becomes a source of security during infancy through a process in which the child invests the object with meaning.[7] Parents and teachers can have very little direct effect on a child's imaginative play, but they can contribute to an environment that is conducive to it. Playing "let's pretend" games, discussing dreams, and making up stories convey to the child the message that imaginative stories are acceptable.

Kornei Chukovsky shows that children who have been deprived of traditional fairy tales and other imaginative stories will create their own.[8] Adults who fear that too much fantasy will affect a child's sense of reality need not worry; a lively imagination is a central part of the developmental process. Imaginative stories provide a source of pleasure as well as a focal point for children's developing imagination and sense of story.

Some of the most distinguished literature for children builds upon the imaginative life of the central characters. In these stories stuffed animals come to life, fancy runs free, imaginary friends are real, and creatures hide under beds. Dr. Seuss created the fantastic parade Marco envisions in *And to Think That I Saw It on Mulberry Street* (P), a story that entrances millions across time and place. Other favorites include the characters in A. A. Milne's work, especially Christopher Robin's imaginary friend, Binker, his supportive alter ego:

> Binker, what I call him—is a secret of my own,
> And Binker is the reason why I never feel alone.[9]

Profile

MAURICE SENDAK

If I had been lucky I would have been a Renaissance child living in Florence. I would have been up early every morning to watch Michelangelo chiseling away in his backyard.

Maurice Sendak in an interview with Justin Wintle from The Pied Pipers

This statement captures Maurice Sendak's feeling about his art, which is central to his life, the early part of which was closely observed, not in Michelangelo's Florence, but from a doorstep on a Brooklyn street. Sendak says that his stories and pictures stem from his early life on this Brooklyn street, delineated clearly in his *Really Rosie* (where even the address on the door is that of his childhood home). In a television interview, Sendak stated:

As a metaphor you might say that I've been doing that continuously. I mean everything has come out of that doorstep or that door. It ends up by having been one theme that you repeat endlessly ("An Interview with Maurice Sendak," writ. Bernice E. Cullinan, *Teaching Critical Reading and Thinking to Children and Adolescents,* taught by Bernice E. Cullinan, dir. Roy Allen, New York University's Sunrise Semester, CBS, 1 May 1978).

Maurice Sendak is a self-taught artist and storyteller who studied formally only briefly—at the Art Students League in New York City. He celebrates the old masters as better teachers than contemporary ones. An indefatigable worker, he competes with himself to perfect his skill. Sample work-pages in his *Maurice Sendak Fantasy Sketches* reflect how he practices his craft—at breakneck speed, and often to a boisterous classical-music accompaniment.

Maurice Sendak and Walt Disney's Mickey Mouse celebrated their fiftieth birthdays recently. Disney's art (and the images evoked by William Blake's poetry) made a lasting impression on him. The forces influencing Sendak's style crystallized in *Where the Wild Things Are.* There was never any doubt, as he was

---

Perhaps the best known fantasy story of all is Maurice Sendak's *Where the Wild Things Are* (P). Max is sent to bed without his supper for being naughty and, in his isolation, creates one of the most marvelous experiences contained in children's literature. The slender text flows like music while the illustrations grow in size as Max's imagination grows. Sendak's classic tale echoes the child's feelings of rejection, his journey from a safe home, and the creation of a fantasy world in which

the child is king: "And when he came to the place where the wild things are they roared their terrible roars and gnashed their terrible teeth and rolled their terrible eyes and showed their terrible claws till Max said 'BE STILL!' "[10] Eventually Max tires of being king of all the wild things and wants to be where someone loves him best of all, and so he returns "across days and in and out of weeks" to his very own room. The supper waiting for him, with the tag phrase "and it was still hot," restores Max

growing up, about what Maurice Sendak wanted to do, and, even while still in high school, he worked for All-American Comics on the "Mutt and Jeff" strip. Winner of the Caldecott Medal and the Hans Christian Andersen Award, as well as the Lewis Carroll Shelf Award, numerous citations of merit, and other national and international awards, Sendak has gained worldwide acclaim.

Sendak is the first to say that art alone is not enough to make a good children's book. He doesn't appreciate compliments solely about his pictures because, for his work, the text is vital. He says that while good pictures are imaginative, pictures must come from the text. Illustrations for a bad book will be bad pictures. A really good book brings out the best in him; he has to be truly excited by the words to create illustrations. He says, "I'm a reader primarily, secondly I'm an illustrator."

Sendak's *In the Night Kitchen* was his goodbye to New York when he moved from the city to his present home in some quiet woods in Connecticut. The book was drawn from remembrances of early childhood. Images—such as the bottle of milk (Sendak's transformation of the Empire State Building) and Mickey and his plane (reminiscent of the shooting of King Kong in the film)— come from the movies and comics of childhood; these remain indelible in his memory.

When asked what one should look for in a picture book, Sendak replied:

Originality of vision. Someone who has something to say that might be very commonplace, but who says it in a totally original and fresh way, who has a point of view, who has a genius for expressing the prosaic in a magical way. Do not look for pyrotechnics, for someone who can make a big slambang picture book out of very little, but look for the genuinely talented person who thinks originally (Kenneth Marantz, "The Picture Book: A Call for Balanced Reviewing," *Wilson Library Bulletin*, 52, No. 2 [Oct. 1977], 157).

to a safe home and his mother's love, made visible in her provision of warm food. Sendak's *In the Night Kitchen* (P) and *Outside Over There* (P) also embody memorable imaginative journeys.

Chris Van Allsburg, in *The Garden of Abdul Gasazi* (P), makes a visual statement with his illustrations that carry the major theme of the book. In a story that hinges on the ability of Abdul Gasazi to make magic, the final, full-page dramatic panorama alone affirms that, indeed, he is a magic maker. Allsburg's gift in design parallels the magic he portrays in story.

Some imaginative stories create humor through exaggeration and slapstick and involve people who blatantly disregard normal behavior. Some primary-age children to whom a librarian read *The Stupids Step Out* (P), by Harry Allard, thoroughly enjoyed the ridiculous characters and their antics. The children giggled when they heard the Stupids name their dog "Kitty" and laughed outright when

"There's your Fritz," says magician Abdul Gasazi, pointing out the lost dog he has turned into a duck in *The Garden of Abdul Gasazi.*
(From *The Garden of Abdul Gasazi* by Chris Van Allsburg, published by Houghton Mifflin Company. Copyright © 1979 by Chris Van Allsburg. Reprinted by permission.)

the Stupids wanted to avoid the funny-looking people they saw in a mirror. When the Stupids ate a mashed potato and butterscotch sundae, the children's laughter drowned out the librarian's. Allard continues the adventures of this outrageous family in *The Stupids Have a Ball* (P), in which the Stupids celebrate their children's horrendously bad report cards. Such imaginative tales encourage fantasy-making and playfulness in children's own stories.

IMAGINATIVE STORIES (P) Establishing an environment in which children tell stories contributes to language development and encourages the developing imagination. Unfortunately, children are sometimes admonished not to make up stories and are not given opportunities to recognize the place for "real" and the place for "make believe." Teachers' attitudes toward storytelling and fantasy affect children's willingness to take risks in making up fanciful tales; an inviting smile or a twinkle in the eye can tell children that it is safe to tell a wild tale. Reading many stories in which a character's imagination runs rampant further verifies for them the appropriateness of imaginative storytelling.

DRAGONS AND MONSTERS (P) A dragon-and-monster theme provides many opportunities for children to exercise their imaginations. Ogden Nash's poem *Custard the Dragon*, illustrated by Linell Nash (P, Little, Brown, 1961), about the "realio, trulio, little pet dragon," can be read along with several books about dragons, including:

The Dragon in the Clockbox (P) by M. Jean Craig. Illustrated by Kelly Oechsli. Norton, 1962.
The Dragon of an Ordinary Family (P) by Margaret Mahy. Watts, 1967.
Everyone Knows What a Dragon Looks Like (P-I) by Jay Williams. Illustrated by Mercer Mayer. Four Winds-Scholastic, 1976.
How Droofus the Dragon Lost His Head (P) by Bill Peet. Houghton Mifflin, 1971.
There's No Such Thing As a Dragon (P) by Jack Kent. Golden Press-Western Publishing, 1975.

THE CHILD'S FAMILY WORLD

The first school is the home; it has a lasting influence on the child's social and personal development. In this section, we look at children's picture books that portray the traditional nuclear family, with a father, mother, and one or more children. In these books, the family itself is seldom the issue but merely a backdrop. Books in which the family is non-nuclear, however, most often have the family structure as the major concern, just as books that have some element that departs from the norm—for example an adopted child or divorced parents—will have their focus on the adoption and on the divorce. Both family-related and family-centered books are described and these include stories about adoption, divorce, new babies, siblings, and grandparents. Each cluster of books reflects the child's expanding world.

In our culture the family is the cornerstone of all relationships, and the way children view the family and their role within it influences their affective development. The traditional family unit, however, is changing in our society. Whereas a working father, a homemaker mother, and two children were once the norm, a variety of family styles is now evident. Donald Hall's *Ox-Cart Man* (P), exquisitely illustrated by Barbara Cooney, recalls a simpler time for the family. The cycle of the changing seasons and the attendant activities bind a New England family to the soil and to each other. In October the ox-cart man fills his cart with everything he and his family have made or grown during the year and takes it to Portsmouth Market. He sells the shawl his wife made, mittens his daughter knitted, birch brooms made by his son, shingles he split himself, and even his cart and, after kissing him goodbye on the nose, his ox. The pastoral scenes evoke the simple beauty of time and place.

The role of grandparents, too, has changed as the mobility of today's society often requires that families be separated by thousands of miles. Children's books reflect the changes in family structure; traditional units appear frequently, but so, too, do those affected by divorce, single-parent families, and adoptive families.

Nuclear Families

Judith Viorst presents life from the viewpoint of the child at the center of a nuclear family. In *Alexander Who Used to Be Rich Last Sunday* (P), Grandma comes to visit and gives a dollar to Alexander, who also appears in *Alexander and the Terrible, Horrible, No Good, Very Bad Day* (P). She also gives a dollar each to Nick and Anthony, who save, invest, and work to make their dollars grow. But Alexander loses and spends his bit by bit. He is fined for saying a word boys are not supposed to say and for kicking things boys are not supposed to kick. He loses a bet that he can "hold his breath 'till 300," flushes three cents down the toilet, and loses five cents down a crack in the porch. He sees the rest of his money disappear at a garage sale where he buys a candle stub, a one-eyed bear, and a deck of cards. He tries to make more money by pulling one of his teeth, checking coin-return slots in public telephones, and returning non-returnable bottles to the store. Finally, broke, he invites his grandma and grandpa to come back soon. In this book, as in many with traditional families, the action centers on the child's activities, not on family structure.

In Robert McCloskey's *Blueberries for Sal* (N-P), a parallel plot develops as Sal and her mother, berry picking along a hillside, meet a mother bear and her baby who are eating the berries. Little Sal and the little bear wander off, then meet up with each others' mothers, who are "old enough to be shy" of each other. When mothers and children are appropriately sorted, they all go home, "eating blueberries all the way." This classic tale continues to be a favorite with young children.

Although very few books deal with adoption, the ones that do show it in a positive way—the adopted child being much wanted and much loved. In *Abby* (P), for example, Jeannette Caines writes of a child who begs to look at her baby book to see her first words and the names of her first visitors. Abby asks questions about her brother's reaction to her, where she came from (Manhattan), how old she was when they adopted her, and what she was wearing. Her mother discusses her adoption openly and describes her brother's reactions in a realistic way. When Kevin tells Abby that he will share her for show and tell at school, Abby wants to know what he will say about her. Kevin answers "that you're adopted, that we get to keep you forever, and that I gave you my fire engine for your birthday." This openly loving story reassures listeners that adoption is a desirable thing.

Mothers and fathers, important people in children's lives, are important people in children's books. Both are portrayed as providers or playmates, and friends or taskmasters, who mete out rewards and punishments. Some overpower and protect while others encourage independence, but all show loving concern for the central child character.

Lucille Clifton captures a child's unfounded fears of being discarded in *Amifika* (N-P). Amifika hears his mother preparing for his father's return from years in the Army and planning to get rid of something the father won't miss in the crowded apartment. Amifika worries to himself: "If I don't remember him, how he gon' remember me? . . . I be what Mama get rid of. Like she said, he can't miss what he don't remember. I be the thing they get rid of." Amifika tries to avoid the inevitable by hiding: "If they get rid of me, they have to find me first." He hides in the yard in a space between a tree and a fence, his eyes wet and tired as he lies against the tree feeling forlorn and unloved. He

awakens in the strong, loving arms of his father who covers him with kisses and says, "Wake up, boy. Do you remember me?"

And all of a sudden the dark warm place came together in Amifika's mind and he jumped in the man's arms and squeezed his arms around the man's neck just like his arms remembered something. "You my own Daddy! My Daddy!" he hollered at the top of his voice and kept hollering as his Daddy held him and danced and danced all around the room.[11]

The warm-hearted family that surrounds Amifika is sensitively portrayed in the chalklike illustrations by Thomas Di Grazia.

Mothers are returning to work outside the home in greater numbers than ever. Often, the resulting strain on family life manifests itself in the children, who have a hard time adjusting to the changes. An ever-increasing phenomenon is that of children being raised by other children; young people themselves are often responsible for the primary care of their younger brothers and sisters. This affects the children's school work as well as their social and emotional life. A discussion with classmates and with a teacher who may herself be a working mother may have far-reaching positive effects both at school and at home.

Teaching Idea

CHANGING FAMILIES (P-I) Read Marge Blaine's *The Terrible Thing That Happened at Our House* illustrated by John C. Wallner (P-I, Parents, 1975). Mother, "who used to be a real mother and stayed home all the time," goes back to being a science teacher. The father begins to help with the household chores, but that interferes with the fun he used to have with the children. The young narrator finally explodes and tells everyone how she feels. They have a family meeting to discuss the problem and come up with a variety of suggestions that enable them to enjoy being a family again. The illustrations in this book are particularly funny; when chaos reigns in the house the pictures spill all over the page. On a long strip of craft paper have students make a mural of the "terrible things" that happen in their houses.

Being a big sister who can hold the new baby can make up for unwelcome changes his arrival brings.
(From *We Are Having a Baby* by Vicki Holland. Copyright © 1972 by Vicki McCabe Holland. Reprinted by permission of Charles Scribner's Sons.)

New Baby

Reaction to a new baby in the family is not a new subject in children's books, but authors continue to treat it with ingenuity. A typical plot involves the excitement surrounding the new baby, the gradual disenchantment with this interloper who takes center stage, and eventual acceptance.

Ezra Jack Keats gives a vital spark to the age-old problem in *Peter's Chair* (N-P). Peter feels that his rights and possessions are usurped by the new baby girl: every time he turns around something that has always been his is turned over to the baby. In a last-ditch effort to keep something, he grabs his favorite chair and runs away to camp on the front step. Surprised to find that he no longer fits in his chair, he finally accepts the role of big brother and even helps his father paint his special chair a bright pink for the new baby sister.

Vicki Holland's photodocumentary *We Are Having a Baby* (N-P) covers the period from before the birth through acceptance of the new baby by a sibling. The young narrator describes events and feelings from her point of view—not always a happy one. A caring father steps in to soothe and reassure her when fears and jealousies overwhelm her. The final photo shows the child holding the baby in her arms with the caption, "He's my brother." This book is used repeatedly to smooth

MY EXPANDING FAMILY (N-P)   Children often feel tremendous disappointment when a new baby turns out to be a great deal less than what they imagine the parents had promised. Someone to play with? Hogwash! The baby is just a lump that screams, cries, and demands too much attention. It can't even look at a book, as is shown so well in Dorothy Aldis's poem:

LITTLE

I am the sister of him
And he is my brother.
He is too little for us
To talk to each other.

So every morning I show him
My doll and my book;
But every morning he still is
Too little to look.

DOROTHY ALDIS[12]

Teachers of primary-grade children will want to keep a collection of "new baby" books in their classrooms. Some of the best include:

A Baby Sister for Frances (P) by Russell Hoban. Illustrated by Lillian Hoban. Harper & Row, 1964.
Everett Anderson's Nine Month Long (N-P) by Lucille Clifton. Illustrated by Ann Grifalconi. Holt, Rinehart & Winston, 1978.
Go and Hush the Baby (N-P) by Betsy Byars. Illustrated by Emily Arnold McCully. Viking, 1971.
The Knee Baby (P) by Mary Jarrell. Illustrated by Symeon Shimin. Farrar, Straus & Giroux, 1973.
Nobody Asked Me If I Wanted a Baby Sister (N-P) by Martha Alexander. Dial, 1971.
She Come Bringing Me That Little Baby Girl (P) by Eloise Greenfield. Illustrated by John Steptoe. Lippincott, 1974.
When the New Baby Comes, I'm Moving Out (N-P) by Martha Alexander. Dial, 1979.

Activity: Teacher to Student

NEW BABY BOOKS (N-P)   Can you remember when your younger brother or sister was a new baby? What did your parents tell you before the baby was born? What did you think the new baby would be like? Were you right? How did you feel when the new baby came home?

After you discuss your experiences, take a sheet of drawing paper and make a picture of something a new baby does. Write a one- or two-line caption describing your picture. Your teacher can make a book of all the pictures and keep it in the classroom library.

the ruffled feathers of a child who feels displaced by a new baby in the family.

Brothers and Sisters

Anyone who has a brother or a sister knows that the relationship is a love/hate one—at times fun and wonderful, but at other times awful. Siblings as adversaries and siblings as friends appear frequently in children's books. Judith Viorst, who builds stories upon the boisterous lives of her own sons, captures the humor and hostility in *I'll Fix Anthony* (P). A younger brother brags about how he is going to fix his arrogant big brother, Anthony, who makes life miserable. Even though his mother says that Anthony really loves him, he is more inclined to believe Anthony, who says he stinks. In his fantasizing, Anthony will get German measles, then mumps, and then a virus. And Anthony will lose all races, games, and contests, and will sink to the bottom of the swimming pool; even if he stays afloat he'll go "glug glug." And he'll sit home by the phone while the popular hero storyteller accepts sleep-over invitations. "But right now," he says, "I have to run. . . . When I'm six I'll fix Anthony."

Barbara Shook Hazen sensitively shows the humorous side of the inconvenience of being a member of a large family in *Why Couldn't I Be an Only Kid Like You, Wigger?* (P). Wigger, an only child, spends all of his time at his friend's house, where there is a large and disruptive family. The disadvantages of having so many brothers and sisters— wearing hand-me-downs, standing in line for the bathroom, sharing the television—are contrasted with the imagined delights of being an only child —getting all the Christmas presents, eating out with parents because it is cheaper than getting a sitter. Suddenly the realization dawns—if being an only child is so great, why does Wigger spend all his time visiting the big, hectic family?

Brothers and sisters are notorious rivals. They bicker, they fight, they tease, they whine, they complain, and they criticize. They hate—and they love. Shel Silverstein captures the feelings of one sibling who offers to sell his sister:

FOR SALE

One sister for sale!
One sister for sale!
One crying and spying young sister for sale!
I'm really not kidding,
So who'll start the bidding?
Do I hear a dollar?
A nickel?
A penny?
Oh, isn't there, isn't there, isn't there any
One kid who will buy this old sister for sale,
This crying and spying young sister for sale?

SHEL SILVERSTEIN[13]

Divorce

Children of divorce often feel that they are different from other children; they feel that one parent or the other does not love them, and sometimes they feel responsible for the divorce. A decade ago we had very few books that mirrored life for them in any way, but now there are several. Jeannette Caines's *Daddy* (P), one of the best, shows none

Activity: Teacher to Student

FOR SALE (P-I)   After reading "For Sale," letter a large copy of the poem on craft paper and make it the center of a bulletin board. Write your own advertisement for your brother or sister. You may follow the format and create a new poem, or perhaps add a personalized second verse to this one. You might have fun writing an imaginary lost-and-found ad for your brother or sister. For example:

Lost: One sister who hogs the bathroom and the telephone, who refuses to lower her stereo and never shares her Milky Way. If found, do NOT return.

of the bitterness surrounding divorce, but only Windy's joy when she sees her father on Saturdays:

> Before Daddy comes to get me
> I get wrinkles in my stomach.
> Sometimes I have wrinkles every night
> and at school, worrying about him.
> Then on Saturday morning
> he rings one short and one long,
> and my wrinkles go away.[14]

Windy's father teases, plays, and romps with her to make each Saturday a joyous time. Paula, her fa-ther's new wife, joins in the fun in an openly lov-ing way that avoids the stereotypic portrayal of a stepmother.

Grandparents

Grandparents are alive and well in children's books; they are no longer vague shadows merging with the background. Barbara Williams gives grandmothers a new image in *Kevin's Grandma* (P). A child tells his friend Kevin about his grand-mother: she gives him piano lessons, drives a sta-tion wagon, belongs to a music club, and leads an active life. But Kevin counters each conventional

Teaching Idea

FIND OUT ABOUT FAMILIES (P-I) Projects about families engage children in many ways; they willingly talk about the people and events close to them. Drawing upon personal experiences brings the child's world to the center of the curriculum. Read aloud the following poem:

AFTERNOON WITH GRANDMOTHER

I always shout when Grandma comes,
But Mother says, "Now please be still
And good and do what Grandma wants."
And I say, "Yes, I will."

So off we go in Grandma's car.
"There's a brand new movie quite near by,"
She says, "that I'd rather like to see."
And I say, "So would I."

The show has horses and chases and battles;
We gasp and hold hands the whole way through.
She smiles and says, "I liked that lots."
And I say, "I did, too."

"It's made me hungry, though," she says,
"I'd like a malt and tarts with jam.
By any chance are you hungry, too?"
And I say, "Yes, I am."

Later at home my Mother says,
"I hope you were careful to do as bid.
Did you and Grandma have a good time?"
And I say, "YES, WE DID!!!"

BARBARA A. HUFF[16]

Ask your students to talk about the things they do with a grandparent or another spe-cial relative.

Activity: Teacher to Student

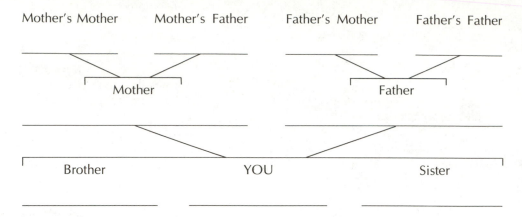

PLANT YOUR FAMILY TREE (P-I) Fill in names in the blanks to make your family tree:

Now fill in the missing words:
1. Your mother's parents and your father's parents are your _____.
2. Your parents' brothers and sisters are your _____ and _____.
3. If your aunts and uncles have children, they are your _____.
4. Your parents' other children are your _____ and _____.

activity with the off-beat things *his* grandmother does: Kevin's grandmother teaches him to arm wrestle, drives a motorcycle, studies karate, scuba dives, and climbs mountains. There is no rocking chair and knitting image here—grandmothers are active people.

Tomie de Paola refers to his old-fashioned Italian grandmother in *Watch Out for the Chicken Feet in Your Soup* (P). From the moment Joey and his friend arrive at Joey's grandmother's door and hear her welcome "Joey, mio bambino! How nice you come to see grandma" through "Zuppa, nice chicken soup," the demonstrative, affectionate grandma prevails. Tomie de Paola says he wrote this book in honor of his Italian grandmother shortly after writing one about his Irish grandmother—*Nana Upstairs and Nana Downstairs* (P). He jokingly confides, "She came to me in a dream

and said, 'A-when you write a book about me?'" With such nice tributes to his forebears, readers may be sorry Tomie de Paola has only two grandmothers.

There are fewer books about grandfathers than about grandmothers, although some good ones do exist. One, Charlotte Zolotow's *My Grandson Lew* (P), is based on a child's memory of a close relationship with his grandfather. Lew awakens one night to talk with his mother about his grandfather, recalling pleasant things they had done together. Lew remembers visits, being carried through a museum, and his grandfather's scratchy whiskers. Lew's mother tells him that his grandfather has died—she had not told him before because she thought he did not remember him. Lew and his mother share their memories and talk about how much they miss him. "But now we will remember him together and neither of us will be so lonely as it would be if we had to remember him alone."[15]

THE CHILD'S SOCIAL WORLD

Social development intersects all other areas of growth; it is both dependent on and necessary to the child's total development. Friendships with others develop slowly and may not really be possible until children develop an identifiable self-concept. Until about the age of two, children often engage in solitary play even when other children are present. Later, in "parallel" play, they are aware of other children and may even play alongside them, with the same toys, but remain independently engaged. Recent research suggests that children at this age are socially aware even though there is little interaction between them.

By the time children enter school they are beginning to interact socially; it is here that group play is common. Identification with and success in a peer group follows as children slowly begin to sort out special friends from within the group.

Friends

Friendship is a mixture of good and bad times and usually encounters many stumbling blocks. Many young children become notorious as fighters as they try simultaneously to declare their independence and develop relationships with others. Children's books reflect the trials as well as the joys of friendship and enable children again to see their feelings mirrored in others.

John Steptoe's *Stevie* (P) portrays a friendship between two boys. Stevie stays with Robert's mother while his own mother works. The older boy's resentment toward Stevie is evident from the beginning and it grows as Stevie intrudes upon Robert's possessions and his independence. When Stevie's mother abruptly takes him away, Robert realizes that the relationship had been important. The strong line illustrations heighten the emotional impact of the sensitive story.

Few other books for children about friendship are so solemn; the great majority focus on the humorous foibles of the characters. In *George and Martha* (P) and several subsequent books, James Marshall created an endearing pair of hippopotamus friends who engage in ridiculously funny antics. Marshall's *Yummers* (P) is a delightful story about Emily Pig and her friend Eugene Turtle. Emily makes all the usual resolutions of any plump nibbler, and Eugene tries to help by diverting her attention from food. Unfortunately, each diversion is strenuous and produces extreme hunger pangs, so that Emily is forced to eat to recover her strength. Her understanding friend stands by her through all her problems.

In Marjorie Weinman Sharmat's *I'm Not Oscar's Friend Anymore* (P), the hero, having had a disagreement with Oscar, goes through a recital of all the afflictions Oscar deserves. Eventually, he decides to give Oscar one more chance to apologize and finds that Oscar doesn't even remember the incident that started all the trouble. Children readily identify with the situation and are able to give many examples from their own short-lived disagreements with their friends.

There are several stories that focus on an unusual aspect of friendship and take their form from Jean de La Fontaine's fable *The Lion and the Rat* (P-I). In each, a small animal helps a larger one in a way that no other one can. In the original fable, a lion becomes hopelessly entangled in a rope net and is freed only after a rat chews through the ropes. This theme of the small helping the big is also found in *Amos and Boris* (P-I), by William Steig, and *The Ant and the Elephant* (P), by Bill Peet.

School

Going to school expands the child's social world, and the excitement of first days at school is recreated in many children's books. Children's questions—Will I have a friend? Who is my teacher? What will I do?—appear as titles and subjects of favorite picture books. Children have pictures of the world different from the ones adults have, but ingenious authors present the world as a child might see it.

Activity: Teacher to Student

ALL CREATURES GREAT AND SMALL (P-I) After reading some stories in which a small animal helps a big one, write your own fable. Discuss some possibilities with your classmates. Start by making a list of some small animals and insects—spiders, grasshoppers, and moles, for example—who might do helpful things. Brainstorm with each other the kinds of special things these creatures could do: the spider spins a web, the grasshopper hops and sings, and the mole builds a tunnel. You can also make a list of big animals and the kinds of situations they might get into that would require the help of smaller animals.

Teaching Idea

MY FRIEND IS SPECIAL (P-I) Children—and indeed all of us—are more at ease with handicapped persons when we know something about them apart from their handicaps. Being able to communicate with a deaf person requires that we learn to sign or finger-spell. The manual alphabet is reprinted in many books; one of the best—*Handtalk: An ABC of Finger Spelling and Sign Language,* by Remy Charlip and Mary Beth Miller (P-I, Parents, 1974)—contains color photographs that clearly demonstrate the signs and is a valuable resource. After reading about and discussing the lives of Helen Keller and Laura Bridgman, as well as other books about the deaf, children eagerly master the skill of sign language. (See Chapter 11 for books about children with special needs.)

Activity: Teacher to Student

LEARN TO SIGN (P-I) Use the American sign language or another hand alphabet and practice signing to each other. As you learn to communicate in sign language, show your skill. Perform at a school assembly by signing the words to a song while the band students play the music. You can also learn to sign a poem.

Invite deaf children to your class to share activities and fun. Tell a story in sign language for them.

Through a slender text and magnificent drawings Rachel Isadora conveys a child's love for her teacher and for drawing in *Willaby* (P). Panoramic scenes of the classroom show all the other children writing, but Willaby is drawing; others are playing, but Willaby is drawing. When Miss Finney, her teacher, is absent, the substitute has the children write get-well notes to her, but Willaby is so engrossed in drawing a picture of a firetruck that she forgets to write a note. When the substitute collects the notes, Willaby hurriedly stuffs the unsigned firetruck picture into the packet. She worries

She is busy drawing a fire truck
she saw on her way to school.

Willaby draws a fire truck seen on the way to school when she is supposed to be writing a get-well card to her teacher. (Reprinted with permission of Macmillan Publishing Co., Inc., from *Willaby* by Rachel Isadora. Copyright © 1977 by Rachel Isadora.)

throughout the weekend that Miss Finney will not know she sent her a card. When Willaby reluctantly arrives at school, however, a note on her desk assures her that Miss Finney did indeed recognize her mark of distinction—her drawing.

Isadora's art carries so much of the story line and characterization that the story would be greatly diminished without it. Touches of pink make Willaby and her work stand out in the otherwise monochromatic charcoal scenes. Subtle humor, as when Willaby wears decorated rain boots while everyone else has plain ones, pervades the appealing illustrations.

Harry Allard's *Miss Nelson Is Missing* (P-I) tells about one teacher's solution to a disruptive class. The children throw spitballs and paper airplanes, whisper, giggle, and do not do their work. Miss Nelson says that something will have to be done about the situation, and the next morning a stern substitute, Miss Viola Swamp, arrives. Miss Swamp loads the children with work, forbids all foolishness, and makes them toe the line so firmly that they long for their sweet and loving Miss Nelson. The children promise to reform when they realize that the mean, crotchety teacher is really Miss Nelson in disguise.

THE CHILD'S NATURAL WORLD

Children learn about nature as they explore their ever-widening worlds. First-hand experiences are primary, of course, but books can deepen and extend children's awareness of the natural world.

Nature

Books can draw attention to nature in sensitive and thoughtful ways; many do not tell a story as much as establish a mood or celebrate natural beauty.

Byrd Baylor and Peter Parnall combine their talents in several picture books that explore the close relationship between people and their land. *The Desert Is Theirs* (P-I) speaks quietly in text and eloquently in illustration about the harmony of birds, insects, animals, and men—"Desert People who call the earth their mother."

Uri Shulevitz conveys images evoked by an ancient Chinese poem with breathtaking simplicity in *Dawn* (P). Here, an old man and his grandson awaken at the edge of a lake as the day slowly gathers light. The miracle of dawn breaks over the lake, and the sun suddenly bursts forth over a mountain that stands guard over the water. The poetic text relates how the lake shivers, and how vapors slowly and lazily begin to rise. It is when the two row to the center of the lake that the startling light spreads over their world in a vivid moment of dawn. The serenity of morning breaking in Shulevitz's book is a stark contrast to Ianthe Thomas's *My Street's a Morning Cool Street* (P). Here, as a young boy makes his way to school, he observes the awakening city. He walks slowly, wiping the sleep out of his eyes as cars whiz by, flapping his coat. A fruit seller prepares his stand for the day's business as a cloud of flies hovers near. Morning breaking in the city carries with it a feeling of intensity, energy, and excitement; this is the natural world for countless children.

Books about clouds suggest new ways for children to experience their world. In Brinton Turkle's *The Sky Dog* (P), a child lies on the sand watching the fluffy white clouds. One resembles a dog, and when a stray dog appears on the beach, the boy is convinced that the "sky dog" has come to him. Tomie de Paola laces fact with humor in *The Cloud Book* (P). This introduction to common clouds contains considerable, hilarious nonsense alongside the scientific information.

Seasons

Young children's sense of time is marked by events more than hours, and their understanding of seasons hinges on observation of falling leaves, snow, spring flowers, or holidays. When we talk with children about spring, summer, fall, and winter, they gradually relate their experiences to the labels we use. Lucille Clifton describes a child at a beginning level of understanding of seasons in *The Boy Who Didn't Believe in Spring* (P). King Shabazz has never seen spring and scoffs when his mother talks about crops coming up. Determined to find the mysterious thing, he and his friend begin to search their urban neighborhood looking for spring. In a vacant lot strewn with debris and an old abandoned car, they find a yellow crocus and a bird's nest holding four small, blue eggs. Finally, spring has become a meaningful concept for them.

John Burningham's *Seasons* (P), an unusually beautiful treatment of the four seasons, gives added meaning to abstract words. Summer seems to shine from the pages in vivid contrast to the stark coldness of the winter scenes. Aileen Fisher's *I Like Weather* (P), a lilting story poem, extols the glories of the many faces of nature—"with different kinds of smells and sounds and looks and feels and ways." Such poems and picture books supply images that can help children conceptualize intangible experiences.

Many phenomena of nature leave exciting substances for children to explore. The first snow of a season is an occasion that never fails to excite children with its endless possibilities for creative play. In Ezra Jack Keats's *The Snowy Day* (N-P), Peter crunches through the snow making intriguing patterns of tracks with his feet. He uses a stick to make a new design and then smacks the stick against a snow-covered tree to plop snow on his head. Readers understand his disappointment when he discovers that the snowball he saves in his pocket melts inside the warm house.

Raymond Briggs's *The Snowman* (N-P), a beautiful wordless book with soft pastel illustrations, blends fantasy and reality. A small boy carefully builds a snowman, which comes to life in the magic of the night and his dreams. The two explore the gadgetry of the house before they go off on a marvelous flight, to return only as the warming sun appears on the horizon.

Mud is another exciting phenomenon of nature —to children if not to their parents. Polly Chase Boyden's poem "Mud," which begins, "Mud is

SNOWMEN AND MUD PUDDLES (P)   Create a three-dimensional scene, or diorama, that shows nature's bounty. Turn a cardboard carton or shoe box on its side to house your diorama, or build your scene on a flat sheet of poster board. Crumpled newspapers form hills and valleys, an aluminum pie tin holds a pond or puddle, and sticks and twigs become trees. Cover everything with a fluffy mixture made with whipped soap flakes to resemble snow, or use real soil to create a muddy paradise. Ivory flakes, or a similar soap product, mixed with just a little water turns to a fluffy paste when beaten with a mixer. Add small figures to your diorama to make the scene realistic. Find (or make from clay) little dolls and animals that look like the characters in snowmen and mud puddle books. Make background scenes on the walls of the diorama. Display the diorama with the book to advertise it to other readers.

The scene in which Peter knocks snow from a tree, in Ezra Jack Keats's *The Snowy Day,* is given a third dimension in this diorama of the event. The illustration on which this is based is shown in the color section for this chapter.

very nice to feel all squishy-squash between the toes!"[17] is fun to read after the first heavy spring rain. Charlotte Pomerantz's story *The Piggy in the Puddle* (P) is a rollicking rhyme that vividly details a baby pig's frolic in a mud puddle. When her family fails to persuade her to come out, they give up and join her—"so they all dove way down derry, and were very, very merry" in the middle of the "puddle, muddle puddle."

Animals

Children have a natural curiosity about the creatures in the natural world, from the tiniest bugs to the biggest elephants. They look at things with the intensity of a poet, the way Mary Ann Hoberman looks at insects in her collection of poems, *Bugs* (P-I). Each poem focuses on some special characteristic—for example, the sound of the beetle in "Click Beetle, Clack Beetle." The poems, a pleasure in themselves, cause us to carefully examine the creepy-crawlers of the earth.

Berniece Freschet's series of nature stories presents scientific concepts in picture books for young children. Her deep respect for nature and wildlife radiates from the pages. *Bear Mouse* (P) sympathetically records the hazardous quest of a mother mouse who eludes many enemies in pursuit of food for herself and her young. Children gain insights about the creatures of the world and begin to understand the precarious balance of nature when they read Freschet's compassionate accounts.

Squirrels, familiar to city and rural children as bushy-tailed little animals that scamper up trees and around bushes, are clever creatures according to Brian Wildsmith in his *Squirrels* (N-P). His spectacular pictures accompany a simple text in which he gives accurate information, including a fascinating description of how the squirrel uses its tail in jumping, swimming, running, and sleeping. Wildsmith calls attention to squirrels as delightful little creatures, but also shows that they can be destructive in their search for food and shelter.

Aileen Fisher, honored by the National Council of Teachers of English for her significant contribution to poetry for children, combines poetic vision with a true regard for nature. Her profound sense of wonder underlies the many story poems she writes for children, in which they see the natural world through her words. It is difficult to choose a favorite from the wealth she gives us, but *Listen, Rabbit* (P-I), from which the following verse is taken, stands out as one of the best:

> My heart went thump!
> And do you know why?
> 'Cause I hoped that maybe
> as time went by
> the rabbit and I
> (if he felt like me)
> could have each other
> for company.[18]

The young boy who watches a rabbit from a distance through an entire year yearns for companionship but understands the need for wild creatures to remain free. Each of Fisher's poems stresses communion with nature, its balance and integrity.

Activity: Teacher to Student

NATURE IN POETRY (P-I) Collect poems, by Aileen Fisher and others, that help us see the inner qualities of the natural world. Choose your favorites and illustrate them with natural objects such as pressed leaves, weeds, dried flowers, feathers, and sticks. Make a group booklet or classroom display to feature book jackets, copies of the poems, and related art work.

Mary and the other children have their chores to do through the long, austere winters of frontierlike northern British Columbia.
(Reproduced from *Mary of Mile 18.* © Ann Blades 1971, published by Tundra Books.)

Children who own pets learn something of the role of a parent, caring for the pet's physical needs, disciplining it, and showing it love and affection, and those who tame an animal from the wilds often learn that it is better for it to return to its natural world. In both cases, children begin to put another's welfare above their own whims. They also learn to respect the creatures of their natural world.

Three books by Carol and Donald Carrick, *Sleep Out* (P), *Lost in the Storm* (P), and *The Accident* (P), revolve around Christopher and his dog Bodger. In the stories, the boy and the dog, cast against dramatic seascapes and storm scenes, play and romp as boys and dogs do. In *Lost in the Storm,* Christopher, involved in playing with his friends, does not realize that Bodger is lost, and suffers remorse because of his neglect. In *The Accident,* Bodger is killed by a truck when he is responding to Christopher's call. Christopher's anger, denial, and final acceptance follow a realistic course of grief. The magnificent scenes by Donald Carrick show not only the work of a fine artist but the work of a man who respects and observes nature closely. Children profit from seeing the natural world depicted in these sympathetic portraits as the backdrop for stories involving pets.

The natural setting for Ann Blades's story *Mary of Mile 18* (P) is northern Canada, where the temperature drops to forty below zero and snow covers the ground for seven months of the year. When the Northern Lights brighten the sky Mary

THE CHILD'S NATURAL WORLD

Teaching Idea

PET SHOW (P) Plan an afternoon with students to show off their pets. Make it clear that every pet is to be kept under the control of its owner at all times, lest there be dog fights, cat fights, lost turtles, or devoured birds. Encourage children who do not have pets to adopt one for the day—a cricket, cockroach, ant, or ladybug. Be sure to have a ribbon to be awarded for every pet—the smallest, the largest, most unusual, and other categories you and your students will create.

Fehr knows that they are a sign that something exciting will happen in her rural, isolated life. The exciting thing does happen—she finds a wolf-pup that she wants to keep as a pet—but her father declares that they will keep only animals that work or provide food. Readers learn about life in northern Canada as they follow the story.

THE CHILD'S AESTHETIC WORLD

As children's interests broaden, the aesthetic environment—art, music, dance, and literature—can add immeasurably to their overall sense of belonging. It is through literature that many children first encounter the cultural arts. Often the first lullabies ("Rock-a-Bye Baby") and the first games ("Pat-a-Cake," "This Little Piggy") are traditional songs of antiquity that appear in well-illustrated books. Moreover, through books children can be introduced to great works of art at an early age. Early and continued exposure to the arts lays a firm foundation on which children build an ever-spiraling appreciation for their aesthetic world.

Art

Children see in their picture books some of the best products of artistic talent they may ever encounter. In fact, one critic claims that picture books are more a form of visual art than they are literature.[19]

Mitsumasa Anno is a superb artist whose talent is evident in *Anno's Journey* (P-I), a magnificent adventure of the imagination. The meticulous watercolor illustrations trace the wanderings of a man through the European countryside, where he meets a fascinating array of people absorbed in their work and play. Anno fills the pages with details and subtly includes many literary and historical figures one can search for amidst the bustling scenes.

John Goodall paints a similarly exquisite picture in *The Story of an English Village* (P-I). Shown from the same perspective over six centuries, the countryside undergoes a gradual differentiation in architecture and life style. The artist skillfully uses half pages (which permit changes to parts of a field of view) to depict the continuous panorama of history; distant castle walls crumble and the house interiors are transformed to meet changing needs. Both of these beautiful books are wordless; through their alluring illustrations they evoke a mood of quiet contemplation. One does not glance casually at them, but pores over them time and again, appreciating the pure joy of discovery.

The art in picture books for children tells a story; it may evoke pensive moods or irrepressible laughter. Graham Oakley achieves a superlative blend of text and pictures in *The Church Mouse* (P), which is one of a series. The church in the English village of Wortlethorpe is home to a large family of mice and their feline companion, Sampson. Each story is a riotous adventure in chaos, in which the extravagant illustrations add comedy to the rather droll, understated text. For example, in

It was a stick

(*Top*) The bright colors and simple forms Leo Lionni uses in *Fish Is Fish* make an apt vehicle for his lighthearted story about a fish with amusingly distorted views of other creatures. (From *Fish Is Fish* by Leo Lionni. Copyright © 1975 by Leo Lionni. Reprinted by permission of Pantheon Books, a Division of Random House, Inc.)

(*Left*) Ezra Jack Keats's work often employs collage, paints, and ink in a single composition. Here he achieves an elegant simplicity in a picture from *The Snowy Day*. (Reprinted by permission of Viking Penguin Inc. from *The Snowy Day* by Ezra Jack Keats. Copyright © 1962 by Ezra Jack Keats.)

(*Above left*) A page from *Brian Wildsmith's Puzzles* demonstrates his typical use of brilliant color and richly organized composition that mixes bold representation and playful abstraction. (From *Brian Wildsmith's Puzzles.* Copyright © 1970. Used by permission of Franklin Watts, Inc.)

(*Above right*) Susan Jeffers pen-and-ink and muted acrylic tones produce delicate and artful interpretations of poetry and folk literature that are reminiscent of Arthur Rackham. (Excerpted from the book *Thumbelina.* Illustrated by Susan Jeffers. Copyright © 1979 by Susan Jeffers. Used by permission of The Dial Press.)

(*Right*) Barbara Cooney selects medium and technique according to the demands of the story. Here, for a tale of early New England, she uses an early American technique of painting on wood. (Reprinted by permission of Viking Penguin Inc. from *The Ox-Cart Man* by Donald Hall, illustrated by Barbara Cooney. Illustrations copyright © 1979 by Barbara Cooney Porter.)

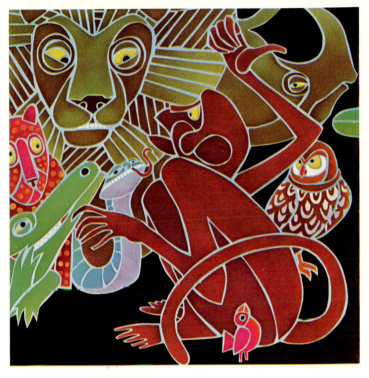

(*Above left*) Ample, lumpy figures, rosy cheeks, and bulbous noses—all rendered in muted water colors and black line—are elements in Margot Zemach's sophisticated and earthy interpretations of character. (Illustration reproduced by permission of Farrar, Straus & Giroux, Inc. from *Duffy and the Devil* by Harve and Margot Zemach. Copyright © 1973 by Farrar, Straus & Giroux, Inc.)

(*Above right*) Leo and Diane Dillon's luminous, stylized work employs freshet (a kind of stencil), line, pastels, airbrush, and bleaching. (Excerpted from the book *Why Mosquitoes Buzz In People's Ears: A West African Tale* by Leo and Diane Dillon. Copyright © 1975 by Leo and Diane Dillon. Used by permission of The Dial Press.)

(*Left*) Nonny Hogrogian, adept at many media and techniques, uses oils in this picture with a flowing, vigorous line from *One Fine Day*. (Reprinted with permission of Macmillan Publishing Co., Inc. from *One Fine Day* by Nonny Hogrogian. Copyright © 1971 by Nonny Hogrogian.)

(*Right*) Simultaneously witty and warm, Arnold Lobel's illustrations—as here, for his *Fables*—convey the human through anthropomorphic animals. (Illustration from *Fables,* written and illustrated by Arnold Lobel. Copyright © 1980 by Arnold Lobel. By permission of Harper & Row, Publishers, Inc.)
(*Below*) Brilliant color and the bold lines of Ed Emberley's woodcuts for *Drummer Hoff* produce a striking effect. (From the book *Drummer Hoff* by Barbara and Ed Emberley. Copyright © 1967 by Edward R. Emberley and Barbara Emberley. Published by Prentice-Hall, Inc., Englewood Cliffs, New Jersey 07632.)

In *The Church Mice at Bay* the new rector, here shown on his arrival, is not quite what the parishioners expected.
(From *The Church Mice at Bay* by Graham Oakley. Copyright © 1978 by Graham Oakley. Reprinted by permission of Atheneum Publishers.)

The Church Mice at Bay (P) the text states that the mice had hoped the vicar's summer replacement would be "a nice quiet young chap." The next page has only two words—"He wasn't"—but a picture that is a panorama of outlandish jumble; a car decorated with flowers, butterflies, and peace doves tears into the driveway leaving scattered pedestrians, shattered milk bottles, an overrun bicyclist, and startled mice in its wake.

The overall effect, the way the illustrations work with the words to tell a story, is of primary concern in picture books. Children are quick to judge and respond intuitively; they either like the pictures or they don't. The style, the medium used, and the images produced combine for an effect that can alone make a book acceptable or unacceptable to the reader.

As children become discriminating in their tastes, they begin to develop an aesthetic awareness. Understanding how the lines and colors work together to form pictures they like comes gradually to children given a great deal of expo-

Activity: Teacher to Student

ART BASED ON BOOKS (P-I)   Find a book or an illustrator's work you like. Use the same medium and techniques to create a work of your own. Ask the art teacher to help you develop projects based on your favorite books.

1.   Brian Wildsmith's animal books, *Fishes* (Watts, 1968), *Wild Animals* (Watts, 1967), and *Birds* (Watts, 1967), are a good model for watercolors. Try to make animal, bird, or fish pictures the way he does.

2.   Ezra Jack Keats uses marbelized paper in several books, including *The King's Fountain,* by Lloyd Alexander (Dutton, 1977), and his own *Hi Cat!* (Macmillan, 1970). You can make marbelized paper by filling a large rectangular cake pan with water and adding a few drops of oil-based paint. Stir the paint just a bit to make an interesting swirl pattern. Carefully place the paper on top of the water until it absorbs the paint, then remove it, and lay it flat to dry. Keats's collages are also good to imitate. Collect scraps of fabric, cotton balls, and paper and make your own collage by arranging shapes and textures.

3.   Marcia Brown's *Once a Mouse* (Scribner's, 1961) shows you how one artist uses woodcuts. Carve designs in soft pine to make printing blocks. Potatoes and cardboard are easier to carve than wood, but sharp tools make it possible to use linoleum blocks or soft wood.

4.   *Ed Emberley's Great Thumbprint Drawing Book* (Little, Brown, 1977) and Ruth Krauss's *This Thumbprint* (Harper & Row, 1967) can give many ideas for using fingerprints in art. You can make personalized note paper, or write a story to accompany thumbprint creatures.

5.   Natalie Babbitt's *The Something* (Farrar, Straus & Giroux, 1970) shows how one child molded a creature from clay. You can also make a "something" with plasticene or modeling clay.

---

sure to art and illustrations of all kinds. As they learn to be sensitive to design and artistic effect, a study of techniques can add to their appreciation.

Music

Music is an integral part of an aesthetic life. Almost from the time they hear their first lullaby, young children can hum or follow along with favorite melodies. Every culture is replete with songs of its people; many are illustrated and published in single-edition picture books—that is, a book in which a single rhyme or song is the basis for lavish illustration.

Margot Zemach illustrates some rollicking folk songs in her characteristically earthy and old-fashioned style. *Mommy, Buy Me a China Doll* (N-P) and *Hush Little Baby* (N-P), two cumulative songs, are augmented by Zemach's jovial interpretations. Aliki also illustrates familiar old songs in a charming style. Her rendition of *Hush Little Baby* (N-P) differs from Zemach's in that Aliki's family is more restrained, well-groomed, and younger than the roguish one Zemach portrays. Aliki's full-page scenes, filled with antiques of the period that gave rise to the song, contain luxurious details. Similarly, in *Go Tell Aunt Rhody* (N-P), she preserves an image of the sentiment of the period in which the song originated. A patchwork quilt design on the endpapers alludes to an early American farm life setting.

Many Mother Goose songs appear in single-edition picture books. For example, Janina Domanska illustrated *I Saw a Ship A-Sailing* (N-P) in unique stylized pictures. Stark lines and vivid colors reflect the movement and rhythm of the song. Susan Jeffers uses pastel shapes contrasted with bold lines to show a young girl's dream-like vision in *All the Pretty Horses* (N-P). The flowing cadence and pensive mood of the song lulls sleepy heads to pleasant dreams when parents read it at bedtime; read aloud during the school day, it can soothe irritable, tired children.

Peter Spier has created at least two books for "The Mother Goose Library," in which he illustrated well-loved songs and rhymes. One of them, *London Bridge Is Falling Down* (N-P), shows the famous old bridge amidst the magnificent panorama of its Thames river environs. Spier's precision and detail invite the child to explore new aspects of the song each time the favorite tune is sung. The entire song is repeated with the musical score at the end of the book, along with a history of the bridge.

Several musical compositions are skillfully transcribed into picture book format; as children visualize the scenes and learn the stories, they build a foundation for appreciation of the original musical scores. One of these, Serge Prokofieff's

Bright, bold illustrations tell the story of the old song.
(Reprinted with permission of Macmillan Publishing Co., Inc., from *Go Tell Aunt Rhody* by Aliki Brandenberg. Copyright © 1974 by Aliki Brandenberg.)

THE CHILD'S AESTHETIC WORLD

Peter and the Wolf (P-I), a well-loved classic, is illustrated with meticulous scratchboard drawings by Frans Haacken. The menacing wolf and the forest creatures provide a vivid accompaniment to the recording of the music. Beni Montresor uses his experience as a theatrical set designer to create illustrations for several operas. His sets and costumes for Rossini's *Cinderella* (P-I), adapted by him, and Mozart's *The Magic Flute* (P-I), adapted by Stephen Spender, give children the opportunity to visualize the elaborate spectacle of a production of these works. These books are not, of course, substitutes for the actual musical experiences children need. However, using them with recordings provides concrete visual images to strengthen appreciation of the music.

Dance and Movement

Expressive movement is natural to children; they sway, tap their feet, and bounce, impelled by the pure joy—or frustration—of being. Music, stories, and poems invite movement; who can sit still while singing the traditional rhymes Humpty Dumpty, Sing a Song of Sixpence, or Ring Around a Rosy?

Four children find delight in a summer night frolic in Janice May Udry's *The Moon Jumpers* (P): "And we all dance, barefooted. Over and over the grass! We play tag in and out. With the wind and with each other. . . . We make up songs. And poems. And we turn somersaults all over the grass."[20] The magic of night compels a joyful romp expressing their feelings and fancies. Elinor Horwitz evokes a similar mood in *When the Sky Is Like Lace* (P). The mystical splendor of a "bimulous" night brings out joy, dance, and movement.

The structured movement that is ballet is shown in Jill Krementz's *A Very Young Dancer* (P-I), a photodocumentary biography of a young ballet student chosen to dance the role of Clara in "The Nutcracker." The strenuous work of the dancer is evident, as is the reward of the thrill and excitement of opening night. Through excellent black-and-white photographs, Krementz skillfully tells the story of the ballet within the story of a dancer learning her craft.

Literature

A love for literature begins early if young children are given pleasurable book experiences. Children who read and are read to develop an intuitive awareness of the kinds of books they like. They also single out favorite characters and recognize similarities in illustrations. If authors and illustrators are talked about as real people, children will seek out other books by their favorites. Knowing books, and knowing about the people who create them, provides a solid beginning for a lifelong love of literature.

The names of some authors and illustrators are synonymous with good children's books; their work outlived the generation for whom it was written and has become classic because of its continued appeal. Children learn to associate a style of writing or illustrating with its creator when they encounter many works by the same person. Beatrix Potter is someone many children know through her miniature books with delicate illustrations of quaint and lovable animals. Although *The Tale of Peter Rabbit* (N-P) is the most famous, the tales of *Benjamin Bunny* (N-P), *Jemima Puddleduck* (N-P), *Mrs. Tiggy Winkle* (N-P), *Tom Kitten* (N-P), *Jeremy Fisher* (N-P), *Squirrel Nutkin* (N-P), and others written by this shy English woman nearly one hundred years ago still appeal to children today. *The Tale of Peter Rabbit* alone sells over 200,000 copies each year. Figurines, stuffed toys, biographies, art exhibits, and films related to her creations attest to their continued popularity. *Nothing Is Impossible: The Story of Beatrix Potter* (I), by Dorothy Aldis, is a biography for older children who fondly remember the animal tales. Margaret Lane's *The Tale of Beatrix Potter* (adult) tells of her early life and contains facsimiles of Potter's original manuscripts.

Another English author children learn to love is A. A. Milne, creator of *Winnie the Pooh* (I). Milne's books, discussed in detail in other sections of this book, warrant mention here for their classic appeal. Two poetry collections, *When We Were Very Young* (P) and *Now We Are Six* (P), appeal to children in the primary grades, while the subtle humor in *Winnie the Pooh* (I) and *The House at Pooh Cor-*

THE CREATORS OF PICTURE BOOKS (P-I) Children who repeatedly hear stories and view illustrations by the same artist grow to feel as if they know that person. Teachers and librarians can encourage children to learn about these people by making them the subjects of study.

An author and/or illustrator of the month soon becomes a popular attraction and consistently boosts circulation of the featured person's books. A bulletin board and a table with not only the books, but realia associated with them, children's reviews of the books, projects based on books made by children, and photographs of the person draw attention to the creator. Children's favorite authors and illustrators can be featured, as well as others the teacher wants to introduce. Information about authors and illustrators can be obtained directly from their publishers, as well as from several books about authors:

Books Are by People by Lee Bennett Hopkins. Citation Press, 1969.
The Junior Book of Authors, edited by Stanley Kunitz and Howard Haycraft. H. W. Wilson, 1951.
More Books by More People by Lee Bennett Hopkins. Citation Press, 1974.
More Junior Authors, edited by Muriel Fuller. H. W. Wilson, 1963.
Something About the Author, Vols. 1–18, edited by Anne Commire. Gale Research, 1971–1980.
Third Book of Junior Authors, edited by Doris De Montreville and Donna Hill. H. W. Wilson, 1972.

A new series involves authors and illustrators discussing their work; *Self-Portrait: Margot Zemach* (P-I, Addison-Wesley, 1978) is the first. In addition, several audio-visual packets present authors and illustrators describing how they work. Steven Kellogg's *The Island of the Skog* (P, Dial, 1973) is accompanied by a sound filmstrip (Weston Woods) in which Kellogg explains the creation of the book.

Holling Clancy Holling's *Pagoo* (P-I, Houghton Mifflin, 1957) is featured in the sound filmstrip "The Story of a Book," part of the Literature for Children series (Pied Piper). Other companies, including Miller Brody and Spoken Arts, produce various materials in which authors and illustrators are featured.

Have your students write to living authors and illustrators. Children who receive a response, even a form letter or printed material about the person, develop an understanding that authors are real people. Children's letters often include their interpretations of the story or pictures, as well as questions. Young children may dictate what they want to say into a recorder and have it transcribed by parent volunteers or older children, although authors and illustrators usually have great understanding of their young audiences and like to hear from children directly. Letters can be sent to authors or illustrators in care of their publishers. (See Appendix for addresses.)

Information about authors and illustrators can be shared by displaying the material with their books. Since every author or illustrator cannot be expected to answer every child, and because children should keep their own letters, preserve them by making copies for others to read—unless, of course, they are private.

Activity: Teacher to Student

LEARN ABOUT YOUR FAVORITE AUTHOR OR ILLUSTRATOR (P-I) Learn about the people who make your favorite books. Read all of their books, read articles written by or about them, and look at filmstrips and clippings about them.

Write a letter to your favorite authors or illustrators. Be sure to make your letter interesting by talking about their books and by telling them something about yourself. Authors receive many letters, so make yours one they will want to read and answer.

Make a collection of all the works of one person. Feature the person in an exhibit, in a notebook, or in a sales talk to your class.

---

ner, (I) makes them more suitable for children in the intermediate grades.

Madeline (P), by Ludwig Bemelmans, is a perennial favorite. "In an old house in Paris that was covered with vines, lived twelve little girls in two straight lines. The smallest one was Madeline."[21] Bemelmans's five books about the sprightly little girl who is a vexation to Miss Clavel were precursors to the non-sexist children's books of today. Madeline is one of the earliest derring-do females; her exploits continue in *Madeline's Rescue* (P), *Madeline and the Bad Hat* (P), *Madeline and the Gypsies* (P), and *Madeline in London* (P).

A Frenchman, Jean DeBrunhoff, wrote *The Story of Babar* (P) in 1937; the story, concerning the life and mishaps of a lovable elephant family, continues in many books. Several publishers rejected DeBrunhoff's manuscripts about Babar because they were written in the present tense. Eventually published, they quickly became a hit, and remain popular with children today, partially because of the sense of immediacy achieved by the use of the present tense. Children feel as if they are observing on-the-spot action in the lives of Babar, his wife Celeste, and their children.

Wanda Gág's *Millions of Cats* (N-P), written in 1928, was the first picture book published in America for children. The delightful rhythmic story of the little old man who brought home "hundreds of cats, thousands of cats, millions and billions and trillions of cats," followed by *Nothing at All* (P) in 1941, continues to be a favorite today.

The Velveteen Rabbit (P-I), written in 1922 by Margery Williams, also remains popular, with its tender story of the relationship between a stuffed animal and a child. The symbolic story concerning the question of what is real can be read on several levels of meaning and holds its rank among the best-loved books.

CRITERIA FOR SELECTING PICTURE BOOKS

There are several qualities one should look for in selecting picture books. Since learning is a continuous reaching out and integrating of both direct and vicarious experiences, in general one should select books that reflect, extend, or enrich the child's expanding world. As a basis for selection, the illustrations are of prime importance. One should look for illustrations (1) that catch and hold the reader's interest, and (2) that have an attraction as art in themselves (as well as those that work with the text to amplify the story).

Young children's language is heavily influenced by the language they read and hear. Children are word collectors; they like to play with words and have fun with their sounds. On hearing John Burningham's *Mr. Gumpy's Outing* (N-P), children will echo Mr. Gumpy's "mucking about." The "bimulous" of "bimulous night," from Elinor Horwitz's *When the Sky Is Like Lace* (P), will also find echoes in the group. Hence, books selected should contain (1) intrinsically interesting words used in interesting ways that build excitement and drama, and (2) language that has an internal rhythm, a melody, and a natural beat.

Young children find it natural to identify with storybook characters. They giggle when the heroine in Ludwig Bemelmans's *Madeline* (P) walks on the rail of the bridge rather than on the beaten path with the other girls; they pull up their shirts and look at their own stomachs when she shows off her appendectomy scar. Through simple fantasy play they become Madeline as she dares to do the things they pretend to do. Thus, we look for (1) characters well developed in text and illustration, who stand out as clearly identifiable human beings or animals, and (2) characters who actively make things happen.

Children do not favor long, descriptive monologues; they want things to happen. Their own re-telling of stories is essentially a moving from one action to the next via connective phrases such as "and then." Young children find it difficult to follow complex, convoluted plots with flashbacks and subplots and are bored with lengthy scene setting and descriptions of the setting. They also want to know the time—present, past, or future—in which the tale is laid, and they want a definite recognizable ending. We look, then, for (1) a clearly identifiable plot—one visible in both text and illustration and that moves forward logically, and (2) a clearly identifiable climax and resolution.

Theme and mood are important aspects of any children's books. The underlying message, the main idea the author is trying to convey, a theme, may be interpreted differently by different readers; there is no one right answer. But although good themes are neither blatantly stated nor so subtle they elude the reader, picture books should have (1) a readily identifiable theme that evolves naturally from plot and character and is integrated with the illustrations, and (2) a theme and adjunct illustrations that are understandable.

Notes

1. William Carlos Williams, "The Red Wheelbarrow," in *Collected Earlier Poems* (New York: New Directions, 1938), p. 277.
2. Frank Smith, *Comprehension and Learning: A Conceptual Framework for Teachers* (New York: Holt, Rinehart & Winston, 1975), p. 2.
3. Ed Emberley, "Caldecott Medal Acceptance," in *Newbery and Caldecott Medal Books: 1966–1975,* ed. Lee Kingman (Boston: Horn Book, 1975), p. 200.
4. Felice Holman, "Leave Me Alone," in *At the Top of My Voice and Other Poems,* illus. Edward Gorey (New York: Norton, 1970), p. 45.
5. A. A. Milne, "The End," in *Now We Are Six,* illus. Ernest H. Shepard (1927; New York: Dutton, 1955), p. 104.
6. A. A. Milne, "Us Two," in *Now We Are Six,* p. 35.
7. Such objects are called *transitional objects.* For further information about the role of security symbols, see Simon A. Grolnich and Leonard Barkin, eds., *Between Reality and Fantasy* (New York: Aronson, 1978); D. W. Winnicott, "Transitional Objects and Transitional Phenomena," *International Journal of Psychoanalysis,* 34, Part II (1953), 89–97; Marion Milner, "Aspects of Symbolism in Comprehension of the Not-Self," *International Journal of Psychoanalysis,* 33, Part II (1952), 181–95; and D. W. Winnicott, "The Location of Cultural Experience," *International Journal of Psychoanalysis,* 48 (1966), 368–72.

8. Kornei Chukovsky, *From Two to Five,* trans. and ed. Miriam Morton (Berkeley and Los Angeles: Univ. of California Press, 1963), p. 119.

9. A. A. Milne, "Binker," in *Now We Are Six,* p. 17.

10. Maurice Sendak, *Where the Wild Things Are* (New York: Harper & Row, 1963), unpaged.

11. Lucille Clifton, *Amifika,* illus. Thomas DiGrazia (New York: Dutton, 1977), unpaged.

12. Dorothy Aldis, "Little," in *All Together* (New York: Putnam's, 1952), p. 89.

13. Shel Silverstein, "For Sale," in *Where the Sidewalk Ends* (New York: Harper & Row, 1974), p. 52.

14. Jeannette Caines, *Daddy,* illus. Ronald Himler (New York: Harper & Row, 1977), unpaged.

15. Charlotte Zolotow, *My Grandson Lew,* illus. William Pène du Bois (New York: Harper & Row, 1974), unpaged.

16. Barbara A. Huff, "Afternoon with Grandmother," in *Favorite Poems Old and New,* ed. Helen Ferris, illus. Leonard Weisgard (New York: Doubleday, 1957), p. 42.

17. Polly Chase Boyden, "Mud," in *Arbuthnot Anthology of Children's Literature,* 4th ed., ed. Zena Sutherland et al. (New York: Lothrop, Lee & Shepard, 1976), p. 103.

18. Aileen Fisher, *Listen Rabbit,* illus. Symeon Shimin (New York: Crowell, 1964), unpaged.

19. Kenneth Marantz, "The Picture Book as Art Object: A Call for Balanced Reviewing," *Wilson Library Bulletin,* 52, No. 2 (Oct. 1977), 148–51.

20. Janice May Udry, *The Moon Jumpers,* illus. Maurice Sendak (New York: Harper & Row, 1959), unpaged.

21. Ludwig Bemelmans, *Madeline* (New York: Viking, 1939), unpaged.

Professional References

Chukovsky, Kornei. *From Two to Five.* Trans. and ed. Miriam Morton. Univ. of California Press, 1963.

Grolnich, Simon A., and Leonard Barkin, eds. *Between Reality and Fantasy.* Aronson, 1978.

"An Interview with Maurice Sendak." Writ. Bernice E. Cullinan. *Teaching Critical Reading and Thinking to Children and Adolescents.* Taught by Bernice E. Cullinan. Dir. Roy Allen, New York University's Sunrise Semester. CBS, 1 May 1978.

Kingman, Lee, ed. *Newbery and Caldecott Medal Books: 1966–1975.* Horn Book, 1975.

Lane, Margaret. *The Tale of Beatrix Potter: A Biography,* 2nd ed. Warne, 1968.

Marantz, Kenneth. "The Picture Book as Art Object: A Call for Balanced Reviewing," *Wilson Library Bulletin,* 52, No. 2 (Oct. 1977), 148–51.

Milner, Marion. "Aspects of Symbolism in Comprehension of the Non-Self," *International Journal of Psychoanalysis,* 44 (1952), 181–94.

Smith, Frank. *Comprehension and Learning: A Conceptual Framework for Teachers.* Holt, Rinehart & Winston, 1975.

Winnicott, D. W. "The Location of Cultural Experience." *International Journal of Psychoanalysis,* 48 (1966), 368–72.

––––––––. "Transitional Objects and Transitional Phenomena," *International Journal of Psychoanalysis.* 34, Part II (1953), 89, 97.

Wintle, Justin, and Emma Fisher. *The Pied Pipers.* Paddington, 1975.

Children's Books Cited in Chapter

Aardema, Verna. *Why Mosquitoes Buzz in Peoples Ears: A West African Tale.* Illus. Leo and Diane Dillon. Dial, 1975.

Aldis, Dorothy. *Nothing Is Impossible: The Story of Beatrix Potter.* Illus. Richard Cuffari. Atheneum, 1969.

Alexander, Martha. *I'll Protect You from the Jungle Beasts.* Dial, 1973.

Aliki, illus. *Go Tell Aunt Rhody.* Macmillan, 1974.

––––––––. *Hush Little Baby: A Folk Lullaby.* Prentice-Hall, 1968.

Allard, Harry. *Miss Nelson Is Missing.* Illus. James Marshall. Houghton Mifflin, 1977.

––––––––. *The Stupids Have a Ball.* Illus. James Marshall. Houghton Mifflin, 1978.

––––––––. *The Stupids Step Out.* Illus. James Marshall. Houghton Mifflin, 1974.

Andersen, Hans Christian. *Thumbelina.* Retold by Amy Ehrlich. Illus. Susan Jeffers. Dial, 1979.

Anno, Mitsumasa. *Anno's Journey.* Collins-World, 1978.

Baylor, Byrd. *The Desert Is Theirs.* Illus. Peter Parnall. Scribner's, 1975.

Bemelmans, Ludwig. *Madeline.* Viking, 1939.

––––––––. *Madeline and the Bad Hat.* Viking, 1957.

_____. *Madeline and the Gypsies*. Viking, 1959.

_____. *Madeline in London*. Viking, 1961.

_____. *Madeline's Rescue*. Viking, 1953.

Blades, Ann. *Mary of Mile 18*. Tundra, 1971.

Briggs, Raymond. *The Snowman*. Viking, 1978.

Brown, Margaret Wise. *Goodnight Moon*. Illus. Clement Hurd. Harper & Row, 1947.

Burningham, John. *Mr. Gumpy's Outing*. Holt, Rinehart & Winston, 1971.

_____. *Seasons*. Bobbs-Merrill, 1970.

Caines, Jeannette. *Abby*. Illus. Steven Kellogg. Harper & Row, 1973.

_____. *Daddy*. Illus. Ronald Himler. Harper & Row, 1977.

Carrick, Carol. *The Accident*. Illus. Donald Carrick. Seabury, 1976.

_____. *Lost in the Storm*. Illus. Donald Carrick. Seabury, 1974.

_____. *Sleep Out*. Illus. Donald Carrick. Seabury, 1973.

Clifton, Lucille. *Amifika*. Illus. Thomas Di Grazia. Dutton, 1977.

_____. *The Boy Who Didn't Believe in Spring*. Illus. Brinton Turkle. Dutton, 1973.

Crowe, Robert L. *Clyde Monster*. Illus. Kay Chorao. Dutton, 1976.

D'Aulaire, Ingri and Edgar Parin. *Abraham Lincoln*, rev. Doubleday, 1957.

De Brunhoff, Jean. *The Story of Babar*. Random House, 1960.

De Paola, Tomie. *The Cloud Book*. Holiday House, 1975.

_____. *Nana Upstairs and Nana Downstairs*. Putnam's, 1973.

_____. *Oliver Button Is a Sissy*. Harcourt Brace Jovanovich, 1979.

_____. *Watch Out for the Chicken Feet in Your Soup*. Prentice-Hall, 1974.

Domanska, Janina, illus. *I Saw a Ship A-Sailing*. Macmillan, 1972.

Emberley, Barbara. *Drummer Hoff*. Illus. Ed Emberley. Prentice-Hall, 1967.

Feelings, Muriel. *Jambo Means Hello: Swahili Alphabet Book*. Illus. Tom Feelings. Dial, 1974.

_____. *Moja Means One: Swahili Counting Book*. Illus. Tom Feelings. Dial, 1971.

Fisher, Aileen. *I Like Weather*. Illus. Janina Domanska. Crowell, 1963.

_____. *Listen, Rabbit*. Illus. Symeon Shimin. Crowell, 1964.

Freeman, Don. *Corduroy*. Viking, 1968.

_____. *Dandelion*. Viking, 1964.

_____. *A Pocket for Corduroy*. Viking, 1978.

Freschet, Berniece. *Bear Mouse*. Illus. Donald Carrick. Scribner's, 1973.

Gág, Wanda. *Millions of Cats*. Coward, McCann & Goeghegan, 1928.

_____. *Nothing at All*. Coward, McCann & Goeghegan, 1941.

Goodall, John. *The Story of an English Village*. Atheneum, 1979.

Hall, Donald. *Ox-Cart Man*. Illus. Barbara Cooney. Viking, 1979.

Hazen, Barbara Shook. *Why Couldn't I Be an Only Kid Like You, Wigger?* Illus. Leigh Grant. Atheneum, 1975.

Hoban, Tana. *Look Again*. Macmillan, 1971.

Hoberman, Mary Ann. *Bugs: Poems*. Illus. Victoria Chess. Viking, 1976.

Hodges, Margaret. *The Wave*. Illus. Blair Lent. Houghton Mifflin, 1964.

Hogrogian, Nonny. *One Fine Day*. Macmillan, 1971.

Holland, Vicki. *We Are Having a Baby*. Scribner's, 1972.

Holman, Felice. *At the Top of My Voice*. Illus. Edward Gorey. Scribner's, 1976.

Horwitz, Elinor Lander. *When the Sky Is Like Lace*. Illus. Barbara Cooney. Lippincott, 1975.

Hutchins, Pat. *Happy Birthday, Sam*. Greenwillow, 1978.

_____. *Titch*. Macmillan, 1971.

Isadora, Rachel. *Willaby*. Macmillan, 1977.

Jeffers, Susan, illus. *All the Pretty Horses*. Macmillan, 1974.

Keats, Ezra Jack. *Peter's Chair*. Harper & Row, 1967.

_____. *The Snowy Day*. Viking, 1962.

Knotts, Howard. *Great-Grandfather, the Baby and Me*. Atheneum, 1978.

Krementz, Jill. *A Very Young Dancer*. Knopf, 1976.

La Fontaine, Jean de. *The Lion and the Rat*. Illus. Brian Wildsmith. Watts, 1963.

Lent, Blair. *John Tabor's Ride*. Little, Brown, 1966.

Lionni, Leo. *Alexander and the Wind-Up Mouse*. Pantheon, 1967.

_____. *Fish Is Fish*. Pantheon, 1970.

Lobel, Arnold. *Fables*. Harper & Row, 1980.

McCloskey, Robert. *Blueberries for Sal*. Viking, 1948.

McDermott, Gerald. *Arrow to the Sun: A Pueblo Indian Tale*. Viking, 1974.

Marshall, James. *George and Martha*. Houghton Mifflin, 1972.

_____. *Yummers*. Houghton Mifflin, 1973.

Mayer, Mercer. *There's a Nightmare in My Closet*. Dial, 1968.

Milne, A. A. *The House at Pooh Corner*. Illus. Ernest H. Shepard. Dutton, 1928.

_____. *Now We Are Six*. Illus. Ernest H. Shepard. Dutton, 1927.

_____. *When We Were Very Young*. Illus. Ernest H. Shepard. Dutton, 1924.

_____. *Winnie the Pooh*. Illus. Ernest H. Shepard. Dutton, 1926.

Montresor, Beni, illus. *Cinderella*. Knopf, 1965.

Mosel, Arlene. *The Funny Little Woman*. Illus. Blair Lent. Dutton, 1972.

Ness, Evaline. *Sam, Bangs and Moonshine*. Holt, Rinehart & Winston, 1966.

Nic Leodhas, Sorche. *Always Room for One More*. Illus. Nonny Hogrogian. Holt, Rinehart & Winston, 1965.

Oakley, Graham. *The Church Mice at Bay*. Atheneum, 1979.

_____. *The Church Mouse*. Atheneum, 1972.

Peet, Bill. *The Ant and the Elephant*. Houghton Mifflin, 1972.

Pomerantz, Charlotte. *The Piggy in the Puddle*. Illus. James Marshall. Macmillan, 1974.

Potter, Beatrix. *The Tale of Benjamin Bunny*. Warne, 1904.

_____. *The Tale of Jemima Puddleduck*. Warne, 1908.

_____. *The Tale of Jeremy Fisher*. Warne, 1906.

_____. *The Tale of Mrs. Tiggy Winkle*. Warne, 1905.

_____. *The Tale of Peter Rabbit*. Warne, 1902.

_____. *The Tale of Squirrel Nutkin*. Warne, 1903.

_____. *The Tale of Tom Kitten*. Warne, 1907.

Prokofieff, Serge. *Peter and the Wolf*. Illus. Frans Haacken. Watts, 1961.

Sendak, Maurice. *In the Night Kitchen*. Harper & Row, 1970.

_____. *Outside Over There*. Harper & Row, 1981.

_____. *Where the Wild Things Are*. Harper & Row, 1963.

Seuss, Dr. *And to Think That I Saw It on Mulberry Street*. Vanguard, 1937.

Sharmat, Marjorie Weinman. *A Big Fat Enormous Lie*. Illus. David McPhail. Dutton, 1978.

_____. *I'm Not Oscar's Friend Anymore*. Illus. Tony De Luna. Dutton, 1975.

Shulevitz, Uri. *Dawn*. Farrar, Straus & Giroux, 1974.

Silverstein, Shel. *Where the Sidewalk Ends*. Harper & Row, 1974.

Skorpen, Liesel Moak. *Charles*. Illus. Martha Alexander. Harper & Row, 1971.

Spender, Stephen, adapt. *The Magic Flute*. Illus. Beni Montresor. Putnam's, 1966.

Spier, Peter. *London Bridge Is Falling Down*. Doubleday, 1967.

_____. *Noah's Ark*. Doubleday, 1977.

Steig, William. *Amos and Boris*. Farrar, Straus & Giroux, 1971.

Steptoe, John. *Stevie*. Harper & Row, 1969.

Thomas, Ianthe. *My Street's a Morning Cool Street*. Illus. Emily A. McCully. Harper & Row, 1976.

Turkle, Brinton. *The Sky Dog*. Viking, 1969.

Udry, Janice May. *The Moon Jumpers*. Illus. Maurice Sendak. Harper & Row, 1959.

Van Allsburg, Chris. *The Garden of Abdul Gasazi*. Houghton Mifflin, 1979.

Viorst, Judith. *Alexander and the Terrible, Horrible, No Good, Very Bad Day*. Illus. Ray Cruz. Atheneum, 1972.

_____. *Alexander, Who Used to Be Rich Last Sunday*. Illus. Ray Cruz. Atheneum, 1978.

_____. *I'll Fix Anthony*. Illus. Arnold Lobel. Harper & Row, 1969.

Waber, Bernard. *Ira Sleeps Over*. Houghton Mifflin, 1972.

_____. *"You Look Ridiculous," said the Rhinoceros to the Hippopotamus*. Houghton Mifflin, 1966.

Ward, Lynd. *The Biggest Bear*. Houghton Mifflin, 1952.

Wildsmith, Brian. *Brian Wildsmith's Puzzles*. Watts, 1971.

_____. *Squirrels*. Watts, 1974.

Williams, Barbara. *Kevin's Grandma*. Illus. Kay Chorao. Dutton, 1975.

Williams, Margery. *The Velveteen Rabbit*. Illus. William Nicholson. Doubleday, 1958 (1922).

Zemach, Harve. *Duffy and the Devil*. Illus. Margot Zemach. Farrar, Straus & Grioux, 1973.

_____. adapt. *Mommy, Buy Me a China Doll*. Illus. Margot Zemach. Farrar, Straus & Giroux, 1975.

Zemach, Margot, illus. *Hush, Little Baby*. Dutton, 1976.

Zolotow, Charlotte. *My Grandson Lew*. Illus. William Pène du Bois. Harper & Row, 1974.

_____. *Someone New*. Illus. Eric Blegvad. Harper & Row, 1978.

Recommended Reading

The Child's Inner World

Many books develop the theme of a child's self-worth and show young readers that each person is important. Leo Lionni's *Pezzetino* (P, Pantheon, 1975) discovers that his size does not make him unworthy. Eve Rice's characters in *Ebbie* (N-P, Greenwillow, 1975) and *Oh, Lewis!* (N-P, Macmillan, 1974) learn that their limitations make them special, while Diane Massie's *Dazzle* (P, Parents, 1969) learns an important lesson when his bragging leads to disaster. Eric Carle's *The Mixed-Up Chameleon* (P, Crowell, 1975) changes his appearance so that he can look like all the other animals, but eventually decides that it is better to be himself. Leo Lionni's *Fish Is Fish* (P, Pantheon, 1970) tries to live outside the water, while the animals in Helen Oxenbury's *Pig Tale* (P-I, Morrow, 1973) give up their comfortable life to pursue worldly wealth; all learn it is better to be themselves.

Dorothy Aldis's poetry in *All Together* (N-P, Putnam's, 1952) speaks directly to the young child struggling to find self-identity, especially the poems "Everybody Says," "The Secret Place," "See, I Can Do It," "Big," "Hiding," "Ho," "Mouths," "Bad," and "After My Bath."

Children's fears are explored in many books, where they often take the shape of scary monsters. Dick Gackenbach's *Harry and the Terrible Whatzit* (P, Seabury, 1977) takes place in a dark, damp cellar, while Ellen Conford's *Eugene the Brave*, illustrated by John Larrecq (P, Little, Brown, 1978), shows a young possum who is afraid of the dark forest. Nighttime fears are explored in Manus Pinkwater's *Around Fred's Bed*, illustrated by Robert Mertens (P, Prentice-Hall, 1976), Russell Hoban's *Bedtime for Frances*, illustrated by Garth Williams (P, Harper & Row, 1960), and Judi Barrett's *I Hate to Go to Bed*, illustrated by Ray Cruz (P, Four Winds-Scholastic, 1977), in all of which the characters sometimes use monsters as an excuse for not going to bed.

Although most any story is suitable for bedtime reading, there are many that soothe and quiet active children. Jean Marzollo's *Close Your Eyes*, illustrated by Susan Jeffers (P, Dial, 1978), and Claudia Fregosi's *The Happy Horse* (P, Greenwillow, 1977) both have outstanding illustrations that show happy characters ending a joyful day. Leland B. Jacobs's *Good Night, Mr. Beetle,* illustrated by Gilbert Riswold (N-P, Holt, Rinehart & Winston, 1963), and Nancy Jewell's *Calf, Goodnight,* illustrated by Leonard Weisgard (N-P, Harper & Row, 1973), are gentle sleepytime stories, as are Stella Farris's *The Magic Teddy Bear* (N, Harper & Row, 1979) and M. B. Goffstein's *Sleepy People* (N, Farrar, Straus & Giroux, 1979).

Susan Russo's *The Moon's the North Wind's Cooky: Night Poems* (N-P, Lothrop, Lee & Shepard 1979) and Siv Cedering Fox's *The Blue Horse and Other Night Poems,* illustrated by Donald Carrick (P, Seabury, 1979), are filled with quiet poems. In addition, many bedtime poems can be found in the standard poetry anthologies.

A book that encourages children to think for themselves and to be responsible is Kay Chorao's *Molly's Moe* (P, Seabury, 1976), in which a young girl must track down her lost, beloved stuffed animal. A young badger child, who appears in several stories, learns the hard way that more than one kind of food tastes good in Russell Hoban's *Bread and Jam for Frances,* illustrated by Lillian Hoban (P, Harper & Row, 1964). Responsibility to other people is the theme as Leo Lionni's *Swimmy* (P, Pantheon, 1963) shows the other small fish how to swim together to save themselves from the larger fish.

Imagination and the imaginative worlds of children's lives are treated in many worthwhile books. Ruth Krauss tells about *A Very Special House,* illustrated by Maurice Sendak (N-P, Harper & Row, 1953), that a child makes up in the "moodle" of his head, while Beatrice Schenk De Regniers shows how you can create *A Little House of Your Own,* illustrated by Irene Haas (P, Harcourt Brace Jovanovich, 1955). Maurice Sendak is a master of imaginative wanderings as evidenced in *In the Night Kitchen* (P, Harper & Row, 1970) and many other books. John Burningham's *Come Away from the Water, Shirley* (P, Crowell, 1977) compares a young girl's imaginative world with the more practical one of her parents'. David McPhail sees into the young child's pretend world in several books, including *The Train* (P, Little, Brown, 1977) and *The Cereal Box* (P, Little, Brown, 1974).

Annette Wynne's poem "I Keep Three Wishes Ready" (*The Arbuthnot Anthology of Children's Literature*) stirs imaginations, as do many poems by Shel Silverstein, Ogden Nash, and Jack Prelutsky.

The Child's Family World

Many books for children show a warm, loving family. Ann Herbert Scott's *Sam,* illustrated by Symeon Shimin (P, McGraw-Hill, 1967), and Elizabeth Starr Hill's *Evan's Corner,* illustrated by Nancy Grossman (P-I, Holt, Rinehart & Winston, 1967), are both about young black boys whose families sustain them.

Books with especially strong mother-child relationships include Robert Kraus's *Whose Mouse Are You?* illustrated by Jose Aruego (N-P, Macmillan, 1970), Margaret Wise Brown's *The Runaway Bunny,* illustrated by Clement Hurd (N-P, Harper & Row, 1942), Crescent Dragonwagon's *Will It Be Okay?,* illustrated by Ben Shecter (P, Harper & Row, 1977), Ann Tompert's *Little Fox Goes to the End of the World,* illustrated by John Wallner (P, Crown, 1976), Marjorie Flack's *Ask Mr. Bear* (N-P, Macmillan, 1932), and Charlotte Zolotow's *Mr. Rabbit and the Lovely Present,* illustrated by Maurice Sendak (P, Harper & Row, 1962).

Adoption is the subject of several books, including Susan Lapsley's *I Am Adopted,* illustrated by Michael Charlton (N-P, Bradbury, 1974), Catherine and Sherry Bunin's *Is That Your Sister?: A True Story of Adoption* (P, Pantheon, 1976), and Valentina P. Wasson's *The Chosen Baby,* illustrated by Glo Coalson (N-P, Lippincott, 1977).

That brothers and sisters can work together is the theme of Peter Spier's *Oh, Were They Ever Happy!* (P, Doubleday, 1978), a marvelous tale of fun and surprise. On the other hand, rivalry and jealousy are dealt with in Lucille Clifton's *My Brother Fine with Me,* illustrated by Moneta Barnett (P, Holt, Rinehart & Winston, 1975), Steven Kellogg's *Much Bigger than Martin* (P, Dial, 1976), Barbara Williams's *If He's My Brother,* illustrated by Tomie de Paola (P, Harvey House, 1976), and Charlotte Zolotow's *If It Weren't for You,* illustrated by Ben Shecter (P, Harper & Row, 1966)—all chronicles of imagined injustices.

Divorce is the subject of several books for young children, including Patricia Perry and Marietta Lynch's photodocumentary, *Mommy and Daddy Are Divorced* (P, Dial, 1978), Joan Lexau's *Me Day,* illustrated by Robert Weaver (P, Dial, 1971), Charlotte Zolotow's *A Father Like That,* illustrated by Ben Shecter (P, Harper & Row, 1971), and Ianthe Thomas's *Eliza's Daddy,* illustrated by Moneta Barnett (P, Harcourt Brace Jovanovich, 1976).

Grandparents are special people, especially understanding one's like the grandmother in *William's Doll,* illustrated by William Pène du Bois (P, Harper & Row, 1972), a sensitive story by Charlotte Zolotow. Other stories of grandparents and grandchildren include Kathryn Lasky's *My Island Grandma,* illustrated by Emily McCully (P, Warne, 1979), and *I Have Four Names for My Grandfather,* illustrated by Christopher G. Knight (N-P, Little, Brown, 1976), Franz Brandenberg's *A Secret for Grandmother's Birthday,* illustrated by Aliki (P, Greenwillow, 1975), Aliki's *The Two of Them* (P, Greenwillow, 1979), and two classic stories by Helen Buckley, *Grandmother and I,* illustrated by Paul Galdone (N-P, Lothrop, Lee & Shepard, 1961), and *Grandfather and I,* illustrated by Paul Galdone (N-P, Lothrop, Lee & Shepard, 1959).

The Child's Social World

Friendship is fragile but survives when people learn to share in Crosby Bonsall's *It's Mine* (N-P, Harper & Row, 1964) and Janice Udry's *Let's Be Enemies,* illustrated by Maurice Sendak (N-P, Harper & Row, 1961). The silly things friends do are humorously shown in Judith Viorst's *Rosie and Michael,* illustrated by Lorna Tomei (P, Atheneum, 1974), and Lucille

Clifton's *Three Wishes,* illustrated by Stephanie Douglas (P, Viking, 1976). Fears about meeting new friends are examined in Miriam Cohen's *Will I Have a Friend?* illustrated by Lillian Hoban (P, Macmillan, 1967), and Lucille Clifton's *Everett Anderson's Friend,* illustrated by Ann Grifalconi (P, Holt, Rinehart & Winston, 1976).

Marjorie Weinman Sharmat's young hero, a personified animal, invites the whole neighborhood to a party, hoping to make just one friend. After he has greeted *The 329th Friend,* illustrated by Cyndy Szekeres (P, Four Winds-Scholastic, 1979), he realizes that he can be his own best friend. Rosemary Wells's *Benjamin and Tulip* (P, Dial, 1973) remain good friends through many arguments, as do the various animals in Dick Gackenbach's *Hound and Bear* (P, Seabury, 1976), Russell E. Erickson's *Warton and Morton,* illustrated by Lawrence Di Diori (P, Lothrop, Lee & Shepard, 1976), and Judy Delton's *Two Is Company,* illustrated by Giulio Maestro (P, Crown, 1976). Leo Lionni's *Little Blue and Little Yellow* (N-P, Astor Honor, 1959) is a classic tale of the genuine togetherness of two good friends.

Many poems celebrate the joy of friendship, including several—"Some People," by Rachel Field, "Different Bicycles," by Dorothy Baruch, and "The Child Next Door," by Rose Fyleman—found in Helen Ferris's anthology, *Favorite Poems Old and New,* illustrated by Leonard Weisgard (P-I, Doubleday, 1957).

Several books show the concerns and apprehensions of going to school for the first time. Among them are Gunilla Wolde's *Betsy's First Day at Nursery School* (N-P, Random House, 1976), Petronella Breinburg's *Shawn Goes to School,* illustrated by Errol Lloyd (N-P, Crowell, 1974), and Harlow Rockwell's *My Nursery School* (N-P, Greenwillow, 1976). Anne Rockwell's *I Like the Library* (N-P, Dutton, 1977) depicts preschool story hours at the public library that introduce children to some of the things they will meet in school. Miriam Cohen's *When Will I Read?* illustrated by Lillian Hoban (N-P, Greenwillow, 1977), expresses a question asked by most young children. Dorothy Joan Harris's *The School Mouse,* illustrated by Chris Conover (P, Warne, 1977), shows how a pet mouse helps a young boy adjust to school.

Teachers receive fair attention in children's books, too. Patricia Reilly Giff shows how an understanding teacher reassures a young boy when *Today Was a Terrible Day,* illustrated by Susanna Natti (P, Viking, 1980), while Miriam Cohen's *The New Teacher,* illustrated by Lillian Hoban (P, Macmillan, 1972), understands her children's concerns when their old teacher must leave. That there is time for fun in school is shown in Clyde Watson's *Hickory Stick Rag,* illustrated by Wendy Watson (P, Crowell, 1976), Franz Brandenburg's *No School Today,* illustrated by Aliki (P, Macmillan, 1975), and Peggy Parish's *Teach Us, Amelia Bedelia,* illustrated by Lynn Sweat (P, Greenwillow, 1977).

School Is Not a Missile Range, illustrated by Ron Martin (P-I, Abingdon, 1977), declares Norah Smaridge with her collection of poems, but the wild antics will bring forth much laughter from knowing children. Several poems in Sara and John E. Brewton and G. Meredith Blackburn's *My Tang's Tungled and Other Ridiculous Situations,* illustrated by Graham Booth (I, Crowell, 1973), poke fun at school; these include Eleanor Farjeon's "All Schools Have Rules," Anna Maria Pratt's "A Mortifying Mistake," Annette Wynne's "The Teacher," Marie Hall Ets's "Grammar," and the anonymous "The Old School Scold."

The Child's Natural World

Byrd Baylor shows a profound sense of respect for nature in her books, including *Hawk, I'm Your Brother,* illustrated by Peter Parnall (P-I, Scribner's, 1976), and *We Walk in Sandy Places,* photographs by Marilyn Schweitzer (P-I, Scribner's, 1976). Kathryn F. Ernst uses subtle humor to show the ecological importance of *Mr. Tamarin's Trees,* illustrated by Diane de Groat (P, Crown, 1976). Robert McCloskey's *Time of Wonder* (P, Viking, 1957) and Bette Lamont's *Island Time* (P, Lippincott, 1976) are both beautifully descriptive celebrations of nature.

The wind is personified in several stories. Judith Barrett's *The Wind Thief,* illustrated by Diane Dawson (P, Atheneum, 1977), and Christian Garrison's *Little Pieces of the West Wind,* illustrated by Diane Goode (P, Bradbury, 1975), show this force of nature in its many forms. Pat Hutchins's *The Wind Blew* (P, Macmillan, 1974) is a humorous look at the wind's mischievous and unpredictable effects, while Uri Shulevitz describes the many qualities of *Rain Rain Rivers* (P, Farrar, Straus & Giroux, 1969). Joanne Ryder tells of a small girl's lovely adventure on the beach on *A Wet and Sandy Day,* illustrated by Donald Carrick (P, Harper & Row, 1977), and Charlotte Zolotow traces a summer rain in *The Storm Book,* illustrated by Margaret Bloy Graham (P, Harper & Row, 1952).

William Binzen uses photographs to illustrate the elusive patterns of the seasons in *Year after Year* (Coward, P-I, McCann & Geoghegan, 1976), while Alice and Martin Provensen show the seasonal changes in *The Year at Maple Hill Farm* (N-P, Atheneum, 1978). Dick Gackenbach tells about *Ida Fanfanny* (P, Harper & Row, 1978), a funny little woman who uses magic to bring different seasons to her land. Eleanor J. Lapp says *The Mice Came in Early This Year,* illustrated by David Cunningham (P, Whitman, 1976)—a sure sign of a hard winter, and Anne Eve Bunting tells about the nature signals that foretell *Winter's Coming,* illustrated by Howard Knotts (P, Harcourt Brace Jovanovich, 1977). Two classic books that focus on winter are Alvin Tresselt's *White Snow, Bright Snow,* illustrated by Roger Duvoisin (P, Lothrop, Lee & Shepard, 1947), and Berta and Elmer Hader's *The Big Snow* (P, Macmillan, 1948). Snow hides treasured objects in Steven Kellogg's *The Mystery of the Missing Red Mitten* (N-P, Dial, 1974), and Ruth Craft's *The Winter Bear,* illustrated by Erik Blegvad (P, Atheneum, 1975), spends a long, cold time in a bare treetop until a young child discovers the stuffed animal.

There are many picture books that give accurate information about animals and show them in their natural environment.

Irene Brady does an outstanding job of developing in young children a respect for wild creatures. *Beaver Year* (P, Houghton Mifflin, 1976) and *Wild Mouse* (P, Scribners, 1976) chronicle the lives of these animals and create a sense of wonder about their growth and survival. In a similar manner, Roger Caras discusses the habits and behavior of *Skunk for a Day,* illustrated by Diane Paterson (P, Windmill-Dutton, 1976). Aileen Fisher's *Sing, Little Mouse,* illustrated by Symeon Shimin (P-I, Crowell, 1969), and Faith McNulty's *Mouse and Tim,* illustrated by Marc Simont (P, Harper & Row, 1978), both show young boys who learn that it is best to let wild animals go free.

There are probably more poems about nature and animals than any other subject; any good anthology will offer many choices. Good supplements are Adrienne Adams's *Poetry of Earth* (P-I, Scribner's, 1972), William Cole's *A Book of Animal Poems,* illustrated by Robert Andrew Parker (P-I, Viking, 1973), and *An Arkful of Animals,* illustrated by Lynn Munsinger (P-I, Houghton Mifflin, 1978), Elizabeth Coatsworth's *The Sparrow Bush,* illustrated by Stefan Martin (P-I, Norton, 1966), and Harry Behn's *The Golden Hive* (P-I, Harcourt Brace Jovanovich, 1966).

The Child's Aesthetic World
First-hand experiences with fine art, music, dance and literature can be supplemented with vicarious exposure through books. Leo Lionni shows us that poetry is important to life when a mouse shirks his responsibilities to study words: *Frederick* (P, Pantheon, 1967) spends his time dreaming while the other mice gather food for the winter, but they learn to appreciate him when he brightens the long, cold days by reciting poetry. Lionni created another artist in *Geraldine, the Music Mouse* (P, Pantheon, 1979), who discovers the joy of creating music. Rachel Isadora's *Ben's Trumpet* (P, Greenwillow, 1979) shows a young child who dreams of making music of the kind he hears coming from the neighborhood jazz club.

Many illustrated song books are avilable, including Peter Spier's *The Star Spangled Banner* (all ages, Doubleday, 1973), *The Erie Canal* (P, Doubleday, 1970), and John Langstaff's *Oh, A-Hunting We Will Go,* illustrated by Nancy Winslow Parker (N-P, Atheneum, 1974), and *Frog Went A-Courtin',* illustrated by Feodor Rojankovsky (N-P, Harcourt Brace Jovanovich, 1955), and Robert Quackenbush's *Clementine* (N-P, Lippincott, 1974) and *Go Tell Aunt Rhody* (N-P, Lippincott, 1973).

Books that would be a shame to miss are Virginia Lee Burton's *The Little House* (P, Houghton Mifflin, 1942), *Mike Mulligan and His Steam Shovel* (P, Houghton Mifflin, 1939), and *Katy and the Big Snow* (P, Houghton Mifflin, 1943); Roger Duvoisin's several stories about *Petunia* (P, Knopf, 1950); Marjorie Flack's *The Story About Ping,* illustrated by Kurt Wiese (N-P, Viking, 1933); Hardie Gramatky's *Little Toot* (N-P, Putnam's, 1939); Munro Leaf's *The Story of Ferdinand,* illustrated by Robert Lawson (N-P, Viking, 1936); Robert McCloskey's *Make Way for Ducklings* (N-P, Viking, 1941); Watty Piper's *The Little Engine That Could,* illustrated by George and Doris Hauman (N-P, Platt & Munk, 1930); H. A. Rey's stories about *Curious George* (N-P, Houghton Mifflin, 1941); and many of Dr. Seuss's stories, including *The 500 Hats of Bartholomew Cubbins* (N-P, Vanguard, 1938) and *Horton Hatches the Egg* (N-P, Random House, 1940).

five

SHEL SILVERSTEIN *INVITATION*

If you are a dreamer, come in,
If you are a dreamer, a wisher, a liar,
A hope-er, a pray-er, a magic bean buyer . . .
If you're a pretender, come sit by my fire
For we have some flax-golden tales to spin.
Come in!
Come in![1]

Folklore

Folklore, the body of literature with no known authors, has been passed down through the generations by word of mouth, embellished with variations bestowed by the many storytellers. The legacy of this literature includes Mother Goose and nursery rhymes, folk tales, fables, myths, legends and tall tales, and folk songs. Each type is distinctive, but all echo the beliefs, customs, and eternal dreams that appeal to people across time.

ORIGINS OF FOLKLORE

Theories about the origin and function of folklore come from the work of social anthropologists, who study beliefs, celebrations, and ceremonies of primal societies. Ruth Sawyer, a well-known twentieth-century storyteller, draws upon collections of such materials in her description of the beginning of storytelling: "The first primitive efforts at conscious storytelling consisted of a simple chant, set to the rhythm of some daily tribal occupation such as grinding corn, paddling canoe or kayak, sharp-ening weapons for hunting or war, or ceremonial dancing."[2]

In addition to composing songs and tales about their daily work, their hunting, and their warfare, primal societies were fascinated by the natural world about them. Wonder and awe at the power of nature, and speculation as to the supernatural forces that might be at work behind it, led to still more stories, those that we classify as myths. And as the tribes grew, so did the impulse to preserve the stories of their ancestors. Legends and hero tales of the mighty deeds of those who had gone before were passed from one generation to the next.

The roots of folklore exist in all societies from all times. The story of civilization shows a continual quest to shape a harmonious balance between the physical world and the mortal's place in it. Through creative imagination, people transform outer reality into a vision of life that they control through analogy and metaphor. The lore they create is a rich source of literature for children.

An ageless art form, folklore is best shared orally—with a live storyteller and audience. Folklore was never intended to be written down, and survived for ages before any of it was captured in print. It springs to life again with a gifted story-teller. Nursery rhymes and folk tales in picture book format are natural for oral storytelling to young children. As they mature, however, children often select anthologies for their own reading, and the vivid images they paint in their own minds become more important than those of any illustrator.

THE ROLE OF FOLKLORE

Children's thinking parallels the intuitive vision of life and simple explanation of the world of primal groups. This vision, not yet governed by logic, is structured first out of children's own awareness of themselves and, next, from perceptions of the world around them. Many psychologists believe that the emergence of emotions, thoughts, language, and literature in primal societies is analogous to that of individual human development. Discussing the development of logical processes in children, Piaget says, "Of course the most fruitful, most obvious field of study would be reconstituting human history—the history of human thinking in prehistoric man."[3] Because there is a parallel between the development of folklore and the development of thought in the child, folklore is the natural literature of childhood.

In the same way that folklore explained the world to early people, it helps children understand their world at early stages in their development and offers an occasional necessary relief from the world of reality they are discovering. Up to about the age of seven, children explain things they cannot understand as occurring by magic; they attribute human characteristics to inanimate objects artlessly. André Favat says:

. . . the characteristics of the child and the characteristics of the fairy tale permit a fairly clear observation: just as magic and animism suffuse the world of the fairy tale, so do they suffuse the world of the child; just as a morality of constraint prevails in the fairy tale, so does it prevail in the moral system of the child; just as the fairy tale world and its hero become one in achieving his ends, so do children believe their world is one with them; and

just as causal relations remain unexpressed in the fairy tale, so do they remain unexpressed in the child's communication.[4]

Because of the correspondence between the assumptions of child and tale, this literature has strong appeal at a specific age, generally five to seven. Although children gradually change their conception of the world as they mature, the logic of the fairy tale is both necessary and sufficient at early developmental levels. As scientific explanations become comprehensible, the need for fairy tales decreases.

Innumerable interpretations are given to the role of folklore: according to Freud, fairy tale characters symbolize subconscious urges during a child's emotional development; Jung sees the mythical figures and conflicts as archetypes of racial memories. Bettelheim's views, much like Freud's, are that fairy tales tap deep unconscious wishes and desires—the wellsprings of repressed emotions. Bettelheim reasons that fairy tales help children deal with emotional insecurities by suggesting images—more easily dealt with—for their fantasies.

It is here that fairy tales have unequaled value, because they offer new dimensions to the child's imagination which would be impossible for him to discover as truly on his own. Even more important, the form and structure of fairy tales suggest images to the child by which he can structure his daydreams and with them give better direction to his life.[5]

According to Jung, the collective unconscious is a part of the mind from which come dream, fantasy, imagining, and vision. Jung perceived this as a substratum of mind common to all people, and he attributes the commonality of mythic imaginings of diverse peoples to the universal nature of the unconscious. Whatever the explanation, it is clear that similar elements are found in the myths, legends, and folk tales of all people across time and place. The reappearing themes, or archetypes, are clearly visible in folklore. For example, the archetype of the hero's quest—slaying a dragon or winning a princess—is seen as the psychological expression of the normal process of maturing. The good mother (fairy godmother), the bad mother (wicked stepmother or old witch), and the shadow (evil underside in every person) are vivid examples of archetypes familiar to us all.

Arthur Applebee explains children's fascination with stories from another perspective.[6] He sees children engaged in a search for meaning, a search for structures and patterns that will suggest order and consistency in the world around them. The patterns of meaning they find are transmitted by a range of social devices—stories among many others. Pleasure comes through mastery of the rules, a particularly important factor in highly patterned, stereotyped formula stories such as folk and fairy tales.

ARCHETYPES IN FOLKLORE

Ask a child to tell you what a folk tale or a fairy tale is and you will probably hear: "They begin 'once upon a time' and end 'they lived happily ever after,' the good people win, and the youngest son gets the princess." This response shows that children recognize the motifs, themes, story conventions, and recurring patterns that are so plentiful in folklore. Awareness of motifs, themes, and conventions develops through repeated experience and becomes the foundation for building a literary education.

Good teachers salt the sands of literature with folklore to give children opportunities to discover recurring patterns; they do not *tell* them what to recognize. Understanding children's sense of story, and knowing labels for conventions, informs good teaching; but for the child being taught, it can in no way substitute for having the literary experience itself. By introducing folklore, then, with its abundance of repeatable patterns, teachers can facilitate students' discovery of archetypes; as the patterns are absorbed, they become the structural framework for viewing all literature as one story.

Themes

Themes, the central and dominating ideas in stories, evolve around topics of universal human concern. The struggle between good and evil is played out time and again in folklore. Hate, fear, and greed are opposed to love, security, and generosity in stories attempting to explain the universe. The themes are developed in folk tales through stereotypical characters who personify good and evil. The characters, portrayed without ambiguity, constitute polarizations of the two forces and provide the structure against which behavior is clearly seen. The bad fairy in "Sleeping Beauty," the witch in "Hansel and Gretel," the stepmother who orders the huntsman to kill Snow White—all are unambiguous representations of evil. In each story, the evil one is destroyed and the virtuous one rewarded—satisfying endings that reaffirm that goodness prevails and evil is crushed—providing necessary reassurance for young children.

The theme contrasting surface appearance and deeper qualities of goodness is a variation on the struggle between good and evil. An enchantment is cast upon a handsome prince who must then live as a monstrous beast, frog, donkey—as in "Beauty and the Beast," "The Frog Prince," and "The Donkey Prince." The loathsome spell is broken by love—that of a beautiful princess who sees the goodness of the prince hidden beneath the gruesome exterior. In other stories, the entire world is under an evil spell, veiled and hidden from clear view until goodness conquers all.

The search for happiness or lost identity in order to restore harmony to life is a recurrent quest theme. In many stories, the hero succeeds only after a long journey, repeated trials (some by fire), much suffering, and extended separation. In Grimm's *The Seven Ravens* (P-I), a young girl travels far and faces difficult trials before she rescues her seven brothers. In *The Angry Moon* (P-I), by William Sleator, Lapin shoots a ladder of arrows to the sky and, with the help of three magic objects, rescues Lapowinsa from the moon, who had been holding her captive. In both stories, characteristically, the journey—from home through alienation, suffering, and trials— has a satisfying ending, with happiness restored.

Hurdles are overcome, trials are met, dragons are slain, and the hero is always victorious. In

Grimm's *The Twelve Dancing Princesses* (P-I), illustrated by Adrienne Adams, the soldier must undergo many trials to discover where the princesses dance nightly. When, with the help of a cloak of invisibility, he discovers the secret, he marries the eldest daughter and inherits the kingdom. In Tomie de Paola's *The Clown of God* (P-I), a juggler travels through a lifetime making people laugh, but when he grows old and inept they taunt him. Desiring to present an offering to Mary and the Christ Child, he gives his greatest and final performance. The theme of giving of oneself permeates the folk tale.

Motifs

A motif is an element that has something distinctive about it; it may be a symbol, an image, a device—a thread that runs through a story to accentuate the theme. Familiar motifs appear in stereotypic characters—gods, witches, fairies, noodleheads, or stepmothers. A second kind of motif—magical objects, spells, curses, or wishes—serves as a chief mechanism of the plot. This can also be an unusual incident—setting out on a quest, snaring the sun, transforming a cinder girl into a beautiful princess or a prince into a frog.

In many stories of conflicting fortunes, the basis for the plot is three wishes. In *The Fisherman and His Wife* (P), translated by Elizabeth Shub, the first two are used to acquire power and wealth, and the third to restore life to its original state. In Paul Galdone's *The Three Wishes* (P), the woodsman wishes for a sausage, in anger his wife spitefully wishes it onto the end of his nose, and they must use the third wish to get it off again. Frequently, the result of wishing is the revelation of the happiness of the original state. Home is appreciated only after it is lost, a simple life is recognized as good only after the complexity of another life style is known.

Another motif that also appears frequently is the noodlehead character—one who is pure-hearted but lacks good judgement. In Grimm's *Hans in Luck* (P), Hans starts out with a bag of gold but ends with nothing after a series of bad trades.

In *Noodlehead Stories* (I), M. A. Jagendorf describes a noodlehead as a simple, blundering person who does not use good sense or learn from experience. Jagendorf includes stories of the noodlehead who loses because he tries to grab too much, has too much pride, or uses big words he does not understand. One noodlehead story appears in several versions—*Turnabout* (P), by William Wiesner, *The Man Who Was Going to Mind the House* (P), by David McKee, and an adaptation from Joseph Jacobs, *Hereafterthis* (P), illustrated by Paul Galdone. Every cultural group has its noodlehead stories: the wise men of Gotham in England, the fools of Chelm in Poland, Juan Bobo in Puerto Rico, the Connemara man in Ireland, and the Montieri in Italy. Children enjoy the good-natured fun and laugh heartily at the stupid blunders of noodlehead characters.

Conventions

Conventions, ever apparent in folk tales, contribute to a child's sense of story. The repeated use of three, the happy ending, and the story frame are conventions that children adopt in the stories they tell. Such conventions are vividly apparent in folk tales. Characters appear in groups of three: three sons, three daughters, three bears, three billy goats gruff, or three little pigs. Events occur in groups of three: three adventures, three tasks, three magical objects to rescue the hero, three trials, or three wishes (which helps prolong the tension).

Children recognize the story frames of "once upon a time" and "they lived happily ever after" early in their literary education. Tales set within these frames contribute to the child's developing concept of story and suggest that this event that once happened may recur. Arthur Applebee examined stories children tell for their use of a formal opening or title, a formal closing, and a consistent past tense. He found that even two-year-olds begin to set off their stories with story frames and that, by age five, nearly all children tell stories marked by at least one of these characteristics; nearly half of the stories are marked by the use of all three conventions. Children's expectations about stories and

Books have always been important to me. I remember way back in the early '40s when I was a young child, a poster (for Book Week, I imagine) of a ship made out of books. At least, I remember it that way, sailing off to "faraway places" with loads of book characters—Alice, Jo March, Robinson Crusoe, Puss-in-Boots, Cinderella, you name 'em—all around. I just can't imagine life without books (*Harcourt Brace Jovanovich promotional material*).

To see the world through the eyes of Tomie de Paola is to see a world of laughter, love, and hope. His ingenuity with words and illustrations places him at the forefront of the *Zio narratori* of the world.

A prolific creator of original stories, de Paola also recasts old tales, making them appeal to children of today as they have for countless years past. *The Clown of God,* a retelling of the ancient French legend of the juggler giving his final performance before the Lady and the Holy Child, is set in medieval Italy. *The Prince of the Dolomites,* an old Italian tale resembling the mythic creation stories, explains how the beautiful Dolomite mountains were changed from black peaks to glimmering pastels by the powerful force of love; a similar feeling of awe and wonder is conveyed in *The Lady of Guadalupe.*

A favorite retold tale, *Strega Nona,* a variant of the magic porridge pot tale (this time with pasta) is set in Calabria, while *Helga's Dowry,* from Scandinavian folklore, is a delightful story about how one troll maiden earns her dowry and the king's love at the same time. In all of these retellings, Tomie de Paola acknowledges the influence of pre-Renaissance Italian masters on his art.

When asked if he fears running out of ideas, de Paola says:

Of course, I do. . . . But I have a trick. I always try to come up with new projects before I finish the one I'm working on. Sort of like sourdough bread, you take a little dough to start your new batch (*Harcourt Brace Jovanovich promotional material*).

Born in Meriden, Connecticut, and of Irish-Italian descent, he now lives in New Hampshire in a 100-year-old white frame farmhouse with a remodeled barn for a studio. He teaches at New England College.

TOMIE DE PAOLA

characters develop early. Applebee asked five-, six-, and seven-year-olds about the nature of stories:

> "What happens in stories?" we asked Ernest: "They live happily ever after."—Who does?—"Poor people."
>
> The patterns of the stories are quickly sensed by children, just as they are by adults; even the characters have their appointed roles: "If you are reading a story about a rabbit, what is the rabbit usually like?"—"Fast."—What about a fox?—"Fast. He wants to eat someone."—What about a witch?—"Cook someone."—What about fairies?—"Fairies? They don't do nothing."—What are they usually like?—"Flying." (Stephen)
>
> And Charles in a similar vein: "What does a lion do in a story?"—"Kills people."—What about an elephant? —"He drinks water. He don't kill people. He just runs about."[7]

Such answers are reexpressions of the symbols and images built into myths and fairy tales; they bear little relation to the real nature of the animals involved, but then they were never intended to. These early expectations, coupled with children's intuitive grasp of the universal dreams of humankind, show the important position of folklore in a literary education.

Gradually, children recognize the cumulative pattern of folk tales—such as the particularly conspicuous one of "This Is the House that Jack Built" —wherein each incident grows from the preceding one. Cumulative folk tales are characterized by their structure and are often called chain tales, since each part of the story is linked to the next. The initial incident reveals both central character and problem; each subsequent scene builds onto the original one. The accumulation continues to a high point, or climax, and then unravels in an identical reverse order or stops with an abrupt or surprise ending. "Henny Penny" and "The Old Woman and Her Pig" exemplify the repetition and chaining, whereas "The Three Little Pigs" and "The Three Bears" use the repetition of scenes and phrases more subtly. "The Gingerbread Boy" and its variant "Johnny Cake" illustrate the chain tale

Children to whom tales are read time and again begin to recognize story patterns. (Photograph by Mike Mazzaschi/STOCK, Boston, Mass.)

RECOGNIZING STORY FORM. (I) Ian Serraillier, in a story poem, spoofs the traditional fairy tale format by reversing it completely. Children who have a background in folklore will respond with delighted recognition as they realize what the poet has done. Before reading "After Ever Happily" aloud to your class, you may want to hint that they should listen for a "trick." Read it slowly and with expression. After one reading, pause for discussion. You might ask students who were able to figure out what the poet had done to identify the point in the poem where they realized what was happening. After the class discussion, read the poem once again so that all may hear it with more understanding and enjoy it together.

AFTER EVER HAPPILY
OR
THE PRINCESS AND THE WOODCUTTER*

And they both lived happily ever after . . .
The wedding was held in the palace. Laughter
Rang to the roof as a loosened rafter
Crashed down and squashed the chamberlain flat—
And how the wedding guests chuckled at that!
"You, with your horny indelicate hands,
Who drop your haitches and call them 'ands,
Who cannot afford to buy her a dress,
How dare you presume to pinch our princess—
Miserable woodcutter, uncombed, unwashed!"
Were the chamberlain's words (before he was squashed).
"Take her," said the Queen, who had a soft spot
For woodcutters. "He's strong and he's handsome. Why not?"
"What rot!" said the King, but he dare not object;
The Queen wore the trousers—that's as you'd expect.
Said the chamberlain, usually meek and inscrutable,
"A princess and a woodcutter? The match is unsuitable."
Her dog barked its welcome again and again,
As they splashed to the palace through puddles of rain.
And the princess sighed, "Till the end of my life!"
"Darling," said the woodcutter, "will you be my wife?"
He knew all his days he could love no other,
So he nursed her to health with some help from his mother,
And lifted her, horribly hurt, from her tumble.
A woodcutter, watching, saw the horse stumble.
As she rode through the woods, a princess in her prime
On a dapple-grey horse . . . Now, to finish my rhyme,
I'll start it properly: Once upon a time—[8]

* This is a love story from the Middle Ages. The poet obviously knew his subject backwards.

with a repetitive phrase—in this case, "Run, run as fast as you can. You can't catch me. I'm the Gingerbread man."

One Fine Day (P), by Nonny Hogrogian, and *Drummer Hoff* (P), by Barbara and Ed Emberley, are written in cumulative style. In *One Fine Day*, an old woman chops off the tail of a fox who has drunk her pail of milk. The fox begs the old woman to give back his tail, but she agrees to do so only if the fox gives back the milk. The story builds as the fox bargains for the milk and suddenly reverses when he is finally granted a request that unlocks all previous ones. "The Cat and the Mouse" in Joseph Jacobs's *English Fairy Tales* (I) is a variant of the same story. *Drummer Hoff* is based on an English folk rhyme in which the story accumulates as additional people help to fire a cannon. The time-honored text, with illustrations that extend the content, combine several layers of meaning in the story.

MOTHER GOOSE AND NURSERY RHYMES

There is no conclusive evidence about the exact origin of the Mother Goose rhymes nor about the existence of an actual person with that name. Iona and Peter Opie, authors of two definitive works, *The Oxford Nursery Rhyme Book* and *The Oxford Dictionary of Nursery Rhymes,* display a healthy skepticism about the origin of the anonymous rhymes and the diverse referents ascribed to them:

Much ingenuity has been exercised to show that certain nursery rhymes have had greater significance than is now apparent. They have been vested with mystic symbolism, linked with social and political events, and numerous attempts have been made to identify the nursery characters with real persons. It should be stated straightway that the bulk of these speculations are worthless. Fortunately the theories are so numerous they tend to cancel each other out.[9]

Some rhymes may have been composed to teach children to count, to learn the alphabet, or to say their prayers, while others—riddles, tongue twisters, proverbs, and nonsense—were simply for amusement.

The name Mother Goose seemingly was first associated with an actual collection of tales in 1697 with Charles Perrault's publication of *Histoires ou contes du temps passé, avec des moralities* (Stories or tales of times past, with morals). The frontispiece shows an old woman spinning and telling stories, and is labeled *"Contes de ma Mère l'Oye"* (Tales of Mother Goose). The exact origin of the name, like the authors of the verses, is lost in the past, but the vitality of the rhymes makes them as fresh as today's bread.

Characteristics

The dominant feature of this type of folklore is the powerful rhythm of the verses; the strong beat resounds in the ear and invites physical response. In the earliest days of a child's life, "Rock-a-bye baby" is an accompaniment for rocking in a chair. Long before meaning is attached to the sounds, the cadence of the language and bounce of an adult's knee undergird a child's developing rhythm. Northrop Frye emphasizes this physical aspect:

Ideally, our literary education should begin, not with prose, but with such things as "this little pig went to market"—with verse rhythm reinforced by physical assault. The infant who gets bounced on somebody's knee to the rhythm of "Ride a Cock Horse" does not need a footnote telling him that Banbury Cross is twenty miles northeast of Oxford. He does not need the information that "cross" and "horse" make (at least in the pronunciation he is most likely to hear) not a rhyme but an assonance. He does not need the value judgment that the repetition of "horse" in the first two lines indicates a rather thick ear on the part of the composer. All he needs is to get bounced.[10]

Both adult and child know that toes are tweaked in "This little piggie went to market" and that hands are clapped for "Pat-a-cake, pat-a-cake, baker's man."

The pronounced beat of the Mother Goose rhymes reinforces the child's developing sense of body rhythm and is even more crucial to the child's developing sense of rhythm in language. The audible beat, stress, sound, and intonation patterns establish themselves in memory and contribute to rhythm in the child's developing language. A regularly repeated accent pattern is often accompanied by assonance, rhyme, or alliteration, all of which are important to the child who is developing speech. In addition, an early introduction to Mother Goose sensitizes the child to poetry, the main body of which is in verse, and this serves as part of the foundation of a literary education.

A second major characteristic of Mother Goose is the imaginative use of words and ideas. Nothing is too preposterous or ridiculous to form the content of a verse. Children delight in the images suggested by the "Three wise men of Gotham who went to sea in a bowl," and by "There was an old woman tossed up in a basket, nineteen times as high as the moon." The fanciful visions spark creativity and enrich the mythic springs of the developing imagination. Nothing is impossible, anything can happen in the young child's unfettered world, and the verses feed the fancy.

A third characteristic of Mother Goose rhymes is the compact structure. The scene is established quickly and the plot divulged at once. Undoubtedly, as in all folklore, the consolidation of action and the economy of words result from being said aloud for many generations before being set down in print. As they were passed from one teller to the next, they were honed to their present simplicity.

Another quality that accounts for the wide popularity and long life of Mother Goose verses is the wit and cleverness, or the laughable stupidity, of the characters. Nonsense is so obvious that the child is in on the joke. The humor appeals to both children and the adults who share the verse with them. Surprise endings with a clever twist leave no question about the outcome.

> Peter, Peter, pumpkin eater,
> Had a wife and couldn't keep her
> He put her in a pumpkin shell,
> And there he kept her very well.

Selecting Nursery Rhyme Books

The most natural way of sharing Mother Goose and other nursery rhymes is by reciting them. There are many books available to provide a rich collection of verses to jog the memory or to expand our repertoire. One of the major criteria for choosing a Mother Goose book is the selection of verses it contains. The verses should maintain the original poetic and robust language characteristic of them. Editions that include verses with simplified language should be avoided, for the value lies in the quality and vigor of the language. Poet Walter De La Mare attests to the importance of language and action in his statement that Mother Goose rhymes

> . . . free the fancy, charm the tongue and ear, delight the inward eye, and many of them are tiny masterpieces of word craftsmanship. . . . Last, but not least, they are not only crammed with vivid little scenes and objects and living creatures, but, however fantastic and nonsensical they may be, they are a direct short cut into poetry itself.[11]

Because the essence of the Mother Goose rhymes lies in the words, language is a crucial factor in selecting a collection. Most editions, however, are illustrated, and the quality of the art should also be considered.

In the case of Mother Goose, the normal function of illustrations—to help visualize the action and characters and to amplify and extend the verses—is no simple task, according to the discerning Maurice Sendak:

> This elusive quality of the verses—that something more than meets the eye—partially explains the unique difficulty of illustrating Mother Goose. While it is true that the great children's literature is always underlaid with deeper shades of meanings which the perceptive illustrator must interpret, the Mother Goose rhymes stubbornly offer still further resistance. For a start, they have about them a certain blandness that betrays the unwary artist into banalities; the deceptively simple verse seems to slip just out of reach, leaving the illustrator with egg on his face. Another difficulty is related to that quality of the verses De La Mare described as "delighting the inward eye." Characteristic of the best imaginative writing, they evoke their own images, thus placing the artist in the embarrassing position of having to contend with Mother Goose the illustrator as well as the poet.[12]

Some illustrators create an entire book around a single Mother Goose rhyme. Maurice Sendak, for example, uses five simple lines as the basis for the

Hector Protector rhyme in *Hector Protector and As I Went Over the Water* (N-P):

> Hector Protector was dressed all in green.
> Hector Protector was sent to the queen.
> The queen did not like him,
> No more did the king.
> So Hector Protector was sent back again.[13]

By playing with the ambiguity in the text, Sendak creates a fanciful picture story that extends the boundaries of the rhyme. Hector is given a cake to carry to the queen, but he kicks it away. On his way he tames both a ferocious lion and a snake, and they accompany him to the palace. The frightened court immediately sends Hector and his companions on their way again, and Sendak then illustrates the homeward journey, without words, until Hector is sent off to his room as punishment.

Contemporary in mode and mischievous in spirit, the illustrations in Susan Jeffers's *Three Jovial Huntsmen* (N) add to the delight of the verse. She captures in beautiful illustrations a less familiar rhyme:

> There were three jovial huntsmen,
> As I have heard men say,
> And they would go a-hunting
> Upon St. David's day.
> All the day they hunted,
> And nothing could they find,
> But a ship a-sailing,
> A-sailing with the wind.[14]

As the three huntsmen amble through the wintry woods, clad in bright colors and gazing about, they are unaware that they are surrounded by animals, which the artist has hidden in the muted line drawings of the woods. The ship "a-sailing with the wind" is a visual illusion made of sun and shadow. This book becomes a hide-and-seek game for children who readily spot the animals that are unseen by the gullible hunters.

Peter Spier has illustrated several individual songs and nursery rhymes with visual worlds full of meticulously rendered detail. In one, *Fox Went Out on a Chilly Night* (N-P), the adventures take place in autumn near a New England village where the fox ran many miles through the picturesque countryside, across a covered bridge, "before he reached the town-o." The foxes' cozy home is a "nice warm den" with an open hearth and a great round table, on which "the fox and his wife cut up the goose with a fork and knife" so the little ones can partake of the bounty. The complete text of the rhyme, with music (provided at the end of the book), a filmstrip (Weston Woods), and the catchy pattern of the refrain encourage children to sing along with vigor. In another, *Hurrah, We're Outward Bound* (N-P), a nineteenth-century French sailing ship, *La Jeune Francaise*, voyages from France to New York and returns by way of England to the rhythms of several nursery songs. Peter Spier bases the intricate illustrations on historical documents and supplements them with historical notes and a map at the end of the book.

Books offering collections of Mother Goose rhymes are more abundant than books based on the individual verses, but they vary in quality of selections and illustrations. Ideally, the illustrations extend the verses without overpowering them. An outstanding example—Marguerite de Angeli's *Book of Nursery and Mother Goose Rhymes* (N-P) —combines a comprehensive collection of verses with exquisite illustrations. The verses are a mixture of pathos, joy, and nonsense, and they retain the rhythmic language of the old versions. The adult reader and child viewer share a thing of beauty as they look at spacious pages graced with finely crafted illustrations. De Angeli captures both the warmheartedness of some verses and the ugliness and grotesqueness of others.

In a totally different style, *Brian Wildsmith's Mother Goose* (N), with characteristic purple, blue, and fuschia geometric patterns, shows no timid shrinking from the malice in the verses. Wildsmith vividly portrays the cruelty of the farmer's wife, preparing to cut off the tails of the three blind mice, and the devilish excitement of Little Johnny Green who puts Pussy in the well. The bold designs and colors create a sophisticated version of the traditional verses.

MOTHER GOOSE AND LANGUAGE PLAY (N-P) We can no longer assume that all children come to school knowing Mother Goose rhymes; unfortunately, this basic literature is neglected for many children, so we need to share it ardently. Sing the verses, recite them, dance them, dramatize them, and play with them, and children will make them their own.

Show a filmstrip, for example, Raymond Briggs's *The Mother Goose Treasury* (N-P, Weston Woods). As you view each frame, children can join in on the verses. Sing along with Peter Spier's *Fox Went Out on a Chilly Night* (N-P, Weston Woods) and John Langstaff's *Over in the Meadow* (N-P, Weston Woods).

Play a recording such as the one in a kit of material called *Mother Goose Songs* (N-P, Bowmar). Use the mini-books, large photo prints, word strip cards, filmstrip, and guidebook available in the kit. Sing along with the verses.

Children enjoy making their own oversized rhyme book, using huge, spiral-bound pages or flip charts for verse and illustration. Choral speaking follows naturally, and can include group singing, movement, and choruses. Have children clap and skip to the rhythm, dramatize a rhyme, and play the many games based on the verses.

Activity: Teacher to Student

FRONT PAGE MOTHER GOOSE (I) Here are some newspaper headlines for nursery rhyme events. Can you guess them?

1. Arachnid Struggles Up Waterspout
2. John Stout Rescues Drowning Cat
3. Violinists at Command Performance
4. Boy Kisses Girl, then Flees
5. Pastry Taste Denied Simon
6. Girl Frightened by Friendly Spider

Make up your own Mother Goose front-page headline about Humpty Dumpty, Little Bo Peep, Old Mother Hubbard, Mary and her lamb, and others. Remember that headlines are meant to be terse attention grabbers.

If your telephone service does not include a "dial-a-story," a letter to the company could persuade them to start one—with Mother Goose rhymes and simple folk tales as the recorded story.

FOLK AND FAIRY TALES

Until the end of the eighteenth century, traditional fairy tales formed, almost by accident, the greater part of storytelling for very young children: uneducated nurses and servants told children the old stories they had been told themselves, because they were the only stories they knew. It was in the nineteenth century that writers came to realize "that there was a natural affinity between the childhood of the race and the childhood of the individual human being."[15]

For centuries children and adults shared and enjoyed the same literature. Folk tales and folk songs were handed down from one generation to the next, and, even in the homes of those who could afford to buy books, children were entertained with folklore by their nursemaids. Folk tales first appeared in print in 1697, with the French publication of the above mentioned *Histoires ou contes du temps passé*, by Charles Perrault. Among the tales included were "The Sleeping Beauty," "Little Red Riding Hood," "Cinderella," and "Puss in Boots." During the course of the eighteenth century, La Fontaine's *Fables,* Countess d'Aulnoy's *Fairy Tales,* and *Beauty and the Beast* by Madame de Beaumont were among the earliest folk tales presented in book form.

Toward the end of the eighteenth century, antiquarians and philologists began to examine folklore as a primary source of information about the customs and languages of peoples. In Germany, two brothers who were making a study of the history and grammar of the German language went out into the countryside to study the use of language in the oral folk tradition. These brothers, Jakob and Wilhelm Grimm, traveled through the country listening to the stories and writing them down. They did eventually write both a dictionary and a book of grammar, but their most famous works are the retellings of the stories they heard. The two volumes of the first edition of *Kinder- und Hausmärchen* were published in 1812 and 1815, respectively.

Many of the tales collected by the brothers Grimm were translated into English in 1823 in a book with the prophetic title, *Household Tales;* there is probably no other children's book that has become so widely known. Over the years, hundreds of translations of their stories have been published, not all of the highest quality. One hundred and fifty years later, Lore Segal and Maurice Sendak selected 27 (from the 210 in the complete collection) for *The Juniper Tree* (I), an outstanding two-volume book. The tales (some translated by Lore Segal, some by Randall Jarrell) are not cut or bowdlerized and retain the vigor and charm of the original language. Sendak's illustrations capture the strength and mystery of the stories.

Enthusiasm for collecting folklore spread around the world: Joseph Jacobs and Andrew Lang collected folk tales in England, and Norse scholars Peter Christian Asbjørnsen and Jorgen E. Moe collected most of the Scandinavian tales we have today. Asbjørnsen and Moe published a notable collection, *East O' the Sun and West O' the Moon* (I), during the 1840s. These tales were rendered into English by George Webbe Dasent in translations that retained the vitality of the spoken language. Many of the same tales appear in Ingri and Edgar Parin d'Aulaire's *East of the Sun and West of the Moon* (I), in which the illustrations are suggestive of Norwegian folk art.

Characteristics

Folk tales are story narratives circulated informally in which heroes and heroines demonstrate cleverness, bravery, or other virtues to triumph over adversaries. They have an artistic, yet simple, form attributable to their oral tradition. The plot lines are clean and direct: the first paragraph establishes characters and setting, the body develops the problem and moves toward the climax, the ending resolves the problem without complications.

There is little ambiguity in folk tales: the good are supremely good, the evil are outrageously evil, and justice prevails without compromise. The problem is identified early and only incidents that build the problem or add complexity have survived oral transmission. The problem resolution is decisive, with little denouement thereafter. Characters live happily ever after, and that is that.

Characters in folk tales are delineated economically, with intentional stereotyping to quickly identify character traits. Subtleties are seldom found, since folk tales are concerned more with situation than character. The foolish, the wise, the wicked, or the virtuous immediately crystallize as characters who will perform in predictable ways. These little-developed characters are stock figures, either altogether good or altogether bad, who seldom change during a story. Names represent a group—Jack, for example, for any lad, or Goldilocks for fair-haired girls.

Themes in folk tales, obvious, although not stated explicitly, express the values of the people who created them and, pieced together, reflect their philosophy of life. The language is simple, direct, vivid vernacular uncluttered by awkward constructions or convolutions. Colloquialisms add to the flavor and reflect the heritage of the tale; they are tempered to the tongue, having been pruned and polished through centuries. With folk tales, language is supreme because all lies in the telling. They have been called "primers of the picture language of the soul."

The setting of folk tales is geographically vague, leaving an impression of worlds complete in themselves. Stories occur at unidentified times in places defined by the minimal physical detail necessary to the events. Because children accept the idea that there was a different range of possibilities in the past, the stories are more believable to them. Young children may know that giants do not live in today's world, but they readily accept the possibility that they lived at one time. A six-year-old boy, asked when the events in "Little Red Riding Hood" happened, replied, "A long time ago when I was a baby, they happened. There was witches and that, a long time ago. . . ."[16]

Fairy tales, like all folk tales, are structured by an unvarying sequence of episodes, but they are unique among folk tales in the deeply magical character of their events. In some, the action of the story is carried forward by the intervention of the wee people or a fairy godmother. Filled with enchantment, these stories nonetheless present a vision of life based on fundamental truths. Children see courage, hard work, and resourcefulness rewarded and the good living happily ever after.

Motifs, recurrent phrases, words, situations, or symbols that run through a tale heighten and accentuate the theme. Motifs that run through folk tales include the quest (a long journey with many trials, but happiness achieved), the struggle between good and evil (evil spells broken by love), the small outwitting the big (Jack takes treasures from the giant), trickery (Brer Rabbit tricks Brer Wolf into throwing him into the briar patch), and sudden reversals of fortune (Cinderella is raised from the ashes when the glass slipper fits).

Trickery or outwitting another is an oft-played element in many tales. For example, a spider man is the trickster in African and Caribbean tales, as in Gail Haley's *A Story, A Story* (P-I). Anansi, the spider man, outwits the Sky God by accomplishing the three tasks he is assigned—the price he must pay for the Sky God's stories. Anansi is crafty and wise in other stories such as Gerald McDermott's *Anansi the Spider* (P-I), in which Anansi encounters trouble far from home. Using their special talents, Anansi's six sons save him and, when he is home again, Anansi wants to give the moon to the son who rescued him. When he cannot decide which son deserves the prize, Nyame, the God of all things, takes the moon up into the sky, to hold it there to this day.

Trickery and cunning also appear in French and Swedish folk tales, as in Marcia Brown's *Stone Soup* (P) and in Harve Zemach's *Nail Soup* (P). In the first story, three soldiers trick an entire village into feeding them when they pretend to make soup from stones. The soldiers ask for a bit of meat, a few potatoes, some vegetables, just to add to the pot of soup made from their stones. In the second story, an old man plays the same trick on an old woman as he makes magical soup from a nail, enriched, of course, by the bits of food she adds to the pot.

Variants of Fairy Tales

Although the origins of folk tales are clouded in prehistory, variants of a tale can be traced. It is certain that the tales are of immense antiquity, dating

(Opposite) Nancy Ekholm Burkert views the queen, Snow White's mother, from outside the castle window. An atmosphere of medieval times in the austere castle walls and the remote and ermine-gowned queen set the time and place of the story before the reader reaches the first page.
(Illustration reproduced by permission of Farrar, Straus and Giroux, Inc. From *Snow White and the Seven Dwarfs, A Tale from the Brothers Grimm.* Translated by Randall Jarell. Pictures by Nancy Ekholm Burkert. Copyright © 1972 by Nancy Ekholm Burkert.)

from a period of wild fancy, and whether they were transmitted from one country to another by word of mouth or started independently in several different parts of the world, we cannot know. Marian Roalfe Cox traced the variants of the Cinderella story and uncovered an amazing number of them. She gives brief excerpts and comparisons in *Cinderella: Three Hundred and Forty-Five Variants* (adult). In a foreword to this collection, Andrew Lang states:

The märchen [fairy tale] is a kaleidoscope: the incidents are the bits of coloured glass. Shaken, they fall into a va-

Trina Schart Hyman portrays Snow White's mother, the queen, from inside the room and as a dreaming, wistful young woman. (From *Snow White* by the Brothers Grimm, translated by Paul Heins, illustrated by Trina Schart Hyman. Translation copyright © 1974 by Paul Heins; illustrations copyright © 1974 by Trina Schart Hyman. By permission of Little, Brown and Company in association with the Atlantic Monthly Press.)

VERSION

	Grimm/Hyman* (Germany, 1812)	Grimm/Le Cain* (Germany, 1812)	Perrault/Walker* (France, 19th Century)
Name	Briar Rose	Thorn Rose	The Princess
Setting	Feast	Feast	Christening banquet
Characters	13 fairies	13 fairies	8 fairies
Prediction	Frog predicts daughter	Crab predicts daughter	No prediction
Onset of spell	15th birthday	15th birthday	16th birthday
Spell	Sleep 100 years	Sleep 100 years	Sleep 100 years
Action	All fall asleep	All fall asleep	Princess falls asleep (Good fairy puts others to sleep)
Obstacle	Thorny briar roses	Hedge of thorns	Briars and brambles
Ending	Lived in peace and joy until they died	Lived happily	Married; at birth of their child princess no longer had memory of 100-year sleep.
Illustration quality	Powerful, sense of gloom, subtle carvings	Exquisite detail, foreboding darkness, tapestry borders, opulent, majestic	Romantic, dreamlike, bright color

* Illustrator.

riety of attractive forms; some forms are fitter than others, survive more powerfully, and are more widely spread.[17]

Folklorists continue to search for different versions, tracing elements in stories found elsewhere. Students like to discover the story parallels for different reasons. It is like finding an old friend when they recognize a favorite tale in different dress.

In *Once Upon a Time: On the Nature of Fairy Tales,*[18] Max Lüthi presents an insightful analysis of the many variants of "Sleeping Beauty." Lüthi speaks of fairy tales as remnants of primal myths, playful descendants of an ancient, intuitive vision of life and the world. For example, Sleeping Beauty, mysteriously threatened and suffering a sleep similar to death but then awakened, parallels the story of death and resurrection. In much the same vein, the awakening of the sleeping maiden can represent the earth's awakening from winter to live and blossom anew when touched by the warmth of spring.

Lüthi shows that the story of Sleeping Beauty is more than an imaginatively stylized love story portraying a girl whose love breaks a spell. The princess is an image for the human spirit: the story portrays the endowment, peril, and redemption, not of just one girl, but all of humankind. Sleeping Beauty's recovery symbolizes the human soul that, suffering repeated setbacks, is yet revived, healed, and redeemed. Human feelings, like longing, grief, and joy, are expressed in the story. The fairy tale is a universe in miniature that not only reflects the wisdom of the ages, but also presents that wisdom in an enchanting tale. Although such elaborate analysis is not for children, it informs a teacher's presentation.

Students can read several versions of Sleeping Beauty to discover the differences in text and illustrations, as shown in the above chart, which was worked out by a group of third-grade students.[19] The list on pages 178–79 shows variants of other folk tales also suitable for this kind of investigation.

When a fine artist turns her hand to children's books, book people rejoice. Nancy Ekholm Burkert's work, rooted in the tradition of master artists, is cause for celebration. She states her intent to illuminate and expand the words of a story and will not work on a book unless it meets her high standards of literary excellence. It must be written by an author who articulates verbally a message Nancy Burkert can respond to artistically. She shocked the children's book world by saying that she thought no more than a hundred of the two thousand books published annually would be of lasting value.

Nancy Ekholm Burkert has been drawing since childhood. In the introduction to *The Art of Nancy Ekholm Burkert,* she says:

I have been drawing all my life, filling the reams of paper my father brought to me, drawing many hours as I listened to the radio. Unlike television, radio did not supply the pictures and therefore in one way stimulated the visual imagination much more (David Larkin, ed., *The Art of Nancy Ekholm Burkert* [New York: Harper & Row, 1977], p. 2).

NANCY EKHOLM BURKERT

The first children's book she illustrated, Roald Dahl's *James and the Giant Peach,* was followed by Eva La Gallienne's translation of Hans Christian Andersen's *The Nightingale.* Later, Edward Lear's *The Scroobius Pip* became memorable because of Burkert's illustrations. Through her perceptive brush she creates unforgettable visions. Snow White has never appeared more alive than she does in Nancy Burkert's reality. The attention to detail—as in scenes showing Snow White alone in the great forest surrounded by birds and animals hidden in the underbrush, or serving the dwarfs' dinner in a medieval cottage furnished with authentic household objects—reflects superb craftsmanship and painstaking work. She says:

When I work I compose on a piece of tracing paper, and then compose and compose again, until I have what I want. And then I transfer it to a piece of Strathmore paper, and work out a full pencil study . . . I use a brush—a small brush—and colored inks—and then I erase the underdrawing. Thus it is a method employing many preparatory sketches, studies on overlays, much reworking, and then transferring them to the final paper (Larkin, ed., *The Art of Nancy Ekholm Burkert,* p. 6).

Her diligence enhances the personal images children create for themselves.

Nancy Ekholm Burkert uses her own children extensively as models in her work. Born in Sterling, Colorado, she now lives in Milwaukee, Wisconsin, with her artist husband, Robert Burkert. Claire and Rand, their children, are nearly grown.

THE BREMEN TOWN MUSICIANS

The Bremen Town Musicians. Illustrated by Paul Galdone. McGraw-Hill, 1968.

The Bremen Town Musicians. Retold by Ruth Gross. Illustrated by Jack Kent. Scholastic, 1975.

The Traveling Musicians. Illustrated by Hans Fischer. Harcourt Brace Jovanovich, 1955.

CINDERELLA

Cinderella. Illustrated by Marcia Brown. Scribner's, 1954.

Cinderella. Retold by C. S. Evans. Illustrated by Arthur Rackham. Viking, 1972.

Cinderella. Illustrated by Errol Le Cain. Bradbury, 1972.

Cinderella: From the Opera by Gioacchino Rossini. Illustrated by Beni Montresor. Knopf, 1965.

Tattercoats. Illustrated by Flora Annie Steel. Bradbury, 1976.

THE FROG PRINCE

The Donkey Prince. Retold by M. Jean Craig. Illustrated by Barbara Cooney. Doubleday, 1977.

The Frog Prince. Illustrated by Paul Galdone. McGraw-Hill, 1974.

The Frog Prince. Retold by Edith Tarcov. Illustrated by James Marshall. Four Winds-Scholastic, 1974.

THE GINGERBREAD MAN

The Bun: A Tale from Russia. Illustrated by Marcia Brown. Harcourt Brace Jovanovich, 1972.

The Gingerbread Boy. Illustrated by Paul Galdone. Seabury, 1975.

Johnny Cake. Illustrated by William Stobbs. Viking, 1973.

Journey Cake, Ho! Retold by Ruth Sawyer. Illustrated by Robert McCloskey. Viking, 1953.

GOLDILOCKS AND THE THREE BEARS

Deep in the Forest. Illustrated by Brinton Turkle. Dutton, 1976. (reversal of traditional tale)

The Three Bears. Illustrated by Paul Galdone. Seabury, 1972.

HANSEL AND GRETEL

Hansel and Gretel. Illustrated by Adrienne Adams. Scribner's, 1975.

Hansel and Gretel. Translated by Elizabeth D. Crawford. Illustrated by Lisbeth Zwerger. Morrow, 1979.

Hansel and Gretel. Retold by Ruth Gross. Illustrated by Margot Tomes. Scholastic, 1974.

Hansel and Gretel. Illustrated by Arnold Lobel. Delacorte, 1971.

Hansel and Gretel. Illustrated by Susan Jeffers. Dial, 1980.

Teeny Tiny and the Witch Woman. Retold by Barbara Walker. Illustrated by Michael Foreman. Pantheon, 1975.

HENNY PENNY

Chicken Licken. Retold by Kenneth McLeish. Illustrated by Jutta Ash. Bradbury, 1974.

Henny Penny. Illustrated by Paul Galdone. Seabury, 1968.

Henny Penny. Retold by Veronica S. Hutchinson. Illustrated by Leonard B. Lubin. Little, Brown, 1976.

Henny Penny. Illustrated by William Stobbs. Follett, 1970.

JACK AND THE BEANSTALK

The History of Mother Twaddle and the Marvelous Achievement of Her Son Jack. Illustrated by Paul Galdone. Seabury, 1974.

Jack and the Beanstalk. Illustrated by Margery Gill. Walck, 1975.

Jack and the Beanstalk. Illustrated by William Stobbs. Delacorte, 1969.

Jack and the Wonder Beans. Retold by James Still. Illustrated by Margot Tomes. Putnam's, 1977.

Jim and the Beanstalk. Retold and illustrated by Raymond Briggs. Coward, McCann & Geoghegan, 1970. (parody)

LITTLE RED HEN

Little Red Hen. Illustrated by Janina Domanska. Macmillan, 1973.

The Little Red Hen. Illustrated by Paul Galdone. Seabury, 1973.

LITTLE RED RIDING HOOD

The Gunniwolf. Retold by Wilhelmina Harper. Illustrated by William Wiesner. Dutton, 1967.

Little Red Riding Hood. Illustrated by Paul Galdone. Seabury, 1974.

Little Red Riding Hood. Illustrated by William Stobbs. Walck, 1973.
Little Red Riding Hood. Illustrated by Bernadette Watts. World Publications, 1968.
Red Riding. Retold by Jean Merrill. Illustrated by Ronni Solbert. Pantheon, 1968. (parody)
Red Riding Hood. Retold by Beatrice Schenk De Regniers. Illustrated by Edward Gorey. Atheneum, 1972.

THE MAGIC PORRIDGE POT
The Magic Porridge Pot. Illustrated by Paul Galdone. Seabury, 1976.
Strega Nona. Retold and illustrated by Tomie de Paola. Prentice-Hall, 1975.

RAPUNZEL
Rapunzel. Illustrated by Felix Hoffmann. Harcourt Brace Jovanovich, 1961.
Rapunzel. Retold and illustrated by Bernadette Watts. Crowell, 1975.

RUMPELSTILTSKIN
Duffy and the Devil. Retold by Harve Zemach. Illustrated by Margot Zemach. Farrar, Straus & Giroux, 1973.
Rumpelstiltskin. Illustrated by William Stobbs. Walck, 1970.
Rumpelstiltskin. Retold by Edith Tarcov. Illustrated by Edward Gorey. Four Winds-Scholastic, 1973.
Tom Tit Tot. Illustrated by Evaline Ness. Scribner's, 1965.

THE SHOEMAKER AND THE ELVES
The Elves and the Shoemaker. Illustrated by Katrin Brandt. Follett, 1967.
The Elves and the Shoemaker. Illustrated by Brinton Turkle. Four Winds-Scholastic, 1975.
The Shoemaker and the Elves. Illustrated by Adrienne Adams. Scribner's, 1960.

THE SLEEPING BEAUTY
Briar Rose. Illustrated by Margery Gill. Walck, 1972.
The Sleeping Beauty. Retold by C. S. Evans. Illustrated by Arthur Rackham. Viking, 1972.
The Sleeping Beauty. Illustrated by Warwick Hutton. Atheneum, 1979.
The Sleeping Beauty. Retold and illustrated by Trina Schart Hyman. Little, Brown, 1977.
The Sleeping Beauty. Illustrated by David Walker. Crowell, 1976.
Thorn Rose. Illustrated by Errol Le Cain. Bradbury, 1975.

SNOW WHITE AND ROSE RED
Snow White and Rose Red. Illustrated by Adrienne Adams. Scribner's, 1964.
Snow White and Rose Red. Illustrated by Barbara Cooney. Delacorte, n.d.

SNOW WHITE AND THE SEVEN DWARFS
Snow White. Illustrated by Trina Schart Hyman. Little, Brown, 1974.
Snow White and the Seven Dwarfs. Illustrated by Nancy Ekholm Burkert. Farrar, Straus & Giroux, 1972.
Snow White and the Seven Dwarfs. Illustrated by Wanda Gág. Coward, McCann & Geoghegan 1938.

THE THREE BILLY GOATS GRUFF
The Three Billy Goats Gruff. Illustrated by Susan Blair. Holt, Rinehart & Winston, 1963.
The Three Billy Goats Gruff. Illustrated by Marcia Brown. Harcourt Brace Jovanovich, 1957.
The Three Billy Goats Gruff. Illustrated by Paul Galdone. Seabury, 1973.
The Three Billy Goats Gruff. Illustrated by William Stobbs. McGraw-Hill, 1968.

THE THREE LITTLE PIGS
The Three Little Pigs. Illustrated by Paul Galdone. Seabury, 1970.
The Three Little Pigs. Illustrated by William Pène du Bois. Viking, 1962.

TOM THUMB
Tom Thumb. Illustrated by Felix Hoffmann. Atheneum, 1973.
Tom Thumb. Illustrated by Otto S. Svend. Larousse, 1976.
Tom Thumb. Illustrated by William Wiesner. Walck, 1974.

The story of the little man who, for a cruel fee, helps the poor girl spin straw or flax into skeins of gold is a well-loved folk tale that has many variants in as many countries. From Germany, comes the best-known version, Grimm's *Rumpelstiltskin* (P), a tale in which the dwarf spins straw into gold. In the version from Suffolk, England, an impet (dwarf) spins five skeins of gold from flax in the story called *Tom Tit Tot* (P), retold by Evaline Ness. In Devonshire and Cornwall, England, the devil knits stockings, jackets, and other clothing for the Squire, as recounted in the tale *Duffy and the Devil* (P), illustrated by Margot Zemach. The corresponding character of Rumpelstiltskin is called Trit-a-Trot in Ireland and Whuppity Stoorie in Scotland.

In one of Evaline Ness's artful woodcuts, the king watches the impet spin straw into gold in *Tom Tit Tot*.
(From *Tom Tit Tot* by Evaline Ness. Illustrations copyright © 1965 by Evaline Ness. Reprinted by permission of Charles Scribner's Sons.)

Arthur Rackham's gleeful Rumpelstiltskin celebrates the bargain he has made with the miller's daughter.
(Reprinted by permission of Viking Penguin Inc.: From *Grimm's Fairy Tales,* illustrated by Arthur Rackham. Published by the Viking Press, Inc., in 1973.)

COMPARING VARIANTS OF RUMPELSTILTSKIN (P-I) Students who read several versions of the Rumpelstiltskin story can compare the different names the little man is called, the chants and refrains used, and the price the dwarf demands for his services. A group may enjoy making a chart as they read, similar to the following:

Tom Tit Tot	Rumpelstiltskin	Duffy and the Devil
	Names guessed	
Bill, Ned, Mark, Sammle, Methusalem, Solomon, Zebedee, Tom Tit Tot	Timothy, Benjamin, Bandylegs, Hunchback, Crookshanks, John, Tom, Rumpelstiltskin	Does not tell
	Chants or refrains	
Nimmy, nimmy not My name is Tom Tit Tot and Well, that won't do no harm, if that don't do no good.	Little does my lady dream Rumpel-stilts-kin is my name	Tomorrow! Tomorrow! Tomorrow's the day! I'll take her! I'll take her I'll take her away! Let her weep, let her cry let her beg, let her pray— She'll never guess my name is . . . Tarraway.
	Price	
("You shall be mine")	First-born child	("I'll take you away")
	Characterization	
Impet	Gnome	Devil

EXPLORING ONE FOLK TALE (I) Students may enjoy one folk tale so much that they want to try various activities to extend their appreciation. Familiar folk tales are an excellent base for drama, art, written and oral-language experiences. "The Three Billy Goats Gruff" is a favorite of children, and they enjoy dramatizing it. Volunteers

(CONTINUED)

can play the roles of each of the billy goats and the troll. (There will be many requests for this part!) Scenery is minimal: the teacher's chair can serve as the bridge under which the troll hides. A narrator may tell the story, with characters speaking their lines, or children can play the scene with dialogue only.

Compare the well-done illustrations in the versions by William Stobbs (N-P, McGraw-Hill, 1968), Susan Blair (N-P, Holt, Rinehart & Winston, 1963), Marcia Brown (N-P, Harcourt Brace Jovanovich, 1957), and Paul Galdone (N-P, Seabury, 1973). Making judgments about illustrations is a particularly useful area in which to exercise discrimination. Ask: Which troll looks meanest? Which is scariest? Which one shows the fiercest battle between the third billy goat and the troll? Which one shows best the size relationship between the smallest, middle-sized, and biggest billy goats? Also useful is to have children draw their impressions of what the troll looks like.

When written language is the focus, children should be able to read the stories for themselves. Discuss the differences in the texts of the four versions. Ask: How is the troll described? What words tell you about him? What words tell you what happened to him when he was pushed off the bridge? How does each story end? Why do you think the stories use the phrase, "Snip, Snap, Snout, this tale's told out"?

A further way to explore this folk tale is through poetry. Try using the following humorous poem, by X. J. Kennedy, for reading aloud and dramatization. (Try saying the title ten times rapidly.)

TERRIBLE TROLL'S TOLLBRIDGE

"Aw, enough is enough!"
Said the Billygoats Gruff,
    And their neighbor the Terrible Troll
Said, "You're welcome to pass
To the hill to crop grass
    If you'll pay me a reasonable toll."

Now they screech to a stop
At his toll bridge and drop
    Goatsmilk cheeses between the troll's choppers.
Old Troll charges a cheese
For a little goat, please—
    Two for mediums, three for big whoppers.[20]

Activity: Teacher to Student

CHANGING THE POINT OF VIEW (P-I)   Try telling "The Three Billy Goats Gruff" the way the troll might. Remember, that the bridge is the troll's and that the goats could seem to be very thoughtless. You might begin: "I was sitting at home one day, calmly minding my own business under my bridge, when some noisy goat came tromping over it. . . ."

Assuming a different point of view is a difficult task for young children. Until about eight or nine years of age, they have not yet reached the level of thought required for taking another's perspective and simply cannot remove themselves from egocentric thinking characteristic of the preoperational stage. Telling a story from a different point of view is a good language activity for them and one that provides some insights for the teacher. The following are excerpts from two retellings by children of "The Three Billy Goats Gruff" from the point of view of the troll.

Matt (age 5):
"The Three Little Billy Goats—up on a hill—uh—eating some grass. He want to cross the water and get some more grass—and get big and fat—and they found a bridge and they wanted to go cross. They better not 'cause the mean old troll is under it. . . . [Later] I'm gonna come and eat you up. He knocked the—the troll got—lost his balance and—crashed in the water. And the troll dropped—and he drownded."

Steve (age 7½):
"Once these three goats wanted to cross a bridge and the—um—Should I say me?—Um—um—I came up and started to scream at him. He said—and the goat said —um—to wait for his other brother. . . . [Later] I better get this one. . . . and he said 'Oh, no, you're not going to eat me up' and then he hit him with his horns and he fell into the water. [Teacher: Who did he hit?] . . . Oh, me. Then, uh, uh, I fell in the water and the other—he started tramping across the bridge and they ate all the grass they wanted."

Neither five-year-old Matt nor seven-and-a-half-year-old Steve can maintain the troll's point of view. Even though both manage to assume it fleetingly, they revert to the third-person narrator—the form they hear most often. You will need to know your students well before asking them to tell a story from a different point of view; you also need to remember that taking another role is a developmental task that is learned naturally—it is *not* something you teach.

Folk tales adapted by different cultural groups show corresponding differences in language and setting. Many Americanized versions of Old World tales are known as "Jack Tales," and revolve around a boy named Jack. One of the most familiar is a variant of "Jack and the Beanstalk" and is known as "Jack's Bean Tree," found in Richard Chase's *The Jack Tales* (I). *Jack and the Wonder Beans* (P-I) is another variant, by James Still. Appalachian dialect permeates these versions of the familiar tale. For example, the giant's refrain in *Jack and the Wonder Beans* is "Fee, fie, chew tobacco, I smell the toes of a tadwhacker."

Simple props set the stage for a re-enactment of *Three Billy Goats Gruff*. As one of the goats crosses the table/bridge, the troll hides beneath.
(HBJ Photograph by Richard C. Polister.)

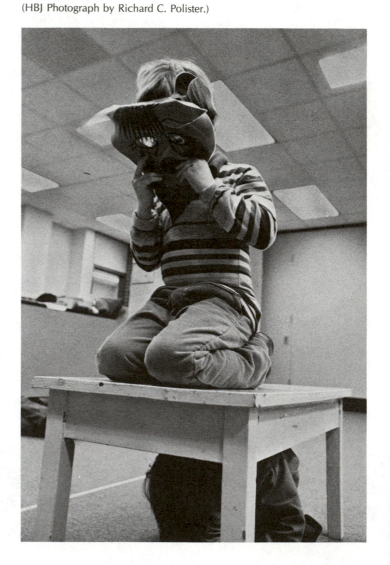

Activity: Teacher to Student

JACK AND THE WONDER BEANS (P-I) When you have finished reading *Jack and the Wonder Beans,* select the words and phrases that reflect the Appalachian dialect. Some examples are ''way back yonder,'' ''poor as Job's turkey,'' ''feet like cornsleds,'' ''meanest eye ever beheld,'' ''sizzled like a red-hot horseshoe in a cooling tub,'' and ''couldn't be trusted to pack slops to a sick bear.'' How would you say these?

Look at the illustrations. How does the artist show the homey mountain atmosphere of this tale? What things do you see in the illustrations that you don't see around your neighborhood? Did you notice Mam smoking a pipe?

Read and compare other Jack Tales such as Richard Chase's *Jack and the Three Sillies* Houghton Mifflin, 1950), *Grandfather Tales* (Houghton Mifflin, 1948), and *The Jack Tales* (Houghton Mifflin, 1943).

Illustration in Folk Tales

The earthy, regal, noodlehead, and other characters, along with the undefined sense of place and time, offer inventive illustrators opportunities for unusual visual interpretations. Some of our most beautifully illustrated books are folk tales. Nearly every year at least one or more folk tales are selected for honor by the Caldecott Medal committee. Among the winners and honor books are

Big Anthony learned Strega Nona's chant for starting the magic pot but not for stopping it. His desperate measure fails to stem the flow of pasta.
(From the book *Strega Nona* by Tomie de Paola. Copyright © 1975 by Tomie de Paola. Published by Prentice-Hall, Inc., Englewood Cliffs, New Jersey 07632.)

numerous folk tales chosen because of their visual distinction. Arlene Mosel's *The Funny Little Woman* (P), illustrated by Blair Lent, Tomie de Paola's *Strega Nona* (P), and Nonny Hogrogian's *One Fine Day* (P) are but a few of the highly recommended books chosen for their excellence in art. These illustrators create a world born of imagination and explore character from within—each in a unique style. Peter Spier's *Noah's Ark* (P), Isaac Bashevis Singer's *Why Noah Chose the Dove* (P-I), illustrated by Eric Carle, and Warwick Hutton's *Noah and the Great Flood* (P-I) contain imaginatively varied images of the same ancient story. Compassion, pathos, and humor are combined in illustrations filled with narrative skill.

FABLES

The fable is a brief didactic comment on the nature of human life presented in dramatic action to make the idea memorable. One factor that distinguishes the fable from other traditional literature forms is that it illustrates a moral, which is stated explicitly at the end. Many common sayings and phrases come from fables: "Better beans and bacon in peace than cakes and ale in fear," "Slow and steady wins the race," "Sour grapes," and "cry (or don't cry) wolf." Such injunctions, explicitly stated as morals, are taught by allegory; animals or inanimate objects represent human traits in stories that clearly show the wisdom of the simple lessons.

Folklorist Joseph Jacobs relates the fable to the beast-tales (in which characters are animals with human characteristics), which were used for satiric purposes and, in some cases, to teach a moral truth. In the single-incident story typical of the fable, we are told not to be vain, not to be greedy, and not to lie. Jacobs traces the origins of fables to both Greece and India. Supposedly, a Greek slave named Aesop used fables for political purposes, and though some doubt that he ever lived, his name has been associated with fables since an-

Though engraver's tools of the time were relatively crude, Wenceslaus Hollar's 1665 engraving of the plight of the lion in Aesop's "The Lion and the Mouse" achieves a sense of the lion's strength and the intricacy of the net.
(The Lion and the Mouse, engraving by W. Hollar for John Ogilby, *The Fables of Aesop*, Thomas Roycroft, London, 1665. The Metropolitan Museum of Art, Rogers Fund.)

cient times. Early collections made in the East derive from the "Panchatantra" (Five Tantras, or Books), a famous collection from India known to English readers as the Fables of Bidpai and Jataka Tales. The Jatakas are stories of Buddha's prior lives as various animals—each tale told to illustrate a moral principle. A seventeenth-century French poet, Jean de La Fontaine, adapted many of the early fables into verse form.

Noted illustrators of children's books have chosen to interpret fables artistically, although there are only a few in single editions. Marcia Brown's subtle yet powerful woodcuts enable *Once a Mouse* (P-I) to stand as a classic among illustrated fables. *The Hare and the Tortoise* (P) and *Three*

Aesop Fox Fables (P-I) are illustrated by Paul Galdone in a flamboyant style that makes clear the subtle humor. In *Two Roman Mice* (P), Marilynne Roach retells and illustrates a version written in 29 B.C. by Horace. In this retelling, Rusticus, the country mouse, tells Urbanus, the city mouse, that it is better to have seeds in the woods than feasts in a trap. Unfortunately, several excellent editions of La Fontaine's fables illustrated by Brian Wildsmith are out of print. *The Lion and the Rat, The North Wind and the Sun,* and *The Rich Man and the Shoemaker* (all P) will enrich any fable collection.

Jack Kent illustrated two collections, *Jack Kent's Fables of Aesop* (P) and *More Fables of Aesop* (P), for younger children. There is very little evidence, however, that primary-grade children

Brian Wildsmith's lion, in *The Lion and the Rat,* occupies almost all the space of the page to convey the strength of the trapped animal.
(From *The Lion and the Rat* by Brian Wildsmith. Copyright 1963. Used by permission of Franklin Watts, Inc.)

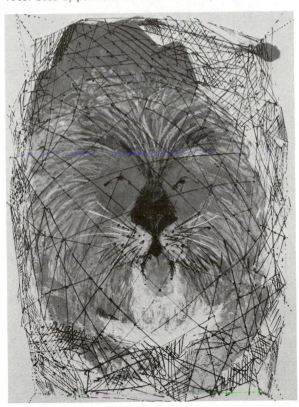

ALLUSIONS FROM FABLES (I-A) Our language is replete with allusions to fables. Students enjoy looking for allusions, matching the morals to the fables, writing their own fables, and illustrating favorite ones. Compile a list of morals used as common sayings in our language and encourage students to find the fable that illustrates the moral.

Activity: Teacher to Student

FIND THE FABLES (I) Match the following maxims with the fable.

_____1. It's just sour grapes.
_____2. You're a dog in the manger.
_____3. Slow and steady wins the race.
_____4. Are you crying wolf?
_____5. Who will bell the cat?
_____6. Don't bite the hand that feeds you.
_____7. Better beans and bacon in peace than cakes and ale in fear.
_____8. Vanity cometh before a fall.

a. The City Mouse and the Country Mouse
b. Belling the Tiger
c. The Fox and the Crow
d. The Dog in the Manger
e. The Boy Who Cried Wolf
f. The Fox and the Grapes
g. The Hare and the Tortoise
h. Once a Mouse

If you are especially interested in fables, extend the list of common sayings and search for their origins in folklore. Russian and Chinese proverbs are especially picturesque; search for some that have counterparts in our common sayings.

understand the subtle abstractions on which the fables hinge. Because fables are very short and their language simple, many teachers give fables to children who are too young to comprehend or fully appreciate them. Since fables are constructed within the oblique perspective of satire, allegory, and symbolism, their intent may elude the literalness of young children's understanding.

Ruth Spriggs collected over 140 fables in *The Fables of Aesop* (I), which appeal to students in the intermediate grades, where the subtleties are more likely to be understood. Certainly the wit and satiric meanings of fables are more fully appreciated by sophisticated readers. The republication of Charles H. Bennett's 1857 edition, *Bennett's*

Fables from Aesop and Others Translated into Human Nature (I), restores an excellent collection filled with biting sarcasm and sardonic wit. Bennett's wry humor is reflected in the retelling, and comic art illustrates the cynical tales. The portrayal of beings simultaneously animal and human, most often the body of a human with an animal's head, makes obvious the image of humans as animals.

Students in intermediate grades quickly recognize the inadequacy (as guides for behavior) of morals stated simplistically in fables. They observe that "slow and steady" does not always win the race and that grapes beyond reach are not always sour. Such responses indicate healthy skepticism toward the brief and witty stories.

SONNET

I thought the Grecian gods were dead and gone,
Their marble forms and faces left to mark
The naive worship of an antique dawn
That scattered far the spirits of the dark.
I thought that Zeus and laughing Aphrodite
Were only bitter wraiths, haunting the mind;
Although they once had homes beside that sea
Where restless waves called out to Homer blind.

But when within a garden plot one night
The moon had covered trees and leaves with frost,
I saw the pity of an ancient sight:
Demeter tearful for her daughter lost.
And then I knew that in this haunted place
An ancient goddess walked, and showed her face.

PAUL HEINS[21]

The images created in Paul Heins's poem echo an emotional response to mythology that we would hope our students experience. The great myths, majestic stories that elude simple analysis, are an important part of the literature curriculum in the late elementary and middle school years.

Myths are said to be prescientific explanations of natural phenomena, the descriptions primal societies made up to explain why the seasons change, why there are storms, and why the sun rises and sets. (These examples are explained in myth as follows: Persephone, the goddess of spring, is captured and taken to the underworld of Hades, where she must stay during the long cold winter months. Zeus and Odin are gods who control the sky: when they are angry they throw lightning bolts and make the thunder roar. Apollo, god of the sun, drives across the sky in a golden chariot.)

Myths are also explained in terms of symbolic expressions of the forces within human nature that we do not fully understand; supposedly such description of the unknown in human terms conferred a sense of control, through analogy and metaphor. Freudians see the myths representing sexual anxieties, jealousies, and psychic struggle between parents and children.

Students do not read the myths for their deep levels of symbolic meaning, however. They read them because they are compelling stories of love, carnage, revenge, and mystery. In Winifred Rosen's forthcoming novel (as yet untitled),[22] a young high-school teacher announces to her class that they will now read about killings, orgies, diabolical plots, child eating, and blood baths—in other words, the Greek myths. Needless to say, the gory details catch the students' interest.

Jung calls myths the memories of the human race that represent in each of us conflicts between the rational mind and the subconscious. Ursula Le Guin, in *A Wizard of Earthsea* (a fantasy discussed in Chapters 1 and 6), personifies these subconscious forces within the youthful hero, Ged, and in the Shadow that follows him and threatens to overwhelm him until he can meet and embrace it. Le Guin discussed the significance of the subconscious, the shadow, in a recent address:

The shadow is the other side of our psyche, the dark brother of the conscious mind. It is Cain, Caliban, Frankenstein's monster, Mr. Hyde. It is Vergil who guided Dante through Hell, Gilgamesh's friend Enkidu, Frodo's enemy Gollum. It is the Doppelgänger. It is Mowgli's Grey Brother; the werewolf; the wolf, the bear, the tiger of a thousand folktales; it is the serpent, Lucifer.[23]

The underside of the human psyche appeared early in mythology.

According to Northrop Frye, as folk tales, fables, songs, and legends develop, a special group of stories, the ones we call myths, crystallize at the center of the verbal culture. The stories are taken seriously because they express the meaning of beliefs and portray visions of destiny. The myths, unlike other stories, relate to each other and together build a mythology of an imaginative world. Literature throughout the ages echoes the themes of the ancient myths; certain motifs, or recurring patterns, are clearly identifiable. Frye traces the origins of all literature, and of the archetypal themes we may identify in it, back to one central story:

. . . how man once lived in a golden age or a garden of Eden or the Hesperides, or a happy island kingdom in the Atlantic, how that world was lost, and how we some day may be able to get it back again. . . .Literature is

still doing the same job that mythology did earlier, but filling in its huge cloudy shapes with sharper light and deeper shadows.[24]

Exploring mythology through recurring themes and motifs leads to endless discoveries.

Elizabeth Cook states that the fixed point of a myth lies in its own concrete nature, not in the things it suggests to different readers, and not in its conjectural origins.[25] She says that a myth ''is'' everything that it has been and everything that it may become; it does not matter that the beautiful and evocative stories may be the product of unconscious misunderstanding and deliberate alteration.

Selecting Myths

Any lack of knowledge concerning myths is easily remedied, for there are many excellent contemporary versions of myths, which do not require an understanding of the complicated lineage of the gods. It is a mistake to neglect myths, for they are crackling good stories and much subsequent literature draws upon them. The chart below is of Greek mythological figures and their Roman counterparts.

A good way for a beginner, whether teacher or student, to select versions of the myths is to turn to recognized translators who are good writers. These include Alfred J. Church, Penelope Farmer, Leon Garfield, Doris Gates, Roger Lancelyn Green, Charles Kingsley, Andrew Lang, Barbara Picard, Ian Serraillier, and Rex Warner, among others. Inclusion of the name of the translator or adaptor on the title page of a book of myths or folklore is an indication that the book is an authentic version.

Myths are seldom appreciated fully until the later years of elementary school, and even then not by all students. The stories of King Midas, Pandora's Box, and Jason and the Golden Fleece are basic material for students' literary education. Good versions of the stories contain interesting, but not flowery, language; the myths have a stately dignity that the language should reflect. Valid retellings do not change the myths from tales of grandeur into sentimental stories. Some retellers interpret characters and events in a unique mode, with variations that illustrate strikingly the effect that style of language can have. In myths, as in all folklore, much depends upon the telling.

Ingri and Edgar Parin d'Aulaire have two beautiful volumes of mythology: *The Book of Greek*

Greek Name	Mythological Figure	Roman Name
Aphrodite	Goddess of love and beauty	Venus
Apollo	God of the sun and youth	Apollo
Ares	God of War	Mars
Artemis	Goddess of the moon and hunt	Diana
Athena	Goddess of wisdom	Minerva
Demeter	Goddess of agriculture	Ceres
Dionysus	God of the vine	Bacchus
Eros	God of love	Cupid
Hades	God of the underworld	Dis
Hephaestus	God of fire	Vulcan
Hera	Wife of Zeus, goddess of women and marriage	Juno
Hermes	Messenger of the gods	Mercury
Hestia	Goddess of home and heart	Vesta
Kronos	God of time and agriculture	Saturn
Persephone	Goddess of spring	Prosperine
Poseidon	God of the sea	Neptune
Zeus	King of the gods, husband of Hera	Jupiter

Myths (I) and *Norse Gods and Giants* (I). Each book contains many well-known myths illustrated with the lithographs for which the d'Aulaires are famous. You can know the d'Aulaires better by seeing them in their home studio in a filmed interview (Weston Woods). Their books remain true to the national cultures of origin of the myths; the Greek myths, for example, have a classic restraint and dignity. The end papers of *Norse Gods and Giants* show the complete conceptual scheme of "high heaven, middle earth, and the underworld." The great tree of life, Yggdrasil, grows up through all these realms, its roots in the underworld and its leafy branches in high heaven. Readers of *The Hobbit* (A), by J. R. R. Tolkien, will recognize middle earth and the underground homes of gnomes and dwarfs. Ingri d'Aulaire, Norwegian by birth, used themes from the folk art of her childhood to make the handsome pages come alive with images of trolls, gnomes, and the heroic figures of the gods.

An Archetypal Theme in Mythology

Penelope Farmer, translator and interpreter of many myths, says:

> . . . myths have seemed to me to point quite distinctly—yet without ever directly expressing it—to some kind of unity behind creation, not a static unity, but a forever shifting breathing one. . . .
> . . . the acquisition by man of life or food or fire has to be paid for by the acceptance of death—the message is everywhere, quite unmistakable. To live is to die; to die is to live.[26]

This great archetypal theme appears again and again throughout all cultures. Children are familiar with the "rebirth" of flowers and trees in the spring. Most of them have buried a seed in the ground and watched for it to sprout, and some may have heard the quotation, "Unless a grain of wheat falls in the ground and dies it remains alone, but if it dies it brings forth much fruit." In image and symbol, these themes reappear under many guises, and children can recognize them through their study of myth.

There are many versions of the story of Perse-phone, goddess of springtime. In addition to those in collections, there are versions in individual picture-book format: *The Story of Persephone* (I), by Penelope Farmer, *Demeter and Persephone* (I), by Penelope Proddow, and *Persephone and the Springtime* (I), by Margaret Hodges. Hodges writes for the younger reader; for example, her version begins, "Everyone everywhere loves the springtime. The ancient Greeks said that spring was a beautiful young girl. Her name was Persephone and she always followed in the footsteps of her mother, Demeter, the earth goddess."[27] Penelope Farmer begins, "She and the goddess of the corn harvest were more like sisters, like lovers even, than a mother and a daughter, wandering the hills together through a world which saw no winter, no autumn, no death or decay, only spring and summer, birth and harvest. Wherever they wandered flowers sprang up, spring flowers for Persephone, summer flowers for the goddess Demeter."[28]

Proddow's version reads, "Now I will sing / of golden-haired Demeter, / the awe-inspiring goddess, / and of her trim-ankled daughter, / Persephone, / who was frolicking in a grassy meadow."[29] Proddow's text is a translation of Hymn Number Two by Homer, and is closest in style to the Greek original. It is complemented with illustrations by Barbara Cooney that capture the classic Greek style with its grace, balance, and dignity.

In the story, the beautiful Persephone, daughter of Demeter, the goddess of earth, is carried off by Hades, god of the underworld, to be his bride. Demeter searches everywhere for her daughter, and finally, in her grief, causes winter to fall over the earth. Finally Persephone's return brings the springtime. It can be useful to children to consider why it was natural for prescientific societies to evolve stories such as Persephone's to explain their world.

All story elements work collectively to create a mood and to develop a theme. The theme may build toward one main idea expressed throughout the story, or there may be a main idea with a minor theme. Mood is the feeling created by the tension, conflict, or joy developed in the story. Awareness of the ways in which the mood reflects the theme

heightens the impact of the story and ensures a richer response.

The illustrations in several versions of Persephone range from somber, dark portrayals to paintings reminiscent of Greek vases. The black horses drawing Hades's fiery chariot, the fields filled with flowers, and the stark contrasts between beauty and the barren earth present strong visual images. The theme that life is carried out in an atmosphere of struggle rather than in a paradise is developed through contrasts in the illustrations. The most satisfying books are those in which the illustrations complement and extend both the theme and the mood of the story.

Creation Myths and Hero Myths

Myths are only tenuously related to historical fact and geographical location and so cannot be taught *as* history. They played an important role, however, in the lives of the ancients, and their influence permeates the art, music, and architecture of Ancient Greece—in fact, all of Greek culture. Myths are an enriching dimension in historical study.

Activity: Teacher to Student

PERSEPHONE (I)   *Before* you read the stories about Persephone, look at all of the illustrations and think about these questions:

1.   How do the illustrations make you feel?
2.   How do you think Persephone feels?
3.   What would life be like in the setting shown?
4.   What is happening to Persephone?
5.   How does the mood of the story change?
6.   How do the colors of the illustrations reflect the changes in mood of the story?

After you read the story discuss some of these questions:

1.   Why didn't Persephone want to stay with Hades?
2.   How did Demeter feel about children? How do you know?
3.   What did Hecate mean by "Not even the owls know where to find her"? How does this make Demeter feel?
4.   What words are used to describe Hades's underworld?
5.   What natural occurrence does the story explain?

Choose activities from the following.

Pretend you are Demeter. Write a letter to Zeus explaining your feelings for your daughter. Tell him what you will do if he does not help you find her.

Write a scene between the river nymph and Demeter in which Demeter discovers that the nymph knows Persephone's whereabouts. Give a dramatic reading or performance of the scene.

Compose a song that tells of Demeter's sadness. Find a suitable melody and write the lyrics for it. Record it on a tape.

Prepare a brief act or pantomime to convey a strong emotion such as love, hate, anger, jealousy, or pain. Build it into a scene with Demeter, Persephone, and Zeus.

Teaching Idea

CYCLE OF SEASONS IN MYTH AND FANTASY (I) In helping students become more sensitive to the idea that "all literature tells one story," ask them to consider other stories in which the seasons of the year mirror the theme. If they have read C. S. Lewis's *The Lion, The Witch, and the Wardrobe* (I, Macmillan, 1951), they will recall that the spell of the White Witch was that it always be winter but never Christmas; with Aslan came the spring. Mole, in Kenneth Grahame's *The Wind in the Willows,* illustrated by Ernest H. Shepard (I, Scribner's, 1933), emerges from his underground home to begin a new life during "spring cleaning." In Hans Christian Andersen's *Thumbelina,* illustrated by Susan Jeffers (P-I, Dial, 1980), the tiny creature spends a long sad winter underground before she is freed and carried off by her friend, the bird, to marry the fairy prince. Likewise, Andersen's duck in *The Ugly Duckling,* retold and illustrated by Lorinda Bryan Cauley (P-I, Harcourt Brace Jovanovich, 1979), suffers through the winter before he is finally recognizable as a swan in the spring. And in *Charlotte's Web* (P-I, Harper & Row, 1952), by E. B. White, Charlotte dies in the fall, but her children are hatched the following spring to bring new friends to lonely Wilbur. Through discussions of such stories, children can be encouraged to look for the interconnections between theme and mood and to begin to build a basis for recognizing recurring themes in all literature.

We group the Greek myths in two broad categories—the creation myths and the hero myths. The Greek creation myths tell how the earth came into being and how the gods, goddesses, and mortals were produced in hierarchical order. In these myths, we learn how the pantheon of gods from Gaea (Mother Earth) to Zeus (Supreme Ruler, Lord of the Sky) came, through a succession of events, to be. Roger Lancelyn Green, in *A Book of Myths* (I-A), intrigues myth readers with both Greek and Norse creation myths: stories of Hyacinthus, in which a flower is born from the blood of Apollo's innocent victim; Clytie, and why the sunflower turns to the sun; the origins of the constellations of Pleiades, Bellerophon, and Pegasus.

Hero myths tell of great adventures, tests, victories, and losses of the gods. They feature the relationships between gods and mortals and show how life must be lived with morality and conscience.

Strong visual images appear in the stories about the master craftsman, Daedalus. Ian Serraillier, in *A Fall from the Sky: The Story of Daedalus* (I), and Penelope Farmer, in *Daedalus and Icarus* (I), present the story of the incarceration and escape of Daedalus and Icarus. The myth suggests that Apollo sought revenge and was angered when Icarus showed excessive pride and dared to emulate a god by flying close to the sun. Thus, the moral: excessive pride (called *hubris*) brings the wrath of the gods.

Jason, Perseus, Theseus, and Hercules are four heroes whose stories are told and retold. The archetypal journey—quest/test/cycle—appears in each hero's tale. Ian Serraillier, in *Way of Danger: The Story of Theseus* (I), *Clashing Rocks: The Story of Jason* (I), and *The Gorgon's Head: The Story of Perseus* (I), traces the exploits of three of these heroes. Theseus learns that his father is King of Athens and fights for his heritage. Jason attempts to

EXPLORING LITERARY COMPONENTS THROUGH MYTHOLOGY (I-A)[30] Through the imaginative and exciting world of mythology, students can develop an understanding of myth as a literary form and enhance their knowledge of the components of narrative fiction. The nature of myths stimulates questions and leads to areas of thought beyond the tales themselves. The objectives of the following activities are to enable the student (a) to recognize plot structure and development in a hero tale, (b) to understand theme and develop an awareness of mood and its impact on theme, (c) to determine how characters are revealed, and (d) to identify and appreciate the recurring theme of creation.

Activity: Teacher to Student

PLOT STRUCTURE AND DEVELOPMENT IN A HERO TALE (I-A) The plot is the story's plan of action—the beginning, the middle, the climax (highest point), and the ending. It tells what the characters do and what happens to them. The plot of a hero tale is based upon a daring quest to accomplish a seemingly impossible goal and is complicated by the obstacles faced during the struggle to reach the goal.

Before you read *The Gorgon's Head* (Walck, 1962) by Ian Serraillier, think about the following questions.

1. How does a person become a hero?
2. What kinds of physical, mental, and spiritual qualities might a hero have? Why might these qualities be necessary?
3. If you were to tell a story about a hero, what are some exciting and daring adventures you would tell? Who are your heroes today?

After reading *The Gorgon's Head,* discuss the following questions with someone who has read the book.

1. What did Perseus set out to prove?
2. What problems and dangers did he face before he accomplished his goal?
3. Why did Athena and Mercury help Perseus?
4. Did the people of his birthplace consider Perseus a hero from the time of his birth?
5. Could any man have accomplished such daring deeds if he had the same gifts as Perseus? Why or why not?
6. What is the climax? Why do you think so?

Choose one of these activities.

1. Rewrite the story of Perseus, the son of Zeus (King of the gods), from Zeus's point of view.
2. Write a dialogue between Danae and the king that shows how Perseus's mother was treated while he was away.

Activity: Teacher to Student

CUPID AND PSYCHE (I-A)[31]   Read Edna Barth's *Cupid and Psyche* (Seabury, 1976) and choose one of the following activities:

1. Write an essay discussing the meaning of the story for you and give some interpretations others might have. (According to some, Psyche represents the human soul. The soul, or psyche, originally in heaven, where all is love, personified by Cupid, is condemned to wander the earth in misery and hardship. Faithful and true, as Psyche was, it eventually returns to heaven and is reunited with love eternal.)

2. Read "Orpheus and Eurydice" and "Echo and Narcissus" in *Mythology,* by Edith Hamilton (Little, Brown, 1942), in order to compare other love stories with Cupid and Psyche's. Discuss the way love is portrayed in the three stories.

3. Psyche, as the representation of the human soul, provides the name for an entire branch of science. Use the dictionary to define the following words as they relate to the story of Cupid and Psyche: psychic, psychedelic, psychiatry, psychology, psychosis, psychosomatic, psychotherapy, cupid's bow, cupidity. Discuss why cupids, hearts, arrows, and love signs are symbols in the celebration of St. Valentine's Day.

---

reclaim his rightful kingdom and makes a quest for the Golden Fleece. Perseus is sent on a dangerous mission—to fetch the head of the snake-haired Gorgon—and, with the help of Athena, cuts off the head of Medusa, sister of three grisly Gorgons.

Hercules (also called Heracles), born to Alcmene, was sired by Zeus. Hercules demonstrates his prodigious strength by strangling two snakes that Hera has maliciously placed in his cradle. Heracles's story is told in *The Labors of Hercules* (I), by Paul Hollander, *The Twelve Labors of Hercules* (I), by Robert Newman, and *Heracles the Strong* (I-A), by Ian Serraillier. The visual images of Hercules slaying a lion whose skin no weapon could pierce, killing a nine-headed Hydra, and cleaning the huge Augean stables in a single day will remain with the reader years after having read the stories.

Love stories interest people of all times; countless myths concern love between a god or goddess and a mortal. The unusual love story of Cupid and Psyche is well known. Psyche, a mortal, incurs the wrath of Venus because she is declared the more beautiful. Venus, in a jealous rage, summons her son Cupid to destroy Psyche by having her fall in love with a monster. Instead of following his mother's orders, Cupid falls in love with Psyche.

The myth of Daedalus and Icarus helps to develop an understanding of the Greek and Roman respect for the human spirit and intellect and the relationship between a father and a son. The story also explains the Greek philosophy of life exemplified in the terms "hubris" and "nemesis." Daedalus, a brilliant engineer, is exiled from Athens for killing his nephew, Talos, because the boy's skill became a threat to him. Proud Daedalus takes his son, Icarus, whom he idolizes, with him to Crete. Daedalus acts as if he invented his son, not merely fathered him, and such excessive pride, called hubris, is unacceptable in the Greek tradition. Minos, King of Crete, commissions the famous engineer to build a stronghold to house his monster son, the

Minotaur. Daedalus draws up plans for a labyrinth so complex that no one can escape it. This brilliant achievement makes him even more confident, and he begins to consider himself equal to the gods. Such pride angers the gods. When inventive Daedalus and his son are imprisoned in his own maze, he realizes that the air is his only route of escape and he fashions wings for Icarus and himself. During the escape Icarus flies too near the sun; the wax with which the wings are fastened melts, and he plunges to his death in the sea. The Greeks called a tragic fate such as that of Daedalus and his son "nemesis"—generally "a come-down." Excessive pride is often followed by a fall—nemesis—in Greek myths, when Nemesis, the goddess of retribution, sees to it that pride is put in its proper place.

Once you and your students become readers of the myths, you will never escape their charm and endless fascination. Penelope Farmer, caught in the magic of myth, sums it up eloquently:

It is a curious phenomenon altogether, myth, tough as leather, fragile as glass. Hardly a story bears logical analysis; . . . shattered by a blow from a sharp mind, [they are] the very next minute . . . whole again. In some weird way the illogic of myth has even succeeded in anticipating science. . . . At whatever level you look at it, for whatever reason, psychic, symbolic, scientific— even simply for amusement—if you gaze long enough you may find myth beginning to explode whole systems and reconstructing them for you. . . . [33]

With these words, Penelope Farmer introduces *Beginnings: Creation Myths of the World* (I-A), a collection of myths from all cultures set forth one after another without commentary. Readers can see for themselves the recurrent themes and motifs. It is a fine starting point for your appreciation of mythology.

Activity: Teacher to Student

DAEDALUS AND ICARUS (I-A)[32] Read Penelope Farmer's *Daedalus and Icarus,* illustrated by Chris Connor (Harcourt Brace Jovanovich, 1971), and choose one of the following activities:

1.   Find and read other myths in which mortals defied the gods or showed hubris and met their nemesis. The myths of Prometheus, Tantalus, and Sisyphus are examples.

2.   Discuss the joyous feeling of freedom Icarus felt (probably much like that felt in modern-day hang-gliding), which may have made him too daring.

3.   Make a scaled replica or diagram of the wings worn by Daedalus and Icarus.

4.   Hold a Saturnalian Festival commemorating the Roman feast of Saturn and the winter solstice. Research the event, which started around 217 B.C. Design a program and list your famous guest speakers—enacted by classmates. The following, written by a ninth-grader, is a good example of the kind of speech the "guests" might make:

What a thrill it was for me to be flying high up and away, far from all cares! But I got so carried away, I forgot to pay attention to my Dad's instructions. Oh, well, you know the rest of the story. So take it from me. If you're flying, driving, or whatever, obey the rules and you won't end up like me. Thank you for inviting me to the Saturnalia.

THERESA ORSINI

Ed Emberley's Paul Bunyan, mighty logger, looms over an ordinary-sized figure to emphasize size by contrast. American tall tales, epitomized by the Bunyan stories, tend to stress great strength and size.
(From the book *The Story of Paul Bunyan* by Barbara and Ed Emberley. Copyright © 1963 by Prentice-Hall, Inc. Published by Prentice-Hall, Inc., Englewood Cliffs, New Jersey 07632.

LEGENDS AND TALL TALES

Legends are folk stories about real or imaginary people; they may have some basis in fact, but they are largely embroidered with fancy. It is difficult to tell where fact stops and imagination takes over because the stories come to us by the vehicle of all folklore—word of mouth. What may have started as a report of what nearly happened, soon became a report of what *did* happen; many storytellers elaborated reports of a hero's exploits until they became full-blown legends. The result is an intricate interweaving of fact and fiction. A grain of truth then, however small, lies at the core of legends.

Each country has its folk heroes, who exemplify character traits its people value. The discussion here centers on stories of American legendary heroes[34] that are called tall tales because the truth is stretched so much in them that they surpass belief. No human could possibly accomplish the deeds attributed to their protagonists. The characters in some tall tales are people who really lived, and many are fictions, but all have grown larger than life in the tales.

American tall tales are a combination of history, myth, and fact. For example, Davy Crockett, Johnny Appleseed, and Daniel Boone were real people, but their stories have made them larger than life, accomplished in feats no mortal would dare. On the other hand, Paul Bunyan is supposedly the creation of a Madison Avenue advertising agency. Mythic men like John Henry (who represents all steel drivers, not just the one), Pecos Bill, and Mike Fink vivify the Yankee work ethic, the brawn and muscle required to develop America. Such folk heroes were created by people who needed idols and symbols of strength as they built a new country. Thus, their heroes are the mightiest, strongest, most daring lumberjacks, railroad men, coal miners, riverboat drivers, and steelmakers possible.

Although tall tales gave early settlers symbols of strength, they also served another need, offsetting the harsh realities of an untamed land. The exaggerated humor and blatant lies in tall tales added zest to and lightened a life of hard labor.

Children, too, love the exaggerated humor and lies that mark the tall tales. They laugh when Paul Bunyan's loggers tie bacon to their feet and skate across the huge griddle to grease it. The thought of Slue-Foot Sue bouncing skyward every time her bustle hits the ground produces giggles. And when Pecos Bill falls out of the covered wagon, children can picture the abandoned infant scrambling toward the coyote mother who eventually raises him with the rest of the coyote pack. Paul Bunyan's folks couldn't rock his cradle fast enough so they put it in the ocean; the waves there are still especially rough because of the strength of Paul's kicking. Because the hero in tall tales is all-powerful, readers know that he will overcome any problem. The suspense is created, then, in *how* the problem will be solved.

Teaching Idea

HERO TALES (I-A) There are many different stories and variants about the adventures of the American tall tale heroes. Reading them aloud, telling them, and having children tell them are happy literary experiences with which to acquaint them with their own folk heroes. Children will look for the zaniest exaggerations and wildest portrayals of character, for it is one time that lying is condoned and the person who tells the most outlandish whopper is applauded.

Activity: Teacher to Student

LEGITIMATE LIES OR SWAPPING WHOPPERS (I) Read *Whoppers: Tall Tales and Other Lies Collected from America Folklore* by Alvin Schwartz (Lippincott, 1975). Form a group to explore tall tales. There are many things you can do to make your learning exciting. Choose some from the following:

1. Make a papier-mâché model of your hero. (Be certain the clothes are appropriate for the occupation.)

2. Draw a picture of your hero to place on a large map of the United States in the area where he lived.

3. Using a corrugated carton, create a diorama of one of your hero's wildest adventures.

4. Write a new adventure for your hero. (Remember to exaggerate wildly.) What would happen if your hero met another tall tale hero?

5. Have a contest to see who can tell the biggest whopper involving a folk hero.

6. Put the story of your character on slides and recite the story. Use a recording for background music.

7. Make up a ballad about your folk character. Sing it or say it as a group.

8. Although women do not appear as frequently as men in American folklore, some are becoming folk heroines. Select a famous woman, such as Harriet Tubman, Annie Christmas (longshorewoman), Annie Oakley, Sacajawea, or Pocohantas, and create a tall tale about her.

9. Make up a game board using symbols associated with the various characters in tall tales.

Teaching Idea

FOLK HEROES IN AMERICAN LITERATURE (I-A)   American folk heroes reflect the values, aspirations, and fears of the pioneer people by whom they were created; knowing about the folk heroes gives a fine understanding of American history during the time when democracy was being established, geographic frontiers were being explored, and complex industrialization was emerging. Reading about folk heroes shows that a culture may be studied through its literature as well as through its history or social studies texts.

Activity: Teacher to Student

DANIEL BOONE (I-A)   There are many things to do to enjoy Daniel Boone tall tales more. You can locate a reproduction of the painting *Daniel Boone Coming through the Cumberland Gap,* by George Bingham. Look at it carefully to see if Boone's strength of character is seen in his face.

Examine a map of the territory Daniel Boone explored. Blazing the "Wilderness Trail," which extended three hundred miles through mountainous terrain from Virginia to Kentucky, was a heroic accomplishment. The danger from Indians and physical elements were not too much for Daniel Boone. Read some biographies of Daniel Boone and think about some of these questions:

1.   In what way was Daniel Boone's early training related to the greatness he achieved as a skilled hunter and woodsman?

2.   Although Daniel Boone developed into a great hero, what events in his life serve to remind us that he was a real human being with normal human needs?

3.   What qualities did Daniel Boone possess that indicate his greatness? Why do you think he was not a vengeful man?

4.   What was Daniel Boone's impression of himself? Do you think he ever showed signs of weakness?

Read the poem "Daniel Boone" by Stephen Vincent Benét (in *The Gift Outright: America to Her Poets,* edited by Helen Plotz, Greenwillow, 1977). Working with others, from your knowledge of Daniel Boone, write additional verses.

In 1830, the first steam engine built to run on tracks lost a race to a horse-drawn wagon. Yet, a network of railroads soon developed east of the Mississippi and, as the West became settled, need for a cross-country railroad emerged. After the Civil War, one crew of railroad workers started building west and another crew worked eastward. When they met, in 1869, transcontinental railroad transportation began. Among the stories that grew up around railroad men, that of Casey Jones is

JOHN HENRY. (I-A) Read several of the versions of the John Henry legend. Read *A Man Ain't Nothin' But a Man*, by John Killens (Little, Brown, 1975). Use the following questions to guide your thinking:

1. What did John Henry think about the relation between humans and machines?

2. What did John Henry's daddy mean when he said, "The battle is over but the war just started"?

3. How was John Henry interviewed for his jobs loading bales of cotton onto a steamboat, at the railroad camp, and at Big Bend?

4. What differences, if any, did John Henry's marriage to Polly Anne make in his life?

5. What did John Henry mean when he referred to himself as a "natural man"?

6. Why did John Henry have to die? In what ways does the author help us to feel that John Henry still lives?

After you have discussed John Henry's life, form a committee to collect verses for a ballad of John Henry and conduct a group songfest. Refer to "John Henry" in *As I Walked Out One Evening: A Book of Ballads,* selected by Helen Plotz (Greenwillow, 1976). After you have read about his life, write more verses to sing about tunnel drilling, his life with Polly Anne, or more adventures that you invent.

---

probably the most widely known. Of those about steel-driving workers, John Henry's is undoubtedly the best known.

FOLK SONGS AND WORK SONGS

Work songs, often developed as a diversion from boring work, capture the rhythm and spirit of the labor in which their creators were engaged. The songs sing of the values and the life styles of the people who laid the railroads, dug the tunnels and canals, and toted that bale. In addition, ballads were used to inform and to persuade, to foster agreement and unify people.

Artemus Ward, in 1863, said, "Let me write the songs of a nashun and I don't care a cuss who goes to the legislator." The truth underlying this statement remains unchanged to this day. Civil Rights marchers, led by Martin Luther King, Jr. singing "We Shall Overcome," were united in spirit and intent by the song's moving words. The power of the song and its singers focused our nation's attention on the march toward equality. Songs are powerful persuasion in both shaping and preserving our cultural heritage.

Excellent single editions of nursery songs, folk songs, and patriotic songs are available. The best include guitar or piano musical scores, historical notes, and good illustrations coordinated with the text. Robert Quackenbush, Aliki, Glen Rounds, John Langstaff, and Peter Spier offer many excellent sources.[35]

Teaching Idea

TRACING THE ORIGINS OF WORK SONGS (I)   Glen Rounds illustrates a number of work songs and folk ballads that can serve as an adjunct to social studies courses. Use *Casey Jones: The Story of a Brave Engineer* (P-I, Childrens Press, 1968), *Sweet Betsy from Pike* (I, Childrens Press, 1973) and *The Strawberry Roan* (I, Golden Gate, 1970). Each book reflects the regional flavor and occupational trappings of the group responsible for the origin of the song. Farmers, cowboys, railroad hands, and gold miners convey the spirit and the humor of the words. Ask your students to match songs with historic events. The rhythm of beating hoofs, pounding hammers, chugging trains, and lifting bales of cotton underlies the words from the world of work in which they grew.

Activity: Teacher to Student

SONGFEST (I)   For the people who were building our nation—digging canals, laying rails, working the mines—a popular pastime at the end of their hardworking day was to sit around campfires and spin yarns. During these times, and while they worked, they sang.

After reading and learning some of the famous folk songs, plan a songfest for your school. Accompany the singing with piano, guitar, or recordings. Make songbooks or songsheets with the words of each song so that everyone in the audience may join in. Before the introduction of each song, say a few words about the role it played in the lives of the people pioneering our nation. Erie Canal, Clementine, Sixteen Tons, and I Been Workin' on the Railroad are learned quickly.

CRITERIA FOR SELECTING FOLKLORE

The qualities one should look for in folklore are numerous and subtle. Authenticity is perhaps the primary criterion, for the old tales are best in pure form. In addition, look for language (1) that retains the flavor of the oral form—with natural, easily spoken rhythms—and (2) that maintains the dignity of the early retellings. (Rewritten, simplified, controlled-vocabulary versions are inadequate.)

Illustrated versions of folklore are abundant; this is often because the materials have the economic attraction for publishers and others of being copyright- (and, hence, royalty-) free. Look for (1) versions by talented artists—comic strip versions that portray Zeus as a Superman hero destroy the genius of the ancient lore—and (2) versions with illustrations that portray the traditional character of the folk heroes—simpering sex symbols and comic dwarfs insult the literary heritage of the tales.

1. Shel Silverstein, *Where the Sidewalk Ends* (New York: Harper & Row, 1974), p. 9.
2. Ruth Sawyer, *The Way of the Storyteller* (New York: Viking, 1962), pp. 45–46.
3. Jean Piaget, *Genetic Epistemology* (New York: Columbia Univ. Press, 1970), p. 13.
4. F. André Favat, *Child and Tale: The Origins of Interest* (Urbana, Ill.: National Council of Teachers of English, 1977), pp. 38, 50.
5. Bruno Bettelheim, *The Uses of Enchantment: The Meaning and Importance of Fairy Tales* (New York: Knopf, 1976), p. 6.
6. Arthur Applebee, "Children and Stories: Learning the Rules of the Game," *Language Arts,* 56, No. 6 (Sept. 1979), 645.
7. Arthur Applebee, "Where Does Cinderella Live?" in *The Cool Web: The Pattern of Children's Reading,* ed. Margaret Meek, Aidan Warlow, and Griselda Barton (New York: Atheneum, 1978), p. 54.
8. Ian Serraillier, "After Ever Happily," in *A Flock of Words,* comp. David McKay (New York: Harcourt Brace Jovanovich, 1970), p. 145.
9. Iona and Peter Opie, *The Oxford Dictionary of Nursery Rhymes* (New York: Oxford Univ. Press, 1951), p. 27.
10. Northrop Frye, *The Well-Tempered Critic* (Bloomington, Ind.: Indiana Univ. Press, 1963), p. 25.
11. Walter De La Mare as quoted in William S. Baring-Gould and Cecil Baring-Gould, *The Annotated Mother Goose* (New York: Bramhall House, 1962), p. 21.
12. Maurice Sendak, "Mother Goose's Garnishings," *Book Week,* Fall Children's Issue, *Chicago Sun Times,* 31 Oct. 1965, pp. 5, 38–40.
13. Anon., "Hector Proctector," in *Book of Nursery and Mother Goose Rhymes,* ed. Marguerite de Angeli (New York: Doubleday, 1954), p. 111.
14. Susan Jeffers, *Three Jovial Huntsmen: A Mother Goose Rhyme* (Scarsdale, N.Y.: Bradbury, 1973), unpaged.
15. Elizabeth Cook, *The Ordinary and the Fabulous* (Cambridge: Cambridge Univ. Press, 1969), p. 7.
16. Arthur Applebee, *The Child's Concept of Story* (Chicago: Univ. of Chicago Press, 1978), p. 44.
17. Marian Roalfe Cox, *Cinderella: Three Hundred and Forty-Five Variants* (n.p.: published for the Folklore Society by David Nutt, 1893), p. x.
18. Max Lüthi, *Once Upon a Time: On the Nature of Fairy Tales,* trans. Lee Chadeayne and Paul Gottwald (New York: Unger, 1970), pp. 21–34.
19. Cited in *The Web,* An Ohio State Univ. Publication (Winter 1978), pp. 3–4.
20. X. J. Kennedy, *The Phantom Ice Cream Man: More Nonsense Verse,* illus. David McPhail (New York: Atheneum, 1979), p. 31.
21. Paul Heins, "Sonnet," *Horn Book Magazine,* Feb. 1979, p. 115.
22. Winifred Rosen. Work in progress.
23. Ursula Le Guin, "The Child and the Shadow," *Quarterly Journal of the Library of Congress,* 32, No. 2 (April 1975), 139–48.
24. Northrop Frye, *The Educated Imagination* (Bloomington, Ind.: Indiana Univ. Press, 1964), pp. 53, 57.
25. Cook, *The Ordinary and the Fabulous, p. 3.*
26. Penelope Farmer, *Beginnings: Creation Myths of the World* (New York: Atheneum, 1979), p. 4.

27. Margaret Hodges, *Persephone and the Springtime* (Boston: Little, Brown, 1973), unpaged.
28. Penelope Farmer, *The Story of Persephone* (New York: Morrow, 1973), unpaged.
29. Penelope Proddow, *Demeter and Persephone* (New York: Doubleday, 1972), unpaged.
30. Plan developed by Charlene Colbert-Manning, Elementary Language Arts Teacher. Orange, N.J.
31. Plan developed by Elizabeth Marcellaro. Hackensack, N.J.
32. Ibid.
33. Farmer, *Beginnings: Creation Myths of the World,* pp. 3–4.
34. The legends of King Arthur and Robin Hood, magnificent legends from England, are discussed in Chapter 9.
35. See Linda Leonard Lamme, "Song Picture Books: A Maturing Genre of Children's Literature," *Language Arts,* 56, No. 4 (April 1979), 400–47, for further titles.

Professional References

Applebee, Arthur. *The Child's Concept of Story*. Univ. of Chicago Press, 1978.

————. "Children and Stories: Learning the Rules of the Game." *Language Arts,* 56, No. 6 (Sept. 1979), 641–46.

Baring-Gould, William S., and Ceil Baring-Gould. *The Annotated Mother Goose: Nursery Rhymes Old and New*. Illus. Walter Crane, Randolph Caldecott, Kate Greenaway, et al. Clarkson Potter, 1962.

Bettelheim, Bruno. *The Uses of Enchantment: The Meaning and Importance of Fairy Tales*. Knopf, 1976.

Cook, Elizabeth. *The Ordinary and the Fabulous*. Cambridge Univ. Press, 1969.

Cox, Marian Roalfe. *Cinderella: Three Hundred and Forty-Five Variants*. Published for the Folklore Society by David Nutt, 1893.

Favat, F. André. *Child and Tale: The Origins of Interest*. National Council of Teachers of English, 1977.

Frye, Northrop. *The Educated Imagination*. Indiana Univ. Press, 1964.

————. *The Well-Tempered Critic*. Indiana Univ. Press, 1963.

Heins, Paul. "Sonnet." *Horn Book Magazine,* 55, No. 1 (Feb. 1979), 115.

Hepler, Susan Ingrid. "Profile: Tomie de Paola: A Gift to Children. *Language Arts,* 56, No. 3 (March 1979), 296–301.

Lamme, Linda. "Song Picture Books: A Maturing Genre of Children's Literature." *Language Arts,* 56, No. 4 (April 1979), 400–07.

Larkin, David, ed. *The Art of Nancy Ekholm Burkert*. Harper & Row, 1977.

Le Guin, Ursula. "The Child and Shadow." *Quarterly Journal of the Library of Congress,* 32, No. 2 (April 1975), 139–48.

Lüthi, Max. *Once Upon a Time: On the Nature of Fairy Tales*. Trans. Lee Chadeayne and Paul Gottwald. Frederick Ungar, 1970.

Meek, Margaret, Aidan Warlow, and Griselda Barton, eds. *The Cool Web: The Pattern of Children's Reading*. Atheneum, 1978.

Opie, Iona, and Peter Opie, eds. *The Oxford Dictionary of Nursery Rhymes*. Oxford Univ. Press, 1951.

————. *The Oxford Nursery Rhyme Book*. Oxford Univ. Press, 1955.

Piaget, Jean. *Genetic Epistemology*. Columbia Univ. Press, 1970.

Sawyer, Ruth. *The Way of the Storyteller*. Viking, 1962.

Sendak, Maurice. "Mother Goose's Garnishings." *Book Week,* Fall Children's Issue, *Chicago Sun-Times,* 31 Oct. 1965, pp. 5, 38–40.

Children's Books Cited in Chapter

Aesop. *The Fables of Aesop: 143 Moral Tales Retold*. Selec. and ed. Ruth Spriggs. Illus. Frank Baber. Rand, 1976.

————. *The Fables of Aesop*. Trans. Sir Roger L'Estrange. Selec. John J. McKinley. Metropolitan Museum of Art, 1964 (London, 1665).

————. *Jack Kent's Fables of Aesop*. Illus. Jack Kent. Parents, 1972.

————. *More Fables of Aesop*. Illus. Jack Kent. Parents, 1974.

Adams, Adrienne, illus. *The Twelve Dancing Princesses*. Holt, Rinehart & Winston, 1966.

Andersen, Hans Christian. *The Nightingale*. Trans. Eva La Gallienne. Illus. Nancy Ekholm Burkert. Harper & Row, 1965.

Asbjørnsen, Peter Christian, and Jorgen E. Moe. *East of the Sun and West of the Moon*. Illus. Ingri and Edgar Parin d'Aulaire. Viking, 1938.

————. *The Three Billy Goats Gruff*. Illus. Susan Blair. Holt, Rinehart & Winston, 1963.

_____. *The Three Billy Goats Gruff.* Illus. Marcia Brown. Harcourt Brace Jovanovich, 1957.

_____. *The Three Billy Goats Gruff.* Illus. Paul Galdone. Seabury, 1973.

_____. *The Three Billy Goats Gruff.* Illus. William Stobbs. McGraw-Hill, 1968.

Bennett, Charles H. *Bennett's Fables: From Aesop and Others Translated into Human Nature.* Viking, 1978.

Briggs, Raymond. *Jim and the Beanstalk.* Coward, McCann & Geoghegan, 1970.

Brown, Marcia, illus. *The Bun: A Tale from Russia.* Harcourt Brace Jovanovich, 1972.

_____. *Once a Mouse.* Scribner's, 1961.

_____. *Stone Soup.* Scribner's, 1947.

Chase, Richard. *The Jack Tales.* Illus. Berkeley Williams. Houghton Mifflin, 1943.

Dahl, Roald. *James and the Giant Peach.* Illus. Nancy Ekholm Burkert. Knopf, 1961.

D'Aulaire, Ingri and Edgar Parin. *Book of Greek Myths.* Doubleday, 1962.

_____. *Norse Gods and Giants.* Doubleday, 1967.

De Beaumont, Madame. *Beauty and the Beast.* Bradbury, 1978.

De Paola, Tomie. *The Clown of God.* Harcourt Brace Jovanovich, 1978.

_____. *Helga's Dowry.* Harcourt Brace Jovanovich, 1977.

_____. *The Lady of Guadalupe.* Holiday House, 1980.

_____. *The Prince of the Dolomites.* Harcourt Brace Jovanovich, 1980.

_____. *Strega Nona.* Prentice-Hall, 1975.

De Regniers, Beatrice Schenk. *Red Riding Hood.* Illus. Edward Gorey. Atheneum, 1972.

Domanska, Janina, illus. *Little Red Hen.* Macmillan, 1973.

Emberley, Barbara. *Drummer Hoff.* Illus. Ed Emberley. Prentice-Hall, 1967.

_____. *The Story of Paul Bunyan.* Illus. Ed Emberley. Prentice-Hall, 1963.

Farmer, Penelope. *Beginnings: Creation Myths of the World.* Atheneum, 1979.

_____. *Daedalus and Icarus.* Illus. Chris Connor. Harcourt Brace Jovanovich, 1971.

_____. *The Story of Persephone.* Illus. Graham McCallum. Morrow, 1973.

Galdone, Paul, illus. *The Gingerbread Boy.* Seabury, 1975.

_____. *The Hare and the Tortoise.* McGraw-Hill, 1962.

_____. *Henny Penny.* Seabury, 1968.

_____. *The History of Mother Twaddle and the Marvelous Achievement of Her Son Jack.* Seabury, 1974.

_____. *The Little Red Hen.* Seabury, 1973.

_____. *The Magic Porridge Pot.* Seabury, 1976.

_____. *Three Aesop Fox Fables.* Seabury, 1971.

_____. *The Three Bears.* Seabury, 1972.

_____. *The Three Little Pigs.* Seabury, 1970.

_____. *The Three Wishes.* McGraw-Hill, 1961.

Green, Roger Lancelyn, ed. *A Book of Myths.* Illus. Joan Kiddell-Monroe. Dutton, 1965.

Grimm, Jakob and Wilhelm. *The Bremen Town Musicians.* Illus. Paul Galdone. McGraw-Hill, 1968.

_____. *The Bremen Town Musicians.* Retold by Ruth Gross. Illus. Jack Kent. Scholastic, 1975.

_____. *Briar Rose: The Story of the Sleeping Beauty.* Illus. Margery Gill. Walck, 1972.

_____. *The Donkey Prince.* Adapted by M. Jean Craig. Illus. Barbara Cooney. Doubleday, 1977.

_____. *The Elves and the Shoemaker.* Illus. Katrin Brandt. Follett, 1967.

_____. *The Elves and the Shoemaker.* Retold by Freya Littledale. Illus. Brinton Turkle. Four Winds-Scholastic, 1975.

_____. *Fairy Tales.* Illus. Arthur Rackham. Viking, 1973.

_____. *The Frog Prince.* Illus. Paul Galdone. McGraw-Hill, 1975.

_____. *Hans in Luck.* Illus. Felix Hoffmann. Atheneum, 1975.

_____. *Hansel and Gretel.* Trans. Elizabeth D. Crawford. Illus. Lisbeth Zwerger. Morrow, 1979.

_____. *Hansel and Gretel.* Retold by Ruth B. Gross. Illus. Margot Tomes. Scholastic, 1974.

_____. *Hansel and Gretel.* Illus. Susan Jeffers. Dial, 1980.

_____. *Hansel and Gretel.* Illus. Arnold Lobel. Delacorte, 1971.

_____. *Hansel and Gretel.* Trans. Charles Scribner, Jr. Illus. Adrienne Adams. Scribner's, 1975.

_____. *The Juniper Tree and Other Tales from Grimm.* 2 vols. Selec. Lore Segal and Maurice Sendak. Trans. Lore Segal and Randall Jarrell. Illus. Maurice Sendak. Farrar, Straus & Giroux, 1973.

_____. *Kinder- und Hausmärchen.* 1812.

_____. *Rapunzel.* Illus. Felix Hoffmann. Harcourt Brace Jovanovich, 1961.

_____. *Rapunzel.* Illus. Bernadette Watts. Crowell, 1975.

_____. *Rumpelstiltskin.* Illus. William Stobbs. Walck, 1970.

_____. *Rumpelstiltskin.* Retold by Edith Tarcov. Illus. Edward Gorey. Four Winds-Scholastic, 1973.

_____. *The Seven Ravens.* Illus. Felix Hoffmann. Harcourt Brace Jovanovich, 1963.

_____. *The Shoemaker and the Elves.* Illus. Adrienne Adams. Scribner's, 1960.

_____. *The Sleeping Beauty.* Illus. Warwick Hutton. Atheneum, 1979.

_____. *The Sleeping Beauty.* Illus. Trina Schart Hyman. Little, Brown, 1977.

_____. *Snow White.* Trans. Paul Heins. Illus. Trina Schart Hyman. Little, Brown, 1974.

_____. *Snow White and Rose Red.* Trans. Wayne Andrews. Illus. Adrienne Adams. Scribner's, 1964.

_____. *Snow White and Rose Red.* Illus. Barbara Cooney. Delacorte, n.d.

204

_____. _Snow White and the Seven Dwarfs._ Illus. Wanda Gág. Coward, McCann & Geoghegan, 1938.

_____. _Snow White and the Seven Dwarfs: A Tale from the Brothers Grimm._ Trans. Randall Jarrell. Illus. Nancy Ekholm Burkert. Farrar, Straus & Giroux, 1972.

_____. _Thorn Rose._ Illus. Errol Le Cain. Bradbury, 1977.

_____. _Tom Thumb._ Trans. Anthea Bell. Illus. Otto S. Svend. Larousse, 1976.

_____. _Tom Thumb._ Illus. Felix Hoffmann. Atheneum, 1973.

_____. _Tom Thumb._ Illus. William Wiesner. Walck, 1974.

_____. _The Traveling Musicians._ Illus. Hans Fischer. Harcourt Brace Jovanovich, 1955.

Haley, Gail E. _A Story, A Story: An African Tale._ Atheneum, 1970.

Harper, Wilhelmina, reteller. _The Gunniwolf._ Illus. William Wiesner. Dutton, 1967.

Hodges, Margaret. _Persephone and the Springtime: A Greek Myth._ Illus. Arvis Stewart. Little, Brown, 1973.

Hogrogian, Nonny. _One Fine Day._ Macmillan, 1971.

Hollander, Paul. _The Labors of Hercules._ Illus. Judith Ann Lawrence. Putnam's, 1965.

Hutchinson, Veronica S. _Henny Penny._ Illus. Leonard Lubin. Little, Brown, 1976.

Hutton, Warwick, illus. _Noah and the Great Flood._ Atheneum, 1977.

Jacobs, Joseph, ed. _English Fairy Tales._ Illus. John D. Batten. Dover, 1967.

_____. _Hereafterthis._ Illus. Paul Galdone. McGraw-Hill, 1973.

_____. _Jack and the Beanstalk._ Illus. Margery Gill. Walck, 1975.

_____. _Jack and the Beanstalk._ Illus. William Stobbs. Delacorte, 1969.

_____. _The Three Little Pigs._ Illus. William Pène du Bois. Viking, 1962.

Jagendorf, Moritz A. _Noodlehead Stories from Around the World._ Illus. Shane Miller. Vanguard, 1957.

Jeffers, Susan, illus. _Three Jovial Huntsmen: A Mother Goose Rhyme._ Bradbury, 1973.

Kennedy, X. J. _The Phantom Ice Cream Man: More Nonsense Verse._ Illus. David McPhail. Atheneum, 1979.

La Fontaine, Jean de. _The Lion and the Rat._ Illus. Brian Wildsmith. Watts, 1963.

_____. _The North Wind and the Sun._ Illus. Brian Wildsmith. Watts, 1964.

_____. _The Rich Man and the Shoemaker._ Illus. Brian Wildsmith. Watts, 1965.

Lear, Edward, and Ogden Nash. _The Scroobius Pip._ Illus. Nancy Ekholm Burkert. Harper & Row, 1968.

Le Guin, Ursula. _A Wizard of Earthsea._ Illus. Ruth Robbins. Parnassus, 1968.

McDermott, Gerald. _Anansi the Spider: A Tale from the Ashanti._ Holt, Rinehart & Winston, 1972.

McKee, David. _The Man Who Was Going to Mind the House._ Abelard Schuman, 1972.

McLeish, Kenneth, reteller. _Chicken Licken._ Illus. Jutta Ash. Bradbury, 1974.

Merrill, Jean. _Red Riding._ Illus. Ronni Solbert. Pantheon, 1968.

Montresor, Beni. _Cinderella: From the Opera by Gioacchino Rossini._ Knopf, 1965.

Mosel, Arlene. _The Funny Little Woman._ Illus. Blair Lent. Dutton, 1972.

Ness, Evaline. _Tom Tit Tot._ Scribner's, 1965.

Newman, Robert. _The Twelve Labors of Hercules._ Illus. Charles Keeping. Crowell, 1972.

Nichols, Ruth. _Marrow of the World._ Illus. Trina Schart Hyman. Atheneum, 1972.

Perrault, Charles. _Cinderella._ Illus. Marcia Brown. Scribner's, 1954.

_____. _Cinderella_ Illus. Errol Le Cain. Bradbury, 1972.

_____. _Cinderella._ Retold by C. S. Evans. Illus. Arthur Rackham. Viking, 1972.

_____. _Histoires ou contes du temps passe; avec des moralities._ 1697.

_____. _Little Red Riding Hood._ Illus. Bernadette. World, 1968.

_____. _Little Red Riding Hood._ Illus. Paul Galdone. McGraw-Hill, 1974.

_____. _Little Red Riding Hood._ Illus. William Stobbs. Walck, 1973.

_____. _The Sleeping Beauty._ Retold by C. S. Evans. Illus. Arthur Rackham. Viking, 1972.

_____. _The Sleeping Beauty._ Trans. and illus. David Walker. Crowell, 1977.

Proddow, Penelope, trans. _Demeter and Persephone._ Illus. Barbara Cooney. Doubleday, 1972.

Roach, Marilynne. _Two Roman Mice._ Crowell, 1975.

Sawyer, Ruth. _Journey Cake, Ho!_ Illus. Robert McCloskey. Viking, 1953.

Sendak, Maurice, illus. _Hector Protector and As I Went Over the Water._ Harper & Row, 1965.

Serraillier, Ian. _Clashing Rocks: The Story of Jason._ Illus. William Stobbs. Walck, 1964.

_____. _A Fall from the Sky: The Story of Daedalus._ Illus. William Stobbs. Walck, 1966.

_____. _The Gorgon's Head: The Story of Perseus._ Illus. William Stobbs. Walck, 1962.

_____. _Heracles the Strong._ Illus. Rocco Negri. Walck, 1970.

_____. _Way of Danger: The Story of Theseus._ Illus. William Stobbs. Walck, 1963.

Shub, Elizabeth, trans. _The Fisherman and His Wife._ Illus. Monika Laimgruber. Greenwillow, 1979.

Silverstein, Shel. _Where the Sidewalk Ends._ Harper & Row, 1974.

Singer, Isaac Bashevis. _Why Noah Chose the Dove._ Trans. Elizabeth Shub. Illus. Eric Carle. Farrar, Straus & Giroux, 1974.

Sleator, William. *The Angry Moon*. Illus. Blair Lent. Little, Brown, 1970.

Spier, Peter. *Fox Went Out on a Chilly Night*. Doubleday, 1961.

_____. *Hurrah, We're Outward Bound*. Doubleday, 1968.

_____. *Noah's Ark*. Doubleday, 1977.

Spray, Carole. *Will O' the Wisp: Folk Tales and Legends of New Brunswick*. Brunswick Press, 1979.

Steel, Flora Annie, reteller. *Tattercoats: An Old English Tale*. Illus. Diane Goode. Bradbury, 1976.

Still, James. *Jack and the Wonder Beans*. Illus. Margot Tomes. Putnam's, 1977.

Stobbs, William, illus. *Henny Penny*. Follett, 1970.

_____. *Johnny Cake*. Viking, 1973.

Tarcov, Edith, reteller. *The Frog Prince*. Illus. James Marshall. Four Winds-Scholastic, 1974.

Tolkien, J. R. R. *The Hobbit*. Houghton Mifflin, 1938.

Turkle, Brinton. *Deep in the Forest*. Dutton, 1976.

Walker, Barbara. *Teeny Tiny and the Witch Woman*. Illus. Michael Foreman. Pantheon, 1975.

Wiesner, William. Illus. *Turnabout*. Seabury, 1972.

Wildsmith, Brian. *Brian Wildsmith's Mother Goose: A Collection of Nursery Rhymes*. Watts, 1964.

Zemach, Harve. *Duffy and the Devil: A Cornish Tale*. Illus. Margot Zemach. Farrar, Straus & Giroux, 1973.

_____. *Nail Soup*. Illus. Margot Zemach. Follett, 1964.

Recommended Reading

Mother Goose and Nursery Rhymes

Many outstanding illustrators have made unique interpretations of the familiar nursery rhymes. Susan Jeffers evokes a dreamlike quality in *If Wishes Were Horses and Other Rhymes* (N-P, Dutton, 1979), while Wallace Tripp uses rollicking humor in his collections: *A Great Big Ugly Man Came Up and Tied His Horse to Me: A Book of Nonsense Verse* (N-P, Little, Brown, 1973) and *Granfa' Grig Had a Pig and Other Rhymes Without Reason from Mother Goose* (N-P, Little, Brown, 1976). Arnold Lobel, too, uses humor in *Gregory Griggs and Other Nursery Rhyme People* (N, Greenwillow, 1978).

There are many good comprehensive collections of Mother Goose verses, including Raymond Briggs's *The Mother Goose Treasury* (N-P, Coward, McCann & Geoghegan, 1966), Alice and Martin Provensen's *The Mother Goose Book* (N-P, Random House, 1976), and Brian Alderson's collection *Cakes and Custard: Children's Rhymes,* illustrated by Helen Oxenbury (N-P, Morrow, 1975). *Nicola Bayley's Book of Nursery Rhymes* (N-P, Knopf, 1977) uses luminous colors to interpret a small collection of well-known verses, while Tasha Tudor's characteristic old-fashioned pastels illustrate her *Mother Goose* (N-P, Walck, 1944). In contrast, Leslie Brooke chose bright colors as well as black and white to provide action in *Ring O' Roses* (N-P, Warne, 1923.)

Each year finds more and more folk and fairy tales on the market; illustrated single tales and new collections abound. Nearly a century ago Andrew Lang compiled traditional stories in a series of color books. These are now being reissued under the editorial eye of folklore authorities; *The Blue Fairy Book,* edited by Brian Alderson (I, Kestrel-Viking, 1978 [1889]) is the first of a planned series. Virginia Haviland selected a large group of stories for Raymond Briggs to illustrate in his whimsical style for *Fairy Tale Treasury* (P-I, Coward, McCann & Geoghegan, 1972). Eric Carle retells and illustrates seven Grimm tales in *Eric Carle's Storybook* (P-I, Watts, 1976), while Anne Rockwell gives us *The Three Bears and Fifteen Other Stories* (P, Crowell, 1975) and *The Old Woman and Her Pig and Ten Other Stories* (P, Crowell, 1979). Brian Alderson translated and compiled an attractive collection of *The Brothers Grimm Popular Folk Tales,* illustrated by Michael Foreman (P-I, Doubleday, 1978).

Several outstanding illustrators are known for their interpretations of familiar tales, among them Felix Hoffmann, whose brilliant colors shine in many books, including *The Bearskinner* (P, Atheneum, 1978). Errol Le Cain, too, has given us many fine books, including *The Twelve Dancing Princesses* (P, Viking, 1978). Margot Tomes draws plain, almost homely characters that add a touch of humor to Wanda Gág's translations of *The Sorcerer's Apprentice* (P, Coward, McCann & Geoghegan, 1979) and *Jorinda and Joringel* (P, Coward, McCann & Geoghegan, 1978). A different interpretation is given to *Jorinda and Joringel,* translated by Elizabeth Shub (P, Scribner's, 1968), by Adrienne Adams's delicate watercolors.

Alan Barrett's illustrations for Philippa Pearce's retelling of *Beauty and the Beast* (P-I, Crowell, 1972) differ dramatically from Mercer Mayer's bold, vividly colored pictures for Marianna Mayer's adaption of the same story (P, Four Winds-Scholastic, 1978). Similarly, for *Puss in Boots,* Paul Galdone's humorous caricatures (P, Seabury, 1976) offer contrast for Marcia Brown's fluid French paintings (P, Scribner's, 1952).

Ruth Manning Sanders compiled several volumes that feature tales about various kinds of folklore characters. *A Book of Monsters,* illustrated by Robin Jacques (I, Dutton, 1976), and *A Book of Giants,* illustrated by Robin Jacques (I, Dutton, 1962), offer yet another avenue for exploring traditional literature.

Virginia Haviland is responsible for an extremely valuable series of books, which includes *Favorite Fairy Tales Told in Denmark,* illustrated by Margot Zemach (I, Little, Brown, 1971), *Favorite Fairy Tales Told in Ireland,* illustrated by Artur Marokvia (I, Little, Brown, 1961), and others that feature the lore of each country. Idris Shah compiled *World Tales* (I, Atheneum, 1977), another excellent collection of stories from around the world.

Each culture offers its own unique tales or variants of universal tales. *It Could Always be Worse: A Yiddish Folk Tale,* retold and illustrated by Margot Zemach (P, Farrar, Straus & Giroux, 1976), and *Could Anything be Worse?: A Yiddish Tale,* retold and illustrated by Marilyn Hirsh (P, Holiday House, 1974), are the same story about a man who seeks help from the Rabbi when the noise and crowding in his home threaten to defeat him. Each illustrator adds her own mark to the humorous story.

Verna Aardema's retellings of several African tales are beautifully illustrated by Leo and Diane Dillon. *Why Mosquitoes Buzz in People's Ears* (P-I, Dial, 1975) and *Who's in Rabbit's House?* (P-I, Dial, 1977) are traditional animal legends. Aardema also retells *The Riddle of the Drum: A Tale from Tizapan, Mexico,* illustrated by Tony Chen (P-I, Four Winds-Scholastic, 1979).

The Clay Pot Boy, adapted by Cynthia Jameson and illustrated by Arnold Lobel (P-I, Coward, McCann & Geoghegan, 1973), is a Russian tale with some of the same characteristics as ''The Gingerbread Boy.'' Another Russian tale, whose message is that even the tiniest creature may be able to help solve a difficult task, is told in *The Turnip,* illustrated by Janina Domanska (P, Macmillan, 1969), and in Alexei Tolstoy's *The Great Big Enormous Turnip,* illustrated by Helen Oxenbury (P, Watts, 1969).

Pura Belpré has retold Puerto Rican tales in *The Dance of the Animals,* illustrated by Paul Galdone (P, Warne, 1972), and in a collection, *Once in Puerto Rico,* illustrated by Christine Price (P-I, Warne, 1973). Ashley Bryan's *The Dancing Granny* (P, Atheneum, 1977) is a West Indian adaptation of the African Anansi tales.

The folklore that became America's had its roots in the traditional literature of the countries from which its people came. Molly Garrett Bang adapted and illustrated *Wiley and the Hairy Man* (P, Macmillan, 1976), a story about a young boy terrorized by a swamp creature until he outwits it. Joel Chandler Harris is known for his collection *The Complete Tales of Uncle Remus* (I, compiled by Richard Chase, illustrated by Arthur Frost et al., Houghton Mifflin, 1955). Ennis Rees retells some of the famous stories about *Brer Rabbit and His Tricks* (P, illustrated by Edward Gorey, Scott, Foresman, 1967) and others in *More of Brer Rabbit's Tricks* (P, illustrated by Edward Gorey, Scott, Foresman, 1968). The familiar Tar Baby story can be compared with the African and Jamaican versions.

Fables

Collections of fables are more plentiful than are single editions, although even the former do not abound. Eve Rice adapted and illustrated *Once In a Wood: Ten Tales from Aesop* (P, Greenwillow, 1979) in easy-to-read format. Among the standard collections are *Aesop's Fables,* illustrated by Boris Artzybasheff (I, Viking, 1933), and *Aesop's Fables,* selected and adapted by Louis Untermeyer, illustrated by Alice and Martin Provensen (I, Golden, 1966). A classic volume that has been reissued is: *The Caldecott Aesop. A Facsimile of the 1883 Edition by Alfred Caldecott,* illustrated by Randolph Caldecott (I-A, Doubleday, 1978).

Myths

Penelope Proddow's *Art Tells a Story: Greek and Roman Myths* (I-A, Doubleday, 1979) is a selection of myths accompanied by photographs of various art works that interpret them. Isaac Asi-

mov explores our language as it reflects *Words from the Myths,* illustrated by William Barss (I-A, Houghton Mifflin, 1961). Bernard and Dorothy Evslin and Ned Hoopes produced a valuable compendium, *Heroes, Gods and Monsters of the Greek Myths,* illustrated by William Hunter (I-A, Four Winds-Scholastic, 1967), while Robert Graves gives a concise overview of *Greek Gods and Heroes,* illustrated by Dimitris Davis (I, Doubleday, 1960). Ann Terry White's *The Golden Treasury of Myths and Legends,* illustrated by Alice and Martin Provensen (I, Golden, 1959), is a large, well-illustrated reference.

Bernard Evslin recounts the epic tales of the Trojan War in *Greeks Bearing Gifts: The Epics of Achilles and Ulysses,* illustrated by Lucy Martin Bitzer (I-A, Four Winds-Scholastic, 1976). Doris Gates provides a valuable series of books, each of which focuses on the stories of one particular god or goddess. *The Golden God: Apollo,* illustrated by Constantinos Coconis (I-A, Viking, 1973), *Lord of the Sky: Zeus,* illustrated by Robert Handville (I-A, Viking, 1972), and *The Warrior Goddess: Athena,* illustrated by Don Bolognese (I-A, Viking, 1972), are among the best.

Penelope Proddow shows her skill as a storyteller in *Hermes, Lord of Robbers,* illustrated by Barbara Cooney (I, Doubleday, 1971), and *Dionysus and the Pirates* (A, Doubleday, 1970). Roger Lancelyn Green retells the stories associated with the mythical founders and rulers of Thebes in *The Tale of Thebes* (I-A, Cambridge Univ. Press, 1977). Other individual myths are retold in *The Serpent's Teeth: The Story of Cadmus,* illustrated by Chris Connor (I, Harcourt Brace Jovanovich, 1971), by Penelope Farmer, and *The Gorgon's Head,* illustrated by Charles Mikolaycak (I, Little, Brown, 1972), by Margaret Hodges.

Norse mythology is recreated less frequently than that of the Greeks, but several good stories do exist. Dorothy G. Hosford's *Thunder of the Gods,* illustrated by Claire and George Louden (I, Holt, Rinehart & Winston, 1952), is a collection of the best of the Viking tales. Ann Pyk's *The Hammer of Thunder,* illustrated by Jan Pyk (P-I, Putnam's, 1972), is told in picture book format, which makes it accessible to younger readers. One of the most popular Norse myths is retold in two books: Edna Barth's *Balder and the Mistletoe: A Story for the Winter Holidays,* illustrated by Richard Cuffari (I, Seabury, 1979), and Margaret Hodges's *Baldur and the Mistletoe: A Myth of the Vikings,* illustrated by Gerry Hoover (P-I, Little, Brown, 1974).

Legends and Tall Tales

There are several collections of tall tales that will provide hours of fun: Walter Blair's *Tall Tale America,* illustrated by Glen Rounds (I, Coward, McCann & Geoghegan, 1944), Adrien Stoutenburg's *American Tall Tales,* illustrated by Richard M. Powers (I, Viking, 1966), Benjamin A. Botkin's *A Treasury of American Folklore* (I, Crown, 1944), Maria Leach's *The Rainbow Book of American Folk Tales and Legends* (I, World, 1958), and Anne Malcolmson's *Yankee Doodle's Cousins,* illustrated by Robert McCloskey (I, Houghton Mifflin, 1941).

Stories of individual heroes are also available, and include Harold W. Felton's *Pecos Bill and the Mustang,* illustrated by

Leonard Shortall (I, Prentice-Hall, 1965), and *New Tall Tales of Pecos Bill,* illustrated by William Moyers (I, Prentice-Hall, 1958). Paul Bunyan is perhaps one of America's most loved legendary heroes; his story is told by Glen Rounds in *Ol' Paul, the Mighty Logger* (I, Holiday House, 1976). Ezra Jack Keats created appropriately bold illustrations for his retelling of *John Henry, an American Legend* (P-I, Pantheon, 1965).

American Indian legends are discussed elsewhere, but two particularly useful retellings are Byrd Baylor's *And It Is Still That Way: Legends Told by Arizona Indian Children* (P-I, Scribner's, 1976) and Richard Erdoes's collection, *The Sound of Flutes and Other Indian Legends,* told by Lame Deer, Jenny Leading Cloud, Leonard Crow Dog, and others, illustrated by Paul Goble (I-A, Pantheon, 1976).

six

e. e. cummings *who knows if the moon's*

who knows if the moon's
a balloon, coming out of a keen city
in the sky —filled with pretty people?
(and if you and i should

get into it, if they
should take me and take you into their balloon,
why then
we'd go up higher with all the pretty people

than houses and steeples and clouds:
go sailing
away and away sailing into a keen
city which nobody's ever visited, where

always
　　　　　it's
　　　　　　Spring) and everyone's
in love and flowers pick themselves[1]

Fantasy and Science Fiction

Fantasy opens doors to worlds of imaginative delight paralleled nowhere in the real world. Yet, the fantastic encounters enrich and illumine children's real experiences and provide new roads to meaning in their own lives.

Fantasy may be defined as fiction in which there is some element not found in the natural world. Like the fairy tale, fantasy hints of the non-natural, of things magical. Size doesn't matter, time doesn't matter, place doesn't matter: the essence of life encapsulated in each being counts. Nonrational phenomena play a significant part in fantasy; scientific explanations are beside the point and natural laws are suspended.

Science fiction is most similar to fantasy in that it is set in worlds that do not correspond to present realities. It differs from fantasy in that the future realities it depicts are often based on extrapolation from scientific principles.

Fantasy may be further categorized as high fantasy and low fantasy, distinctions based on the setting and the type of nonrational phenomenon employed. The setting for low fantasy is the primary world we live in, with nonrational events occurring but unexplained—they simply occur; they are inexplicable. On the other hand, high fantasy occurs in a secondary world where nonrational causality is postulated. The primary world simply does not exist, and the physical and human laws of the secondary world prevail. Time works on a different schedule in secondary worlds, logic functions according to the rules the author spells out, and beings interact and communicate in ways congruous to that world.

It takes time for a lifelong love of fantasy to grow, but there are many times along the way when children respond to fantasy naturally. The rhythms of its language and the subtle images it evokes appeal to readers with special sensibilities to things at once deep and high, elusive and visible.

Fantasy invites wholehearted immersion in its compelling narratives. It is especially important because of the role it plays in the child's imaginative development. Fantasy forges links between language and images, making things unseen seen and making things unknown known. It helps the reader see beyond the concrete world to a world that could be. It helps children deal with what they unconsciously know and feel—those terrors and joys of childhood that are a part of the existential mysteries of life.

Children who never read fanciful stories have a difficult time considering the possibility of fantasy. They seem bound to the literal, the practical, the ordinary. It may be that there is a critical period in which children need to know fantasy in order to be free to suspend disbelief and imagine a world they cannot see. Imagination educated by fantasy leads to visions of worlds beyond the one at hand. Herein lies the necessity of fantasy.

Children cut their teeth on humorous fantasy. Fanciful literature provides them with a number of memorable characters and situations to make them laugh and love to imagine. Some stories offer children the delight of finding that they are smarter than the characters, which makes them feel immensely superior.

An important observation for teachers is that children derive satisfaction from and have their interest sustained by a thread of humor that is common to many books of fancy. Such stories provide a necessary transition, a base for the richness of more sophisticated and complex work by great writers of fantasy.

Great writers of fantasy—J. R. R. Tolkien, C. S. Lewis, Eleanor Cameron, Elizabeth Cook—themselves choose different words to describe the quality peculiar to fairy tale and fantasy. Tolkien uses the word ''faerie'' and takes care to specify that by this he does not mean a small winged creature also called fairy, but rather a quality of feeling called heart's desire—that is, a yearning for a romantic, visionary world. C. S. Lewis describes this quality in terms of the response that certain imaginative works evoke in him. His term is ''joy,'' and in his autobiographical book *Surprised by Joy* he tells of the aesthetic response called forth by such varied works as Beatrix Potter's *The Tale of Squirrel Nutkin,* Norse mythology, and George Macdonald's *Phantasies.* Lewis's joy is neither happiness nor pleasure; rather, he equates it with a Greek word that is translatable into ''Oh, I desire too much.''

Eleanor Cameron describes the response that fantasy evokes in her—in this case, while reading about the death of King Arthur:

His death meant the passing of goodness and courage and idealism, the breaking up of the ring, the scattering of the great knights: all of that gone, perhaps forever. I remember now the almost unutterable poignancy I felt—sadness mixed with longing—yet a sense of exaltation, of having touched something very fine and powerful and strength-giving. For me, as a child, this was equal to the adult experience of Greek or Shakespearean tragedy.[2]

And Elizabeth Cook describes the quality unique to fantasy as ''a sense of the strange, the numinous, the totally Other, of what lies quite beyond human personality and cannot be found in any human relationships.''[3]

The terms we use to try to understand and embrace fantasy—a sense of faerie, heart's desire, joy, unutterable poignancy, a sense of the numinous—are more evocative than definitive. Our purpose as teachers, however, is to understand—rather than to analyze and define—enough aspects of the experience to enable us to start young readers on the path that will lead to a lifetime of delight. We speak with conviction if we have the experience firsthand.

Children move about comfortably in the world of fantasy if they have a secure grasp on what is real and what is make-believe. By about the second grade, children are quite interested in making these distinctions. It is not unusual for a group to become intensely involved in a discussion of what ''could really happen.'' For instance, children break into spontaneous and heated argument about whether Santa Claus, elves, or fairies are real. Teachers aware of the level of development reflected in such discussions may lead children to new insights and help them see that, although fantasy is not real, it can be *true:* it vivifies the truth.

Eventually, distinctions between fantasy and reality become unnecessary; children understand the universal truth that transcends the artificial dichotomy. At this point they are able to move on to that willing suspension of disbelief that imaginative literature evokes, and the wise teacher frees them to do so. A discussion that may have been necessary and desirable at an earlier point in a literary education hampers the appreciation of literature at a later time. Children move effectively in and out of fantasy if granted freedom from explanation; that is, if they are not asked to reconcile the fanciful events with the real world.

To accept the conventions of fantasy, then, becomes a basic rule of the game. The tacit acceptance of make-believe, necessary for the full enjoyment of literature, is illustrated in a scene from Edward Eager's *Half Magic* (I). The incident captures the child's attitude toward fantasizing and seems to say that children know full well that if you have to say what you're doing, it ruins it. As the story opens, four children have just finished reading E. Nesbit's *The Enchanted Castle* (I):

> There was a contented silence when she closed the book, and then, after a little, it began to get discontented.
> Martha broke it, saying what they were all thinking. "Why don't things like that ever happen to *us*?"
> "Magic never happens, not really," said Mark, who was old enough to be sure about this.
> "How do you know?" asked Katharine, who was nearly as old as Mark, but not nearly so sure about anything.
> "Only in fairy stories."
> "It *wasn't* a fairy story. There weren't any dragons or witches or poor woodcutters, just real children like us!"
> They were all talking at once now.
> "They *aren't* like us. We're never in the country for the summer, and walk down strange roads and find castles!"
> "We never go to the seashore and meet mermaids and sand-fairies!"
> "Or go to our uncle's, and there's a magic garden!"
> "If the Nesbit children do stay in the city it's London, and *that's* interesting, and then they find phoenixes and magic carpets! Nothing like that ever happens here!"
> "There's Mrs. Hudson's house," Jane said. "That's a *little* like a castle."
> "There's the Miss Kings' garden."
> "We could *pretend* . . ."
> It was Martha who said this, and the others turned on her.
> "Beast!"
> "Spoilsport!"
> Because of course the only way pretending is any good is if you never say right out that that's what you're doing. Martha knew this perfectly well, but in her youth she sometimes forgot. So now Mark threw a pillow at her, and so did Jane and Katharine. . . .[4]

Fantasy readers, then, know that to say right out that it is pretending is to miss the whole point. If you have to explain—it's lost.

Fantasies seldom reveal their ultimate secrets; they are suggestive and elusive. In some stories, miniature worlds peopled by elves, trolls, and gnomes emphasize the dignity of every little creature. In other stories, human nature is reflected in microcosmic proportion in animal characters. In all fantasy stories, time past and time future may meld into time present, or time may be held still so that a moment in conventional time is years in fantasy time. The quest that is Everyman's takes us to Narnias and Camelots and Prydains.

SMALL WORLDS CLOSE UP

Every cultural group has its traditional sprites, elves, trolls, hobbits, or leprechauns, which go unseen about houses and villages doing their work. Fantasies about toys or miniature beings highlight human emotions by displaying them in action on a miniscule scale. From Arriety in *The Borrowers* (I), by Mary Norton, to Zeee in *Zeee* (P), by Elizabeth Enright, the best and worst in human nature is magnified against a lilliputian backdrop where characters are memorable because of their size.

The soldier in Hans Christian Andersen's *Steadfast Tin Soldier* (P-I) appears all the more heroic because he is a tiny toy with no power over his own fate. Similarly, Thumbelina's dignity blossoms through her search for happiness (*Thumbelina*, P-I). Respect for personhood, woven into the stories, says to children that a person is a person no matter how small.

Pod, Homily, and Arriety, in *The Borrowers*, live under the kitchen floor at Great-Aunt Sophy's and furnish their home with safety pins, postage stamps, and other items carelessly dropped by full-size people. Pod, the father, ventures out collecting whatever the family needs. Borrowing becomes dangerous and supplies run low for them when Aunt Sophy is bedridden, but they survive by their wits. Homily, Pod's wife, believes that humans exist solely to provide the things they need, but, she warns their daughter, Arriety, it is dangerous to be seen by them. Despite her mother's warnings, Arriety makes friends with one of them—the Boy who comes to stay at the old house. When the cook discovers the presence of the Borrowers and calls the rat catcher to exterminate them, it is the Boy who silently helps them escape.

So as not to offend their pride, the Boy helps the Borrowers in ways unknown to them. Eventually, they are forced to find a new home, and their subsequent life is followed in *The Borrowers Afield* (I), *The Borrowers Aloft* (I), and *The Borrowers Afloat* (I), in which they continue their search for a peaceful and safe place to live.

Fantasy worlds inhabited by inanimate objects and fanciful creatures with human thought, language, and feelings become real to young children who know them. Children's thinking goes through an animistic period when favorite toys and stuffed animals take on lives and personalities of their own. Fine fantasy writers create stories on the sub-

stance of a correspondence to these children's beliefs.

In *The Return of the Twelves* (I-A), by Pauline Clarke, Max respects the dignity of the twelve toy soldiers he finds under a loose board in the attic of an old English home once occupied by the Brontës. He realizes the soldiers will be offended if he does not let them conduct their own affairs. Max's attitude toward the Twelves, like the attitude of the Boy toward the Borrowers, underscores the importance of respecting the small and the weak:

He had an instinct that if he were to pick them all up, put them into the shoe box where he kept them, and carry them down, they might think it a terrible insult. They might freeze again at once, to pay him back. What he had to do was to think of some better way and let them discover it.[5]

Through hours of watching and listening Max learns that the soldiers once belonged to Charlotte, Emily, Branwell, and Anne Brontë. The fact of their former ownership leads to a problem when an

In *The Return of the Twelves*, twelve courageous and intrepid toy soldiers find an ingenious means of transport back to their museum home.
(Reprinted by permission of Coward, McCann & Geoghegan, Inc., from *The Return of the Twelves* by Pauline Clark. Illustrations copyright © 1963 by Coward McCann, Inc.)

American museum director wants to buy them for a great deal of money. The soldiers decide to go to their rightful home, Haworth, which has now become the Brontë Museum. Fiercely proud of their competence, they reject being packed up and jostled off to the Museum and plan to go there on their own:

[The] plan was bold and desperate, but if it worked it would enable the noble Young Men to reenter their original home with the kind of dignity which befitted them, and completely . . . under their own steam. This was very important to Max, for he had quite early realized that part of their life depended on their being left to do things by themselves and not being interfered with. He could oversee and suggest, but not dictate. And they had undertaken the whole march without consulting him.[6]

The miniature soldiers make the journey on foot, as any self-respecting infantrymen would. Max realizes that they are beings in their own right and is tactful as he gives the courageous troops the means to leave the attic and travel through rough terrain to the Brontë Museum, which lies far away in toy-soldier miles.

For children there is inevitable humor and delight in being big in relation to worlds made small, but there is also an identification with the small—as they are, relative to the adults around them. At one point in *The Return of the Twelves*, Butter Crashey, separated from his eleven friends, finds himself standing on a mantelpiece in a strange farmhouse. He echoes the belief of many young children in a beneficent being who will come to the rescue. The thought that comforts him is

. . . that the rest would surely tell the Genii of his plight. . . . And if the chief Genii, and the older Genii, and the gentle Genii could not effect his rescue, then what were Genii for?[7]

This affirmation of a shared belief in a benevolent being wins readers to the side of the small soldiers.

Pauline Clarke maintains the integrity of the idiosyncratic personality of each of the toy soldiers, gliding deftly through the unusual blend of reality and fantasy, and of past and present.

The importance of a name to creatures, however small, is shown in Tove Jansson's tales about

A tiny "creep" explains how his recent acquisition of a name —Teety-woo—makes all the difference. Things no longer just happen; now they happen to Teety-woo, a creature with an identity.
(Illustration from *Tales from Moominvalley* by Tove Jansson. 1964. Walck edition. By permission of Ernest Benn Publishers, Kent, England.)

the Moomins, little beings that inhabit the lands of Scandinavia. In *Tales from Moominvalley* (I), Snufkin meets a tiny "creep" during one of his long wanderings through the wilderness and asks his name.

"I'm so small that I haven't got a name," the creep said eagerly. "As a matter of fact, nobody's even asked me about it before. . . ."[8]

Activity: Teacher to Student

DIORAMAS (P-I) Make a diorama of the Borrowers's home. Use the same kinds of items they use to furnish their house. Spools become tables, thimbles become bathtubs, and postage stamps become pictures for the walls. Use miniature dolls for Pod, Homily, and Arriety. See what else you can find around school that people drop carelessly, such as rubber bands and paper clips, that can be turned into useful items for the Borrowers.

Snufkin acceeds to the creep's plea for a name, and thoughtfully selects "Teety-woo" as a good one for him because it has a light melodic beginning and a little sadness to round it off.

Teety-woo, ecstatic about being named, soon makes a name plate and begins truly living a real life rather than drifting around from one place to another. Having a name makes all the difference to the little creep, for later, when he and Snufkin meet again, he says:

Now I'm a person, and everything that happens *means* something. Because it doesn't only happen, it happens to *me*, Teety-woo. And Teety-woo may think this or think that about it, as the case may be—if you see what I mean?[9]

Once he had a name everything about him took on importance, so that even his feelings were worthy of consideration. The reader's satisfaction in this book and the others in the Moomin series comes from such respect for the small and from the brilliant language in which it is cast.

Russell Hoban's *The Mouse and His Child* (I) was relatively unnoticed immediately after its publication in 1967, but the significance of the book is now recognized. The story operates on several levels of meaning: at the surface, it is the story of a clockwork mouse father and son who are tossed onto a garbage dump. Manny Rat, villain, rules the dump kingdom and threatens to take their innards for his spare parts collection. The mouse and his child not only want to avoid Manny Rat's plans for them, but desperately long to become self-winding

and find a permanent home in a doll's house. Adventures, with narrow escapes from the enemy rat, include a bank robbery, battles between armies of shrews, and capture in the claws of a parrot.

On another level, the story explores the meaning of life, the hereafter, happiness, and hope. A label on a dog food can shows a dog carrying a can, which has on it the same label showing the dog carrying the can, and so on, ever smaller, seemingly endlessly. The phrase "beyond the last visible dog," which refers to this illusion, is used symbolically in the story to refer to the search for happiness and meaning in life—embodied in the mouse child's hopefulness and persistence.

ANIMAL FANTASY

Children approximately three to seven years old attribute human thought, feeling, and language to animals dressed like people. Actually, during this period of animistic thinking, anything may be invested with life in the child's mind and become an object upon which he projects fantasies, hopes, and fears. Because books that extend and enrich such normal developmental tendencies strike a responsive chord in children, animal fantasy is a well-loved form among children at this stage. Like the folk tale, it becomes part of children's literary experiences before they make clear distinctions between fact and fancy.

Some of the most memorable characters from children's literature are created in animal fantasies. Wilbur and Charlotte, Peter Rabbit, and Toad of Toad Hall call to mind many of the modern classics of this genre. Some animal fantasies for older readers create an allegorical world in which the human scene is replayed to amuse and, often, to instruct. In adult literature, a community of animals may duplicate the follies of human society in a political allegory or satire. George Orwell's *Animal Farm* (A) is perhaps the best-known example, and often appears on required reading lists for junior and senior high-school students. *Watership Down* (A), by Richard Adams, also reflects human society allegorically in warrens of rabbits.

For young children, as well, animals that appear in *The Tale of Peter Rabbit* (N-P) or *The Tale of Squirrel Nutkin* (N-P), both by Beatrix Potter, have some human quality, as they know it, "writ small." Sophisticated readers detect the sly undertone of humor directed at human foibles, while naive readers enjoy the lively action and fun inherent in the situations.

A. A. Milne creates a believable personality in the form of a stuffed animal, Winnie the Pooh. Winnie, the Silly Old Bear, shines with the love and adoration that millions of children have poured upon him. Pooh, Piglet, Eeyore, Kanga, Tigger, Owl, and Rabbit romp through warmhearted adventures in the 100-Aker Wood with their owner, Christopher Robin. These toy animals from the Milne nursery attained immortality in *Winnie the Pooh* (I) and *The House at Pooh Corner* (I). *Now We Are Six* (P-I) and *When We Were Very Young* (P-I), poetry collections, are enjoyed by very young children who delight in repeating parts of the verses spontaneously. The two collections of stories are probably best understood by children above the third grade because of the subtle word play and innuendos. (The actual stuffed toys, which belonged to Christopher Milne, are now displayed at the offices of Milne's publisher, E. P. Dutton & Co.)

Christopher Robin Milne's original nursery toys, on which the characters in A. A. Milne's Pooh stories were based, on permanent display at the offices of publisher E. P. Dutton & Co., Inc. (Photograph courtesy E. P. Dutton.)

When we try to identify the basis of the strong appeal of Milne's menagerie, we note the strong characterization of Winnie the Pooh and each of the other animals. Eeyore's gloomy outlook as the eternal pessimist, Piglet's excitability and copycat tendencies, and Pooh's naive but loving nature endear them to the reader. In "In Which Eeyore Has a Birthday and Gets Two Presents," a deflated red balloon and an empty honey pot, birthday gifts from the two well-intentioned friends, are sources of great tongue-in-cheek hilarity.

Paddington is another lovable English bear whose name comes from the London train station where he is found after arriving there from darkest Peru. His stories, told by Michael Bond, appear in *A Bear Called Paddington* (I), *More About Paddington,* (I), *Paddington Takes to TV* (I), *Paddington at Large* (I), and many others. Paddington wears a deplorably shabby hat and a tag with a request, "Please take care of this bear." Children laugh at his clumsiness and bungling independence. Paddington behaves as if he were just another child in the Brown family with which he lives; the incongruity of the resulting situations is the source of the fun.

A stuffed animal that has gained nearly the popularity of Pooh and Paddington, but who is more sentimental, is *The Velveteen Rabbit* (P-I). In Margery Williams's fine story, the rabbit of the title, given to the Boy for Christmas, is cast aside after a few hours of play. Another member of the nursery, the Skin Horse, explains to the rabbit about nursery magic and what it means to be real:

"Real isn't how you are made," said the Skin Horse. "It's just a thing that happens to you. When a child loves you for a long, long time, not just to play with, but REALLY loves you, then you become Real."

"Does it hurt?" asked the Rabbit.

"Sometimes," said the Skin Horse, for he was always truthful. "When you are Real you don't mind being hurt."[10]

The Boy eventually grows to love the rabbit but the time comes when it must be burned because the Boy has played with it while ill with scarlet fever. Providentially, a flower fairy turns the toy into a real rabbit, so that it is free to dwell with others of its kind. This gentle fantasy appeals to many, who are touched by its strong portrayal of the meaning and power of love.

The Wind in the Willows (I), by Kenneth Grahame, is one of the finest animal fantasies. Originally published in 1908, it has appeared in many editions over the years; two of the most notable are those illustrated by Ernest Shepard and by Arthur Rackham. Adrienne Adams illustrated the first chapter for a picture-book edition, *The River Bank* (P-I), and Beverly Gooding illustrated the second chapter for *The Open Road* (P-I); both are accessible to an audience younger than that appropriate to the complete work, and can serve as introductions to it. As with all great literature, however, presenting it to an audience too young to appreci-

Teaching Idea

ANIMAL WORLDS (I)   Children develop a sense of place when they visualize and concretize the setting of a story. The endpapers of *Winnie the Pooh* by A. A. Milne, illustrated by Ernest H. Shepard (I, Dutton, 1926), show the map of the 100-Aker Wood. Project the map (use an opaque projector) onto a classroom wall to make, in effect, a mural on which children can, as you read the stories aloud, plot the routes the characters take.

ate it can spoil for them the truly rich experience it embodies.

Kenneth Grahame's style is as leisurely and poetic as the meanderings of the river where most of the action takes place. The story begins with Mole in the middle of spring cleaning, dusting, and whitewashing his little house.

. . . Spring was moving in the air above and in the earth below and around him, penetrating even his dark and lowly little house with its spirit of divine discontent and longing. It was small wonder, then, that he suddenly flung down his brush on the floor, said "Bother!" and "O blow!" and also "Hang spring-cleaning!" and bolted out of the house without even waiting to put on his coat.[11]

Mole discovers the river:

Never in his life had he seen a river before—this sleek, sinuous, full-bodied animal, chasing and chuckling, gripping things with a gurgle and leaving them with a laugh, to fling itself on fresh playmates that shook themselves free, and were caught and held again. All was a-shake and a-shiver—glints and gleams and sparkles, rustle and swirl, chatter and bubble. The Mole was bewitched, entranced, fascinated.[12]

When Mole meets Rat, he decides that life on the river bank is preferable to life in tunnels, and the two friends set up housekeeping together.

In succeeding chapters, Badger and Mr. Toad of Toad Hall enter the story and the thread of plot winds in and about their fantastic adventures. The story is an idyllic evocation of human emotions from wanderlust to homesickness at Christmas time.

In the most poetic chapter of all, "The Piper at the Gates of Dawn," Mole and Rat set out upon the river in search of lost Baby Otter. They find him asleep at the feet of Pan, the diety of forests and animals. The religious emotions of love and awe are captured in a scene where the animals are drawn in expectation to the sound of the pipes played by their god:

. . . suddenly the Mole felt a great Awe fall upon him, an awe that turned his muscles to water, bowed his head, and rooted his feet to the ground. It was no panic terror —indeed he felt wonderfully at peace and happy—but it was an awe that smote and held him and, without seeing, he knew it could only mean that some august Presence was very, very near. With difficulty he turned to look for his friend, and saw him at his side cowed, stricken, and trembling violently. And still there was utter silence in the populous bird-haunted branches around them; and still the light grew and grew.

Perhaps he would never have dared to raise his eyes, but that, though the piping was now hushed, the call and the summons seemed still dominant and imperious.[13]

The serious strands are counterbalanced with hilarious comedy in the form of Toad's boastful songs in praise of himself, written in a mock-heroic style that is great fun.

E. B. White's *Charlotte's Web* (P-I), a song in praise of barnyard creatures sung by a sensitive observer, tells of the friendship between Wilbur the pig and Charlotte the spider. It is a eulogy to all friendships. In a letter to readers, White describes the inspiration for the book, which remains a children's all-time favorite.

As for *Charlotte's Web,* I like animals and my barn is a very pleasant place to be, at all hours. One day when I was on my way to feed the pig, I began feeling sorry for the pig because, like most pigs, he was doomed to die. This made me sad. So I started thinking of ways to save a pig's life. I had been watching a big grey spider at her work and was impressed by how clever she was at weaving. Gradually I worked the spider into the story that you know, a story of friendship and salvation on a farm. Three years after I started writing it, it was published.[14]

When Charlotte first speaks to Wilbur during the night he can hardly wait until morning to find out who she is.

"Attention, please!" he said in a loud, firm voice. "Will the party who addressed me at bedtime last night kindly make himself or herself known by giving an appropriate sign or signal."[15]

Charlotte eventually speaks to him, but after she describes the way she makes her living Wilbur is not certain about her.

Wilbur was merely suffering the doubts and fears that often go with finding a new friend. In good time he was to discover that he was mistaken about Charlotte. Underneath her rather bold and cruel exterior, she had a kind heart, and she was to prove loyal and true to the very end.[16]

Charlotte *is* loyal and true, and through her friendship and creative spinning of words in her spiderweb above Wilbur's pen she saves his life. Wilbur depends upon Charlotte's friendship, and although he is unable to save *her* life, he assures a place for her progeny.[17]

This book is often misused and overused. In addition to being presented to children too young to understand some of the subtleties, it is sometimes read aloud in every grade from kindergarten through grade six.

Richard Adams's *Watership Down* (A), another animal fantasy, contains extended metaphor, imagery, and a delineation of the struggle between good and evil, suggesting that it is also an allegorical work. A visionary rabbit, Fiver, foresees his hillside home covered with blood. Those he persuades to leave their warren and search for safety are subjected to many trials, which test their ingenuity during the journey. When they arrive at Watership Down and find a measure of security, they still raid rival warrens because they must have female rabbits among them if they are to survive.

No synopsis can do justice to this beautiful and moving story; it must be read and savored in its entirety. Richard Adams, an astute observer of nature, involves his reader in a true work of art. Only good readers in the upper elementary grades will persist through its 429 pages; for those who do, the involvement is complete. Reading it aloud will allow more children to relish its richness.

William Steig's books are subject to several levels of interpretation. In *Dominic* (I), a restless hound of that name packs his piccolo and collection of hats to set off in search of adventure—aiming only for wherever he gets and whatever he finds. William Steig spoofs the fairy tale tradition itself when Dominic meets the Doomsday Gang, an assortment of evil foxes, weasels, and cats. Dominic nurses an ailing pig and inherits his treasure, provides music for fairy mice, and rescues a widow goose in distress. Finally, he finds a beautiful bride, Eleanor, sleeping in an enchanted garden, waiting patiently for her prince. Dominic, the hero of many faces, changes moods and roles as he changes hats.

In a later story, *Abel's Island* (I), about Abel, an intrepid mouse, William Steig spoofs the Victorian novel. Abel and his lovely wife Amanda are caught in a torrential storm on a picnic, and when Amanda's scarf blows away, gallant Abel runs to rescue it. While chasing the scarf, Abel is swept away in a flood of water to a river island from which he cannot escape. During a year of isolation on the island, Abel learns to fend for himself and turns to sculpture and literature to create a pleasant and endurable life.

Abel's adjustment to the primitive life is not an easy one, for he is obviously a gentleman mouse of culture and refinement. The understated nature of William Steig's style is particularly well shown when, after a year of hardship, suffering, and emotional strain, Abel returns home to an empty house. He places Amanda's scarf on the table and, when she returns, says simply, "I've brought you back your scarf." This story of gallantry and commitment leaves many telling gaps for the adult reader, but the humor and pathos hold even young readers who miss the subtle parody.

William Steig's stories are replete with transformations, some of them magical but others changes of character or situation. In *Sylvester and the Magic Pebble* (P), Sylvester makes an ill-advised wish that turns him into a stone. In *Tiffky Doofky* (P), the witch turns herself into a pair of old sneakers, and Caleb in *Caleb and Kate* (P) is unrecognizable to his beloved wife as a dog. The transformation in *Abel's Island* is not a magical transformation but rather the transformation of Abel himself as an individual. He changes from soft and genteel to self-sufficient and hardmuscled, so that, when he tries to put on his velvet smoking jacket, he finds it no longer fits comfortably.

Many of William Steig's books contain verses or magical incantations, and almost all contain marvelous lists of items, lists that are made humorous by the very disparity of the objects. For example, Sylvester's parents take alfalfa sandwiches,

They started homeward at noon, having drunk quarts of sarsaparilla to quench their thirst. If all went well—and why shouldn't it?—they'd be back at the farm by three o'clock, as Farmer Palmer had promised.

It was August and the hot sun glittered through a haze. They chatted as they moved along. Ebenezer opined that rain would have a cooling effect, and Farmer Palmer was of the same opinion.

Farmer Palmer's Wagon Ride

WILLIAM STEIG

Something always seems not to go well for the animals in William Steig's colorful books. But the mishaps that befall Farmer Palmer, Abel's estrangement from Amanda, the bamboozling of Minstrel Roland by the fox, and Sylvester's metamorphosis are all just so many disasters that are reversed by endurance and perseverance. William Steig's stories affirm for children the place of persistence and patience in winning things not easily won. In his acceptance speech for the Caldecott Medal, he said:

Art, including juvenile literature, has the power to make any spot on earth the living center of the universe; . . . it helps us to know life in a way that still keeps before us the mystery of things. It enhances the sense of wonder. And wonder is respect for life. Art also stimulates the adventurousness and the playfulness that keep us moving in a lively way and that lead to useful discovery (Lee Kingman, ed., *Newbery and Caldecott Medal Books: 1966–1975* [Boston: Horn Book, 1975], p. 219).

William Steig's art has the power to keep the mystery of things before us as it promotes a sense of wonder in illustrations that extend his unpretentious wit. Children sense the playfulness that permeates the text and is sprinkled generously throughout the illustrations.

Steig says that his books often start as visual images; when he wrote *Roland the Minstrel Pig,* for example, he imagined a picture of a pig hanging on a string. *Sylvester and the Magic Pebble* was to be a book with magic in it because children like magic, and he does too.

Born in Manhattan and educated in the New York City public schools, Steig had a formidable career as a magazine cartoonist before he started writing books for children. His work is seen frequently in *The New Yorker.*

Teaching Idea

EXPLORING ONE AUTHOR'S WORK (I)[18] William Steig's animal fantasies in picture-book format, because they are so manageable, provide a convenient way for intermediate-grade students to trace theme, motif, and characterization. Shadings of human love and avarice are seen in the relationships between his animals. Amos, the mouse, and Boris, the whale, are the closest of friends in *Amos and Boris* (P), despite the fact that neither can long survive in the other's atmosphere. Violet, a most feminine little pig, develops a close friendship with a bone that talks and sings—and ultimately rescues her from a wolf—in *The Amazing Bone* (P). In *Caleb and Kate* (P), the principal characters display deep conjugal tenderness, and the title character in *Tiffky Doofky* (P) searches for the love of his life. A panorama of human emotions is presented in animal disguise. As one child commented, "It's a way of getting us to think better about other people's feelings."

In *Farmer Palmer's Wagon Ride* (P), Farmer Palmer's thoughts of his wife and children give him the strength to continue on his ill-fated homeward journey.

"If I could only lay my own weary form on the dear, green ground and sleep like my friend Ebenezer," thought Farmer Palmer. But a vision of the beloved round faces and small sweet eyes of his wife and children gave him the heart to go on.[19]

In the space of an hour, all the books can be read or re-read. Ask your students to compile a chart to compare the books. The following chart, begun by fifth-grade students, will give them a start. These students included *Abel's Island,* a longer novel.

THEMES, MOTIFS, LANGUAGE, AND CHARACTERS IN BOOKS BY WILLIAM STEIG

Themes	Motifs	Language features	Characters	Title
Right prevails	Journey to find fame		Villainous fox	*Roland, the Minstrel Pig*
Love conquers all	Sylvester becomes a magic pebble	Picnic list	Burro family	*Sylvester and the Magic Pebble*
Friends help	Journey for adventure	List of supplies; large and small contrast	Mouse and whale	*Amos and Boris*
Bone helps	Magic bone		Naive child	*The Amazing Bone*
Master rescues servant	Journey to market		Man and donkey	*Farmer Palmer's Wagon Ride*
Love awaits Caleb	Caleb becomes a dog			*Caleb and Kate*
Trials before finding true-love	Magic arrow	List of garbage	Boy dog meets girl dog	*Tiffky Doofky*
Love waits at home	Journey to rescue scarf	List of picnic items	Abel, gallant hero	*Abel's Island*

pickled oats, sassafras salad, and timothy compote with them on their picnic. Abel and Amanda enjoy delicate sandwiches of pot cheese and watercress, hard-boiled quail egg, onions, olives, black caviar, and bright champagne on their ill-fated picnic. Alert readers will notice the counterpart in Kenneth Grahame's *The Wind in the Willows* when Rat packs coldtonguecoldhamcoldbeefpickledgherkinssaladfrenchrollscresssandwichespottedmeatgingerbeerlemonadesodawater for his picnic.

Each of William Steig's books also deals with a journey away from or toward home and beloved persons or objects and, in some, with efforts to communicate with a beloved one. Sometimes the obstacle is distance, sometimes a transformation that makes them unrecognizable and mute.

Robert O'Brien's *Mrs. Frisby and the Rats of NIMH* (I) is a story of a group of rats used for experimental purposes in the laboratories of NIMH. They are given DNA and steroid injections in tests to see if these substances raise intelligence. The injections are effective: the bright rats discover that they can open their own cages. They do not use their new-found skill hastily, however, but carefully plot their escape from the building and plan their survival. In a parallel plot, which intersects the story of this highly intelligent rat society, Mrs. Frisby, a widowed mouse mother, is in danger of having her family home, in which her son is recuperating from pneumonia, destroyed by spring plowing of the garden. Mrs. Frisby goes to the highly developed rat society to seek help. Through her conversations with them the reader learns that her dead husband was one of the experimental rats. Although Mrs. Frisby goes to the rat society to seek aid for herself, she helps them by warning of their forthcoming extermination by cyanide gas. O'Brien's story leads to serious discussions about how our society deals with groups that differ from the dominant one.

TIME FANTASY

In time fantasy, time is the element that is carried beyond the world of everyday experience. The author, by using time symbolically, is making a statement about the meaning of time itself. Eleanor Cameron, in the title essay in *The Green and Burning Tree*, describes a globe of time, in which all time—past, present, and future—is perceived as a whole. For writers such as Eleanor Cameron, past and future are present in time now.

Cameron opens her essay with words from T. S. Eliot's "Burnt Norton":

. . . say that the end precedes the beginning,
And the end and the beginning were always there
Before the beginning and after the end . . .[20]

The implication of time being held still, coupled with the image of the green and burning tree from Welsh mythology (similar to the biblical image of Moses and the burning bush) suggest that in a timeless world of myth and magic, the ordinary laws of the natural world are set aside.

Authors of time fantasy invent a dazzling variety of devices to permit their characters to move in and out of conventional time. For example, Madeleine L'Engle in *A Wrinkle in Time* (I-A) moves her characters from the here and now to other parts of the universe by "tessering" or "wrinkling time." In a conversation among Mrs. Whatsit, Mrs. Who, Meg and Charles Wallace, the author explains the fantastic phenomenon:

"You see," Mrs. Whatsit said, "if a very small insect were to move from the section of skirt in Mrs. Who's right hand to that in her left, it would be quite a long walk for him if he had to walk straight across."
Swiftly Mrs. Who brought her hands, still holding the skirt, together.
"Now, you see," Mrs. Whatsit said, "he would *be* there, without that long trip. That is how we travel."[21]

Meg complains that she does not understand.

"That is because you think of space only in three dimensions," Mrs. Whatsit told her. "We travel in the fifth dimension. This is something you can understand, Meg. Don't be afraid to try."[22]

Madeleine L'Engle's trilogy of space and time fantasies, *A Wrinkle in Time, A Wind in the Door* (I-A), and *A Swiftly Tilting Planet* (I-A), is partially set in a place and a time that are within the conventional universe and partially in an imagined time and place.

C. S. Lewis chronicles the events in Narnia with human characters who move in and out of a fantasy universe existing beyond human constraints. Narnia stands in another time, so that one may live hundreds of years there and return to the ordinary world without any time having passed. In *The Lion, the Witch and the Wardrobe* (I), a skeptical Peter and Susan discuss Lucy's stories about Narnia with the Professor:

"Well, Sir, if things are real, they're there all the time."

"Are they?" said the Professor; and Peter did not know quite what to say.

"But there was not time," said Susan. "Lucy had had no time to have gone anywhere, even if there was such a place. She came running after us the very moment we were out of the room. It was less than a minute, and she pretended to have been away for hours."

"That is the very thing that makes her story so likely to be true," said the Professor. "If there really is a door in this house that leads to some other world (and I should warn you that this is a very strange house, and even I know very little about it)—if, I say, she had got into another world, I should not be at all surprised to find that that other world had a separate time of its own; so that however long you stayed there it would never take up any of *our* time. . . ."[23]

In other stories, fantastic journeys take place within dreams, as in *Through the Looking Glass* (I-A), by Lewis Carroll, or in *Peter* (A), by Anne Holm. Frequently, either time or place, or both, are altered when the characters go through a particular door or follow a special path. The children in *The Lion, the Witch and the Wardrobe* go through the wardrobe, and the children in *A Walk Out of the World* (I), by Ruth Nichols, go down a slope through a certain stretch of woods.

Some characters simply experience altered consciousness as they go into times past. In the five volumes of Susan Cooper's series, *The Dark Is Rising* (I-A), the Old Ones, servants of the Light—immortals dedicated to keeping the world free of evil—are born with a special wisdom and power. Will Stanton, the last of the Old Ones, discovers his heritage on his eleventh birthday. In one scene, Will goes back into the historical time of an etching that depicts construction at an ancient Roman site in England. Many times within the story, Will Stanton communicates with the Old Ones, who have endured across the ages. Readers respond to the ancient struggle between light and dark, or good and evil, cast into a time-slipped frame.

The concept of the "eternal now" that fascinates Eleanor Cameron is developed in her own book, *The Court of the Stone Children* (I-A). The plot of the story, set in present-day San Francisco, centers on Nina's attempt to solve the mystery surrounding nineteenth-century Dominique, whose portrait hangs in the French Museum. Nina visits the museum's furnished rooms, to which Dominique's ghost returns for a time among the pieces that had once been part of her home. Together, the girls reconstruct the events of a scandal surrounding Dominique's father. When Nina is in the museum, particularly when she is in the rooms recreated from the furnishings of times gone by, she has what she calls her "Museum Feeling"—a sense of the continuity over time of these rooms, "with their massive pieces of furniture, carved, worn by thousands of hands, by innumerable brushings of cloth and flesh—all gone, gone long since."[24] Another facet of the fused nature of time is evoked by a painting—"Time Is a River Without Banks," by Chagall—that Nina discovers in the museum. As the fairytale-like painting reappears in her dreams, she perceives that "if there are no banks, there is nothing for time to pass."[25] The time motif appears again in a friend's notebook, which is filled with quotations about the paradox of time, and in the faded landlady who gazes into mirrors, hoping that she might once again catch sight of the girl she used to be. Eleanor Cameron says:

In almost any fantasy of time travel, or of the mingling of different times, there inevitably arises the intriguing question of who, rightfully, is a ghost to whom, it being usually a matter of whose time the scene is being played in, though this is not invariably easy to decide— . . . . the mood or feeling being often ambiguous or even wittily paradoxical. . . . [26]

In *The Court of the Stone Children,* we recognize that Dominique knows she is a ghost to Nina.

After the mystery of Dominique's father is solved, Nina realizes that the ghostly Dominique will not return to this time. In other novels, characters go back in time to live in the bodies and lives of people in ages past. For example, the title character in *Peter* lives the lives of his own ancestors. Much the same device is found in Madeleine L'Engle's *A Swiftly Tilting Planet,* where Charles Wallace, through his ability to kythe—that is to understand the thoughts of another being—is able to live in and think with the minds of several persons in the past. In Margaret Anderson's *To Nowhere and Back* (I), Elizabeth becomes one with a girl named Ann, who lived one hundred years earlier. While watching children play near an old cottage, Elizabeth notices Ann, loses sight of her, then sees her again. But when "the strange girl" seems about to get away again, Elizabeth acts:

"Wait! Wait!" shouted Elizabeth in a shrill voice. But the girl walked toward the cottage. "Wait!" said Elizabeth, and started to run after her. She caught her at the cottage door.

Elizabeth could never understand what happened at the moment when she reached the girl, although it was to happen again and again. She reached out and touched the child—and they became one person. Elizabeth disappeared and only Ann walked in through the door, but Elizabeth was still there, thinking and looking and feeling as Ann did.[27]

Teaching Idea

WHO IS THE GHOST TO WHOM? (I-A)[28]   As children read a number of fantasies and accumulate a background of reading experience, they will enjoy discussing and comparing how the characters move back and forth in time and deciding who is the ghost to whom. After assembling a selection of books of time fantasy, have the class compile a chart that lists the title of the fantasy, the device for time travel, and the names of the ghost and the real person. If this is done as a mural or a bulletin board, all children can discuss and add to the chart as it grows. The chart might resemble the sample given here:

TIME FANTASIES AND GHOSTS

Title	Time device	Who is the ghost?
The Court of the Stone Children	Dominique appears in Nina's time but they cannot touch	Nina is real; Dominique is ghost.
Peter	In dreams, Peter goes back to time of his ancestors	Peter becomes someone else in the past.
Tom's Midnight Garden	Tom is drawn into Hattie's childhood when she dreams of him	Tom is real; Hattie is a real woman. They meet as children in Hattie's dreams.
The Children of Green Knowe	Tolly meets children from a painting	Tolly is real. Children from the painting lived at an earlier time.

Lucy M. Boston weaves fantasies that lie just at the edge of reality. The transition from real to unreal is so subtle that the illusion is easy to believe. By the time fanciful elements are drawn into the story in *The Children of Green Knowe* (I), readers are so intensely involved that they, too, almost see and hear the children in the painting playing hide and seek. We are never quite certain whether the fantasy elements are a part of the imagination or whether they are real. In this story, Toseland, called Tolly, comes to live with his great grandmother, Mrs. Oldknow, at the intriguing ancient manor house called Green Knowe. They talk about the children in the painting who had lived at Green Knowe 400 years earlier. The presence of the children in the house and garden seems very possible.

Tolly discovers a key that opens a long-untouched toy box in which he finds objects the children in the painting are holding. His great-grandmother tells Tolly stories of how the children received the treasured objects. The love with which she speaks about the family brings a sense of those from the past into the present. When Tolly feels the children's presence, and Mrs. Oldknow shares his awareness of them, there is a willing suspension of disbelief for readers, who also want it to be true.

QUEST STORIES

Archetypal themes from folklore become vividly evident in quest fantasies. Here again is the same misty outline of a story in which we search again for the golden age or lose—and seek to regain—our identity. Victory in the battle between good and evil depends upon finding the missing heir, recognizing a prince in disguise, or achieving utopia under the rule of a king whose coming has been foretold. Titles of popular contemporary fantasies—*The High King* (I-A), *The Lord of the Rings* (A), *The Once and Future King* (A)—reverberate with overtones of such a glorious kingdom, or reflect the quest that must be undertaken before the golden time is ushered in: *Over Sea, Under Stone*

(I-A), *The Farthest Shore* (I-A), *The Great and Terrible Quest* (A).

Many quest tales are structured within—in fact, draw explicitly upon—the framework of the Arthurian legends. In *Steel Magic* (I), by André Norton, three children who have ventured to an island "out of time" fight against powers that oppose the return of the age of Arthur using the "steel magic" in the knife, fork, and spoon in their picnic basket. In *The Dark Is Rising*, by Susan Cooper, Merlin—wizard of the Arthurian legend—appears in various incarnations across different periods of time to fight against the dark. In the final battle, the forces of light in every age join with those who fight against the dark.

Quest stories that are most memorable describe characters' outer and inner struggles, and may involve Herculean journeys where overcoming obstacles vanquishes evil. Quests become a search for an inner, rather than outer, enemy. Inner strength is required as characters are put to a variety of tests that oftimes seem endless and unconquerable. It is the indomitable goodness of character that prevails.

Weaving legends from Arthurian days into the fabric of modern life, Susan Cooper dramatizes the risks of not standing up for what is right and just. The multilayered reality of her series, *The Dark Is Rising*, epitomizes tales dealing with the interconnection between visible and sensed reality. Although discussed as time fantasy, its subject may also be viewed as a quest. Susan Cooper bases the stories on English and Celtic myth, beginning with *Over Sea, Under Stone* and continuing with *The Dark Is Rising, Greenwitch* (I-A), *The Grey King* (I-A), and *Silver on the Tree* (I-A). The stories start realistically as Simon, Jane, and Barney Drew find an old manuscript with a maplike drawing through which they learn of a grail associated with King Arthur. Unlocking the inscription on the grail is a major problem, and the story becomes more complex as it reveals, in *The Dark Is Rising*, more about the struggle between the forces of light and dark. Eleven-year-old Will Stanton, seventh son of a seventh son, learns that he is called upon to carry the burden of power of the Old Ones, who fight across the centuries to ward off the powers of the Dark. Will also appears in *Greenwitch* where Jane becomes involved in a spring ritual of weaving a huge sacrifical figure (a greenwitch) from hazel, rowan, and hawthorne branches. This is cast into the sea to welcome summer and bring blessings of good crops and a good catch of fish to the small Cornwall village. The Dark in the village wears many faces and works through weak people to overpower the Light. In *The Grey King* Will is sent to North Wales to recuperate from a serious illness and there continues his quest for the Signs that will finally overcome the Dark. Forces of evil appear in many forms: a wicked sheep owner, a chimerical fox, and the Grey King. Will meets Bran, an albino child who knows nothing of his origins. Together they find the golden harp, awaken the Six Sleepers of the past, and discover Bran's parentage: he is Arthur's son, the Pendragon, brought forward in time to the present when he is needed most. Clues from Celtic lore intrigue the reader already caught in a web woven of everyday reality and mythic elements.

Finally, in *Silver on the Tree,* the story strands are braided dextrously as all the major characters are brought forward to the present for the ultimate confrontation with the Dark, embodiment of prejudice, hatred, and cruelty. In the memorable farewell of Bran to Arthur, human affection merges with the universal pain of being mortal.

Cooper's skillful manipulation of myth and reality is unparalleled. Based on ancient verses drawn from Arthurian legends, which foretell significant events, people, and places, the meaning of the myths is revealed gradually to Will Stanton and the reader.

That modern stories often echo symbolic meanings from Arthurian legends—a quest, an unacknowledged king, a Camelot—shows the continuity of much literature. For example, Ged's inner and outer struggles with the evil shadow that would possess his soul—in Ursula Le Guin's *A Wizard of Earthsea* (I-A)—is both physical and emotional, as was King Arthur's quest. The idea of a high king in the Le Guin story also derives from the social structure of the sixth century A.D., when

Will Stanton, one of the "Old Ones," who, across the ages, work to protect the world from the ever-threatening forces of evil.
(Illustration by Alan E. Cober from *The Dark Is Rising* by Susan Cooper. A Margaret K. McElderry Book. Illustration copyright © 1973 by Alan E. Cober. Reprinted by permission of Atheneum Publishers.)

a WIZARD OF EARTHSEA

URSULA K. LE GUIN DRAWINGS BY RUTH ROBBINS

The stark, bold line drawing of Ged suggests the strength he must show in his encounters with evil.
(From *A Wizard of Earthsea* by Ursula K. Le Guin. Illustrated by Ruth Robbins. Parnassus Press, 1968.)

a loose confederation of nobles rallied under the banner of a high king in order to protect themselves against a common enemy. Even in fantasies where there is no direct connection with the Arthurian legends, such as C. S. Lewis's "Chronicles of Narnia," it seems entirely right that there be a medieval setting with the trappings of chivalry. Thus the four children of Lewis's stories are destined to become kings and queens reigning from the four thrones in Cair Paravel when the golden age arrives in Narnia.

High fantasy—that is, fantasy that inhabits a secondary world created with high poetic seriousness—is most impressively realized in what we call quest literature. The finest authors of such works create whole worlds—with geographies, histories, languages, mythologies, and genealogies of their own. The names of the fantasy kingdoms—Narnia, Prydain, Middle Earth, Earthsea—have an irresistible allure that links them with the old names of Celtic and Saxon myths and legends. Of all fantasy, this type works the strongest enchantment. The greatest for many readers, the Ring trilogy by J. R. R. Tolkien, has inspired so devoted a following that we still see the legend "Frodo lives" on sidewalks and subway walls—attesting to nostalgia for a golden age.

June S. Terry says that children assimilate quest tales "into the bloodstream," unconsciously absorbing the values of human society past and present.[29] Values inherent in quest tales, shaped by generations of human experience, emerge consistently and are widely accepted. Because most children unconsciously learn from experience that goodness is generally rewarded and wickedness punished, quest tales provide affirmation of their unconscious knowledge. Further, fantasy readers learn a lesson common to most literature—that human nature has two sides and that life holds bitterness as well as happiness. Eternal hope is also conveyed in fantasy's almost always buoyant resolutions—offering the promise that despite repeated setbacks good fortune is ultimately assured.

One of the key volumes in C. S. Lewis's "Chronicles of Narnia," *The Magician's Nephew* (I), describes the creation of Narnia. In the "prequel" (introduction) to the six other volumes, young Digory Kirke and Polly Plummer gain entrance to other worlds with the help of three magic rings. In *The Magician's Nephew,* Digory, lonely and unhappy in his uncle's house, and with his mother seriously ill, seeks happiness and good. Under the guidance of Aslan, he learns that life may be harsh before it is happy and that one must always be on guard against tyrants. Although few children enjoy all seven stories of the series equally (for, though great in conception, some are less than great in execution), many love and remember the passages describing Aslan singing Narnia into existence:

The Lion was pacing to and fro about that empty land and singing his new song. It was softer and more lilting than the song by which he had called up the stars and the sun; a gentle, rippling music. And as he walked and sang the valley grew green with grass. It spread out from the Lion like a pool. It ran up the sides of the little hills like a wave. In a few minutes it was creeping up the lower slopes of the distant mountains, making that young world every moment softer. The light wind could now be heard ruffling the grass. The higher slopes grew dark with heather.[30]

As they read this, some children see the parallel with the opening chapters of Genesis, which Lewis, a distinguished scholar and theologian, intended. Some children will attend to the religious symbolism (which will be meaningful only if they discover it for themselves); others, who do not detect it, will still experience a sense of the numinous from the representation of a beneficent providence in the figure of Aslan. For students who would not appreciate the equation of Aslan with Christ, stressing the image could spoil the literary experience.

Lloyd Alexander's "Chronicles of Prydain" begins in *The Book of Three* (I-A), where readers meet memorable characters—the foundling Taran, an Assistant Pig-Keeper; Princess Eilonwy of the red-gold hair; Gwydion, the good; and Arawn, Fflewddur Fflam, Gurgi, Dallben, and others. Five books catalogue Taran's quest, a quest that changes from story to story. First, he searches for Hen-Wen, the oracular pig in *The Book of Three,* then for the cauldron in *The Black Cauldron* (I-A), and later for the kidnapped Princess Eilonwy in *The Castle of Llyr* (I-A). Finally, he sets out, in *Taran Wanderer* (I-A), to discover his identity, and, in *The High King* (I-A), learns that greatness is not a

Endpaper map of the territory in which the heroes of *The High King* search for their identity and contend with evil forces.
(From *The High King* by Lloyd Alexander. Map by Evaline Ness. Copyright © 1968 by Lloyd Alexander. Copyright © 1968 by Holt, Rinehart and Winston. Reproduced by permission of Holt, Rinehart and Winston, Publishers.)

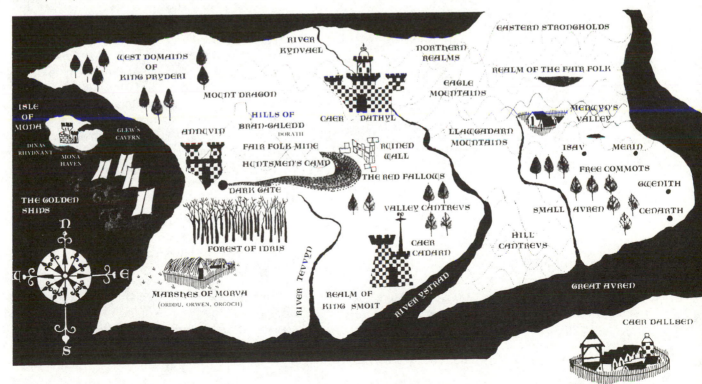

QUEST STORIES

Linda and Philip, protagonists in *The Marrow of the World,* in which good and evil struggle for Linda's soul in a world beneath a lake in the Georgian Bay area of Canada. (Illustration by Trina Schart Hyman from *The Marrow of the World* by Ruth Nichols. A Margaret K. McElderry Book. Copyright © 1972 by Ruth Nichols. Reprinted by permission of Atheneum Publishers.)

matter of birth but of wisdom, humility, and responsible choice.

Taken together, the stories show an evolution of Taran's inner growth. In the final book, *The High King,* Taran, now a hero, finds that many of the things he sought seem insignificant, and his understanding of heroism has changed drastically;

what he sought at the beginning no longer interests him at the end. In this story of one seeking identity, Taran steadily progresses toward maturity in a quest as much internal as external. Throughout the chronicles, humor is sprinkled generously to lighten the seriousness of Taran's search and his struggles with evil along the way. Each book can be read for the excitement, battles, mystery, and intrigue it contains, and, for the thoughtful reader, subtle meanings are to be found in Taran's quest.

Children frequently complete reading a book disappointed that it has ended. A child who reads Tolkien's *The Hobbit* (I-A), can look forward to reading, as an adolescent, his complex, 1300-page, multivolume *The Lord of the Rings* (A), to which *The Hobbit* is a prelude. Bilbo Baggins is the timid, insular hobbit that Gandalf the Wizard singles out as having the greatest potential for heroism and most capable of recovering the thirteen dwarfs' long lost treasure from the dragon Smaug. Bilbo is understandably reluctant to undertake this quest for it is much easier to live in his comfortable burrow, eating six meals a day. Discovering resources he didn't know he had, this small, determined, self-sacrificing creature rises to the challenge of the personal and spiritual quest.

With the aid of Gollum's little gold ring, Bilbo attains the power of invisibility and the confidence to undertake more difficult tasks. Bilbo has no desire to be a hero and, in the final fierce battle of the Five Armies, uses the magic ring to protect his head from being chosen for a sweeping stroke by a goblin swordsman.

Upon his return to Hobbiton, Bilbo is considered somewhat strange by his neighbors, for he writes poetry and is often visited by dwarfs and wizards. Nonetheless, he remains very happy to the end of his days, which ''were extraordinarily long.'' Tolkien's work has become the standard by which all other fantasies are judged; it is a cornerstone in a literary education.

Ruth Nichols creates a vivid sense of place in a quest novel, *The Marrow of the World* (I-A), which deals with a search for identity in the midst of a struggle between good and evil. Set against (and integrated with) the terrible beauty of the deep Canadian forests and lakes, the story tells of Philip and his strangely remote cousin Linda, whose birth and origins are clouded in mystery. Linda, from another world, and Philip, from our natural one, are summoned into that other world by a witch who would use Linda to achieve immortality. Philip accompanies Linda on a perilous search for her identity that leads them deep into an underwater world controlled by evil to which Linda seems irrevocably bound. The theme that individual courage is needed despite the intervention of higher powers is effectively dramatized, although a scene in which Linda arrives at the source of the "marrow" is cut disconcertingly short.

LITERARY LORE

All fantasy is rooted in folklore, a verity evident in some stories more than others. Mollie Hunter's fine novels acknowledge the "chain of communication through the centuries—the long, unbroken line of folk memory stretching . . . from Megalithic times to the present day. . . ."[31] So, too, do stories from Hans Christian Andersen and Natalie Babbitt and Isaac Bashevis Singer.

We call literary lore those stories that have a haunting mythic quality and echo the sounds from storytellers' tongues of ages past. In *A Stranger Came Ashore* (I), Mollie Hunter captures, on the very first page, a timeless moment reflecting this quality:

It was a while ago, in the days when they used to tell stories about creatures called the Selkie Folk. A stranger came ashore to an island at that time—a man who gave his name as Finn Learson—and there was a mystery about him which had to do with these selkie creatures. Or so some people say, anyway. . . . [32]

Haunting images of stories past return in the scene she sets and in the stories she tells.

Hans Christian Andersen was the first to use the classic fairy tale form to write stories of his own, which are often confused with the traditional ones because he emulates them so well. One of the most prolific writers of modern fantasy during his lifetime (1805–1875), Andersen worked as a cobbler in Denmark and was loved by the children who listened to his stories long before they were written down. *The Ugly Duckling*, said to be an autobiographical account in allegorical form, describes the indignities and heartaches Andersen suffered.

Many of Hans Christian Andersen's stories have been illustrated by outstanding artists and appear in picture-book format. *The Emperor's New Clothes* (P-I), illustrated by Virginia Lee Burton, Jack and Irene Delano, and others, strikes out at hypocrisy and pretentiousness. In this well-known story, two weavers tell the emperor that only wise men fit for high office can see the magic cloth they weave. No high official wants to admit that he cannot see the cloth and, thereby, to testify to his unfitness for the job. So each pretends to see the beautiful fabrics the two weavers describe. At a royal parade in which the emperor wears "robes" made of the non-existent cloth, a small child exposes the hoax by calling out, in his innocence, that the emperor is, indeed, naked.

Andersen's *The Nightingale* (P-I), translated by Eva Le Gallienne and illustrated by Nancy Ekholm Burkert, is the story of a jeweled mechanical bird that so intrigues the emperor that he banishes the real nightingale despite its beautiful song. In a dramatic scene the emperor realizes his mistake and asks to have the real nightingale returned, acknowledging that the beauties of nature are more precious than the most elaborate and lifelike objects made by man.

Following in the same tradition, Natalie Babbitt builds on the classic forms of literature to create fresh and original fantasies. In an artistically written literary tale, *Tuck Everlasting* (I), she presents the advantages and drawbacks of eternal life. The Tuck family, who had unwittingly drunk from a magic spring that gives everlasting life, remain forever the same age. Ten-year-old Winnie Foster discovers the magic spring and through it comes to know the Tucks. Pa Tuck tells Winnie about life as an immortal in the midst of a changing world. He describes life as a wheel: "But dying's part of the wheel, right there next to being born. You can't

Profile

NATALIE BABBITT

It's a wheel, Winnie. Everything's a wheel, turning and turning, never stopping. The frogs is part of it, and the bugs, and the fish, and the wood thrush, too. And people. But never the same ones. Always coming in new, always growing and changing, and always moving on. That's the way it's supposed to be. That's the way it *is*.

Tuck Everlasting

In *Tuck Everlasting*, Natalie Babbitt asks if the dream of an eternal life is really a blessing. For Tuck, who is explaining the cyclical nature of life to young Winnie Foster, there is no spoke on the wheel, for he has drunk from the spring granting everlasting life. Many of Natalie Babbitt's stories blur the line between fantasy and reality, leaving the reader to ponder the nature of truth.

Speaking of children and literature, Natalie Babbitt has said:

I have the greatest respect for the intelligence, sensitivity, and imagination of young people. They are the true and unfettered audience, and as such deserve the best efforts of everyone who writes for them. Nothing can be good enough, but we can try (*Farrar, Straus & Giroux promotional material*).

Natalie Babbitt was born and grew up in Ohio. During her childhood, she spent many hours reading fairy tales and myths. She would often pretend that she was a librarian, stamping her books and checking them in and out to herself. She also liked to draw and, since her mother was an amateur landscape and portrait artist, had access to lots of paints, paper, and pencils. She studied art at Laurel School in Cleveland and at Smith College. Soon after graduation she married Samuel Fisher Babbitt, who later became president of Kirkland College. The Babbitts have three children—Christopher, Tom, and Lucy—all now grown.

Natalie Babbitt collaborated on her first book with her husband, but then decided to write and illustrate on her own. In addition to the several books she has written, she has illustrated books of poems by Valerie Worth and the book jackets of her own novels. Told by a child interviewer how beautiful he thought the jacket illustration for *The Eyes of the Amaryllis*, Natalie Babbitt answered, "That's the nicest thing anyone ever said to me."

Children's literature is enriched by Natalie Babbitt's work.

pick out the pieces you like and leave the rest. Being part of the whole thing, that's the blessing."[33] The Tucks give Winnie a vial of the water to keep so that she can make a choice when she reaches womanhood. Bestowing the magical agent verifies the connection between this turn-of-the-century story and folklore traditions. Strong characterization, poetic prose, and careful plotting build a story that haunts the thoughtful reader.

In his first book for children, *Zlateh the Goat* (I), Isaac Bashevis Singer, a masterful storyteller, retells seven middle-European Jewish tales of yesteryear that sound as if they are of today. Maurice Sendak's pictures enrich the book, and Weston Woods has recreated the title story as a beautiful film. Money is running low for Reuven and his family as Chanukah nears. He decides to sell the beloved family goat, Zlateh, to the butcher. Aaron, the oldest son, is charged with the heartbreaking job of delivering the goat. A sudden blizzard causes them to lose their way, forcing Aaron and Zlateh to take refuge in a haystack:

For three days Aaron and Zlateh stayed in the haystack. Aaron had always loved Zlateh, but in these three days he loved her more and more. She fed him with her milk and helped him keep warm. She comforted him with her patience. He told her many stories, and she always cocked her ears and listened. When he patted her, she licked his hand and his face. Then she said, "Maaaa," and he knew it meant, I love you too.[34]

Isaac Singer's recreations of images from the lore of the old country are embellished with sprightly wit. *Naftali the Storyteller and His Horse, Sus* (I-A), about a man very much like Singer himself, contains eight stories that echo traditional values and practices so meaningful during the Diaspora. "A Hanukkah Eve in Warsaw" is the story of a boy, not yet seven, who, craving independence, leaves *cheder* (school) to walk home alone. Always before an assistant teacher had accompanied him, but the boy wants to boast to his friends that he is grown up enough to go alone. A sudden snowstorm causes him to lose his way, but his eventual return and the forgiveness that awaits him makes Chanukah even sweeter. Follies of vanity, the vul-

nerability of being human, and faith in the ultimate goodness of life shine through Singer's stories.

Mollie Hunter's novels describe the struggle between good and evil in a manner that makes readers feel the author is speaking directly to them, for there is an immediacy and timelessness in her tales. Folklore and legend reverberate in them, and they encompass the best of the old tales cast in the present. They carry a sense of continuity that what is has always been and evermore shall be. In *The Walking Stones* (I) the reader goes with Donald into an ancient circle of stones used for worship by the ancient Druids and feels the aura of the place and of the primordial rituals once performed there. In the above mentioned *A Stranger Came Ashore*, Hunter sings the legends of the Selkie Folk (seals in human form) into life as she tells of unusual events in a village in the Shetland Isles. A young sailor, Finn Learson, washed ashore after a shipwreck on a stormy night, is not what he seems, but only twelve-year-old Robbie Henderson senses the evil and mystery about him. Robbie's dying grandfather questions Finn Learson's identity, and with the help of his raven-like schoolmaster, Yarl Corbie, Robbie learns the truth. Suspense works beneath the surface of routine occurrences in the isolated village, where rumor, myth, and legend blend. When the tale is told, the author suggests that, while some may opt for conventional explanations of the events, those who see with the third eye and allow the imagination a life of its own will find more powerful symbols.

Mollie Hunter alludes to the factual base that underlies folklore; she shows the connections between such and the fanciful tales that grow out of the repeated retelling of the stories. Her work vividly illustrates the idea that "all literature is but one story," for in it fantasy, reality, and folklore intermix.

Two books, because they show their traditional parentage proudly, deserve special mention: Robin McKinley's *Beauty* (I-A)—a loving rendition of the Beauty and the Beast tale, and Shirley Rousseau Murphy's *Silver Woven in My Hair* (I)—an intermingling of several Cinderella tales. From the moment you discover how Beauty acquires her

BEAUTY

A RETELLING OF THE STORY OF

Beauty & the Beast

by Robin McKinley

Echoes from folklore reverberate through a poetic retelling of the story of "Beauty and the Beast."
(From *Beauty: A Retelling of the Story of Beauty and the Beast* by Robin McKinley. Harper & Row, 1978.)

nickname, you know that you are embarking on an old story you have heard before, but Robin McKinley's compelling and poetic language keeps you bound to the pages to savor once more the engaging narrative. Beauty's father is a wealthy merchant who falls on hard times and moves his family to the country near a dark, forbidding forest. The father, who becomes lost in the woods, is saved by a gruesome monster who allows him to go free on condition that he hand over one of his daughters in his place. It is Beauty who willingly goes to the Beast to fulfill her father's bargain. The

terror of her early encounters with the Beast, the gradual recognition of his kindness and love for her, and the eventual release of the handsome prince from his imprisonment in the repulsive body of the Beast is played out in captivating prose. After several months at the castle, Beauty begs to visit her family but is refused by the gentle Beast. In a fit of anger, Beauty faints, then returns to consciousness unaware that she is lying in the Beast's arms:

My memory began to return. I had been unhappy because I was homesick. The Beast had said that he could not let me go home. Then I must have fainted. It occurred to me that the velvet my face rested on was heaving and subsiding gently, like someone breathing, and my fingers were wrapped around something that felt very much like the front of a coat. There was a weight across my shoulders that might have been an arm. I was leaning against the whatever-it-was, half sitting up. I turned my head a few inches, and caught a glimpse of lace, and beneath it a white bandage on a dark hand; and the rest of my mind and memory returned with a shock like a snowstorm through a window blown suddenly open.[35]

The entire story strikes with the freshness of new-blown snow.

Literature study reveals numerous variants of the Cinderella theme; Shirley Rousseau Murphy's *Silver Woven in My Hair* puts the rags-to-riches tale in a story set in the Middle Ages. Thursey, a kitchen maid in an inn in the village of Geis, comforts herself with the stories she collects and secretly records from wandering minstrels. One such story is played out in her own life. Her friend Gillie, the goatherd, is really the Prince in disguise.

Criteria for Selecting Fantasy

As with all books, fantasy must tell an interesting story, have a well-developed plot that holds the reader, and contain an identifiable theme. Standards for all other categories of children's books of course apply to fantasy as well. The following criteria, however, apply uniquely to fantasy:

1. The fanciful world described and the events taking place in it are plausible.

2. Characters and events stay within the framework of the created world.

3. Story elements create awe and wonder in such a way that they compel suspension of disbelief.

4. Characterization, archetypal themes, and poetic seriousness are such that they reinforce believability of setting and causality.

SCIENCE FICTION

Science fiction, with its quasi-predictive themes, is a natural literature for our rapidly changing, technological society. It is a futuristic literature in an age that itself is future oriented. By extrapolating from scientific knowledge, authors follow to their extremes the paths society is taking. Science fiction authors deal seriously with possibilities for the future, but make no pretense of predicting it.

Science fiction is emerging as a respectable genre with a readership continually growing and boosted by the popularity of such films as ''Star Wars'' and ''Close Encounters of the Third Kind.'' There was a time when the Buck Rogers type of gimmickry dominated this kind of writing. The concern then was less with serious characterization and theme than with ingenious inventions, the story serving largely as a backdrop for exotic gadgetry, the characters merely puppets pasted against a paltry plot.

With the emergence of higher quality science fiction, it has become necessary for teachers to recognize that the possibility of true fact can become the factually true. There was a time when we felt secure in believing George Orwell's *1984* and Aldous Huxley's *Brave New World* remote. The visions they presented could only be found in books. But some of the things they prophesied have already come true. Yesterday's creative science fiction writers forecast many of today's scientific discoveries.

Some futurists say that the age when death will be obsolete is near; that ''telebodies'' or ''telehumans'' with electronic parts, quasi-humans who are maintained through telemonitoring, will be commonplace; that versatile and durable replacements for our fragile or deteriorated body parts will be readily available. Genetic intervention will make hereditary diseases obsolete and life-support suits will continuously monitor our internal body functions. Indeed, these ideas do not seem as far-fetched as they once did: much of what was once in the future is here with us today.

Michael Wood says that ''science fiction is a mirror in the house of intellect raised not by pride or passion or the urging of the gods but by the curiosity and the capacity for invention.''[36] Gifted writers such as Isaac Asimov, Arthur C. Clarke, Robert Heinlein, H. M. Hoover, John Christopher, and Anne McCaffrey have harnessed this curiosity and capacity for invention to elevate science fiction to an art form dealing with serious themes.

A strong and oft-repeated theme is the effect of technological developments on human beings. For example, innovations in warfare, in communications and locomotion could shrink the world so that the behavior of one person might affect the lives of countless others. A science fiction writer, using this as a basis, might depict an individual or small group attempting to take power over the world.

In better science fiction, moral issues are not neglected. Stories set in worlds never known deal with problems we may someday face—the rights of extra-terrestrials whose planets are colonized, the ethics of allocation of limited resources, the sharing of diminishing resources in a world of rapidly growing populations—and cause us to rethink the choices and directions of our society. Science fiction, so appropriate for a changing world, is a literature about change and the attendant moral issues change brings.

There is much science fiction in a lighter vein that is filled with exciting adventure and humor. Some writers adhere strictly to the facts of science whereas others take artistic license with them. Certainly, a child's introduction to the genre should be through some of the lighter, suspenseful stories. Science fantasy, a blend of fantasy and science fiction, often set in other worlds and uncomplicated by elaborate scientific theories, provides a good entrée for beginning science fiction readers.

Robert Heinlein, dean of science fiction writers, illuminates the social implications of science

Today's children have access to devices resembling some once found only in science fiction. (Photograph by Patricia Hollander Gross / STOCK, Boston, Mass.)

and technology for life by critically examining the power and danger of modern technology. Heinlein was among the outstanding science fiction writers of the 1950s and 1960s who moved the genre to a place worthy of esteem. In an early work, *Farmer in the Sky* (A), he recreates the experience of taking off in a spaceship, the Bifrost:

> The Bifrost tilted over a little and the speaker said, "Minus three minutes!"
> And then "Minus one minute!" and another voice took up the count: "Fifty-nine Fifty-eight Fifty-seven."
> My heart started to pound so hard I could hardly hear it. But it went on: "Thirty-five Thirty-four. . . ."
> "And three."
> "And two. . . ."
> I never did hear them say "one" or "fire" or whatever they said. About then something fell on me and I thought I was licked. Once, exploring a cave with the fellows, a

bank collapsed on me and I had to be dug out. It was like that—but nobody dug me out. My chest hurt. My ribs seemed about to break. I couldn't lift a finger. I gulped and couldn't get my breath. I wasn't scared, not really, because I knew we would take off with a high "g," but I was awfully uncomfortable. I managed to turn my head a little and saw that the sky was already purple. While I watched, it turned black and the stars came out, millions of stars. And yet the sun was still streaming in through the port.[37]

This kind of writing, though accurate for its day, doesn't burn as brightly for sophisticated Trekkies of the 1980s as more recent works.

John Christopher's trilogy about extraterrestrial invaders of Earth appeals to today's readers in the upper elementary grades. *The White Mountains* (I-A), *The City of Gold and Lead* (I-A), and *The Pool of Fire* (I-A) are set in the twenty-first century in a world ruled by the Tripods, dreaded robots. When humans are fourteen, the Tripods implant steel caps in their skulls that operate to keep them submissive, docile, and helpless. Will and his two friends learn that free people live in the White Mountains and make a hazardous journey to join them. Humane characters are pitted against hostile aliens in a series of bizarre encounters. Christopher's narrative will impel readers to ponder the values of life and science.

Set on the planet of Pern, where the major threat to the inhabitants is Threadfall, a recurrent rain of life-devouring threadlike spores, Anne McCaffrey's *Dragonsong* (I-A) is the first book in an excellent science fiction trilogy. The Pernese, living in cavelike "Holds," have trained giant flying dragons with riders to burn from the skies the dreaded Threadfall. Menolly, daughter of a dour, uncompromising man, wants to become one of the Harpers—singers and musicians whose songs are a means of educating the children in the traditions of Pern. Her father refuses to allow this because making music is traditionally men's work. Miserable, Menolly runs away but is caught outside the Holds during Threadfall; she finds refuge in a cave that is the hatching ground for the eggs of fire lizards, small versions of the huge dragons. When the eggs hatch, Menolly teaches the new lizards to sing, and thus is finally recognized for her song-making talents.

Dragonsinger (I-A), sequel to *Dragonsong*, describes Menolly's life as she studies at Harper Hall, the only girl apprentice in a craft dominated by males. Unanticipated problems await Menolly amid the pleasures of a rewarding musical life. In the final book, *Dragondrums* (I-A), masterharper Menolly's protegé, Piemur, is the protagonist. His life changes when his voice does, and in the guise of an apprentice message-drummer, he serves as a spy for the Masterharper. The series presents a wholly conceived fantasy world populated by strong characters who confront universal human problems that are lightened with touches of humor.

Sylvia Engdahl examines anthropological and sociological aspects of life in the future in her short stories and novels. One of the best, *Enchantress from the Stars* (A), is written from the perspective of the three central characters, each of whom is a member of one of three groups whose fortunes intertwine. Elana joins the Anthropological Service of the Federation of Planets, a group made up of the most advanced people in the universe. Georyn lives in primitive Andrecia, a world that still believes in enchanted forests and dragons. Jarel is one of the Imperialists invading Andrecia to place colonists on this rich virgin land.

Elana, only a First-Phase student at the Academy for Anthropological Service, does not qualify for a starship exploration to any of the Youngling

Activity: Teacher to Student

SCIENCE FICTION TIME CAPSULES (I-A) Many fine science fiction series have the same central characters—for example, those written by John Christopher and Anne McCaffrey. Read the first dozen pages in the first book of the series and, in a few brief paragraphs, predict what you think the story will be about and what will happen to the central figures. Seal your prediction and those of your classmates in a secret envelope. Bury them in a time capsule cigar box to be unearthed after all of you have finished reading the series. Form a small group to discuss your endings as compared with the author's.

planets. She tries to persuade her father, the Senior Agent, to allow her to join him when problems arise in Andrecia, especially since her bethrothed, Evrek, is a member of the crew. Failing to persuade her father, she stows away on the starship.

The Andrecians live on a beautiful Youngling planet but have advanced only to the stage of a feudal society and are in danger of being taken over by the Imperialists. The Imperialists, more advanced technologically, do not share the humanitarian values of the Federation. The power of love and faith are triumphant in Engdahl's examination of the interaction between cultures at different levels of development. This story and its sequel, *The Far Side of Evil* (A), raise significant questions, which leave readers pondering their own society and its values.

In all of her work, Engdahl is suggesting hypotheses about humankind's future and the nature of the universe. She forces her characters (and her readers) to consider questions of individual commitment and ethical behavior. In the foreword to a collection of four of her stories, *Anywhere, Anywhen: Stories of Tomorrow* (A), Engdahl decries the tendency to assign books about the future automatically to the category of science fiction:

Personally, I do not believe that the future is something that should be set apart and mentioned only in literature of one particular type, directed to one specific audience. To me, past, present, and future are all parts of an unbroken thread, the thread of human experience. Almost everybody is interested in the future.[38]

Engdahl pinpoints the problematic nature of strict classifications, which her work transcends inasmuch as she focuses on the universality of human problems.

H. M. Hoover envisions an alien race that conquered Earth centuries ago in *The Delikon* (A). A violent revolution is brewing that will cast out the Delikon from Earth and their headquarters at Kelador. Varina, a young Delikon teacher, age 307, who has been restructured in human form to teach two human children, is torn between loyalties to her people and to the Earthlings in her charge.

When she and the two children go on a camping trip they are caught between the battle lines of the revolutionaries and the Delikon. Varina, repelled by the brutality of war, wants to return to her native home, but when she finally reaches Kelador she finds the Delikon defeated and the last starship gone, stranding her on Earth. In a final touching scene, when Varina has run across a lawn and disappeared behind a hedge, the children call, "Are you coming back?" But, though Varina hears the question, she cannot answer, because she does not know. The larger questions of finding one's purpose and place in life are considered in this engrossing novel.

Arthur C. Clarke, a nationally recognized scientist, sets *Dolphin Island* (I-A) in the twenty-first century and incorporates scientific conjecture based on research that has been done with dolphins. Johnny floats on a raft after his ship, the Santa Anna, is wrecked:

Something jolted the raft, and he awoke with a start. For a moment he could hardly believe that he had been sleeping and that the sun was now almost overhead. Then the raft jerked again—and he saw why.

Four dolphins, swimming side by side, were pushing the raft through the water. Already it was moving faster than a man could swim, and it was still gaining speed. Johnny stared in amazement at the animals splashing and snorting only inches away from him; was this another of their games?

Even as he asked himself that question, he knew that the answer was No. The whole pattern of their behavior had changed completely; this was deliberate and purposeful. Playtime was over. He was in the center of a great pack of the animals, all now moving steadily in the same direction. There were scores, if not hundreds, ahead and behind, to right and left, as far as he could see. He felt that he was moving across the ocean in the midst of a military formation—a brigade of cavalry.[39]

The dolphins push Johnny to the waist-high water surrounding Dolphin Island, then leave. His new home and life on Dolphin Island provide fascinating reading for children.

Children also find it fascinating that dolphins communicate with each other, and they are intrigued by scientists' efforts to teach chimpanzees and apes to "talk." One such animal, an ape named Washoe, after years of confinement and training, finally generated her first words: "Let . . . me . . . out."

John Donovan uses experimentation with apes as the basis of his story *Family* (I-A). The story, told from Sasha's point of view, describes the demeaning process used by scientists to teach the apes human language. The apes have a language of their own, which they use with each other throughout experiments they think ridiculous. Four of the apes, Sasha, Dylys, Lollipop, and Moses, escape from the laboratory and live together in a wooded area where, as friendship and love grow among them, they truly become a family. One day, deer hunters shoot Moses and Lollipop. In a bittersweet ending, Sasha and Dylys return to the laboratory, for Dylys now carries Moses' child, and they know that only within these confines will its safety be assured. Despite their experiences, the apes nurture the hope that humankind's better impulses will ultimately assert themselves.

Donovan's story throws a creative and questioning light on scientific experiments with animals.

A holocaust in which civilization is destroyed is a frequent science fiction theme. Few have developed the theme more convincingly than Robert C. O'Brien in *Z for Zachariah* (I-A). A lone sixteen-year-old girl, Ann Burden, survives nuclear radiation that seemingly has destroyed all other human, animal, and vegetable life. Her desperation is recorded in her diary:

At first when all the others went away, I hated being alone, and I watched the road all day and most of the night hoping that a car, *anybody*, would come over the hill from either direction. When I slept, I would dream that one came and drove on past without knowing I was here; then I would wake up and run to the road looking for the taillights disappearing. Then the weeks went by and the radio stations went off, one by one. When the last one went off and stayed off, it came to me, finally, that nobody, no car, was ever going to come. . . .[40]

When hope is gone that any other human lives, a man in a "safe-suit" walks into the valley. Delight and fear are mixed in Ann's relationship with the strangely aloof Mr. Loomis. She dreams of companionship but finds terror and eventually must hide when he threatens to kill her. There is no hope for mutual trust, making life in the valley intolerable; Ann steals the safe-suit and leaves the valley to go we know not where.

The story evokes a cry for decency essential to the survival of the last humans on earth. Ann Bur-

Activity: Teacher to Student

A RACE OF THE FUTURE (A) What do you think society will be like in the twenty-first century? Will it be one grand global village? Will there still be families as we know them? Assuming that technological advances continue, what will your community be like? To what will humanity have been reduced or elevated—or will it be unchanged?

With these questions in mind draw upon examples from the science fiction you have read to describe the people who will be walking where you walk 1,000 years from now. Tell about their appearance, the things they do in their leisure time, and the things that make them happy and sad. You might bind your essays in an original book called "Future World."

In the hardbound edition (left) of *Z for Zachariah,* Ann Burden scans the horizon in her search for another living person in a world devastated by nuclear war. The paperback cover (right) shows Ann and the person she eventually discovers. (Hardcover jacket design by James and Ruth McCrea from *Z for Zachariah* by Robert C. O'Brien. Copyright © 1974 by Sally Conly. Reprinted by permission of Atheneum Publishers. Paperback cover design by Boris Vallejo from *Z for Zachariah* by Robert C. O'Brien. Dell Publishing Co., Inc., 1977.)

den, a vulnerable human being, looks for and hopes for the best in Mr. Loomis, but she does not find it. She refuses to compromise her dream, and escapes with the hope that she will find others alive in the world. Part of the beauty of Robert O'Brien's work is his sensitive and exquisite observation of details in things around us that we normally take for granted. Through Ann's words in a diary, O'Brien's perceptions shine strong.

A positive byproduct of reading science fiction is the flexibility of imagination that it can encourage. Reading science fiction aloud, a good way to entice students to read it independently, also engages the interests of those literal minded students who disparage this genre. Some avid readers, so involved in the here-and-now, have little patience for reading about a make-believe future. These same children, of course, are the very ones who may some day turn science fiction into science fact. They are intuitive in perceiving relations and, by exposure to science fiction, become more imaginative in approaching solutions to problems. Perhaps they are the ones who need it most.

Criteria for Selecting Science Fiction

Elements of plot, style, theme, and characterization are fully developed in good science fiction as in all good fiction. In addition, technological and scientific information is presented accurately, for good science fiction uses elements that are extensions of known physical laws. Such information is presented in a way that is understandable to the reader, and explanations do not interfere with the story line. The story causes readers to consider values about life and science thoughtfully. It critically examines the power and danger of modern technology and illuminates the social impact of science on life.

ON BEYOND ZACHARIAH (I-A) When Ann Burden, in Robert C. O'Brien's *Z for Zachariah* (Atheneum, 1975), leaves her valley home she carries along the diary in which she records the terrifying days with Mr. Loomis. Now, finally free, Ann searches for the children she wants to teach. Write the daily entries in the diary that you think Ann would have written. You need to decide whether she realizes her goal or finds something else as satisfying.

Here is a sample written by a fifth-grade student:

August 24. I have been walking for almost twenty days and have not found any life. Still, I have hope.

August 30. It is so hot in the safe-suit sometimes I want to take it off. Today I was walking and found a giant tree, an oak I think. I decided to climb it. I grabbed a branch and it broke off easily. It was dead, of course. I had forgotten. The tree may have been dead, but inside was something alive. Bugs, small but alive and if there are birds alive, I know what they are eating. I have more hope than ever.

September 3. Last night I had a dream. Not my usual dream of finding a valley, but a truly horrible dream. I dreamed Mr. Loomis was following me. I don't know how he could, because I have the safe-suit. Maybe he lied to me and could make another one. I don't know.

September 13. It is Friday the thirteenth. Believe it or not, it is my lucky day. I saw the birds, I actually saw the birds. I followed them five miles, I think. Now they are sleeping on a tree. I am going to watch them all the time so I don't lose them like Mr. Loomis did. They are flying west. I am very tired. I have not had my terrible dream again. I don't even think he could make another safe suit, even if he wanted to. I am very happy.

September 17. I followed the birds into another town. Too bad it is deserted and brown. In this town there is a library. I went inside and took three books. I would have taken more but they were too heavy. When I came out the birds were gone. I feel like crying. All my hopes and dreams are gone.

September 19. The birds are back!

May 3. I have not written for a long time and I don't think I will ever write again. I have found my valley, my kids. They were waiting for me just like in my dreams. Two days after I came, another wanderer came—without a safe suit. He came from the west and was looking for others. He will stay with me and my kids. I am very, very happy.[41]

Notes

1. e. e. cummings, "who knows if the moon's," in *Bring Me All of Your Dreams,* selected by Nancy Larrick (New York: M. Evans, 1980), p. 76.
2. Eleanor Cameron, *The Green and Burning Tree* (Boston: Little, Brown, 1969), pp. 3–4.
3. Elizabeth Cook, *The Ordinary and the Fabulous* (Cambridge: Cambridge Univ. Press, 1969), p. 5.
4. Edward Eager, *Half Magic* (New York: Harcourt Brace Jovanovich, 1954), pp. 8–9.
5. Pauline Clarke, *The Return of the Twelves* (New York: Coward, McCann & Goeghegan, 1963), p. 30.
6. Ibid., pp. 221–22.
7. Ibid., p. 216.
8. Tove Jansson, *Tales from Moominvalley* (New York: Walck, 1964), p. 16.
9. Ibid., p. 21.
10. Margery Williams, *The Velveteen Rabbit* (New York: Doubleday, 1958), p. 17.
11. Kenneth Grahame, *The Wind in the Willows* (New York: Avon, 1965), p. 9.
12. Ibid., p. 11.
13. Ibid., p. 121.
14. E. B. White, *Letter to Readers* (pamphlet available from Harper & Row, Dept. 363, 10 East 53rd Street, New York, N.Y. 10022).
15. E. B. White, *Charlotte's Web* (New York: Harper & Row, 1952), p. 34.
16. Ibid., p. 41.
17. Teachers can read *Letters of E. B. White* (ed., Dorothy Lobrano Guth, Harper & Row, 1976) and *Essays of E. B. White* (Harper & Row, 1977) for personal insights into his life and beliefs.
18. Developed by Lillian Brightly, King's Road School, Madison, N.J.
19. William Steig, *Farmer Palmer's Wagon Ride* (New York: Farrar, Straus & Giroux, 1974), unpaged.
20. Eleanor Cameron, *The Green and Burning Tree,* p. 71.
21. Madeleine L'Engle, *A Wrinkle in Time* (New York: Farrar, Straus & Giroux, 1962), pp. 75–76.
22. Ibid., p. 76.
23. C. S. Lewis, *The Lion, the Witch and the Wardrobe* (New York: Macmillan, 1951), pp. 45–46.
24. Eleanor Cameron, *The Court of the Stone Children* (New York: Dutton, 1968), p. 5.
25. Ibid., p. 30.
26. Eleanor Cameron, *The Green and Burning Tree* p. 90.
27. Margaret Anderson, *To Nowhere and Back* (New York: Knopf, 1975), pp. 40–41.
28. Developed by Margaret Anzul, Madison Elementary School, Madison, N.J., 1979.
29. June S. Terry, "To Seek and to Find: Quest Literature for Children," in *Children's Literature: Criticism and Response,* ed. Mary Lou White (Columbus, Ohio: Merrill, 1976), p. 139.
30. C. S. Lewis. *The Magician's Nephew,* illus. Pauline Baynes (New York: Macmillan, 1955), p. 92.
31. Mollie Hunter, *Talent Is Not Enough* (New York: Harper & Row, 1976), p. 65.
32. Mollie Hunter, *A Stranger Came Ashore* (New York: Harper & Row, 1975), p. 1.
33. Natalie Babbitt, *Tuck Everlasting* (New York: Farrar, Straus & Giroux, 1975), p. 63.
34. Isaac Bashevis Singer, *Zlateh the Goat,* illus. Maurice Sendak (New York: Harper & Row, 1966), p. 86.
35. Robin McKinley, *Beauty* (New York: Harper & Row, 1978), p. 168.
36. Michael Wood, "Coffee Break for Sisyphus: The Point of Science Fiction," *New York Review of Books,* 2 Oct. 1975, pp. 3–4, 6–7.
37. Robert Heinlein, *Farmer in the Sky* (New York: Scribner's, 1950), pp. 33–34.

38. Sylvia Engdahl, ed., *Anywhere, Anywhen: Stories of Tomorrow* (New York: Atheneum, 1976), p. viii.
39. Arthur C. Clarke, *Dolphin Island: A Story of People of the Sea* (New York: Holt, Rinehart & Winston, 1963), pp. 30–31.
40. Robert C. O'Brien, *Z for Zachariah* (New York: Atheneum, 1975), p. 5.
41. Diane Litvak, student, Worthington Hills School, Worthington, Ohio.

Professional References

Alexander, Lloyd. "High Fantasy and Heroic Romance." *Horn Book Magazine,* 47, No. 6 (Dec. 1971), 577–84.

Bova, Ben. *Through Eyes of Wonder: Science Fiction and Science.* Addison, 1975.

Boyer, Robert H., and Kenneth J. Zahorski, eds. *The Fantastic Imagination: An Anthology of High Fantasy.* Avon, 1977.

Cameron, Eleanor. *The Green and Burning Tree: On the Writing and Enjoyment of Children's Books.* Little, Brown, 1969.

_____. "High Fantasy: *A Wizard of Earthsea*." *Horn Book Magazine,* 47, No. 2 (April 1971), 129–38.

Cook, Elizabeth. *The Ordinary and the Fabulous.* Cambridge Univ. Press, 1969.

Engdahl, Sylvia. "The Changing Role of Science Fiction in Children's Literature." *Horn Book Magazine,* 47, No. 5 (Oct. 1971), 449–55.

Frye, Northrop. *The Educated Imagination.* Indiana Univ. Press, 1964.

Higgins, James E. *Beyond Words: Mystical Fancy in Children's Literature.* Teachers College Press, Columbia Univ. 1970.

Hunter, Mollie. *Talent Is Not Enough: Mollie Hunter on Writing for Children.* Harper & Row, 1976.

Kingman, Lee, ed. *Newbery and Caldecott Medal Books: 1966–1975.* Horn Book, 1975.

Lewis, C. S. *Surprised by Joy: The Shape of My Early Life.* Harcourt Brace Jovanovich, 1966.

Tymn, Marshall B., Kenneth J. Zahorski, and Robert H. Boyer. *Fantasy Literature: A Core Collection and Reference Guide.* Bowker, 1979.

White, E. B. *Essays of E. B. White.* Harper & Row, 1977.

_____. *Letters of E. B. White.* Ed. Dorothy Lobrano Guth. Harper & Row, 1976.

White, Mary Lou, ed. *Children's Literature: Criticism & Response.* Merrill, 1976.

Wood, Michael. "Coffee Break for Sisyphus: The Point of Science Fiction." *New York Review of Books,* 2 Oct. 1975, pp. 3–4, 6–7.

Children's Books Cited in Chapter

Adams, Richard. *Watership Down.* Macmillan, 1974.

Alexander, Lloyd. *The Black Cauldron.* Holt, Rinehart & Winston, 1965.

_____. *The Book of Three.* Holt, Rinehart & Winston, 1964.

_____. *The Castle of Llyr.* Holt, Rinehart & Winston, 1966.

_____. *The High King.* Holt, Rinehart & Winston, 1968.

_____. *Taran Wanderer.* Holt, Rinehart & Winston, 1967.

Andersen, Hans Christian. *The Emperor's New Clothes.* Illus. Virginia Lee Burton. Houghton Mifflin, 1949.

_____. *The Emperor's New Clothes.* Illus. Jack and Irene Delano. Random House, 1971.

_____. *The Nightingale.* Trans. Eva Le Gallienne. Illus. Nancy Ekholm Burkert. Harper & Row, 1965.

_____. *The Steadfast Tin Soldier.* Illus. Paul Galdone. Seabury, 1979.

_____. *Thumbelina.* Illus. Adrienne Adams. Scribner's, 1961.

_____. *The Ugly Duckling.* Illus. Lorinda B. Cauley. Harcourt Brace Jovanovich, 1979.

Anderson, Margaret J. *To Nowhere and Back.* Knopf, 1975.

Babbitt, Natalie. *The Eyes of the Amaryllis.* Farrar, Straus & Giroux, 1977.

_____. *Tuck Everlasting.* Farrar, Straus & Giroux, 1975.

Bond, Michael. *A Bear Called Paddington.* Illus. Peggy Fortnum. Houghton Mifflin, 1958.

_____. *More About Paddington.* Illus. by Peggy Fortnum. Houghton Mifflin, 1962.

_____. *Paddington at Large.* Illus. Peggy Fortnum. Houghton Mifflin, 1963.

_____. *Paddington Takes to TV.* Illus. Ivor Wood. Houghton Mifflin, 1966.

Boston, Lucy M. *The Children of Green Knowe.* Illus. Peter Boston. Harcourt Brace Jovanovich, 1955.

Cameron, Eleanor. *The Court of the Stone Children.* Dutton, 1973.

Carroll, Lewis. *Through the Looking Glass.* Illus. John Tenniel. St. Martin's Press, 1977.

Christopher, John. *The City of Gold and Lead.* Macmillan, 1967.

_____. *The Pool of Fire.* Macmillan, 1968.

_____. *The White Mountains.* Macmillan, 1967.

Clarke, Arthur C. *Dolphin Island: A Story of People of the Sea.* Holt, Rinehart & Winston, 1963.

Clarke, Pauline. *The Return of the Twelves.* Illus. Bernarda Bryson. Coward, McCann & Geoghegan, 1963.

Cooper, Susan. *The Dark Is Rising.* Illus. Alan E. Cober. Atheneum, 1973.

_____. *Greenwitch.* Atheneum, 1974.

_____. *The Grey King.* Illus. Michael Heslop. Atheneum, 1975.

_____. *Over Sea, Under Stone.* Illus. Marjorie Gill. Harcourt Brace Jovanovich, 1966.

242

_____. *Silver on the Tree*. Atheneum, 1977.

Donovan, John. *Family*. Harper & Row, 1976.

Eager, Edward. *Half Magic*. Illus. N. M. Bodecker. Harcourt Brace Jovanovich, 1954.

Engdahl, Sylvia, ed. *Anywhere, Anywhen: Stories of Tomorrow*. Atheneum, 1976.

_____. *Enchantress from the Stars*. Illus. Rodney Shackell. Atheneum, 1970.

_____. *The Far Side of Evil*. Illus. Richard Cuffari. Atheneum, 1971.

Enright, Elizabeth. *Zeee*. Illus. Irene Haas. Harcourt Brace Jovanovich, 1965.

Grahame, Kenneth. *The Open Road*. Illus. Beverly Gooding. Scribner's, 1980.

_____. *"The River Bank": From The Wind in the Willows*. Illus. Adrienne Adams. Scribner's, 1977.

_____. *The Wind in the Willows*. Illus. Ernest H. Shepard. Scribner's, 1908.

Heinlein, Robert. *Farmer in the Sky*. Illus. Clifford Geary. Scribner's, 1950.

Hoban, Russell. *The Mouse and His Child*. Illus. Lillian Hoban. Harper & Row, 1967.

Holm, Anne. *Peter*. Trans. L. W. Kingsland. Harcourt Brace Jovanovich, 1968.

Hoover, H. M. *The Delikon*. Viking, 1977.

Hunter, Mollie. *A Stranger Came Ashore*. Harper & Row, 1975.

_____. *The Walking Stones*. Harper & Row, 1970.

Huxley, Aldous. *Brave New World*. Harper & Row, 1932.

Jansson, Tove. *Tales From Moominvalley*. Trans. Thomas Warburton. Walck, 1964.

Larrick, Nancy, selector. *Bring Me All of Your Dreams*. M. Evans, 1980.

Le Guin, Ursula. *The Farthest Shore*. Illus. Gail Garraty. Atheneum, 1972.

_____. *A Wizard of Earthsea*. Illus. Ruth Robbins. Parnassus, 1968.

L'Engle, Madeleine. *A Swiftly Tilting Planet*. Farrar, Straus & Giroux, 1977.

_____. *A Wind in the Door*. Farrar, Straus & Giroux, 1973.

_____. *A Wrinkle in Time*. Farrar, Straus & Giroux, 1962.

Lewis, C. S. Chronicles of Narnia Series. 7 bks. Macmillan.

_____. *The Lion, The Witch and the Wardrobe*. Illus. Pauline Baynes. Macmillan, 1950.

_____. *The Magician's Nephew*. Illus. Pauline Baynes. Macmillan, 1955.

Lovett, Margaret. *The Great and Terrible Quest*. Holt, Rinehart & Winston, 1967.

McCaffrey, Anne. *Dragondrums*. Atheneum, 1979.

_____. *Dragonsinger*. Atheneum, 1977.

_____. *Dragonsong*. Atheneum, 1976.

McKinley, Robin. *Beauty: A Retelling of the Story of Beauty and the Beast*. Harper & Row, 1978.

Milne, A. A. *The House at Pooh Corner*. Illus. Ernest H. Shepard. Dutton, 1928.

_____. *Now We Are Six*. Illus. Ernest H. Shepard. Dutton, 1927.

_____. *When We Were Very Young*. Illus. Ernest H. Shepard. Dutton, 1924.

_____. *Winnie the Pooh*. Illus. Ernest H. Shepard. Dutton, 1926.

Murphy, Shirley Rousseau. *Silver Woven in My Hair*. Illus. Alan Tiegreen. Atheneum, 1977.

Nesbit, E. *The Enchanted Castle*. Illus. H. R. Millar. Ernest Benn, 1956.

Nichols, Ruth. *The Marrow of the World*. Illus. Trina Schart Hyman. Atheneum, 1972.

_____. *A Walk Out of the World*. Illus. Trina Schart Hyman. Harcourt Brace Jovanovich, 1969.

Norton, André. *Steel Magic*. Illus. Robin Jacques. Archway, 1978.

Norton, Mary. *The Borrowers*. Illus. Beth and Joe Krush. Harcourt Brace Jovanovich, 1953.

_____. *The Borrowers Afield*. Illus. Beth and Joe Krush. Harcourt Brace Jovanovich, 1955.

_____. *The Borrowers Afloat*. Illus. Beth and Joe Krush. Harcourt Brace Jovanovich, 1959.

_____. *The Borrowers Aloft*. Illus. Beth and Joe Krush. Harcourt Brace Jovanovich, 1961.

O'Brien, Robert. *Mrs. Frisby and the Rats of NIMH*. Atheneum, 1971.

_____. *Z for Zachariah*. Atheneum, 1975.

Orwell, George. *Animal Farm*. Harcourt Brace Jovanovich, 1954.

_____. *Nineteen Eighty-four*. Harcourt Brace Jovanovich, 1949.

Pearce, Philippa. *Tom's Midnight Garden*. Illus. Susan Einzig. Lippincott, 1959.

Potter, Beatrix. *The Tale of Peter Rabbit*. Warne, 1902.

_____. *The Tale of Squirrel Nutkin*. Warne, 1903.

Singer, Isaac Bashevis. *Naftali the Storyteller and His Horse, Sus, and Other Stories*. Illus. Margot Zemach. Farrar, Straus & Giroux, 1976.

_____. *Zlateh the Goat and Other Stories*. Illus. Maurice Sendak. Harper & Row, 1966.

Steig, William. *Abel's Island*. Farrar, Straus & Giroux, 1976.

_____. *The Amazing Bone*. Farrar, Straus & Giroux, 1976.

_____. *Amos and Boris*. Farrar, Straus & Giroux, 1971.

_____. *Caleb and Kate*. Farrar, Straus & Giroux, 1977.

_____. *Dominic*. Farrar, Straus & Giroux, 1972.

_____. *Farmer Palmer's Wagon Ride*. Farrar, Straus & Giroux, 1974.

_____. *Roland the Minstrel Pig*. Harper & Row, 1968.

_____. *Sylvester and the Magic Pebble*. Windmill-Dutton, 1969.

_____. *Tiffky Doofky*. Farrar, Straus & Giroux, 1979.

Tolkien, J. R. R. *The Hobbit*. Houghton Mifflin, 1938.

_____. *The Lord of the Rings*. Houghton Mifflin, 1974.

White, E. B. *Charlotte's Web*. Illus. Garth Williams. Harper & Row, 1952.

White, Terence H. *The Once and Future King*. Putnam's, 1958.

Williams, Margery. *The Velveteen Rabbit*. Illus. William Nicholson. Doubleday, 1922.

Recommended Reading

Small Worlds Close Up

Carol Kendall created the miniature world of the Minnipins, a group of conforming people who face a challenge from a group of rebels who would break tradition in *The Gammage Cup,* illustrated by Erik Blegvad (I, Harcourt Brace Jovanovich, 1959), and *The Whisper of Glocken,* illustrated by Imero Gabbato (I, Harcourt Brace Jovanovich, 1965), which can be read as social commentaries on false values within a community. Stephen Krensky's *A Troll in Passing* (I, Atheneum, 1980) tells a similar story about an army of giant trolls who seek to evict a lower tribe from its cozy mountain caves.

Rumer Godden wrote a series of stories, including *The Doll's House,* illustrated by Tasha Tudor (P-I, Viking, 1962 [1947]), and *Impunity Jane,* illustrated by Adrienne Adams (P-I, Viking, 1954), in which dolls lead interesting, albeit uncertain, lives at the mercy of the human children who own them. *Miss Hickory,* by Carolyn Sherwin Bailey, with illustrations by Ruth Gannett (I, Viking, 1962 [1946]), is about a doll of apple twigs with a hickory nut head who lives with her friends Crow, Frog, Squirrel, and Ground Hog, while *Hitty, Her First Hundred Years,* by Rachel Field, with illustrations by Dorthy P. Lathrop (I, Macmillan, 1938), tells about the adventures of a doll (made from the wood of a mountain ash) as she travels the world. In Patricia Clapp's *King of the Dollhouse,* illustrated by Judith Gwyn Brown (P-I, Lothrop, Lee & Shepard, 1974), a young girl discovers that a miniature royal family has moved into her doll house for the summer. William Sleator's *Among the Dolls,* illustrated by Trina Schart Hyman (I, Dutton, 1975), is a psychological study of a troubled young girl's investment of her dolls with a malevolent reality that boomerangs.

Lewis Carroll's *Alice's Adventures in Wonderland,* illustrated by Tove Jansson (I-A, Delacorte, 1977), is, of course, the classic story of a young girl's entrance into an extraordinary world. Norton Juster writes of another curious land in *The Phantom Tollbooth,* illustrated by Jules Feiffer (I, Random House, 1961), a world where language is carried to fantastic extremes. Children who understand and enjoy word play will be fascinated with such characters as King Azoz the Unabridged, the ruler of Dictionopolis.

Poems of Lewis Carroll, selected by Myra Cohn Livingston (I-A, Crowell, 1973), contains poems from his two classic stories, as well as "The Hunting of the Snark" and various parodies, puzzles, and riddles. Several of Shel Silverstein's poems in *Where the Sidewalk Ends* (P-I, Harper & Row, 1974), including "Invitation," "One Inch Tall," and the title poem, will help attune children to the fantasy of small worlds.

Animal Fantasy

Humorous animal fantasies are often children's first introduction to worlds where impossible things are made believable. Beverly Cleary's *The Mouse and the Motorcycle,* illustrated by Louis Darling (P-I, Morrow, 1965), and *Runaway Ralph,* illustrated by Louis Darling (P-I, Morrow, 1970), tell about the exciting adventures of a small mouse who discovers that a toy motorcycle can be the beginning of a new career. In a similar story,

Roger W. Drury's *The Champion of Merrimack County,* illustrated by Fritz Wegner (P-I, Little, Brown, 1976), O Crispin gains the support of a small girl and her mother when he crashes his racing bicycle during a practice run around the rim of an antique bathtub. E. B. White's *Stuart Little,* illustrated by Garth Williams (P-I, Harper & Row, 1945), is the mouse-son of a human family who makes his place in their giant world.

Michael Bond is best known for his stories about Paddington, the bear, but he also created a series of stories about an engaging guinea pig whose vivid imagination often leads her into trouble. *The Tales of Olga da Polga,* illustrated by Hans Helweg (P-I, Macmillan, 1971), and *Olga Carries On,* illustrated by Hans Helweg (P-I, Hastings, 1977), are full of funny episodes that seem perfectly reasonable to young readers.

Robert Lawson's *Rabbit Hill* (P-I, Viking, 1944) and *The Tough Winter* (I, Viking, 1954) are classic stories about rabbits who depend upon people for food. The first book opens with the excited discovery that "new folks" are coming to live in a long-deserted house, and may be "planting people."

George Selden writes about a cricket who was transported from Connecticut to a subway station in *The Cricket in Times Square,* illustrated by Garth Williams (I, Farrar, Straus & Giroux, 1960). Chester is befriended by a boy who provides a cage for the cricket in his family's newsstand far below the sidewalks of New York. In a sequel, *Tucker's Countryside,* illustrated by Garth Williams (I, Farrar, Straus & Giroux, 1969), Chester goes with his new friends, Tucker Mouse and Harry Cat, on a needed vacation to the Connecticut countryside. *Harry Cat's Pet Puppy,* illustrated by Garth Williams (I, Farrar, Straus & Giroux, 1974), further describes the adventures of the animal friends.

Deborah and James Howe's *Bunnicula: A Rabbit Tale of Mystery,* illustrated by Alan Daniel (I, Atheneum, 1979), is a very funny story about a pet rabbit thought to be a vampire by his human family.

While many animal fantasies are humorous, several explore, on a deeper level, the foibles and cares of all creatures. Randall Jarrell's *The Bat-Poet,* illustrated by Maurice Sendak (I, Macmillan, 1965), tells about a small brown bat who writes poetry to tell the other bats about the wonders of the daytime. Alan Arkin's *The Lemming Condition,* illustrated by Joan Sandin (I, Harper & Row, 1976), is a haunting story about Bubber, a sensitive young lemming who questions the instinctive suicidal migration of his community. This nature parable speaks strongly about the effects of unquestioned conformity.

Walter Wangerin wrote a complex animal story about the conquest of evil by Chaunticleer the Rooster, ruler of the barnyard. *The Book of the Dun Cow* (A, Harper & Row, 1978) can be compared with Richard Adams's *Watership Down* in its exploration of society and the forces that would destroy it.

Many poems place animals in imaginary situations and allow children to visualize strange and fantastic delights. Rose Fyleman's "Mice," Elizabeth Coatsworth's "The Mouse," and Patricia Hubbells' "Message from a Mouse, Ascending In a Rocket", all in *The Arbuthnot Anthology of Children's Literature,* 4th ed., edited by Zena Sutherland et al. (Lothrop, Lee & Shepard, 1976), can be read together with stories about animals that do strange and yet believable things.

REFERENCES

Lucy Boston's stories about her majestic old house, Green Knowe, provide readers with a marvelous opportunity to think about what might have been. In *The Stones of Green Knowe,* illustrated by Peter Boston (I, Atheneum, 1976), the author draws together characters from eight hundred fifty years of the fictional history she created for the house in *The River at Green Knowe,* illustrated by Peter Boston (I, Harcourt Brace Jovanovich, 1959), *The Treasure of Green Knowe,* illustrated by Peter Boston (I, Harcourt Brace Jovanovich, 1958), and others.

Many different devices are used to transport characters into other times and other worlds. In Edward Ormondroyd's *Time at the Top,* illustrated by Peggie Bach (I, Parnassus, 1963), and *All in Good Time,* illustrated by Ruth Robbins (I, Parnassus, 1975), Susan discovers that the elevator in her apartment building goes beyond the top floor and delivers her into the world of a century ago. Penelope Farmer uses a bed in a boarding school to transport characters in *Charlotte Sometimes,* illustrated by Chris Connor (I, Harcourt Brace Jovanovich, 1969), while Julia Sauer has her character, Greta, walk through a strange fog to enter the world of Blue Cove in her book, *Fog Magic,* illustrated by Lynd Ward (I, Viking, 1943).

An herb garden near her aunt's old Maine home leads Rosemary back into the eighteenth century in Jane Louise Curry's *Parsley Sage, Rosemary and Time* (I, Atheneum, 1975), while a fireplace, a concealed staircase, and some eerie sounds send Roger back into the time of the former residents of an old house in Curry's *Poor Tom's Ghost* (I-A, Atheneum, 1976).

William Mayne's *Earthfasts* (I-A, Dutton, 1967) is an intriguing story about two boys who discover a stranger from the past, who emerges from beneath the earth and whom they identify as the legendary Nellie Jack John, seeker of King Arthur's treasure.

English manors and cottages are the settings for many exciting time fantasies. A house in the Cotswolds, which was destroyed by fire in 1902, becomes visible to two modern teenagers when they find an old pendant on the grounds of *Romansgrove,* by Mabel Esther Allan, illustrated by Gail Owens (I-A, Atheneum, 1975). In Eileen Dunlop's *Elizabeth, Elizabeth,* illustrated by Peter Farmer (I-A, Holt, Rinehart & Winston, 1977), a young girl spends a lonely summer with her historian aunt until she happens upon an old looking glass that transforms her into a girl with the same name from the distant past.

Betony Dovewood, who discovers a miniature china cottage in a cupboard in her grandfather's home, finds that *The Other Face* (I, Dutton, 1976) belongs to one of her forebears of a century and a half earlier. In Nancy Bond's *A String in the Harp* (I-A, Atheneum, 1976), twelve-year-old Peter becomes involved in the life of a sixth-century bard in an experience that enables him to sort out his life in the present.

Margaret J. Anderson's characters move both into the past and into the future in two stories set in Scotland. *In the Keep of Time* (I, Knopf, 1977) and *In the Circle of Time* (I, Knopf, 1979) include historical information about the abandoned tower and the ancient circle of stones that form the basis for the stories. Penelope Lively has written several compelling time-shift fantasies including *Going Back* (I, Dutton, 1975) and *The Ghost of*

Thomas Kempe, illustrated by Antony Maitland (I, Dutton, 1973). In her *The House in Norham Gardens* (I, Dutton, 1974), Clare, who lives in an English Victorian house with two elderly aunts, becomes able, through her dreams, to realize her place in the present.

Poetry about different times and different places abounds. Several poems by Walter De La Mare, including "Sam," "Tillie," and "The Little Green Orchard," all in *The Arbuthnot Anthology of Children's Literature,* 4th ed., edited by Zena Sutherland et al. (Lothrop, Lee & Shepard, 1976), will stir children's imaginations concerning the past and the future.

Quest Stories

Alan Garner combines time warp, superstition, and conflict in several intriguing stories about overcoming evil that might be categorized as "high fantasy," in view of their depth and complexity. *Elidor* (I-A, Walck, 1967) is a land threatened by the powers of darkness into which four children drop as they explore an abandoned church. Garner's *The Owl Service* (I-A, Walck, 1968) and *Red Shift* (I-A, Macmillan, 1973) combine legend with time travel to create difficult but fascinating stories.

Betsy Gould Hearne's *South Star,* illustrated by Trina Schart Hyman (I-A, Atheneum, 1977), tells about Megan, the last surviving daughter of a family of giants of long ago who is separated from her parents during a terrible storm. A sequel, *Home,* illustrated by Trina Schart Hyman (I-A, Atheneum, 1979), continues Megan's story as she searches for her father.

Patricia A. McKillip begins a trilogy with *Riddle-Master of Hed* (A, Atheneum, 1976), in which young Prince Morgan must abandon his plan to rule his land of simple, peace-loving farmers to follow his destiny. Morgan's story is continued in *Heir of Sea and Fire* (A, Atheneum, 1977) and *Harpist in the Wind* (A, Athenum, 1979) where he finally learns the answers to the riddles of the universe and of his own identity.

Diana Wynne Jones explores the theme of the struggle against oppressive forces in *Cart and Cwidder* (I-A, Atheneum, 1977) and its companion *Drowned Ammet* (I-A, Atheneum, 1978). In both books dangerous and repressive conditions force young people to flee their homelands. A third book, *The Spellcoats* (I-A, Atheneum, 1979), set in the fantasy land of Dalemark, takes place at an earlier time than the others and again involves the escape from hostile forces in their native village.

Literary Lore

The stories of Hans Christian Andersen, known as the father of the modern fairy tale, have survived and are now enjoying a new popularity in part because of the beautiful picture book editions that have been created by outstanding artists. Among the best are *Thumbelina,* adapted by Amy Ehrlich and illustrated by Susan Jeffers (P, Dial, 1979), *The Snow Queen,* illustrated by Marcia Brown (P, Scribner's, 1972), *The Little Match Girl,* illustrated by Blair Lent (P, Houghton Mifflin, 1968), *The Fir Tree,* illustrated by Nancy Ekholm Burkert (P, Harper & Row, 1970), and *The Princess and the Pea,* illustrated by Paul Galdone (P, Seabury, 1978).

Mary Norton provides an unusual speculation of what happens to fairy tale characters in a story about a practical, matter-of-fact young boy named James who dreams of a land where the familiar giants and princesses are all living together in a state of suspended time. *Are All the Giants Dead?* illustrated by Brian Froud (I, Harcourt Brace Jovanovich, 1975), is an amusing look at the grown-old Jack the Giant Killer and Jack (of Beanstalk fame), as well as the daughter of Beauty and the Beast, who is under a spell that, it seems, nobody is working on.

The lore of devils and monsters is made richer by Natalie Babbitt. Her *The Devil's Storybook* (I, Farrar, Straus & Giroux, 1974) is a collection of short stories, while *Knee Knock Rise* (I, Farrar, Straus & Giroux, 1970), an exciting story about the power of tradition, tells of young Egan who, though he bravely discovers that the eerie noise that terrorizes his village has a natural cause, is not believed by the villagers.

Mollie Hunter is a master at combining the folklore of the ages with skilled storytelling to produce marvelous tales of fantasy. *The Wicked One* (I, Harper & Row, 1977) is a huge, ugly, sometimes evil, supernatural creature in the hills of Scotland. It causes hot-tempered Colin Grant so much trouble that he flees to America, only to discover that the creature has relentlessly followed him. The natural and the mythical are elements in Mollie Hunter's stories of her native Scotland, including *The Kelpie's Pearls,* illustrated by Stephen Gammell (I, Harper & Row, 1976), a drama revolving around the mystery of the Loch Ness monster. Penelope Lively, too, develops her stories with a deft combination of history, legend, and fantasy. *The Whispering Knights,* illustrated by Gareth Floyd (I, Dutton, 1976), are a circle of ancient stones near the legendary haunt of Morgan le Fay, King Arthur's evil sister. Three modern children concoct a witch's brew that arouses the wrath of the famous enchantress, sending a quiet Cotswold valley into a fearful summer.

Elizabeth Pope's *The Perilous Gard,* illustrated by Richard Cuffari (I-A, Houghton Mifflin, 1974), skillfully blends folk myth and superstition with the history of Tudor England. Kate Sutton, exiled because of her sister's criticism of Queen Mary, unlocks the mystery of an old castle, last stronghold of the Fairy Folk.

John Gardner writes original fairy tales with a deft blend of enchantment and humor. His *Dragon, Dragon and Other Tales,* illustrated by Charles Shields (I-A, Knopf, 1975), is set in the land of dragons, giants, and fairy godmothers who play wry tricks on hapless villagers. Jane Yolen, too, is a master of the original fairy tale. One of her books, *Shape Shifters: Fantasy and Science Fiction Tales About Humans Who Can Change Their Shapes* (I-A, Seabury, 1978) is a collection of unusual stories that will lead students into a study of this legendary phenomenon.

Daisy Wallace edited several collections of poems, including *Monster Poems,* illustrated by Kay Chorao (P-I, Holiday House, 1976), and *Witch Poems,* illustrated by Trina Schart Hyman (P-I, Holiday House, 1976), that contain traditional chants, curses, and spells as well as contemporary poems. William Cole collected *Poems of Magic and Spells,* illustrated by Peggy Bacon (P-I, World, 1960), while Lee Bennett Hopkins collected ghostly stories and poems in *A-Haunting We Will Go* (P-I, Whitman, 1977). Jack Prelutsky's *Nightmares: Poems to Trouble Your Sleep,* illustrated by Arnold Lobel (P-I, Greenwil-

low, 1976), is a hit with children, who squeal with delight at the eerie spooks.

Science Fiction

While many science fiction books are filled with complex concepts and ideas making them suitable for older readers, there are several science fantasy stories for younger children who are developing the speculative abilities required by the more difficult books. Ellen MacGregor and Dora Pantell have written a series of books about an eccentric old lady, *Miss Pickerell,* who becomes involved in a variety of quasi-scientific explorations. Louis Slobodkin begins a series with *The Space Ship Under the Apple Tree* (P-I, Macmillan, 1952), while Eleanor Cameron's *The Wonderful Flight to the Mushroom Planet,* illustrated by Robert Henneberger (I, Little, Brown, 1954) is the first of a group of books about space exploration. Jerome Beatty's Matthew Looney stories, and Jay Williams's Danny Dunn adventures are other books for young science fiction buffs.

Alexander Key's *Escape to Witch Mountain,* illustrated by Leon B. Wisdom, Jr. (I, Westminster, 1968), is the story of two children who seek a home in a mysterious land. Carl Biemiller's *The Hydronauts* (I, Doubleday, 1970) and Ben Bova's series, which begins with *Exiled from Earth* (I, Dutton, 1973), are also appropriate for intermediate-grade children.

John Christopher writes of possible world crises and the power struggles that threaten deterioration of society. *Wild Jack* (I, Macmillian, 1974) and *Empty World* (I, Dutton, 1978) offer provocative looks at future worlds.

Peter Dickinson's series of books deal not with the technological impact of a future society, but with a world that has returned to a feudal state. His *The Weathermonger* (I-A, Little, Brown, 1969), *Heartsease,* illustrated by Nathan Goldstein (I-A, Little, Brown, 1969), and *The Devil's Children* (I-A, Little, Brown, 1970) show how a group of children try to fight prejudice and fear in a world nearly destroyed by machines. In Penelope Lively's *The Voyage of QV 66,* illustrated by Harold Jones (I, Dutton, 1979), only animals survive a massive flood.

H. M. Hoover sets *Return to Earth* (I-A, Viking, 1980) in the year 3307, when the administrator of another planet comes back to an earth governed by corporations. Hoover's *The Lost Star* (A, Viking, 1979) speculates about life in the far future on a distant planet inhabited by imagined life forms. In both books the author probes the idea of the responsibility humans have for cultures they discover. John Rowe Townsend explores the same idea in *The Creatures* (I-A, Lippincott, 1980), in which a small colony of superior beings lives under a protective dome and controls the lowly creatures on the outside.

Frank Bonham presents a frightening look at the effects of technology in *The Forever Formula* (A, Dutton, 1979), a story about life after cryogenic storage. Jean Karl looks at a future in which the Clordians, from another part of the galaxy, have projected deadly rays to the earth. *The Turning Place: Stories of the Future Past* (A, Dutton, 1976) recounts episodes of human survival in a world of chaos.

Ted Hughes wrote *Moon-Whales and Other Moon Poems,* illustrated by Leonard Baskin (I-A, Viking, 1976), a collection of haunting visions of a grotesque, disquieting place.

seven

MARK STRAND   *EATING POETRY*

Ink runs from the corners of my mouth.
There is no happiness like mine.
I have been eating poetry.

The librarian does not believe what she sees.
Her eyes are sad
and she walks with her hands in her dress.

The poems are gone.
The light is dim.
The dogs are on the basement stairs and coming up.

Their eyeballs roll,
their blond legs burn like brush.
The poor librarian begins to stamp her feet and weep.

She does not understand.
When I get on my knees and lick her hand
she screams.

I am a new man.
I snarl at her and bark,
I romp with joy in the bookish dark.[1]

Poetry and Verse

There is little consensus about the nature of poetry. Poetry means something different to each poet and each person, the individual definition arising from the uniqueness of the individual. Poetry is personal and, in a sense, it is beyond explanation. We find it easier to appreciate poetry than to define it. Perhaps we should not try to say what it is, but rather what it does to us, what it evokes in us so that we see an experience afresh.

Yet, we need at least a provisional understanding of what poetry is. Most definitions focus on surface distinctions such as elements, form, or the way it looks on a page, and many think that poetry is distinguished by the use of rhyme or meter. Indeed, children often remark, "It looks different." These are superficial distinctions, the most salient aspect of poetry being its highly charged, condensed, and concentrated language, which uses so few words to say so much. Poetry is filled with words artistically organized and pressurized in ways that call our attention to experiences we have not known or fully recognized. Poetry is a poet's intuition of truth.

Myra Cohn Livingston cites fellow poet May Swenson's distinction between poetry and other modes of expression:

Poetry doesn't tell; it shows. Prose tells.
Poetry is not philosophy; poetry makes things be, right now.
Not an idea, but a happening.
It is not music, but it sounds while showing.
It is mobile; it is a thing taking place—active, interactive, in a place.
It is not thought; it has to do with senses and muscles.
It is not dancing, but it moves while it remains.[2]

Although poetry's words can be familiar ones, they are carefully chosen and placed in such a way as to capture the imagination, that faculty that births miracles. The poetic experience is qualified by precise selection and ordering of words. Exceptional poets shape an ordinary, everyday experience into an emotional universal. As Northrop Frye says, "The poet's job is not to tell you what happened, but what happens: not what did take place, but the kind of thing that always does take place."[3]

247

The contribution of poetry to the growth and enrichment of the imagination is immense. Poetry, even more than other literature, can help keep the sense of wonder alive in children. It can provoke dreams of possibility and visions of miracles. It is totally different from television, for example, whose images are presented full-blown for the passive viewer. Poetry makes you work! The concepts presented in television or film are largely what the artist imagines, requiring little imaginative collaboration from the audience. When children read or hear poetry, on the other hand, they create the images for themselves.

Children appreciate the vivid images conveyed by poetry; they are able to see the

> Narrow hats high
> Above yellow bead eyes,
> The tatter-haired witches
> Ride through the skies[4]

suggested by Karla Kuskin in "The Witches' Ride." They are able to feel

> Curtains of seaweed,
> Blankets of mist,
> Walls of coral bank
> Sea-foam kissed[5]

in "Sea Spirit" by Patricia Hubbell. They almost smell the lavender, tobacco, Listerine, and hot buttered toast in Christopher Morley's "Smells (Junior)"[6] and hear the clatter of wheel on track in David McCord's "Song of the Train."[7] They can all but taste the "Animal crackers, and cocoa to drink/That is the finest of suppers" in Christopher Morley's "Animal Crackers."[8]

Children at different stages of development appreciate different kinds of verse and poetry. At developmentally early stages, nursery rhymes, jingles, and simple verse are an enchantment; at later stages, linguistically complex—even adult—poetry can be a joy. From the young child's early delight with chants, nursery songs, and verse, springs the older child's subsequent thirst for more sophisticated poetic works.

The complexity of the poetry and verse in this chapter varies, as does children's grasp of it.

Young children don't cut their teeth on Wallace Stevens; instead, their best experiences with poetry begin with Mother Goose (Chapter 5), the groundwork from which we build.

With this in mind we include much that is essentially rhyme—skillful, even touching, often funny, and usually pertinent—but not, in any rigorous sense, poetry. Our goal is to surround children with appealing verse, and ultimately fine poetry, for every occasion and activity. Poetry is not just saved for rare times on Friday afternoons. When poetry is an essential part of the school day, totally enjoyed for itself, the pervading spirit facilitates dialogue between poets, children, and teachers.

Poetry feeds the imagination through its words and images. Just as we are concerned with giving children the best food for a healthy body, so are we concerned with giving their minds the best words to grow on. Undoubtedly, some of the best words are found in poetry.

We include the words of poets whose work has endured as well as those of new poets just making their mark; we give the most attention to contemporary poets whose work breathes the life of today.

We include poetry with every topic in every chapter of this book to emphasize that poetry is a part of life and that all should share it. In *Beauty: A Retelling of the Story of Beauty and the Beast* (I-A), by Robin McKinley, the child, Honour, says, "I was the only one who read poetry for pleasure." Ideally, all students would experience poetry as Honour does.

Good teachers think of poetry in terms of sharing rather than teaching, in terms of enjoying rather than analyzing, in terms of delight rather than duty. If ever there existed an area of literature where enthusiasm is contagious, it is within poetry. When poetry experiences are infused with pleasure they take root and become an aesthetic and intellectual wellspring for children. We should take every opportunity to discover and enjoy poetry along with our students.

Poetry is essential to the full development of the child's imaginative faculties, and since memory is both receptive and tenacious in the early years, it is good to have some poetry in every school day. Poetry can enrich a variety of classroom activities that cut across curriculum areas. Poetry should be presented not in isolation, but in relation to children's experiences, which can consist of enjoying the sounds and feeling the sweetness of the words even without understanding them—a point for teachers to remember. Annis Duff, in a description of how she shared poetry with her two children, says:

Meaning, *per se,* is a rather secondary consideration in our choice of poetry for sharing, for it is one of the subtlest and most valuable properties of great poetry that it speaks to the feelings rather than to the intellect. What for the moment has no applicable meaning for the child, because of his limited experience, is often committed readily and joyously to memory for the music of the words and the haunting quality of the images. Years later, it will flower in all the nobility of its intention, to illuminate and enrich experience.[9]

In this spirit, Robert Frost's poem "Stopping by Woods on a Snowy Evening" speaks to all ages at several levels. In order to live this poem, children do not need to know all of the implications in the words:

> The woods are lovely, dark, and deep,
> But I have promises to keep,
> And miles to go before I sleep,
> And miles to go before I sleep.[10]

It is enough to sense the wonder that the words evoke. The picture book version by Susan Jeffers, illustrated mainly with frosty black-and-white New England scenes, treats children to an intimate perception, one that invites a literal interpretation. Although there is more than the prospect of a long trip ahead in the poet's words, children do not need to know this to apprehend it in their terms. The value in beautiful versions such as Jeffers's is that they help children to make the first step into poetry at a simple and perhaps literal (but nonetheless authentic) level from which they can go on to fuller and richer meaning once experience has broadened.

Children are more apt to love poetry if they are not compelled to memorize it, but choose to memorize it for themselves instead. A permanent distaste for poetry often results from meaningless analysis and required memorization.

The teacher's personality, approach, and attitude are crucial to successful experiences with poetry. At the elementary level, it is best to go the way of intuition and not analysis. Once poetry has captured its children, knowledge of poetic devices, elements, and forms may become important. Although there is debate about the value of formal lessons in poetic techniques, there is little disagreement that appreciation *is* expanded when one knows about sound, rhythm, meaning, and form—the how and the what of poetry. In developing awareness of poetic techniques, however, the elementary school teacher treads softly, avoiding overemphasis.

Children learn to know poetry and to love it when they are exposed to it in positive ways. In the case of poetry, familiarity breeds appreciation. How many of us were schoolchildren who thought that all poems began with a brief paragraph of introduction and explanation and ended with a list of related questions? This isolation of the subject need not be the rule; poetry should permeate the curriculum and be not just a means to other ends; otherwise, the spirit of poetry flies out the window. If reading a story about dogs, one might also read poetry about dogs. When studying an aspect of nature, include poetry about nature. Poetry coordinated with topics of study and events throughout the school day illuminates experience. Read for itself, it is sheer joy. Children learn, by absorption, that poetry can apply to every aspect of life. Although you don't always need to relate poetry to some curricular end, you do need to use poetry in such a way as to permit glimpses of the unicorn.

The more experience children have with poetry, the more pleasure they accumulate. The child is the source from which our direction is taken: ask questions wisely and explain meanings at the child's request. In most instances, wait until children want to know. Questions expand the meaning and extend the enjoyment of a poem, but, in this area particularly, teachers need to know when to stop teaching. We need to know how to tell

250 children what to look for without telling them what to see.

The teacher's goal is to guide discussion while allowing leeway for children to find their own (and the poet's) meanings and insights. The means of achieving this goal come more easily the more we share poetry with children and listen to their responses.

Recent studies show that neither children's preferences for poetry nor teachers' practices in teaching it have changed significantly over the years. We know that teachers tend to continue to read their old favorites without keeping up with the many new and beautiful books of poetry published each year. We know, too, that teachers of upper elementary grades do not devote as much time to poetry as do their colleagues in the lower grades.

Chow Loy Tom's national survey shows, among other things, that most teachers in the middle grades read neither poetry *nor* prose aloud more than once a month. Ann Terry, who extended Tom's study, concludes that children's poetry choices remain stable and consistent over the years. Many children today, like those of 50 years ago, prefer humorous poems. Most children do not like sentimental and serious poetry, or poems difficult to understand. Poetry with clear-cut rhyme and rhythm is well liked; poetry that depends heavily upon imagery is not. When given a choice, children overwhelmingly favor contemporary poems with modern content written in today's language.

Carol Fisher and Margaret Natarella found that content influences the preferences of first-, second-, and third-grade children, and that humor is an important factor. Favorite topics are familiar experiences and animals. The narrative is the most popular poetic form, especially those specimens that are rhymed and have a strong meter.

We believe, then, that poetry offers education of the imagination and pure joy. Children come to each poetry experience prepared to enjoy, to explore, and to extend understanding. Children's understanding is outstripped by their imagination; their emotions are not circumscribed by their intelligence. Poetry enables them to see unicorns, miracles, and the dew glistening on spider webs.

THE ELEMENTS OF POETRY

Poets manipulate the elements of sound, rhythm, and meaning to distinguish their work from prose.

The discussion in this section and the one that follows (Forms of Poetry) is intended to provide a basic understanding of these elements for teachers so that they may be better informed when sharing poetry with children. In no way is it intended that these be taught to children sequentially, element by element or form by form. Instead, through the illustrative activities, children can construct meaningful experiences for themselves.

Words as Sound

Of all the elements of poetry, sound offers the most pleasure to children. The choice and arrangement of sounds make the music of poetry and, at the same time, serve to reinforce meaning. Alliteration, assonance, onomatopoeia, and rhyme are among the language resources of sound.

Poets' ears are tuned to the repetition of consonants, vowels, syllables, words, phrases, and lines, separately and in combination. Anything may be repeated to achieve effect. Alliteration refers to the repetition of the initial consonant sounds of words at close intervals, such as "thin spaghettis softly scream/and curdle quarts of quiet cream,"[11] or "Timothy Tompkins had turnips and tea./The turnips were tiny./He ate at least three."[12]

Mary Ann Hoberman plays with the sounds of language in *A House Is a House for Me* (P):

> And envelopes, earmuffs and eggshells
> And bathrobes and baskets and bins
> And ragbags and rubbers and roasters
> And tablecloths, toasters and tins.[13]

Assonance, the repetition of vowel sounds at close intervals, is sprinkled in this verse.

Rhoda W. Bacmeister uses assonance and alliteration in the verses of "Galoshes":

There's a line in *The Night Before Christmas* that will stay in my head forever because when I first learned it, I didn't understand all the words.

As dry leaves before the wild hurricane fly,
When they meet with an obstacle, mount to the sky,
So up to the housetop the coursers they flew,
With the sleigh full of toys, and St. Nicholas too.

I didn't know *hurricane;* I didn't know *obstacle;* I didn't know *coursers;* but I just loved the way they sounded (Alvina Treut Burrows, "Profile: Karla Kuskin," *Language Arts,* 56, No. 8 [Nov./Dec. 1979], 935–37).

Karla Kuskin's fascination with words began in childhood, when her parents and teachers read poetry to her and listened to her read aloud. Her love of language and poetry grew over the years, and she writes for children as a means of sharing her deep feeling with them.

Karla Kuskin illustrates her own books, extending the poetic images with visual ones. In *Near the Window Tree* she wishes for three things: a chair, a book to read, and a tree to let the sun sift through. Opposite each poem in this book are capsule descriptions of how and why each was written. Her unique view, evident in all her work, is vividly expressed in *Any Me I Want to Be,* in which thirty animals and things describe themselves and their surroundings.

Karla Kuskin is a native of New York City, where she now lives with her husband and two children. She has said:

Instead of building a fence of formality around poetry I want to emphasize its accessibility, the sound, rhythm, humor, the inherent simplicity. Poetry can be as natural and effective a form of self-expression as singing or shouting (*Harper & Row promotional material*).

This belief enhances her style and has won for her the 1979 National Council of Teachers of English Award for Poetry for Children.

KARLA KUSKIN

Susie's galoshes
Make splishes and sploshes
And slooshes and sloshes,
As Susie steps slowly
Along in the slush.[14]

Repetition is like meeting an old friend again; children find it reassuring. Repetition of words underscores meaning, establishes a sound pattern, and is a source of humor in many nursery rhymes, as in the anonymous *If All the Seas* (N-P):

If all the seas were one sea,
What a *great* sea that would be!
If all the trees were one tree,
What a *great* tree that would be!
And if all the axes were one axe,
What a *great* axe that would be!

And if all the men were one man,
What a *great* man that would be!
And if the *great* man took the *great* axe,
And cut down the *great* tree,
And let it fall into the *great* sea,
What a splish-splash that would be![15]

Onomatopoeia is the creation of a word from natural sounds associated with the thing or action designated, or the use of such words. For example, the word "murmur" resembles somewhat the sound of murmuring. Other words that sound like what they mean are bang, snap, and hiss. Shel Silverstein plays with onomatopoeia in "The Fourth":

Oh
CRASH!
my
BASH
it's
BANG!
the
ZANG!
Fourth
WHOOSH!
of
BAROOOM!
July
WHEW![16]

Onomatopoeia in combination with other sound resources can achieve poetic effect to light up any child's eyes.

Although poetry need not rhyme, most research in children's preferences indicates that rhyme is preferred. An example of end rhyme—in which the rhyming words are at the ends of lines—is Dennis Lee's popular "I Eat Kids Yum Yum!"

A child went out one day.
She only went to play.
A mighty monster came along
And sang its mighty monster song:

"I EAT KIDS YUM YUM!
I STUFF THEM DOWN MY TUM.
I ONLY LEAVE THE TEETH AND CLOTHES.
(I SPECIALLY LIKE THE TOES.)"

The child was not amused.
She stood there and refused.
Then with a skip and a little twirl
She sang the song of a hungry girl:

"I EAT MONSTERS BURP!
THEY MAKE ME SQUEAL AND SLURP.
IT'S TIME TO CHOMP AND TAKE A CHEW—
AND WHAT I'LL CHEW IS YOU!"

The monster ran like that!
It didn't stop to chat.
(The child went skipping home again
And ate her brother's model train.)[17]

Shel Silverstein's "Tree House" illustrates internal rhyme, in which the rhymed words occur within the line:

A tree house, a free house,
A secret you and me house.
A high up in the leafy branches
Cozy as can be house.

A street house, a neat house,
Be sure and wipe your feet house
Is not my kind of house at all—
Let's go live in a tree house.[18]

When rhyme spills over from the end of one line to the beginning of the next it is called *runover*. David McCord gives us a beautiful example of this (together with end rhyme) in his "Runover Rhyme":

Down by the pool still fishing,
Wishing for fish, I fail;
Praying for birds not present,
Pheasant or grouse or quail.

Up in the woods, his hammer
Stammering, I can't see
The woodpecker, find the cunning
Sunning old owl in the tree.

Over the field such raucous
Talk as the crows talk on!
Nothing around me slumbers;
Numbers of birds have gone.

Even the leaves hang listless,
Lasting through days we lose,
Empty of what is wanted,
Haunted by what we choose.[19]

If children are provided with many opportunities to experience a variety of rhyme schemes, the chances are that they will then come to see how the use of rhyme can add to and enhance the meaning of a poem.

THINGS TO DO AND NOT TO DO (ALL AGES)   Poetry can be regarded as an oral art form and can often be appreciated most when it is spoken or read aloud. Long before children learn to read and long after they are reading alone, they should hear poetry read. Some guidelines for reading poetry aloud include:

1. Read it silently first, to grasp its meaning for yourself.

2. Read it aloud to yourself several times to determine where pauses will affect the sense. Thus, you will not necessarily stop at the end of a line, but carry over from one to the next to complete the thought. Poets use punctuation purposefully to guide our reading.

3. Listen to recordings of poets reading their own work to gain a feeling for phrasing.

4. Read with expressiveness appropriate to the poem. The content determines the tone.

5. Read poems in a natural, not sing-song or stagelike, voice.

6. Give children time to enjoy the words of the poem. In poetry's condensed language every word can carry much meaning.

7. Read the same poem aloud to the class more than once.

8. Invite children to join in so they can savor the words, too.

The primary purpose in sharing poetry with children is to extend their understanding and increase their pleasure and enjoyment of it. In order to insure success—that is, to instill a love of poetry in children—avoid these common pitfalls, which might be called ten ways to make children hate poetry:

1. Make everyone memorize a classic poem and ask individual children to recite it alone before the class.

2. Read only the Romantic and Victorian poetry that you remember from your childhood about truth, beauty, and wisdom.

3. Read poetry in a sing-song or dramatic voice.

4. Have children analyze the deeper meaning of every poem.

5. Pick out similes, metaphors, and symbols in every poem.

6. Test children on the metrical pattern and rhyme scheme of poems.

7. Read poetry only once a month.

8. Read only poems that teach a lesson, and make children learn the moral.

9. Require children to copy long tedious poems into their notebooks.

10. Make February "poetry month" and ask every student to read a collection of poems and write a book report.

Activity: Teacher to Student

A POETRY PAGEANT (P-I) Poetry is fun when you share it with your friends. One way to do that is through choral speaking. Select some of your favorite poems and divide them into parts as music is divided for singing by a chorus. Use the natural rhythm of the language and the swinging cadence of the lines to help in dividing the poem into parts. High and low voices can be blended to emphasize poetic sounds just as instruments are used in an orchestra. There can be solos, duets, boys alone, girls alone, boys and girls together, and whatever other variations the poem suggests. Some poems about unusual and imaginative animals, and especially good for choral speaking, can be found in X. J. Kennedy's *The Phantom Ice Cream Man: More Nonsense Verse* (Atheneum, 1979); Mary Ann Hoberman's *The Raucous Auk* (Viking, 1973); Jack Prelutsky's *The Pack Rat's Day and Other Poems* (Macmillan, 1974); and William Cole's *An Arkful of Animals* (Houghton Mifflin, 1978).

Rehearse until your production is polished. You might want to make simple animal costumes or face masks. Take a troupe of "troubadors" around the school, dropping into classrooms for about ten minutes to share your interpretations.

Words as Rhythm

Rhythm is everywhere in life; think of ocean waves, the tick of a clock, hoofbeats, one's pulse. In poetry, rhythm refers to recurrences of syllables and accents, in the rise and fall of words spoken or read. All good poetry is rhythmical just as other forms of high art are. The rhythm in painting, sculpture, and other visual arts is seen in the repetition of line, form, or color. Rhythm in dance is apparent in the flow of the body movements and the graceful flow of motion. In music it is evident in the beat. Well-written prose has rhythm, too, although it is less evident or regular than in poetry.

Rhythm is usually manifest in poetry as accented and unaccented syllables are alternated. It is what Eve Merriam calls "the repeat of a beat . . . an inner chime that makes you want to tap your feet or swerve in a curve."[20]

The rhythm in poetry is most often metrical. Meter is ordered rhythm, in which certain syllables are regularly stressed or accented in a more or less fixed pattern. "Meter" means "measure," and metrical language in poetry can be measured. The meter in poetry can run from that of tightly structured verse patterns to loosely defined free verse. Whatever it is, rhythm helps to create and then reinforce a poem's meaning. In *Circus* (N-P), Jack Prelutsky adjusts his rhythms to the subject:

> Over and over the tumblers tumble
> with never a fumble
> with never a stumble,
> top over bottom and back over top
> flop-flippy-floppity-flippity-flop.

But the tumblers pass, and are followed by the elephants, whose plodding walk echoes in the new rhythm:

> Here come the elephants, ten feet high,
> elephants, elephants, heads in the sky.
> Eleven great elephants intertwined,
> one little elephant close behind.[21]

and the rhythm plods along in the way elephants walk.

David McCord captures the rhythmic chant of children's playground behavior in "Bananas and Cream":

Bananas and cream,
Bananas and cream:
All we could say was
Bananas and cream.

We couldn't say fruit,
We wouldn't say cow,
We didn't say sugar—
We don't say it now.[22]

When Robert Louis Stevenson writes:

Faster than fairies, faster than witches,
Bridges and houses, hedges and ditches;
And charging along like troops in a battle
All through the meadows the horses and cattle[23]

he is using a rapid rhythm that suggests what the view would be like "From a Railway Carriage."

Word order, too, contributes to the rhythm of poetry. Arranging words is central to the making of a poem. Teachers, and perhaps some special students, should be aware of the ways poets manipulate syntax to make poetry distinctive from prose. One noticeable feature of poetic language is the way it varies from the straight declarative sentence. In Robert Louis Stevenson's "Where Go the Boats?" the poet states:

Dark brown is the river
    Golden is the sand.
It flows along forever,
    With trees on either hand.[24]

The literal meaning of the poem could probably be communicated in this way:

The river is dark brown,
    The sand is gold.
The river keeps on flowing forever,
    With trees on both sides.

But it is immediately recognized that something is lost. Retaining most of Stevenson's words but rearranging the word order totally distorts the visual image. Poets manipulate syntax until they find an order and rhythm pleasing to them and one that communicates more than the literal message. For children, the inverted sentence order used for poetic effect can at first interfere with meaning; how-

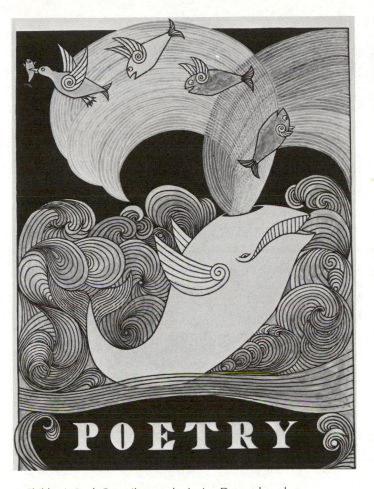

A Children's Book Council poster by Janina Domanska celebrates the joy of poetry. The exuberant, swirling forms capture the richness and song of much poetry for children. ("Poetry" poster by Janina Domanska for the Children's Book Council, Inc., New York, N.Y. Used by permission.)

ever, children grow in their ability to comprehend inverted sentences as they hear poetry read aloud.

Words as Pictures

Poets frequently position the lines of their verse to produce an effect that helps convey rhythm (and even content). Two classic examples are David McCord's "The Grasshopper"[25] and A. A. Milne's "Halfway Down."[26] One that children especially like is "Serpent," by Eve Merriam.

sliding over stones
a silent spill

sleek as silk
iridescent

appearing and
disappearing

slipping soundless out of sunlight
to seek dark-wooded sanctuary

sequestered
surreptitious

slithering round
underground secretive roots

Narcissus

spun in upon
its sinuous self

ancient synonym for
sibylline
mystery

The slithering form and hissing consonants add to the sense
of a serpent.
("Serpent" from *Out Loud* by Eve Merriam. Copyright ©
1973 by Eve Merriam. Published by Atheneum. By permission of the author.)

fog smog	fog smog
tissue paper	tissue paper
clear the blear	clear the smear
fog more	fog more
splat splat	downpour
rubber scraper	rubber scraper
overshoes	macintosh
bumbershoot	muddle on
slosh through	slosh through
drying up	drying up
sky lighter	sky lighter
nearly clear	nearly clear

clearing clearing veer
clear here clear

Eyes compelled to reciprocate like a windshield wiper help
make the image vivid in the reader's mind.
("Windshield Wiper" from *Out Loud* by Eve Merriam. Copyright © 1973 by Eve Merriam. Published by Atheneum. By
permission of the author.)

It is easy to see the words slithering down the page. In another verse, "Windshield Wiper," the rhythm swishes back and forth as you read from the left column to the right.

Poetry calls attention to itself by its shape on the page. We might find the following statements interesting if we read them in the continuous line of regular prose: "Neatness, madam, has nothing to do with the Truth. The Truth is quite messy like a wind blown room." But when we see the words arranged as William J. Harris arranges them in "The Truth Is Quite Messy," the impact is stronger:

Neatness, madam, has
nothing to do
with the Truth.
The Truth
is quite messy
like
a wind blown room.[27]

Awareness of the linguistic structures poets choose and manipulate develops gradually. Children grow in their understanding of how rhythm and shape contribute to meaning in a poem by hearing and reading a great deal of poetry.

Words as Meaning

Poetry often carries many layers of meaning and, as in other literature, is subject to many different interpretations. I. A. Richards demonstrates in *Practical Criticism* that the level of sophistication and experience in reading poetry affect the meaning the reader obtains. The meaning children create is directly proportionate to what experience has prepared them to understand.

One teacher read William Jay Smith's "The Toaster"[29] to children of varying levels of development and asked them to draw a picture of what the

Teaching Idea

PARALLEL POEMS (I-A) Having students write poems as homework is a sure-fire way to make them dislike poetry. None of us would want to be told to go home and write a poem tonight, as if the creative spark could be ignited on request. The ability to write poetry that is not doggerel develops gradually; some never achieve it.

Students can be eased into poetry writing when they perceive it as fun and not as assigned work. Sometimes it can be done collaboratively, with two or three students working together; sometimes it can be done by using an established poet's work as a guide. Here it is suggested that students experiment with writing parallel poems— poems that have a subject and a style similar to an existing poem used as a model. Before sending them out on their own, you may want to begin with a whole-class collaboration. A poetry worksheet can be used to brainstorm for descriptive words about the subject and related words that rhyme with these. Preliminary planning eases poetic expression of ideas.

Activity: Teacher to Student

SPINNING OFF WITH SPECIES AND SEEDS (I-A) Read David McCord's "Glowworm" in *One at a Time* (Little, Brown, 1977), which begins with the line "Never talk down to a glowworm." Work with one or two other students to write a parallel poem (a poem that has a subject and a form like McCord's) about a bumblebee, gypsy moth, mosquito, or firefly. Try to use the pattern of the opening line. For example, you could begin, "Never light up with a firefly."

Or read David McCord's "Pumpkin Seeds" (in *One at a Time*) to spark poems about apple seeds, avocado seeds, or peach pits. Ask yourself and your writing partners what kind of imaginary special thing could grow from your seed. What word would you substitute for "pumpkin" in the opening lines, "There is a man who says he may/Have on the market any day/A pumpkin of tremendous size"?[28] Or accept Shel Silverstein's poem "The Toucan" (in *Where the Sidewalk Ends,* Harper & Row, 1974) as an invitation to continue writing with the same rhythm and shape. Continue adding clever verses about this broad-billed bird.

Once you begin, you will find many poems to parallel.

Children often appreciate creative efforts of their peers as much as those of adults. (Photograph by Susie Fitzhugh.)

poem was about. The poem describes the toaster as a "silver-scaled dragon who sits at my elbow and toasts my bread." Children in the concrete-operations stage interpreted the poem as an actual dragon and drew fiery-mouthed dragons showing that they understood the poem at the literal, concrete level. Older children, above the fourth grade, drew pictures of toasters that resembled dragons, suggesting that they understood the figurative language Smith used in the poem.

Not all poems have hidden meanings that can be recognized only by those who can ferret out the relationship between symbols and details about the poet's view of life. It is true that some poems bear subtle messages; however, most are descriptions of character, expressions of emotions, or accounts of events. We chance losing our students if we continually send them searching for hidden messages. It is perfectly acceptable to assert, as Alice did, after reading "Jabberwocky": "Somehow it seems to fill my head with ideas, only I don't know exactly what they are."

Among the poetic devices used to convey meaning are figurative language, imagery, and de-

notation and connotation. Through them poets suggest that more is meant than meets the ear. What is left unsaid is often as important as what is put down on the page.

Figurative language produces a meaning other than the literal one of the words used. In poetry, figurative language is used frequently and affects meaning in unique ways. Metaphor, simile, and personification make the language of poetry different from that of prose. As poets create vivid experiences, they use language metaphorically; they help us to see or feel things in new ways. It is not enough just to have the idea; poets must also have the words. Carl Sandburg says: ". . . the right words, the special and particular words for the purpose in view, these must come. For out of them the poem is made."[30] The special and particular words often involve figurative language.

Children need experience in using and understanding figurative language before they can fully appreciate the poetry that relies on it. Whether they will understand this use of language in a poem depends upon their background. Young children understand the comparisons made on a physical plane but not at a psychological one. Bushes that look like popcorn balls and cars that look like big, fat raisins are more likely to be meaningful to these children than a prison guard's heart of stone. Young children interpret such a prison guard's heart as being physically of stone. When they are more mature, they recognize that the comparison refers to a psychological state.

Once children gain some understanding of how figurative language contributes to meaning, poetry assumes a deeper dimension. Recognizing contrast, comparison, and exaggeration on a psychological plane affords children richer interpretations.

Metaphor and simile are two devices used to compare one thing to another, or to view something in terms of something else. The comparison in a simile is stated and uses the words "like" or "as" to draw the comparison. A comparison in a metaphor is inferred—something is stated as something else.

In David McCord's "Tiger Lily," the comparison is a metaphor since the tiger lily *is* a panther:

> The tiger lily is a panther,
> Orange to black spot:
> Her tongue is the velvet pretty anther,
> And she's in the vacant lot.[31]

Again, Charles Simic, in "Watermelons," likens a watermelon to a buddha in the unannounced comparison of a metaphor:

> Green Buddhas
> On the fruit stand.
> We eat the smile
> And spit out the teeth.[32]

Eve Merriam makes it unmistakable, entitling her equation of morning with a new sheet of paper, "Metaphor":

> Morning is
> a new sheet of paper
> for you to write on.
>
> Whatever you want to say,
> all day
> until night
> folds it up
> and files it away.

The bright words and the dark words
are gone
until dawn
and a new day
to write on.[33]

Personification refers to the representation of a thing or abstraction as a person. When we say "Fortune smiled on us" or "If the weather permits," we are giving human qualities to an idea like fortune or a force of nature like the weather. Poets often give human feelings or thoughts to plants and animals. Hilda Conkling uses personification to make the ideas more vivid or unusual in "Dandelion":

> O little soldier with the golden helmet,
> What are you guarding on my lawn?
> You with your green gun
> And your yellow beard,
> Why do you stand so stiff?
> There is only the grass to fight![34]

Langston Hughes's "April Rain Song" employs personification:

> Let the rain kiss you.
> Let the rain beat upon your head with silver liquid
>   drops.
> Let the rain sing you a lullaby.[35]

In "Chairs" Valerie Worth adds human characteristics to her description of chairs:

> Chairs
> Seem
> To
> Sit
> Down
> On
> Themselves, almost as if
> They were people,
> Some fat, some thin;
> Settled comfortably
> On their own seats,
> Some even stretch out their arms
> To
> Rest.[36]

Laurence Perrine, in *Literature: Structure, Sound, and Sense*, defines imagery in poetry as "the representation through language of sense ex-

Activity: Teacher to Student

PORTRAITS IN PERSONIFICATION (I-A) Collect poems in which personification is used. (You may want to work in groups.) When you have found several poems, read them aloud to each other. Draw or paint what you think the personified object would look like if you could see it. Compare the different interpretations and select several for a classroom bulletin board. Be sure to include a copy of the poem that inspired the pictures.

---

perience.[37] Poets create imagery through the use of words in ways that arrest our senses; we can imagine that we almost see, taste, touch, smell, or hear what they describe. Little escapes the poet's vision; nothing limits the speculations upon what he sees. In just such speculation, Robert Frost makes a seemingly commonplace incident memorable:

DUST OF SNOW

The way a crow
Shook down on me
The dust of snow
From a hemlock tree

Has given my heart
A change of mood
And saved some part
Of a day I had rued.[38]

Ted Hughes's uncompromising imagery in "Moon Whales" evokes an emotion solitary and existential:

They plough through the moon stuff
Just under the surface
Lifting the moon's skin
Like a muscle
But so slowly it seems like a lasting mountain
Breathing so rarely it seems like a volcano
Leaving a hole blasted in the moon's skin . . .[39]

Denotation refers to the literal or dictionary definition of a word or phrase. Connotation refers to the suggested meaning associated with the literal one—the overtones of meaning. Connotations can vary with the individual person. Water,

for instance, may have connotations of refreshment, cooling, beauty, or pleasure, depending on which of its many aspects you are thinking of, and where you have enjoyed water the most. But it might also arouse feelings of terror in a person who had been in danger of drowning.

Poetry makes use of both denotative and connotative meaning, saying what it means but saying much more. Connotation enriches meaning. Sometimes the sounds of words combine with their connotations to make a very pleasing pattern. The following poem, "Names," by Dorothy Aldis, is made almost entirely from the names of particularly colorful flowers.

Larkspur and Hollyhock,
Pink Rose and purple Stock,
Lovely-smelling Mignonette,
Lilies not quite opened yet,
Phlox the favorite of bees,
Bleeding Heart and Peonies—
Just their names are nice to say,
Softly,
On a summer's day.[40]

The connotations associated with the names suggest a floral collage.

"Reflections on a Gift of Watermelon Pickle Received from a Friend Called Felicity," by John Tobias, carries both denotative and connotative meanings, with several possibilities for interpretation. Trying to arrive at consensual validation of "one right meaning," as with most poems, is counterproductive.

During that summer
When unicorns were still possible;
When the purpose of knees
Was to be skinned;
When shiny horse chestnuts
   (Hollowed out
   Fitted with straws
   Crammed with tobacco
   Stolen from butts
   In family ashtrays)
Were puffed in green lizard silence
While straddling thick branches
Far above and away
From the softening effects
Of civilization;

During that summer—
Which may never have been at all;
But which has become more real
Than the one that was—
Watermelons ruled.

Thick pink imperial slices
Melting frigidly on sun-parched tongues
Dribbling from chins;
Leaving the best part,
The black bullet seeds,
To be spit out in rapid fire

Against the wall
Against the wind
Against each other;

And when the ammunition was spent,
There was always another bite:
It was a summer of limitless bites,
Of hungers quickly felt
And quickly forgotten
With the next careless gorging.

The bites are fewer now.
Each one is savored lingeringly,
Swallowed reluctantly.

But in a jar put up by Felicity,
The summer which maybe never was
Has been captured and preserved.
And when we unscrew the lid
And slice off a piece
And let it linger on our tongue:
Unicorns become possible again.[41]

The sensory images evoked by the phrases "green lizard silence," "thick pink imperial slices," or "sun-parched tongues" paint pictures in the mind's eye as vivid as any that a painter creates on canvas.

Teaching Idea

A POETRY FESTIVAL (ALL AGES) A poetry festival celebrates the primacy of poetry in our lives. It is an undertaking limited only by the wingspan of our imagination. Children should participate in planning every step; brainstorm with them to determine what different attractions and exhibits they want to have.

An entire school day might be set aside to celebrate the many faces of poetry. Select a site that is spacious. Some teachers use the entire school, but you may want to begin with the gymnasium or playground. Mark off areas for game booths and exhibits. The entrance can be a large archway decorated with poetry book jackets. Would you like a yellow brick road leading up to it?

Invitations made by children can be sent out. They could contain favorite poems accompanied by original drawings. Good choices for the invitations might be "Eating Poetry" by Mark Strand, which opens this chapter, and "How to Eat a Poem" by Eve Merriam:

Don't be polite.
Bite in.
Pick it up with your fingers and lick the juice that may run down your chin.
It is ready and ripe now, whenever you are.[42]

(CONTINUED)

To this can be added the invitation, such as "Come join us for a Poetry Festival," with date, time, and place indicated.

Among the attractions you might have an audio-visual booth with cassettes, records, or films of poets reading or discussing their work, or original tape recordings of children reading well-loved poems. This could be in a quiet area set apart from the rest of the festival.

Other booths may feature actual poets surrounded by their books. The Children's Book Council provides lists of local authors and poets, and the National Council of Teachers of English has a "Poets in the Schools" program to help you organize this part of the festival. Meeting an author is an unforgettable childhood experience.

There could be a food booth where you serve some of the gastronomical delights of poetry, such as "watermelon pickle," "bananas and cream," "rice pudding," or "chicken soup with rice." Your students will be able to come up with lots of good ideas when it comes to food. Copies of "food poems" can be used to decorate the area.

A game booth might include a dart wall filled with several rows of inflated balloons containing poems like the fortune in a fortune cookie. The child who bursts the balloon keeps the poem as the prize. Children are an excellent source of original games.

A graffiti wall can be made from huge sheets of craft paper on which children write statements about their favorite poems and poets. They might even include original verses. Have lots of felt-tipped pens available.

You can also set up an entertainment or show-time booth where barbershop quartet entertainers perform poems from song picture books. There are many, and among those from which children particularly enjoy singing are *When I First Came to this Land,* by Oscar Brand (P-I-A, Putnam's, 1974); *Sweet Betsy from Pike,* by Robert A. Parker (P, Viking, 1978); *Mommy, Buy Me a China Doll,* by Harve Zemach (N-P, Farrar, Straus & Giroux, 1975); and *The Star-Spangled Banner,* by Peter Spier (P-I, Doubleday, 1973). Encourage children to make up new verses. A prize can be awarded for the best.

Remember to take pictures of your Poetry Festival. It is sure to be something children will remember for many years. To make the memory last, you can have a hallway bulletin board on which to share the photos with all of the school.

The possibilities for this type of celebration are unlimited. It is an undertaking that takes energy and entails much planning, but the fun children experience with it and the positive ways in which they share poetry bring immeasurable joy.

FORMS OF POETRY

It is evident to the beginning reader of poetry that it comes in many forms. Poems look different; the visual form, which reflects the pattern, affects the way the poem is to be read and contributes to meaning. Poetic patterns are clearly defined, although poets manipulate the conventional patterns as often as they manipulate word meanings. Children need not pay attention to form to enjoy poetry, but when they begin to write poetry they will recognize and use some of its conventions.

In poetry, perhaps more than in any other area, children need to discover. Instead of starting with definitions of poetic forms and moving to illustrations of them, it is best to expose children to many examples of a form and allow them to deduce the commonalities. Reading many poems in the same form gives children a feel for and a sense of it in use.

The true expression of real feelings is far more important than form in creative writing. Myra Cohn Livingston, in *When You Are Alone/It Keeps You Capone,* describes the relation between technical aspects and creative ideas in children's poetry writing:

One encourages expression, true and meaningful expression (as distinguished from factual statement); reads poetry, introduces forms, and speaks about the elements and tools of poetry and how meaning is to be found in poetry, so that each child will, we hope, find a form that best expresses his own thoughts and feelings.[43]

Knowing about the many possibilities of poetic form, however, *can* help in selecting poetry wisely.

Poetry as Story: Narrative Poems

Children love a good story and, since they also respond to rhythm and rhyme, like stories in narrative verse. Narrative poetry sets a story—with characters, plot, and theme, like any other story—into a poetic framework, which can make even a humble story memorable. A. A. Milne and Aileen Fisher are among many poets whose narratives appeal to young children. Milne's work is collected in *When We Were Very Young* (P) and *Now We Are Six* (P). "Sneezles," "Binker," and "Forgiven," all in *Now We Are Six,* are favorites, but "Bad Sir Brian Botany" is even more popular.

Sir Brian had a battleaxe with great big knobs on;
He went among the villagers and blipped them on the head.
On Wednesday and on Saturday, but mostly on the latter day,
He called at all the cottages, and this is what he said:
"I am Sir Brian!" (ting-ling)
  "I am Sir Brian!" (rat-tat)
"I am Sir Brian, as bold as a lion—
  Take that!—and that—and that!"[44]

Aileen Fisher writes narrative poems that have been produced in picture-book format and that often focus on exploring nature. They include *Listen, Rabbit* (P), *Going Barefoot* (P), *Like Nothing at All* (P), and *Sing, Little Mouse* (P). In the last, the poem story describes a boy's search for a mouse that sings:

"Josie," I said,
"and Jerry, too,
told me that someone
their uncle knew
had a singing mouse.
Do you think it's true?"

It is only after he gives up the search that his wish comes true. To his surprise and delight, a white-footed mouse hides in his camping gear. He makes a cage for the mouse, puts it in it, and then:

"You're free again,
and away you go . . .
and I've had my wish
so at last I know
that it's a perfectly
possible thing
for a light-footed
flight-footed
left-footed
right-footed
White-Footed Mouse
to *sing.*"[45]

Activity: Teacher to Student

APPRECIATING NARRATIVE POEMS (I-A) The best way to appreciate the unfolding of the plot in narrative poetry is to read it aloud. Don't be concerned about vocabulary that is unfamiliar. Unfamiliar words can usually be understood from context—the way they are used in a line or sentence.

Choose some poems to read from the following:

1. *The Pied Piper of Hamelin,* by Robert Browning, illustrated by C. Walter Hodges (Coward, McCann & Geoghegan, 1971). This story is fun to tape-record dramatically. Pay special attention to the lines:

> Great rats, small rats, lean rats, brawny rats,
> Brown rats, black rats, grey rats, tawny rats.[46]

Recite them slowly and dramatically to paint a vivid and memorable picture.

Write what you think of the story's moral, summed up in the statement, "So, Willy, let's keep our promise to all men—especially pipers"? Locate the edition that Kate Greenaway illustrated and compare her pictures with those of Hodges. In what way does this narrative poem document the dramatic conflict between greed and honor?

2. *The Rime of the Ancient Mariner,* by Samuel Taylor Coleridge (Coward, McCann & Geoghegan, 1971). Investigate the ballad form, which has the rhyme scheme used in 107 of *Rime*'s 142 stanzas. The conclusion of each of the seven parts emphasizes the shooting of the albatross. Discuss what you think this might mean. When you finish reading the poem, think about some of the words we use today that might be obsolete one hundred years from now—for example, disco, psychedelic, UFO. Start a collection of "Archaic Words to Come" and share them on a bulletin

---

When poetry is read aloud the words can truly sing, and the musical quality of the verse may be fully savored; narrative poetry is most appreciated in oral presentations. This form of poetry usually describes a single event and tells a tale in the figurative language of adventure. Listening to story poems helps children develop a sensitivity to the charm of the spoken word and the tune of verse.

With increasing frequency, single editions of narrative poems beautifully illustrated are available. No longer need we settle for the simple, dull, and standard verses of textbooks.

Fun and Nonsense: Humorous and Concrete Poems

Well-loved contemporary poems for children contain a clearly discernible strand of humor. Young children gleefully seize on the nonsense rhymes and older ones savor a more irreverent brand of humor, the blacker the better. With the exception of the limerick, which has an exceptionally clear-cut rhyme scheme and form, humorous poems are discussed below according to their content. Concrete poems, innovative poetic variations, are discussed too.

board. Make a class newspaper in which you rewrite the poem in prose reportorial style to describe an exciting local event. Which form leaves a more lasting impression? Discuss why you think so. Collaborate with some classmates to write a sequel to the lines:

Water, water every where,
And all the boards did shrink;
Water, water every where,
Nor any drop to drink.[47]

3. *The Highwayman,* by Alfred Noyes (Prentice-Hall, 1969). The ominous tone of this narrative is set forth in the first stanza:

The wind was a torrent of darkness among the gusty trees,
The moon was a ghostly galleon tossed upon cloudy seas,
The road was a ribbon of moonlight over the purple moor,
And the highwayman came riding—riding—riding—
The highwayman came riding, up to the old inn-door.[48]

Some questions to think about after reading are:
How does Noyes make us sympathetic to Bess and to the outlaw, who is really nothing more than a thief?
Can you find similarities here to the famous outlaws Bonnie and Clyde?
How does the illustrator's use of pastel shades of blue, indigo, and violet influence the poem's mood?
What events have you seen reported in the news that concern love, betrayal, and death? How could they be described in poetic verse?

Fortunately, we have many poets who turn to humor for poetry ideas; Shel Silverstein, William Cole, and X. J. Kennedy are among the best. Silverstein's collection *Where the Sidewalk Ends* (P-I) is credited with bringing more converts to poetry than any other volume; for many it is the turning point at which they first become poetry lovers. When a teacher reads aloud from it, children who think they don't care for poetry may listen suspiciously at first, then cautiously ask to "see that book." *Where the Sidewalk Ends* contains verse and illustrations that tickle the reader in weird and ridiculous ways: for "Jumping Rope," a gangly girl is shown completely entangled in a jumping rope from head to foot. "Band-Aids" describes all the places a child needs band-aids, and the illustration shows head and torso covered with them. Silverstein shows no restraint in the situations he mocks to make things laughable. He tells of a king whose mouth is stuck tight with peanut butter, gives a recipe for a hippopotamus sandwich, describes a dreadful situation in which someone eats a baby, and warns about the dangers of picking one's nose. Anything becomes the butt of Silverstein's humor, and he's on target about what makes children laugh.

In the gooey, smelly poem "Sarah Cynthia Sylvia Stout/Would Not Take the Garbage Out," Silverstein piles up the pits, the rinds, the crusts, and bones to show what happened to a girl who would not take the garbage out:

> Sarah Cynthia Sylvia Stout
> Would not take the garbage out!
> She'd scour the pots and scrape the pans,
> Candy the yams and spice the hams,
> And though her daddy would scream and shout,
> She simply would not take the garbage out.
>
> And so it piled up to the ceilings:
> Coffee grounds, potato peelings,
> Brown bananas, rotten peas,
> Chunks of sour cottage cheese.
>
> It filled the can, it covered the floor,
> It cracked the window and blocked the door
> With bacon rinds and chicken bones,
> Drippy ends of ice cream cones,
> Prune pits, peach pits, orange peel,
> Gloppy glumps of cold oatmeal,
> Pizza crusts and withered greens,
> Soggy beans and tangerines,
> Crusts of black burned buttered toast,
> Gristly bits of beefy roasts . . .
>
> The garbage rolled on down the hall,
> It raised the roof, it broke the wall . . .[49]

By the time you finish reading the graphic details of Sarah's overflowing garbage pail, students are gagging and groaning in mock horror. Despite their pretense of utter disgust, the comment heard most often is, "Read it again."

Although not as bizarre or graphic as Silverstein's work, *Beastly Boys and Ghastly Girls* (I), a collection by William Cole (of work from A. A. Milne, Hilaire Belloc, William Jay Smith, A. E. Housman, Ted Hughes, John Ciardi, Lewis Carroll, and James Whitcomb Riley, among others), also celebrates children's antics, mocking adult strictures with such advice as "put some mustard in your shoe," "spill broth on the tablecloth," "never stew your sister," and "beat him when he sneezes."

Other collections show Cole's zest for ridiculous situations, inane nonsense, and general, all-around silliness. *Oh, That's Ridiculous!* (P-I) and *Oh, What Nonsense* (P-I) are appropriate for both younger and older children.

The work of X. J. Kennedy is now attracting Silverstein and Cole poetry fans. Kennedy, too, has a sense of fun that appeals to intermediate-grade students. In "A Big Deal for the Tooth Fairy" he plans to hit pay dirt:

> Tooth Fairy, hear! Tonight's the night
> I've dreamed about for ages,
> For haven't we kids got a right
> To rake in living wages?
>
> I've tried to work my back teeth loose,
> Tied doorknobs (threads—what cop-outs!),
> But gosh! my jaws just won't produce
> A quick cash crop of dropouts.
>
> So come prepared to lose a heap
> In larger trading ventures.
> Tonight I lay me down to sleep
> On top of Grandpap's dentures.[50]

The idea Kennedy proposes is not such a far-fetched notion; it must pass through the minds of countless enterprising children.

Young children respond to the humor in the many works of Dr. Seuss, as substantiated by continuous large sales, televised versions of some works, and huge audiences whenever he speaks. His early works, *And to Think That I Saw It on Mulberry Street* (P), *The 500 Hats of Bartholomew Cubbins* (P), and *McElligot's Pool* (P), show the original sparks of creativity that he continues to replay to the delight of young children.

Wallace Tripp's work also appeals to young children. In *A Great Big Ugly Man Came up and Tied His Horse to Me* (N-P), some traditional rhymes and some by modern poets are illustrated in a hilarious way. The illustrations for the title verse show a tiny, bewildered animal completely entangled in a horse's reins. Although the verses themselves are funny, Tripp's illustrations exaggerate the humor and bring out giggles, as clever details are discovered. Looking through this book once is not enough to catch all the fun; new jokes are discovered on each rereading. In *Granfa' Grig Had a Pig and Other Rhymes without Reason from*

Mother Goose (N-P), Tripp continues with whimsical poems about animals.

Limericks appeal to children because they poke fun and have a definite rhythm and rhyme. Edward Lear (1812–1888) is given credit for making the limerick popular, although he did not create it. His *Book of Nonsense* (I) was published in 1846 and is still popular today. Part of the lasting appeal of limericks lies in their tendency to lampoon and spoof those who take themselves too seriously.

Edward Lear's association with the limerick form is insoluble; a typical Lear effort is:

> There was an Old Lady whose folly,
> Induced her to sit in a holly;
> Whereon by a thorn,
> her dress being torn,
> She quickly became melancholy.[51]

Learning Lear's work is essential to an exploration of the limerick. *The Complete Nonsense of Edward Lear* (I) and *Whizz!* (P) are required reading. In *Whizz!* the "old man in a tree who was horribly bored by a bee" is portrayed by Janina Domanska as crossing a bridge. Characters from other limericks are added in cumulative fashion until the entire bridge collapses and everyone falls into the river.

Limericks are devoured by the many students who enjoy this brand of humor. Some limericks are in the stream of folklore, where original authorship is lost. One such is:

> A flea and a fly in a flue
> Were imprisoned, so what could they do?
> Said the fly, "Let us flee."
> Said the flea, "Let us fly."
> So they flew through a flaw in the flue.[52]

Children laugh at the nonsense primarily because the verses break the conventions of language; they encapsulate a joyful absurdity.

Poets use parody to ridicule work that is sentimental and moralistic or that may have a plodding, overused meter or meaningless refrain. Longfellow is a frequent butt of parody, perhaps because much of his poetry is sentimental and because he uses the same rhythms relentlessly. Several parodies of Longfellow's "The Song of Hiawatha" appear in Myra Cohn Livingston's *Speak Roughly to Your Little Boy* (I), a collection of parodies and bur-

Teaching Idea

WRITING LIMERICKS (I) Limericks are fun to write, although, of course, not all children will want to write them. It is well to remember that writing is not always fun and easy for students; for many it is hard and tedious. When children do enjoy writing, it is usually about themselves—their thoughts and their feelings—although, they enjoy writing about real and/or imaginary animals or pets.

Those who want to try limericks should know the rhyme scheme—a a b b a—and that the third and fourth lines are shorter than the rest. Before asking children to set out on their own, it is good to read several limericks aloud and to have them create one as a group. Come prepared with three or four starting sentences and let children choose a favorite. You might find it helpful to prepare a simple list of rhyming words.

Activity: Teacher to Student

PICK-A-POEM BULLETIN BOARD (I) A Pick-a-Poem Bulletin Board is a good way to share limericks. Cut out paper flowers and write a limerick on the stem of each. Put each flower in a slit cut into a large sheet of construction paper or cardboard, as shown in the diagram. The part of the stem on which the limerick is written should not be visible. Pick a flower and enjoy a chuckle. Of course, remember to replant your garden frequently!

lesques presented with the original poems. One of these is "The Modern Hiawatha," by George A. Strong:

> When he killed the Mudjokivis
> Of the skin he made him mittens,
> Made them with the fur side inside,
> Made them with the skin side outside,
> He, to get the warm side inside,
> Put the inside skin side outside;
> He, to get the cold side outside,
> Put the warm side fur side inside.
> That's why he put the fur side inside,
> Why he put the skin side outside,
> Why he turned them inside outside.[53]

Parodies, often written anonymously, appeal to mature students who recognize the connection to the original poem. They are funny only when the reader is in on the joke.

A contemporary, innovative form, which combines graphic elements with language, is called concrete poetry. Concrete verses do not use words alone to make a statement; instead they use the appearance of the thing described as well. Children call them shape (or picture) poems. The actual physical form of the words is used to depict the subject, so that the whole becomes an ideogrammatic statement; the work illustrates itself as the shapes of words and lines take form.

Myra Cohn Livingston's *O Sliver of Liver and Other Poems* (I) has some fine concrete poems. Children take delight in deciphering the poetic architecture of her "Winter Tree" and of Shel Silverstein's funny giraffe poem in *Where the Sidewalk Ends* (both shown on the facing page). Richard Lester's cello (p. 271) is also delightful.

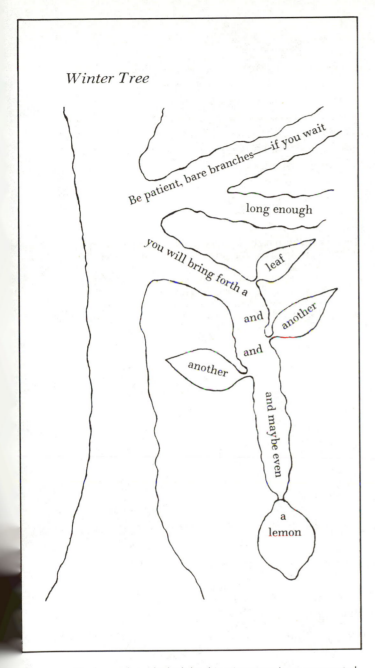

Winter Tree

Be patient, bare branches—if you wait

long enough

you will bring forth a

leaf

and

another

and

another

and maybe even

a
lemon

PLEASE
DO NOT
MAKE F
UN OF
ME AN
D PLEAS
E DON'T
LAUGH
IT ISN'T
EASY T
O WRIT
E A PO
EM ON
THE NE
CK OF
A RUN
NING
GIRA
FFE.

The lemon brought forth by this winter tree is an unexpected delight for young readers.
("Winter Tree" from *O Sliver of Liver and Other Poems* by Myra Cohn Livingston, drawings by Iris Van Rynbach (A Margaret K. McElderry Book). Copyright © 1979 by Myra Cohn Livingston. Reprinted by permission of Atheneum Publishers.)

In this poem, in which form and subject merge, simply the act of deciphering the words on the neck of Silverstein's giraffe provokes laughter.
("Poem Written on the Neck of a Running Giraffe" from *Where the Sidewalk Ends: The Poems and Drawings of Shel Silverstein*. Copyright © 1974 by Shel Silverstein. By permission of Harper & Row, Publishers, Inc.)

Teaching Idea

CREATING CONCRETE POETRY (I)   Robert Froman's *Street Poems* (P-I, Dutton, 1971) and *Seeing Things: A Book of Poems* (I, Crowell, 1974), and Ian Finlay's *Poems to Hear and See* (I, Macmillan, 1971) are enjoyable collections.

Froman's work often motivates students to experiment with concrete poetry and to visualize words in new ways. Giose Rimanelli and Paul Pimsleur also create concrete poetry in *Poems Make Pictures Pictures Make Poems* (P-I, Pantheon, 1972). A careful examination of these books can be useful.

To inspire children to try their hand at creating concrete poetry, show them the poems that follow—two were made by students.[54]

something around it. Zero is a ring that is nothing with

Zero is more than nothing in this concrete poem. Children can be made sensitive to words where meaning and form interact.
("Zero" from *Poems Make Pictures Pictures Make Poems* by Giose Rimanelli and Paul Pimsleur. Text copyright © 1972 by Giose Rimanelli and Paul Pimsleur. Illustrations copyright © 1972 Ronni Solbert. Reprinted by permission of Pantheon Books, a Division of Random House, Inc.)

chairs are for sitting not but you can sit not for knitting in a chair and knitting

Experiencing concrete poems and seeing some (like these) that their peers have created make most children eager to write their own.

Snakes are long and scaly and sometimes even bite

My
y cello big and fat
makes
the sound
of a screeching
rat. It plays F
double sharp
when I want
it to play
B flat. It
sounds like
a bad com-
position when
I play in the 4th
position. If I try
to play vibrato my
bow goes all
s-t-a-c-c-
ato
!

RICHARD
LESTER

Reading this cello is clearly more fun than playing it.
(Illustration by Satomi Ichikawa from *From Morn to Midnight: Children's Verses Chosen by Elaine Moss.* Illustrations
copyright © 1977 by Satomi Ichikawa. By permission of Thomas Y. Crowell, Publishers.)

Statements of Mood and Feeling: Lyric Poetry

Lyric poetry offers a direct and intense outpouring of thoughts and feelings. Any subjective, emotional poem can be called lyric, but most so designated are songlike and expressive of a single mood. The verses are especially musical.

Many of Christina Rossetti's poems are lyrics. Her "Who Has Seen the Wind?" leaves the question drifting in the mind.

Who has seen the wind?
Neither I nor you:
But when the leaves hang trembling,
The wind is passing through.

Who has seen the wind?
Neither you nor I:
But when the trees bow down their heads,
The wind is passing by.[55]

In "Mothers," Nikki Giovanni expresses an intensity difficult to match as she really sees her mother for the first time:

the last time i was home
to see my mother we kissed
exchanged pleasantries
and unpleasantries pulled a warm
comforting silence around
us and read separate books

i remember the first time
i consciously saw her
we were living in a three room
apartment on burns avenue

mommy always sat in the dark
i don't know how i knew that but she did

that night i stumbled into the kitchen
maybe because i've always been
a night person or perhaps because i had wet
the bed
she was sitting on a chair
the room was bathed in moonlight diffused through
those thousands of panes landlords who rented
to people with children were prone to put in
    windows

she may have been smoking but maybe not
her hair was three-quarters her height
which made me a strong believer in the samson myth
and very black

i'm sure i just hung there by the door
i remember thinking: what a beautiful lady[56]

Nearly all children's poems can be called lyrical in the sense that they have a singing quality and are personal expressions of feeling. Older students, with a richer understanding of symbolism, have a better appreciation for this type of poetry. Lyric poems above all others are not a one-time thing; they are for reading many times over. That children must come to trust their own feelings and learn that there is no right answer when it comes to poetry is particularly the case with the lyrical mode.

Poetry in Symbol and Image: Haiku and Cinquain

The word *haiku* means beginning. It is a Japanese poetry form that today enjoys great popularity in America. Each haiku usually consists of seventeen syllables arranged in a five-seven-five pattern and generally refers to nature, a particular event happening at the moment, and an attendant emotion or feeling, often of the most fragile and evanescent kind.

Although haiku is a favorite with teachers, Ann Terry's study of children's preferences in poetry shows that it is *not* always a favorite with them—a signal for teachers to handle with care. Myra Cohn Livingston, noted children's poet, deplores the fact that haiku is given the status of a game by many teachers. She recommends that teachers who want to know the essence of haiku read *Wind in My Hand, The Story of Issa* (I), by Hanako Fukuda. Collections of haiku by Issa and others in *Don't Tell the Scarecrow* (P-I) provide excellent examples for children.

The haiku form is both abstract and tightly constructed. Ann Atwood, collector and author, in *Haiku: The Mood of Earth* (I-A), says:

The haiku form itself, bound within the limitations of approximately seventeen syllables, is paradoxical in nature. It is both simple and profound, constrictive and expansive, meticulously descriptive and yet wholly suggestive. And it is the very limitations of haiku that demand the discipline necessary to all art. For with this meagre allowance of words, the poet must not be tempted to stop at the right word, but must enlarge his search until the *only* word is within his grasp.[57]

Atwood's work has features that should make haiku interesting to students. First, she parallels the words with magnificent color photographs to extend the images. She does with photography what haiku does with words; detailed close-ups of each subject help reveal the essence of her poem. Second, she refers to concrete things students can identify, such as a sea creature's shell, the "hand" of a leaf, and a piece of driftwood. (An excellent sound filmstrip, which extends the function of the book's photographs, is also available.) Atwood's

In *Haiku: The Mood of Earth,* color photographs enhance the poetry in an unusual and exciting combination. (From *Haiku: The Mood of Earth* by Ann Atwood. Copyright © 1971 by Ann Atwood. Reprinted by permission of Charles Scribner's Sons.)

273

On wood returning

from a long sea journey

the deeper print of waves.

In a sea creature's shell

flashing in waves of sunlight

—the waking of wings!

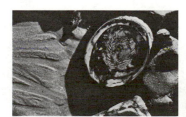

Activity: Teacher to Student

DESIGNING A HAIKU CARD (I-A)   No matter what the season of the year, plan an outing with some classmates. Collect bits and pieces of nature such as a smooth stone, a grasshopper, a flowerless branch, a cocoon, an abandoned nest, a colorful leaf. Arrange these specimens on a table in the poetry corner of your classroom. Take a quick-developing snapshot of your favorite and mount it on a piece of construction paper. You might want to write a haiku to accompany the picture. Give the card to someone special.

---

several books illustrate her belief that seeing and feeling are fused in haiku poetry and haiku photography. Teachers should look at: *Haiku-Vision: In Poetry and Photographs* (I-A), *My Own Rhythm: An Approach to Haiku* (I-A), *Haiku: The Mood of Earth* (I-A), and *Fly with the Wind, Flow with the Water* (I-A). The photographs in each are especially exciting for the counterpoint they provide.

A cinquain consists of five unrhymed lines that are usually made up of two, four, six, eight, and two syllables, in that order. A simplified variation that has five lines of one, two, three, four, and one words is manipulated easily by children in the intermediate grades. The pattern can be as follows:

Line 1: One word, the title, usually a noun
Line 2: Two words describing the title
Line 3: Three words that show action
Line 4: Four words that show feeling or emotion
Line 5: One word, a synonym for the title

The cinquain and other verse forms such as the diamante are useful when children begin writing their own poetry and, although they should not be compelled to adhere to a rigid structure, children sometimes find a set pattern helpful.

A sixth-grade boy using the original cinquain syllable count to convey his father's injunction on the subject of poetry produced the following.

Poem
Read it good son
It's educational

People everywhere having fun
Writing.[58]

Haiku and the cinquain are probably the most abstract poetry that children will experience. Since their symbolism and imagery are elusive for many children, wide exposure to other forms is needed before they meet these.

Ballads and Sonnets

Ballads are relatively short narrative poems that are adapted for singing or give the effect of a song. Usually written in stanzas, ballads are characterized by lyricism and a story line relating a single incident or subject. The so-called folk or popular ballads are of unknown authorship, while the authors of literary ballads are known.

Generally speaking, ballads sing of heroic deeds and of murder, unrequited love, feuds. Carl Sandburg's *The American Songbag* (A) is a classic collection of the ballads of railroad builders, lumberjacks, and cowboys. Use of dialogue in the telling of the story, and repetition in the refrains, characterize this form.

One teacher uses ballads by contemporary songwriters to introduce his jaded junior high-school students to poetry. He plays Simon and Garfunkel songs—"I Am a Rock" and "Sounds of Silence"—in his classroom to make the statement that poetry is song. Gradually, he exposes students to the words of songs written as poetry and eventually discusses the metaphoric statements the poem-songs make.

Helen Plotz presents 150 ballads in *As I Walked Out One Evening: A Book of Ballads* (A) that tell of love, death, work, war, and fairy folk. She cites individual authors, although many of the pieces are folksongs, changed by the singer as they are passed along. In the introduction, Plotz discusses origins, characteristics, and types of ballads:

Ballads are elemental, stark, outspoken. Words are simple, direct, few. Ballads tell of faithfulness and faithlessness, of revenge, jealousy and murder, of transcending love and blinding hate. The story is stripped to the bare bone—there is no probing, no explanation. Often we must guess at what went before and this very spareness gives tremendous force to the climax.[60]

Plotz includes traditional ballads that tell of supernatural happenings: the changeling child, the demon lover, and the young man enticed by the Queen of Elfland. She also describes the broadside, a ballad that tells about a political happening, a murder, or other sensational event. Some broadsides still exist in the folk songs of today, although political ballads seldom outlive their day; "The Wearin' o' the Green" and "Yankee Doodle," however, are two that did. Her collection enriches the study of past and present, providing material for happy songfests.

Unlike ancient poetic forms that became archaic, such as the rondeau and the triolet, sonnets continue to live. These fourteen-line poems follow two models—the Petrarchan, an eight-line stanza followed by a six-line stanza; and the Shakespearean, three four-line stanzas followed by a rhyming couplet. Perennial themes for sonnets—love, friendship, time, and the meaning of life—are skillfully expressed within the rigidity of the rhyme scheme and meter. The lineage of some of our most famous sonneteers, W. H. Auden, Louise Bogan, John Berryman, and Edna St. Vincent Millay, can be traced to Wordsworth, Shelley, and Keats. Helen Plotz, foremost anthologist, has collected one hundred thirty poems in *This Powerful Rhyme: A Book of Sonnets* (A). The title comes

Teaching Idea

RECITING CONTEMPORARY BALLADS (A)   Older students love the ballads of Billy Joel, John Denver, and other contemporary troubadours. Billy Joel's song "Just the Way You Are" is a poem that has been set to music.

Don't go changing to try and please me
You never let me down before
Don't imagine you're too familiar
And I don't see you anymore

I would not leave you in times of trouble
We never could have come this far
I took the good times, I'll take the bad times
I'll take you just the way you are.[59]

Encourage your students to read the words with, and then without, thinking of the music. Have them form committees to plan reciting contemporary ballads as dramatic readings, with the lines of the lyrics divided for the various male and female voice parts.

from Shakespeare's sonnet that begins "Not marble, nor the gilded monuments/Of princes, shall outlive this pow'rful rhyme."

The lure of this fragile form is as durable as Circe's enchantment. Phyllis McGinley's "Good Humor Man" seems up to the minute with this classical form as she likens the ice-cream man to the Pied Piper:

> So, long ago, in some such shrill procession
> Perhaps the Hamelin children gave pursuit
> To one who wore a red-and-yellow fashion
> Instead of white, but made upon his flute
> The selfsame promise plain to every comer:
> Unending sweets, imperishable summer.[61]

Students nurtured on poetry can make meaningful experiences from linguistically complex adult forms such as ballads and sonnets. Like Wordsworth's "Michael," building stone by stone, students building poem by poem can reach a gratifying eminence, for poetry once possessed is forever a wellspring of joy.

ANTHOLOGIES

To provide variety in poetry while holding collections to manageable size, teachers and librarians need anthologies. Poems are also sometimes easier to locate and select in these collections than when shelved individually by author.

Three types of anthologies have proven particularly useful in the classroom: the specialized anthology, with work by several poets on one subject; the generalized anthology, with works by many poets on many subjects; and the anthology of the work of only one poet. Although limited in number, there is an ever increasing supply of anthologies for reference.

Specialized anthologies seem to be gaining in popularity. The recent spate of books of poems and verses on witches, monsters, fairies, and other fanciful creatures bears witness to this. Noted anthologist Nancy Larrick brings the visions of some fine poets to *Bring Me All of Your Dreams* (I-A). This collection includes poetry of well-knowns such as Langston Hughes, Walter De La Mare, e. e. cummings, and Carl Sandburg, as well as the work of lesser-knowns—all bound together by the filament of dreams. The organization of the book is enhanced by an index of first lines, an index of poets and poems, and a biographic section, "Meet the Poets."

Humor is the strand that ties together David Kherdian's collection *If Dragon Flies Made Honey* (P-I). The lively poems by Jack Kerouac, Ruth Krauss, and William Carlos Williams take on hilarity with José Aruego and Ariane Dewey's exuberant illustrations. Although at first glance the book appears to be for the very young, its subtleties make it equally appealing to more mature children as well.

The classic generalized anthology, May Hill Arbuthnot's *Time for Poetry*, now incorporated into *The Arbuthnot Anthology of Children's Literature*, is a complete volume with verse on many subjects. Best-loved poems of childhood include those about people, animals, adventures, games, jokes, magic and make-believe, wind and water, holidays and seasons, and wisdom and beauty. The anthology is essential for any teacher who considers poetry central to children's lives.

A Flock of Words: An Anthology of Poetry for Children and Others (I-A), an additional fine resource, began as David MacKay's personal poetry collection made while he was a teacher. In his teaching, MacKay used poems clipped from newspapers and magazines, and was a pioneer in encouraging children to emulate the work of great poets by examining closely the many ways poets use evocative language.

A most beautiful book, one of today's classics, *Reflections on a Gift of Watermelon Pickle . . . and Other Modern Verse* (I-A) was compiled by Stephen Dunning, Edward Lueders, and Hugh Smith. The compilers began with 1200 poems considered good and, by testing them with students, gradually refined the collection to 114 poems. The broad spectrum of poetic statements, on subjects from a bud to a steamshovel, to advice to travelers, or arithmetic, is augmented with dramatic black-and-white photographs. A brief section of interpretive comments and questions concerning some of the poems is appended. Dunning, Lueders, and Smith used the same process of field-testing poems to produce another excellent anthology, *Some Haystacks Don't Even Have any Needles: And Other Complete Modern Poems* (A).

David McCord's *One at a Time* (all ages) is an anthology comprised solely of his work. An impressive volume, it is a collection of all of his poetry. McCord's wit and thoughtful perception sing in the music of his words. *One at a Time,* more than any other single volume, is a key to cultivating poetic taste—to produce children who will read poetry for pleasure.

When you find a poem that delights you and your students, look for others by the same poet; you may be surprised to find an entire anthology devoted to your favorite poet. Brewton's *Index to Poetry* will hasten the search. Every classroom needs several specialized, generalized, and individualized anthologies of poetry. Teachers who know and love poems can do justice to the privileged task of passing on the beauty of langauge from one generation to the next.

CRITERIA FOR SELECTING POETRY FOR CHILDREN

It is a sign of strength when teachers search out new poems instead of relying upon the ones they were required to memorize when children. Furthermore, what speaks to one generation may not speak to another. This suggests that wise teachers will not pass on the poetry of their youth unless it is of exceptional quality. Instead, they will select the best that gives children a sense of their own time. What speaks most directly to children is the poetry that is geared to their level of intellectual development and that falls within the parameters of their experience.

We may not always know why a particular poem appeals to children but we do know that the ones read aloud with enthusiasm are likely to become their favorites. In making your selections, remember that poetry for children appeals primarily to their emotions and intensifies them. It can make them happy or sad, proud or self-critical, and angry or compassionate. The very best that there is in poetry for children calls attention to experience in ways not seen or felt before.

Thinking about the poems we loved best may provide clues to what will appeal to children today. Some may have had strong, readily identifiable rhythms, others a unique patterning of language. Patterns that catch the melody and rhythm of familiar language help children accept the sounds of poetry. Repetition of key words and rhyming patterns, subtle cement that hold a poem together, appeal to children's innate sense of rhythm.

Some loved poems may have used interesting words or ordinary words in interesting ways; David McCord does both in "Goose, Moose, Spruce":

> Three goose: geese.
> Three mooses: meese?
> Three spruces: spreece?
>
> Little goose: gosling.
> Little moose: mosling?
> Little spruce: sprosling?[62]

As research has repeatedly shown, children prefer humorous poems with strong rhythm and rhyme over free verse with abstract symbolism. They enjoy narrative poetry because it is based on their natural love of story. In "Mummy Slept Late and Daddy Fixed Breakfast," by John Ciardi, Daddy fixes waffles. The child speaks:

> I tried to cut it with a fork:
> The fork gave off a spark.
> I tried a knife and twisted it
> Into a question mark.

At the end of this delightful story, the child concludes,

> The next time Dad gets breakfast
> When Mommy's sleeping late,
> I think I'll skip the waffles
> I'd sooner eat the plate![63]

We cannot, however, let what research says about the past circumscribe what might be. This is to say that although we know that many children

Profile

DAVID McCORD

. . . poetry, like rain, should fall with elemental music, and poetry for children should catch the eye as well as the ear and the mind. It should delight; it really has to delight (Lee Bennett Hopkins, "David McCord," in *Books Are by People* [New York: Citation Press, 1969], p. 169).

David McCord was born near Greenwich Village in New York City. When he was twelve years old, he moved with his parents to a ranch on the Rogue River in Oregon where he learned about nature and wildlife. He studied the constellations and chose Orion as his favorite skymark. Although as a child he learned to shoot a rifle, McCord has never aimed at a living thing since he was fifteen because his love of all life is far too deep.

McCord graduated from Harvard University, where he worked as an alumni editor and fund raiser for many years; he has written a history of Harvard, *In Sight of Sever*. The first honorary degree of Doctor of Humane Letters granted at Harvard was conferred on him, at the same ceremonies at which President John F. Kennedy received an LL.D. Queen Elizabeth II of England invited David McCord to join the Royal Institute of Arts and Letters, and, when she visited the United States during the bicentennial, he wrote a sestina in her honor.

Author or editor of nearly fifty books of poetry, essays, history, medicine, light verse, and verse for children, his work appears in more than 300 anthologies. Also an artist, he has had several one-man shows of watercolor landscapes. He lives in Boston and is a Boston Red Sox fan.

One of David McCord's teachers once told him never to let a day go by without looking on three beautiful things; he tries to live by that precept. Each day the sky, in all kinds of weather, is the first of the three.

McCord frequently talks with groups of children in elementary schools as a means of dispelling a misconception that once was his: "I learned when I was young that all poets had to be dead. . . . the fact that there were living poets never surfaced until high school" (David McCord, Acceptance Speech for the NCTE Award for Poetry for Children, NCTE National Meeting, New York City, 29 Nov. 1977).

David McCord's books of poetry for children include *All Day Long, Away and Ago, Everytime I Climb a Tree, Far and Few, For Me to Say, The Star in the Pail, Take Sky;* there are many others. His collected poems for children, published in *One at a Time,* appeared in 1977, the year he was awarded the National Council of Teachers of English Award for Poetry for Children.

respond to rhyme, humor, and story, there are those who can appreciate a much wider range of forms and elements in poetry. We need to be prepared to point their way.

David McCord says, "poetry, like rain, should fall with elemental music, and poetry for children should catch the eye as well as the ear and the mind."[64] Though the criteria direct us to poems that catch eye, ear, and mind, only teachers with a developing love for poetry will catch the heart.

Summing Up

Understanding poetry is a long and continual process built only upon experiences that are both wide and broad. Children develop better understanding the more they internalize poetry. They profit little from verbal definitions and descriptions. It is firsthand experience with listening to, reading, writing, and discussing poetry that contributes the most to fostering their love of it. Children who live with poetry in their homes and in their schools turn to poems again and again for pleasure.

Close attention to children's comments can supply a basis for thought-provoking questions that will lead children to discover the substance of poetry for themselves. The object is to develop a child's liking for the music of words; detailed analysis divests poetry of its splendor. Misconceptions may be of greater value than the explanation that

---

NCTE AWARD FOR POETRY FOR CHILDREN

Each year more than sixty awards are given for children's books. Until 1977, when the National Council of Teachers of English established the first award for poetry, all these awards were for prose works. The NCTE Award for poetry for children is given to a poet for the entire body of work produced, not for individual poems or books. A national committee of professionals makes the selection.

The first recipient of the award was David McCord; recipients in 1978, 1979, and 1980 were Aileen Fisher, Karla Kuskin, and Myra Cohn Livingston, respectively. Books by these poets carry the seal shown below.

Seal of the National Council of Teachers of English Award for Poetry for Children, designed by Karla Kuskin.

destroys it. The magic that the words exercise on the imagination, more valuable than accuracy at beginning stages, leaves a telling mark. Appropriate discussions of poetry take children back to the poem, not away from it and into discussions of values, moral judgments, or personal opinion.

Poetry is valuable for the full realization of life. Only by hard work can we participate in the imaginative experience of others—and thereby get to know our own better. The more readers participate, the more they themselves create, and the more personal and enjoyable the experience of poetry becomes. The rewards are more than worth the effort.

Teachers can help children trust their own feelings about poetry, to free their thinking about it so that it becomes flexible as it can be. They can help them to not think in a predictable manner.

Experience with the fun of verse is all that is needed for children to develop discrimination. Teachers can use the special pleasure inherent in poetry to extend the imagination, contribute new sensations, and enhance past experiences. This is most readily achieved by teachers whose enthusiasm shows, who read good poetry aloud in such a way as to show the value and worth they themselves place in it. It is a most important first step toward making a love of poetry catching.

Notes

1. Mark Strand, "Eating Poetry," in *Beach Glass & Other Poems,* ed. Paul Molloy (New York: Four Winds-Scholastic, 1970), p. 7.
2. Myra Cohn Livingston, *When You Are Alone/It Keeps You Capone: An Approach to Creative Writing with Children* (New York: Atheneum, 1973), p. 237.
3. Northrop Frye, *The Educated Imagination* (Bloomington, Ind.: Indiana Univ. Press, 1964), p. 63.
4. Karla Kuskin, "The Witches' Ride," in *Witch Poems,* ed. Daisy Wallace, illus. Trina Schart Hyman (New York: Holiday House, 1976), p. 9.
5. Patricia Hubbell, "Sea Spirit," in *To Look at Any Thing,* ed. Lee Bennett Hopkins, photographs by John Earl (Harcourt Brace Jovanovich, 1978), p. 41.
6. Christopher Morley, "Smells (Junior)," in *Time for Poetry,* comp. May Hill Arbuthnot, illus, Arthur Paul (Chicago: Scott, Foresman, 1952), p. 3.
7. David McCord, "Song of the Train," in *One at a Time,* illus. Harry B. Kane (Boston: Little, Brown, 1977), p. 107.
8. Christopher Morley, "Animal Crackers," in *Time for Poetry,* comp. May Hill Arbuthnot, p. 154.
9. Annis Duff, *Bequest of Wings: A Family's Pleasures with Books* (New York: Viking, 1944), pp. 76–77.
10. Robert Frost, *Stopping by Woods on a Snowy Evening,* illus. Susan Jeffers (New York: Dutton, 1978), unpaged.
11. Jack Prelutsky, "The Ghostly Grocer of Grumble Grove," in *Ghost Poems,* ed. Daisy Wallace, illus. Tomie de Paola (New York: Holiday House, 1979), p. 12.
12. Karla Kuskin, "The Meal," in *Alexander Soames: His Poems* (New York: Harper & Row, 1962), unpaged.
13. Mary Ann Hoberman, *A House Is a House for Me,* illus. Betty Fraser (New York: Viking, 1978), unpaged.
14. Rhoda W. Bacmeister, "Galoshes," in *The Arbuthnot Anthology of Children's Literature,* 4th ed., ed. Zena Sutherland et al. (New York: Lothrop, Lee & Shepard, 1976), p. 103.
15. *If All the Seas Were One Sea,* illus. Janina Domanska (New York: Macmillan, 1971), unpaged.

16. Shel Silverstein, "The Fourth," in *Where the Sidewalk Ends* (New York: Harper & Row, 1974), p. 15.
17. Dennis Lee, "I Eat Kids Yum Yum!" in *Garbage Delight,* illus. Frank Newfield (Boston: Houghton Mifflin, 1977), p. 37.
18. Shel Silverstein, "Tree House," in *Where the Sidewalk Ends,* p. 79.
19. David McCord, "Runover Rhyme," in *One at a Time,* p. 410.
20. Eve Merriam, "Inside a Poem," *It Doesn't Always Have to Rhyme* (New York: Atheneum, 1964), p. 3.
21. Jack Prelutsky, *Circus,* illus. Arnold Lobel (New York: Macmillan, 1974), unpaged.
22. David McCord, "Bananas and Cream," in *One at a Time,* p. 129.
23. Robert Louis Stevenson, "From a Railway Carriage," in *A Child's Garden of Verses,* illus. Jessie Willcox Smith (New York: Scribner's, n.d.), p. 45.
24. Robert Louis Stevenson, "Where Go the Boats?" in *A Child's Garden of Verses,* p. 16.
25. David McCord, "The Grasshhopper," in *One at a Time,* p. 28.
26. A. A. Milne, "Halfway Down," in *When We Were Very Young* (New York: Dutton, 1924), p. 83.
27. William J. Harris, "The Truth Is Quite Messy," in *Poems Here and Now,* ed. David Kherdian, illus. Nonny Hogrogian (New York: Greenwillow, 1976), p. 20.
28. David McCord, "Pumpkin Seeds," in *One at a Time,* p. 218.
29. William Jay Smith, "The Toaster," in *Laughing Time,* illus, Juliet Kepes (Boston: Little, Brown, 1955), p. 20.
30. Carl Sandburg, "Short Talk on Poetry," in *Early Moon* (New York: Harcourt Brace Jovanovich, 1958), p. 19.
31. David McCord, "Tiger Lily," in *One at a Time,* p. 33.
32. Charles Simic, "Watermelons," in *The Other Side of a Poem,* ed. Barbara Abercrombie (New York: Harper & Row, 1977), p. 41.
33. Eve Merriam, "Metaphor," in *It Doesn't Always Have to Rhyme,* p. 27.
34. Hilda Conkling, "Dandelion," in *Shoots of Green: Poems for Young Gardeners,* ed. Ella Bramblett (New York: Crowell, 1968), p. 26.
35. Langston Hughes, "April Rain Song," in *The Dream Keeper* (New York: Knopf, 1932), p. 8.
36. Valerie Worth, "Chairs," in *Small Poems,* illus. Natalie Babbitt (New York: Farrar, Straus & Giroux, 1972), p. 6.
37. Laurence Perrine, *Literature: Structure, Sound, Sense* (New York: Harcourt Brace Jovanovich, 1978), p. 594.
38. Robert Frost, "Dust of Snow," in *Robert Frost's Poems,* introduction and commentary by Louis Untermeyer (New York: Washington Square Press, 1960), p. 240.
39. Ted Hughes, "Moon Whales," in *Moon Whales and Other Poems* (New York: Viking, 1976), p. 1.
40. Dorothy Aldis, "Names," in *Sung Under the Silver Umbrella,* comp. Association for Childhood Education International, illus. Dorothy P. Lathrop (New York: Macmillan, 1935), p. 105.
41. John Tobias, "Reflections on a Gift of Watermelon Pickle," in *Reflections on a Gift of Watermelon Pickle and Other Poems,* comp. Stephen Dunning et al. (Chicago: Scott, Foresman, 1966), pp. 142–43.
42. Eve Merriam, "How to Eat a Poem," in *It Doesn't Always Have to Rhyme,* p. 79.
43. Myra Cohn Livingston, *When You Are Alone/It Keeps You Capone,* p. 5.
44. A. A. Milne, "Bad Sir Brian Botany," in *When We Were Very Young,* p. 94.
45. Aileen Fisher, *Sing, Little Mouse,* illus. Symeon Shimin (New York: Crowell, 1969), unpaged.

46. Robert Browning, *The Pied Piper of Hamelin,* illus. C. Walter Hodges (New York: Coward, McCann & Geoghegan, 1971), unpaged.

47. Samuel Taylor Coleridge, *The Rime of the Ancient Mariner,* illus. C. Walter Hodges (New York: Coward, McCann & Geoghegan, 1971), unpaged.

48. Alfred Noyes, *The Highwayman,* illus. Gilbert Riswold (Englewood Cliffs, N.J.: Prentice-Hall, 1969), unpaged.

49. Shel Silverstein, "Sarah Cynthia Sylvia Stout/Would Not Take the Garbage Out," in *Where the Sidewalk Ends,* pp. 70–71.

50. X. J. Kennedy, "A Big Deal for the Tooth Fairy," in *The Phantom Ice Cream Man,* illus. David McPhail (New York: Atheneum, 1979), p. 38.

51. Edward Lear, *The Complete Nonsense Book* (New York: Dodd, Mead, 1958), p. 31.

52. *Golden Treasury of Poetry,* comp. Louis Untermeyer, illus. Joan Walsh Anglund (New York: Golden Press, 1963), p. 241.

53. George A. Strong, "The Modern Hiawatha," in *Speak Roughly to Your Little Boy,* ed. Myra Cohn Livingston, illus. Joseph Low (New York: Harcourt Brace Jovanovich, 1971). p. 6.

54. Nancy, age twelve, wrote the poem on chairs, and Stephanie, also age twelve, wrote the poem on snakes; both are students at Worthington Hills School in Worthington, Ohio.

55. Christina Rossetti, "Who Has Seen the Wind?" in *Arbuthnot Anthology,* p. 99.

56. Nikki Giovanni, "Mothers," in *Celebrations: A New Anthology of Black American Poetry,* comp. and ed. Arnold Adoff (New York: Follett, 1977), pp. 32–33.

57. Ann Atwood, *Haiku: The Mood of Earth* (New York: Scribner's, 1971), unpaged.

58. Adam, age 12, Worthington Hills School, Worthington, Ohio.

59. Billy Joel, "Just the Way You Are," in *The Stranger* (New York: Bradley Publications, 1977), p. 28.

60. Helen Plotz, *As I Walked Out One Evening: A Book of Ballads* (New York: Greenwillow, 1976), p. xiii.

61. Phyllis McGinley, "Good Humor Man," in *This Powerful Rhyme,* selected by Helen Plotz (New York: Greenwillow, 1979), p. 28.

62. David McCord, "Goose, Moose, Spruce," in *One at a Time,* p. 221.

63. John Ciardi, "Mummy Slept Late and Daddy Fixed Breakfast," in *You Read to Me and I'll Read to You,* illus. Edward Gorey (New York: Lippincott, 1961), p. 18.

64. Lee Bennett Hopkins, "David McCord," in *Books Are by People* (New York: Citation Press, 1969), p. 169.

Professional References

Brewton, John E., G. Meredith Blackburn, III, and Lorraine A. Blackburn, comps. *Index to Poetry for Children and Young People 1970–1975.* H. W. Wilson, 1978.

Burrows, Alvina T. "Profile: Karla Kuskin." *Language Arts,* 56, No. 8 (Nov./Dec. 1979), 935–37.

Duff, Annis. *Bequest of Wings: A Family's Pleasures with Books.* Viking, 1944.

Fisher, Carol J., and Margaret A. Natarella. "Of Cabbage and Kings: Or What Kinds of Poetry Young Children Like." *Language Arts,* 56, No. 4 (April 1979), 380–85.

Frye, Northrop. *The Educated Imagination.* Indiana Univ. Press, 1964.

Hopkins, Lee Bennett. *Books Are by People.* Citation Press, 1969.

_____. *Pass the Poetry, Please!: Using Poetry in Pre-Kindergarten–Six Classrooms.* Citation Press, 1972.

Koch, Kenneth. *Rose, Where Did You Get That Red?: Teaching Great Poetry to Children.* Random House, 1973.

_____. *Wishes, Lies and Dreams: Teaching Children to Write Poetry.* Random House, 1971.

Krogness, Mary Mercer. "Imagery and Image Making." *Elementary English,* 51, No. 4 (April 1974), 488–90.

Lewis, Marjorie. "Why Is Poem a Four-Letter Word?" *School Library Journal,* 23, No. 9 (May 1977), 38–39.

Livingston, Myra Cohn. "But Is It Poetry?" *Horn Book Magazine,* 51, No. 6 (Dec. 1975), 571–80. Part II in 52, No. 1 (Feb. 1976), 24–31.

_____. *When You're Alone / It Keeps You Capone: An Approach to Creative Writing With Children*. Atheneum, 1973.

Perrine, Laurence. *Literature: Structure, Sound, and Sense*. 3rd ed. Harcourt Brace Jovanovich, 1978.

Richards, I. A. *Practical Criticism: A Study of Literary Judgment*. Harcourt Brace Jovanovich, 1956 (1929).

Sutherland, Zena, et al., eds. *The Arbuthnot Anthology of Children's Literature*. 4th ed. Lothrop, Lee & Shepard, 1976.

Terry, Ann. *Children's Poetry Preferences: A National Survey of the Upper Elementary Grades*. National Council of Teachers of English, 1974.

Tom, Chow Loy. "Paul Revere Rides Ahead: Poems Teachers Read to Pupils in the Middle Grades." *The Library Quarterly*, 43, (Jan. 1972), 27–38.

Children's Books Cited in Chapter

Abercrombie, Barbara, ed. *The Other Side of a Poem*. Illus. Harry Bertschmann. Harper & Row, 1977.

Adoff, Arnold, comp. *Celebrations: A New Anthology of Black American Poetry*. Follett, 1977.

Arbuthnot, May Hill, ed. *Time for Poetry*. Illus. Arthur Paul. Scott, Foresman, 1961.

Association for Childhood Education International, comps. *Sung Under the Silver Umbrella*. Illus. Dorothy Lathrop. Macmillan, 1935.

Atwood, Ann. *Fly with the Wind, Flow with the Water*. Scribner's, 1979.

_____. *Haiku: The Mood of Earth*. Scribner's, 1971.

_____. *Haiku-Vision in Poetry and Photography*. Scribner's, 1977.

_____. *My Own Rhythm: An Approach to Haiku*. Scribner's, 1973.

Bramblett, Ella, ed. *Shoots of Green: Poems for Young Gardeners*. Crowell, 1968.

Ciardi, John. *You Read to Me, I'll Read to You*. Illus. Edward Gorey. Lippincott, 1961.

Cole, William, ed. *Beastly Boys and Ghastly Girls*. Illus. Tomi Ungerer. Collins-World, 1964.

_____. *Oh, That's Ridiculous!* Illus. Tomi Ungerer. Viking, 1972.

_____. *Oh, What Nonsense!* Illus. Tomi Ungerer. Viking, 1966.

Domanska, Janina. *If All the Seas Were One Sea*. Macmillan, 1971.

Dunning, Stephen, Edward Lueders, and Hugh Smith, comps. *Reflections on a Gift of Watermelon Pickle and Other Modern Verse*. Lothrop, Lee & Shepard, 1967.

_____. *Some Haystacks Don't Even Have Any Needles: And Other Complete Modern Poems*. Lothrop, Lee & Shepard, 1969.

Ferris, Helen, ed. *Favorite Poems Old and New*. Illus. Leonard Weisgard. Doubleday, 1957.

Fisher, Aileen. *Going Barefoot*. Illus. Adrienne Adams. Crowell, 1960.

_____. *Like Nothing at All*. Illus. Leonard Weisgard. Crowell, 1962.

_____. *Listen, Rabbit*. Illus. Symeon Shimin. Crowell, 1964.

_____. *Sing, Little Mouse*. Illus. Symeon Shimin. Crowell, 1969.

Frost, Robert. *Robert Frost's Poems*. Washington Square Press, 1960.

_____. *Stopping by Woods on a Snowy Evening*. Illus. Susan Jeffers. Dutton, 1978.

_____. *You Come Too: Favorite Poems for Young Readers*. Illus. Thomas Nason. Holt, Rinehart & Winston, 1959.

Fukuda, Hanako. *Wind in My Hand*. Ed. Mark Taylor. Trans. Hanako Fukuda. Illus. Lydia Cooley. Golden Gate-Childrens, 1970.

Hoberman, Mary Ann. *A House Is a House for Me*. Illus. Betty Fraser. Viking, 1978.

Hopkins, Lee Bennett, ed. *To Look at Any Thing*. Photographs by John Earl. Harcourt Brace Jovanovich, 1978.

Hughes, Langston. *Don't You Turn Back*. Selec. Lee Bennett Hopkins. Illus. Ann Grifalconi. Knopf, 1969.

Hughes, Ted. *Moon-Whales and Other Moon Poems*. Viking, 1976.

Issa, Yayū, Kikaku, and other Japanese poets. *Don't Tell the Scarecrow*. Illus. Tālivaldis Stubis. Four Winds-Scholastic, 1969.

Joel, Billy. *The Stranger*. Bradley Publications, 1977.

Kennedy, X. J. *The Phantom Ice Cream Man: More Nonsense Verse*. Illus. David McPhail. Atheneum, 1979.

Kherdian, David. *If Dragon Flies Made Honey*. Illus. José Aruego and Ariane Dewey. Greenwillow, 1977.

_____. ed. *Poems Here and Now*. Illus. Nonny Hogrogian. Greenwillow, 1976.

Kuskin, Karla. *Alexander Soames: His Poems*. Harper & Row, 1962.

_____. *Any Me I Want to Be*. Harper & Row, 1972.

_____. *Near the Window Tree*. Harper & Row, 1975.

Larrick, Nancy. *Bring Me All of Your Dreams*. Evans, 1980.

_____. *Piping Down the Valleys Wild: Poetry for the Young of All Ages*. Illus. Ellen Raskin. Delacorte, 1968.

Lear, Edward. *The Book of Nonsense*. Hale, n.d.

_____. *The Complete Nonsense Book*. Dodd, Mead, 1958 (1912).

_____. *The Complete Nonsense of Edward Lear*. Collected by Holbrook Jackson. Dover, 1951.

_____. *Whizz!* Illus. Janina Domanska. Macmillan, 1973.

Lee, Dennis. *Garbage Delight*. Illus. Frank Newfield. Houghton Mifflin, 1977.

Livingston, Myra Cohn. *O Sliver of Liver and Other Poems*. Illus. Iris Van Rynbach. Atheneum, 1979.

_____, ed. *Speak Roughly to Your Little Boy: A Collection of Parodies and Burlesques, Together with the Original Poems, Chosen and Annotated for Young People*. Illus. Joseph Low. Harcourt Brace Jovanovich, 1971.

Longfellow, Henry Wadsworth. *The Story of Hiawatha.* Houghton Mifflin, 1883.

McCord, David. *All Day Long.* Illus. Henry B. Kane. Little, Brown, 1966.

_____. *Away and Ago.* Illus,. Leslie Morrill. Little, Brown, 1975.

_____. *Every Time I Climb a Tree.* Illus. Marc Simont. Little, Brown, 1967.

_____. *Far and Few.* Illus. Henry B. Kane. Little, Brown, 1952.

_____. *One at a Time.* Little, Brown, 1977.

_____. *The Star in the Pail.* Illus. Marc Simont. Little, Brown, 1975.

_____. *Take Sky.* Illus. Henry B. Kane. Little, Brown, 1962.

McKinley, Robin. *Beauty: A Retelling of the Story of Beauty and the Beast.* Harper & Row, 1978.

MacKay, David. *A Flock of Words: An Anthology of Poetry for Children and Others.* Illus. Margery Gill. Harcourt Brace Jovanovich, 1969.

Merriam, Eve. *It Doesn't Always Have to Rhyme.* Illus. Malcolm Spooner. Atheneum, 1964.

_____. *Out Loud.* Illus. Harriet Sherman. Atheneum, 1973.

Milne, A. A. *Now We Are Six.* Illus. Ernest H. Shepard. Dutton, 1927.

_____. *When We Were Very Young.* Illus. Ernest H. Shepard. Dutton, 1924.

Molloy, Paul. *Beach Glass and Other Poems.* Four Winds-Scholastic, 1970.

Moss, Elaine, selec. *From Morn to Midnight.* Illus. Satomi Ichikawa. Crowell, 1977.

Plotz, Helen, ed. *As I Walked Out One Evening: A Book of Ballads.* Greenwillow, 1976.

_____. *This Powerful Rhyme: A Book of Sonnets.* Greenwillow, 1979.

Prelutsky, Jack. *Circus.* Illus. Arnold Lobel. Macmillian, 1974.

Sandburg, Carl, ed. *American Songbag.* Harcourt Brace Jovanovich, 1927.

_____. *Early Moon.* Illus. James Daugherty. Harcourt Brace Jovanovich, 1958 (1930).

Seuss, Dr. *And to Think That I Saw It on Mulberry Street.* Vanguard, 1937.

_____. *The 500 Hats of Bartholomew Cubbins.* Hale, 1938.

_____. *McElligot's Pool.* Random House, 1947.

Silverstein, Shel. *Where the Sidewalk Ends.* Harper & Row, 1974.

Smith, William Jay. *Laughing Time.* Illus. Juliet Kepes. Little, Brown, 1955.

Stevenson, Robert Louis. *A Child's Garden of Verses.* Illus. Jessie Willcox Smith. Scribner's, n.d.

_____. *A Child's Garden of Verses.* Illus. Brian Wildsmith. Watts, 1966.

Sutherland, Zena, et al., eds. *The Arbuthnot Anthology of Children's Literature.* 4th ed. Lothrop, Lee & Shepard, 1976.

Tripp, Wallace, comp. *Granfa' Grig Had a Pig and Other Rhymes Without Reason from Mother Goose.* Little, Brown, 1976.

_____. *A Great Big Ugly Man Came Up and Tied His Horse to Me: A Book of Nonsense Verse.* Little, Brown, 1973.

Untermeyer, Louis, selec. *The Golden Treasury of Poetry.* Illus. Joan Walsh Anglund. Golden Press-Western, 1959.

Wallace, Daisy, ed. *Ghost Poems.* Illus. Tomie de Paola. Holiday House, 1979.

_____. *Witch Poems.* Illus. Trina Schart Hyman. Holiday House, 1976.

Worth, Valerie. *Small Poems.* Illus. Natalie Babbitt. Farrar, Straus & Giroux, 1972.

Recommended Reading

Elements of Poetry

Sound

The delights of sound abound in books of poetry and verse about animals and insects. William Cole, in *Dinosaurs and Beasts of Yore* (P-I, Collins, 1979), sings of the eohippus, brachiosaurus, and pterodactyl, while Norma Farber, in *Never Say Ugh to a Bug,* illustrated by Jose Aruego (P-I, Greenwillow, 1979), considers spittlebugs and spiders, wasps and water-skaters. Creatures as different as the herring and osprey, and the ichthyosaurus and quinquemaculatus, are Robert S. Oliver's subjects in *Cornucopia* (P-I, Atheneum, 1978).

Repetition of words underscores meaning and establishes sound pattern and humor in Eve Merriam's "A Round" in *Finding a Poem* (P-I, Atheneum, 1970). A. A. Milne's "The King's Breakfast," when the king asks for "a little bit of butter for my bread," or his "Rice Pudding," in which Mary Jane has a tantrum because she is served "rice pudding again," both in *When We Were Very Young,* illustrated by Ernest H. Shepard (P-I, Dutton, 1924), sound joyful to young listeners.

In *Our Fathers Had Powerful Songs* (N-P, Dutton, 1974), Natalie Belting's collection of American Indian poetry, songs of the world's creation, of daily living, and of dead spirits are ear-appealing. Faith Hubley's pictures and Elizabeth Swados's words in *Lullaby* (N, Harper & Row, 1980) are music for the young child. Written in two languages, *The Tamarindo Puppy and Other Poems,* by Charlotte Pomerantz, illustrated by Byron Barton (P-I, Greenwillow, 1980), speaks in one—the language of love.

Rhythm

Hoofbeats make a special kind of rhythm. Among the books capturing the beat of horses are William Cole's *The Poetry of Horses* (P-I, Scribner's, 1979) and Lee Bennett Hopkins's *My Mane Catches the Wind,* illustrated by Sam Savitt (I, Harcourt Brace Jovanovich, 1979). Cole's compilation has sections on foals and colts; workers, wild horses, and war horses; and certain special horses. There are poems by Coatsworth, Frost, De La Mare, and Nash.

Siv Cedering Fox's *The Blue Horse and Other Night Poems* (P-I, Seabury, 1979), a collection of fourteen poems about sleeping, dreaming, and waking, begins with the question ". . . and what do you think of before you fall asleep?" The rhythms of night are collected by Susan Russo in *The Moon's the North Wind's Cooky* (N-P, Lothrop, Lee & Shepard, 1979). In addition to Lindsay's title poem, Aiken's "Night Landscape," Guiterman's "Nocturne," and Stevenson's "Windy Nights" show the many faces of night. The rhythm of hours beats faster and lighter in two collections by Lee Bennett Hopkins, *Go to Bed! A Book of Bedtime Poems* (N-P, Knopf, 1979) and *Morning Noon and Nighttime, Too* (N-P, Harper & Row, 1980).

Arnold Adoff writes song poems with rhythm and melody. *Big Sister Tells Me That I'm Black,* illustrated by Lorenzo Lynch (N-P, Holt, Rinehart & Winston, 1976) resounds with an exuberantly rhythmic chant: "we shout out loud / hip hip / hip hooray / hip hip / we Black today." *Black Is Brown Is Tan,* illustrated by Emily McCully (N-P, Harper & Row, 1973), is a rhythmic story-poem about the beauty of the family that is all the colors of the human race. It is also a gentle celebration of the strength of family love, as is *Make a Circle, Keep Us In: Poems for a Good Day,* illustrated by Arnold Himler (N-P, Delacorte, 1975). The text here rambles all over the page in roughly circular fashion, underscoring the theme ideographically; the circle of love that makes a family is visible in text form, and illustration.

Meaning

The poems and verses in Lilian Moore's *Go With the Poem* (I, McGraw-Hill, 1979), an anthology in a contemporary spirit of work by well-known and soon-to-be known poets, paint vivid pictures for students in middle grades. The section titles are lines from poems: "I'm the Driver and the Wheel" is taken from "On the Skateboard," by Lillian Morrison; "What Shall I Do With the Seed?" is from "There Came a Day," by Ted Hughes; and "When a Friend Calls to Me" is from "A Time to Talk," by Robert Frost. A vivid picture emerges from the words in "The Wind" in Kaye Starbird's *The Covered Bridge House and Other Poems* (I, Four Winds-Scholastic, 1979).

Daisy Wallace's collections help fuel the pictures fashioned in the imagination of a child reading. In addition to ghost, giant, witch, and monster poem editions, she edited *Fairy Poems,* illustrated by Trina Schart Hyman (P-I, Holiday House, 1980), in which the words conjure visions of leprechauns, goblins, elves, and winged fairies. Verse to prickle the skin is collected in two books by Lee Bennett Hopkins—*A-Haunting We Will Go* (I, Whitman, 1977) and *Monsters, Ghoulies, and Creepy Creatures* (I, Whitman, 1977). This inveterate collector has most recently gathered poems for believers and non-believers in *Elves, Fairies, & Gnomes,* illustrated by Rosekrans Hoffman (P-I, Knopf, 1980). His merry melange includes verse by both classic and contemporary poets. Aileen Fisher, in *Out in the Dark and Daylight,* illustrated by Gail Owens (P-I, Harper & Row, 1980), shows why she is the 1978 recipient of the NCTE Award for Poetry for Children. This book includes 140 new poems in which young readers will discover ant villages under rocks, daisy worlds, and sounds of spring.

Edna St. Vincent Millay's Poems Selected for Young People (I-A, Harper & Row, 1979) will augment the experience in reading and listening to poetry that improves students' ability at ferreting out deeper layers of meaning. There are sixty long poems, sonnets, and nature poems for mature students. "The Ballad of the Harp-Weaver" treats life and devotion in a poem about a mother's love for her son.

Ashley Bryan's *I Greet the Dawn: Poems by Paul Laurence Dunbar* (A, Atheneum, 1978) includes, for the most part, poems in standard English, with only a few of the Black-dialect poems for which Dunbar is known. The poet sings of life, love, and God, of Lincoln and of Harriet Beecher Stowe. Bryan introduces the collection with a fine biography.

Other intense poetry for more mature readers is found in Ted Hughes's *Selected Poems 1957–1967* (A, Harper & Row, 1973). The book's more than sixty poems by this major English poet have been gleaned from his first three books: *The Hawk in the Rain* (1957), *Lupercal* (1960), and *Wodwo* (1967). Hughes's other recent work includes *Season Songs,* illustrated by Leonard Baskin (A, Viking, 1975), *Moon-Whales and Other Moon Poems,* illustrated by Leonard Baskin (A, Viking, 1976), and *Poetry Is* (I-A, Doubleday, 1970).

Stark contrasts sharpen meaning for young children in David Kherdian's *Country Cat, City Cat* (N-P, Four Winds-Scholastic, 1978), which includes poems about the city, the country, and cats. Frank Asch's *City Sandwich* (N-P, Greenwillow, 1978) and *Country Pie* (N-P, Greenwillow, 1979) have black-and-white drawings with many details and textures. In *Somebody Spilled the Sky,* illustrated by Eleanor Hazard (N, Greenwillow, 1979), Ruth Krauss presents verse for the very youngest listeners. The illustrations lend meaning to the words and, in the verse "Where," delicately portray the enormousness of the world for a curious youngster.

Forms of Poetry
Poetry as Story

Narrative poetry's ability to make a story (with a beginning, middle, end, characters, plot, theme, and setting) memorable by adding meter and rhyme is exemplified by Natalie Babbitt's *Phoebe's Revolt* (P-I, Farrar, Straus & Giroux, 1968) and Mildred Howells's *The Woman Who Lived in Holland,* illustrated by William Curtis Holdsworth (N-P, Farrar, Straus & Giroux, 1973), both in picture book format. The latter tells about the woman who scrubbed everything in sight and even wanted to shine up the stars in the sky. Mary Ann Hoberman's *I Like Old Clothes,* illustrated by Jacqueline Chwast (N-P, Knopf, 1976), is the story of hand-me-down clothes: "Clothes with a history, Clothes with a mystery." Some of the wild costumes worn by the characters suggest that other people's old clothes are fun to wear.

Collections of story poems include many that relate to a single theme or topic. William Cole selects verse dealing with strange and mysterious happenings, stories at sea, stories about fighting men, and odd and funny tales in *The Poet's Tales: A New Book of Story Poems,* illustrated by Charles Keeping (I-A, Collins-World, 1971). Mary O'Neill writes about *People I'd Like to Keep,* illustrated by Paul Galdone (I, Doubleday, 1964.)

Lucille Clifton writes about Everett Anderson, who is six years old, Black, and "runs and loves to hop." *Some of the Days of Everett Anderson,* illustrated by Evaline Ness (N-P, Holt, Rinehart & Winston, 1970) describes the urban Black child who delights in activities of universal interest. Other story-poems by her are *Everett Anderson's Year,* illustrated by Ann Grifalconi (N-P, Holt, Rinehart & Winston, 1974), and *Everett Anderson's Friend* (N-P, Holt, Rinehart & Winston, 1976).

The lines of "*I Am Cherry Alive,*" *The Little Girl Sang,* by Delmore Shwartz (I, Harper & Row, 1979), must have sung to Barbara Cooney to inspire the celebration and emotion of her illustrations. The poem is an adventure best shared individually with children because the artist's candid interpretation of rapturous identification with nature may catch some off guard. In a lighter vein, Karla Kuskin's *Herbert Hated Being Small* (P, Harper & Row, 1979) celebrates growing up. We learn that size is relative; it is related to whom you are standing beside.

Elinor Parker's *100 More Story Poems,* illustrated by Peter Spier (I, Crowell, 1960), includes many old standards. Parker concentrates upon narrative poetry about people, magic, history, heroes, the sea, and animals. In *Callooh! Callay! Holiday Poems for Young Readers* (P-I, Atheneum, 1978), Myra Cohn Livingston collects verse about more than a dozen holidays, blending the subtleties of Walt Whitman and e.e. cummings with the simpler appeal of Hilda Conkling and Valerie Worth.

Arnold Adoff's *Where Wild Willie,* illustrated by Emily Arnold McCully (N-P, Harper & Row, 1978), describes the loneliness and excitement of a young girl running away. His other picture books include *Ma nDa LA,* illustrated by Emily McCully (N-P, Harper & Row, 1971), and *I Am the Running Girl,* illustrated by Ronald Himler (I, Harper & Row, 1979).

Two poems that interest students in the middle grades are "Annabel Lee," by Edgar Allan Poe, in *Anthology of Children's Literature,* by Edna Johnson, Evelyn R. Sickels, and Frances C. Sayers (A, Houghton Mifflin, 1970), and "Elegy Written in a Country Churchyard," by Thomas Gray, in *Anatomy of Literature,* by Robert Foulke and Paul Smith (A, Harcourt Brace Jovanovich, 1972). *Paul Revere's Ride,* illustrated by Joseph Low (I-A, Windmill-Dutton, 1973) is Henry Wadsworth Longfellow's famous version of the event. The galloping hoofbeats, the martial rhythm, and the stirring words of this poem—"defiance and not of fear"—remind readers to be ever alert in defense of freedom.

Fun and Nonsense

Of the many verse forms children find entertaining, few compare in popularity with the limerick. In *A Lollygag of Limericks* (I-A, Atheneum, 1978), Myra Cohn Livingston shows her enchantment with such English places as Skittle, Chipping, Needles-on-Stoor, Yately, and Barnby Moor. N. M. Bodecker's *A Person from Britain Whose Head Was the Shape of a Mitten and Other Limericks* (I-A, Atheneum, 1980) introduces readers to "A Maid in Old Lyme" and "A Bride of North Conway." Sara and John Brewton collect limericks that appeal to children's raucous sense of humor in *Laughable Limericks,* illustrated by Ingrid Fetz (P-I, Crowell, 1965), and Leland B. Jacobs does the same in *Funny Folk in Limerick Land,* illustrated by Raymond Burns (P-I, Garrard, 1971), and *Animal Antics in Limerick Land,* illustrated by Edward Malsberg (P-I, Garrard, 1971). William Cole's *The Book of Giggles,* illustrated by Tomi Ungerer (P-I, Collins-World, 1970), includes illustrations that add to the limericks' sense of ridiculousness.

Ogden Nash, noted writer of much humorous verse for children, extends Edward Lear's use of the limerick and uses other forms to delight both children and adults. In the classic *The Moon Is Shining Bright as Day: An Anthology of Good Humored Verse,* illustrated by Rose Shirvanian (I-A, Lippincott, 1953), Nash collects 180 poems by ninety-three authors. Heinrich Hoffmann's "The Story of Augustus Who Would Not Have Any Soup," Walter De La Mare's "Miss T," Norman Gale's "Bobby's First Poem," and Nash's "Adventures of Isabel" appear in this collection. Lear's *The Owl & the Pussy-Cat & Other Nonsense,* illustrated by Owen Wood (P-I, Viking, 1979), is a whimsical picture book with magnificent and elaborate artwork. It is an edition worthy of Lear's eccentricities.

In *Custard and Company: Poems by Ogden Nash* (P-I, Little, Brown, 1980), Quentin Blake adds cartoonlike drawings to accompany Nash's funny pieces about usual and unusual animals and insects, and cowardly Custard, the dragon.

The work of N. M. Bodecker echoes the familiar rhythm of the traditional nursery rhymes in combination with his own unique nonsense. "*Let's Marry,*" *Said the Cherry: And Other Nonsense Poems* (I, Atheneum, 1974) and *Hurry, Hurry, Mary Dear! and Other Nonsense Poems* (I-A, Atheneum, 1976) are two of his collections. Bodecker's syllabic nonsense, word play, and nonconforming view of people, combine to create flies that keep multiflieing and a wife who must up the storms and down the screens. Idioms are taken literally and when someone loses his head, children see the event in Bodecker's illustrations.

Animals frequently appear in humorous verse. Poets create fantastic animals, characterize some aspect of their sound, or caricature some physical feature. Jack Prelutsky views the world from the animal's perspective. In *Toucans Two and Other Poems,* illustrated by Jose Aruego (N-P, Macmillian, 1970), he quips about animals in a mischievous way that enables readers to see them or think of them in never-before ways. In *The Pack Rat's Day and Other Poems,* illustrated by Margaret Bloy Graham (P-I, Macmillan, 1974), Prelutsky describes the habits of the Pack Rat. He uses tongue-tangling nonsense with strong rhythm and rhyme to describe fanciful creatures in *The Snopp on the Sidewalk and Other Poems,* illustrated by Byron Barton (I, Greenwillow, 1977). "The Locomotive Sloth" and "The X Bird" are two of X. J. Kennedy's animals in *The Phantom Ice Cream Man: More Nonsense Verse* (I, Atheneum, 1979).

Theodore Roethke describes some humorous animals in *Dirty Dinky and Other Creatures: Poems for Children* (I, Doubleday, 1973). There is "a most odious Yak who took toads on his back" and a Bat who seems to be a mouse with wings and wears a human face. Mary Ann Hoberman is a perceptive observer of animal behavior in *The Raucous Auk: A Menagerie of Poems,* illustrated by Joseph Low (P-I, Viking, 1973).

There are many anthologies of humorous verse for children. William Cole's collections number a dozen, including *Oh, How Silly!* illustrated by Tomi Ungerer (I, Viking, 1970), and *Oh, That's Ridiculous!* illustrated by Tomi Ungerer (I, Viking, 1972). His own poem "The Panteater" appears in *Oh, Such Foolishness!* (I, Lippincott, 1978) with other poems for fans of Dennis Lee and Shel Silverstein.

Leland B. Jacobs selects humorous poetry in two books children enjoy: *Funny Bone Ticklers in Verse and Rhyme,* illustrated by Edward Malsberg (P-I, Garrard, 1973), and *Poetry for Chuckles and Grins,* illustrated by Tomie de Paola (P-I, Garrard, 1968). Another funny collection, by Myra Cohn Livingston, is *What a Wonderful Bird the Frog Are: An Assortment of Humorous Poetry and Verse* (I, Harcourt Brace Jovanovich, 1973). Livingston does not include any of her own poetry in this book in which she selects, with the eye and ear of the poet, subjects ranging from television programs to historical figures.

There are surprises, word plays, humorous twists, and exaggeration calling attention to the lighter side of life in John Ciardi's *Fast and Slow: Poems for Advanced Children and Beginning Parents,* illustrated by Becky Gaver (N-P, Houghton Mifflin, 1975). Some of the poems poke fun at serious themes while others are pure tongue-in-cheek nonsense. In all of the poems about the problems children cause, there is a glow of warmth and love and pride in their antics. Sedate children, who would not create even a bit of havoc, do not appeal to Ciardi. X. J. Kennedy relates the dire events for the mother who threatened to dive into the stove if her child slammed the door just one more time. Shoelaces are made out of spaghetti by the child who uses his noodle, and snowflake souffle makes a tasty dish. In *One Winter Night in August and Other Nonsense Jingles,* illustrated by David McPhail (P-I, Atheneum, 1975), Kennedy combines wry humor with outright silliness.

In *Rolling Harvey Down the Hill,* illustrated by Victoria Chess (P-I, Greenwillow, 1980, Jack Prelutsky is his usual hilarious self. This funny collection is about a group of boys— Lumpy, Tony, Will, Harvey, and the narrator—and their misadventures. They smoke in the cellar, eat worms, break a window, and scare girls. A delightful gang!

Tales of Adventure

Among the ballads popular with children are Stephen Vincent Benét's *The Ballad of William Sycamore,* illustrated by Brinton Turkle (I, Little, Brown, 1972), and Ernest Lawrence Thayer's *Casey at the Bat: A Ballad of the Republic, Sung in the Year 1888,* illustrated by Wallace Tripp (I, Coward, McCann & Geoghegan, 1978). The latter illustrates well that poetry contains humor and pathos, telling stories of people in their greatest and most inglorious moments. Alfred Lord Tennyson's *The Charge of the Light Brigade,* illustrated by Alice and Martin Provensen (I, Golden Press-Western, 1964), has been shared with youngsters to show how hearty and strong poetry can be.

Two modern ballads that are enjoyable reading and listening are Caroline D. Emerson's "A Modern Ballad: The Ups and Downs of the Elevator Car," in *My Tang's Tungled and Other Ridiculous Situations,* by Sara and John E. Brewton, illustrated by Graham Booth (I, Crowell, 1973), and Charlotte Pomerantz's *The Ballad of the Long-Tailed Rat,* illustrated by Marian Parry (N-P, Macmillan, 1975). In its last verse, everyone takes credit for catching the long-tailed rat, but the rat only admits to losing a "pinch of an inch."

eight

RANDALL JARRELL From *CHILDREN SELECTING BOOKS IN A LIBRARY*

What some escape to, some escape: if we find Swann's
Way better than our own, and trudge on at the back
Of the north wind to —to —somewhere east
Of the sun, west of the moon, it is because we live

By trading another's sorrow for our own; another's
Impossibilities, still unbelieved in, for our own . . .
'I am myself still?' For a little while, forget:
The world's selves cure that short disease, myself,
And we see bending to us, dewy-eyed, the great
CHANGE, dear to all things not to themselves endeared.[1]

Contemporary Realism

Is a story a window, through which we see the world, or a mirror, in which we see ourselves? For most of us, it is both window and mirror, endlessly expanding our experience beyond a life lived in one time and one place.

Eleven-year-old Christine, discussing what made Judy Blume's books seem so real, said, "Her books are about life the way it really is—not fairy tale endings. Her books don't have happy endings; they're just like real life. Some have sad endings and some just sort of stop and you know things will go on just the way they are. That's the same way it really is." Christine's reading of the works of this author has left her with the mirror concept of literature. Evan, another child discussing Blume's books, said, "I really don't like to tell people, but I pretend I am the person in the book not only while I'm reading it but for a long time after. If it's rainy or boring, I go to my room and I just play that I'm Margaret or Harriet." ("Margaret" is protagonist of *Are You There, God? It's Me, Margaret* (I), by Judy Blume, and "Harriet" the title character of *Harriet the Spy* (I), by Louise Fitzhugh.) Thus Evan experiences literature as a window.

Realistic fiction has a strong sense of actuality; its plausible stories seem almost reports of what is happening or what could happen any place. Such stories are both mirrors and windows of life; they cause us to reflect on life and they show us lives that may not be attainable by us in reality. The many experiences they allow us can be had safely; we can sail around the world without fear of shipwreck or suffer blindness without loss of sight, while still probing the emotions of the moment. We can also rehearse experiences we might someday have; we can fall in love, undergo a job interview, experience the birth of a child. These practice sessions with story help prepare us for reality, creating expectations and models that influence our reactions to real events.

We live by trading another's sorrows and impossibilities for our own; as we read we move between fantasy, dream, and reality to ponder our own lives while living vicariously in others'.

While reading, we unconsciously participate in a story, all the while composing similar stories to deal with our own wishes and fears. We draw analogies between stories we read and stories that, in

Profile

JUDY BLUME

School isn't as boring as it used to be. Wendy and Caroline made copies of their *How To Have Fun With Blubber* list and on Monday morning they passed them out.

We made Linda say, *I am Blubber, the smelly whale of class 206.* We made her say it before she could use the toilet in the Girls' Room, before she could get a drink at the fountain, before she ate her lunch and before she got on the bus to go home. It was easy to get her to do it. I think she would have done anything we said. There are some people who just make you want to see how far you can go.

Blubber

The things Judy Blume remembers, such as being afraid of thunderstorms, or wanting a first bra, are the concerns of many children today, and she captures these experiences in stories that fast become children's favorites. In a letter to her readers, Judy Blume says:

Most of you want to know where I get my ideas. That's a scary question because I'm not sure. Ideas seem to come from everywhere. In *Blubber* I drew heavily on an incident that took place in my daughter's classroom. The idea for *Deenie* came from a woman whose daughter had scoliosis. I wrote *It's Not the End of the World* because I knew many families who were suffering the pains of divorce. Since that time I have experienced divorce myself and while it wasn't easy, it wasn't the end of the world for any of us. The idea for the book *Tales of a Fourth Grade Nothing* came from a news article about a real toddler who actually swallowed a pet turtle. I based the character of Fudge on my son, Larry, when he was that age (*Bradbury Press promotional material*).

Judy Blume's ideas have become a dozen books that children adore. She is high on their list of best-loved authors because her books deal with first experiences that carry strong personal and emotional meaning. Her readers often ask, "How do you know all our secrets?"

It's because I remember just about everything from third grade on, and many things that happened before that. I can tell you exactly what I was wearing on the spring day that one of my kindergarten classmates stepped on my little finger while I was sketching on the floor. And how embarrassing it was when I cried in front of the whole class (*Bradbury Press promotional material*).

Judy Blume was a very quiet little girl who lived an exciting life inside her head. Today she lives in the mountains of northern New Mexico with her daughter Randy and son Larry. The scenery is so beautiful she has to turn her back to the window to keep her mind on what she is writing.

effect, we tell ourselves. Pleasure arises when a story transforms our wishes and fears from unconsciousness into conscious, manageable, and coherent forms. Bruno Bettelheim, in *The Uses of Enchantment,* describes the process for young children as being one in which the experiences of the symbolic figures portrayed in fairy tales become surrogate experiences that embody the child's unconscious fears. For example, fears of being abandoned may find expression in the story of Hansel and Gretel and, since Hansel and Gretel ultimately return to a safe home, the child finds reassurance in the story. Older children continue the process with other types of literature.

National surveys and librarians' reports have repeatedly shown that intermediate-grade students choose realistic stories far more than any other type. Perhaps children at this age, searching for an identity and looking for a yardstick against which to measure themselves, turn to realistic fiction to help them define the person they want to become.

No definition of realism is simple, and to say that realism is fiction that could happen in the real world—as opposed to fantasy, which could not—is simplistic. Every work of fiction, like the stories we tell ourselves, is part fantasy and part reality. As we create the myth we call reality, we selectively remember and reshape events of our past and present; the same thing happens in books.

The realistic books we discuss—which have contemporary settings, as distinct from fiction set in the historical past or in the future—touch upon nearly every facet of life that students see reported in the newspapers and on television. The best of them illumine life, whereas the news merely reports it. Good literature presents social and personal concerns in a fully human context, not as sensationalistic news items. Children who read widely, testing and tasting from alternate life styles, have many opportunities to try out roles vicariously through realistic books.

Realistic books today do not ask young people to believe in a perfectly run world. When headlines proclaim that some schools are more dangerous than the streets, harsh reality strikes close.

Children know that the world is not entirely safe. Good literature does not resolve complex problems with easy answers. There is no such thing as a "no pain, no remorse" abortion, and good literature does not pretend there is. Literature reflects the society that creates it and, as our world changes, so do children's books.

Realistic books serve children in countless ways, one of which is by showing that, although

Pleasingly plump Linda's school report on whales includes a description of "blubber," a nickname with which she then becomes tagged.
(From the book *Blubber* by Judy Blume. Laurel Leaf Edition, 1978. Used by permission of Dell Publishing Co., Inc.)

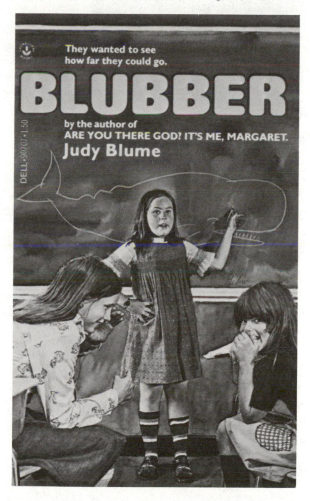

Profile

PAUL ZINDEL

TILLIE'S VOICE: The Conclusion: My experiment has shown some of the strange effects radiation can produce . . . and how dangerous it can be if not handled correctly. Mr. Goodman said I should tell in this conclusion what my future plans are and how this experiment has helped me make them.

For one thing, the effect of gamma rays on man-in-the-moon marigolds has made me curious about the sun and the stars, for the universe itself must be like a world of great atoms—and I want to know more about it. But most important, I suppose, my experiment has made me feel important—every atom in me, in everybody, has come from the sun—from places beyond our dreams. The atoms of our hands, the atoms of our hearts. . . . Atom. *Atom*. What a beautiful word.

The Effect of Gamma Rays on
Man-in-the-Moon Marigolds

Tillie's growing awareness of her self worth and the need she sees for a change in her life are important issues to Paul Zindel. They are recurring themes with variations in all of his books; almost all his protoganists endure the absence of parental love.

In *The Pigman,* John and Lorraine try to ease their guilt for their unintentional part in the death of Mr. Pignati, the only adult who had been a friend. Chris Boyd, in *Confessions of a Teenage Baboon,* faces his father's absence and his mother's domination; Marsh Mellow, in *Pardon Me, You're Stepping on My Eyeball,* suffers an alcoholic mother and a missing father. In speaking about teen-agers and writing, Paul Zindel has said:

I'm trying to tell the kids to examine self-hate and any feelings of inadequacy and to act to stop the process. I'm telling the kids that I love the

---

values and norms may change from generation to generation, basic emotions do not. Realistic fiction, serving up new experiences, can be a factor in helping children mature. To be sure, this does not deny the roles of fantasy, biography, or poetry as conveyers of truth; we need them all.

A moment of reflection about our own reading can clarify how books help us try on roles, define identity, and expand our understanding by increasing our repertoire of experience.

THE REALISTIC BOOK AS MIRROR

Literature mirrors our perception of life; we see in stories reflections of our own values, disappointments, and dreams. In what an author creates, a reader sees parts of his own inner and outer world. This is necessarily so because we create the images for the words the author gives us—and we know that the eye finds what the mind seeks.

Of Self-Determination

"Read a book and discover yourself" conveys the essence of the appeal realism carries for its readers. Children unabashedly ask for books "about someone just like me." The comparability between the book and the reader does not hinge upon age, time, or place, however, but upon the validity of the emotions presented. Feelings must ring true in the reader's view; they are more important than surface actuality. When children read books that show others searching for self, they find underdog and sympathize with his struggle because that's what I was and am in many ways still. I want my kids to feel worthy, to search for hope against all odds as they travel the plots of my books. I'm trying to tell all kids that they don't have to consider themselves misfits, that they deserve hopes and dreams and the technique and patience to make those dreams reality. I tell the kids that my books have a secret—a very useful secret—and to read them to find the lessons they teach, or to examine the problems they pose. . . . I tell the kids that tomorrow becomes today through self-inspection and action and belief, that their minds come equipped by God or Nature with the spirit and means to be joyful and intimate with their fellow human beings. I tell them life can be sort of fun, but it isn't easy. I tell them in my novels to take good care of themselves, to be self-ish if they must in order that their souls stay intact and their hearts never lie (Audrey Eaglen, "Of Life, Love, Death, Kids, and Inhalation Therapy: An Interview with Paul Zindel," *Top of the News*, 34, No. 2 [Winter 1978], 182).

Readers seem to know that Paul Zindel is on their team for they continue to snap up his books. When adolescents speak, Paul Zindel listens; he catches their lingo and appeals to their weird sense of humor through his sense of the ridiculous. The essentially tragic themes are laced with wit in stories that give readers hope and reassurance. Written from the adolescent's point of view, it is clear why, when Paul Zindel speaks, adolescents listen.

Paul Zindel was a high-school chemistry teacher for ten years in New York City before he turned to writing. A talented playwright, he, his wife, Bonnie, and their two children divide their time between the East and West coasts.

---

that they are not alone and learn that life will be what they make of it.

Because our society has few of the ritualized rites of passage of primal societies, the way is less clear for our preadolescents; they must mark their own paths. Books that portray a character struggling toward adulthood allow such readers to see themselves reflected, and provide a rehearsal for real life.

Bette Greene shows a girl grappling with the feelings of first love and self-determination in *Philip Hall Likes Me. I Reckon Maybe.* (I). Eleven-year-old Beth is the second-best arithmetic solver, the second-best speller, and the second-best reader in her class. Philip Hall is first, but perhaps shouldn't be. Beth's mother asks, "Beth, honey, you is so smart about most things. How come the good Lord made you so dumb about Philip Hall?" Philip is the number-one best in everything but, Beth wonders, Is he number one only because I let him be? Am I afraid he wouldn't like me if I were best? Though she considers such thoughts preposterous, they gnaw at her, and eventually she has the courage to test them.

Beth fluctuates between loving and hating Philip Hall. She wins and then lets him win; she does his work for him while he plays the guitar for her. When they prepare to enter their calves in the same 4-H Club contest, Philip tries to dissuade her, and Beth clarifies her feelings:

. . . The dumb bum! Where in the good book is it written that a girl's calf can't be in the same contest with a boy's calf? Well, Mister Philip Hall, for too long I've worried that you wouldn't like me if I became the number-one best student, ran faster in the relay race, or took the blue ribbon for calf-raising. . . . Well, I reckon I'm still worried, but with a difference. Now I'm worried that I might not win and that would give you entirely too much satisfaction.[2]

Although Beth's determination wavers, she eventually enters the calf in the contest. When she takes the blue ribbon, Philip admits that losing is a hard

Chris Boyd's only memento of his father was an old Chesterfield coat, which he figuratively and literally tried to fill. (From *Confessions Of a Teenage Baboon* by Paul Zindel. Harper & Row, 1977.)

thing to get used to. He is able to accept it after pouting awhile and finally admits, "Sometimes I reckon I likes you, Beth Lambert."[3] Beth's innocence and heartwarming ambivalence toward a boy are captured as authentic feelings.

Many readers outside the Appalachian setting of Virginia Hamilton's *M.C. Higgins the Great* (I-A) find that the emotions ring true as an adolescent makes decisions about his life. The finely crafted story centers on thirteen-year-old M.C., the oldest son, and is told from a perspective of respect for the culture's diversity and richness. Further, the author imbues with symbolic meaning objects native to the environment and captures the local dialect adroitly.

M.C.'s family has lived for three generations on Sarah's Mountain, now scarred by strip-mining bulldozers that leave a spoil heap of uprooted trees and earth plastered together by rain hanging like a huge boil over his home.

A forty-foot pole in the front yard stands in contrast to the spoil heap. M.C. climbs the pole to sit and look at the Ohio River Valley and avoid the chore of caring for the younger children. Sitting atop the pole, he rises above his environment literally and figuratively. The pole is associated with freedom, escape from problems, and a finer life:

Forty feet up, he was truly higher than everything on the outcropping. Higher than the house and higher than the trees. Straight out from Sarah's Mountain, he could see everything in a spectacular view. He occasionally saw people clearly walking the hill paths nine miles away. Thinking they were absolutely alone, they had no inkling his eyes were upon them.[4]

It is from atop the pole that M.C. sees two strangers enter the hill country. One is a Chicago "dude" whom M.C. thinks will make his mother a country-and-western singing star. The other is Lurhetta Outlaw, at first just a stranger, but eventually a girl who inspires M.C. to take charge of his life. M.C. sees, by her example, that he has choices and is responsible for determining his own future.

For many adolescents the message of our culture is to stand up for what they believe and to take pride in being different; Robert Cormier's *The*

A PANEL OF PAUL ZINDEL'S CHARACTERS (A)   In the spirit of Steve Allen's "Meeting of the Minds" television program where discussants must respond according to character (as recorded in history or fiction), organize a panel on which two students take the role of each of the following Zindel couples:

> Sean and Liz from *My Darling, My Hamburger*
> Marsh and Edna, in *Pardon Me, You're Stepping on My Eyeball*
> Lorraine and John from *The Pigman*
> Dewey and Yvette from *I Never Loved Your Mind*

Questions for discussion might be the following:

> 1. What is most difficult about being an adolescent?
> 2. What conditions must exist for parents and teen-agers to get along well with each other?
> 3. When and why do teen-agers' parties need adult supervision?

Chocolate War (A) shows that in some cases a person who stands up for his beliefs may stand alone. In this novel, Jerry refuses to participate in a fund-raising school sale of chocolate bars on assignment from the powerful school gang leader, Archie. Each morning the tension mounts as students report their sales for the preceding day, and Jerry continues to report "None." The social pressure for Jerry to participate grows and, with it, his resolve to act according to his beliefs. Archie, who sees Jerry's refusal as a personal affront, joins with Brother Leon, power-hungry headmaster of the school, to break Jerry's resistance, and between them they give Jerry a physical and psychological beating. The poster Jerry keeps in his locker, "Do I dare disturb the universe?" symbolizes his dare to question the stifling atmosphere of the school and to stand against the tyranny of peer pressure.

As their age and experience increase, students read authors whose work is of greater complexity. Paul Zindel writes about complicated and sometimes controversial issues for advanced readers. Zindel says that his perennial theme is that life will be what we make of it; he casts that theme in compelling stories.

Of Peer Relations

You may remember reading books as a child that pictured friendships as idyllic relationships of loyalty and noble sacrifice. Not so books today. A wide range of relationships among peers is explored, with some characters noble, some loyal, but most simply human—warts and all.

Because teens and preteens value acceptance by their peers highly, they are very susceptible to peer pressure. Their literature reflects their vulnerability and their strengths. Louise Fitzhugh, in *Harriet the Spy* (I), was one of the earliest novelists to sketch the fuller dimensions of childhood, with its unbecoming parts and its passions. Harriet M. Welsch's passion is to become a writer, and in order to practice her craft, she routinely records her observations in a journal. Here she is riding on the subway with her friend Sport:

> "What are you writing?" Sport asked.
> "I'm taking notes on all those people who are sitting over there."
> "Why?"
> "Aw, Sport"—Harriet was exasperated—"because I've *seen* them and I want to *remember* them." She turned back to her book and continued her notes: MAN

Intrepid Harriet runs into some problems on her "spy route," a means of practicing her writing craft.
(Illustration from *Harriet the Spy,* written and illustrated by Louise Fitzhugh. Copyright © 1964 by Louise Fitzhugh. By permission of Harper & Row, Publishers, Inc.)

WITH ROLLED WHITE SOCKS, FAT LEGS. WOMAN WITH ONE CROSS-EYE AND A LONG NOSE. HORRIBLE LOOKING LITTLE BOY AND A FAT BLONDE MOTHER WHO KEEPS WIPING HIS NOSE OFF.[5]

Harriet writes her frankest opinions in her notebook, many not complimentary to her classmates. One horrible day her notebook is missing and terror strikes her heart:

When she got back to where they had started she saw the whole class— . . . all sitting around a bench while Janie Gibbs read to them from the notebook. Harriet descended upon them with a scream that was supposed to frighten Janie so much she would drop the book. But Janie didn't frighten easily. She just stopped reading and looked up calmly. The others looked up too. She looked at all their eyes and suddenly Harriet M. Welsch was afraid. They just looked and looked, and their eyes were the meanest eyes she had ever seen.[6]

The mean eyes are only the beginning of Harriet's classmates' retaliation; they refuse to speak to her, spill ink on her, steal her tomato sandwich, and shove her around. The resolution of Harriet's problems with her peers is tinged with a little heartache but is relieved by wit and humor. She is embarked on the voyage of growing up to become the person she wants to be even though the trip is not an easy one.

Adolescents often set goals for themselves that strain their emotions and disrupt relationships. They keenly sense the inconsistencies in their goals and vacillate among their choices. In Marilyn Sachs's *A Summer's Lease* (I-A), Gloria Rein's

Activity: Teacher to Student

OBSERVE AND DESCRIBE PEOPLE (I)   Keep a journal similar to Harriet's that you carry with you every place you go. Describe the people you see and speculate about what they are like, what their lives are like, and what they like or don't like to do. Be sure to include your feelings about them. Star the entries that you might not say out loud. Think about why you would not say these things in public.

RENEWING A SUMMER'S LEASE (I-A)   Gloria's opening paragraph for her story "Shadows" begins:

SHE LAY ON THE LUMPY COUCH in the living room, looking up at the cracks in the ceiling. Through the tightly closed window the sun streamed, dabbing golden streaks on the dusty furniture (Marilyn Sachs, *A Summer's Lease,* p. 9).

After finishing *A Summer's Lease* and learning a great deal about Gloria's self-centeredness, finish writing the story for her.

When Gloria says, "I can't take anything from him, from anybody, for nothing" (p. 123) she tells a great deal about herself. Discuss this statement as it relates to her attempts to deny Jerry his co-editorship of *Wings.* What is the significance of her feeling that she has to be "Better than . . . better than . . . better than!" (p. 94). Would you choose Gloria as a friend? Why? Explain why you think Gloria has or has not changed by the end of the story.

The June issue of *Wings* is outlined in part in the text. Write articles for the titles listed in the Table of Contents.

---

goal—editorship of the high-school literary magazine—is a praiseworthy one that becomes undesirable when the ambition is magnified to unrealistic proportions that distort the sense of right and wrong. Talented, fifteen-year-old Gloria's ambition blinds her to positive qualities in other people. Gloria knows she isn't beautiful—"my skin was bad, my hair was ugly, I had hairy arms and legs. . . . But I could get along without being beautiful because I was a genius, and geniuses didn't have to be beautiful."[7] Gloria's behavior is a defense against an intolerable home life and her practical mother's insistence that she take a commercial program in school in order to become a secretary.

As Mrs. Horne, her sensitive English teacher, observes, Gloria makes everything into an epic experience. She tells her "It's a better world, Gloria, if you let your compassion grow bigger than your jealousy."[8] Despite Mrs. Horne's advice, Gloria makes little progress toward understanding and accepting her peers. She wins the title of editor but loses a valued friend.

Walter Dean Myers portrays merrymaking coupled with a sense of responsibility among peers in *The Young Landlords* (A). Fifteen-year-old Paul and a group of his Harlem friends, organized into a spur-of-the-moment "Action Group," complain to the owner of a run-down apartment building on their street:

"You got forty-eight hours to give us some action," Gloria said, "or we'll be down here with our picket signs. And you can smile all you want to, but we'll see who'll be smiling in the end."

"Who is the spokesman for your group?" Mr. Harley asked. . . . "Well, who's the oldest?"[9]

Paul discovers that he is the oldest and must serve as the contact person for the Action Group.

. . . So I gave him my name and address, although I knew I didn't want to. But as soon as everybody else found out that I was the oldest, they jumped right on my case.

"Go on and give it to him," Omar said. "He can't do nothing."

THE YOUNG ^LAND^ LORDS

WALTER DEAN MYERS

Walter Dean Myers emphasizes the strengths of the black community in a story in which teenagers become the unwilling owners of a run-down apartment building.
(Jacket art from Walter Dean Myers's *The Young Landlords* done by Diane de Groat. Copyright © 1979 by Viking Penguin Inc.)

"Now, sir, do you have a dollar?" Mr. Harley said to me.

"A dollar?"

"Surely, if you're really interested in the building and the improvements you're suggesting, you won't mind investing a dollar?"[10]

Paul learns that by giving the owner a dollar, his group has just purchased the building, and the problems of improving it are now theirs. They discover that answers are a lot easier to come by when you stand across the street from the problem and—even harder to accept—that there are not good answers to every problem. They learn to make do the best they can.

In a subplot to the learning-to-be-landlords theme, Myers tells a story of peer loyalty: when a friend of the group is falsely accused of theft, all work actively to prove his innocence. The bittersweet story told from Paul's point of view in modern teen-age language shows a boy on his way to manhood, learning to be loyal, learning to be responsible, and learning to accept his parents.

Of Families

Contemporary children's books present a varied picture of family life and probe new dimensions of realism. Not only are traditional families portrayed, but also communal, one-parent, and extended families, as well as families headed by divorced or separated parents, and children living alone without a family. Although Louisa May Alcott's 1868 classic *Little Women* (I-A) has Jo express the conventional view when she says "families are the most beautiful things in all the world," Jo's own daring in stepping out of her traditional role signaled changes to come (in the way of views expressed) in children's books.

Although there have always been books like Sydney Taylor's *All-of-a-Kind Family* (I), a nostalgic account of a Jewish family in New York in the 1930s in which each member stays in culturally assigned roles, books about nontraditional households appear with ever increasing frequency, answering the child's need to see life as it really is. Modern readers find both mirrors and windows in the wealth of family stories today.

In *Mama* (I), Lee Bennett Hopkins presents a single-parent family, a structure well known to many children. Mama and her two sons live alone —Dad walked out long ago. The family is dependent upon Mama for food, clothing, and shelter. The boys certainly do not want for love: Mama swathes them with love. And even though they are poor, they do not lack material things. Mama sees to it that they get everything they need—and a bit more besides. The eleven-year-old narrator, however, is often quite worried about the way his

Mama manages to get everything she wants for her boys. For example, she has the boys sneak into the restroom to avoid paying for a ticket on the train, and she asks them to carry unpaid-for clothing and Christmas decorations out of the stores she works in. Whatever Mama's techniques, they are clearly acts of love in providing for her sons. The conflict grows as the narrator worries that his Mama will be caught stealing and will be put in jail, leaving him and his brother alone. He also worries about the influence her behavior has on his younger, impressionable brother.

In M. E. Kerr's *Dinky Hocker Shoots Smack* (I-A) the traditional family has contemporary problems. Susan (Dinky) Hocker's mother is so involved in social service, especially the rehabilitation of drug addicts, that she has no time for her daughter. Dinky's own problem involves not drugs but food; she is very overweight. Her attempts to get her parents' attention are futile until the night her mother is recognized as the outstanding volunteer of the year. When Mrs. Hocker leaves the community hall glowing from the praise for all her work with former drug addicts, she finds "Dinky Hocker Shoots Smack" painted over walls and sidewalks in her path. Desperate, Dinky herself had painted the signs as a way of saying, "Hey, look at me!"

Richard Peck in *Representing Super Doll* (A), delineates yet another kind of mother, one who forces her own unfulfilled dreams and unrealized fantasies upon her daughter. Richard Peck jokes about the origin of this book: several hours waiting back stage at a television studio with a teen-age beauty contest winner and her mother.

Verna tells the story about Darlene Hoffmeister, a dumb but beautiful blonde beauty contest winner she calls Super Doll. When Mrs. Hoffmeister, who controls Darlene's life, cannot go with her to New York, she chooses Verna to go in her place. Choosing Verna is exemplary of Mrs. Hoffmeister's tendency to make all her daughter's decisions for her: she chooses her clothes, her friends, and her dreams. There are surprises when Verna pretends to be Super Doll on a television show, but the real coup comes when Darlene begins to think for herself.

This Cinderella story in reverse vividly characterizes Darlene's mother by words as well as deeds. Darlene finally realizes that she cannot continue letting her mother live her life and tells Verna:

"Mother is so mad at me," she said finally, "that she's practically freaked out. . . . I told her I wasn't going to Las Vegas and compete for National Super Doll. And I

Teaching Idea

THREE MOTHERS (I-A)[12] We know that mothers come in all shapes and sizes and that degrees of interest in their children vary as much as physical diversity. The mothers portrayed in Lee Bennett Hopkins's *Mama* (I, Knopf, 1977), M. E. Kerr's *Dinky Hocker Shoots Smack* (I-A, Harper & Row, 1972), and Richard Peck's *Representing Super Doll* (A, Viking, 1974) are as different as different can be. Although there is little question about the mothers' love, each expresses it in unique extremes.

In the activities on the following page, students are given the opportunity to explore a variety of moral and ethical questions. As they compare the issues in the three books, they can also ask themselves: What would my mother do in these situations? How do I know?

Activities: Teacher to Student

MAMA (I)   Suppose that, when Mama plays the "Christmas tree game," the store detective catches her and that she is arrested and told that a trial will be held.

Conduct a mock trial. Invite volunteers to play Mama, the narrator, the police officers, store detective, judge, and lawyers. The rest of the group can be the jury.

Mama tells her story first. The narrator testifies in defense of Mama next.

In presenting their verdict, in writing or discussion, the members of the jury should consider these questions: Should the court take the children away from Mama? Should Mama be put in jail? What should be said to Mama?

DINKY HOCKER SHOOTS SMACK (I-A)   There are times in this story when it seems that Mrs. Hocker hasn't the vaguest idea of what makes her daughter tick. She shows her insensitivity when she asks Dinky to pick up pies: "To ask someone like Dinky to go into Woerner's Restaurant just to pick up pies was like asking a wino to pick up something at a liquor store."[13]

Pretend you are Dinky. Write a Dear Abby letter to explain your feelings about your mother.

Do you think you got your mother's attention when you painted the town with the words "Dinky Hocker Shoots Smack"?

Was this act enough of a shock for her?

Do you think things will really change when you come home from Europe?

Create a collage on your mirror—not your reflection, but what is inside of you.

REPRESENTING SUPER DOLL (A)   A young boy who lives on my block is a pretty good baseball player. From the minute he could walk his parents were out in the schoolyard teaching him to catch and hit a ball. He is now in high school and stopped by to talk to me. "You know," he began, "I don't even like baseball; all my life my father has been pushing me into it, and now when I want to get into a good college, he's pushing me out to go practice baseball."

What advice would you give him?

Why do some parents push their children into something they want themselves?

---

wasn't having her enter me in any more contests or anything. That whatever she thought up for me to do next, I wasn't going to do it. . . . I told her she'd have to settle for living her own life and not mine too. And she said so this is the thanks she gets for sacrificing everything and did I suppose for a minute I was going to get any place at all without her doing the thinking.[11]

Books about children in foster homes depict adults ranging from child molesters to all-loving parent figures. Children are portrayed as victims of child abuse, abandonment, alcoholism, neglect, and a whole range of society's ills. The children themselves are oftentimes cynical, bitter, disillusioned, and despondent, but sometimes courageous and strong.

The interaction between foster parents and homeless children reveals a mixture of motivations and human conflicts. For some foster children, the

Can this do any harm to their children?

How does the example relate to *Representing Super Doll?*

At the end of the book Darlene tells Verna that she has finally gotten through to her mother. Do you agree?

Do you think Mrs. Hoffmeister realized even at this point what she had created?

When Verna was chosen as Super Doll on the television panel show, were you shocked? Didn't the author give little hints, in certain scenes with Hal and Verna's mother, that this was what the story was leading up to?

COMPARING THREE MOTHERS (I-A) In making decisions we select one plan of action over another. Each of the mothers in the three books discussed made choices, too. The paths they chose had certain results and may not have been the ones you would have chosen. Make a chart like the one below, fill in the problems each character faced, the alternatives they had, and the action you believe they should have taken.

CHARACTER	PROBLEM	ALTERNATIVES	ACTION
Mama			
Mrs. Hocker			
Mrs. Hoffmeister			

Which central character would you most like to have known? Why? Do you feel you have anything in common? Decide on a list of things you would do together the day you met.

Author Richard Peck, who wrote *Representing Super Doll,* has said that "young people are liable to choose books as they choose friends, more as mirrors than as windows." What do you think he means by that? Do you agree or disagree? Are any of the characters in these books mirrors for you?

---

memories of the natural parents may be rightfully idealized, whereas for others, the memories are haunting nightmares.

That such themes will engage the interest of certain readers—even those not normally oriented toward books—is emphatically confirmed by the experience of a student teacher in a residential treatment center for emotionally disturbed children. She was reading aloud to a group of young-

sters, aged ten to fifteen, from Eleanor Clymer's *Luke Was There* (I-A). The lunch bell rang at the tense moment in the story at which Julius, the child who trusts no adults because they always let him down, is trying to decide whether to go back to a children's home. (Julius had run away from the home when Luke, the counselor he loved, was drafted.) The class refused to leave the room until the story was completed, and so the teacher read on to reveal that Julius does go back to the home and, when he arrives careworn and hungry, finds Luke there. The students clapped, yelled, and cheered at the happy ending, their identification and involvement unmistakable.

Katherine Paterson tells about a self-proclaimed genius in *The Great Gilly Hopkins* (I) who is determined to hate Maime Trotter as much as she has hated all of her other foster parents. She believes her stay with Maime is only temporary, to be ended when her beautiful mother, Courtney (a flower child gone to seed) comes to get her.

Gilly scorns the fat, illiterate Maime as well as the strange seven-year-old William Ernest who lives with them, and she wonders what it is that Mr. Randolph, the blind black man who lives next door, wants. Slowly and reluctantly Gilly learns to love these people.

Eventually, Gilly's grandmother takes Gilly home with her. Gilly, unhappy there, is convinced by Maime Trotter to stay, because her grandmother, lonely all the years since her daughter Courtney disappeared, needs her. In a bittersweet ending Gilly recognizes the responsibilities of love.

Betsy Byars paints a vivid description of three foster children with bitter memories, who come to live with Mr. and Mrs. Mason in *The Pinballs* (I). First to arrive is Harvey, who has two broken legs —acquired when his drunken father ran over him

Activity: Teacher to Student

"MEET THE CHARACTER" RADIO SCRIPT (I)   Interview Carlie and Gilly on a "radio talk show." Needed are someone to play the announcer, M.C., Carlie, and Gilly. Others can write book commercials for the station breaks. They can be advertisements for the books *The Pinballs,* by Betsy Byars (Harper & Row, 1977), and *The Great Gilly Hopkins,* by Katherine Paterson (Crowell, 1978). Use the following script as a model for the interview, filling in the blanks, of course.

Announcer: Hello folks! Welcome to "Meet the Character." Today's special guests are Gilly Hopkins and Carlie who come directly to us from Katherine Paterson and Betsy Byars. Now, let's give a warm welcome to our genial M.C., _____.

M.C.: Well, I'm certainly happy to be here. Today we're going to chat with two unusual young women. By the time the show is over, you'll know more about foster homes and what it feels like to live in them. Both of our guests have spent most of their lives in foster homes and have strong feelings about them. But, first, a word from our sponsor.

Announcer: (book commercial)

M.C.: Let's begin with you, Carlie. Tell us a little about the circumstances under which you were placed in a foster home. How did you feel about your foster parents?

Carlie: _____.

M.C.: Gilly, I understand that you were in about four or five homes before you got to Maime Trotter's. Did you ever think any of those places were permanent or were they all temporary?

Gilly: _____.

in his haste to get to his poker game. Next is Thomas J., left on the doorstep of eighty-two-year-old twins who kept him for six years, then gave him up when they were incapacitated. Finally there is Carlie, a scrappy, television-addicted girl who fought pitched battles with her most recent stepfather. On her arrival she heads for the television set saying, "Don't talk to me when 'Young and Restless' is on." When Mrs. Mason protests that she just wants to welcome her, Carlie snaps back, "Welcome me during the commercial."

The three children gradually learn to respect themselves and each other. Carlie confers the name "pinballs" on them because they get knocked around by others and can't help what happens to them. But they come to realize that they do have some control over their lives; the book ends hopefully as the three resolve that they will no longer be pinballs.

Fathers are portrayed in fiction sporadically—not on a par with mothers. More often than not, the father's image is negative. With problem-laden books popular now, good fathers don't seem to be newsworthy. Paula Fox portrays a father who lies, in *Blowfish Live in the Sea* (I), and John Ney describes a father with too much money and too few principles in a series that begins with *Ox: The Story of a Kid at the Top* (I-A). The father in Richard Peck's *Father Figure* (A) is exceptional; he does his best to regain his rightful place with his sons, al-

---

M.C.: Carlie, we know you called yourself and the other foster children pinballs. What do you mean by that? Do you think you have any control over what happens to you now?

Carlie: _____.

M.C.: Gilly, we know for a fact that you think you're brilliant and that you said that you are too clever and too hard to manage. What do you think Maime Trotter thought about you when you first arrived? How does she feel now that you're living with your grandmother?

Gilly: _____.

M.C.: Here's a question for both of you. You both had foster brothers that you had mixed feelings about when you first met. What are they doing and how do you feel about them now?

Gilly: _____.

Carlie: _____.

M.C.: What hopes do you two girls have for the future? I know, Carlie, that you want to be a nurse.

Carlie: _____.

Gilly: _____.

M.C.: Well, our time is almost up. What advice do you have for the foster children who might be listening to us today?

Carlie: _____.

Gilly: _____.

M.C.: We'd like to thank you both for being our guests.

THE REALISTIC BOOK AS MIRROR

304 though he had left them in leaving a bad marriage years before. Contemporary realistic fiction, in its neglect of fathers, seems to be derelict in fulfilling its role of reflecting the real world.

Of Personal Integrity

Students are engaged in a process of trying to find out who they are, what they like and don't like, and what they will and will not do. They are passionately preoccupied with themselves and look to literature for solutions to or escape from their pre-

Discovering a fictional counterpart in a book can help and comfort a troubled child, alone with his problems. (Photograph by Anna Kaufman Moon / STOCK, Boston, Mass.)

occupations. They enter into books in ways they cannot with television because of the differences, discussed previously (Chapter 3), between the two mediums: television offers full-blown images, literature gives characters but not their height and weight, dialogue, but not intonation. Readers must supply something of themselves in a literary experience, making it a more personal and creative one than watching television; in reading, images are personally shaped in the live, closed circuit between reader and book.

When students who want to understand themselves and to make use of their understanding create, as they read, images of themselves behaving nobly, they are left with important memories. Stories that hinge upon the personal integrity of a character draw readers instinctively into grappling with envisaged tests of their own mettle.

Mildred D. Taylor's story of Cassie Logan, *Roll of Thunder, Hear My Cry* (I-A) contains repeated occasions that require personal integrity in the face of blatant racism. One episode revolves around the distribution of textbooks in a rural black school in Mississippi in the 1930s. Cassie's little brother, a proud first-grade student who is already reading and anxious to have his own book, is heartsick when the teacher gives him a book with soiled covers and marred pages. He hesitantly asks his teacher for another, pointing out that his is dirty:

"Dirty!" Miss Crocker echoed, appalled by such temerity. . . . "Dirty! And just who do you think you are, Clayton Chester? Here the county is giving us these wonderful books during these hard times and you're going to stand there and tell me that the book's too dirty? Now you take that book or get nothing at all!"[14]

Clayton tries to explain, but then, overcome with anger, throws the tattered book to the floor and stamps madly on it. When Cassie receives her own book, she sees immediately the cause of his fury. Stamped inside the cover is a chart showing the race of the twelve previous owners and the condition of the book each year. During the first eleven years the book had been issued to a "white," but it was only when the condition of the book had declined to "very poor," that it was issued to a

. . . by the time I entered high school, I was confident that I would one day be a writer. . . . once I had made up my mind to write, I had no doubts about doing it. It was just something that would one day be. I had always been taught that I would achieve anything I set my mind to (*Dial promotional material*).

MILDRED TAYLOR

In a talk cosponsored by the International Reading Association and the Children's Book Council, Mildred Taylor described her childhood memories of a vibrant countryside and the vitality of black community life, with its revivals and courtings, prayer meetings and picnics. Where there was beauty, however, there was also insufferable hatred and bigotry. She and her sister attended local schools, and she recalls how each book was marked, not only with previous owners' names, but with their race as well. Even as a child she sensed some wrong, which she tried to efface by scratching out the information.

As a child, Mildred Taylor wondered why the history books contained no stories about blacks, when the stories from her own family's past were filled with heroic men and women who fought against oppression and indignities with valor. Her desire to tell the story of strong black families facing difficulties heroically and with integrity led her to write *Song of the Trees* (I) and *Roll of Thunder, Hear My Cry,* winner of the 1977 Newbery Medal and 1977 National Book Award.

She decries the depiction of black ghettos only as slums. The ghetto in which she grew up was not a slum, and she has no recollection of fatherless families; rather she remembers the protective presence of strong adults—somewhat like the Logan's protection of Cassie and her brothers in the *Roll of Thunder* series.

From her Peace Corps experience in Ethiopia, Taylor learned the price independence exacts from the individual. Although her writing carries powerful themes about survival in a hostile society, Taylor's messages radiate rather than pummel:

It is my hope that to the children who read my books, the Logans will provide those heroes missing from the schoolbooks of my childhood; Black men, women, and children of whom they can be proud (*Dial promotional material*).

Throughout, the strength and importance of the family is central. She credits her father, a master storyteller, with having a powerful influence on her life. Her values and principles were shaped in a wholesome and loving family with strong and sensitive parents. Pride in one's heritage is a universal theme meaningful for all readers.

306 "nigra." Cassie is well aware of the consequences when she also returns her book and gets in line behind her brother to feel the sting of the teacher's switch.

Cassie Logan evinces personal integrity and maturity often in the story: she trounces a snippy white girl who humiliates her; she refuses to continue a friendship with T.J., who is instrumental in getting her mother fired from her teaching job; she helps prevent a lynching; and she grieves for T.J. when he is jailed. Cassie's love for her family, their land and their trees rings throughout her story. Her quiet dignity nurtured by an upright, proud, and independent family, attests to the strength of the human spirit.

Words by Heart (I-A), by Ouida Sebestyen, sketches yet another kind of integrity in her story of Lena, a twelve-year-old girl with an exceptional capacity for memorizing beautiful passages from the Bible and Walt Whitman, and the words of her father. Lena knows that her only competition in a Scriptures-quoting contest will be Winslow Starnes, recognized champion in her town, but she is determined to outstrip him in the face of obvious favoritism toward him from the judge. When it is clear that Lena cannot be denied as the winner, the judge hesitantly hands her the prize he holds wrapped in his hand.

"You win the prize, Miss Lena." He handed it out abruptly. "I wish it could have been just what you wanted, because you deserve . . ." Then he sat down as if *his* memory had failed *him* too.
Lena held it in her trembling hand and said, "Thank you, Mr. Kelsey." She unwrapped the paper.
Inside was a tie, a blue bow tie with a little celluloid hook at the back that was supposed to fit over a collar button. A boy's prize.[15]

Lena rejects the prize obviously meant for Winslow Starnes but she worries that her father is disappointed by her seemingly haughty act. It is Papa, disappointed in his ambition to become a preacher, who teaches Lena to love beautiful words and to aspire to live by them, and who sustains her by his resolute faith. Through her father's example, she learns to love her enemies even in the face of shattering loss and maintains the integrity he modeled for her:

She knew, with a heavy sinking, how Papa would answer, whom he would quote. Love your enemies and do good to those who hate you. Give to them that asketh thee. The words that had been so beautiful to say, so easy, turned to stone. No one had told her, not Papa, not the preacher, that they could change like that when they had to be lived, and crush her with their weight.[16]

Ouida Sebestyen wraps her story in poetry and vivifies the clear distinction between saying beautiful words and living them.

Becky's integrity is tested in conflicts concerning her loyalty to her religion and her right to choose her future in Barbara Cohen's *Bitter Herbs and Honey* (A). Becky's parents expect her to maintain her orthodox Jewish life in the midst of a gentile community—as they do, and to "marry Jewish" as soon as she graduates from high school. They have even selected the young man they think she should marry.

Becky's ideas differ from her parents', not only about the mate they choose for her but about her future in general. Her friendship with Peter van Ruysdaal creates consternation in her parents, and ensuing discussions take on a familiar ring:

"I don't see why you won't let me go to the van Ruysdaals' Christmas party," I always said.
"A Jewish girl doesn't belong at a Christmas party," she always replied.
"Oh, Mama, don't be ridiculous. No one's going to say any prayers or anything. Christmas is just an excuse for having a party."
"There's no reason for you to go to a party in a *goyishe* house any time."
"Solly's going. Abe and Lilly are going."
"If their parents don't care what happens to them," Mama answered firmly, "that's not my business. But you are my business."[17]

The important choices about Becky's life are hers, shaped by the firm grounding in the teachings from the Torah and her unyielding sense of purpose. As she sits singing with her friends and neighbors, she is aware that her life is changing. She listens to the singers flanking the six scrolls in their purple velvet, gold-embroidered wrappers resting in the satin-lined ark. The meaning of the song sounded clear:

I have given you good teaching;
Forsake not My Torah.
It is a tree of life to them that hold fast to it,
And everyone that upholds it is happy.[18]

Becky's integrity does not allow her to forsake the teachings of the Torah nor does it allow her to forsake her destiny.

THE REALISTIC BOOK AS WINDOW

An author invites us to look through her window, and we respond, to see the world through another's eyes. Literature gives us many windows from which to view the world: through some, we see landscape—a countryside, a skyline, the sea—through others, we see bustling activity or quiet contemplation; sometimes the view is stormy and sorrowful. Literature's windows on the world look upon the full range of human experience, including our joys and sorrows, our virtues and vices.

On Laughter

To fully reflect the world, realistic books must present all its dimensions. From the plethora of problem books in recent years, it would seem that it is *only* a problem world, all grimness and sordid facts. As we know, the real world has both laughter and tears, both happiness and sadness; children's books reflect them all. A world made up of problems and no joy is just as unrealistic as the Panglossian vision or the happily-ever-after world we gave children a generation ago, when so many books displayed the happy-ending syndrome.

Children like humorous books. Each year in "Children's Choices," a joint project of the International Reading Association and the Children's Book Council, they appear more frequently than any other kind.

Helen Cresswell's British humor crosses the Atlantic with few problems in the Bagthorpe saga. The Bagthorpe family first appears in *Ordinary Jack* (I-A), then in *Absolute Zero* (I-A), and again in *Bagthorpes Unlimited* (I-A) and *Bagthorpes v. the World* (I-A). This wacky, hilarious, ludicrous family is a source of delight. Characterization is so strong that readers know exactly how each member of the zany family will react to every crisis. For example, in *Bagthorpes Unlimited*, Grandma prepares a list of the family's most prized possessions, totally worthless things to anyone else, instructing any robber to leave them alone. She gives the exact location of the items and, of course, in due time, the items are stolen. Grandma is so unnerved by this catastrophe that she wants her nearest and dearest close by. This brings some unwanted relatives into the house whom the Bagthorpe children try to drive away by insidious means, such as placing maggots in a box of chocolate candy. Each member of the family is gifted and feels that it is his duty to "add strings to his bow." Father is a television script writer, Mother writes the "Agony Column" for the local newspaper, and each child has his own talents to perfect. Grandma is unquestionably the ruler of the family, while Grandpa remains hazily in the background using his hearing aid to be selectively deaf. All the children are precocious, except for Ordinary Jack, who is eclipsed by this outgoing, gregarious family.

In Ellen Raskin's *The Westing Game* (I), Turtle Wexler is one of sixteen rather strange people who are invited to the reading of Sam Westing's will. The group is divided into eight pairs, given different sets of clues, and $10,000 per team. All the partners have to do is find the answer—but no one knows the question. The teams play the Westing Game through one hilarious escapade after another. Competition is strong and alliances are soon made (though no one trusts anyone else) and disasters ensue as they try to outwit each other. Readers are as much in the dark as the participants until the very end. The zany word play and intrigue in the puzzle-knotted, word-twisting plot show off Ellen Raskin's special brand of ingenuity.

THE WESTING GAME GAME (I)   Make a board game for Ellen Raskin's *The Westing Game* (Dutton, 1978). Go through the book and write the clues on game cards—for example, "FRUITED PURPLE WAVES FOR SEA" (p. 44) and "SKIES AM SHINING BROTHER" (p. 82). Draw a twisting path that runs around the board and is divided into spaces. You might ornament this with a picture of a rolled up will at the start and the Westing house at the end. Put the clues on the board at various spaces. Some clues can turn out to be dead ends, while others lead to the solution of the story's puzzle. Make a set of markers to represent the characters and use a spinner to determine how far each one moves on a turn. Make up rules, such as: dead-end clues require the player to go back three spaces; valid clues allow the player to skip ahead three spaces. The winner is the first player to reach the Westing house.

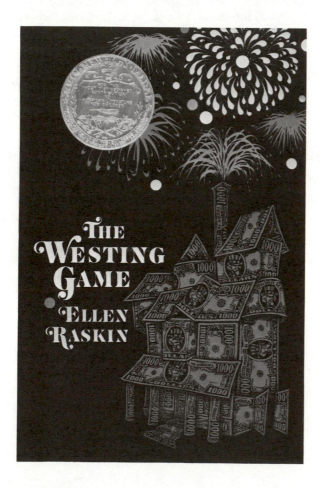

Sam Westing's house seems to be made of money when he plays a zany game with his heirs.
(From *The Westing Game* by Ellen Raskin. Copyright © 1978 by Ellen Raskin. Reprinted by permission of the publishers, E. P. Dutton.)

On Courage

Although many realistic novels are problem laden, and critics who read them cry out, "Please deliver me from yet another book with the cracked ceiling syndrome," realism contains stories of courage in which people are not beaten down by life, but transform it into something splendid through inner strength. If we are to examine life adequately through realistic literature, we need to share the inspirational books with our students as well as the dismal ones. In a day when we have few heroes in real life, it can be good to look to literature for lives to emulate.

Discussing *The Third Eye* (I-A), Mollie Hunter declared that "courage needs witness," and her uplifting theme is vivified in this book. The gripping story is a fitting testament to her belief that courageous acts should be recognized.

Jinty and her sisters visit Toby, a lonely blind boy, through the fence that surrounds his yard. He begs Jinty to bring flowers so he can see them in his mind's eye. Jinty tries to describe the colors to him:

"Jaggedy-hot" for "red." That was easy. "A sunny day that's still cold." That was easy, too, for "yellow." But what could she say for "purple"?

"It's like a taste," she decided eventually. "You think it's going to be jaggedy-hot, like red; but when you do taste it, it slides away into something smoother, and really cold."

Toby laughed at this, and fanned his hand across his eyes as if to make himself see purple, stuck out his tongue as if he were tasting it.[19]

In this kind of vivid language, which makes you see, Mollie Hunter tells the story of Jinty who witnesses courage. In *The Third Eye* we first meet Jinty on her way to give evidence to the Procurator Fiscal, an attorney or judge taking pretrial testimony. Through a series of flashbacks we find the reason for her appearance: she was the last person to see the Earl of Ballinford alive. The Earl, wealthy landowner and acknowledged lord of the village, lived under the Ballinford doom—a prophetic curse that meant an oldest son would never outlive his father. The Earl lived and died courageously trying to change the pattern that had cursed his family for generations. Jinty recognizes the brand of courage the Earl portrays but aches that it is such a lonely one.

Jinty's story involves much more: her two sisters display a certain kind of courage as they defy parental rules in order to shape the lives they choose to live. Jinty's mother, seemingly hardened and determined to raise her three daughters according to her unbending standards, personifies the courage of endurance.

In the midst of conflict and tension, Jinty herself characterizes yet another kind of courage, the quiet kind that causes her to see and to know strengths and weaknesses of those around her and to acknowledge their humanness.

Vera and Bill Cleaver document courage in a different setting in *Where the Lilies Bloom* (I-A) and its sequel, *Trial Valley* (I-A). Mary Call Luther lives in the Great Smoky Mountains, where people are free, proud, and achingly poor. She is a plucky girl who uses all of her resources to maintain the raw dignity and independence of her poverty-stricken and problem-plagued family. One of Mary Call's heartaches is her eighteen-year-old sister, Devola, who is "cloudy in the head." Another is Roy Luther, her father, who is desperately ill from "worms in the chest." Ima Dean and Romey, a younger sister and brother, complete her family; the mother is long dead.

The family survives by collecting medicinal herbs from the mountain slopes and selling them at the general store. When Roy Luther dies, Mary Call keeps a promise to her father, which means that she and Romey must drag his body to the top of the mountain to bury him so that officials and nosy neighbors, unaware of his death, will not send the children to the county home. She keeps another promise to hold the family together and never take charity.

And I get scared and I think, but how am I going to do this? Who will show me how and who will help me?

And then I get madder and I say to myself, Aw, quit your bellyaching. There's a way; all you have to do is find it.[20]

Mary Call finds the way but it tests her mettle and courage every step along the mountain path she climbs.

On Heroism

Readers build expectations about literature and about the world by accumulating experience in both. They explore life and plumb its depths through first-hand, but also virtual, experiences. Heroism lies on the horizon of expectations in literature and in life.

Not many children have the opportunity—or would want—to live alone on a frozen tundra, say, or beneath the ground in a subway. They can have these and much more as virtual experiences through books.

Readers meet a hero in Felice Holman's *Slake's Limbo* (I). A street gang taunts and chases thirteen-year-old Aremis Slake through the alleys and junkyards of his neighborhood. He expects to be beaten, as always, but this time he escapes into a subway. Once there he discovers, in the wall of the subway tunnel, a hole that becomes his refuge for one hundred and twenty-one days.

Slake's survival depends upon his wit and cunning; Slake's heroism lies in the tenacious determination through which he overcomes the terror and the desperation that bind him to his dark molelike subsistence: "He turned and started up the stairs and out of the subway. Slake did not know exactly where he was going, but the general direction was up."[21] Though afraid, he was going to face life.

Jean George's *Julie of the Wolves* (I-A) is an example of contemporary realism that can be read at

Julie, a courageous girl alone in the Alaskan tundra, insinuates herself into a wolf pack in order to survive.
(From *Julie of the Wolves* by Jean Craighead George. Pictures by John Schoenherr. Harper & Row, 1972.)

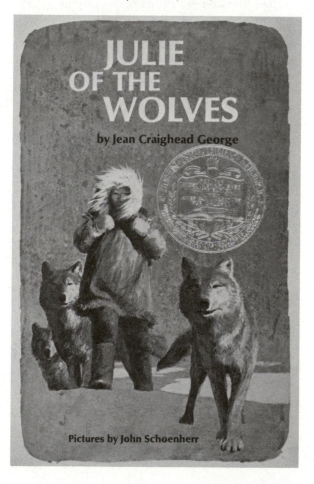

JULIE OF THE WOLVES
by Jean Craighead George

Pictures by John Schoenherr

several levels of meaning. It can be a story of a girl's search for identity, a journey from a safe home through danger and hardship toward maturity, a commentary about the destruction of nature and earlier ways of life, a fight for individualism, initiation rites and loss of innocence, or an adventure story about wolves. It could even be read as propaganda against the use of guns or a plea for the enforcement of game laws to protect wildlife. The theme or major thought that readers take from the book depends entirely upon the transaction between their unique experiences and the narrative created by Jean George. The power of the reader's emotional response is related to the strength of the identification made with the central character.

Julie, the English name for the Eskimo girl Miyax, is the heroine; all other characters are known through their relationship with her. Kapugen, Miyax's father, does not enter the story in person until the final pages, and yet his power and guiding influence are felt throughout the story. Amaroq, untamed leader of the wolf pack, becomes a father figure for Miyax, and his cub, named Kapu by the girl, becomes something close to a brother. Miyax's devotion to her father is seen in several ways: in her frequent references to things he taught her; in her naming of the young son of Amaroq, Kapu, a shortened form of her father's name; the changes in her life when she hears that Kapugen is lost forever; and the overwhelming gratitude she experiences when she believes he may still be alive.

The story engages the reader from the outset, with Miyax's desperate situation clearly stated:

. . . she was frightened, not so much of the wolves, . . . but because of her desperate predicament. Miyax was lost. She had been lost without food for many sleeps . . . and . . . the very life in her body . . . depended upon these wolves for survival. She must somehow tell him [the wolf] that she was starving and ask him for food.[22]

The novel is divided into three sequences: the present, the past, and, again, the present. Part I chronicles Miyax's strategy as she learns the ways of the wolves in order to gain entry to their world and obtain food. Part II presents Miyax's memories

DWELLERS OF THE TUNDRA (I-A) After you have read Jean George's *Julie of the Wolves* (Harper & Row, 1972), study wolves and the habits of the Alpha leader. The author's description of the relationships within the wolf pack may lead you to wonder about control and leadership in other animal families.

Investigate the hunting laws in your state and trace the legislation on endangered species.

Study the geography of the Arctic tundra and make a map to trace Miyax's journey. You may want to use some of the following books:

Dwellers of the Tundra: Life in an Alaskan Eskimo Village, by Aylette Jenness. Macmillan, 1970.
Wolf Run: A Caribou Eskimo Tale, by James Houston. Harcourt Brace Jovanovich, 1971.
Wonders of the World of Wolves, by Jacquelyn Berrill. Dodd, Mead, 1970.
The Wounded Wolf, by Jean George. Illustrated by John Schoenherr. Harper & Row, 1978.

---

of the days following her mother's death, endless days spent with her father learning the Eskimo ways. In this part Miyax's reasons for running away become evident. The present resumes in Part III, when the wolf pack moves on and Miyax is left alone on the tundra.

Various devices heighten the drama. Dramatic foreshadowing concerning Miyax's father establishes the importance of a father figure for Miyax. There are hints about a white house in San Francisco that seems to reflect an unexpressed dream of finding friends, a home, and a family in a gussak (white man's) world. After an unknown and uncaring pilot shoots Miyax's beloved wolf-father, Amaroq, the gussak world comes to symbolize killing, guns, and other horrors. The small caribou bone replica that Miyax carves in the image of Amaroq and the golden plover she rescues now become far more meaningful to her.

The author's use of Eskimo words and traditions establishes an authentic tone. Time is measured by the number of "sleeps" and by the signs in nature Miyax reads. The behavior of the wolves and the means that Miyax uses to establish communication with them are described graphically.

Perplexing questions remain in the reader's mind long after the book has been read. Julie's father had become a hunter in a gussak world. Was it actually he who shot the wolves? Did Julie leave her Eskimo ways behind and accept the changes that her father had accepted? The skillful novelist "halve[s] this matter amicably [with her reader] and leave[s] him something to imagine, in his turn."[23]

On Compassion

Pity can diminish its object, but true compassion ennobles and stengthens. Through literature, children can see models of many kinds of emotional response. During childhood, when values are crystallizing, fiction with windows on compassion is imperative.

Jill Paton Walsh, noted English writer, seemingly balances two stories against each other in *Unleaving* (A), a story that takes its inspiration from Gerard Manley Hopkins's poem "Spring and Fall." The reader first meets Gran making her way downstairs falteringly to join her daughter, son-in-law, and their three children for tea. In the second paragraph, the reader meets Madge in a school uni-

Activity: Teacher to Student

AN AUTHOR INTERVIEW (I-A) Plan with your class to invite an author whose books you enjoy. Discuss before the visit questions you might ask, such as:

Were there experiences in your own life that led you to write this book?

Did you think you were going to be a writer when you were our age?

Do you have a special place to write?

When do you write?

What are you working on now?

Record the interview so that you can enjoy it again; then share it with others.

Names and addresses of authors are available from publishers, who will discuss arrangements with you. If it is not possible to have an author visit, you might consider a phone call. The telephone company can help arrange for a conference call so that everyone can take part.

---

form, traveling alone on a night train to Goldengrove, the scene of Gran's tea party.

Before long, the reader learns that Madge inherited Goldengrove, but the point-counterpoint of Madge's story and Gran's story continues until we discover eventually that the stories are one, separated only by time. The muted, interlacing stories center the narrative on one consciousness while avoiding a first-person narration.

After the tea party, the children beg their grandmother to take them to the beach, and although the others protest, she agrees.

"I'll take them this time," says Gran, getting up from her chair, both hands down on the chair arms to raise herself. . . . "I can manage," says Gran. "I had a rest this afternoon. I can get down the path if I take my time, you know. . . ." Their voices, as they descend the cliff path, fade; and left behind in the peace among the crumbs and jam and unwashed teacups—someone has licked the cream spoon cloudy clean—the grownups smile and sigh.[24]

Back again with schoolgirl Madge as she is summoned to the headmistress's study, we find that arrangements are being made for a university professor to take a reading party to Goldengrove for the summer. When the professor and his wife arrive, Madge is there to greet them.

"You must be Madge Fielding," says Mrs. Tregeagle. "This is Molly. Say hello, Molly."

Madge stoops toward the child, hands held out, and smiling. "Hello, Molly," she says.

The child looks up. Its face is very ruddy, with almond-shaped pale blue eyes, and hardly any lashes. It smiles, and as it does so the smile fills with spittle, which overflows and oozes down its chin. The eyes swim inward into a squint. Madge sickens for an instant, then realizes, then covers up and steadies her smile. Forcing herself, she bends and picks up the child, staggered at its solidity and weight.[25]

There is another Tregeagle child, Patrick, who is Madge's age; he observes her revulsion at meeting Molly and hates her for it. Later, Madge shows compassion for Molly but, eventually, far greater compassion is asked of her for Patrick.

The professor and the reading party discuss profound philosophical questions related to moral and ethical issues. The students staunchly defend their logic as long as their discussions remain in the abstract, but when a tragedy strikes, their profound statements seem hollow. They are unable to make the link between their scholarly talk and compassion when Patrick desperately needs it. Madge, who feels herself an outsider in the lofty discussions, is the only one able to help ease his pain.

Natalie Babbitt fuses fantasy and realism with skill in several books, each more enchanting than the last. In *The Eyes of the Amaryllis* (I)—a story of faith, love, and compassion—she makes us believe in Geneva's search for a sign from the sea and in the vision of a man who walks the shore unseen by others. She also makes us feel the compassion of Geneva's eleven-year-old granddaughter, Jenny, and helps us to see through her eyes and her hopes the possibility of life and death overlapping, of past and present intermingling. Jenny believes and sees with her grandmother; she respects the woman's sturdy dignity and independence that even her father ignores.

On Aging

Older people are gaining a new respect in our society. Once content to shunt the over 65s off to rocking chairs and retirement centers, we are now beginning to realize the vast resources the elderly constitute, and the personal value of continuing an active, contributing life. Medical experts explore the process of aging while others study the psychological impact of reduced mental and physical capacities. At the same time families cope with the aging person's fierce desire for independence in the face of health and safety factors.

Children often see their families in conflict over the problem of what to do with grandparents who no longer can care for themselves.

Norma Fox Mazer creates a thought-provoking story about aging in *A Figure of Speech* (I). A harsh, insensitive atmosphere pervades the Pennoyer's home where Grandfather Carl lives in the basement, out of the way of the rest of the family. Gradually Grandpa is being divested of his independence: he is asked to promise not to cross streets alone, and he is told "at eighty-three nobody expects you to be a hundred percent" and "if you move out of your basement apartment you'll be upstairs with all of us watching you." Only thirteen-year-old Jenny, herself feeling unwanted, is compassionate toward her grandfather, who is considered a burden by everyone else and referred

Time shared with the elderly can be an illuminating experience, one that may be had through the surrogate of a book as well. (Photograph by Betsy Cole / STOCK, Boston, Mass.)

THE REALISTIC BOOK AS WINDOW

to as an "old guy" and a "senior citizen," which makes him feel like a "figure of speech." When Jenny's older brother brings his new wife home, they move into the basement apartment and Grandpa is forced to share a room with the teenage son, a situation that leads to further tension in the uncaring family.

Grandpa finally tires of living as a fourth-class citizen and returns to his former home to salvage his dignity. Unknown to her parents, Jenny goes with him to share his final days. After his death, the family persists in platitude and cliché: Grandpa "didn't suffer a bit"; "it's a real comfort to us that he went so easily." The devastating cruelty and indifference of this family stimulate important discussion among readers.

Stephanie S. Tolan tells a similar story in *Grandpa—and Me* (I), although here the grandfather remains an important member of the family. Kerry, narrator of the story, is at first embarrassed by her grandfather's senile behavior. She becomes increasingly distressed when her parents discuss the possibility of putting him in a nursing home. "Does *he* have a choice?" she asks when they talk about the alternatives. Grandpa's alertness is intermittent: he lives in the past but then returns to lucid moments in the present. Near the end of the summer when it becomes obvious that a solution must be found, Grandpa goes through his personal belongings, sorting and distributing mementos to his family. He speaks to Kerry as if she were his older sister, but Kerry knows that although he is talking as if crazy, he isn't. One morning he leaves the house, and walks into the neighborhood swimming pool and drowns. Kerry goes to his room where she finds the bed has been made and the remaining items from his closet neatly labeled with the names of those who are to receive them and arranged around the room. Grandpa had, after all, made his own choice about his future.

Activity: Teacher to Student

COMPARING STORIES ABOUT AGING (I) Both Stephanie Tolan, in *Grandpa—and Me* (Scribner's, 1978), and Norma Mazer, in *A Figure of Speech* (Delacorte, 1973), tell stories about an aging grandfather from the point of view of a granddaughter who has a special relationship with him. Discuss why the authors chose compassionate girls as their narrators. Also answer the following questions.

1. What alternate ways of caring for the aging parent did each family explore? Was the person about whom the decisions were being made involved in the decision process? What do you think the grandfathers would have chosen for themselves?

2. Which author evokes the grandfather's feelings most vividly? (Read aloud the parts of the stories that support your choice.)

3. Can you imagine how a fiercely independent person feels when he is treated like a small child and given rules to follow? Describe the reactions of the two men in these stories and try to guess how your own grandparents would cope with similar treatment.

4. You might also pretend that you are Jenny or Kerry and write a eulogy for your grandfather. Try to capture the loving and sensitive part of his nature while avoiding clichés. Include tranquil recollections that involve other members of your family so that the eulogy has a direct impact upon them.

On Death

The death of a family member or a friend is something no one wishes to experience but something most of us do experience at some time in our lives. Children begin to discover that people and animals are not immortal as soon as a beloved pet dies, grandparents grow old, or children themselves fall ill. Impermanence is an idea we all find hard to acknowledge, especially when death involves the young.

Constance Greene's *Beat the Turtle Drum* (I) treats the theme of impermanence. Thirteen-year-old Kate and her eleven-year-old sister Joss are having a wonderful summer. Joss's savings and a birthday check from her grandmother allow her to rent a horse for a week, fulfilling a cherished dream. The horse, Prince, is delivered on her birthday. Joss is supremely happy and, because of her love for her sister, so is Kate.

The birthday week is filled with joy, and, at its end, Kate and Joss are picnicking in a favorite tree. Prince is grazing peacefully below when Joss falls, breaks her neck, and dies instantly. There are foreshadowings of the tragic event, especially Ian Serraillier's poem at the beginning of the book, but the suddenness and terrible finality of Joss's death shock the reader.

Ann, a young reader of *Beat the Turtle Drum,* said of the story: "in . . . just one second the whole thing shifts, like very instantly. The whole book changes and everybody's personality changes completely."[26]

Ann was explicit about her use of this story as a "practice" session in experiencing life:

When I wasn't reading, I was thinking what it would be like if that really happened, because it's such a big thing that happened, I was thinking what would happen if it really did happen . . . like if it happened to me or something. Like if I had a sister, or if my mother died or something, how that would affect me.[27]

Ann's comments reveal the role this story can play in a child's life.

Katherine Paterson's *Bridge to Terabithia* (I) also contains the unexpected and shocking death of a child. Jess is in the fifth grade and not very

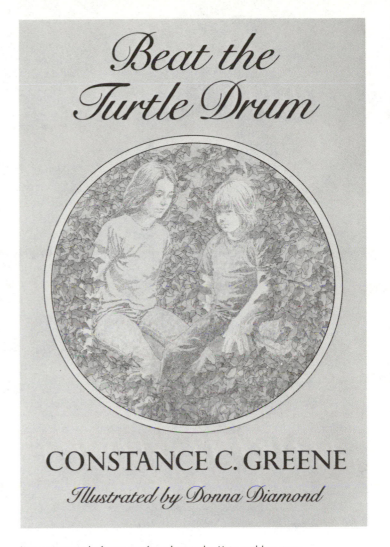

Just a moment before a profound tragedy, Kate and her younger sister Joss sit in a tree observing the horse Joss has rented with her birthday money.
(Jacket art from Constance Green's *Beat the Turtle Drum* done by Donna Diamond. Copyright © 1976 by Viking Penguin Inc.)

happy. He does not get along with his older sisters or his mother. His father is not often at home and he has no really close friends. When Leslie moves in next door Jess's world changes. The two create the magic kingdom of Terabithia, and Leslie's knowledge and imagination expand Jess's world and his self-confidence.

Profile

KATHERINE PATERSON

I never meant to hurt them. I just wanted—what had she wanted? A home—but Trotter had tried to give her that. Permanence—Trotter had wanted to give her that as well. No, what she wanted was something Trotter had no power over. To stop being a "foster child," the quotation marks dragging the phrase down, almost drowning it. To be real without any quotation marks. To belong and to possess. To be herself, to be the swan, to be the ugly duckling no longer—Cap O' Rushes, her disguise thrown off—Cinderella with both slippers on her feet—Snow White beyond the dwarfs—Galadriel Hopkins, come into her own.

The Great Gilly Hopkins

Galadriel, called Gilly, wants to be with her mother despite the fact that Maime Trotter provides her with a loving home. Katherine Paterson expresses Gilly's longing in literary allusions from folklore that conjure images that help readers visualize inner feelings. Her alternation of short terse sentences and long complex ones heightens tension and expands the dramatic action. Like the protagonist in her *The Master Puppeteer,* she is a master of her craft, her memorable stories are marked with imagery evoked by vivid language and with a believability that derives from her use of many characters and incidents drawn from life.

In her acceptance speech for the 1977 National Book Award, Katherine Paterson said:

I don't write for children. . . . I write for myself and then look in the catalog to see how old I am. But it's not true that I simply write for myself. I do write for children. For my own four children and for others who are faced with the question of whether they dare to become adult, responsible for their own lives and the lives of others. . . . I want to become a spy like Joshua and Caleb. . . .

I have crossed the river and tangled with a few giants but I want to go back and say to those who are hesitating, Don't be afraid to cross over. The promised land is worth possessing and we are not alone. I want to be a spy for hope (*Crowell promotional material*).

Readers take strength from her dramatic stories, rich with feeling, to face heartache in their own lives.

Winner of the 1977 National Book Award and the 1978 Newbery Medal, Katherine Paterson was born in China, the daughter of American missionary parents from the American South. She attended schools in China, Virginia, North Carolina, West Virginia, and Tennessee. In fact, she went to thirteen different schools during her first eighteen years. As a young woman, she lived in Japan for four years, but now lives with her minister husband and their four children in Maryland.

CONTEMPORARY REALISM

The story is full of small meaningful events, school encounters, and the beautiful growth of the friendship between Leslie and Jess. The magic kingdom of Terabithia lies across a gully that they reach by swinging on a rope. When they are in Terabithia, they are its king and queen and rule their imaginary subjects with royal dignity and grace. One day, crossing to Terabithia alone over a rain-swollen creek, Leslie falls, is knocked unconscious, and drowns. Jess's world ends that day, too.

Jess cannot accept Leslie's death. He returns to the place Terabithia had once been, taking her dog, one of their subjects.

> He landed upstream from Terabithia. If it was still Terabithia. . . . They went into the castle stronghold. It was dark and damp, but there was no evidence there to suggest that the queen had died. He felt the need to do something fitting. But Leslie was not here to tell him what it was. . . .
> . . . "C'mon, Prince Terrien," he said quite loudly. "We must make a funeral wreath for the queen."[28]

While Jess works a pine bough and flowers into a symbolic offering, a bird hops close to him.

> "It's a sign from the Spirits," Jess said quietly. "We made a worthy offering."
> He walked slowly, as part of a great procession, though only the puppy could be seen, slowly forward carrying the queen's wreath to the sacred grove. He forced himself deep into the dark center of the grove and, kneeling, laid the wreath upon the thick carpet of golden needles.
> "Father, into Thy hands I commend her spirit." He knew Leslie would have liked those words. They had the ring of the sacred grove in them.
> The solemn procession wound its way through the sacred grove homeward to the castle. Like a single bird across a stormcloud sky, a tiny peace winged its way through the chaos inside his body.[29]

Eventually Jess finds strength in himself, and as a tribute to Leslie's life, the kingdom of Terabithia continues.

Three fifth-grade girls, discussing this story, appreciated the sense of hope evident in the ending: "Only at one little part it made you sad. But the very ending I loved because it made you feel, like, happy again."[30] Another response to the ending:

". . . if you feel sad about something, you shouldn't try to forget it, but you should try to get over it as much as you can so you can enjoy things, because life shouldn't be something where you can't enjoy anything."[31] All three felt that the story showed them that you could, and should, "get over" the death of a friend and that Jess was a good model of how they might react if they were in similar circumstances.

Ronald Kidd's *That's What Friends Are For* (I-A) considers a different problem concerning death. Scott is dying of leukemia, and his friend Gary knows it. Gary, frightened both of death and of Scott's appearance, does not visit Scott as often as he could, rationalizing his behavior with feeble excuses. When Scott dies, Gary is left with a terrible burden of guilt about deserting his friend. In the poignant last chapter, Gary talks about his concept of eternal life as being remembered by your friends, but when he tries to remember Scott his memories fade, just as the picture of Scott has that Gary keeps next to his window. He gets angry still, angry at Scott for dying, angry at himself for letting his friend down.

A sister's lingering death from leukemia and the problems of growing up are mingled in Lois Lowry's *A Summer to Die* (A). The story is told by Meg, thirteen years old, who shares a room with her older sister Molly, prettier and neater than Meg. In order to reduce the number of squabbles, Molly draws a line with chalk right down the center of their room:

> "There. Now be as much of a slob as you want, only keep your mess on your side. *This* side is *mine*."[32]

From Meg's perspective, Molly did everything right; she always knew what to say, she was full of fun and enthusiasm, and she was gorgeous. She acquired a figure and boyfriends the same year that Meg was given her outgrown winter coat.

Then Molly fell sick. At first problems were minor, but then the terrible test results arrived foretelling that she would never come home from the hospital. During the summer that Molly slowly dies, Meg begins to mature and discover her adult strengths. The warmth of a close family and good friends help sustain Meg through the traumatic summer. She grows in the knowledge that her world must change and that those she loves may not always be with her.

On Caring

Though we share the earth with other creatures, in our preoccupation with our dominion of it we often fail to think about the balance of nature and the contribution animals make to it. Children find it easy to love animals and respond to stories about them—whether wild creatures or pets.

Jean George's *Julie of the Wolves* (I-A), already discussed in the section "On Heroism," provides a vivid picture of the complex structure of a wolf pack. It is only by observing and imitating the wolves' actions that Julie gets them to accept her into their group and, so, survives on the frozen Alaskan tundra.

Children have a special affinity for animals—creatures that neither scold nor pass judgment. Unquestioning loyalty and devotion from an animal can sometimes help a child progress toward maturity. Children who devote themselves to nurturing and caring for an animal begin to recognize another's needs—the first step toward compassion.

Realistic animal stories often involve a child who grows in understanding and caring. In Betsy Byars's *The Midnight Fox* (I), nine-year-old Tom dreads the two months he must spend at his Aunt Millie's farm while his parents vacation in Europe. His parents are outdoorsy people who cannot understand Tom's fear of animals or his distaste for farm life. His mother enthusiastically describes the fun he will have climbing trees, watching the cows and horses, and gathering eggs, but Tom only imagines being attacked by an angry chicken if he goes near the hen house. Unhappily settled on the farm, Tom mopes and gets in everyone's way. The only bright spot in his day is the walk to the mailbox where there is often a letter from Petie, a friend who shares his misery. The outlook for the summer is dismal until the day he sees a black fox. The

Young children identify readily with animals, and so respond to stories about them. (Photograph by Susie Fitzhugh.)

fox's black fur is tipped with white, "as if it were midnight and the moon were shining on her fur, frosting it." Tom is enchanted and sits quietly watching the fox until it bounds away.

During the next few weeks, Tom tracks the fox, awed by its grace and poise. One day she appears with her cub and Tom watches as the two romp and play unaware that they are watched. Caught up in observing the fox, Tom forgets his misery until Aunt Millie informs her husband that a fox has taken her turkey. Tom, stunned, begins to sense that tragedy for his fox is near. Compassion for the animal and understanding of the need for balance between freedom and responsibility create conflict for the sensitive child.

Although wild animals are within the experience of relatively few children, pets are important to many. Wilson Rawls's *Where the Red Fern Grows* (I-A), an autobiographical account, tells about Billy Colman, who lives in the Arkansas mountains during the Great Depression. In a family with scarcely enough money for food, Billy has to scrimp and save for two years before he accumulates the $50 dollars needed to purchase the two coon hounds he wants. Billy dreams of the day he can start training the coon hounds, which he had to have because, "there I was sitting right in the middle of the finest hunting country in the world" and so no other kind of dog would do. Billy's faithful long training of the two dogs is repaid when they win the gold cup in the annual

Tom learns much about himself when he tracks a fox, then saves her and her cub from destruction.
(From *The Midnight Fox* by Betsy Byars. Avon Books, 1975.)

Teaching Idea

WILD ANIMALS IN LITERATURE (I) Read Betsy Byars's *The Midnight Fox* (I, Viking, 1968) aloud to your students, and encourage them to read similar stories on their own, such as Keith Robertson's *In Search of a Sandhill Crane* (I, Viking, 1973), Lee Kingman's *The Year of the Raccoon* (I-A, Houghton Mifflin, 1966), and Betsy Byars's *The House of Wings* (I, Viking, 1972). Discuss the books and compare the protagonists' attitudes and feelings before and after their encounters with the animals. Discuss how animals sometimes help people discover something about themselves.

coon hunting contest. But their training works against the dogs when they refuse to give up the chase for a savage bobcat. Billy's grief as he buries his beloved dogs where the red fern grows is shared by child and adult readers.

Dogs are the subject of many books for children in stories full of adventure, excitement, and often pathos. Meindert DeJong's *Hurry Home, Candy* (I) describes, from the point of view of a dog, its lonely search for security. Repeatedly beaten with brooms, the dog grows increasingly fearful of humans. Separated from his owners, he searches for a new home, but the brooms or images of them continually plague him and prevent his finding one. Eventually he finds a home with a man who senses the dog's fear. This story draws forth empathy.

Two memorable classics center upon a dog's search for security. Eric Knight's *Lassie Come Home* (I), well known to children through television and movies, is an account of a perilous journey a beloved collie takes to return to his master. Sheila Burnford's *The Incredible Journey* (I) is a story about a young Labrador retriever, an old bull terrier, and a Siamese cat who make a similar, 250-mile journey to their home. Starvation, always threatening, recedes into the background when the three encounter a bobcat, a bear, a tribe of Indians, storms, dangerous terrain, and other seemingly insurmountable obstacles. Children find the animals' shared responsibility and concern believable.

Several authors write about horses with a deep sense of compassion. In the forefront is Marguerite Henry, who thoroughly researches the stories of actual animals and events to bring dramatic reality to her writing. In *King of the Wind* (I), she traces the life of the beautiful horse, Sham, from a small stable in Morocco to France and then to England. A white spot on the horse's foot symbolizes speed, and the mark of the wheat ear on his chest, misfortune. Orphaned at birth, Sham is raised by a mute boy, Agba, whose devotion to the horse endures through bitter trials. Sham and Agba survive and, at the close of the story, Sham's quality, recognized at his birth by Agba, is acknowledged by the Earl of Godolphin.

Marguerite Henry fills her stories with a sense of caring and appreciation for animals, as *Misty of Chincoteague* (I), *Stormy, Misty's Foal* (I), and *Sea Star, Orphan of Chincoteague* (I), based in fact, bear out. The first story begins as a shipwreck leaves a cargo of Spanish horses floundering in a stormy sea. A few of the horses reach Assateague Island, where they survive and live for hundreds of years. The other two stories follow the Chincoteague line to the present. The island of Chincoteague, just off the coast of Virginia and Maryland, is today the scene of an annual Pony Penning Day, in which the wild descendants of those first Spanish horses are herded across a channel from their island refuge.

CRITERIA FOR SELECTING BOOKS OF CONTEMPORARY REALISM

There is more concern about selecting books of merit in the realm of realistic fiction than any other genre. The reason for this is the vast range of sensitive topics with which realistic fiction is concerned. Many adults prefer to shield children from the explicit language and subject matter of many of these books. Others, however, believe that experiences in reality once removed have a rightful place in children's lives.

The one universal for wise selection is that books be in keeping with a community's standards. With this in mind, other criteria of literary quality can be applied.

Modern realistic books are different from realistic books of the past because their readers are different. Today's social and psychological environment impinges upon young people in ways that their literature also reflects. Jacqueline Peters summarizes part of the life style of the present generation of children.

It watched mom and dad staying in bed on Sunday morning instead of attending church; it sat for hours in front of a television set watching the make-believe world come to life. It read magazine covers which announced that God was dead. It found stacks of *Playboy* under dad's bed. It saw the inhabitants of the earth being beaten, lynched, robbed, murdered and bombed.[33]

Whether or not we agree with this, it is the case that books that are realistic cannot avoid dealing with urgent issues. We can expect, however, that they not offend our personal sense of what is proper.

In choosing, we cannot deny that the young reader carries a world in his head that is different from ours. For those who think that some of the harshness in realistic books is burdensome for children, La Rochefoucauld's observation may be pertinent: "We *all* have sufficient strength to endure the misfortunes of others." When children read about reality in these books, they are shielded by the fact that the misfortune befalls a character in a book. The veil of fiction protects them, although the situations do reflect real life. Children intuitively distance themselves from scenes they find emotionally distressing; they push away books that hurt too much. Nevertheless, to give children only problem books is just as unrealistic as it is to shield them from all problems.

We should identify books that are relevant but not relentlessly so—books in which reality is relieved by wit and humor. Since taboos are now infrequent, the content and language of books cover a wide spectrum, and almost any subject in adult novels may appear in children's books. Hence, if you want to be sure that books you select conform to community standards of taste, you need to read them before introducing them to your students.

What we must demand of realistic books is that their insights into life not be slick or preachy; rather, that they have emotional validity, that they be honest and discerning without distorting or misleading or offending. We need to require the same high standards of sensitivity to the emotions and feelings of the character that we expect of adult novels.

Notes

1. Randall Jarrell, "Children Selecting Books in a Library," cited by Barbara Hardy, "Narrative As a Primary Act of Mind," in *The Cool Web: The Pattern of Children's Reading*, ed. Margaret Meek, Aidan Warlow, and Griselda Barton (New York: Atheneum, 1978), p. 14.
2. Bette Greene, *Philip Hall Likes Me. I Reckon Maybe* (New York: Dial, 1974), pp. 118–19.
3. Ibid., p. 135.
4. Virginia Hamilton, *M.C. Higgins, the Great* (New York: Macmillan, 1974), p. 26.
5. Louise Fitzhugh, *Harriet the Spy* (New York: Harper & Row, 1964), pp. 10–11.
6. Ibid., p. 180.
7. Marilyn Sachs, *A Summer's Lease* (New York: Dutton, 1979), p. 3.
8. Ibid., p. 88.
9. Walter Dean Myers, *The Young Landlords* (New York: Viking, 1979), p. 8.
10. Ibid., p. 9.
11. Richard Peck, *Representing Super Doll* (New York: Viking, 1974), pp. 182–83.
12. Adapted from plans developed by Susan Marinoff, Walt Whitman School, Brooklyn, New York.
13. M. E. Kerr, *Dinky Hocker Shoots Smack* (New York: Harper & Row, 1972), p. 18.
14. Mildred D. Taylor, *Roll of Thunder, Hear My Cry* (New York: Dial, 1976), p. 23.
15. Ouida Sebestyen, *Words by Heart* (Boston: Little, Brown, 1979), pp. 14–15.
16. Ibid., p. 148.
17. Barbara Cohen, *Bitter Herbs and Honey* (New York: Lothrop, Lee & Shepard, 1976), p. 70.
18. Ibid., p. 159.
19. Mollie Hunter, *The Third Eye* (New York: Harper & Row, 1979), p. 67.
20. Vera and Bill Cleaver, *Where the Lilies Bloom* (Philadelphia: Lippincott, 1969), p. 15.

21. Felice Holman, *Slake's Limbo* (New York: Scribner's, 1974), p. 117.
22. Jean George, *Julie of the Wolves* (New York: Harper & Row, 1972), pp. 5–6.
23. Laurence Sterne, *Life and Opinions of Tristram Shandy, Gentleman* (New York: Pocket Books, 1957), p. 83.
24. Jill Paton Walsh, *Unleaving* (New York: Farrar, Straus & Giroux, 1976), p. 9.
25. Ibid., p. 24.
26. S. Lee Galda, "Three Children Reading Stories: Response to Literature in Preadolescents," Diss. New York University 1980, p. 103.
27. Ibid., p. 109.
28. Katherine Paterson, *Bridge to Terabithia* (New York: Crowell, 1977), p. 119.
29. Ibid., p. 120.
30. S. Lee Galda, "Three Children Reading Stories," p. 111.
31. Ibid., p. 75.
32. Lois Lowry, *A Summer to Die* (Boston: Houghton Mifflin, 1977), p. 2.
33. Jacqueline Peters, "Life Styles of Today and Tomorrow: A Scenario," *National Association of Women Deans and Counselors Journal,* 36, No. 3 (Spring 1973), 103.

Professional References

Bettelheim, Bruno. *The Uses of Enchantment: The Meaning and Importance of Fairy Tales*. Knopf, 1976.

De Montreville, Doris, and Donna Hill, eds. *Third Book of Junior Authors*. H. W. Wilson, 1972.

Eaglen, Audrey. "Of Life, Love, Death, Kids, and Inhalation Therapy: An Interview with Paul Zindel, *Top of the News,* 34, No. 2 (Winter 1978), 178–85.

Galda, S. Lee. "Three Children Reading Stories: A Developmental Approach to Response to Literature in Preadolescents." Diss. New York University, 1980.

Hopkins, Lee Bennett. *More Books by More People*. Citation Press, 1974.

Meek, Margaret, Aidan Warlow, and Griselda Barton, eds. *The Cool Web: The Pattern of Children's Reading*. Atheneum, 1978.

Peters, Jacqueline. "Life Styles of Today and Tomorrow: A Scenario." *National Association of Women Deans and Counselors Journal,* 36, No. 3 (Spring, 1973), 102–05.

Sterne, Laurence. *Life and Opinions of Tristram Shandy, Gentleman*. Oxford Univ. Press, n.d.

Children's Books Cited in Chapter

Alcott, Louisa May. *Little Women*. Little, Brown, 1968 (1868).

Babbitt, Natalie. *The Eyes of the Amaryllis*. Farrar, Straus & Giroux, 1977.

Blume, Judy. *Are You There, God? It's Me, Margaret*. Bradbury, 1970.

————. *Blubber*. Bradbury, 1974.

————. *Deenie*. Bradbury, 1973.

————. *It's Not the End of the World*. Bradbury, 1972.

————. *Tales of a Fourth-Grade Nothing*. Illus. Roy Doty. Dutton, 1972.

Burnford, Sheila. *The Incredible Journey*. Illus. Carl Burger. Little, Brown, 1961.

Byars, Betsy. *The Midnight Fox*. Illus. Ann Grifalconi. Viking, 1968.

————. *The Pinballs*. Harper & Row, 1977.

————. *Summer of the Swans*. Illus. Ted CoConis. Viking, 1970.

Cleaver, Vera, and Bill Cleaver. *Trial Valley*. Lippincott, 1977.

————. *Where the Lilies Bloom*. Illus. James Spanfeller. Lippincott, 1969.

Clymer, Eleanor. *Luke Was There*. Illus. Diane de Groat. Holt, Rinehart & Winston, 1973.

Cohen, Barbara. *Bitter Herbs and Honey*. Lothrop, Lee & Shepard, 1976.

Cormier, Robert. *The Chocolate War*. Pantheon, 1974.

Cresswell, Helen. *Absolute Zero: Being the Second Part of the Bagthorpe Saga*. Macmillan, 1978.

————. *Bagthorpes Unlimited: Being the Third Part of the Bagthorpe Saga*. Macmillan, 1978.

————. *Bagthorpes v. the World: Being the Fourth Part of the Bagthorpe Saga*. Macmillan, 1979.

————. *Ordinary Jack: Being the First Part of the Bagthorpe Saga*. Macmillan, 1977.

DeJong, Meindert. *Hurry Home, Candy*. Illus. Maurice Sendak. Harper & Row, 1958.

Fitzhugh, Louise. *Harriet the Spy*. Harper & Row, 1964.

Fox, Paula. *Blowfish Live in the Sea*. Bradbury, 1970.

George, Jean Craighead. *Julie of the Wolves*. Illus. John Schoenherr. Harper & Row, 1972.

Greene, Bette. *Philip Hall Likes Me. I Reckon Maybe*. Dial, 1974.

Greene, Constance C. *Beat the Turtle Drum*. Illus. Donna Diamond. Viking, 1976.

Hamilton, Virginia. *M.C. Higgins, the Great*. Macmillan, 1974.

Henry, Marguerite. *King of the Wind.* Illus. Wesley Dennis. Rand McNally, 1948.

_____. *Misty of Chincoteague.* Illus. Wesley Dennis. Rand McNally, 1947.

_____. *Sea Star, Orphan of Chincoteague.* Illus. Wesley Dennis. Rand McNally, 1949.

_____. *Stormy: Misty's Foal.* Illus. Wesley Dennis. Rand McNally, 1963.

Holman, Felice. *Slake's Limbo.* Scribner's, 1974.

Hopkins, Lee Bennett. *Mama.* Knopf, 1977.

Hunter, Mollie. *The Third Eye.* Harper & Row, 1979.

Kerr, M. E. *Dinky Hocker Shoots Smack.* Harper & Row, 1972.

Kidd, Ronald. *That's What Friends Are For.* Nelson, 1978.

Knight, Eric. *Lassie Come Home.* Illus. Marguerite Kirmse. Holt, Rinehart & Winston, 1978 (1940).

Lowry, Lois. *A Summer to Die.* Illus. Jenni Oliver. Houghton Mifflin, 1977.

Mazer, Norma Fox. *A Figure of Speech.* Delacorte, 1973.

Myers, Walter Dean. *The Young Landlords.* Viking, 1979.

Ney, John. *Ox: The Story of a Kid at the Top.* Little, Brown, 1970.

Paterson, Katherine. *Bridge to Terabithia.* Illus. Donna Diamond. Crowell, 1977.

_____. *The Great Gilly Hopkins.* Crowell, 1978.

_____. *The Master Puppeteer.* Illus. Haru Wells. Crowell, 1976.

Peck, Richard. *Father Figure.* Viking, 1978.

_____. *Representing Super Doll.* Viking, 1974.

Raskin, Ellen. *The Westing Game.* Dutton, 1978.

Rawls, Wilson. *Where the Red Fern Grows: The Story of Two Dogs and a Boy.* Doubleday, 1961.

Sachs, Marilyn. *A Summer's Lease.* Dutton, 1979.

Sebestyen, Ouida. *Words by Heart.* Little, Brown, 1979.

Taylor, Mildred. *Roll of Thunder, Hear My Cry.* Dial, 1976.

_____. *Song of the Trees.* Illus. Jerry Pinkney. Dial, 1975.

Taylor, Sydney. *All-of-a-Kind Family.* Illus. Helen John. Follett, 1951.

Tolan, Stephanie S. *Grandpa—and Me.* Scribner's, 1978.

Walsh, Jill Paton. *Unleaving.* Farrar, Straus & Giroux, 1976.

Zindel, Paul. *Confessions of a Teenage Baboon.* Harper & Row, 1977.

_____. *The Effect of Gamma Rays on Man-in-the-Moon Marigolds.* Harper & Row, 1971.

_____. *Pardon Me, You're Stepping on My Eyeball.* Harper & Row, 1976.

_____. *The Pigman.* Harper & Row, 1968.

Recommended Reading

Of Self Determination

Characters in children's books often face seemingly insurmountable odds in achieving a sense of personal worth. Robert Burch's *Queenie Peavy,* illustrated by Jerry Lazare (I, Viking, 1966), is a feisty young girl who believes that all her problems will be solved when her father is released from prison. Discovering that he is neither able nor willing to help her leads her to the decision that she is herself able to make something better of her life. When young Jeremy says *Good-by to Stony Crick,* by Kathryn Borland and Helen Speicher, illustrated by Deanne Hollinger (I, McGraw-Hill, 1975), and moves with his family to the city, he has an overwhelming desire to return to the security of his former home. This is soon replaced with the urgent need to cope with the problems of daily living in the hard times of the Depression. In Sue Ellen Bridgers's *Home Before Dark* (I-A, Knopf, 1976) fourteen-year-old Stella resolves to create a better life for herself than that of her family of migrant farm workers. Robbie Branscum tells of another determined young girl in *Toby, Granny and George,* illustrated by Glenn Rounds (I-A, Doubleday, 1976). A spirited thirteen-year-old, Toby uses cleverness, courage, and persistence to rise above the smothering atmosphere of her small Arkansas community.

Tough Chauncey, by Doris Buchanan Smith (I-A, Morrow, 1974), is a troublemaker, the product of a broken home and mistreatment by the grandparents with whom he lives. He runs away and eventually learns that in a foster home he will get the help he needs to make something of his life. In Betsy Byars's *The Cartoonist,* illustrated by Richard Cuffari (I, Viking, 1978), Alfie ignores the sharp criticism of his widowed mother and is happy only when he is in his attic retreat. *Arilla Sun Down,* by Virginia Hamilton (I-A, Greenwillow, 1976), feels insignificant when compared to her older brother, who seems to have no difficulty accepting his mixed Indian/black heritage. Only after she bravely rescues him following his fall from a horse does she gain a sense of her own importance.

Some stories depict humorous struggles for independence. Emma knows that *Nobody's Family Is Going to Change,* by Louise Fitzhugh (I-A, Farrar, Straus & Giroux, 1974), without some prodding. Emma's lawyer father is strongly opposed to his daughter's aim to become an attorney and horrified that his son wants to become a tap dancer. When Emma becomes involved in a children's rights organization her father slowly comes to realize that his prejudices will not stop his children from seeking their own way. Claudia, in E. L. Konigsburg's *From the Mixed Up Files of Mrs. Basil E. Frankweiler* (I, Atheneum, 1967), feels her family is unfair and runs away with her younger brother to the Metropolitan Museum of Art, where they become involved in an intriguing mystery.

Langston Hughes's *The Dream Keeper and Other Poems,* illustrated by Helen Sewell (A, Knopf, 1932), contains many verses that speak to children seeking their identities. So, too, do several collections by Arnold Adoff, including *I Am the Darker Brother: An Anthology of Modern Poems by Black Americans* (I-A, Macmillan, 1968) and *Black Out Loud: An Anthology of Modern Poems by Black Americans,* illustrated by Alvin Hollingsworth (I-A, Macmillan, 1970).

Of Peer Relations

Jean Little's *Look Through My Window,* illustrated by Joan Sandin (I, Harper & Row, 1970), tells of the developing friendship between two girls who had been content to lead relatively solitary lives with their books and poetry. *Kate* (I, Harper & Row, 1971), a sequel, explores the jealousies that arise when other friends threaten to come between two with a special relationship.

Constance C. Greene's *A Girl Called Al,* illustrated by Byron Barton (I, Viking, 1969), *I Know You, Al,* illustrated by Byron Barton (I-A, Viking, 1975), and *Your Old Pal, Al* (I-A, Viking, 1979) describe the adventures of two pre-adolescents who share clothes, problems, fears, and all the worries of growing up.

In Robin F. Brancato's *Something Left to Lose* (A, Knopf, 1976), Rebbie, a frightened, insecure teenager uses the idea of the sanctity of friendship to browbeat her friends into wild and dangerous escapades until one of the girls learns to assert herself. Frank Bonham's *Durango Street* (A, Dutton, 1965) and Paula Fox's *How Many Miles to Babylon?* illustrated by Paul Giavanopoulos (I-A, D. White, 1967), describe the difficulties faced by youngsters caught in the demands of gang life. Susie Hinton, too, shows how teenagers must fight for individuality and independence within a gang in *That Was Then, This Is Now* (A, Viking, 1971) and in *The Outsiders* (A, Viking, 1967). Walter Dean Myers presents a more positive look at peer influence in *Fast Sam, Cool Clyde and Stuff* (I-A, Viking, 1975), a reminiscence of the author's childhood on the streets of New York.

Mary O'Neill's *People I'd Like to Keep,* illustrated by Paul Galdone (I, Doubleday, 1964), is a collection of poems that show the special relationships and feelings between friends. "My Friend Leona" is especially appropriate to share after reading Eleanor Estes's *The Hundred Dresses,* illustrated by Louis Slobodkin (P-I, Harcourt Brace Jovanovich, 1944), a bittersweet story about a girl who lies to gain the acceptance of her friends.

Of Families

Although there are many outstanding books in which nuclear families live quite normal lives, these stories often feature some other aspect by which they are classified. Certainly, typical families exist in books as well as in real life, but so, too, do families facing unusual or otherwise unique situations.

Although the arrival of a new baby is more frequently treated in picture books for younger children, older siblings, long used to parents' undivided attention, may face greater difficulties in adjusting to family changes. Lois Lowry's *Anastasia Krupnik* (I, Houghton Mifflin, 1979), a spunky ten-year-old who keeps a list of "Things I Love" and "Things I Hate," immediately enters the expected baby on the latter list. Norma Klein's *Confessions of an Only Child,* illustrated by Richard Cuffari (I, Pantheon, 1974), tells a similar story, as does Marilyn Sachs's *Dorrie's Book,* illustrated by Anne Sachs (I-A, Doubleday, 1975). Dorrie's school assignment to write a "real book . . . a long one with chapters" becomes the vehicle through which she expresses her feelings concerning expected triplets. Dorrie's perceptions are extremely funny at times, and her journal reflects a reluctant, but growing acceptance of the new babies. All of these books show a warm, loving family unit and the special feelings each girl develops toward her new sibling.

Just as divorce is becoming commonplace in our society, it also serves as background for some books without actually being the focus of the story. Of books that deal with the effects of divorce on children, Annabel and Edgar Johnson's *The Grizzly,* illustrated by Gilbert Riswold (I, Harper & Row, 1964), was one of the first. David dreads the camping trip he is to take with a father he has not seen for many years. His lack of physical stamina and fear of wild animals nearly cause a permanent split between them but David's courage and strength in a sudden emergency surprise both the boy and his father.

In Stella Pevsner's *A Smart Kid Like You* (I, Seabury, 1974), Nina, bitter about her parents' divorce, tries to sabotage her new math teacher, who is also her father's new wife. Nina slowly comes to terms with her disappointment and finds that she likes her new step-mother and has a better relationship with her mother. Noel, in Anne Alexander's *To Live a Lie* (I-A, Atheneum, 1975), finds it easier to tell people that her mother is dead than to admit that her mother has left home to pursue a college education. In Hilma Wolitzer's story, Teddy can't understand how two people can fall *Out of Love* (I-A, Farrar, Straus & Giroux, 1976). Her discovery of old love letters written by her father to her mother rekindle hope that her father will return, and she begins a new effort to make her mother more attractive. Her slow acceptance of the inevitable is coupled with her own growing friendship with a boy.

In Betsy Byars's *The Night Swimmers,* illustrated by Troy Howell (I-A, Delacorte, 1980), Retta, after the death of her mother, feeling that she must now take charge of the family, undergoes the painful realization that she, too, needs comfort and leadership. In Isabelle Holland's *Now Is Not Too Late* (I, Lothrop, Lee & Shepard, 1980) Cathy has been told that her mother is dead. The discovery that her new friend and art teacher is really her mother, a recovering alcoholic, shakes her trust in her relationships with the rest of her family, but her understanding grandmother helps her to new understanding.

Adoption is another subject becoming more visible in children's books. Ten-year-old Peter accepted his adoption until his friendly school bus driver remarked that he wouldn't want *Somebody Else's Child,* by Roberta Silman, illustrated by Chris Conover (I, Warne, 1976). Natalie, too, is happy in her adopted home, but still cannot resist the urge to find her natural mother in Lois Lowry's *Find a Stranger, Say Goodbye* (I-A, Houghton Mifflin, 1978). Her family supports her search, and stands lovingly by when she finds that her natural mother has no place for this daughter.

Several poems in David MacKay's collection, *A Flock of Words,* illustrated by Margery Gill (I-A, Harcourt Brace Jovanovich, 1969), deal with family relationships, including Stephen Spender's "My Parents," Robert Frost's "The Span of Life," and e.e. cummings's "Nobody Loses All the Time."

Of Personal Integrity

Julia Cunningham has written several powerful stories in which characters face extreme deprivation and hardship yet maintain their integrity. *Come to the Edge* (I-A, Pantheon, 1977) tells about an abandoned fourteen-year-old boy who, devastated by rejection, continually flees personal relationships. Eventually he finds an acceptable life with the only person who will allow him freedom to be himself. Cunningham's *Dorp Dead,* illustrated by James Spanfeller (I-A, Pantheon, 1965), is the story of a similar young boy torn between the desire for independence and the need for security. An orphan, Gilly is sent to live with a strange man, Kobalt, who exhibits increasingly odd behavior, until Gilly realizes that his very life is at stake.

Florence Parry Heide, too, writes of lonely children caught between personal integrity and social involvement. In *When the Sad One Comes to Stay* (I, Lippincott, 1975) Sara is forced to choose between the friendship of a lonely old woman and the materialist snobbery of her mother. In *Growing Anyway Up* (I, Lippincott, 1976) a very intense, private young girl finds that she must make an accommodation with her emotional needs in order to get on with the business of living.

Paula Danziger writes of a different kind of integrity in *The Cat Ate My Gymsuit* (I-A, Delacorte, 1974), the story of an overweight, insecure girl who learns to stand up for her convictions. When her favorite English teacher is fired, Marcy leads those agitating for her reinstatement, and is suspended from school. Danziger's sequel, *There's a Bat in Bunk Five* (I-A, Delacorte, 1980), follows Marcy to summer camp. M. E. Kerr writes of a similar incident in *Is That You, Miss Blue?* (A, Harper & Row, 1975). When one of the teachers in her private boarding school is found to be incompetent, Flanders objects not as much to the dismissal as to the lack of compassion for the troubled woman.

On Laughter

In addition to books by Beverly Cleary, Robert McCloskey, Keith Robertson, and others, children will especially enjoy Barbara Robinson's *The Best Christmas Pageant Ever,* illustrated by Judith Gwyn Brown (I, Harper & Row, 1972), a marvelously funny account of the havoc wrought by the six Herdman children when they become involved in a church Christmas play.

Humorous poetry abounds, and children will soon be caught up in the hilarious verses of Shel Silverstein's *Where the Sidewalk Ends* (P-I, Harper & Row, 1974). In addition, the work of William Cole provides many laughs. His collections include *Beastly Boys and Ghastly Girls,* illustrated by Tomi Ungerer (P-I, Collins-World, 1964,), *Oh, How Silly!* illustrated by Tomi Ungerer (P-I, Viking, 1970,), *Oh, That's Ridiculous!* illustrated by Tomi Ungerer (P-I, Viking, 1972), *Oh, Such Foolishness,* illustrated by Tomie de Paola (P-I, Lippincott, 1978), and many others. Myra Cohn Livingston edited *What a Wonderful Bird the Frog Are: An Anthology of Humorous Poetry and Verse* (I, Harcourt Brace Jovanovich, 1973) and Ogden Nash is responsible for *The Moon Is Shining Bright as Day: An Anthology of Good Humored Verse* (I, Lippincott, 1953.)

On Courage

Courage can be shown against physical and environmental trials as well as emotional and psychological ones. Armstrong Sperry's classic story, *Call It Courage* (I, Macmillan, 1940), is a strong narrative about a young Polynesian boy who struggles to overcome his fear of the sea. Criticized by his peers and re-

jected by his father, Mafatu sets out alone to face the hazards of the sea, conquers his fear, and returns to take his place in the tribe.

Another outstanding survival story is Scott O'Dell's *Island of the Blue Dolphins* (I-A, Houghton Mifflin, 1960), a true account of one girl's solitary existence on an island off the coast of California. Left alone after her brother is killed by wild dogs, Karana tames the animals and begins to face the task of living alone for eighteen years. A sequel, *Zia* (I, Houghton Mifflin, 1976), is a bittersweet end to Karana's story. Rescued at last, she is unable to adjust to life in a mission house, and eventually dies.

William Armstrong's *Sounder,* illustrated by James Barkley (I, Harper & Row, 1969), tells of a different kind of courage. The father of a black family risks his life to steal food for his starving family and is sent to an oppressive prison. The cruelty shown man and animal alike stuns readers and introduces them to depths of life unsuspected by many.

Willo Davis Roberts tackles child abuse in *Don't Hurt Laurie!* illustrated by Ruth Sanderson (I-A, Atheneum, 1977). Discouraged from having friends, wary of her mother's temper, and constantly forced to change schools to evade prying questions, Laurie lives on the edge of a fearful overwhelming loneliness. Irene Hunt's *The Lottery Rose* (I-A, Scribner's, 1976) tells of a small boy who suffers at the hands of his mother's sadistic boyfriend. Both stories are grim, but end on a realistically affirmative note—as the problem becomes more widely recognized, there is growing hope for such children.

Courage in facing serious illness is the subject of Victoria Poole's *Thursday's Child* (A, Little, Brown, 1980), in which seventeen-year-old Sam will die if a heart transplant operation is unsuccessful. Doris Lund writes about her son *Eric* (A, Lippincott, 1974), a superb athlete who put up a courageous battle before his death from leukemia.

On Heroism

James Houston's *Frozen Fire* (I, Atheneum, 1970) is based on the true and dramatic ordeal of two boys lost in the Arctic wilderness. Twelve-year-old Matthew depends upon his Eskimo friend to lead him through seventy-five miles of whirling snow and bitter cold. Another story based on fact, Alan Eckert's *Incident at Hawk's Hill,* illustrated by John Schoenherr (I, Little, Brown, 1971), tells how an emotionally disturbed young boy survives for nearly a year in a badger den and is eventually adopted by the animals.

The boy in Jean George's *My Side of the Mountain* (I, Dutton, 1959) displays a different heroism when he runs away from home to live by himself in the Catskill mountains. Sam builds a home in a tree and survives by scavenging for food.

On Compassion

Irene Hunt tells an absorbing story about an extended family formed out of need and love. *William* (A, Scribner's, 1977) lives with his terminally ill mother and two sisters next door to a sixteen-year-old girl who has run away to have her baby. Soon after the baby's birth William's mother dies, leaving a group of frightened young people who stay together because the alternative is no family at all. Another lonely child, not so fortunate, is Zeke, in Mary Weik's *The Jazz Man,* illustrated by Ann Grifalconi (I, Atheneum, 1966). Zeke's destitute family, unable to face their responsibilities to their crippled son, abandon him, and he is left alone, except for the musician across the alley—the "Jazz Man"—whose music gives him strength. A haunting, dreamlike ending leaves the reader to decide whether Zeke survives.

A child who resents her placement in a foster home learns to show compassion for a younger child in Marion Bauer's *Foster Child* (I-A, Seabury, 1977). Renny views her placement as only temporary and is astounded to discover that the other children are far less optimistic. Being molested by Pop Beck, the foster parent, turns her thoughts from her own problems to the needs of a younger girl in the family.

A fourteen-year-old boy develops a close relationship with Justin McLeod, *The Man Without a Face,* by Isabelle Holland (A, Lippincott, 1972), who agrees to tutor him. The boy, who wants to get into a boarding school to escape his demanding family, precipitates an emotional encounter when he presses for an explanation of the man's horribly scarred face.

Meet the Austins (I, Vanguard, 1960) was Madeleine L'Engle's first book about the warm, loving Austin family, who take in Maggy, an orphan. Strains that develop because of the girl's behavior are resolved when the parents show their children that kindness and understanding can change Maggy. One of the children, Vicky, confronts questions of love and death, dependence and responsibility in a fourth book about the Austins, *A Ring of Endless Light* (A, Farrar, Straus & Giroux, 1980). Vicky is now almost sixteen, and struggling with the knowledge that her beloved grandfather is dying. Her work—studying communication with dolphins—and her poetry enable her to come to terms with the frailty of life. Madeleine L'Engle shows deep compassion in all of her writing.

On Aging

Seeing a beloved grandparent sicken and decline can be traumatic for children. In Barbara Corcoran's *The Faraway Island* (I, Atheneum, 1977), painfully shy Lynn chooses to spend the year with her grandmother rather than go with her family to Belgium. Her idyll is shattered, however, when the old woman begins to grow senile and Lynn must take on more and more responsibilities. Another young girl faces similar circumstances in Vera and Bill Cleaver's *Queen of Hearts* (I-A, Lippincott, 1978). Wilma resents having to spend her summer caring for her grandmother but, even more, she resents the subtle changes she sees in her grandmother's behavior. Her acceptance of the changes in her life and in her grandmother's enables her to resolve her conflicts.

Peter Hartling's *Oma,* translated by Anthea Bell, illustrated by Jutta Ash (I, Harper & Row, 1970), is a feisty, hard-working German grandmother who struggles against the problems of aging as well as the unique difficulties of raising her orphaned grandson. Finally, increasing frailty raises the question of what will become of the boy after her death.

Robert Burch has written a bittersweet story, *Two That Were Tough,* illustrated by Richard Cuffari (I, Viking, 1976), about the relationship between an aging man and his tough old rooster, Wild Wings. Although the old man eventually has to move to his daughter's home, the rooster stays on at the homestead, symbolically maintaining the independence both had desired.

David Ignatow's poem "Two Friends," in *The Arbuthnot Anthology of Children's Literature,* 4th ed., edited by Zena Sutherland et al. (Lothrop, Lee & Shepard, 1976), is a plea for compassion among aging friends. Eve Merriam's *Rainbow Writing* (I-A, Atheneum, 1976) includes "Grandmother Rocking" and "Say Nay," two poems about aging.

On Death

Doris Buchanan Smith's *A Taste of Blackberries,* illustrated by Charles Robinson (I, Crowell, 1973), a simple story of a young boy who dies from an allergic reaction to bee stings, has a dramatic impact on young readers. Jean Little's *Home from Far,* illustrated by Jerry Lazare (I, Little, Brown, 1965) also tells of the death of a child. Jenny's adjustment to her twin brother's death is difficult and the foster children her parents take in only add to her grief. Sympathetic parents eventually encourage Jenny to accept the reality of her life.

Terminal illness is the subject of Alfred Slote's *Hang Tough, Paul Mather* (I-A, Lippincott, 1973). Paul, hospitalized with leukemia, refuses to give in to the disease, sneaks from the hospital and pitches one more game of Little League baseball before he finally comes to terms with his impending death. Paige Dixon tells about a teenage boy who suffers from "Lou Gehrig's" disease in *May I Cross Your Golden River?* (A, Atheneum, 1975). A sequel, *Skipper* (A, Atheneum, 1979), focuses on the surviving younger brother, who has difficulty adjusting to his brother's death. In Virginia Lee's beautiful story, *The Magic Moth* (I, Seabury, 1972), the entire family gathers around ten-year-old Maryanne's bed as she nears death. Six-year-old Mark-o watches in wonder as the caterpillar he had brought to Maryanne's bedside leaves its cocoon and flies out the window, symbolizing the release of death.

The death of a parent is realistically portrayed in several books. In June Jordan's *His Own Where* (A, Crowell, 1971), a teenager keeps a vigil at the bedside of his dying father, as does young Corrie in Carol Farley's *The Garden Is Doing Fine,* illustrated by Lynn Sweat (I-A, Atheneum, 1975). The title of this book echoes the reassurance she gives her father who, dying of cancer, does not know that it is winter and that his garden is gone. Cancer also takes the father in Jan Greenberg's *A Season In-Between* (I, Farrar, Straus & Giroux, 1979) and the mother in Isabelle Holland's *Of Love and Death and Other Journeys* (I-A, Lippincott, 1975). In this story fifteen-year-old Meg is puzzled by her mother's insistence that she get to know the divorced father she has never met until she realizes that her mother is dying and is planning for her daughter's future without her. A young boy discovers that his broken arm is not the most terrible thing that can happen in Peggy Mann's *There Are Two Kinds of Terrible* (I-A, Doubleday, 1977). His mother's cancer is immeasurably worse, and Robbie's stages of anguish and his reactions of fear, anger, and grief are realistically portrayed.

Fourteen-year-old Orin takes on the burden of caring for his family when his father, unable to accept the death of his wife in an automobile accident, becomes an alcoholic in Mary Stolz's *The Edge of Next Year* (I, Harper & Row, 1974). Orin gradually accepts his new responsibilities and, although he knows he will always miss his mother, also recognizes that eventually he must relinquish her.

Mollie Hunter's *A Sound of Chariots* (I-A, Harper & Row, 1972) tells of the special relationship young Bridie McShane shared with her father. After his death she refuses to use her writing talents, remaining bitter and withdrawn, until a loving friend convinces her that she can make her father live on through her talents.

Robert Frost's "The Span of Life," in David MacKay's *A Flock of Words* (I-A, Harcourt Brace Jovanovich, 1970), is a poem that will add depth and understanding to any account of death.

On Caring

Children often learn about responsibility and respect through their relationships with animals. In Isabelle Holland's *Alan and the Animal Kingdom* (I-A, Lippincott, 1977) a frightened young boy, living alone after the death of his guardian, rejects all aid until, fearful for his cat's life, he gratefully accepts the friendship of adults who can help him.

Chester Aaron writes a compelling story in *Spill* (I-A, Athe-neum, 1977). When an oil tanker collision spills thousands of gallons of oil onto the beach near his California home, Jeff, who has become involved with a gang of pot-smoking musicians, joins the volunteer efforts to save the wildlife. In the process, he rejects his friends and re-establishes his commitment to ecological work. Jean George has written many books dealing with the balance of nature and man's place in preserving the earth. In *Going to the Sun* (I-A, Harper & Row, 1976) she shows how a young man changes from predator to protector as he slowly gains respect for the mountain goat he had sought to kill. In *The Cry of the Crow* (I-A, Harper & Row, 1980) Jean George writes about the wildlife of the Florida Everglades. A young girl secretly trains her pet crow to imitate human speech. Fearful that her father and brothers will kill the pesky bird, she finds a unique way to prevent it.

Colin Thiele is an Australian author who shows deep respect for the environment. *Storm Boy,* illustrated by John Schoenherr (I, Harper & Row, 1978), takes place on an isolated coast where a young boy prefers his simple existence with his father and pet pelicans to the frightening unknown world of school in the big city. Only after one of his pets is killed is he able to think toward a future that will certainly be richer for his childhood experiences. Thiele's *Fight Against Albatross Two* (I-A, Harper & Row, 1976) deals with the conflict between the need to preserve nature and the world's need for oil. When an oil rig is set up off the coast of a quiet Australian fishing village, the people take sides in a bitter fight in which the animals' welfare is sometimes forgotten amidst the political uproar.

nine

ARTHUR GUITERMAN   *ANCIENT HISTORY*

*I hope the old Romans
Had painful abdomens.*

*I hope that the Greeks
Had toothache for weeks.*

*I hope that the Arabs
Were bitten by scarabs.*

*I hope that the Vandals
Had thorns in their sandals.*

*I hope that the Persians
Had gout in all versions.*

*I hope that the Medes
Were kicked by their steeds.*

*They started the fuss
And left it to us!*[1]

Historical Fiction and Biography

In the epigraph, Arthur Guiterman expresses the feelings of many students who come away from a study of history with a sense of revulsion. They may memorize names of kings and dates of battles, but the terms and numbers remain sterile, the people merely shadows, the events meaningless.

History is made by people—what they did, what they said, and what they were, people with strengths and weaknesses who experienced victories and defeats. Authors of historical books want children to know historical figures as human beings who have shortcomings as well as great strengths. Overblown heroes and stale rhetoric diminish our real heritage.

For children, history becomes exciting when the people who made it seem to arise alive from the pages. Historical fiction and biography add the human dimension to the historical facts presented in nonfiction. As Madeleine L'Engle says, we may go to encyclopedias for facts, but we go to stories and poetry for truth. Historical fiction extends the fragments of history reported in textbooks and helps students view history not as in Guiterman's mocking verse, but as a story of life as it was lived by real people.

Supplementing history textbooks with historical fiction brings advantages not possible by using a single textbook. First of all, access to multiple resources enables learners to make choices about what they learn and empowers them to make judgments about what they read. Secondly, a single textbook can provide only limited coverage of a topic; the array of trade books is virtually unlimited. Trade books undergird the social studies by adding experiences on which children build concepts.

A plan for relating literature to the curriculum will vary according to a teacher's style. One fifth-grade teacher begins a study of the Revolutionary War period by asking students to brainstorm "facts" about George Washington, Betsy Ross, and Paul Revere. He writes the offered information and misinformation on charts, which are referred to frequently during the study. Inevitably, there are conflicting reports, and the students revise their original statements as they locate additional information.

Another teacher works with her third-grade children to develop a study plan for a unit on early settlers in America. She fills the room with many sources of information, including books, records, films, realia, and pictures. The students spend several days exploring the material and making suggestions about topics that interest them, which the teacher writes on the chalkboard. The list might include Pilgrims, Plymouth Rock, the Mayflower, the first Thanksgiving, and witch trials. The group organizes the ideas into reasonably logical categories, and students then choose topics they want to pursue, identify sources of information, and begin the research for the study. Examining the past in this way helps students begin to understand human behavior, the ways that people and societies interact, the concept of humans as social beings, and the values that make people human.

The books discussed in this chapter show that history is created by people, that people living now are tied to those who lived in the past through a common humanity, and that human conditions of the past shape our lives today. By relating trade books to topics in the social studies, we enrich children's understanding with a wealth of material that far exceeds the limited view of any single text. Historical fiction and biographies are read for insights into the panoply of history; they are a lively and fascinating way to transmit the story of the past to the guardians of the future.

Historical fiction, though it is set in a time prior to the one in which we live, is like contemporary realism in that it relates human experiences in the natural world. In essence, a historical novel is an imaginative story anchored by some historical fact. Historical biography tells primarily the life story of an actual person, with the times in which he or she lived in a secondary role. Reading about one person brings the wide scope of history to a focus in a single life, showing the interaction between that person (and, perhaps, close relatives and associates) and events. Nonfiction about the past aims to report what is known objectively, some authors using primary sources and original documents to do so. Certain poetry, too, can be a way of conveying a vision of people and events of the past.

When do contemporary events become historical? Unlike the condition "antique," which takes one hundred years to achieve, the classification "historical" does not have a formal basis in time. Hence, it is difficult to tell where to draw the line, because what may seem contemporary to us may seem to be historical to our younger students.

Some of the stories discussed in Chapter 8— Mildred Taylor's *Roll of Thunder: Hear My Cry* (I-A) and Sydney Taylor's *All-of-a-Kind Family* (I), for example—could easily be placed in the present chapter, since they are set in the Depression of the 1930s. In this case, since other qualities in them were more important to our purposes than historical setting, they were treated as specimens of "contemporary realism"—reinforcing the point that literature can be approached in many ways. As you examine the past through literature with your students, you may want to extend the period considered historical; on the other hand, you may want to explore historical novels from other perspectives.

Historical fiction and biography are grounded in facts but not restricted by them. An author may use historical records to document events, but the facts merely serve as a scaffolding for the story. Jean Lee Latham, before she undertakes the actual writing, prepares a meticulously detailed time line of documented events from historical records as background for her story. Milton Meltzer uses primary sources and first-person narratives based on letters, memoirs, and interviews. His re-creations let people of the past speak for themselves. In early books, Meltzer simply recorded material from primary sources, but in later ones he interwove this with narrative to establish context and interpret the significance of events.

The best historical stories come from authors well acquainted with the facts. Two works exemplifying a good combination of historical knowledge and storytelling ability are books by Esther Forbes and by two brothers—James Lincoln Collier, a writer, and Christopher Collier, a historian. While researching information for an adult biography of Paul Revere, Esther Forbes became intrigued with stories of the young apprentices who lived in eighteenth-century Boston. When she completed the biography, she told their story in *Johnny Tremain* (I-A), maintaining a level of historical accuracy like that of the biography. The Colliers combined their talents to produce a bittersweet story of a family caught between loyalty to the English crown and desire for independence in *My Brother Sam Is Dead* (I-A).

PREHISTORIC TIMES

Scientists theorize about the daily life and culture of ancient peoples in ways very much like the process children use in building an ever-expanding knowledge of their world. Both child and scientist observe fragments of life and make inferences about those fragments to intuit what else must be true. Children are intrigued with the idea that much of what we know about prehistoric times is based on bits of pottery, weapons, or scraps of bone painstakingly reassembled to reconstruct a skull or a skeleton or a whole culture. Intermediate-grade children respond to the study of prehistoric people and animals more or less as they respond to story, and this is entirely compatible with the way most children's books on the prehistoric present their accounts of the time. Older children become actively involved in distinguishing what is hard fact from what is theory and become interested in theorizing on their own.

Several books present imaginative conceptions of life before recorded history. One of the stories, *Fire Hunter* (I-A), portrays James Kjelgaard's view of the way in which several important human advances may have come about. For example, as the story opens, Hawk, chief spear maker for a nomadic tribe, is experimenting with a new weapon he believes will help in the dangerous hunt for game. Because he is flouting custom, Hawk incurs the suspicions of his fellow tribesmen and is abandoned by the tribe together with a young woman, Willow, who is wounded and unable to travel further. By their ingenuity the two young people manage to survive, and in doing so evolve a new way of life:

Until now his life had been a nomadic one. The tribe to which he had belonged had always found it necessary to wander, to follow the game herds upon which they depended for food. Often they passed one season hundreds of miles from where they had spent the previous one. There was no such thing as a settled or permanent home. . . .

But Hawk knew that he could not possibly wander now. Even if he were not accompanied by the wounded Willow, one man alone was no match for all the dangers of traveling. He must have a haven, some place of safety, and the fire was the safest place he knew. He hauled more wood and built his fire up. Then he looked restlessly about.[2]

Hawk and Willow drive a great bear from its cave and make a home there. Hawk experiments with new ways of making weapons; he perfects darts that he can throw with great skill and finally designs a bow that sends his darts even farther. As the students read, they share his sense of excitement in discovery:

Experimentally he pulled at the sinew, and when he did the stick bent. As soon as he released it, the stick straightened. The quivering sinew seemed to sing softly to him. . . .

Hawk forgot everything else. . . .

A green stick itself had great power, a mysterious force that belonged to things that grew, but did not move freely by themselves. And animal sinew, Hawk reasoned, so useful to both beasts and men, who could move as they pleased, must contain some magical element of its own. Combined, the two seemed to possess a power greater than either alone. Hawk drew the sinew again, and again, and let the stick snap itself back to its former shape.[3]

In the end, curiosity and ingenuity are vindicated when remnants of the tribe return to take shelter with Hawk and Willow in the cave stronghold. The momentum of this dramatic story carries children along to an understanding of anthropological theory, of the ways people established a life pattern long before history was written.

A useful supplementary reference when reading stories set in prehistoric times is *The Epic of Man* (I-A), by Leften Stavrianos. The illustrations, in double-page spreads, depict fire hunts, rituals, and scenes of prehistoric tribes at work. Illustrations of ceremonies in the caves of the great hunters include reproductions of the famous drawings of animals in the Lascaux Caves, which adds an "I-was-there" quality to the stories. Ceremonies of initiation and preparation for a hunt form a dramatic backdrop for stories of prehistoric people.

D. Moreau Barringer's *And the Waters Prevailed* (I-A) is an imaginative story that intrigues readers. Set in prehistory, it opens with a manhood ceremony in which Andor the Little must go forth —on his "manhood hunt"—into the wilds to defend, feed, and clothe himself for a month. Later, on another expedition, he reaches the shores of the gray restlessness of the Atlantic Ocean at the place now known as the Strait of Gibraltar. Andor sees that the time may come when the rock wall there will not be able to hold back the battering sea, and that it will break through and flood the plain where his tribe makes its home. His warning is ignored because his people are unable to comprehend what Andor describes.

As an aid to comprehension, the endpapers of *And the Waters Prevailed* show a map of the area around the Mediterranean Sea as it might have looked at the beginning of the story and as it looks today. Also, in a note, the author discusses the

This endpaper map from *And the Waters Prevailed* helps readers follow this story set in prehistoric southern Europe. (From *And the Waters Prevailed* by D. Moreau Barringer. Copyright © 1956 by E. P. Dutton & Co., Inc. Reprinted by permission of the publisher, E. P. Dutton.)

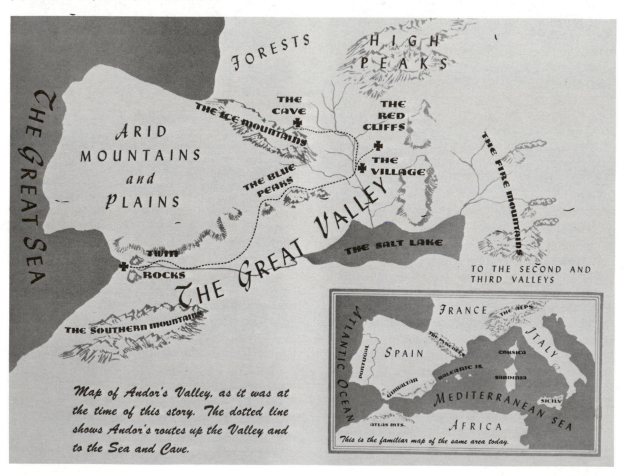

Map of Andor's Valley, as it was at the time of this story. The dotted line shows Andor's routes up the Valley and to the Sea and Cave.

This is the familiar map of the same area today.

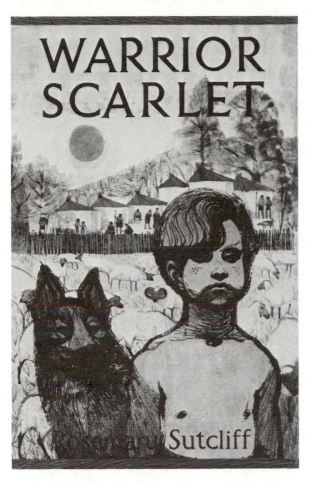

In Ancient Britain, Drem, because he has failed his test of manhood, lives in exile from his tribe.
(From *Warrior Scarlet* by Rosemary Sutcliff, illustrated by Charles Keeping, published by Oxford University Press. © Oxford University Press 1958.)

probable event that gave rise to his fiction—the creation of the Mediterranean Sea by the flooding of the area when the Atlantic breached the barrier at what is now the Strait of Gibraltar. Against this background, the author paints a fascinating re-creation of what prehistoric village life might have been like and an even more fascinating tale of one man's lonely courage.

Rosemary Sutcliff, an artist whose novels of ancient Britain are masterful evocations of their time, provides sensitive insights into the human spirit. In *Warrior Scarlet* (A), set in prehistoric Britain, Drem One-Arm, crippled since birth, spends all his years in the Boys' House training and struggling to learn a warrior's skills in spite of his handicap. As a result of an accident, he fails his wolf-slaying task and is not permitted to complete the initiation ceremonies. Instead, he is considered dead and is banished to live with the shepherd people in the hill country. Toward the end of the famine winter that follows, the wolf that Drem failed to kill returns to attack an aged shepherd, and this time Drem is triumphant. He returns to wear the warrior scarlet of his tribe, but with an understanding of the vicissitudes experienced by those who live different lives.

The best fiction about prehistoric people does more than re-create possible settings and events of the past. It engages itself with themes basic to all persons everywhere—the will to survive, the need for courage and honor, the growth of understanding, the development of compassion.

Teaching Idea

RECONSTRUCTING THE PAST (I) Using both fiction and nonfiction in a study of prehistoric people is rewarding because each form enriches the other. It is good to begin a unit with the discoveries of the Leakeys at Olduvai Gorge in Africa. Use the following articles from the *National Geographic* magazine for reading aloud or retelling in your own words.

''Adventures in the Search for Man'' by Louis S. B. Leakey. Photos by Hugo van Lawick. Jan. 1963, pp. 132–52.

(CONTINUED)

"Exploring 1,750,000 Years Into Man's Past" by Louis S. B. Leakey. Photos by Robert F. Sisson. Oct. 1961, pp. 564–89.

"Finding the World's Earliest Man (*Zinjanthropus boisie*)" by Louis S. B. Leakey. Photos by Des Bartlett. Sept. 1960, pp. 420–35.

"The Leakey Tradition Lives On" by Melvin M. Payne. Jan. 1973, pp. 143–44.

"The Leakeys of Africa: Family Search of Prehistoric Man" by Melvin M. Payne. Feb. 1965, pp. 194–231.

"Preserving the Treasures of Olduvai Gorge" by Melvin M. Payne. Photos by Joseph J. Scherschel. Nov. 1966, pp. 701–09.

Also useful are the television film "Dr. Leakey and the Dawn of Man," produced under the auspices of the National Geographic Society, and the biography *The White Kikuyu: Louis S. B. Leakey* (I-A), by Anne Malatesta and Ronald Friedland (McGraw-Hill, 1978).

For the children the chief appeal of articles on prehistory lies in the photographs and drawings that usually accompany them. Children are fascinated by the picture of a reconstruction of a skull in which the actual pieces discovered at the site are contrasted with sections supplied through scientific speculation. Photographs of Louis Leakey and his crew lying on the ground, working with painstaking care to uncover a fragment without damaging it, show something of the patience this work demands. The articles can be supplemented by the sound filmstrip *Man on the Move: An Introduction to Anthropology*, by Ethel J. Alpenfels (Miller Brody). The accompanying teacher's guide contains time charts, glossaries, a bibliography for further reading, and a wealth of teaching aids.

Activity: Teacher to Student

TIME LINES AND MAPS (I)   Gather information to make a classroom time-line mural to help see more clearly the possible times various groups of prehistoric peoples might have existed. The time line can be constructed so that the dates of eras run across the top, and the titles of stories set in the various periods appear along the bottom. In some cases, of course, you may need to infer when the story is to have taken place.

Make a series of world maps—one for each story read. On each map, locate the setting of the story, either stated or implied, and fill in the location of other prehistoric peoples known to exist at the time. Julian May's *Before the Indians*, illustrated by Symeon Shimin (Holiday House, 1969), is a good reference work for the project. Maps show the locations of tribes known to have existed in North and South America and also provide illustrations of artifacts and plant and animal life that you could use to decorate your maps.

Museum trips can help children visualize the world of prehistory and generate interest in books dealing with it. (Photograph © 1980 by Marjorie Pickens.)

ANCIENT EGYPT AND GREECE

Children are fascinated by the pyramids and mummies of ancient Egypt. Viewing museum treasures such as those from the tomb of Tutankhamun can heighten this interest. Children who can visit the Metropolitan Museum of Art in New York City and explore the Temple of Dendur, which occupies its own hall in the museum, will delight in the mysteries of Egypt firsthand. There are also several beautiful books on Egyptian culture, particularly on the Tutankhamun excavations.

Several years after the discovery of Tutankhamun's tomb and its treasures in 1922, a novel for young people was published that was inspired by the fascination for the civilization of Akhenaten (at Tell el-Amarna) that then swept the world. The book, *The Lost Queen of Egypt* (A), by Lucile Morrison, tells of the childhood of the royal princess Ankhsenpaaten, later to be queen, in the court of Akhenaten and Nefertiti. The author paints an idyllic picture of the sun-filled city and of the spirit of mystical idealism that pervades the court and domestic life. As the royal princess grows up, however, the political uncertainties and intrigues emanating from the old capitol of Thebes combine with the defeats of the pharaoh's armies abroad to cast threatening shadows over the kingdom. When Tutankhamun and his bride Ankhsenpaaten ascend the throne, as child rulers, they are forced to return to Thebes, where in their youth and inexperience they are unable to withstand the power of the high priest Ay. When Tutankhamun dies, presumably poisoned, his queen is spirited out of the palace (to save her from marriage to the aged Ay) and hidden on a river boat. From there she disappears into the safety of anonymity—truly the lost queen of whom history has no trace.

One of the appeals of the el-Amarna period is the beauty and naturalness of its art. The murals, furniture, and jewelry that were actually found in the tomb appear in the story as the work of the character Kenofer, a young artist who works with his goldsmith brother. The famous throne, the shrine in which the coffins rested, and Tutankhamun's funerary mask are among the famous treasures that appear in this fascinating story. In the end, it is Kenofer, whose love for the young royal couple shines through the beauty his hands created for the delight of the queen, who provides the way of escape to a new life. This is a book rich in historical reconstruction, dramatic incident, and characterization. Mature readers who are able to manage its length and complexity will be rewarded with an unforgettable story.

The Golden Goblet (I-A), by Eloise Jarvis McGraw, is set in the city of Thebes during the reign just prior to that of Akhenaten, and tells of Ranofer, an orphaned artisan whose dream is to become a goldsmith. Forced by his cruel half brother, Gebu, to serve as an apprentice in the stone-cutting shop, Ranofer stumbles upon evidence that Gebu and his sinister comrades may be tomb robbers. In an exciting climax, Ranofer shadows the robbers to the Valley of the Kings, where the tombs of dead pharaohs are cut into the stone of the cliffs, and follows them into the terrifying blackness of a royal tomb. His discovery of the thieves frees him from his brother's power so that he can give his life a new shape and fulfill his dream of becoming an apprentice to a master goldsmith.

Mara, Daughter of the Nile (A), also by Eloise Jarvis McGraw, is a longer, more difficult novel with a somewhat melodramatic sweep and the excitement of a romance in which a slave girl is instrumental in protecting a pharaoh and winning the love of a lord. Egypt fans will like it.

Children who discover the mysteries of ancient Egypt through books will find labyrinths to probe and set their minds imagining. Many fine books tell them what the great Sphinx might say if only it would speak.

Studying prehistoric and ancient civilizations through literature about archaeology can breathe life into a distant past and provide a bridge to the present. In his *Gods, Graves, and Scholars* (A), C. W. Ceram evokes the sense of excitement and mystery that impels some archaeologists to dig into the past. Historians had paid little attention to the epic poems of the Iliad and the Odyssey except as records of early Greek society and religion when a German businessman, Heinrich Schliemann, following his hunch that the siege of Troy described by Homer had been an actual event, began excavating a mound near the Dardanelles in 1870. There he uncovered layer upon layer of settlements, one of which was a fortified city that had

Activity: Teacher to Student

READING THE PAST (I-A) Research the subject of archaeology in the library. Books about the earliest discoveries might include Hans Baumann's *The Caves of the Great Hunters* (Pantheon, 1962) and *In the Land of Ur: The Discovery of Ancient Mesopotamia* (Pantheon, 1969), or Leonard Cottrell's *Reading the Past* (Macmillan, 1971). The books tell about discoveries that have given us information about a previously unknown past. Major strides in learning about ancient civilizations such as the Mesopotamian were made by deciphering their writing systems. Report your findings on this and other aspects of archaeological discoveries.

been destroyed around 1200 B.C. Ceram graphically describes the process:

The hill was like a tremendous onion, which he proceeded to dismember layer by layer. Each layer seemed to have been inhabited at a different period. Populations had lived and died, cities had been built up only to fall into decay. Sword and fires had raged, one civilization cutting off another, and again and again a city of the living had been raised on a city of the dead. . . . The question now arose which of these nine cities was the Troy of Homer, of the heroes and the epic war. . . . Schliemann dug and searched. In the second and third levels from the bottom he found traces of fire, the remains of massive walls, and the ruins of a gigantic gate. He was sure that these walls had once enclosed the palace of Priam. . . .[4]

Schliemann then went to Mycenae, in southern Greece, to locate the legendary home of the Greek leader Agamemnon. From there he went on to discover other civilizations, which dated back as far as 1800 B.C. This man, who saw more than an interesting story in Homer's epic poems, led the way to untold discoveries that enlighten our thinking. His deeds make explicit the fact that literature and archaeology can work together to help us uncover the past.

THE MIDDLE AGES

The dissolution of the Roman Empire signaled the beginning of that part of the medieval period sometimes referred to as the Dark Ages. There is little recorded history of these times, which were marked primarily by the battles of the "barbarian" tribes that swept across Europe. Shadowy figures have life breathed into them in novels set in this period—novels that blend fact and legend, as here:

On a summer night in the year 408 a flaming red comet appeared over Europe striking terror into the hearts of all who saw it; a menacing omen, a flaming red comet shaped like a tremendous eagle with a sword in its talons.

In that year, when the walls of Rome were cracking before the onslaught of the Goths led by King Alaric; when the Vandals were invading Hispania led by King Gunderic; when Roman Britain was fighting a losing war against the terrible barbarian pirates, the Saxons—on a summer night of that year was Attilla born.[5]

These words occur near the closing of the stirring saga *The White Stag* (I), by Kate Seredy, a haunting retelling of the legend of the founding of the Hungarian nation, unique in literature for children. It opens in an uncharted land of the East, filled with echoes of the Biblical stories of the beginning of human history. Legend touches history as the bloody armies of Attila the Hun push back the borders of the Roman Empire. One group of the many comprising the great Hun migrations has been seeking a "promised land." When the group's wanderings lead it to the sheer, seemingly impassable walls of the Carpathian Mountains, the White Stag of Hungarian mythology appears in a wintry storm and leads it through a mountain pass into the land promised to the fathers.

Kate Seredy grew up in Hungary before World War I and came to the United States after the war to continue her career as an artist and illustrator. Her drawings of both children and animals in all of her stories are filled with vitality and a strong sense of movement, but the illustrations for *The White Stag* have even greater strength and sweep than those of any of her other books; they are entirely in keeping with the poetic majesty of the tale. Reading this story aloud makes manifest the poetic beauty of its language.

The symbol of civilization as a light quenched by barbarian forces is a motif woven through Rosemary Sutcliff's *The Lantern Bearers* (A). The story opens with the youthful hero, Aquila, watching the last of the Roman legions leave Britain, sailing out from Rutupiae Light. Aquila lights the signal fire in the lighthouse for the last time as a farewell gesture. Events move with dramatic swiftness as Saxon marauders burn his home, kill his father, capture his sister, and carry him off. Aquila escapes to the camp of the youthful Ambrosius, leader of the British tribes, who holds to the ways of Rome. Many historical figures—Vortigern, Hengest and Horsa, Ambrosius—move through the pages of this novel. Aquila gradually overcomes his hatred of the Saxons and achieves a measure of contentment building a new life for himself. An intriguing element is introduced as the story draws to a climax with the introduction of a new war lord, the youthful Artorius—whom his men call Artos the Bear and whom later legends would call King Arthur.

The Artos of these pages, though not the Arthur of legend but a historical figure reflective of the times, is nonetheless much like the Arthur about whom legends would arise. It was said that Artos, base-born nephew and ward of Ambrosius, would never become high king. Instead, Artos achieved fame as a war lord, a cavalry commander of brilliance and courage who held back the Saxon hordes. Artos is described as tall, with mouse-fair hair, a somewhat ingenuous young man who would rather relax among his comrades in arms after battle than retire to his own quarters in lonely dignity, a man to whom people would always matter too much. After the coronation feast for Ambrosius, Aquila, in discussion with Eugenus concerning whether future generations will remember their deeds of valor, says:

> "I wonder if they will remember us at all, those people on the other side of the darkness."
> Eugenus was looking back towards the main colonnade, where a knot of young warriors . . . had parted a little, and the light of a nearby lantern fell full on the mouse-fair head of the tall man who stood in their midst, flushed and laughing, with a great hound against his knee.
> "You and I and all our kind they will forget utterly, though they live and die in our debt," he [Eugenus] said. "Ambrosius they will remember a little; but *he* [Artos] is the kind that men make songs about to sing for a thousand years."[6]

This thread of Artos's story is picked up again by Rosemary Sutcliff and woven into an outstanding historical novel for adults, *The Sword at Sunset*.

The search for the "real" Arthur is the subject of a number of recent books. In *King Arthur in Fact and Legend* (A), Geoffrey Ashe discusses the excavation of several possible Arthurian sites. Chief among these are Cadbury Castle, a hill fortification that may have been the site of Camelot, and Glastonbury Abbey, where Arthur was thought to have

been buried. The hill fort near Glastonbury looks out over a marshy area, in the midst of which the legendary island of Avalon was said to have risen. Excavations on the hill show remnants of a small Dark Ages stronghold, where someone lived in much the same style as the Welsh chieftains. Equally ancient sites excavated in Wales are associated with a war lord, much like the Arthur of legend. Historical documents also describe the excavation of a tomb (by the monks of Glastonbury in 1190) thought to contain the remains of Arthur and Guinevere.

Macaulay's detailed drawings and clear text provide explicit information on the building of a medieval castle. (From *Castle* by David Macaulay, published by Houghton Mifflin Company. Copyright © 1977 by David Macaulay. Reprinted by permission.)

MIDDLE AGES (I-A)   After reading many books on the subject, show what you learned about the Middle Ages by doing one of the following projects.

Heraldry   Make a banner, shield, or coat of arms using paper, fabric, or wood. Find illustrative designs in reference books and use them as models to create your own distinguishing marks of honor.

Castles   Build a replica of a medieval castle or cathedral from balsa wood, sugar cubes, or blocks. Use David Macaulay's *Castle* (Houghton Mifflin, 1977) and *Cathedral: The Story of Its Construction* (Houghton Mifflin, 1973) for models and detailed designs.

Clothing and Customs   Make clothing for dolls or miniature figures in the fashions of medieval times. Use Joe Lasker's *Merry Ever After* (Viking, 1976) for ideas about the dress of nobility and serfs. Re-enact a wedding celebration such as Lasker describes. Design clothing for knights and their ladies, serfs, and noblemen to show how one's position determined dress.

Stained Glass   Make small replicas of stained-glass windows and decorative panels from cellophane or plastic.

Scrolls   Make a scroll or proclamation using Old English lettering.

Chess   Out of clay, pâpier-maché, or wood, make a chess board and its pieces, which are like a feudal population—king, queen, knights, pawns (serfs), etc. Research the origin of the game of chess. Have a chess tournament in your classroom.

DISTINGUISH HISTORY AND LEGEND (I-A)   Select one of the many stories about the Middle Ages and do research using fiction and nonfiction to separate history from legend.

Read Marguerite de Angeli's *The Door in the Wall* (Doubleday, 1949); Elizabeth J. Gray's *Adam of the Road* (Viking, 1942); Rosemary Sutcliff's *Knight's Fee* (Walck, 1960); or another book set in medieval times. Compare events and characters with corresponding ones in history textbooks and reference books. Read *The Sword of King Arthur,* by Jay Williams (Crowell, 1966), Clyde Robert Bulla's *The Sword in the Tree* (Crowell, 1956), *The Story of King Arthur and His Knights,* by Howard Pyle (Scribner's, 1954), and other books about King Arthur and compare the different authors' visions of him.

Research (and report on) a topic, such as barbarians, serfs, knights, ladies of the court, Crusades, guilds, or apprentices. Find out about customs and dramatize a scene of everyday life that might have occurred in medieval times.

Read the play "Camelot," by Alan Jay Lerner and Federick Lowe, and listen to the recording of that Broadway musical. Use the musical background for special effects while you enact the play in readers' theater style—each actor reading aloud one character's part from a script.

EXPLORATIONS

Whether in real life or in books, explorations of the unknown, where the explorers find danger and mystery, mesmerize. Accounts of the navigators of the earlier world are as intriguing to today's children as travels to the moon or to Mars. Explorers of the past and those of the present need the same kind of courage and willingness to face the unknown.

Although there are innumerable books from which to choose, we focus on an adventurous people, the Vikings, and a courageous man, Christopher Columbus, as representative of the exploring spirit of the many others.

Vikings

The cadences of an ancient saga permeate Erik Haugaard's novel *Hakon of Rogen's Saga* (I) and its sequel *A Slave's Tale* (I). In the first person, Hakon tells of his exile and his struggle to regain the birthright stolen by a cruel uncle. Helga, a slave girl, continues the story of the harsh but heroic Viking people from *her* point of view in *A Slave's Tale*. Themes of slavery of the mind and slavery of power are interwoven in both stories. Haugaard states that he has not blunted his pen in writing for young people and asks to be judged by adult standards; even when judged by the highest standards, he succeeds. Readers savor the metaphorical language: disasters lurk behind each day, pride makes a poor shield. Images of the Vikings crystallize in such prose.

Tales of the Vikings often tell about coastal raids to conquer new lands as well as the never-ending struggle for power among themselves. Leif Erickson's life, representative of the Viking explorer, is the basis of Ingri and Edgar Parin d'Aulaire's picture biography *Leif the Lucky* (P-I). The d'Aulaire's excellent stone lithography illustrations convey the strength and valor of a man who roamed the seas hundreds of years ago.

In Clyde Robert Bulla's *Viking Adventure* (P-I), a follow-up of Leif Erickson's exploration to Vineland is described as it might have occurred. Sigurd, a young Norwegian boy, hears from his father stories of the distant Vineland discovered by Leif and to which his father dreams of returning. Sigurd fulfills his father's dream by making the journey —one in which human treacheries prove to be as great as those from the uncharted seas. Adroitly, Bulla establishes strong characterization to build high tension in the plot. (One third-grade class, after reading the story, became enamored of Viking lore and produced several projects, including a journal of Sigurd's journey, a model of his ship, and a map of the route taken.)

Scandinavian folklore, especially the sagas, provides additional insights concerning the Viking age and, combined with other sources, supplements and modifies interpretations made by archaeologists and historians. In *The Vinlanders' Saga* (I), Barbara Schiller rewrites a saga dealing with the discovery and exploration of North America five hundred years before Christopher Columbus. She cautions that, though the facts of history in the saga may not be accurate, the humanity of history can be heard in the voices of the Vikings and seen through their eyes. That Scandinavian folklore embodied much authentic history is borne out by the records kept by Icelandic scribes, which verifies the idea that much history (perhaps disguised and transformed) is reflected in the literature of a culture.

Columbus and After

During the years 1415 to 1550, explorations of the world were in full swing, with the Portuguese, Spanish, and English dominating the seas. In many schools, that Christopher Columbus discovered America in 1492 is parroted as fact. Such a closed-minded approach to history is untenable; recent books keep the question open. Frances FitzGerald, in *American History Revisited* (adult), comments on some of the changes in viewpoint:

Poor Columbus! He is a minor character now, a walk-on in the middle of American History. Even those books that have not replaced his picture with a Mayan temple or an Iroquois mask do not credit him with discovering America—even for the Europeans. The Vikings, they say, preceded him to the New World, and after that the

NORSE MYTHS (I)   The Norse myths, a part of the Viking culture, provided models of strength and power for their hearers, just as the sagas of valorous deeds also inspired some to strike out for far-off lands. The stories about the powerful gods and men of the Vikings, as told in the Norse myths and sagas, are subtle integrations of literature and history.

Reading Ingri and Edgar Parin d'Aulaire's *Norse Gods and Giants* is a good way to begin a study of Norse mythology as a part of a study of the Vikings. As you read the myths, examine the illustrations and the endpapers, which illustrate the nine Norse worlds.

Identify the major Norse gods and tell which domains they ruled. In what ways are Greek gods similar or different? Identify story threads, and the ideas of a cycle of life and death and of the relatedness of fertility and seasons, which appear in both Greek and Norse myths.

Most of the names of the days of the week derive from Norse gods—Tuesday is named for Tiu; Wednesday, Odin; Thursday, Thor; and Friday, Freya. Research the stories of these gods and their characteristics. Find other allusions in our language to the Norse myths.

Dramatize and read in chorus a Viking saga. What events do the sagas tell about that were later verified by archaeological findings?

Use these sources in investigating Norse myths:

Baldur and the Mistletoe: A Myth of the Vikings by Margaret Hodges. Little, Brown, 1974.
The Hammer of Thunder by Ann Pyk. Putnam's, 1972.
In the Morning of Time: The Story of the Norse God Baldur by Cynthia King. Four Winds-Scholastic, 1970.
Norse Gods and Giants by Ingri and Edgar Parin d'Aulaire. Doubleday, 1967.

Europeans, having lost or forgotten their maps, simply neglected to cross the ocean again for five hundred years.[7]

Despite revisions of long-held beliefs, there are some books that treat Columbus's voyages in time-honored fashion. For example, Ronald Syme's comprehensive *Columbus: Finder of the New World* (I) chronicles the mutiny, starvation, and exhaustion plaguing Columbus's voyages. Shortly after returning from his fourth voyage, Columbus died, but left long instructions, maps, and charts of the seas for others to use. Themes of courage and sacrifice permeate this adulatory biography.

Robert Meredith and E. Brooks Smith edited original source material for *The Quest of Columbus* (I) and based their biography on Columbus's son's detailed journals. The tone is understandably laudatory. *The High Voyage* (I), by Olga Litowinsky, recounts the fourth and final voyage to the New World; it, too, is based on the biography by Columbus's son, Fernando.

Other informational books present a more tentative view of Columbus's role in the discovery of

America. Patricia Lauber, in *Who Discovered America?* (I), states that hunters from northeastern Siberia discovered it 25,000 years ago and what has followed has simply been a matter of continuous rediscovery. Lauber describes the way archaeologists, historians, and anthropologists have been working for years to answer a supposedly grade-school question.

Johanna Johnston, in *Who Found America?* (P-I), cites many who can conceivably be called discoverers of America: the Asians, Norsemen, Africans, Native Americans, and Pilgrims, as well as Columbus, Ponce de Leon, Amerigo Vespucci, and Leif Erickson. Johnson superimposes old maps upon present-day ones to emphasize how little of the world was known in 1490.

Ellen Pugh, in *Brave His Soul* (I-A), presents the theory that a Welsh prince, Madog, came to North America in 1170, nearly three hundred years before Columbus. She also discusses evidence that the Mandan Indians were possibly the first discoverers of America. Books such as this, which present conflicting reports, get children to question and not accept uncritically everything they find in

Teaching Idea

EVALUATING FACTS IN HISTORICAL FICTION (P-I)   Any report or account, and certainly those constituting historical fiction or historical biography, is of necessity an interpretation. Children need to learn that what they read in historical books is only one person's view of what happened rather than an incontrovertible account. One way to make this evident is to compare books that present divergent views of the same person or event.

Activity: Teacher to Student

COMPARE FACTS IN FICTION (P-I)   Read several books about Christopher Columbus and the discovery of America: *Columbus,* by Ingri and Edgar Parin d'Aulaire (Doubleday, 1955); *The Columbus Story,* by Alice Dalgleish, illustrated by Leo Politi, (Scribner's, 1955); *Who Found America?* by Johanna Johnston, illustrated by Anne Siberell (Golden Gate-Childrens Press, 1973); and *Following Columbus: The Voyage of the Nina II,* by Robert F. Marx (World, 1964).

Discuss the following:

How does each author describe the discovery of America?
What points differ in the presentations?
What documentation does each author provide?
What would you tell a younger child who asked you who discovered America?

Role-play a discussion between two people in which one person is convinced that Columbus *did* discover America and the other person is convinced that he *did not*.

On the cover of *Who Discovered America?* Leif Erickson and an unknown Native American, together with Christopher Columbus, reflect the book's refutation of the latter's candidacy for the honor.
(Cover illustration from *Who Discovered America* by Patricia Lauber. Copyright © 1970. Reprinted with permission of Random House, Inc.)

books. Authors recognize that they can give children their perceptions of the truth without closing the doors of their minds to alternate explanations.

THE NEW WORLD

Immigrants—in our terms, anyone with a role in the evolution of the nation—were coming to America long before 1620, some escaping religious persecution, some seeking adventure and financial gain, and some seeking political freedom. The greatest number to settle were Puritans, who chose to start a new society based on their own religious convictions rather than remain under a repressive English church. Economic and social conditions in England also made the New World attractive to people who were willing to sacrifice the known for the possibilities of a promising unknown.

The First Colonies

One period that has intrigued many centers around the lost colony of Roanoke. John White, leader of the colony, had returned to England for supplies while the rest—men, women, and children—stayed on in Roanoke, building the settlement. White, delayed because all English ships were in use against the Spanish Armada, finally returned to find that the colony had disappeared; no trace of its people was ever found. Recently, archaeologists uncovered groundworks they believe could have been built by the lost colonists. Sonia Levitin, in *Roanoke* (I-A), embroiders the historical record with her imaginative story of one of the young men who stayed to build the community. Dan Lacy uses a similar tack in his nonfiction book *The Lost Colony* (I). Both authors employ creative imagination based on historical knowledge to fill in what might have happened at Roanoke.

Jean Lee Latham's *This Dear-Bought Land* (I-A) conveys some of the hardship and personal sacrifice of establishing a colony in America. The story begins in England in 1606 and describes young David Warren's attempts to sail with Captain John Smith. David, fifteen and small for his age, wants to carry on his family's tradition as a blustering sea dog, but Smith disparagingly decrees that the difficult journey is not for women or children.

Elizabeth Campbell chronicles the story of Jamestown in *Jamestown: The Beginning* (I). Written from the points of view of the settlers, the ship's crew, the American Indians, and the captain of the expedition, the author, using documented sources, conveys the suspense of the journey and the joy and thankfulness at the long-awaited sighting of land.

Activities: Teacher to Student

ROANOKE AND JAMESTOWN (I-A) Dramatize the scene between David Warren and John Smith—two of the characters of Jean Lee Latham's *This Dear-Bought Land* (Harper & Row, 1957)—in which David pleads with Captain Smith to allow him to go with him to America. Shift the scene to three years later, when David, who has decided to stay in Jamestown rather than return to England, says goodbye to Captain Smith, who, wounded, is returning to England.

Also, research information about Roanoke and Jamestown, and find out what roles were played by John White, Virginia Dare, John Smith, John Rolfe, and Pocohantas.

Write your version of what may have happened to the lost colony at Roanoke.

SETTLERS AT PLYMOUTH ROCK (I) After reading several accounts of the journey aboard the Mayflower, prepare the first edition of the *Plymouth News* to be sent back to England. Include the birth announcement of Oceanus (the child born during the voyage), death notices, advertisements recruiting new settlers, a report of the voyage and progress at the settlement, and social news.

Using Jean Fritz's *Who's That Stepping on Plymouth Rock?* (Coward, McCann & Geoghegan, 1975) as source material, deliver a speech in which you are Plymouth Rock and are speaking to tourists who have come to see you. Tell them what has happened to you over the years. You may feel like complaining a little or expressing your pride in being so famous.

Write entries for Constance's diary, as in *Constance,* by Patricia Clapp (Lothrop, Lee & Shepard, 1968). The entries can be for the period preceding her trip to America, when she has been informed by her father that she must go, even though she does not want to leave England. How does she feel about not having a choice? What nightmares has she about the New World?

Pilgrims at Plymouth

Patricia Clapp uses a diary form to tell the story of the early settlers through the eyes of a young girl in *Constance: A Story of Early Plymouth* (I-A). Constance, the daughter of Stephen Hopkins, is not as enthusiastic as her father about the promise of the new land. Through the personal references in Constance's diary, readers come to know the sprightly people in the settlement. Constance, an opinionated girl, expresses her distaste for certain people freely. Her insights breathe life into the people who appear in her diary, which continues until 1626. In Margaret Hodges's book about Constance's father, *Hopkins of the Mayflower: Portrait of a Dissenter* (I-A), the character of Hopkins is a composite of Elizabethan men who sought profit and adventure in the New World. Because the last sections of this book overlap the years described in *Constance,* they can serve for interesting comparisons.

Jean Fritz takes an unusual approach in *Who's That Stepping on Plymouth Rock?* (P-I), which is, in effect, a biography of the rock. She tells of the number of times Plymouth Rock has been moved, and the discussions that have arisen about its prominence in history; she adds a touch of humor to a subject that has long been treated with reverence.

The First Thanksgiving

The Thanksgiving story, told in so many different ways, is excellent fare for critical reading. Though young children delight in reciting the "facts"—the proceedings, the menu, the guest list of the first Thanksgiving—older children want to know if all this really happened the way they were taught it did.

There are several books that question the traditional image of the first Thanksgiving. Lee Wyndham, in *A Holiday Book: Thanksgiving* (I), states that there was no Thanksgiving festival in Plymouth in 1621 because the harvest was so meager there was nothing left for a feast. Virginia Voight's biography, *Massasoit: Friend of the Pilgrims* (P-I), states that the idea of a thanksgiving feast was not new to the Native Americans. According to her version, Massasoit offers to help his English brothers give thanks in the white men's way. Edna Barth, in *Turkeys, Pilgrims and Indian Corn: The Story of the Thanksgiving Symbols* (P-I), traces the origin of thanksgiving festivals to harvest festivals and states that the feast held in 1621 was not the first celebration of its kind on American soil.

Critical reading—comparing information from many sources, checking documentation, identifying discrepancies, and listing possible conclusions—is worthwhile for all readers, and especially suitable in the case of subjects and treatments such as those discussed above.

Witchcraft at Salem

In Salem Village in 1692, several young girls, bored by their rigid Puritanical life, were titillated by colorful tales recounted by a Barbadian slave. These tales, though they may have started as innocent storytelling, ended ultimately in the death of the twenty people convicted in the famous Salem witch trials.

Activities: Teacher to Student

FACT OR FICTION (P-I)   List all of the facts you know about the first Thanksgiving, and note where you got this information. Research many sources to see how the occasion is reported. Do they all tell the story in the same way? What differences are there? How can you find out which books give the information that is closest to the truth? Look at the qualifications of the author; what resources has the author used? After you've read from many different sources, decide which version you believe. Write your own account of the first Thanksgiving.

WITCH HUNTS (A)   The witchcraft trials in Salem Village in 1692 are reported in fiction and nonfiction. Compare the books and identify points on which they differ.

You may want to draw some tentative conclusions about the causes and outcomes of the witchcraft trials. Also, describe the commonly held view of witches, and look for modern cases that resemble witchcraft trials. What has the phrase "witch hunting" come to mean in our language?

You might also discuss the events of 1692 from the perspectives of people involved: Tituba, Reverend Parris, Cotton Mather. Dramatize one of the trials in which the young girls accuse Tituba of witchery.

346

That calamity still holds political, literary, social, and historical interest, and there are several books that add to an understanding of it. In Elizabeth Speare's *The Witch of Blackbird Pond* (I-A), Kit befriends an old woman living outside the village and discovers the principle of guilt by association when she is accused, together with the old woman, of being a witch. Leonard Everett Fisher's *The Warlock of Westfall* (I-A) adds another perspective on the witchcraft hysteria that swept Massachusetts in 1692. In the story, Samuel Swift, a lonely, eccentric bachelor in his late seventies, is accused, tried, and hanged; Westfall was close enough to Salem Village to be infected by its hysteria. Ann Petry, in *Tituba of Salem Village* (I-A), relates the dramatic Salem story from the point of view of Tituba, a slave woman accused of witchcraft because of her innocent storytelling.

Marion Starkey's books, *The Devil in Massachusetts* (A), *The Visionary Girls* (A), and *The Tall Man from Boston* (A), are based on careful research of the historical record and show meticulous attention to detail. The third of these books focuses on an incident in which Tituba charges a "tall man from Boston" with devil dealing. The terrified villagers need someone to fit Tituba's hysterical description and fall upon John Alden, son of Myles Standish's famous friend.

THE REVOLUTIONARY WAR PERIOD

Neither the beginning nor the end of the American Revolution is clearly marked in time nor is the story clearly told. Some colonists resented paying taxes to England when they were not represented in the English Parliament. Many, however, remained loyal to King George III and fully disapproved of the rebellious leaders who agitated for the independence of the colonies.

Fiction set in this period frequently involves divided loyalties in colonial families or communities. Authors often tell the story through the eyes of a child or an adolescent character who supports the rebels, but whose parents remain loyal to Britain.

The bitter ending of a tale of divided loyalties is revealed in the title of this book about the American Revolution. (Cover illustration from *My Brother Sam Is Dead* by Karl W. Stuecklen. Written by James Lincoln Collier and Christopher Collier. Illustration copyright © by Scholastic, Inc. Reproduced by permission of Four Winds Press, a division of Scholastic, Inc.)

James Lincoln Collier and Christopher Collier tell of one family caught in conflicting loyalties in *My Brother Sam Is Dead* (I-A). The father, a Connecticut tavern-keeper, thinks the colonists have a few legitimate complaints against England but nothing serious enough to cause bloodshed. Twelve-year-old Tim idolizes brother Sam who reports in detail on his debates when he comes home from college. Tim begs for Sam's stories, savoring the clever "telling points" Sam makes against his opponents. Conflict begins when Sam arrives home wearing a rebel uniform, and it increases in intensity as the family becomes enmeshed in the struggle between loyalists and rebels. Sam is accused of stealing cattle, and an ironic turn of events leads to the bitter outcome foretold in the title.

Early Thunder (I), by Jean Fritz, is the story of fourteen-year-old Daniel, who shares his father's loyalist viewpoint at first, but gradually moves toward sympathy with the Rebels. His change in allegiance leads to another family confrontation.

Such stories, by presenting political issues of the Revolution in terms of family and personal conflicts, engage the reader's emotions. Identifying with the fictional characters helps give concreteness to historical figures and to the choices that had to be made.

Robert Newton Peck's stories, set near Fort Ticonderoga, are about Ethan Allen and the Green Mountain Boys. *Hang for Treason* (A), set in 1745, depicts in earthy language some of the conflict and unrest that led to the Revolutionary War. In *Rabbits and Redcoats* (A), Peck shows romantic notions of war evaporating in the midst of battle. Two teen-aged boys who have sneaked into the ranks of the Vermont revolutionaries so they can brag that they fought with Ethan, learn that battles are not glamorous, that honor and dignity depend upon more than fighting.

A briefer book dealing with the Revolutionary period is Patricia Gauch's *This Time, Tempe Wick?* (P-I), which gives a humorous account of American soldiers encamped in New Jersey who confiscate food and horses from farmers. When Tempe Wick learns that her horse Bonny may be one of them, she hides it in her bedroom. The author's note adds authenticity to the story, for there *was* a Bonny, and her hoofprints remain on the bedroom floor to this day. Tempe's creative resolution of the problem adds a spark of life to history.

Revolutionary Leaders

Biographies about the people involved in the American Revolution give a serious view of their beliefs, sometimes a humorous glimpse of their foibles, and, ideally, a feeling that they were real people with blood in their veins. Jean Fritz decries the way we turn people from our past into stone statues to revere. She prefers to enter their world, match their words to their actions, follow the crisscross of their public and private lives, and accept them finally as friends. Jean Fritz feels that a picture that shows a believable human being is preferable to one that idealizes the subject as a saint.[8]

Samuel Adams failed at nearly everything he tried, except being a politician; in this role, he excelled. He was elected to a number of minor offices in Boston and to the Boston Assembly in 1765. Words were his best weapon: he wrote under at least twenty-five different pen names to spread his ideas, and stormed around Boston talking to everyone about the injustice of English treatment of the colonists. Fayette Richardson writes about Adams's early life in *Sam Adams: The Boy Who Became Father of the American Revolution* (P-I), and Margaret Green provides another view in *Radical of the Revolution: Samuel Adams* (I-A).

Benjamin Franklin, with his continuing leadership role in the establishment of the new nation, is a favorite subject for biographers. Jeannette Eaton, in *That Lively Man, Ben Franklin* (I), describes his life from an apprenticeship to a printer through political engagements and involvement with the drafting of the Declaration of Independence. James Daugherty writes about a similar period in *Poor Richard* (I), but also includes Franklin's experiences in London and his role as an inventor, scientist, and patriot.

Jean Fritz contends that humor is one of the most effective keys to appreciating the past and to seeing historical figures as fully human. Instead of stale facts about leaders of the American Revolution, she presents affectionate and well-informed biographical narratives. Each of her titles is a question: *Why Don't You Get a Horse, Sam Adams?, What's the Big Idea, Ben Franklin?, And Then What Happened, Paul Revere?, Where Was Patrick Henry on the 29th of May?, Will You Sign Here, John Hancock?,* and *Can't You Make Them Behave, King George?* (all P-I). Their brevity, humanizing personal insights, and humorous illustrations make these biographical narratives favorites; share

Activities: Teacher to Student

LITERARY ANALYSIS (I-A)   After you finish reading *My Brother Sam Is Dead,* by James L. and Christopher Collier (Four Winds-Scholastic, 1974), use the following questions to rethink and discuss some of the important parts:

1. What did the title suggest before you read the story? What does it reveal about who is telling the story? Where in the story do you begin to realize the full significance of the title?

2. What clues do you find in the first four pages of historic events that set the scene for the story? For example, "went on up to Concord" (p. 2); "the Minute Men hid in the fields" (p. 2); "somebody signalled them from some church steeple in Boston" (p. 4).

3. When do you discover there is family conflict? For example, Sam's father corrects him when he speaks of "lobster backs" (p. 4); and his father's comments: "I will not have treason spoken in my house," and "Nobody wants rebellion except fools and hotheads" (p. 6).

4. How does the conflict become a central theme in the story? How is the conflict affecting Tim when he says: "It made me nervous to listen to Sam argue with Father" (p. 7); and "It seemed to me that everybody was to blame, and I decided that I wasn't going to be on anybody's side any more: neither one of them was right" (p. 167)?

5. Compare this book with Esther Forbes's *Johnny Tremain* (Houghton Mifflin, 1946).

DISPEL THE MYTHS (I-A)   Read several different accounts of a historical legend to discover any differences. Identify statements based on opinion. Look carefully for documentation and for statements that seem direct and factual but are not.

Check for authenticity of an account by asking yourself the following questions:

1. How did the story first get started; when and where was it first told?

2. What documentation or sources does the author provide?

3. What do you think happened? What evidence supports your position?

4. Do any words make it seem that the author is not certain about the truthfulness of the story? For example, are phrases such as "some people say," "there is a story that" used?

5. Does the author make up dialogue for imagined meetings between historical figures? (There may be justification for created dialogue; discuss possible reasons.)

The following reference books can be useful in tracing some of the stories:

Celebrations: The Complete Book of American Holidays by Robert Myers and the editors of Hallmark Cards. Doubleday, 1972.

Dictionary of Misinformation by Tom Burnham. Crowell, 1975.

Forty Million School Books Can't Be Wrong: Myths in American History by L. Ethan Ellis. Macmillan, 1975.

them among a group—with readers assigned one book, describing and explaining it to the others, or presenting their subject in creative impersonation. In *Why Don't You Get a Horse, Sam Adams?* (P-I), Fritz pokes fun at Adams's refusal to ride a horse. Adams finally relents, however, so that his historical image remains untarnished and he appears in sculptured representations, not on foot, but mounted like his contemporaries. Listen to Jean Fritz reading the stories on cassette tapes (Weston Woods) to lure students by her enthusiasm for her subject.

Deborah Sampson, using the name Robert Shurtliff, served for a year and a half as a soldier in the Continental Army. Her masquerade went undiscovered until she was hospitalized for a fever. Patricia Clapp wrote *I'm Deborah Sampson: A Soldier in the War of the Revolution* (I-A) in a lively first-person account of the contribution of this woman. Ann McGovern tells the same story in *The*

Secret Soldier: The Story of Deborah Sampson (I). After Deborah Sampson's identity was disclosed, she left the Continental Army but continued to defy convention by traveling and lecturing—unbecoming behavior for a woman of her day. Her story is also told in Cora Cheney's *The Incredible Deborah* (I). Comparing these different approaches to Deborah Sampson's story can provide an excellent experience in critical reading.

Legends of the Revolution

Legends from the American Revolutionary period are abundant; the national pride and desire to create a legacy gave rise to stories that were quickly embellished. Many of the legends are distortions and exaggerations of actual events. Tracing the origins of the stories, separating fact and fiction, adds adventure and mystery to the study of history.

Fiction says that Betsy Ross made the first flag; fact says that nobody knows who made it. Accord-

Sam Adams envisions how posterity may see him should he fail to learn to ride a horse. (Reprinted by permission of Coward, McCann & Geoghegan, Inc. from *Why Don't You Get a Horse, Sam Adams?* by Jean Fritz. Illustrations copyright © 1974 by Trina Schart Hyman.)

Profile

JEAN FRITZ

Jean Fritz was five years old when she announced to her father that she was going to be a writer; she would write about America. At the time she was living in China, where her parents were missionaries, and spent a good deal of her time defending her country to a neighbor boy who said derogatory things about George Washington.

For her, America represented an ideal—a place where everything was perfect. As an only child she spent a lot of time with books and "learned early that words could get me where I wanted to go, which was simply some place else but most especially America" (Doris De Montreveille and Donna Hill, eds., "Jean Fritz," in *Third Book of Junior Authors* [New York: H. W. Wilson, 1972], p. 95). As soon as she could write she composed stories about children doing all the American things she dreamed of doing—exploding firecrackers on the Fourth of July and going to grandmother's house for Thanksgiving.

After she moved to the United States she continued to pursue her fascination with America. She says that *The Cabin Faced West,* although ostensibly written about her great-great-grandmother's pioneer girlhood, was really her attempt to establish her roots as an American. She has written about other periods in American history, but her favorite is the Revolutionary era.

Jean Fritz bemoans the dull way in which history is usually taught. She believes that stale facts and images should be replaced with studies that show historical characters as real people, and that humorous anecdotes help children relate to history much better than cold dates. Her series of biographies of Revolutionary-era personalities presents fresh insights into the lives of people too often placed on pedestals, beyond understanding and caring.

Jean Fritz lives in Dobbs Ferry, New York, where she takes an active interest in today's national and international concerns. "I join groups, write letters, make phone calls, and have on occasion demonstrated; in short, my life . . . is caught up in the special agonies of the times" (Lee Bennett Hopkins, "Jean Fritz," in *More Books by More People* [New York: Citation Press, 1974], p. 177).

Jean Fritz's deep love for and pride in America enrich yesterday's history, and that of tomorrow.

ing to fiction, George Washington asked Betsy Ross, a seamstress in Philadelphia, to make a flag with thirteen stars and stripes to represent the thirteen colonies. Supposedly, he sketched six-pointed stars, but she suggested five-pointed ones. There is no historical evidence to support the story; Betsy Ross's grandson, William J. Canby, first told it at a meeting of the Philadelphia Historical Society in 1870, almost one hundred years after the supposed event. One of the most comprehensive and carefully documented books on the subject, Thomas Parrish's *The American Flag* (I-A), traces the evolution of the present-day flag from its British origins and totally discounts the Betsy Ross story.

Fiction says that George Washington chopped down a cherry tree when he was six-years-old and, admitting to the offense, said, "I cannot tell a lie." Fact says there is no historical truth to the tale. The story first appeared in a biography of George Washington by Parson Mason Locke Weems who credited George, not with cutting down the tree, but only with cutting through the bark. Biographies of George Washington help to separate the fiction that has been embroidered into the facts. Genevieve Foster's *George Washington's World* (I), and Robin McKown's *Washington's America* (I) are comprehensive biographies that clarify fact and fiction. McKown states that the cherry tree story is the most popular fanciful tale told about Washington, and, true or not, the cherry tree story lives on as a part of American folklore.

Fiction says that Paul Revere took a midnight ride to warn that the British were coming. Fact says that two other men set out with him to warn the colonists and that Paul Revere never reached Concord. Largely because Henry Wadsworth Longfellow's poem does not mention William Dawes or Samuel Prescott, they have been dropped from the historical record of the event.

Jean Poindexter Colby, in *Lexington and Concord, 1775* (I), discusses how the facts about the past can become distorted:

. . . what one writer said might have happened on one day, the next writer said *did* happen on that day. In this way incidents that did not occur became "facts," and people appeared or disappeared on the scene at the will of the historians, essayists, or—in one important instance—a poet. Henry Wadsworth Longfellow, for example, took the events and the characters that appealed to him and made a narrative poem of them. His "Paul Revere's Ride" has been the favorite source of information on the subject for one hundred years even though he omitted such an important man as William Dawes, and had Paul Revere spreading the alarm of the British march in Concord in spite of the fact that he never got there. There are many other historical errors in it but it is still published for children and taken as truth, presumably.[9]

Students need to read Longfellow's poem in conjunction with the many other—and more authentic—reports about the important events of 1775 and 1776.

AMERICAN INDIANS

The history of America is incomplete without chapters on its native inhabitants, American Indians. Often their story was told by white men who characterized them in stereotyped ways—as ferocious savages, or as downtrodden people who suffer nobly. Although many books perpetuate this teepee-and-feathers image, a growing number now give more accurate portrayals of the Native American's culture and a more objective picture of the three-hundred-year clash between the white and American Indian cultures.

Folklore

Anpao: An American Indian Odyssey (I-A), by Jamake Highwater, is one "kind of chronicle of the Indians of America, though it is folk history rather than the presumably objective history of white men."[10] It combines numerous tales passed down through generations, sometimes borrowed by one tribe from another, into a continuous life journey of one hero. The book illustrates a way of knowing history through literature.

When asked to discuss the myths and legends that are its basis, Highwater said: "That is something I would like to discuss but you're using the

Profile

"It is difficult, what you ask of me. But you are good and I have promised to give you what you want." And so, with a motion of his golden fingers, the Sun took the scar from Anpao's face. He was transformed at once. The Sun, the Moon, and Morning Star stared at him in amazement, for he looked exactly like his celestial brother and his great father. He was very handsome and tall and his body was perfectly formed and heavily muscled.

Anpao: An American Indian Odyssey

Thus Anpao recognizes and is recognized by his celestial family in the spellbinding tale-of-tales Jamake Highwater presents. Highwater is special in his ability to share his ancestors' culture, linking Native American and contemporary American experience.

He observes that

Among American Indians the teller of stories is a weaver. His designs are the threads of his personal saga as well as the history of his people. Though the weaver's designs are traditional, the hands which weave them are always new. . . The stories of Anpao's saga belong to everyone, but the words, like the threads of a weaving, are new and belong to me. I created the character of Anpao out of accounts of the boyhood of early Indians and from my own experiences as an Indian youth (Jamake Highwater, *Anpao: An American Indian Odyssey* [New York: Lippincott, 1945], p. 239).

JAMAKE HIGHWATER

The stories that Jamake Highwater weaves continue the river of memory of his people and courageously influence current thinking. His novels and nonfiction are only a part of his contribution to building a heritage for tomorrow, for he also comments on music, dance, and art. Jamake Highwater was born in Montana and lived in Southern California before making New York City his home. He serves as American Indian Consultant to the New York State Council on the Arts and writes articles and critiques for numerous scholarly and popular journals.

wrong words. They are *not* myths and legends, they are an alternate way of viewing reality." He further explains his point in the storyteller's farewell in *Anpao:*

You may have noticed that I am disinclined to refer to "myths" and "legends" when I talk about *Anpao*. This is because these words express the dominant society's disregard for the beliefs of other peoples, just as I would be expressing a nonchalant superiority were I to speak to Christians of their "Jesus myths." *Anpao* is not concerned with myths but with a reality which seems to have escaped the experience of non-Indians.[11]

Jamake Highwater's perspective is undergirded by a Blackfeet/Cherokee heritage and a study of cultural anthropology, comparative literature, and music. The old tales are neither curiosities nor naive fiction; they are alternate visions of the world and reveal an alternate process of history. Indeed, the stories told

. . . exist as the river of memory of a people, surging with their images and their rich meanings from one place to another, from one generation to the next—the tellers and the told so intermingled in time and space that no one can separate them.[12]

Tales, chants, poetry, and song can serve as a bridge to understanding American Indian culture. John Bierhorst, a folklorist, compiled several volumes showing how, in their lore, American Indians pay tribute to the beauty of nature, the power of spirits, and the role of the supernatural. In 1899, Edward Curtis, a photohistorian who realized that the Indian culture might soon disappear, saved the remnants of a vanishing race through photographs and transcriptions. Nine of the tales Curtis preserved appear in *The Girl Who Married a Ghost and Other Tales from the North American Indian* (I-A), edited by John Bierhorst.

We can also learn about American Indian culture from the chants and songs that they believe possess the power to make things happen. For example, their songs describing the beautiful dawn are sung with the aim of making the dawn come again, a song about a horse is both a tribute to it and a means of investing it with the strength about which the song sings.

Ritual occasions—such as daybreak, hunts, festivals, and times of initiation—have their special sounds and rhythms. In *The Trees Stand Shin-ing: Poetry of the North American Indians* (P-I), Hettie Jones selected songs that Robert Andrew Parker illustrated with magnificent full color paintings. In a foreword, Jones explains that the songs show the American Indians' view of their world, their land, and their lives. The song-poems include prayers, stories, lullabies, and war chants.

Conflict of Cultures

Within recent decades we have developed a new consciousness about American Indians and about the differences between their concepts and those of the early settlers. The Native American believed, for example, that the land belonged to all, while the European settlers, of course, brought with them the idea of individual ownership. Staking their claims to lands that the American Indians had roamed freely for hundreds of years set the stage for conflict—from grisly battles, in which hundreds were killed, to inner conflicts in which individuals who had come to know each other as friends had to choose between friendship and loyalty to the violently opposed groups. Several stories, based on true accounts, describe the tur-

Activity: Teacher to Student

ANPAO: AN AMERICAN INDIAN ODYSSEY (A) In order to recapture the spirit of Indian lore, share parts of *Anpao* through dramatic reading or storytelling. Trace variants of the tales in the folklore of other tribes and cultures. For this purpose look at:

The Angry Moon by William Sleator. Illustrated by Blair Lent. Little, Brown, 1970.
The Girl Who Loved Wild Horses by Paul Goble. Bradbury, 1978.

American Indians believe in the wholeness of experience, the interdependence of man and nature, the importance of the quest for love, and the search for one's destiny. During the Westward Expansion, how did the basic beliefs of settlers and natives make conflict inevitable?

Discuss some of the ideas that are uniquely Indian, such as their concepts of time (measured by suns, moons, and seasons) and space, a "contrary" (a person who does and says everything in reverse—as with Oapna in *Anpao*), the river of stars, the relationship with one's horse, the ownership of land, and the meaning of fences.

354 moil of such people, caught between two cultures. In *Betrayed* (A), by Virginia Driving Hawk Sneve, three Sioux Indian boys are beset with a moral dilemma: Should they rescue women and children captives despite the broken promises of the Indian agent? In *Indian Captive: The Story of Mary Jemison* (I-A), by Lois Lenski, a woman tries to escape her Seneca Indian captors but finally chooses to remain with them.

William O. Steele, in *The Man with the Silver Eyes* (I-A), tells of Talatu, an eleven-year-old Cherokee who hates all whites. Sent to live with Benjamin Shinn, a "silver-eyed" Quaker, Talatu grudgingly comes to respect the peace-loving man even as he endures his fate in noble Cherokee tradition. When Shinn is mortally wounded in an attempt to save Talatu's life, the boy learns that Shinn is his natural father.

Evelyn Sibley Lampman conveys a Native American point of view in *Squaw Man's Son* (A), in which Billy Morrison's Modoc Indian mother is sent back to her people by his white father. When his father marries a white woman, who treats Billy

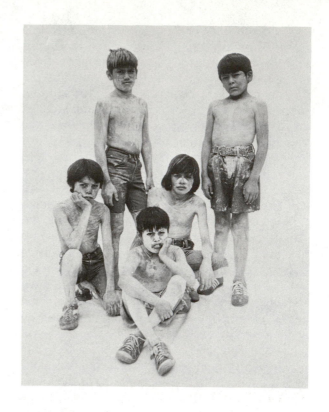

The contemporary Western dress of the Navajo fire dancers in John Running's photograph (top right) is in marked contrast to the traditional style of Edward Curtis's Assiniboin boy (right). (Top right photograph by John Running. Photograph on right by E. S. Curtis of "A Painted Tipi-Assiniboin." © Copyrighted by The University Museum, University of Pennsylvania.)

CLASH OF CULTURES (I-A)[13] People from different cultures perceive the world differently. This was true of Native Americans and of the settlers. Check below which of the following were considered Desirable (D) and which Undesirable (U) by each group.

Native Americans				Early Settlers	
D	U			D	U
___	___	fences		___	___
___	___	fields		___	___
___	___	forests		___	___
___	___	log barns		___	___
___	___	trails		___	___
___	___	men and women equal		___	___
___	___	men working fields		___	___
___	___	sharing land		___	___
___	___	keeping possessions		___	___

What may happen when people disagree about what is desirable and what is undesirable?

Some things to think about after reading *The Light in the Forest,* by Conrad Richter (Knopf, 1953):

1. True Son says, "Nobody can help how he is born" (p. 8). What did he mean? What would you have meant had you said it?

2. At the close of the Vietnam War many Vietnamese children were adopted by families in the United States. What similarities and/or differences do you see between True Son being taken by the Indians, then returned to his natural parents after eleven years, and Vietnamese children being adopted by families with different cultural backgrounds?

INTEGRATING LITERATURE AND THE ARTS (I-A)[14] After you read Scott O'Dell's *Sing Down the Moon* (Houghton Mifflin, 1970), choose from the following activities.

Art Make a large mural showing Canyon de Chelly and the "trail of tears" the Navahos were forced to take to the desolate site of Fort Sumner, or make a diorama of Canyon de Chelly showing the home sites and pastures contrasted with the barren landscape of Fort Sumner.

Written Language Make a crossword puzzle using words from the story: mesa (p. 3), goading (p. 11), hogan (p. 19), hobble (p. 25), haggle (p. 35), omen (p. 37), baile (p. 39), tethered (p. 47), tortillas (p. 57), sheathed (p. 59), mottled (p. 63), pinon (p. 97), pillaged (p. 136).

Drama Dramatize a scene from the novel such as when Tall Boy is taken away to prison, when Bright Morning and Nehana run away, the womanhood ceremony, when the Long Knives come, when the Navahos are forced from the canyon, the Long Walk. Pantomime scenes after listening to a recording of the story.

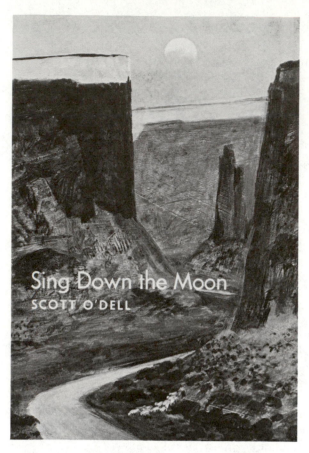

A somber cover reflects the tragic nature of Scott O'Dell's story of the forced resettlement of thousands of Navahos to Fort Sumner, New Mexico.
(From *Sing Down the Moon* by Scott O'Dell, published by Houghton Mifflin Company. Copyright © 1970 by Scott O'Dell. Reprinted by permission.)

he is banished. Values clash for True Son, caught between two cultures. A sequel, *A Country of Strangers* (I-A), tells a comparable story of Stone Girl, who attempts to return to a white community after living with her Indian family.

Some Indian tribes were decimated by the whites' appropriation of their territory. Theodora Kroeber details the disappearance of one such tribe—the Yana Indians—in *Ishi: Last of His Tribe* (A). The author's husband was curator of the Museum of Anthropology and Ethnology at the University of California when Ishi was found wandering near the ruins of his native village. The Kroebers recorded Ishi's memories of the life of his people and pieced together fragments of tribal history. A sequel, *Ishi in Two Worlds* (A), further recounts the history of the Yana and documents in photographs a way of life now extinct. Ishi served as a consultant to the museum staff and added immeasurably to knowledge about the Yana Indians.

Scott O'Dell's *Sing Down the Moon* (I-A) vividly describes the "Long Walk"—an actual event—of the forced resettlement of the Navahos from Canyon de Chelly to Fort Sumner, New Mexico—three hundred miles away. O'Dell relates the story through the eyes of Bright Morning, a courageous Navaho woman who wants to escape the disease, poverty, and spiritlessness of the resettlement and return with her husband to the peace of their home in the canyon.

CIVIL WAR

Slavery was a part of American history until emancipation. Many chapters of American history are grim, but those involving slavery and the Civil War are among the most so; the war was a long, savage contest, costly not the least in human lives. Fiction, biography, nonfiction, and poetry offer students accounts of the turmoil and tragedy of the bloody period and of its reverberations, still felt today.

Slavery

The years immediately before the Civil War, although a bleak period in American history, are marked with acts of heroism. Jean Fritz's *Brady* (I-

with contempt, Billy runs away to live with the Modocs, but finds that they will not accept him. The struggle between the Indians and whites is reflected in conflict both between groups and in the personal life of one boy.

Conrad Richter's *The Light in the Forest* (I-A) is the story of True Son, kidnapped when he is four years old and raised by an Indian chief. When a treaty releases all prisoners, True Son must return to his white home, where he finds the ways of the people intolerable. He returns to his Indian tribe, but, when he refuses to participate in an ambush,

A) tells of a young boy who, because he cannot keep a secret, has not been told by his parents about their activities with the underground railroad. When his father is injured, Brady shows that he can be trusted and carries out the plan for moving a refugee slave to the next haven of safety, courageously driving a wagon, with its hidden human cargo, through a countryside dangerously populated with slave hunters.

As the televised series based on Alex Haley's *Roots* (adult) shows so well, historical biography can personalize the impact of social conditions on individual lives, making facts come alive by focusing on feelings. Elizabeth Yates accomplishes this by tracing the life of an African prince from his capture by slave traders, through his years of bondage, to his death as a free man in *Amos Fortune: Free Man* (I). For Elizabeth Yates, the story began

Teaching Idea

AMOS FORTUNE: FREE MAN (I)   Because of the beauty of the language and the strength of the images it evokes, Elizabeth Yates's *Amos Fortune: Free Man* (I, Dutton, 1967) begs to be read aloud. Use some of the following questions to extend your students' appreciation of Amos Fortune's story.

1. What visual images are suggested by the words used to establish the setting? (For example, "no lingering of daylight," "snuffing out of the sun," "people were gathering for their mystic dance that would welcome in the time of herbage, the time for the planting of corn".)
2. Monadnock means "mountain that stands alone." What significance does the mountain have for Amos Fortune?
3. What does the sentence "He had won his way to equality by work well done and a life well lived" mean to you?
4. What should an obituary about Amos Fortune include?

Activity: Teacher to Student

STUDY THE PAST THROUGH TOMBSTONES (I)   The tombstones in an old cemetery often contain interesting information. Visit a cemetery in your area to see what the tombstones reveal about the past. Are there many deaths in one year, which might indicate a plague or other disaster? Are women buried with infants, suggesting death at childbirth? Do the men tend to have had several wives? Can you tell when there was a war? Did people die young?

Survey the first names that were popular during a period. Look for family names that are still represented in your community. Did any of the people buried here achieve historical significance? Make a rubbing of a symbol or inscription on a tombstone that carries historical significance by placing a sheet of paper on the stone and rubbing the paper lightly with pencil, charcoal, crayon, or chalk.

with two tombstones—those of Amos Fortune and his wife—in the ancient churchyard of her New England village. Although, traditionally, the man's tombstone was higher, Fortune's and his wife's were of the same size. Curiosity about a man who would choose such a striking symbol of equality led her on a search through wills, official documents, indenture papers, and other historical records. She found that Amos Fortune had been sold into slavery in 1725, and worked to buy his freedom, which he achieved, after more than forty years, at the age of sixty. He also bought the freedom of at least four other slaves whose lives touched his own. Readers sense compassion and respect for a man who lived nobly.

Harriet Beecher Stowe's *Uncle Tom's Cabin* (A) was one of the books that aroused abolitionist sentiments—one of the factors that led to the Civil War. The genteel daughter of a New England clergyman, married to a minister, Harriet Beecher Stowe vowed in her anger over the Fugitive Slave Act: "I will write something. I will if I live!" Despite her lack of firsthand knowledge of slavery, she kept her vow, writing a story that influenced thousands. *Uncle Tom's Cabin,* first serialized in an antislavery weekly, sold three hundred thousand copies after it was published in book form in March, 1852.

Woman Against Slavery: The Story of Harriet Beecher Stowe (I), by John Anthony Scott, is a well documented story of the life and beliefs of the author of *Uncle Tom's Cabin.* Students of literature need to know about this occasion, on which a book had obvious and direct impact upon the course of history.

Frances Cavanah gives an account of the man whose life and memoirs were used as a basis for Harriet Beecher Stowe's novel in *The Truth About the Man Behind the Book That Sparked the War Between the States* (I-A). It is exciting to trace the course of real lives reflected in literature and to see the interplay between literature and history.

Julius Lester uses first-person narratives in *To Be a Slave* (I-A), edited verbatim transcripts of accounts by blacks who escaped from the antebellum South. The transcripts were made by workers in the Federal Writers' Project interested in preserving a record of black speech patterns and language. Julius Lester also uses interviews, footnotes to history (such as bills of sale for slaves, letters, marriage registers), and primary sources for six stories about slaves and freedmen in *Long Journey Home* (I-A). He tells the stories of minor figures because he feels that they are the true movers of history, while the famous exist as symbols of their actions. The stories are dramatic, sometimes bitter, always poignant.

Fight for Freedom

Novels set in the Civil War period focus on the horrors of war, especially that of countryman fighting countryman, and, in some cases, brother against brother. Books set in this period do not aim at painting an exciting picture or romanticizing the battles; instead, they focus on injury and death, divided loyalties, and, frequently, the anguish of those who wanted no involvement in the war.

Irene Hunt's *Across Five Aprils* (I-A) describes the tragic involvement of the Creighton family, which has loved ones on both the Confederate and Union sides. Jethro, too young to join either army, experiences the war through his older brothers and a beloved teacher. The five Aprils begin in 1861 with the first incidents of the war and end in 1865 with the death of Lincoln.

Biographies of historical figures enhance the study of the Civil War period and there are many from which to choose; Abraham Lincoln is the subject of more than any other. James Daugherty's *Abraham Lincoln* (I-A) is a lusty account of the man and his concerns. During the war years, Lincoln kept himself informed on every battle, troop movement, and military decision, and often criticized his generals severely. Daugherty's book reveals Lincoln's deep concerns about the causes of the war and his even deeper concern that the North would not win. F. N. Monjo's *Me and Willie and Pa* (P-I) is a refreshing and unusual biography of Lincoln, not a staid account of his greatness but a child's-eye view written as if told by Lincoln's son Tad. Personal glimpses into the Lincoln household are conveyed through Tad's naive comments.

ACROSS FIVE APRILS (I-A) Viewing the issues involved in the Civil War from the perspective of one family gives students an awareness of the complexities that were involved. Because the issues in *Across Five Aprils,* by Irene Hunt (I-A, Follett, 1964), are, indeed, complex, it is advisable to read and discuss the first four chapters before proceeding to the last half of the story. Also, at this stage, students are developing a historical perspective and need help putting events into chronological order; a time line of events in the Civil War or a time line of American history that includes the Civil War can help students create a coherent time frame.

Your class could use this book as a framework for the study of the Civil War, since it begins with the original causes and continues until the death of Abraham Lincoln. The historical background, however, should not be allowed to obscure the vivid character development.

The book also provides an excellent background for discussion of how suffering can change people, as seen in the attitudes of Tom and Eb; the effects of rumor and prejudice, as experienced by Bill's family when he runs away to join the Southern forces; and how the innocent—for example, the father, Matt Creighton—may suffer for the positions others take.

Activity: Teacher to Student

HISTORY THROUGH LITERATURE (I-A) Read Irene Hunt's *Across Five Aprils* (Follett, 1964) and choose one of the following activities.

1. Prepare a bulletin board or a large mural divided to represent the five Aprils covered in the novel. Illustrate each section with pictures and note news events and family events from the story, as begun here:

April, 1861	April, 1862	April, 1863	April, 1864	April, 1865
War begins	Father ill	Eb deserts Yankee army	Turning point of war	War ends; Lincoln shot

2. Select words and phrases from the story that are no longer used in conversation. Write the words or phrases and their meanings on cards; put the cards on a bulletin board labeled "Old Time Talk." If there is a modern counterpart, write it next to the old one in a different color. Some examples from the book: "bedded"

(CONTINUED)

(p. 8), "spent" and "tol'able" (p. 20), "put one's hand in the fire" (p. 25), "take by the britches" (p. 44), "passel" (p. 168). When the list is long enough—say five or six items—make a word-matching game; for example:

1. _____ allow (p. 15)
2. _____ grub (p. 163)
3. _____ mind (p. 131)
4. _____ feathering (p. 9)
5. _____ write a better hand (p. 132)

a. food
b. remember
c. improve handwriting
d. agree, suppose
e. softly rising

3. News of the war, carried mainly by word of mouth, made the war seem much closer than do the ones reported on radio and television. Dramatize a modern newscast about a distant battle and then give an eyewitness report about Jethro's visit to the army camp.

4. Re-enact the scene in which Shad brings the news that the Confederates have fired on Fort Sumter or the scene in which Bill asks John to tell his mother that he was not at Pittsburg Landing (so that she will know he was not involved in Tom's death). Continue the scene as John goes to Mrs. Creighton to carry the message Bill asks him to relay.

There are many comprehensive biographies for the student who wants to learn more about Lincoln and the Civil War. Carl Sandburg's multivolume tome is the definitive work; the first twenty-seven chapters of Sandburg's *Abraham Lincoln: The Prairie Years* (A) are reprinted in *Abe Lincoln Grows Up* (A), which is usually appreciated most by elementary students if it is read aloud by the teacher.

Bruce Catton's work is a vital resource for studying the Civil War. He and the editors of American Heritage Magazine produced *The Battle of Gettysburg* (I-A), an oversize book with excellent photographs, drawings, and engravings. At the three day battle of Gettysburg, turning point of the war, things happened so rapidly that historians still disagree about them; Catton's work helps readers understand the chaos. He gives a more comprehensive view of the war in *This Hallowed Ground* (I-A).

LIFE ON THE FRONTIER: THE PIONEERS

Frontier life required great physical strength and an unlikely counterpart: the ability to endure loneliness. Pioneer families worked hard by necessity, providing their own food, clothing, shelter, and entertainment. Novels evoke the sense of facing life unaided in lands of breathtaking beauty, barren plains, and howling wildernesses.

Of the many good historical novels describing families who endure the hardships of frontier living and find abiding satisfaction in their lives, one series of books stands out above all others—the "Little House" series, by Laura Ingalls Wilder. These autobiographical stories convey the strong feelings of love and companionship in a family facing danger and difficulties. Starting with *Little House in the Big Woods* (P-I) and continuing through seven more books about Laura, Pa, Ma, Mary, Carrie, and Grace, the literary legacy of this series has been renewed through its serialization on television.

The sense of isolation permeates the opening paragraph of the first book in the series:

The great, dark trees of the Big Woods stood all around the house, and beyond them were other trees and beyond them were more trees. As far as a man could go to the north in a day, or a week, or a whole month, there was nothing but woods. There were no houses. There were no roads. There were no people. There were only trees and the wild animals who had their homes among them.[15]

Laura shows how she feels about her life as she describes what she does. She is glad that her world is the way it is, that her father and mother are there, that the warmth of love fills her home. The family saga continues in *Little House on the Prairie, On the Banks of Plum Creek, By the Shores of Silver Lake, The Long Winter, Little Town on the Prairie,* and *These Happy Golden Years* (all I). The eighth book, *The First Four Years* (I), found as a manuscript among Mrs. Wilder's effects after her death at the age of ninety, ends the sensitive chronicles of this pioneer family on the wild prairies of the American West in the 1870s and 1880s.

The televised version has created widespread interest and an opportunity for comparative reading and viewing. Avid Laura Ingalls Wilder fans in one school meet after each program to discuss the differences between the books and the television show. This kind of comparison leads naturally into critical reading and viewing.

Through the Little House books, children can study pioneer life and, in the process, experience some of the best literature for them. The stories, in their evocation of the physical strength and moral fiber needed to face wilderness days, convey a sense of the arduous and precarious nature of pioneer life.

Laura's Pa, source of security and comfort to his pioneer family, enlivens a social gathering with his fiddle. Memories of earlier times permeate Laura Ingalls Wilder's stories.
(Illustration by Garth Williams from *Little House in the Big Woods* by Laura Ingalls Wilder. Copyright, 1953, as to pictures, by Garth Williams. By permission of Harper & Row, Publishers, Inc.)

Activity: Teacher to Student

APPRECIATING PIONEER LIFE (I)   After reading the Little House books, invite your parents to school to share what you have learned about pioneer living. When they arrive, give them a copy of the newspaper from Plum Creek, Minnesota, which you have published. The paper could use events from the books, such as when grasshoppers covered the land and destroyed the Ingalls's crops, or when there was a flood, drought, or blizzard. Report the disaster in front-page stories and headlines. Here is a sample from a fourth-grade class:

PLUM CREEK GAZETTE

GRASSHOPPERS COVER EARTH: CROPS DESTROYED

The Charles Ingalls farm was one of many hit by grasshoppers this week when swarms of the hungry insects

(continued on page 2)

Weather forecast

Hot and dry.

Letters to the Editor

Dear Editor,
The grasshoppers were the last straw. I'm pulling out and going back East to civilization.

Personal: Mrs. Oleson entertained in honor of Nellie's birthday.

Help Wanted: Barn raising, Saturday. Food for all workers.

Treat parent visitors to a pioneer luncheon. Use *The Little House Cookbook,* by Barbara Walker, illustrated by Garth Williams (Harper & Row, 1979), which gives recipes for bread, pancake men, and starling pie, as well as pioneer methods for churning butter, drying blackberries, and making ice cream. Preparing and eating food were central parts of life in pioneer families.

Entertain your guests with square dancing. Learn one of the square dances that Laura watched at Grandpa's house. Use recordings for music and instructions by a caller.

Re-create an evening in Laura's home: Pa's fiddle music can be recaptured with recordings. *The Laura Ingalls Wilder Song Book,* edited by Eugenia Garson and Herbert Haufrecht, illustrated by Garth Williams (Harper & Row, 1968) contains the music and words for many of the songs the family sang. *On the Banks of Plum Creek* (Harper & Row, 1953) includes "Captain Jinks" (p. 338) and "Weevily Wheat" (p. 336). Learn the words to the songs that Pa played on his fiddle and have a songfest.

Use the illustrations from *Pioneer Life on the American Prairie, A Frontier Album* (Scholastic, 1977) to show scenes on the overhead projector as background for your pioneer day.

TWENTIETH-CENTURY AMERICA

At the beginning of the twentieth century, Americans, expansive with high hopes, worked toward technological and industrial progress, one mark of which would be the acquisition, by many people, of labor-saving devices such as sewing machines, typewriters, and telephones. Fathers ruled the families, and most worked long and hard to provide for them. Farming, which required the help of all family members, was the major occupation across most of the country. Child labor was by then illegal but still practiced in subtle ways.

There are many children's books that re-create a sense of those times. In Jacqueline Jackson's *The Taste of Spruce Gum* (I), the time is 1903, and Libby must go to her stepfather's lumber camp in Vermont. She does not want to live in a lumber camp, nor does she want her widowed mother to marry a man—her own uncle—who has proposed by mail. The mill community differs markedly from the life Libby knew in Illinois, and her feelings toward her stepfather are slow to change. The occupational and regional cultures that permeate the novel contrast sharply with the life Libby had known. Slowly, and believably, she adjusts to the people, the work, and the region.

Birdie Boyer, in Lois Lenski's *Strawberry Girl* (I), is an enterprising young lady with determination and grit. She helps the family raise strawberries on their new farm in Florida and struggles with dry weather, grass fires, and roving cattle. The shiftless Slaters, a neighboring family, spell trouble, but in the end Birdie takes one of the Slaters to her school:

"This here is Shoestring . . ." she began. "Oh, no, I mean . . ."
"My name's Jefferson Davis Slater," said the boy. "I come to git book-larnin'."
"You are one of the Slaters?" asked Miss Dunnaway. In her eyes there came a frightened look. "They told me the Slater boys had left school. Was it you and your brothers who . . ."
"Gus and Joe whopped the man teacher," said Shoestring, dropping his eyes. "I wasn't in school then."
"But Shoestring . . . I mean, Jeff's different!" broke in Birdie. "He ain't rough and wild like Gus and Joe."

"You must say 'isn't' not 'ain't,' Berthenia," corrected Miss Dunnaway.
"He isn't rough," said Birdie. "He won't make ary trouble for you, Teacher."
"'Any' trouble, not 'ary,'" said Miss Dunnaway.
"I won't make you no trouble," said Shoestring, looking up at her, "iffen you jest larn me to read and write."
"'Any' trouble, not 'no' trouble, Jefferson. And 'if,' not 'iffen.' 'Teach' me, not 'larn' me. That's fine. I'm proud to welcome a peaceable Slater to my school."[16]

Birdie Boyer, like many of Lois Lenski's other characters, embodies regional and cultural mannerisms in her language and life style. In preparation for each of her regional books, Lois Lenski lived in the community in which she set her novel. Because of her careful research and her ear for the language, her books ring true.

Immigrant life is sensitively portrayed in Marietta Moskin's *Waiting for Mama* (I-A). Because there was only enough money to pay passage for part of the family to come to America, Mama stayed behind. The family works hard to earn the money needed if Mama is to join them. Becky, too young to work, finds a way to help by sewing with her ten-year-old sister late at night. The life of an immigrant family was not easy, but hardship drew its members close together.

World War II

The years 1936 to 1946, encompassing the Second World War, Adolph Hitler's climb to power in Germany, and Japanese military activity in the Pacific, brought to conscious awareness the potential of man's inhumanity. The horrors of the period were so great—"unthinkable"—that, until recently, very little was written for young people about it. In the last few years, however, many stories dealing with the times have emerged.

Santayana's admonition that those who do not know the past are condemned to repeat it is adequate cause for attending to the tragedy, and the books describing Hitler's reign of terror, with its effects ultimately on all people, are a good place to begin. On the positive side, many emphasize a thread—sometimes slender, sometimes strong—running through the literature that in the midst of inhumanity there can be humaneness. Eric Kimmel, in an article about the Holocaust and juvenile fiction, states:

. . . if the Holocaust remains incomprehensible, it will be forgotten. And if it is forgotten, it is certain to recur.[17]

Despite their grimness, some books are affirmative: young people work in underground movements, strive against terrible odds, plan escapes, and struggle for survival. Some show heroic Jewish resistance, in which characters fight back or live with dignity and hope in the face of a monstrous future. There are probably many teachers who will agonize over the place of literature in teaching about the Holocaust. Valid questions for them are: Is mass murder a suitable subject for a children's novel? What is the place of an account of it in the school curriculum? What are the possible consequences of not informing young people about one of the most bitter lessons of history?

EUROPEAN THEATER Nathaniel Benchley's *Bright Candles* (A), an underground-resistance novel, tells the story of the dignified and stoic opposition of the Danes to the Nazi occupation. Sixteen-year-old Jens Hansen works actively to sabotage the Nazis and is interrogated by them; we read of his joy when the blackout curtains are taken down and the candles relit on May 5, 1946.

Judith Kerr's three novels, *When Hitler Stole Pink Rabbit* (I), *The Other Way Round* (I-A), and *A Small Person Far Away* (A), chronicle a life that could be the author's own from days as a refugee from Germany to the present. Anna, daughter of an affluent Jewish journalist, is forced to leave Berlin because her father's views are not acceptable to the Nazis. The family goes first to Switzerland and then to England and, with each move, Anna's resentment grows as life becomes more degrading. In *The Other Way Round,* Anna's family lives in England, but her highly respected writer father has difficulty getting his work published and gradually grows quiet and sad. Mama, by contrast, becomes more excitable and considers the war a personal affront. The third book, *A Small Person Far Away,* finds Anna married and working as a writer for the

BBC, a position the author holds in real life. Anna is called back to Germany to be with her mother, who has tried to commit suicide; the journey brings remembered and current heartaches as she tries to resolve her relationship with her mother and her feelings about her native country.

Consciousness of their racial backgrounds and traditions, slight in most of the Jewish characters in the refugee novels, is not much greater in the novels laid in Germany or the occupied countries. One exception to this appears in Hans Richter's *Friedrich* (I), a story of a friendship between two German boys, one Jewish. Despite the fact that Friedrich did not choose to join Hitler's youth group, the Jungvolk, the boys see no differences between themselves except in religious practice. As the diabolic plan of Nazi persecution slowly unfolds, Friedrich and his family find themselves denied even simple dignities, and, in a bitter ending, Friedrich is forbidden entrance to a bomb shelter during an air raid. Ultimately, his resulting death must seem to him a refuge from the unrelenting hatred.

Fred Uhlman's *Reunion* (A) is also about a friendship, this time one in which one friend feels betrayed. Hans, a shy Jewish adolescent, finds that he shares interests in poetry, music, art, and literature with Konradin, son of a German nobleman. The two friends are forced apart on the eve of the Nazi takeover, and Konradin's behavior leaves Hans embittered at the apparent betrayal of their friendship. When he is asked to contribute to a war memorial for former classmates killed in the Second World War, Hans recognizes that thirty years have not erased the anger that he feels. On the list of war dead, a small notation concerning the manner of Konradin's death is a revelation to Hans.

Stories of Jews forced into hiding show strong and courageous individuals who, although living under terrifying stress, maintained hope for eventual freedom. *Anne Frank: The Diary of a Young Girl* (I-A) is the actual journal of this sensitive girl who, with her family, hid in a secret annex of an office building in Amsterdam for two years. The firsthand chronicles of the fear, hunger, and indignities of their hidden existence are chilling. Only

REUNION (A)[18] The story *Reunion* (Farrar, Straus & Giroux, 1977), by Fred Uhlman, narrows the wide scope of history to the relationship between two boys. Uhlman's writing style and literary craft make the novel worthy of careful study. Discuss some of the following:

Characterization   What do you learn about Hans as he tells the story from his point of view? How does Hans's enthusiastic view of Konradin influence your opinion of the latter?

Setting   What words does the author use to evoke a feeling of time and place? What scenes do you see in your mind's eye?

Plot   How does the author space major events in the story to build your expectations? How does the final revelation influence all that has happened before?

Theme   What is the major thought that you carry away from the story? Does the meaning of the title change after you finish reading the story?

Anne's father survived the Frank's subsequent imprisonment in a concentration camp. Anne's diary was found in 1946.

Johanna Reiss wrote *The Upstairs Room* (I-A), an autobiographical account of her escape to freedom, primarily for her own daughters, but readers everywhere learn about persecution from reading it. Ten-year-old Annie and her older sister expect to be hidden in the upstairs room of the Dutch farm home for only a few weeks, but the weeks stretch into more than two years. Usually the girls are free to move about the farm, but at one point Nazi soldiers make their headquarters in the front of the house and the girls are required to stay in bed day and night to avoid discovery. A sequel, *The Journey Back* (I-A), follows the girls as they make difficult adjustments after the war.

Yuri Suhl's novels embody Jewish characters who, fiercely proud of their traditions, continue to practice their religion in the face of Nazi oppression. In *Uncle Misha's Partisans* (I-A) twelve-year-old Motele finds that knowing how to play the violin leads to ways to help his Jewish comrades. Through his violin playing, Motele infiltrates the German Officers' House where he not only picks up information but, in a final act of retribution, plants a bomb. Suhl's *On the Other Side of the Gate* (I-A) centers on Hershel and Lena, a young married couple who are determined to give birth to the child Lena carries despite a Nazi edict forbidding Jewish procreation. The child's birth and infancy are closely guarded secrets within the Polish ghetto until they smuggle the child to safety.

In an excellent work of nonfiction, Milton Meltzer collects first-person narratives growing out of the Holocaust in *Never to Forget* (A). Letters, diaries, memoirs, eyewitness reports, and autobiographies are excerpted and woven into the fabric of history. Jewish ideals—"Live and die with dignity," and "Not by force but by the strength of the spirit"—emanate from the personal reports.

In striking contrast to the accounts of hatred, death, and betrayal are the stories of those who had the courage to reach out to others across lines of group loyalty or nationality or self-interest. In Jaap ter Haar's *Boris* (I-A), a young boy lives in Leningrad while it is under siege by German troops. His father was killed when his truck carrying food to Leningrad's starving people across the frozen surface of Lake Ladoga broke through the

Profile

MILTON MELTZER

To forget what we know would not be human.
To remember it is to think of what being human means. The Holocaust was a measure of man's dimensions. One can think of the power of evil it demonstrated—and of those people who treated others as less than human, as bacteria. Or of the power of good—and of those people who held out a hand to others. By nature, man is neither good nor evil. He has both possibilities. And the freedom to realize the one or the other.

Never to Forget: The Jews of the Holocaust

Milton Meltzer followed the path to the terror and grief of the Nazi era through eyewitness accounts—letters, diaries, journals, and memoirs. However inadequate words, he says, language is all we have to reach across barriers to understanding. Letting history speak for itself characterizes all his work and provides accuracy and authenticity normally found only in primary sources. His technique brings a sense of immediacy to the past and re-creates a feeling of the time.

Meltzer's more than thirty-five books reveal his love of the American story and his respect for the struggles of our forebears. He portrays turn-of-the-century working-class life in *Bread and Roses,* the hardships of the Depression in *Brother Can You Spare a Dime?,* and, in *Violins and Shovels,* the story of government-supported, Depression-era WPA projects.

Milton Meltzer believes that young people are interested in the past and that it is best discovered through letters, memoirs, journals, and other original documents. He feels it is unnecessary to fabricate stories about historical events since the truth itself is inherently intriguing. One need only read the letters and poems in *Never to Forget: The Jews of the Holocaust* to recognize the validity of his belief.

The son of hard-working immigrant parents, Milton Meltzer was born in Worcester, Massachusetts, and studied to be a journalist. He and his wife, who have two grown daughters, live in New York City, where he devotes himself to scholarly research and writing.

---

ice. Boris and his friend, Nadia, trying to supplement their meager daily ration of watery soup, are digging for potatoes in a barren field in the "no-man's land" between the German and Russian lines, when Nadia collapses. A German soldier takes them back to the Russian lines behind a white flag. The soldiers temporarily lay aside their differences in compassion for the children, and a Russian, speaking to the German soldier through his interpreter, says:

"Tell them they are free to go back, Ivan Petrovitch." He hesitated, as if searching for words. "Say to them that we are grateful; it would be shameful if we, in the brutality of war, should forget all humanity."[19]

In T. Degens's *Transport 7-41-R* (I-A), another gripping story, a thirteen-year-old girl is traveling illegally aboard a crowded cattle car carrying refugees home to Cologne. Observing with distaste the callousness and inconsiderateness of the motley group of passengers, she tries to remain aloof. Eventually, however, she is drawn to an elderly couple, the Lauritzens, who seem especially vulnerable to the brutishness of the group. She learns that Mr. Lauritzen is trying to fulfill a pledge to his critically ill wife that she will be buried near the cathedral in Cologne. When Mrs. Lauritzen quietly

In *Transport 7-41-R* a 13-year-old girl overcomes the bitterness engendered by war to help an aging couple.
(Jacket art from T. Degens's *Transport 7-41-R* done by Barbara Bascove. Copyright © 1974 by T. Degens. Reprinted by permission of Viking Penguin Inc.)

dies while still aboard the train, both the girl and Mr. Lauritzen know that the others will throw the body, in its cumbersome wheelchair, off the train if they discover her death. As the transport is delayed time and time again, keeping the secret of Mrs. Lauritzen's death and fulfilling the promise to her become less realistic. The dedication of the girl to the elderly couple is a touching story, believably told through gradual interweaving of detail.

THE PACIFIC THEATER Despite the fact that American armed forces fought for four years in the Pacific, there are few children's and adolescent novels set in this theater, and the European scene dominates in books of this period.

One novel set in the Pacific during the war—*The House of Sixty Fathers* (I), by Meindert DeJong—tells the story of Tien Pao, son of Chinese refugees, who is swept by floodwaters into Japanese-held territory. During his efforts to make his way through enemy land to find his parents, he meets an American pilot. They eventually reach an American air base, where an entire company of G.I.s adopts Tien Pao and thereby become his "sixty fathers."

Yoshiko Uchida's *Journey to Topaz* (I) describes the life of Japanese-Americans who, following the attack on Pearl Harbor, were shunted by the thousands to internment camps despite lifelong loyalty to America. The FBI arrests the father as an enemy alien, and places the rest of the family in an evacuation center, where they live in converted horse stables.

Farewell to Manzanar (I-A), by Jeanne Wakatsuki Houston and James Houston, begins when Jeanne Wakatsuki is seven years old and is taken with her family to a relocation camp, Manzanar. Release from the camp is nearly as traumatic as the incarceration for, in the process, the family is broken up. The whole experience leaves those subjected to it with a pervasive sense of unworthiness that plagues their lives long after.

Eleanor Coerr's *Sadako and the Thousand Paper Cranes* (P-I) describes lingering death from radiation. Sadako was only two years old when the atomic bomb was dropped on her home city, Hiro-

THE IMPACT OF WORLD WAR II (A)   The death camps in Europe and the atomic bomb in the Pacific theater stand as haunting evidence of the extent of man's capability for inhumanity to man. As you read books on these subjects, keep in mind the following questions and suggestions.

Discussion   How is it possible that a nation that produced great scientists and artists also allowed Dachau, Auschwitz, and Buchenwald? What comparisons can you draw between the death camps in Europe and the bombing of Hiroshima?[20]

Research   Read eyewitness reports of survivors, examine photodocumentaries, and view filmed documentaries of the war-scarred world. (Your local newspaper or library may have files of the war-years issues of newspapers.)

Drama   Conduct a "You Are There" program of the bombing of Pearl Harbor, the bombing of Hiroshima, the Battle of the Bulge, D-Day at Normandy Beach, the Nuremberg trials, the discovery of a Nazi war criminal living in the United States, or an hour in the heart of the Warsaw ghetto.

Writing   Write an essay on what you think we should have learned from the events of the World War II period. Write an opinion on the treatment of war criminals. Write a diary entry as if you had been caught in the midst of a battle area.

---

shima; when she was twelve, she was stricken with leukemia. Restricted to bed, Sadako folded paper cranes because legend says the crane lives for 1,000 years and that sick persons who fold 1,000 of them and keep them at their side will be granted long life. Sadako was able to fold only 644 before her death, but her classmates folded 356 more so that 1,000 paper cranes could be buried with Sadako. Betty Jean Lifton tells how, in Japan, the death of Sadako came to symbolize the death of all children killed by the bomb, and how children collected money to erect a powerful monument, inscribed at the base of which is the plea for all children: "This is our cry, this is our prayer; peace in the world."

WAR ECHOES IN AMERICA   Some stories of the World War II period are not set in the European or Pacific theater, nor do they focus on evacuees or relocation camps. In Janet Hickman's *The Stones*

(I), Garrett McKay's father is missing in action. When Garrett and his friends discover that Jack Tramp, a village recluse who has often borne the brunt of childish pranks, is actually named Adolph —like Hitler—their pranks become more serious. The characters and events in Hickman's novel ring true in this story about the perniciousness of anger and hatred disguised as patriotism.

THE SIXTIES AND SEVENTIES

School integration stories dominated the sixties; some underplayed the bitter encounters in schools and ended on a hopeful note, but others included ugly picket lines and racist slurs. One of the first school integration novels seems mild by comparison with those that followed. *Mary Jane* (I), by Dorothy Sterling, tells of a child exceptional in every way. Her grandfather is a renowned scientist, she is very bright, and her entrance into an all-white school is rather quiet and peaceful. Lorenz Graham's *South Town* (I-A) and its sequels give a more telling picture of riots, bigotry, and blatant racism.

One of the strongest integration stories, Bella Rodman's *Lions in the Way* (A), is set in a Tennessee town that has fought the Supreme Court decision to integrate schools but has finally been forced to comply. Eight students arrive at a previously all-white high school. Robby, the leader of the black students and protagonist of the novel, is embittered by the cruelties of Joel, a white boy who had been his friend as a child. The Army is called in, a minister is injured, and hatred flames in this novel that shows many sides to the integration issues.

Florence E. Randall based *The Almost Year* (I-A) on a true incident. A liberal white family invites a black teenager to live with them because of disruptions in her family. They try very hard to pass off with logical explanations the strange happenings that engulf them during their guest's stay—for example, doorbells ringing with no caller, hailstones beating on their house but not on their neighbors'. The only explanation seems to be that the girl has attracted poltergeists—but many things go unexplained. The story ends realistically—not on a happily-ever-after note—with consistent behavior on the part of the clearly drawn characters.

Stories of the Vietnam War are few, the best being Mary Lois Dunn's *The Man in the Box* (I-A). In Chau Li's village in South Vietnam, the Viet Cong have put a captured American soldier in a small wooden boxlike cage and left him to die, as they had once done to Chau Li's father, who had been the village chief. At great risk to his own life, Chau Li helps the prisoner escape and hides with him in the mountains where they are eventually rescued by helicopter. The boy's act of compassion is a show of humanity in the midst of an inhumane war.

Ann Nolan Clark tells a story of an eleven-year-old Vietnamese boy now in America in *To Stand Against the Wind* (I-A). On the Day of the Ancestors, Em tries to write down all his memories, but he cannot, the memories flowing from his heart, not his pen. The joy and heartache of his life in Vietnam pervades the writing. When circumstance compels him to become head of his household, he feels he is not ready, and then recalls a proverb his father taught him: "It takes a strong man to stand against the wind." A sense of tragedy for the disrupted order of a traditional life style emanates from the novel.

In the midst of an inhumane war a Vietnamese boy risks his life to save *The Man in the Box* from torture by the Viet Cong.
(Jacket design by Nicholas Fasciano for *The Man in the Box* by Mary Lois Dunn. Copyright © 1968 by Mary Lois Dunn. Reprinted with permission of McGraw-Hill Book Company.)

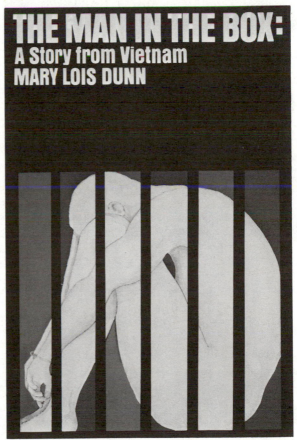

THE MAN IN THE BOX:
A Story from Vietnam
MARY LOIS DUNN

The tumultuous sixties began with the election of John F. Kennedy, the youngest man ever elected President. Kennedy was proficient in politics and felt that there were resources of idealism as yet untapped in the American people. His *Profiles in Courage* (I-A) and Richard Tregaskis's *John F. Kennedy and PT-109* (I) give students an opportunity to know him. Space exploration proceeded during Kennedy's term in office, and, in 1962, John Glenn entered space orbit. In July, 1969, Neil Armstrong became the first man to walk on the moon.

Clearly, the civil rights movement was the outstanding social revolution of the sixties. Martin Luther King, Jr., Medger Evers, Rosa Park, Ralph Bunche, and many others earned a place in history for their courageous acts. Many biographies were written about Martin Luther King, Jr., the best of which is probably James Haskins's *The Life and Death of Martin Luther King, Jr.* (A). Haskins paints an objective yet sympathetic picture of King's beliefs and work. Describing the days immediately before King's assassination, he counterpoints King's activities with those of his murderer, James Earl Ray. Haskins quotes from an extemporaneous speech King gave the day before his death:

And some began to talk about the threats that were out, of what would happen to me from some of our sick white brothers. . . . Well, I don't know what will happen now. We've got some difficult days ahead. But it really doesn't matter to me now. . . . Because I've been to the mountaintop! . . . Like anybody I would like to live . . . a long life. Longevity has its place. But I'm not concerned about that now . . . I just want to do God's will! And He's allowed me to go up to the mountain, and I've seen the Promised Land.[21]

The seventies were tumultuous in a way different from the sixties. The Watergate scandal forced Richard Nixon to resign from the presidency, American troops finally left Vietnam, and women liberationists fought for equality in all areas of life. Changing social values were rapidly reflected in children's books.

Go Ask Alice (A), anonymous, but later acknowledged as the work of Beatrice Sparks, soon became one of the top ten books in popularity, and provoked widespread controversy. Fifteen-year-old Alice thinks that drugs are the way to fun and friends and, despite attempts to kick the habit, becomes a down-and-out junkie. In an interview, Beatrice Sparks reported that there was a real Alice, but as an author she filled out the character with information gained from working as a counselor with several teen-age addicts. Television productions, paperback editions, and translations contributed to the notoriety of Alice, a girl who died of an overdose and left a diary detailing her losing battle with drugs.

Many books captured the spirit of the women's liberation movement, but none more humorously than Lila Perl's *That Crazy April* (I). Mother is an activist in a family that does not go along with her radical feminism. Her daughter does not want to take industrial-arts courses at school or to fulfill in other ways the liberationist role her mother insists upon. She is embarrassed when she finds her mother's name preceded by Ms. on the mailbox and wants to bake cookies despite her mother's objections. The book brings the liberation cause into perspective.

CRITERIA FOR SELECTING HISTORICAL BOOKS

We present only a few of the hundreds of historical books available; as you search for books to enrich your social studies curriculum, keep the following characteristics in mind.

Many books that present historical facts do not qualify as literature. To do so, historical fiction and biography must meet the criteria for *all* literature —tell an engaging story, have well-developed characters, and evolve themes—while, in addition, evoking a historical setting through a well-structured plot. Basic themes, such as comradeship, loyalty, treachery, love and hate, revenge, and the struggle between good and evil run through historical fiction and biography.

Historical fiction and biography should be consistent with historical evidence, the story, though imaginative, remaining within the limits of the historical background chosen, with distortion and anachronism avoided.

Language should be in keeping with the period and place of the setting, particularly in dialogue. A problem arises in the case of words of the past that would be understood today by few readers. This can be dealt with by synthesizing language that has the right sound for a period, but is understandable to contemporary readers. Rosemary Sutcliff says:

I try to catch the rhythm of a tongue, the tune that it plays on the ear, Welsh or Gaelic as opposed to Anglo-Saxon, the sensible workmanlike language which one feels the Latin of the ordinary Roman citizen would have translated into. It is extraordinary what can be done by the changing or transposing of a single word, or by using a perfectly usual one in a slightly unusual way: "I beg your pardon" changed into "I ask your pardon." . . . this is not done by any set rule of thumb; I simply play it by ear as I go along.[22]

Historical fiction and biography should also reflect the values of the period: portraying the sexes as equal, for example, in a story set in Victorian times would be inconsistent with the father-knows-best customs that prevailed.

Good historical books show no revisionism; that is, they do not rewrite history to suit present ways of thinking. For example, Paula Fox, though the attitudes are offensive to her (and probably most of her readers) has characters express racist ones in *The Slave Dancer* (I-A) in order to reflect accurately the temper of the times during slavery.

Historical fiction and biography of quality are first literary works, not thinly veiled attempts to teach history. The spirit of the historical period will emerge from the story; historical facts dare not overpower it. The skillful writer absorbs factual information, which then provides a foundation for the story. As Hester Burton says, "The prime object of writing an historical novel is an exercise of the heart rather than the head."[23] If the research baggage outweighs the story line, the plot sinks.

Finally, noteworthy historical novels do not overgeneralize; they do not lead the reader to believe, for example, that all Native Americans are like the one portrayed in this story. Each character is unique just as each of us is, and while the novelist focuses on one person in a group, it is clear that it *is* only a person, and not an epitome.

Notes

1. Arthur Guiterman, "Ancient History," in *The Arbuthnot Anthology of Children's Literature,* 4th ed., ed. Zena Sutherland et al. (New York: Lothrop, Lee & Shepard, 1976), p. 7.
2. Jim Kjelgaard, *Fire Hunter* (New York: Holiday House, 1951), p. 61.
3. Ibid., pp. 206–07.
4. C. W. Ceram, *Gods, Graves, and Scholars,* rev. ed. (New York: Knopf, 1967), pp. 36–37.
5. Kate Seredy, *The White Stag* (New York: Viking, 1937), p. 67.
6. Rosemary Sutcliff, *The Lantern Bearers* (New York: Walck, 1959), p. 251.
7. Frances, FitzGerald, *American History Revisited* (Boston: Little, Brown, 1979), pp. 8–9.
8. Jean Fritz, "George Washington, My Father, and Walt Disney," *Horn Book Magazine,* 52, No. 2 (April 1976), 191–98.
9. Jean Poindexter Colby, *Lexington and Concord, 1775* (New York: Hastings House, 1975), pp. 87–88.
10. Jamake Highwater, *Anpao: An American Indian Odyssey* (New York: Lippincott, 1977), p. 240.
11. Ibid., p. 242.
12. Ibid., p. 239.

13. Adapted from a plan by Sally Hollaman, Librarian and Reading Laboratory Teacher, Saxe Junior High School, New Canaan, Conn.
14. Adapted from a plan by Diane R. Confer, Kane Public Schools, Kane, Pa.
15. Laura Ingalls Wilder, *Little House in the Big Woods* (New York: Harper & Row, 1953 [1932]), pp. 1–2.
16. Lois Lenski, *Strawberry Girl* (New York: Lippincott, 1945), pp. 189–90.
17. Eric A. Kimmel, "Confronting the Ovens: The Holocaust and Juvenile Fiction," *Horn Book Magazine,* 53, No. 1 (Feb. 1977), 84.
18. Adapted from a plan in Bernice E. Cullinan, *A Penguin Teacher's Guide for Reunion by Fred Uhlman* (New York: Penguin Books), unpaged.
19. Jaap ter Haar, *Boris* (New York: Delacorte, 1966), p. 66.
20. Erika Hess Merems, *The Holocaust Years: Society on Trial, Teacher's Guide* (New York: Bantam, 1978), p. 6.
21. James Haskins, *The Life and Death of Martin Luther King, Jr.* (New York: Lothrop, Lee & Shepard, 1977), pp. 109–10.
22. Rosemary Sutcliff, "History Is People," in *Children and Literature: Views and Reviews,* ed. Virginia Haviland (Chicago: Scott, Foresman, 1973), pp. 307–08.
23. Hester Burton, "The Writing of Historical Novels," in *Children and Literature,* ed. Virginia Haviland, p. 303.

Professional References

Arbuthnot, May Hill. *The Arbuthnot Anthology of Children's Literature,* 4th ed. Ed. Zena Sutherland et al. Lothrop, Lee & Shepard, 1976.

De Montreville, Doris, and Donna Hill, eds. *Third Book of Junior Authors.* H. W. Wilson, 1972.

Fritz, Jean. "George Washington, My Father, and Walt Disney." *Horn Book Magazine,* 52, No. 2 (April 1976), 191–98.

Haviland, Virginia, ed. *Children and Literature: Views and Reviews.* Scott, Foresman, 1973.

Hopkins, Lee Bennett. *More Books by More People.* Citation Press, 1974.

Kimmel, Eric. "Confronting the Ovens: The Holocaust and Juvenile Fiction." *Horn Book Magazine,* 53, No. 1 (Feb. 1977), 84–91.

Merems, Erika Hess. *The Holocaust Years: Society on Trial, Teacher's Guide.* Bantam, 1978.

Children's Books Cited in Chapter

Ashe, Geoffrey. *King Arthur in Fact and Legend.* Thomas Nelson, 1971.

Barringer, D. Moreau. *And the Waters Prevailed.* Illus. P. A. Hutchinson. Dutton, 1956.

Barth, Edna. *Turkeys, Pilgrims, and Indian Corn: The Story of the Thanksgiving Symbols.* Illus. Ursula Arndt. Seabury, 1975.

Benchley, Nathaniel. *Bright Candles: A Novel of the Danish Resistance.* Harper & Row, 1974.

Bulla, Clyde Robert. *Viking Adventure.* Illus. Douglas Gorsline. Crowell, 1963.

Campbell, Elizabeth A. *Jamestown: The Beginning.* Illus. William Sauts Bock. Little, Brown, 1974.

Catton, Bruce. *The Battle of Gettysburg.* American Heritage, 1963.

———. *This Hallowed Ground: The Story of the Union Side of the Civil War.* Doubleday, 1962.

Cavanah, Frances. *The Truth about the Man Behind the Book That Sparked the War Between the States.* Westminster, 1975.

Ceram, C. W. *Gods, Graves, and Scholars.* Rev. ed. Knopf, 1967.

Cheney, Cora. *The Incredible Deborah: A Story Based on the Life of Deborah Sampson.* Scribner's, 1967.

Clapp, Patricia. *Constance: A Story of Early Plymouth.* Lothrop, Lee & Shepard, 1968.

———. *I'm Deborah Sampson: A Soldier in the War of the Revolution.* Lothrop, Lee & Shepard, 1977.

Clark, Ann Nolan. *To Stand Against the Wind.* Viking, 1978.

Coerr, Eleanor. *Sadako and the Thousand Paper Cranes.* Illus. Ronald Himler. Putnam's, 1977.

Colby, Jean Poindexter. *Lexington and Concord 1775: What Really Happened.* Photographs by Barbara Cooney. Hastings House, 1975.

Collier, James Lincoln, and Christopher Collier. *My Brother Sam Is Dead.* Four Winds-Scholastic, 1974.

Curtis, Edward. *The Girl Who Married a Ghost and Other Tales from the North American Indian.* Ed. John Bierhorst. Four Winds-Scholastic, 1977.

Daugherty, James. *Abraham Lincoln.* Viking, 1943.

———. *Poor Richard.* Viking, 1964.

D'Aulaire, Ingri and Edgar Parin. *Leif the Lucky*. Doubleday, 1941.

Degens, T. *Transport 7-41-R*. Viking, 1974.

DeJong, Meindert. *The House of Sixty Fathers*. Illus. Maurice Sendak. Harper & Row, 1956.

Dunn, Mary Lois. *The Man in the Box*. McGraw-Hill, 1968.

Eaton, Jeannette. *That Lively Man, Ben Franklin*. Illus. Henry Pitz. Morrow, 1948.

Fisher, Leonard. *The Warlock of Westfall*. Doubleday, 1974.

Forbes, Esther. *Johnny Tremain*. Illus. Lynd Ward. Houghton Mifflin, 1946.

Foster, Genevieve. *George Washington*. Scribner's, 1949.

Fox, Paula. *The Slave Dancer*. Illus. Eros Keith. Bradbury, 1973.

Frank, Anne. *Anne Frank: The Diary of a Young Girl*. Rev. ed. Trans. B. M. Mooyart. Doubleday, 1967.

Fritz, Jean. *And Then What Happened, Paul Revere?* Illus. Margot Tomes. Coward, McCann & Geoghegan, 1973.

_____. *Brady*. Illus. Lynd Ward. Coward, McCann & Geoghegan, 1960.

_____. *The Cabin Faced West*. Illus. Feodor Rojankovsky. Coward, McCann & Geoghegan, 1958.

_____. *Can't You Make Them Behave, King George?* Illus. Tomie de Paola, Coward, McCann & Geoghegan, 1977.

_____. *Early Thunder*. Illus. Lynd Ward. Coward, McCann & Geoghegan, 1967.

_____. *What's the Big Idea, Ben Franklin?* Illus. Margot Tomes. Coward, McCann & Geoghegan, 1976.

_____. *Where Was Patrick Henry on the 29th of May?* Illus. Margot Tomes. Coward, McCann & Geoghegan, 1975.

_____. *Who's That Stepping on Plymouth Rock?* Illus. J. B. Handelsman. Coward, McCann & Geoghegan, 1975.

_____. *Why Don't You Get a Horse, Sam Adams?* Illus. Trina Schart Hyman. Coward, McCann & Geoghegan, 1974.

_____. *Will You Sign Here, John Hancock?* Illus. Trina Schart Hyman. Coward, McCann & Geoghegan, 1976.

Gauch, Patricia Lee. *This Time, Tempe Wick?* Illus. Margot Tomes. Coward, McCann & Geoghegan, 1974.

Graham, Lorenz. *South Town*. Follett, 1959.

Green, Margaret. *Radical of the Revolution: Samuel Adams*. Messner, 1971.

Haar, Jaap ter. *Boris*. Delacorte, 1966.

Haley, Alex. *Roots: The Saga of an American Family*. Doubleday, 1976.

Haskins, James S. *The Life and Death of Martin Luther King, Jr.* Lothrop, Lee & Shepard, 1977.

Haugaard, Erik Christian. *Hakon of Rogen's Saga*. Illus. Leo and Diane Dillon. Houghton Mifflin, 1963.

_____. *A Slave's Tale*. Illus. Leo and Diane Dillon. Houghton Mifflin, 1965.

Hickman, Janet. *The Stones*. Illus. Richard Cuffari. Macmillan, 1976.

Highwater, Jamake. *Anpao: An American Indian Odyssey*. Illus. Fritz Scholder. Lippincott, 1977.

Hodges, Margaret. *Hopkins of the Mayflower: Portrait of a Dissenter*. Farrar, Straus & Giroux, 1972.

Houston, Jeanne Wakatsuki, and James D. Houston. *Farewell to Manzanar*. Houghton Mifflin, 1973.

Hunt, Irene. *Across Five Aprils*. Follett, 1964.

Jackson, Jacqueline. *The Taste of Spruce Gum*. Illus. Lillian Obligado. Little, Brown, 1966.

Johnston, Johanna. *Who Found America?* Illus. Anne Siberell. Golden Gate-Childrens Press, 1973.

Jones, Hettie, ed. *The Trees Stand Shining: Poetry of the North American Indians*. Illus. Robert Andrew Parker. Dial, 1971.

Kennedy, John F. *Profiles in Courage*. Young Readers Memorial Ed. Harper & Row, 1964.

Kerr, Judith. *The Other Way Round*. Coward, McCann & Geoghegan, 1975.

_____. *A Small Person Far Away*. Coward, McCann & Geoghegan, 1979.

_____. *When Hitler Stole Pink Rabbit*. Coward, McCann & Geoghegan, 1972.

Kjelgaard, James. *Fire Hunter*. Holiday House, 1951.

Kroeber, Theodora. *Ishi In Two Worlds: A Biography of the Last Wild Indian in North America*. Univ. of California Press, 1961.

_____. *Ishi: Last of His Tribe*. Parnassus, 1964.

Lacy, Dan. *The Lost Colony*. Watts, 1972.

Lampman, Evelyn Sibley. *Squaw Man's Son*. Atheneum, 1978.

Latham, Jean Lee. *This Dear-Bought Land*. Illus. Jacob Landau. Harper & Row, 1957.

Lauber, Patricia. *Who Discovered America?* Random House, 1970.

Lenski, Lois. *Indian Captive: The Story of Mary Jemison*. Lippincott, 1941.

_____. *Strawberry Girl*. Lippincott, 1945.

Lester, Julius. *Long Journey Home: Stories from Black History*. Dial, 1972.

_____. *To Be a Slave*. Dial, 1968.

Levitin, Sonia. *Roanoke: A Novel of the Lost Colony*. Atheneum, 1973.

Litowinsky, Olga. *The High Voyage*. Viking, 1977.

McGovern, Ann. *The Secret Soldier: The Story of Deborah Sampson*. Illus. Ann Grifalconi. Four Winds-Scholastic, 1975.

McGraw, Eloise Jarvis. *The Golden Goblet*. Coward, McCann & Geoghegan, 1961.

_____. *Mara, Daughter of the Nile*. Coward, McCann & Geoghegan, 1953.

McKown, Robin. *Washington's America*. Grosset & Dunlap, 1961.

Macaulay, David. *Castle*. Houghton Mifflin, 1977.

Meltzer, Milton. *Bread and Roses: The Struggle of American Labor*. Knopf, 1967.

_____. *Brother, Can You Spare a Dime? The Great Depression*. Knopf, 1969.

_____. *Never to Forget: The Jews of the Holocaust*. Harper & Row, 1976.

_____. *Violins and Shovels: The WPA Art Project*. Delacorte, 1976.

Meredith, Robert, and E. Brooks Smith, eds. *The Quest of Columbus: An Exact Account of the Discovery of America Being the History Written by Ferdinand Columbus*. Illus. Leonard Everett Fisher. Little, Brown, 1966.

Monjo, F. N. *Me and Willie and Pa*. Illus. Douglas Gorsline. Simon and Schuster, 1973.

Morrison, Lucile. *The Lost Queen of Egypt*. Lippincott, 1937.

Moskin, Marietta. *Waiting for Mama*. Illus. Richard Lebenson. Coward, McCann & Geoghegan, 1975.

O'Dell, Scott. *Sing Down the Moon*. Houghton Mifflin, 1970.

Parrish, Thomas. *The American Flag*. Simon and Schuster, 1973.

Peck, Robert Newton. *Hang for Treason*. Doubleday, 1976.

_____. *Rabbits and Redcoats*. Illus. Laura Lydecker. Walker & Co. 1976.

Perl, Lila. *That Crazy April*. Seabury, 1974.

Petry, Ann. *Tituba of Salem Village*. Crowell, 1964.

Pugh, Ellen. *Brave His Soul*. Dodd, Mead, 1970.

Randall, Florence E. *The Almost Year*. Atheneum, 1971.

Reiss, Johanna. *The Journey Back*. Crowell, 1976.

_____. *The Upstairs Room*. Crowell, 1972.

Richardson, Fayette. *Sam Adams: The Boy Who Became Father of the American Revolution*. Crown, 1975.

Richter, Conrad. *A Country of Strangers*. Knopf, 1966.

_____. *The Light in the Forest*. Knopf, 1953.

Richter, Hans Peter. *Friedrich*. Holt, Rinehart & Winston, 1970.

Rodman, Bella. *Lions in the Way*. Follett, 1966.

Sandburg, Carl. *Abe Lincoln Grows Up*. Illus. James Daugherty. Harcourt Brace Jovanovich, 1956.

_____. *Abraham Lincoln: The Prairie Years*. 2 vols. Harcourt Brace Jovanovich, 1926.

Schiller, Barbara. *The Vinlanders' Saga*. Illus. William Bock. Holt, Rinehart & Winston, 1966.

Scott, John Anthony. *Woman Against Slavery: The Story of Harriet Beecher Stowe*. Crowell, 1978.

Seredy, Kate. *The White Stag*. Viking, 1937.

Sneve, Virginia Driving Hawk. *Betrayed*. Illus. Chief Oren Lyons. Holiday House, 1974.

Sparks, Beatrice. *Go Ask Alice*. Prentice-Hall, 1971.

Speare, Elizabeth George. *The Witch of Blackbird Pond*. Houghton Mifflin, 1958.

Starkey, Marion L. *The Devil in Massachusetts: A Modern Inquiry into the Salem Witch Trials*. Knopf, 1949.

_____. *The Tall Man from Boston*. Illus. Charles Mikolaycak. Crown, 1975.

_____. *The Visionary Girls: Witchcraft in Salem Village*. Little, Brown, 1973.

Stavrianos, Leften. *The Epic of Man: A Collection of Readings*. Prentice-Hall, 1971.

Steele, William O. *The Man With the Silver Eyes*. Harcourt Brace Jovanovich, 1976.

Sterling, Dorothy. *Mary Jane*. Illus. Ernest Crichlow. Doubleday, 1959.

Stowe, Harriet Beecher. *Uncle Tom's Cabin*. Dutton, 1972 (1852).

Suhl, Yuri. *On the Other Side of the Gate*. Illus. Diane Martin. Watts, 1975.

_____. *Uncle Misha's Partisans*. Four Winds-Scholastic, 1973.

Sutcliff, Rosemary. *The Lantern Bearers*. Illus. Charles Keeping. Walck, 1959.

_____. *Warrior Scarlet*. Illus. Charles Keeping. Walck, 1958.

Syme, Ronald. *Columbus: Finder of the New World*. Illus. William Stobbs. Morrow, 1952.

Taylor, Mildred. *Roll of Thunder, Hear My Cry*. Illus. Jerry Pinkney. Dial, 1976.

Taylor, Sydney. *All-of-a-Kind Family*. Illus. Helen John. Follett, 1951.

Tregaskis, Richard. *John F. Kennedy and PT-109*. Random House, 1962.

Uchida, Yoshiko. *Journey to Topaz*. Illus. Donald Carrick. Scribner's, 1971.

Uhlman, Fred. *Reunion*. Farrar, Straus & Giroux, 1977.

Voight, Virginia. *Massasoit: Friend of the Pilgrims*. Illus. Cary. Garrard, 1971.

Wilder, Laura Ingalls. *By the Shores of Silver Lake*. Illus. Garth Williams. Harper & Row, 1953 (1939).

_____. *The First Four Years*. Illus. Garth Williams. Harper & Row, 1971.

_____. *Little House in the Big Woods*. Illus. Garth Williams. Harper & Row, 1953 (1932).

_____. *Little House on the Prairie*. Illus. Garth Williams. Harper & Row, 1953 (1935).

_____. *Little Town on the Prairie*. Illus. Garth Williams. Harper & Row, 1953 (1941).

_____. *The Long Winter*. Illus. Garth Williams. Harper & Row, 1953 (1940).

_____. *On the Banks of Plum Creek*. Illus. Garth Williams. Harper & Row, 1953 (1937).

_____. *These Happy Golden Years*. Illus. Garth Williams. Harper & Row, 1953 (1943).

Wyndham, Lee. *A Holiday Book: Thanksgiving*. Illus. Hazel Hoecker. Garrard, 1963.

Yates, Elizabeth. *Amos Fortune: Free Man*. Illus. Nora S. Unwin. Dutton, 1950.

Recommended Reading

Prehistoric Times

William O. Steele's *The Magic Amulet* (I-A, Harcourt Brace Jovanovich, 1979) is an exciting story of a wounded boy's struggle for survival after he is abandoned by his primitive hunting tribe. Joseph Bato's *The Sorcerer* (A, McKay, 1976) is about a boy, forced into exile, who becomes an artist in his Cro-Magnon society.

Some of the finest fiction comes from English authors who capture the history of the British Isles in cameolike vignettes that flesh out the skeletal facts found in history books. Rosemary

Sutcliff is a talented writer and an informed historian who weaves stories of human lives and historical facts in intricate designs. Her books span the full range of English history, beginning with *Warrior Scarlet* (A, Walck, 1966), the story of Drem, a boy with a crippled arm who lived during the Bronze Age.

Ancient Egypt and Greece

The discovery, in 1922, of the tomb of King Tutankhamun heralded a new era of archaeological exploration, which is discussed in Thomas G. H. James's *The Archaeology of Ancient Egypt,* illustrated by Rosemonde Nairac (A, Walck, 1973). David Macaulay's *Pyramid* (I-A, Houghton Mifflin, 1975) explores the engineering and architectural feats involved in the building of a twenty-fifth-century B.C. funerary complex, while Lise Manniche re-creates the culture in *How Djadja-Em-Ankh Saved the Day: A Tale from Ancient Egypt* (I, Crowell, 1977), a fascinating scroll-like book.

Shirley Glubok and Alfred Tamarin's *The Mummy of Ramose: The Life and Death of an Ancient Egyptian Nobleman* (I-A, Harper & Row, 1978) explains the painstaking steps of the mummification process as well as the broad range of ancient funerary practices, while Aliki gives a more simple explanation with detailed drawings in *Mummies Made in Egypt* (P-I, Crowell, 1979).

Miriam Schlein's *I, Tut: The Boy Who Became Pharaoh,* illustrated by Erik Helgerdt (P-I, Four Winds-Scholastic, 1978), and June Reig's *Diary of the Boy King Tut-Ankh-Amen* (I, Scribner's, 1978) attempt to recreate the life of the famous Egyptian, while Shirley Glubok's *Discovering Tut-ank-Amen's Tomb* (I-A, Macmillan, 1968) and Irene and Laurence Swinburne's *Behind the Sealed Door: The Discovery of the Tomb and Treasures of Tutankhamun* (I-A, Sniffen Court-Atheneum, 1978) discuss the famous 1922 excavation and its findings.

George Selden tells the story of *Heinrich Schliemann: Discoverer of Buried Treasure,* illustrated by Lorence Bjorklund (I, Macmillan, 1964), while Hans Baumann's *Lion Gate and Labyrinth* (I-A, Pantheon, 1967) tells about Schliemann's effort to prove that the then only legendary city of Troy had actually existed. I. G. Edmonds's *The Mysteries of Troy* (A, Nelson, 1977) describes Schliemann's excavations of Trojan civilization for the period 3000 B.C. to 400 A.D. Barbara Picard retells the ancient stories of Troy in *The Iliad of Homer,* illustrated by Joan Kiddell-Monroe (I-A, Walck, 1960), and *The Odyssey of Homer,* illustrated by Joan Kiddell-Monroe (I-A, Oxford Univ. Press, 1979), as does Padraic Colum in *The Children's Homer: Adventures of Odysseus and the Tale of Troy,* illustrated by Willy Pogany (I, Macmillan, 1962).

The Middle Ages

Stories set in this period often pit young men and women against hoodlums and bandits, or emphasize the strength and courage of those who would fight to overcome a brutal ruling class. In Gene Wolfe's *The Devil in a Forest* (I-A, Follett, 1976), a young apprentice fights to protect his small village from plundering bandits. Geoffrey Trease's *The Barons' Hostage* (I-A, Nelson, 1975) is an exciting romance set during the Barons' War in the thirteenth century. Barbara Picard captures the feelings of the Middle Ages in several books, including *Lost John,* illustrated by Charles Keeping (I-A, Criterion Press, 1962), and *One Is One* (I-A, Holt, Rinehart & Winston, 1966).

Sir Thomas Malory's *King Arthur and His Knights of the Round Table,* edited by Sidney Lanier and Howard Pyle, illustrated by Florian (I-A, Grosset & Dunlap, n.d.), provides exciting fare for a study of the Middle Ages. Margaret Hodges gives background into the man and the legend in *Knight Prisoner: The Tale of Sir Thomas Malory and His King Arthur,* illustrated by Don Bolognese and Elaine Raphael (I-A, Farrar, Straus & Giroux, 1976).

Barbara Cooney adapted *Chanticleer and the Fox* (P-I, Crowell, 1958) from Chaucer's *Canterbury Tales* in a lovely picture book that captures the proud, handsome rooster as he flees from the sly fox. Ruth Craft brings to life *Pieter Brueghel's The Fair* (I-A, Lippincott, 1976), his panoramic painting of village life.

Students planning a fair to culminate a study of the Middle Ages will find valuable information in Lynn Edelman Schnurnberger's *Kings, Queens, Knights and Jesters: Making Medieval Costumes,* illustrated by Alan Robert Showe, photographs by Barbara Brooks and Pamela Hort (I-A, Harper & Row, 1978).

Several poems pertinent to a study of the Middle Ages can be found in William Cole's *Rough Men, Tough Men: Poems of Action and Adventure,* edited by William Cole, illustrated by Enrico Arno (I-A, Viking, 1969), including Alfred Noyes's "Saint George and the Dragon," Samuel Rowlands's "Sir Eglamor," Edward Rowland Still's "Opportunity," W. S. Gilbert's "The Troubador," Alfred Lord Tennyson's "Sir Galahad," and an English folk ballad, "Robin Hood and Little John."

Barbara Willard captures the spirit of Medieval Sussex in *The Miller's Boy,* illustrated by Gareth Floyd (I-A, Dutton, 1976), in which Thomas experiences prejudices of class and becomes the whipping boy for a high-bred friend.

Mollie Hunter, perhaps best known for her books of fantasy, bases many stories on historical fact and legend that she interweaves intriguingly and imaginatively. In the foreword to one of these, *The Stronghold* (I-A, Harper & Row, 1974), she describes how she stood inside an ancient stone structure in her native Scotland and wondered how, why, and when it had been built; the book is her speculative answer.

Louis Untermeyer's *The Golden Treasury of Poetry,* illustrated by Joan Walsh Anglund (P-I-A, Golden Press-Western, 1959), contains several anonymous related poems, including "Moy Castle," "Robin Hood and Allan a Dale," "Robin Hood and the Widow's Sons," "King John and the Abbot of Canterbury," Robert Browning's "How They Brought the Good News from Ghent to Aix," and Sir Walter Scott's "Lochinvar."

Explorations

Several exciting stories tell about young people who are captured by Viking raiders. Madeleine Polland's *Beorn the Proud,* illustrated by William Stobbs (I, Holt, Rinehart & Winston,

), begins as Viking invaders sack and burn a village on the coast of Ireland; the sole survivor is a young girl who is taken as a slave to Denmark. Bruce Clements's *Prison Window, Jerusalem Blue* (I-A, Farrar, Straus & Giroux, 1977) follows the lives of a brother and sister after their capture, while Rosemary Sutcliff's *Blood Feud* (A, Dutton, 1977) is the story of a freed slave who joins with his former master to avenge the death of the master's father.

Ann McGovern's *Half a Kingdom: An Icelandic Folktale* (I, Warne, 1977) will be useful in a study of the Vikings, as will Catherine Sellew's *Adventures with the Giants* (I, Holt, Rinehart & Winston, 1952), Padraic Colum's *The Children of Odin: The Book of Northern Myths* (I, Macmillan, 1920), Dorothy Hosford's *Thunder of the Gods* (I, Holt, Rinehart & Winston, 1952), and Edna Barth's *Balder and the Mistletoe: A Story for the Winter Holidays,* illustrated by Richard Cuffari (I, Seabury, 1979).

Betty Baker's *Walk the World's Rim* (I-A, Harper & Row, 1965) and Maia Wojciechowska's *Odyssey of Courage: The Story of Alvar Nunez Cabeza de Vaca,* illustrated by Alvin Smith (I, Atheneum, 1965), are two differing fictional accounts of the Spanish settlement of Mexico. Elizabeth Shepherd's *The Discoveries of Esteban the Black,* illustrated by William Steinck (I, Dodd, Mead, 1970), in the form of a biographical journal, is about a slave who is taken from Africa to Florida and then to Mexico.

Among the many biographies of the legendary discoverer of America is Gian Paolo Ceserani's *Christopher Columbus,* illustrated by Piero Ventura (I, Random House, 1979). Biographies of other explorers, numerous and easily located, vary in quality. Among the best are Edith Thacher Hurd's biographical account of Sir Frances Drake's voyage in *The Golden Hind,* illustrated by Leonard Everett Fisher (I, Crowell, 1960), and Jean Lee Latham's *Far Voyager: The Story of James Cook* (I, Harper & Row, 1970).

J. C. Squire's haunting poem "Sonnet," in *Favorite Poems Old and New,* edited by Helen Ferris, illustrated by Leonard Weisgard (P-I-A, Doubleday, 1957), is a tribute to an unknown Indian who watched as Columbus's ships neared his shore. Joaquin Miller's "Columbus," in *This Land Is Mine: An Anthology of American Verse,* edited by Al Hine, illustrated by Leonard Vosburg (P-I-A, Lippincott, 1965), Arthur Hugh Clough's "Columbus," in *America Forever New,* edited by Sara and John E. Brewton, illustrated by Ann Grifalconi (P-I-A, Crowell, 1968), and Rosemary Carr and Stephen Vincent Benét's "Christopher Columbus," in *A Book of Americans,* illustrated by Charles Child (P-I-A, Holt, Rinehart & Winston, 1961), all tell the story of the legendary discoverer of America.

The New World

Elizabeth A. Campbell's *The Carving on the Tree* (P, Little, Brown, 1968) is a fictional account of what might have happened when the original Roanoake settlers disappeared, while Manly W. Wellman's *Jamestown Adventure* (I, Washburn, 1967) speculates on what life might have been like for those early Americans. Ronald Syme's biography gives a picture of *John Smith of Virginia,* illustrated by William Stobbs (I-A, Morrow, 1954). The editors of American Heritage magazine produced *Jamestown: First English Colony* (I-A, Harper & Row, 1965), a beautifully illustrated volume that chronicles the known events of that time and speculates on the lives of those brave settlers.

The story of the Pilgrims began well before the famous voyage of the Mayflower in 1620. F. N. Monjo's *The House On Stink Alley: A Story about the Pilgrims in Holland,* illustrated by Robert Quackenbush (P-I, Holt, Rinehart & Winston, 1977), describes their stopover in Leyden, Holland, from the point of view of the eight-year-old son of William Brewster. Monjo describes the settlers' concern to protect their claim in the new world in *The Secret of the Sachem's Tree,* illustrated by Margot Tomes (P-I, Coward, McCann & Geoghegan, 1972). The story, based on historical fact, tells how the people hid the Connecticut charter in an oak tree in 1667 to keep it from being returned to England. Arnold Lobel shows imaginative humor in the picture book *On the Day Peter Stuyvesant Sailed Into Town* (P-I, Harper & Row, 1971), which describes Stuyvesant's horror at the deplorable condition of the New York colony, and his disbelief of a dream in which it has become a huge metropolis. Peter Spier's *The Legend of New Amsterdam* (P-I, Doubleday, 1979) is a similar spoof, focusing on "Crazy Annie," who looks into the distance shouting "People and stone . . ."—a vision that was, of course, to come true.

Squanto was a Native American who befriended the Pilgrims; Clyde Robert Bulla tells about him in *Squanto: Friend of the White Men,* illustrated by Peter Burchard (P-I, Crowell, 1954), and in *John Billington: Friend of Squanto,* illustrated by Peter Burchard (P-I, Crowell, 1956).

Students who wish to read about witchcraft and the Salem trials will find the following books useful: Shirley Jackson's *The Witchcraft of Salem Village,* illustrated by Lili Rethi (I, Random House, 1956), Clifford L. Alderman's *The Devil's Shadow: The Story of Witchcraft in Massachusetts* (I-A, Messner, 1967), and Alice Dickinson's *The Salem Witchcraft Delusion, 1692: "Have You Made No Contact with the Devil?"* (I-A, Watts, 1974).

Edwin Tunis gives a comprehensive view of social life and customs in *Colonial Living* (I-A, Crowell, 1976). Shirley Glubok presents a similar look at early American life in her adaptation of Alice Morse Earle's *Home and Child Life in Colonial Days,* with special photography by Alfred Tamarin (I, Macmillan, 1969). Elizabeth Schaeffer discusses *Dandelion, Pokeweed, and Goosefoot: How the Early Settlers Used Plants for Food, Medicine and in the Home,* illustrated by Grambs Miller (I, Addison-Wesley, 1972), while Lila Perl tells about *Slumps, Grunts, and Snickerdoodles: What Colonial America Ate and Why,* illustrated by Richard Cuffari (I-A, Seabury, 1975). Leonard Everett Fisher developed a series of books about Colonial American craftsmen, including *The Doctors* (I, Watts, 1968), *The Homemakers* (I, Watts, 1973), *The Blacksmiths* (I, Watts, 1976), *The Schoolmasters* (I, Watts, 1967), and others. Shirley Glubok's *The Art of Colonial America* (I-A, Macmillan, 1970) includes various bits of facts that, with the outstanding illustrations, give a clear picture of life in colonial America. For those who wish to try their hand at some of the handicrafts done by the early settlers, there are Janet and Alex D'Amato's *Colonial Crafts for You to Make* (I, Messner, 1975) and *More Colonial Crafts for You to Make* (I, Messner, 1977).

Marguerite de Angeli, a noted author of outstanding historical fiction for children, sets several of her books in colonial America, including *Skippack School* (P-I, Doubleday, 1939), a story about German settlers in Pennsylvania, and *Elin's Amerika* (P-I, Doubleday, 1941), about Swedish immigrants in the mid-1600s.

Several poems in *This Land Is Mine: An Anthology of American Verse*, edited by Al Hine, illustrated by Leonard Vosburgh (P-I-A, Lippincott, 1965), can be used in a study of early settlers in colonial America, including William Makepeace Thackeray's "Pocahontas," Felicia Dorothea Hemans's "The Landing of the Pilgrim Fathers," and Stephen Vincent Benét's "Cotton Mather." Among the first white children born in America were "Peregrine White and Virginia Dare," in *A Book of Americans*, edited by Rosemary and Stephen Vincent Benét, illustrated by Charles Child (P-I-A, Holt, Rinehart & Winston, 1961). Helen Plotz edited *The Gift Outright: America to Her Poets* (I-A, Greenwillow, 1977), which contains many poems that can be used in a study of early America.

The Revolutionary War Period

Many books of historical fiction are based on actual events and the activities of real people. Judith Berry Griffin's *Phoebe and the General*, illustrated by Margot Tomes (I, Coward, McCann & Geoghegan, 1977), relates a true incident in which a young black girl, posing as a housekeeper in the home where George Washington was staying, discovered the identity of a man who had threatened the general's life. Another true episode is related in F. N. Monjo's *Zenas and the Shaving Mill*, illustrated by Richard Cuffari (I, Coward, McCann & Geoghegan, 1976), which describes the harassment of the neutral Quakers of Nantucket during the Revolution.

Several stories have strong female characters who play important roles in the fight for independence. Mildred Lawrence's *Touchmark* (I, Harcourt Brace Jovanovich, 1975) tells about a resourceful young girl who contrives a way to carry secret messages to the Revolutionary leaders, as does Esther Wood Brady's *Toliver's Secret*, illustrated by Richard Cuffari (I, Crown, 1976), in which a young girl disguises herself as a delivery boy to deliver important information for General Washington. A fourteen-year-old girl's resentment of British soldiers billeted in her home impels her to dedicate herself to the rebel cause in Ann Finlayson's *Rebecca's War* (I, Warne, 1972), while the young heroine in Frances Duncombe's *Summer of the Burning*, illustrated by Richard Cuffari (I-A, Putnam's, 1976) takes over the responsibility for her family after her mother dies and her father is taken prisoner by the British.

Fiction about the Revolutionary period for older readers includes John and Patricia Beatty's *Who Comes to King's Mountain?* (A, Morrow, 1975), James Forman's *Cow Neck Rebels* (A, Farrar, Straus & Giroux, 1969), and Leonard Wibberley's Treegate family saga, which begins with *Peter Treegate's War* (A, Farrar, Straus & Giroux, 1960).

Robert Lawson achieved a unique blend of biography and fantasy in his books, which are told from the point of view of animals. A horse tells the story of *Mr. Revere and I* (I, Little, Brown, 1953), while a mouse is the narrator of *Ben and Me* (I, Little, Brown, 1951). These humourous glimpses of Paul Revere and Ben Franklin add a light touch to a study of these leaders.

There are probably more biographies of George Washington, Benjamin Franklin, Paul Revere, and other Revolutionary War heroes than of any other American except Abraham Lincoln. Burke Davis's peceptive book, *Three for Revolution* (I-A, Harcourt Brace Jovanovich, 1975), focuses on the critical events leading to the war and the roles played by Patrick Henry, Thomas Jefferson, and George Washington. Linda Grant De Pauw's *Founding Mothers: Women in the Revolutionary Era*, illustrated by Michael McCurdy (I-A, Houghton Mifflin, 1975), discusses the contributions of women and develops a historical perspective that emphasizes the role of the common people in shaping history.

Individual biographies are easy to locate and too numerous to list here. For useful insights into how American heroes are treated in books for children, compare several biographies of the same person: for example, Benjamin Franklin's multiple accomplishments are presented in different ways in Ingri and Edgar Parin d'Aulaire's *Benjamin Franklin* (P-I, Doubleday, 1950), F. N. Monjo's *Poor Richard in France*, illustrated by Brinton Turkle (P-I, Holt, Rinehart & Winston, 1973), and Aliki's *The Many Lives of Benjamin Franklin* (P-I, Prentice-Hall, 1977)—all books for primary-grade children. Miriam Anne Bourne views Franklin from the perspective of his young daughter in *What Is Papa Up To Now?* illustrated by Dick Gackenbach (P-I, Coward, McCann & Geoghegan, 1977).

F. N. Monjo adds a great deal of insight and humor to his fictionalized biographies. *Grand Papa and Ellen Arroon*, illustrated by Richard Cuffari (P-I, Holt, Rinehart & Winston, 1974), is told from the point of view of Thomas Jefferson's granddaughter, while *A Namesake for Nathan*, illustrated by Eros Keith (I-A, Coward, McCann & Geoghegan, 1977), is subtitled an *Account of Captain Nathan Hale by His Twelve-Year-Old Sister, Joanna*. Lest we forget the adversary in the Revolutionary War, Monjo writes a humorous eyewitness account of the events preceding the Revolution in *King George's Head Was Made Of Lead*, illustrated by Margot Tomes (P-I, Coward, McCann & Geoghegan, 1974), a reference to the statue of the English king that was knocked down and melted to make American bullets.

Several books will be useful in a critical study of the famous ride made by Paul Revere. Esther Forbes's *America's Paul Revere*, illustrated by Lynd Ward (I-A, Houghton Mifflin, 1946), is a beautifully illustrated volume. Leonard Everett Fisher's *Two If by Sea* (I, Random House, 1970) discusses the roles of William Dawes and others who participated in the events of that night.

Mary Kay Phelan's *Midnight Alarm: The Story of Paul Revere's Ride,* illustrated by Leonard Weisgard (I, Crowell, 1968), is a present-tense account that records the contributions of others. The source of the belief held by many that Revere alone alerted his countrymen to the arrival of the British is, of course, Henry Wadsworth Longfellow's poem *Paul Revere's Ride,* available in a well-illustrated picture book by Paul Galdone (P-I, Crowell, 1963), as well as in many anthologies.

Poetry and songs from the American Revolution praise the men and woman who changed the path of history and provide excellent fare for songfests. Oscar Brand's *Songs of Seventy-Six: A Folksinger's History of the Revolution* (P-I-A, M. Evans, 1973) contains songs that were collected from newspapers, books, and manuscripts in American and British museums and libraries.

Several poetry anthologies include material that covers the entire range of American history, yet are likely to be most useful in a study of this period. Rosemary and Stephen Vincent Benét's *A Book of Americans,* illustrated by Charles Child (P-I-A, Holt, Rinehart & Winston, 1961), is a series of biographical poems about American heroes from Christopher Columbus to Woodrow Wilson, including many from the Revolutionary period. Likewise, Eve Merriam's *Independent Voices,* illustrated by Arvis Stewart (P-I-A, Atheneum, 1968), sketches the lives of famous Americans from this and other periods. Sara and John E. Brewton compiled *America Forever New: A Book of Poems,* illustrated by Ann Grifalconi (P-I-A, Crowell, 1968), and Al Hine edited *This Land Is Mine: An Anthology of American Verse,* illustrated by Leonard Vosburgh (P-I-A, Lippincott, 1965). Lee Bennett Hopkins edited *Beat the Drum, Independence Day Has Come,* illustrated by Tomie de Paola (P-I, Harcourt Brace Jovanovich, 1976), as a part of his series of holiday poetry anthologies.

Patriotic music is an important adjunct to the study of America. C. A. Browne tells *The Story of Our National Ballads,* revised by Willard Heaps (I, Crowell, 1960), and Robert Kraske gives backgound into *America the Beautiful: Stories of Patriotic Songs* (P-I, Garrard, 1972). Our national anthem is beautifully visualized in two picture books: Frances Scott Key's *The Star Spangled Banner,* illustated by Peter Spier (P-I, Doubleday, 1973), and *The Star Spangled Banner,* illustrated by Paul Galdone (P-I, Crowell, 1966).

American Indians

The new awareness of the Native American culture has given rise to many outstanding books that relate the lives and legends of Indians. Christie Harris retells the folklore of the Pacific Northwest Indians in several books about a tiny supernatural creature, including *Mouse Woman and the Muddleheads,* illustrated by Douglas Tait (I, Atheneum, 1979), and *Mouse Woman and the Vanished Princesses,* illustrated by Douglas Tait (I, Atheneum, 1976). Betty Baker has written much about Native Americans, including *At the Center of the World,* illustrated by Murray Tinkelman (P-I, Macmillan, 1973), a collection of Papago and Pima myths. Diane Wolkstein retold *Squirrel's Song:*

A Hopi Indian Tale, illustrated by Lillian Hoban (P, Knopf, 1976), and Gerald McDermott created beautiful illustrations for his adaptation of *Arrow to the Sun: A Pueblo Tale* (P-I, Viking, 1974). Byrd Baylor and Peter Parnall have combined their talents in several elegant picture books that celebrate Indian myth, folklore, and fact. *The Desert Is Theirs* (P-I, Scribner's 1975) focuses on the harshly beautiful setting that controls the lives of the Indians who live there.

Fiction about American Indians often portrays the conflicts resulting from the white man's attempts to develop a new country. Janet Hickman's *The Valley of the Shadow* (I-A, Macmillan, 1974), based on historical diaries and documents, tells the bloody story of the massacre of the Moravian Indian tribe in northeastern Ohio by warring British and American troops during the Revolutionary War.

Conflict of culture became a serious problem for both Indians and whites. William O. Steele's *Wayah of the Real People,* illustrated by Isa Barnett (I-A, Holt, Rinehart & Winston, 1964), tells of a young Indian boy who is sent to the Brafferton School set up in Williamsburg for Indians, while an Indian boy in Evelyn S. Lampman's *The Year of Small Shadow* (I-A, Harcourt Brace Jovanovich, 1971) spends a year with a white lawyer. Eth Clifford explores the conflicts and benefits resulting from the mixing of the races in *The Year of the Three Legged Deer* (I, Houghton Mifflin, 1971), as does Robert Newton Peck in *Fawn* (I-A, Little, Brown, 1975). Weyman Jones's *Edge of Two Worlds* (I, Dial, 1968) is a moving story in which a young white boy, the sole survivor of an Indian attack, learns to respect the venerable Sequoyah, author of the Cherokee syllabary, whom he finds living in a cave.

The music and poetry of Native Americans is beautifully represented in several books, including Nancy Wood's *War Cry on a Prayer Feather: Prose and Poetry of the Ute Indians* (I-A, Doubleday, 1979) and Natalia M. Belting's poetry collections, *Whirlwind Is a Ghost Dancing,* illustrated by Leo and Diane Dillon (P-I-A, Dutton, 1974), and *Our Fathers Had Powerful Songs,* illustrated by Laszlo Kubinyi (P-I-A, Dutton, 1974). John Bierhorst has collected Indian music in *Songs of the Chippewa,* illustrated by Joe Servello (I-A, Farrar, Straus & Giroux, 1974), and *A Cry From The Earth: Music of the North American Indians* (I-A, Four Winds-Scholastic, 1979). *Flint and Feather: The Complete Poems of Pauline Johnson* (I-A, Muson, 1917) contains lyrical poetry surging with the life and love of her Mohawk ancestry.

Indian art is preserved in several books by Shirley Glubok, including *The Art of the North American Indian* (P-I-A, Harper & Row, 1964). Jamake Highwater surveys his people in *Many Smokes, Many Moons: A Chronology of American Indian History Through Indian Art* (I-A, Lippincott, 1978). In *Bear's Heart: Scenes from the Life of a Cheyenne Artist of One Hundred Years Ago with Pictures by Himself* (I-A, Lippincott, 1977), Burton Supree and Ann Ross tell the story of a Cheyenne Indian who, while confined in a military prison, made a pictorial record of his people's captivity; it is a haunting look at what happened to thousands of Indians who fled from the white man.

Civil War

Peter Burchard's *Chinwe* (I-A, Putnam's, 1979) is a young Ibo woman who, like Amos Fortune, is captured in her native Africa and brought to America on a slave ship. Frightful conditions on those ships are described in Paula Fox's *The Slave Dancer*, illustrated by Eros Keith (I-A, Bradbury, 1973), a story about a white boy who is kidnapped and taken aboard such a ship to play his fife when the slaves are brought up from the hold to exercise on deck.

Many books describe attempts to escape slavery by means of the underground railroad. Peter Burchard's *Bimby* (I, Coward, McCann & Geoghegan, 1968) knows that his father had been killed while attempting escape, yet he knows that he, too, must try. Barbara Claassen Smucker's *Runaway to Freedom: A Story of the Underground Railway*, illustrated by Charles Lilly (I-A, Harper & Row, 1978), is the story of a young girl who successfully leads her crippled friend through dangerous territory until they at last achieve freedom in Canada. Several stories tell about white children who play important roles in moving slaves along the underground railroad, including Rhoda W. Bacmeister's *Voices in the Night*, illustrated by Ann Grifalconi (I, Bobbs-Merrill, 1965), Aileen Fisher's *A Lantern in the Window*, illustrated by Harper Johnson (I, Thomas Nelson, 1957), and Enid L. Meadowcroft's *By Secret Railway*, illustrated by Henry C. Pitz (I, Crowell, 1948).

Florence B. Freedman tells about *Two Tickets to Freedom: The True Story of Ellen and William Craft, Fugitive Slaves,* illustrated by Ezra Jack Keats (I, Simon and Schuster, 1971), who disguised themselves and traveled by train to the north.

Harriet Tubman led nearly three hundred people to freedom after her own escape. Her story is told in numerous books, including Ann Petry's *Harriet Tubman: Conductor on the Underground Railroad* (A, Crowell, 1955), Dorothy Sterling's *Freedom Train: The Story of Harriet Tubman* (A, Doubleday, 1964), and Ann McGovern's *Runaway Slave: The Story of Harriet Tubman,* illustrated by R. M. Powers (I, Four Winds-Scholastic, 1965). Jacob Lawrence's extravagant paintings, in his picture story *Harriet and the Promised Land* (I, Simon and Schuster, 1968), have strong impact.

The Civil War affected nearly every family in the United States, even those not directly involved. Janet Hickman's *Zoar Blue* (I-A, Macmillan, 1978) is the story of two young Quakers who disobey their community's stricture against war. William O. Steele's *The Perilous Road,* illustrated by Paul Galdone (I, Harcourt Brace Jovanovich, 1958), is an exciting story about a young southern boy who nearly provokes an attack on a Yankee wagon train on which his brother might be traveling. Peter Burchard's *Jed: The Story of a Yankee Soldier and a Southern Boy* (I, Coward, McCann & Geoghegan, 1960) tells about a Union soldier who risks his life to save a young southern boy. Harold Keith's *Rifles for Watie* (I-A, Crowell, 1957) focuses on a young man who joins the Union Army but, quite by accident, becomes a member of a Rebel unit.

Betty Sue Cummings tells a powerful story about a young girl who sees the war destroy her home, devastate the land, and tear her family apart. *Hew Against the Grain* (A, Atheneum, 1977) is her grandfather's advice, which she tries to take to heart as she struggles to maintain her spirit. Patricia Lee Gauch describes the horrors of battle in *Thunder at Gettysburg,* illustrated by Stephen Gammell (P-I, Coward, McCann & Geoghegan, 1975), in which a young girl is swept into the midst of the fighting and spends three days helping wounded soldiers.

F. N. Monjo uses a familiar device to tell *Gettysburg—Tad Lincoln's Story,* illustrated by Douglas Gorsline (I, Dutton, 1976), in which the President's son relates information he gets from his father, and *The Vicksburg Veteran,* illustrated by Douglas Gorsline (I, Simon and Schuster, 1971), in which General Grant's son tells about that battle.

Biographies of Civil War heroes are numerous. Stonewall Jackson is the subject of Jean Fritz's *Stonewall,* illustrated by Stephen Gammell (I-A, Putnam's, 1979).

Many women played important roles in the Civil War. Patricia Clapp discusses *Dr. Elizabeth: A Biography of the First Woman Doctor* (I-A, Lothrop, Lee & Shepard, 1974), while Adele Deleeuw tells about the *Civil War Nurse: Mary Ann Bickerdyke* (I-A, Messner, 1973).

Poetry about the Civil War speaks dramatically about the people and the times. John Greenleaf Whittier put into verse the true story of *Barbara Frietchie,* illustrated by Paul Galdone (P-I, Crowell, 1965), an old woman who waved the Union flag in defiance of Stonewall's orders as he moved his troops through her town.

Poems about Abraham Lincoln, as numerous as biographies of him, appear in most standard anthologies. Two of the most famous poems are "Nancy Hanks—1784–1818," by Rosemary Carr and Stephen Vincent Benét, in *A Book of Americans,* illustrated by Charles Child (P-I-A, Holt, Rinehart & Winston, 1961), which is a plea for information about her soldier son, and Julius Silberger's "A Reply to Nancy Hanks," in *Time for Poetry,* edited by May Hill Arbuthnot (P-I-A, Scott, Foresman, 1967).

The anthologies of American patriotic poetry listed above for the Revolutionary War period also contain many poems about the Civil War. Paul Glass compiled *Singing Soldiers: A History of the Civil War in Song* (P-I-A, Grosset & Dunlap, 1969), which contains many ballads and songs of this period.

Life on the Frontier: The Pioneers

Accounts of the adventures and dangers surrounding the westward expansion into the forests and wilderness of the thirteen original colonies and beyond appear frequently. Alice Dalgleish's *The Courage of Sarah Noble,* illustrated by Leonard Weisgard (P-I, Scribner's 1954), vividly describes the experiences of an eight-year-old girl who goes with her father to establish a new home on the Connecticut frontier. Indians help Sarah and her father in this and other stories, including Elizabeth Yates's *Carolina's Courage,* illustrated by Nora S. Unwin (P-I, Dutton, 1964), in which a doll given to young Carolina assures safe travel through Indian territory. Anne Colver's *Bread and Butter Indian,* illustrated by Garth Williams (P-I, Holt, Rinehart & Winston, 1964), and *Bread and Butter Journey,* illustrated by Garth Williams (P-I, Holt, Rinehart & Winston, 1970), tell of the friendship between a white girl and an Indian in the New Hampshire wilderness.

Jean Fritz tells about a lonely girl's resentment of her family's move to the Pennsylvania frontier in *The Cabin Faced West,* illustrated by Feodor Rojankovsky (P-I, Coward, McCann & Geoghegan, 1958). Rebecca Caudill's *Tree of Freedom,* illustrated by Dorothy Morse (I, Viking, 1949), is the symbol of a new life for a young girl who journeys to the Kentucky frontier.

Carol Ryrie Brink based her story *Caddie Woodlawn,* illustrated by Trina Schart Hyman (I-A, Macmillan, 1973 [1935]), on her tomboy grandmother's life in the 1860 Wisconsin wilderness, while Ann Nolan Clark describes a young girl's adjustment to the Minnesota wilderness in *All This Wild Land* (I, Viking, 1976). Willa Cather wrote several pioneer stories for adults; her biography is told in Ruth Franchere's *Willa: The Story of Willa Cather's Growing Up* (I, Crowell, 1958). The true story of the Sager family of seven children who, after the deaths of their parents, made the long, hard journey on the Oregon Trail to a new life beyond the Rocky Mountains, is told in several books, including Anna Rutgers Van der Loeff's *Oregon at Last!* (I, Morrow, 1962), Neta L. Frazier's *Stout-Hearted Seven* (I, Harcourt Brace Jovanovich, 1973), and Honore Morrow's *On to Oregon* (I, Morrow, 1946). Evelyn Sibley Lampman tells about a young girl orphaned on the Oregon Trail in *Bargain Bride* (I-A, Atheneum, 1977).

Patricia Beatty wrote several stories about the far western frontier, including *Something to Shout About* (I, Morrow, 1976) and *By Crumbs, It's Mine!* (I, Morrow, 1976).

Although girls appear in the majority of pioneer stories, boys, too, had exciting adventures in the American wilderness. William O. Steele wrote a number of good frontier stories, including *The Year of the Bloody Sevens,* illustrated by Charles Beck (I, Harcourt Brace Jovanovich, 1963), in which a young boy travels to Kentucky with two woodsmen in search of his father. The title is derived from the year in which the story takes place, 1777, which was a very bloody year in the boy's life as well as in the life of the new country.

Many non-fiction books present all aspects of life in the developing western frontier. Edwin Tunis wrote an excellent round-up of *Frontier Living* (I-A, Crowell, 1976), while Lila Perl concentrates on frontier food in *Hunter's Stew and Hangtown Fry: What Pioneer America Ate and Why,* illustrated by Richard Cuffari (I-A, Seabury, 1977).

The poetry and music of the American frontier enriches the study of pioneer life. Oscar Brand compiled *When I First Came to This Land,* illustrated by Doris Burn (P-I-A, Putnam's, 1974), a collection of folk songs celebrating the courage and spirit of the American pioneer.

The abovementioned anthologies of patriotic poetry contain a wealth of material to enhance the study of American pioneer living. In addition, William Cole's anthology, *Rough Men, Tough Men: Poems of Action and Adventure,* illustrated by

Enrico Arno (I-A, Viking, 1969), features such titles as "Whiskey Bill," an American cowboy ballad, Edward Lueders's "Rodeo," and Robert W. Service's "The Shooting of Dan McGrew."

Twentieth-Century America

The early twentieth century brought changes for Americans, who struggled to build their lives in the developing cities as well as in the still-vast open lands. Walter D. Edmonds gives a good description of turn-of-the-century country life in *Bert Breen's Barn* (I-A, Little Brown, 1975), as a young boy rebuilds a barn to help improve his family's run-down farm. Vera and Bill Cleaver always write about spunky characters who survive against great odds: *Dust of the Earth* (I-A, Lippincott, 1975) is no exception as fourteen-year-old Fern Drawn and her family survive the harshness of the Dakotas in the 1920s.

California in the 1920s is the setting for two timeless stories by Eleanor Cameron. *Julia and the Hand of God,* illustrated by Gail Ownes (I, Dutton, 1977), and *A Room Made of Windows* (I, Little, Brown, 1971) follow an imaginative young girl as she struggles to become a writer.

The Depression is the background for many stories about people who fight against great odds merely for survival. Crystal Thrasher's *The Dark Didn't Catch Me* (I, Atheneum, 1975) and its sequel *Between Dark and Daylight* (I, Atheneum, 1979) feature a gritty eleven-year-old girl who sees her mother become increasingly bitter when her father leaves home to find work. Two young brothers take to the road in search of work in Irene Hunt's vivid story *No Promises in the Wind* (I-A, Follett, 1970), while the family in Beth Bland Engel's *Ride the Pine Sapling* (I, Harper & Row, 1978) takes in roomers to help make ends meet. Mildred Taylor's *Song of the Trees,* illustrated by Jerry Pinkney (I, Dial, 1975), and *Roll of Thunder, Hear My Cry* (I, Dial, 1976) tell of the struggle of a poor black family to retain their land as well as maintain their dignity in the face of southern racism during the Depression. Poverty in the rural south is also the background for Robbie Branscum's *For Love of Jody* (I, Lothrop, Lee & Shepard, 1979), in which a family not only struggles against hard times but also has to deal with the problem of a brain-damaged child.

Long after the Depression had ended, sharecroppers and migrant workers lived in poverty, and disappointments and misfortunes were common, yet many books show families constantly seeking a better life. Lois Lenski wrote many stories about poor families including *Cotton in My Sack* (I, Lippincott, 1949), in which a family's dream to settle down and work their own land becomes a reality. Doris Gates tells a similar tale in *Blue Willow,* illustrated by Paul Lantz (I, Viking, 1940). Louisa R. Shotwell's *Roosevelt Grady,* illustrated by Peter Burchard (I, Collins, 1963), is a black boy who dreams of quitting the migrant life and going to school in one place.

Several authors reminisce about their own childhood days in stories set before World War II. Robert Newton Peck writes about the adventures he shared with his friend *Soup,* illustrated by Charles Gehm (I, Knopf, 1974), in several books. Robert

Burch grew up in rural Georgia and writes about his youth in *Skinny,* illustrated by Don Sibley (I, Viking, 1964), and in *Wilkin's Ghost,* illustrated by Lloyd Bloom (I-A, Viking, 1978).

World War II

Joseph Ziemian's *The Cigarette Sellers of Three Crosses Square* (I-A, Lerner, 1976) recounts the true story of a group of Jewish ragamuffins who outwit the Gestapo and survive in the Aryan section of Nazi-occupied Warsaw. Many stories tell of refugees who were forced to leave their homes during the German occupation. Aimee Sommerfelt's *Miriam* (I-A, Criterion, 1963) goes into hiding with her family during the occupation of Norway, while Doris Orgel's *A Certain Magic* (I-A, Dial, 1976) tells about a young Jewish refugee living with an English family. Claire Huchet Bishop's *Twenty and Ten,* illustrated by William Pène du Bois (P-I, Viking, 1964), tells of ten Jewish children who were given refuge in a French boarding school.

Doris Orgel's *The Devil in Vienna* (I-A, Dial, 1978) is an autobiographical account of the occupation of Vienna, when the author suddenly found herself an outcast among her gentile friends. The friendship of unlikely pairs is a common thread in many stories, including two by John R. Tunis *His Enemy, His Friend* (I-A, Morrow, 1967), in which a German sergeant helps a young French boy, and *Silence Over Dunkerque* (I-A, Morrow, 1962), about a young French girl who befriends a British soldier. Children in many places aided refugees and did their share of fighting the Germans. Hilda Van Stockum's *The Winged Watchman* (I, Farrar, Straus & Giroux, 1963) is a windmill that serves as a hiding place in the resistance system, while Marie McSwigan's *Snow Treasure,* illustrated by Mary A. Reardon (I, Dutton, 1942), tells about a group of Norwegian children who secretly move gold bullion on their sleds past the German lines. Robert Westall's *The Machine Gunners* (I-A, Greenwillow, 1976) describes a young boy's attempt to overcome his fear of air raids by fighting back with his machine gun.

Thousands of children were evacuated from their homes during World War II. Noel Streatfield tells about three such children sent to the English countryside in *When the Sirens Wailed,* illustrated by Judith Gwyn Brown (I, Random House, 1976), while Nina Bawden's *Carrie's War,* illustrated by Colleen Browning (I, Lippincott, 1973), describes the feelings of a girl evacuated to a Welsh mining town. Hester Burton's *In Spite of All Terror,* illustrated by Victor G. Ambrus (I-A, Collins, 1969), tells about a girl's uneasiness when sent to live with an aristocratic family in the English countryside. Margaret J. Anderson describes a clever deception when a wealthy girl being sent to Canada trades places with a friend from an orphanage. Each girl is able to experience pleasures she has never known in *Searching for Shona* (I-A, Knopf, 1978). Sheila Garrigue relates her own experiences when *All the Children Were Sent Away* (I, Bradbury, 1976). Charles Hannam's *A Boy in That Situation* (A, Harper & Row, 1978) is another autobiographical account of a spoiled young boy forced to become aware of prejudice, injustice, and responsiblity.

Although most stories for children concerning the Nazi regime do not, some vividly describe the horrors and tortures suffreed by its victims. One such, Esther Hautzig's *The Endless Steppe: Growing Up in Siberia* (I-A, Crowell, 1968), tells about a Jewish family in a German prison camp in Siberia. Marietta Moskin takes the reader inside the death camps in *I Am Rosemarie* (A, John Day, 1972), a survival story of the most important kind. Rosemarie and her family do escape, but only after suffering near starvation, grinding labor, disease, and the brutality of sadistic guards. James D. Forman tells about *The Survivor* (A, Farrar, Straus & Giroux, 1976), the only member of the Ullman family to live through the horrors of Auschwitz. Anne Holm's *North to Freedom* (I-A, Harcourt Brace Jovanovich, 1965) is a moving story about a young boy who wanders across Europe in search of his mother after having spent most of his life in German prison camps.

A few stories tell about German children living in the same period. Ilse Koehn's *Mischling, Second Degree: My Childhood in Nazi Germany* (A, Greenwillow, 1977) is an autobiographical account of a young girl forced to become a member of the Hitler Youth. Ilse is separated from her family in the hope that the officials will not discover that she has a Jewish grandparent. Hilda van Stockum's *The Borrowed House* (I-A, Farrar, Straus & Giroux, 1975) describes a young German girl's feelings when she realizes that she is living in a house that had been confiscated from a Jewish family.

Although the fighting never reached America, many Jewish refugees did. Myron Levoy tells about *Alan and Naomi* (I-A, Harper & Row, 1977), two Jewish children who experience the war in totally different ways. Naomi is a refugee from France who is in shock after seeing her father murdered by the Gestapo. Alan, who has known only the security of life in America, spends countless hours trying to restore the girl to health. Michele Murray's *The Crystal Nights* (I-A, Seabury, 1973) tells about Jewish refugees living with relatives in America, while Harry Mazer's *The Last Mission* (A, Delacorte, 1979) describes the experiences of a Jewish-American boy who enlists. His idealistic view of war is abruptly changed when his aircraft is shot down and he is taken prisoner.

Bette Greene's *The Summer of My German Soldier* (I, Dial, 1973) tells about a young Jewish girl in Arkansas who befriends a German prisoner of war. A sequel, *Morning Is a Long Time Coming* (I-A, Dial, 1978), describes the girl's journey to Europe at the close of the war to find her friend's mother.

M. E. Kerr's contemporary novel *Gentlehands* (A, Harper & Row, 1978) involves the tracking of a war criminal thirty years after the war; the horrors of Auschwitz are recalled when Buddy discovers that his grandfather is that camp's infamous "Gentlehands."

Eve Merriam's poem "Fantasia," in *Finding a Poem,* illustrated by Seymour Chwast (I, Atheneum, 1970), is a stark statement expressing a dream that someday a child may ask, "Mother, what was war?" Other poems in this book include "The Measure of Man" and "The Dirty Word."

ten

KIM WILLIAMS   *REQUIEM FOR A RIVER*

"So we diverted the river," he said,
showing blueprints
and maps
and geological surveys.
"It'll go in this canal now."

The Rio Blanco River starts in a glacier
up the white-capped Andes.
It has run through a green valley
for three million years,
maybe more.

Now in this year
when the Rio Blanco copper mine
at 12,000 feet altitude
gets underway,
the river has to go.

Pick it up,
Move it over —
Anything is possible.
Don't stand in the way
of progress.
And a 90-million-dollar mine.
"We concreted the dam," Bert said.
Thanks.[1]

Informational Books

The elementary school curriculum is comprised of areas of knowledge divided into specific subjects such as mathematics, science, and social studies. Children are taught all of these as separate disciplines, but must learn to integrate them to make sense of the world. Learning is, then, more than the laying on of discrete areas of information; it requires an active response from students, an interpretation or reconstruction of new information in relation to what they already know. Instead of teaching a body of facts for memorization, our goal is to help students learn to think. There are informational books on multitudinous subjects designed to achieve this aim. We use them according to the learner's existing knowledge, interest, and the purpose at hand. Teachers fashion learning activities that cut across the curriculum and that draw upon books of fiction, nonfiction, and poetry in ways that encourage in children an active search for meaning.

Nonfiction (or "informational" books) are distinguished from fiction by their emphasis. Both may tell a story and both may include fact; in fiction, however, the story is uppermost, with facts sometimes used to support it, while in nonfiction the facts are uppermost, with storytelling perhaps used as an expressive technique.

More than 60 to 70 percent of most library collections in elementary schools and in the children's sections of public libraries are informational books; fiction makes up the smallest part—a surprise to most people. Nonfiction writers complain, justifiably, that their work—even though numbers are on their side—receives less attention than fiction. In many good schools the entire curriculum is taught with informational books rather than textbooks.

Because there are too many informational trade books to permit review of them in any comprehensive way, what follows is the merest sampling of the great range and variety of informational books available; selections are given for the primary-, intermediate-, and advanced-grade levels.

LEARNING FROM TRADE BOOKS

Even though the typical school day is segmented according to subjects, we know that learning is not similarly compartmented; children do not learn reading in reading class alone, science in science class alone, history in social studies alone. Children learn best to think, read, write, speak, and listen when instruction in all curriculum areas is integrated—when, for example, a teacher exploring plant life in a science lesson grasps the opportunity to relate "phototropism" to other words with the prefix "photo." This kind of integration in instruction parallels the way children actually learn—not facts in isolation, but rather parts of a meaningful whole.

Reading for information is related to other language uses; it is part of the scheme of the total language system. Children do read to learn in assigned textbooks, but they read to learn with enthusiasm and excitement in specialized trade books of quality. Compared to a textbook, a trade book can reveal the point of view of the author more directly, focus on an individual or a topic with a sharper light, and present specialized information that often gives readers a fuller understanding. For example, a textbook may mention that Carl Linnaeus developed a system or a taxonomy for classifying plants, but Alice Dickinson's biography *Carl Linnaeus: Pioneer of Modern Botany* (A) gives a far more intimate and revealing picture of the man and his work. Or, while a textbook may barely mention that some plants open only during the day or that birds seem to know when to migrate, Seymour Simon's *The Secret Clocks: Time*

Sense of Living Things (I) probes these phenomena thoroughly.

When young children read *Eat the Fruit, Plant the Seed* (P), by Millicent E. Selsam and Jerome Wexler, they learn how to plant fruit seeds that grow into interesting house plants. Photographs show the various stages of growth while the text details the best growing conditions. The limited number of seeds discussed allows full explication for the beginning gardener and/or horticulturist. When intermediate-grade students read Millicent E. Selsam's *How Animals Live Together* (I), they learn how scientists observe the social life of the animal world and about the problems associated with observing animals in their natural habitats. (Behavior of animals in captivity is often uncharacteristic.)

A Frog's Body (P-I), by Joanna Cole, offers simply related facts and clear photographs and diagrams. Because the bullfrog's organs are similar to those of human beings, readers learn by analogy about their own bodies. The magnificent photographs capture for study aspects of a frog's body and behavior that would be difficult to reproduce in real life.

It is probable that you remember, from your

Excellent photographs extend the simple text of *A Frog's Body,* in which readers learn the anatomy and physiology of the frog. (From *A Frog's Body* by Joanna Cole, 1980. Illustrated by Jerome Wexler © 1980. Reprinted by permission of the publisher, William Morrow & Company, Inc.).

elementary-school textbooks, not more than some isolated fragments. It is equally probable that you remember much more associated with some special project that you may have had to research and develop for a presentation, a science fair, or a demonstration. We learn when our emotions are involved, we learn when we are actively engaged, and we learn when we pursue our own—rather than someone else's—interests. Facts are remembered when they are integrated into one's conception of reality, and they are most often learned and retained for use when they are part of a meaningful experience. We all learn by fitting new information into a coherent frame or schema in a process of assimilation and accommodation that is described by Piaget. Nonfiction makes information available to children in ways that facilitate the creation of meaningful category systems and critical schemata. When children seek out information for themselves, identify what is relevant, and use it for meaningful goals, they become more efficient at storing and retrieving facts. The especially fine informational books published today illumine their path. Furthermore, there are trade books on virtually any topic and for almost any level of understanding, and this rich and vast array of materials generates an interest and excitement that encourages students to grow.

LEARNING TO READ CRITICALLY

Taxonomies of critical thinking skills abound, and although there is little support for a hierarchical ordering or rigid sequential development, there is a general developmental progression from the somewhat simple to the complex. Taxonomies include inferring, comparing, attending to detail, distinguishing between fact and opinion, evaluating, verifying information, determining the qualifications of the author, generalizing, analyzing, synthesizing, hypothesizing, and predicting on the basis of what is known. (Concomitantly, students progress in their ability to apply work-study skills such as following directions, using a table of contents, using an index and a glossary, taking notes, using a card catalog, and other library skills.)

Critical reading and thinking are basic to learning for a lifetime. The schemata we develop as we learn to read, and read to learn, influence all subsequent knowledge. Readers who are literate but absorb information passively—rather than thinking and evaluating—become higher illiterates. Thinking readers, sometimes called critical readers, evaluate new information in light of what they already know, compare many sources instead of accepting only one point of view, and make judgments about what they read. They can discriminate fact from opinion. The overarching goal of education—to develop informed, thinking, participating citizens—requires such readers.

The habit of reading critically, then, is invaluable. The child who believes that anything found in print is the truth, the whole truth, is at a disadvantage relative to the one who has learned to check sources, compare reports, and evaluate. Children do not question what they read when they are given one textbook, which is held up as embodying the final and whole truth on its subject. They do learn to question and evaluate as they read if we encourage them to make comparisons among different sources—often nonfiction trade books.

We can engender unquestioning respect for the authority of the textbook by the way we respond to students' questions. Replies such as "Look it up in the book," or "What does the book say?" may inadvertently teach students to pay abject homage to textbooks in general.

Developmental differences in ability to think critically are not so much a matter of kind as of degree. Long before they turn to information found in books, very young children can make comparisons: they can deal with ideas such as who is taller, which coat warmer, which cookie bigger. Listening to stories or looking at books, young children can attend to detail and make comparisons. For example, when looking at the photographs in the portfolios by Jorg Müller, *The Changing City* (P-I-A) and *The Changing Countryside* (P-I-A), they can observe that parts of the landscape such as

386 mountains and rivers may remain the same from one decade to the next, and other parts, such as a new highway, are very different. Older children will make many more inferences about what causes the changes in the landscape when a country road becomes a superhighway with gas stations, shops, restaurants, and motels. Students who are even more mature will draw implications from the scenes about ecology, the quality of life, and the need for planning.

Children of all ages can verify information found in books by checking it against observations made in real life, as, for example, when a forgotten peanut butter sandwich turns up covered with green mold while the class is reading about fungi in Lucia Anderson's *The Smallest Life around Us* (P-I). Young children can hypothesize about the causes of mold, can experiment with different conditions that promote or retard it, see that it grows on bread, lemons, or grass, and can learn about useful molds that help make cheese or bread.

Children verify information found in books in different ways. Some may ask a teacher or parent, others may go to other books or to an authority on the topic. For some fifth-grade students studying transportation, a resource book was *Jet Journey* (I), by Mike Wilson and Robin Scagell. *Jet Journey* is a large well-illustrated book with photographs, diagrams, and scale model drawings that cover the world of flying. It includes sections on knowing planes, how planes fly, and finding the way through the sky. Boxed inserts show how things work, projects to make, and quick experiments to try. Students verified the information in a variety of ways. Some followed the book's directions for determining how far away a plane is in the sky, for making a "visual approach slope indicator," and for building a model Concorde. Thus, they verified the information involved by actually trying the projects and seeing if they worked.

Another section in the book describes safety-first preflight checks. The text states:

The flight engineer walks slowly round the outside of the plane to ensure that nothing is obviously wrong. When he is satisfied, he joins the pilot and first officer on the flight deck. Here the crew checks all the plane's instruments, systems and controls. . . . The crew tests each instrument in turn, checking its reading. Some systems, such as the hydraulics which work the brakes and undercarriage, can only be checked when the engines are running.[2]

The students verified this and a great deal of other information in the text by visiting a local airport. One child's father, a commercial airline pilot, arranged to get the students into an observation deck where he explained what was happening to the jet liner being prepared for takeoff. What the children saw was a beehive of activity: trucks zooming out to the plane with precooked dinners and snacks, fuel trucks lined up pumping fuel into the tanks, baggage carts moving baggage from conveyor belts to plane, and the flight crew checking instruments and talking with people in the control tower. Everything was being done under crisislike conditions, with people running, yelling orders, working within a very tight schedule—all of which made the statement "the flight engineer walks slowly round the outside of the plane to ensure that nothing is obviously wrong" seem ludicrous. The students were able to ask people at the airport about their jobs and verified the information in the book through direct observation. The major discrepancy they noted was that the book did not convey the sense of urgency they observed at the airfield, although the book was accurate in the actual information it contained. Teachers who encourage these kinds of activities help students become more divergent thinkers.

Children of all ages can make evaluative decisions—about what they like and don't like—although the bases for their judgments differ. Young children pressed for their reasons draw from an egocentric base and offer subjective, affective reasons: "Just because I like it." Intermediate-grade students might say they like a book "Because it's good," whereas older students evaluate in terms of the object itself: "It's good because it is well written and has clear illustrations." Each evaluative decision is developmentally appropriate.

Primary-grade children compared and evaluated two books about popcorn—*The Popcorn Book* (P), by Tomie de Paola, and *Popcorn* (P), by

Millicent E. Selsam. Both books tell about varieties of corn and where and when popcorn was discovered. They differ markedly, however, in style of presentation, illustrations, and amount and kind of information given. Selsam's book contains striking color and black-and-white photographs, whereas de Paola's book is illustrated with humorous and whimsical cartoonlike drawings. Selsam devotes a major part of her discussion to germinating seeds, planting and growing corn, the properties of corn plants, and pollenization. De Paola devotes more of his book to the popping process; he has one character read from an encyclopedia some interesting facts about popcorn: how much is eaten each year, which cities are the top popcorn-eating cities, and funny stories about popcorn (such as the popcorn blizzard in the Midwest). After the books had been read aloud, children in one group said: "*The Popcorn Book* is more fun but the other one tells you more stuff." "If you want to know about growing popcorn, you should read *Popcorn* because it tells you what to do."

The children also found a discrepancy between the two books concerning when popcorn was first found. De Paola says, "In a bat cave in New Mexico, archeologists found some popped corn that was 5,600 years old." Selsam says, "Scientists do know that people who lived in caves in New Mexico 2,000 years ago did pop corn, because popped kernels of that age were found there in a cave named Bat Cave." De Paola also states, "and 1,000-year-old popcorn kernels were found in Peru that could still be popped." Selsam adds, "There were also unpopped kernels in the cave, and the scientists studying the corn were able to pop some of these 2,000-year-old kernels." When the children discussed which was right, one said, "Well, I think she's [Selsam] right because we have a lot of other books by both of them and hers are all science books and his are mostly funny books." In further evaluation one child said, "Hers is more like a real science book but his tells you real stuff in a funnier way." Information on the jackets of the two books—if academic credentials can be taken as an index of competence—seem to confirm the children's judgments: Millicent Selsam has several degrees in the sciences, and none is claimed for Tomie de Paola.

These remarks of children show how natural it is for them to make comparisons. They also illustrate the usefulness of informational books in the curriculum to foster growth in critical reading and thinking.

Students in advanced grades deal with topics and use skills at a more complex level than do younger students. For adolescents, personal and social concerns become dominant in the search for information. Numerous books satisfy their curiosity about sexual development and relationships with the opposite sex, and clarify their self-identity as sexual beings. Two books by Eric W. Johnson, *Love and Sex in Plain Language* (A) and *Sex: Telling It Straight* (A), and one by Joan Horvath, *What Girls Want to Know About Boys, What Boys Want to Know About Girls* (I-A), are books that students will want to read, compare, analyze, and evaluate. Another that teachers may want to use with more mature students is William A. Block's *What Your Child Really Wants to Know About Sex* (A).

In *What Girls Want to Know About Boys, What Boys Want to Know About Girls,* Horvath gives basic physiological information and then presents interviews with teens and preteens who describe their feelings about the opposite sex. When the author talks with Andy, she asks him if he would go out with a girl who is captain of the football team. Andy asks if she means the girls' football team or *the* football team, and when she says she means *the* football team, he says, "Not if she was tougher than most of the guys." After probing for reasons Andy feels this way, she finally elicits the comment, "I guess I'd be afraid of getting a razzing from the guys. Boys don't like to think that girls can be more capable than they can be".[3] Many of Andy's responses are based upon what others, especially his peers, would think of him. For example, he says, "Well, nobody in our school would take out someone who was ugly. If a boy took out an ugly girl, the boy would feel inferior. The other boys would think less of him".[4]

In several interviews, students say that "looks" and "personality" are what attract them to the op-

Profile

SEYMOUR SIMON

The sun is far away from Earth and its moon. A spaceship that could travel to the moon in a few days would take more than a year to come close to the sun.

The sun is an average-size star. There is nothing very special about it, except for the fact that it is our star. Life on Earth depends upon the heat and light of the sun.

The Long View into Space

A rare combination of talent and knowledge of children, science, and teaching, Seymour Simon is a believer in the hands-on approach of leading children to discoveries about their world. For example, he used the appeal of making paper airplanes to teach the concepts of aerodynamics in *The Paper Airplane Book*. The diagrams explain thrust, lift, gravity, and how movable wing surfaces, like flaps, affect flight.

The author of over sixty books, Simon builds on twenty years of teaching experience, though he now goes directly to children rather than writing for a school curriculum. He knows what readers are interested in and how to relate science to their interests. He involves the child as scientist as well as reader by providing projects, experiments, and things to observe in every book.

Pets in a Jar and *Look to the Night Sky* are among many of his works named "outstanding science trade books for children" by the National Science Teachers Association. The practical activities that he provides for children to try on their own lead to greater understanding because they make the children active participants in the learning process. Simon knows, and shows that he knows, that children learn by doing.

Seymour Simon was born in New York City, where he attended school and later taught. He lives in suburban Long Island with his wife and two sons. A full-time writer and scholar, he takes time out for tennis and for talks with teachers and students.

posite sex. But when, further along in the interview, they give details about what that means, "personality" usually emerges as shared interests and the capacity to make them (the interviewee) feel important. Students in advanced grades will be able to recognize the real feelings behind the statements, for they certainly have their own opinions about the topic, and will compare the way they feel with the ways portrayed in the book.

They can draw conclusions and check them against the author's. For example, Horvath states:

Another thing that the interviews revealed is the importance of paying attention to your own self-image. Most of the young people I talked to said that their decisions were often shaped by the opinions of their close friends. You have to allow for the natural fact that self-image, at this point in your life, is to a certain extent a reflection of what your friends approve of. But what about the person who constantly conforms to the choices of others?

Always conforming to others is hardly a way for a girl to discover what she really likes or wants.[5]

Adolescent readers will evaluate the author's statements in light of their own experience. They can also compare this book with others and decide which they prefer and why.

Many books encourage the reader to adopt a critical stance based on observing, collecting, and analyzing data; drawing conclusions; making inferences; and testing hypotheses. In *The Secret Clocks: Time Sense of Living Things* (I), Seymour Simon states:

During the summer or during the warmer months of spring and fall, you can do a simple experiment to demonstrate the time sense of bees. Spread out some honey or syrup on a piece of blue paper. Place the paper outdoors each morning at the same time in the same spot. Bees can see blue, yellow, blue-green, and ultraviolet (a color you cannot see). The honey on the paper will attract the bees by its odor. . . . After you are sure that the bees are showing up on schedule, place the same color sheet in the same spot but without any honey smeared on it. Start observing an hour earlier than the regular feeding time and continue for an hour later than the regular time. Record the number of bees that come in fifteen-minute blocks of time. Use a bar graph to show your results. [He gives a sample graph] Keep setting the paper each day at the same time until the bees stop showing up. . . . How do your results compare with those shown on the graph? For how many days did your bees continue to show up at the correct time? Try the same experiment at different seasons or at different times of the day to see if that makes any difference in the results you get.[6]

Simon involves readers as "scientists"—checking information by conducting experiments and observing, interpreting, and comparing their results with his.

ORGANIZING INTEGRATED UNITS WITH INFORMATIONAL BOOKS

There are numerous ways to approach a unit of study with informational books. Much depends upon the children in your group—their developmental level, their interests, and their background in the area of study.

One of the major things a teacher must know is how to locate books on a subject. Several avenues are open: the card catalog and librarians in school and public libraries lead you to books on your topic. There are also specific reference sources that list books by subject—for example, *Subject Guide to Children's Books in Print* and *Children's Catalog,* which are updated each year. Other valuable resources include *The Elementary School Library Collection* and *Index to Children's Poetry.* In addition, professional organizations in several disciplines publish annual lists of outstanding books for children. "Notable Children's Trade Books in the Field of Social Studies" appears in the April issue of the journal of *Social Education,* "Outstanding Science Trade Books for Children" appears in the March issue of *Science and Children,* and "Children's Choices" appears in the October issue of *The Reading Teacher.* Many of the specialized lists are available from the Children's Book Council.

As you locate books, many different ways of organizing a study will become evident. Creating "a web of possibilities" is one favored by some teachers. In this method, you brainstorm a topic for the many ways a unit study might proceed, seeking likely areas of study, and organize materials according to the way you choose. The web of possibilities concept, developed in England and then popularized in America by Charlotte S. Huck, is based on a "schema," or network, of resources and activities emanating from a central theme, topic, or book. The units in this chapter—one each for the primary, intermediate, and advanced levels—are developed around a topic in this fashion.

Networks for units can also be created by groups of children thinking together about avenues they would like to pursue. The unit study for the primary grades—My Body and How It Works—began as a discussion in which children proposed ideas they wanted to explore. These were then written on a chalkboard and added to by children and teachers over several weeks, as they worked through the unit. The group pursued many of the ideas in the actual study but by no means all of them. In fact, one should never try to do everything suggested in a web of possibilities—the elements are simply ideas from which to choose.

The unit for intermediate grades—Using the World's Resources in a More Resourceful Way—was developed by librarians in response to teachers' requests for material on the energy crisis. Books, films, clippings, articles, and speakers offer students ways to research a topic. The collection of materials should be used as a starting point, with students involved in the search. Learning to locate information is a useful skill at any age.

The advanced-grades unit—Endangered Species—grew from a group of student scientists who, interested in ecology, were outraged when an antipollution law failed to be enacted and began writing to their community's representatives. On the assumption that they might be more convincing if they knew their facts, they researched their topic. The unit is, in effect, a trace of their steps along the way.

Each unit is illustrative, not prescriptive. Your students' curiosity and interests lead the way.

The Primary-Grades Unit: My Body and How It Works

Primary-grade children are fascinated and amazed by themselves and see themselves as the center of their world. We can build upon their egocentrism to lead them to discoveries about their bodies and what keeps them healthy. A positive self-concept facilitates learning. Through using the unifying theme of the child's own body, feelings, eating habits, and individual concerns, children can come to see themselves as unique and special. They also need to feel that they are developing normally and that what they are doing is what they should be doing. As they focus on the uniqueness and acceptability of themselves, they also learn to see others as unique and acceptable—though different—beings. (With the "mainstreaming" of handicapped children into regular classrooms, acceptance of differences and uniquenesses becomes an unwritten part of the curriculum for all children.)

The five major sections of the chart "Materials and Activities for a Primary-Grades Unit" are discussed below.

BIRTH (HOW I WAS BORN) Early-childhood teachers who keep gerbils, rabbits, hamsters, mice, or other animals in their classrooms have a head start on helping children make discoveries about the birth process. Much of the mystery is dispelled when children can see animals mating, pregnant, giving birth, and feeding their young.

Several excellent books can help in the discovery. Sidonie Matsner Gruenberg's *The Wonderful Story of How You Were Born* (P-I) is a near classic, with copyright dates of 1952, 1953, 1959, and 1970. The list of grandchildren to whom she dedicates the book has grown over the years and now includes a sizable list of great-grandchildren. Gruenberg speaks directly to the reader as she discusses how we formerly thought children could not understand how babies were born and so made up stories about it:

Sometimes they would say the baby was found under a cabbage leaf, or came in the doctor's little black bag. Or in some countries they would say the baby was brought by a big white stork.
But now we realize that children do think about themselves and can understand the true story of where babies come from. And the true story is far more interesting than any made-up story.[7]

Gruenberg goes on to explain the tiny egg cell called an ovum and the even tinier kind of cell called a sperm. In an account told with warmth and love, she uses words such as fertilized ovum, womb, penis, vagina, and puberty in straightforward ways that relate the information to the child who is reading or listening. The edition illustrated by Symeon Shimin echoes the love surrounding birth in the chalklike pictures that extend every page of text.

Erma Brenner's *A New Baby! A New Life!* (P), also illustrated by Symeon Shimin, can be considered a sequel or a parallel story to Gruenberg's. Brenner focuses on the emotional climate surrounding a child's first year. Again, Shimin's charcoal sketches reflect and extend the text, showing

How I Was Born

● BOOKS

*The Wonderful Story of
  How You Were Born*
*Where Do Babies Come
  From?*
A New Baby! A New Life!
My Backyard History Book
*What Was It Like? When
  Your Grandparents Were
  Your Age*

● ACTIVITIES

Trace your family tree.
Make a book about you.
Bring baby pictures to
  school. (guess who?)
Invite grandparents to tell
  about their childhood.
Write your autobiography.

What Helps Me Grow

● BOOKS

*Peter Rabbit's Natural Foods
  Cookbook*
Wild Foods
Great Bread
The Organic Living Book
How to Eat Your ABC's
Natural Foods
Green Grass and White Milk
*What Happens to a
  Hamburger?*

● ACTIVITIES

Bake bread, try recipes.
List what you eat in one
  day.
Bring raw food snacks to
  school.
Make recipe books of
  healthful foods.

MY
BODY
AND
HOW IT
WORKS

What Is Special About Me

● BOOKS

Faces
Bodies
*I Have a Sister, My Sister
  Is Deaf*
Don't Forget Tom
Janet at School

● ACTIVITIES

Describe what makes you
  special
Make a book about your
  hobbies.
Trace silhouettes of faces
  and bodies.
Make handprints in clay.

What I Like to Do

● BOOKS

*Games and How to Play
  Them*
Everybody's a Winner
A Very Young Dancer
A Very Young Rider
A Very Young Gymnast
*Be a Frog, a Bird, or
  a Tree*

● ACTIVITIES

Plan a gymnastic show.
Learn a new game where
  all play.
Make a board game about
  a book.
Pantomime your favorite
  sport.
Paint a picture of your
  favorite activity.

How I Grow and Learn

● BOOKS

The Moon Walker
Before You Were Three
Leo the Late Bloomer
The Book of Think
*The I Hate Mathematics
  Book*
I Am Not a Short Adult

● ACTIVITIES

Make a graph of your height
  and weight.
Draw pictures of yourself at
  birth, one, two, and
  three years.
Tell how you learned
  something.
List what you want to learn.
Make a "blooming" book.

Teaching Idea

BEGINNINGS (P) After reading from the books described or similar ones, give your students materials to make their own books about themselves. Their books may take many forms and directions. They may want to write it with the help of an adult scribe, who writes as the child talks. They may want parents to write the part that tells about their anticipation of the child's birth. They may want to illustrate the book with actual photographs of themselves from infancy to the present, or to draw themselves at various ages. Whatever the direction and form, each book is certain to become a prized possession of the child who is both its subject and author.

Bringing baby pictures for a school bulletin board is a good way to start a study of birth. Naturally, these photographs should be smuggled into school wrapped and covered so that no one gets a sneak preview. Teachers and others on the school staff who bring their baby pictures, too, add to the fun. When all the photographs are posted on the bulletin board, the guessing game can begin. Who is Number 1, 2 . . . ? After the guessing is over, you can write captions for each photograph. Captions that purposely misinterpret the expressions in the photograph—such as, "Where is my teddy bear?" or "I want my mommy"—add humor and interest for children.

Sibling rivalry is the subject of many books for children. Read aloud June Jordan's *New Life: New Room,* illustrated by Ray Cruz (P-I, Crowell, 1975), to see how one family prepares for a new baby. Also read Russell Hoban's *A Baby Sister for Frances,* illustrated by Lillian Hoban (P, Harper & Row, 1964), to see how a badger-child feels about all the attention that goes to her new baby sister. Ask students to tell how they would feel if a new baby came to their family.

---

fretful babies and harried mothers and fathers, and playful babies, and peaceful happy adults. Children, parents, and teachers who share the book cannot help but feel the love that makes a family.

The teaching ideas described above integrate talking, listening, writing, and reading (language skills) with science.

FOOD (WHAT HELPS ME GROW) Since primary-grade children do not deal with abstractions very well, information about their bodies needs to be made concrete with explicit examples. Words such as "the digestive system," or "the circulatory system" do not have much meaning for them until they can visualize the ways each functions. Plastic models of the body help make the concepts more palpable as do many excellent informational books. Paul Showers writes books for the primary grades in a way that represents the body functions in a concrete and comprehensible fashion. For example, in *What Happens to a Hamburger?* (P), illustrated by Anne Rockwell, he states:

Your stomach is a tube like your gullet.
But there is a difference.
Your stomach can stretch like a balloon.
When you eat, your stomach stretches to hold the food.
It looks something like this when it is full.

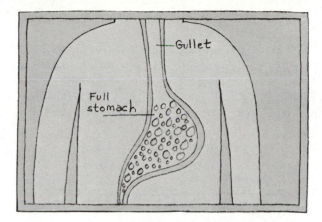

(Illustration by Anne Rockwell from *What Happens to a Hamburger?* by Paul Showers. Illustrations copyright © 1970 by Anne Rockwell. A Let's-Read-and-Find-Out Book. By permission of Thomas Y. Crowell, Publishers.)

Your stomach has muscles like your gullet. They can squeeze together.[8]

The author and illustrator make the information accessible to young children by the way the stomach is compared to a balloon, stretching out when it is full and shrinking or squeezing together when it is empty. The simple line drawings also help make the digestive tract understandable to young children.

Hettie Jones clears up a lot of misinformation and confusion about foods in *How to Eat Your ABC'S: A Book About Vitamins* (I). She calls vitamins the lifeguards of the body and explains that they are nothing new—we have always eaten them but we did not always know about them and which foods contained them. Now that we know,

Teaching Idea

COOKING IN THE CLASSROOM (P) You can find a plethora of good cookbooks for children. One by Aileen Paul, *Kids Cooking without a Stove: A Cookbook for Young Children* (P, Doubleday, 1975) gives thirty easy-to-follow recipes for dishes that can be prepared in the classroom. Another, by The Parents' Nursery School, *Kids Are Natural Cooks,* illustrated by Lady McCrady (P, Houghton-Mifflin, 1974), stresses nutrition. One of the most beautiful, illustrated by Beatrix Potter, is Arnold Dobrin's *Peter Rabbit's Natural Foods Cookbook* (P, Warne, 1977). The recipes are practical and usable, the names delectable. You can make Old Mrs. Rabbit's Hearty Vegetable Soup, Squirrel Nutkin's Banana Nut Loaf, Samuel Whisker's Roly-Poly Pancakes, Cecily Parsely's Smooth Apple Cream, Fierce Bad Rabbit's Carrot-Raisin Salad, or Flopsy, Mopsy and Cottontail's Fresh Blueberry Cobbler. Even if you don't try the recipes, the original illustrations from Beatrix Potter's work makes the book a visual feast.

Activity: Teacher to Student

COOK FROM A BOOK (P) When you read a story in which food is an important part, cook what the story tells about. For example, if you read Maurice Sendak's *Chicken Soup with Rice* (Harper & Row, 1962), make exactly that. If you read Tomie de Paola's *Watch Out for the Chicken Feet in Your Soup* (Prentice-Hall, 1974), make the

(CONTINUED)

braided bread dolls that he gives a recipe for in the book. Naturally, *The Gingerbread Boy* (Seabury, 1975) and *The Little Red Hen* (Seabury, 1973), both illustrated by Paul Galdone, lead to making gingerbread boys and baking bread. Use one of the recipes in Bernice Hunt's *Great Bread: The Easiest Possible Way to Make Almost 100 Kinds,* illustrated by Lauren Jarret (Viking, 1977). Write notes about how you cooked your food and share the food with others. Deliver the notes and the samples to the principal, the librarian, the custodian, and other people in your school.

we can plan to eat the kinds of food that supply the vitamins our bodies need.

The teaching idea "Cooking in the Classroom" and the activity "Cook from a Book" integrate mathematics, science, following directions, reading, speaking to adults, listening, and writing.

EXERCISE (WHAT I LIKE TO DO)   Young children willingly celebrate the joys of their bodies and the physical feats they can perform. They climb trees, jump rope, swing, and hang upside down on jungle gyms and tree limbs for the sheer joy of doing so. Our modern life style, however, could reinforce sedentary tendencies. The more we ride in automobiles, sit endlessly in front of television screens, and talk for hours on the telephone, the

less we spend in more active pursuits. Some researchers show that children today are not as physically fit as they once were, despite the fact that their parents are jogging, playing tennis and golf, and bicycling more than ever.

Tom Schneider, in *Everybody's a Winner* (P-I), describes fantastic new games in which everyone plays, anyone can win, and the emphasis is on fun and participation instead of competition. He explains what goes on inside our bodies during exercise and gives excellent advice about developing our bodies in ways that are fun and involving.

UNIQUENESS   Every child is special and needs to feel so. Many books help them celebrate their uniqueness. (See Chapter 4 for a comprehensive

Teaching Idea

PLAN A GYMNASTIC SHOW (P)   Plan with your students the ways they can demonstrate to others how to develop and keep a healthy body. Rachel Carr's creative yoga exercises for children, *Be a Frog, a Bird, or a Tree* (P-I, Doubleday, 1973) will give you many ideas. Simple instructions encourage children to pretend to be a wheelbarrow, a bridge, or an animal and, at the same time, to develop breathing and muscle control. Creative yoga can easily be combined with creative drama in which children imitate birds, frogs, or animals. Accompany this with musical recordings for rhythmic expression.

discussion.) Barbara Brenner, in *Bodies* (P), combines a simple text with fascinating black-and-white photographs by George Ancona to show the uniqueness of each person's body and what can be done with it. Joy in body movement and physical expression shines through the words and pictures. An earlier book by the same team, *Faces* (P), celebrates the marvel of faces and what we can do with them.

Many recent books focus on the uniqueness of the handicapped child. For example, Hanne Larsen, in *Don't Forget Tom* (P), introduces a mentally handicapped child. After having explained that handicapped may mean "eyes which can't see, ears which can't hear, arms which won't do what you want, or legs that can't walk," the text goes on:

With Tom it's a part of his brain which won't work properly; Tom is mentally handicapped. This means he can't understand as quickly as you or I. He needs more time to learn and to do things.[9]

The beautiful color photographs center on all the things Tom *can* do, with a slender text describing both these accomplishments and the special considerations Tom needs. In this, as in many information books about handicapped children, there is no sentimentality or embarassment—just a straightforward presentation of a child who has special needs.

In *Bodies,* children's spontaneous delight with their bodies is captured in George Ancona's photographs and Barbara Brenner's simple prose.
(Photo © George Ancona 1973. From *Bodies* by Barbara Brenner, E. P. Dutton, publishers.)

Teaching Idea

A GRAFFITI WALL (P) Children like to express themselves through art to state to the world and to themselves, "There's no one else just like me." On large sheets of wrapping paper collect signs and images of what children think makes them special by:

  providing felt pens and letting each create a picture individually
  using finger paints to make individual handprints or footprints
  tracing the outline of each child, and filling it in by painting clothing and hair to
    match

(CONTINUED)

cutting head silhouettes traced from a shadow (use projector light or flashlight)
making cluster pictures of families
using pictures cut from magazines to make collages

To make comparisons, mark children's height on brown paper, then have each one make hand prints or footprints from the bottom of the paper to the mark to see how many "hands" tall she is. This can lead to comparisons, not just of relative height, but of the difference in size of body parts.

Take close-up photographs of children's faces and bodies showing different emotions, poses, and expressions. Write captions and stories to accompany the photographs, or use them to dramatize the amazing flexibility and expressiveness of the body by having one child read the stories or captions aloud while others mime the actions or emotions described.

Activity: Teacher to Student

A BOOK ABOUT ME (P)   Write a story or keep a journal about yourself in a composition book or a handmade book. You might begin: I was born on   (date)   at   (time)   o'clock in   (place).   My   (parents/other)   named me   (name)   because   (reason).   I have   (number)   sister(s) and   (number)   brother(s). The most important thing about me is _____ . The food I like best is _____ and the game I like best is _____ . My favorite TV program is _____ . My favorite book is _____ .

GROWTH AND DEVELOPMENT Young children do not have a well developed sense of time nor do they see changes in themselves over time. They often think they have always looked as they now look, and since growth changes are gradual, they are not aware of them. Several nonfiction titles present concepts of development in a way children can understand. For example, Robie H. Harris and Elizabeth Levy, in *Before You Were Three* (I), show in photographs and text how children grow from birth to age three. The beautifully written text describes changes in walking, talking, thinking, and feeling that occur during this period of rapid growth. Although the book is for intermediate-grade children, primary-grade youngsters can learn a great deal from looking at the pictures and hearing the text read aloud.

Paul Showers describes the first year of development in *The Moon Walker* (P). He compares the infant to a moon walker who must learn to adjust to living and using his body in the different environment of earth, learning to use his hands, mouth, and feet to explore in his first year in the new world.

BENCHMARKS OF GROWING AND LEARNING (P) Read several books to your students that convey the idea that we don't always see the ways we are growing. Some excellent examples include Ruth Krauss's *The Growing Story*, illustrated by Phyllis Rowand (P, Harper & Row, 1947); Charlotte Zolotow's *Someone New*, illustrated by Erik Blegvad (P, Harper & Row, 1978); and Robert Kraus's *Leo the Late Bloomer*, illustrated by José Aruego (P, Windmill, 1971).

Activity: Teacher to Student

BLOOMING (P) Discuss the idea of blooming the way it is used in *Leo the Late Bloomer* (Dutton, 1973)—to mean learning how to do something you have not been able to master. Talk about things you know how to do now and things you are working on. For example, "I bloomed at tying my shoes but I haven't bloomed yet at reading." Work with a group on a "blooming" book—one page for each person—about the things they are blooming at and the things they are working on.

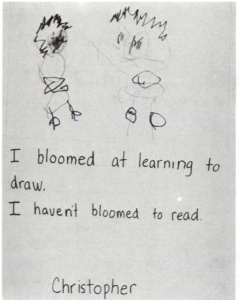

Two creative efforts inspired by Leo's experience in Robert Kraus's *Leo the Late Bloomer*.

**The Intermediate-Grades Unit:
Using the World's Resources
in a More Resourceful Way**

Concern over depletion of the world's resources is growing, and intermediate-grade students, aware of the concern, know that decisions made today affect their present and future lives. Headlines and television specials proclaim the dwindling of energy supplies and their ever greater cost. Many students experience the problem directly when schools close and their homes grow cold when supplies are short.

A scene during a dust storm in the 1930s illustrates a message of Hallie Black's *Dirt Cheap*—that nature ultimately exacts payment for squandered resources.
(From *Dirt Cheap* by Hallie Black, 1979. Illustrated by Arthur Rothstein. Reprinted by permission of the publisher, William Morrow & Company, Inc.)

HALLIE BLACK

DIRT CHEAP THE EVOLUTION OF RENEWABLE RESOURCE MANAGEMENT

Through informational books students can learn firsthand how science affects their lives and can actively gain understanding of attempts to develop new energy sources and to conserve the energy supplies we have. They know that the search for energy sources affects ecology and that much pollution is related to energy use. The unit of study presented here describes some of the many ways we can use informational books to investigate more resourceful ways to use the world's resources.

Because the energy situation is ever-changing, many books become rapidly outdated, causing us to turn to magazines and newspapers for current information. This swiftly changing scene also generates conflicting and contradictory information. In these cases, students learn to check the date of publication to see how recent it is. There are also social and political issues involved so that an article written by a proponent of solar energy will present prospects differently from one by a nuclear energy enthusiast. Students with the misconception that anything in print must be true have trouble dealing with contradictory information. Confronted with such they turn to the teacher and ask which is right. Their question signals that a rare teachable moment has arrived.

THE ENERGY CRISIS Several texts present an introduction to the energy crisis and explore some of the underlying causes. Laurence Pringle, in *Energy: Power for People* (I-A), explains how many Americans who thought resources endless were surprised at the sudden onset of shortages. He examines the status of various types of nonrenewable energy supplies such as oil, coal, and uranium, and previews the renewable sources such as hydroelectricity; geothermal, solar, wind, and ocean energy; and energy from decomposition of garbage (methane). For each type of resource, Pringle discusses problems, progress, dangers, and demand, and concludes with a chapter on the need to conserve and to develop renewable sources. Excellent diagrams and photographs throughout present a clear explanation of the way most of the systems work.

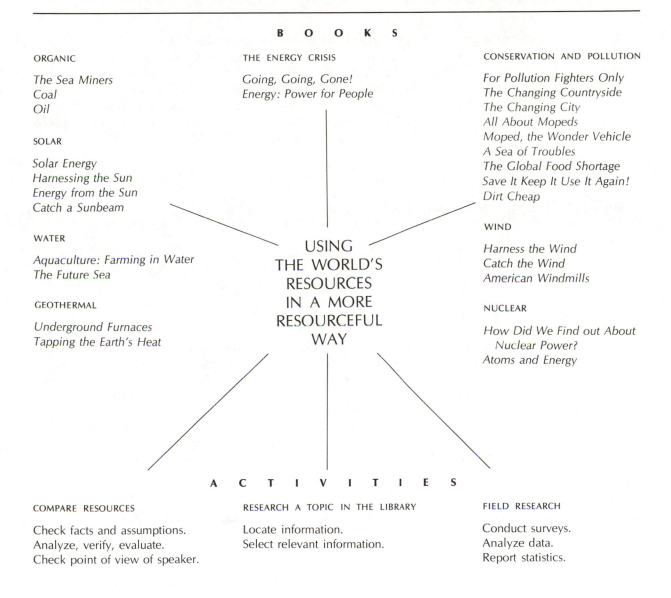

B O O K S

ORGANIC

The Sea Miners
Coal
Oil

SOLAR

Solar Energy
Harnessing the Sun
Energy from the Sun
Catch a Sunbeam

WATER

Aquaculture: Farming in Water
The Future Sea

GEOTHERMAL

Underground Furnaces
Tapping the Earth's Heat

THE ENERGY CRISIS

Going, Going, Gone!
Energy: Power for People

USING
THE WORLD'S
RESOURCES
IN A MORE
RESOURCEFUL
WAY

CONSERVATION AND POLLUTION

For Pollution Fighters Only
The Changing Countryside
The Changing City
All About Mopeds
Moped, the Wonder Vehicle
A Sea of Troubles
The Global Food Shortage
Save It Keep It Use It Again!
Dirt Cheap

WIND

Harness the Wind
Catch the Wind
American Windmills

NUCLEAR

How Did We Find out About Nuclear Power?
Atoms and Energy

A C T I V I T I E S

COMPARE RESOURCES

Check facts and assumptions.
Analyze, verify, evaluate.
Check point of view of speaker.

RESEARCH A TOPIC IN THE LIBRARY

Locate information.
Select relevant information.

FIELD RESEARCH

Conduct surveys.
Analyze data.
Report statistics.

COMPARE INFORMATION FROM RESOURCES, LIBRARY, FIELD RESEARCH

Analyze, compare, determine recency, accuracy, evaluate.

PRESENT WHAT YOU HAVE LEARNED

Have an energy fair.

Teaching Idea

RESEARCHING A TOPIC IN THE LIBRARY (I) An important part of using information is knowing how to find it, and although many resources exist beyond the library, ability to use library resources is of primary importance. As with so many other skills, library skills are *not* learned in the abstract. One lesson each devoted to the card catalog, reference books, and the Dewey decimal system are not enough to teach students to use the library efficiently. It is through direct experience and continued use of library materials to locate, for example, many reports on the same topic, that students acquire the skill.

Activity: Teacher to Student

LOCATING AND SELECTING INFORMATION (I) Find information in the library about energy. Part of the search is like detective work—following one clue to another—but there are some systematic, routine steps that can help:

1. List key words to look for in the subject index of the card catalog. Your list might include the subjects energy, electricity, coal, petroleum, nuclear energy, solar energy, wind power, oceanography.

2. Write down the author, title, and call number of books in the card catalog that sound as if they deal with an aspect of the topic you have listed. When you locate the books, look at their tables of contents for sections of the text that might be helpful. For example, the chapter titles in the table of contents in James Marshall's *Going, Going, Gone?* (Coward, McCann & Geoghegan, 1976) are: 1. The Energy Crisis, 2. Where Our Energy Comes From, 3. The Cost to the Environment, 4. Is Nuclear Energy the Answer? 5. How You Can Save Energy, 6. Conservation for the Nation, 7. Other Sources of Energy, 8. Energy in the Future. Chapters in Laurence Pringle's *Energy: Power for People* (Macmillan, 1975) are: 1. Sorry, no gas, 2. Petroleum and

---

James Marshall's *Going, Going, Gone?* (I-A) contains much of the same information, although the writing style is not as interesting nor do the diagrams and photographs offer as much clear information. A statement made by Marshall in the 1976 edition—"There has not been a serious accident yet in any nuclear reactor"—is considered incorrect by many groups that monitor nuclear incidents; it became indefensible after the Three Mile Island incident in 1979. In this area, as in most topics of current interest, the source of information and the date of publication become important facts to check.

SOLAR ENERGY The discussion of books on solar energy is illustrative of the criteria to be considered in selecting any informational books. Among these are appropriateness of the concepts to the cognitive developmental level of the reader, recency of publication, and qualifications of the author. Thus,

natural gas, 3. Coal comes back, 4. Energy from atoms, 5. Cleaner, safer fuels, 6. Waste not, want not, and a concluding section on "What you can do."

Just from the table of contents, you can see that both authors start with the gas shortage, the crisis that affects people most directly. Both then discuss other sources of energy and ways to save energy. If you are looking for specific suggestions about what each of us can do, Marshall's book seems to be the most useful, since it has a full chapter on saving energy rather than a brief section at the end, as in Pringle's. On the other hand, if you want detailed information on nuclear atomic energy, Pringle's book might be best since its table of contents shows a specific chapter on the subject —"Energy from the Atom." (Actually it does have a thorough, lucid discussion and provides many detailed diagrams to show how a nuclear power plant works.) Once a table of contents has led you into a book, skim the headings and the text to see if the material is about the topics you want to pursue. Read the sections and take notes about the type of energy you are researching. Also, check the publication date of the book to determine if its information is up to date.

3. Use an index of your local (and other) newspapers to find articles about energy production, shortages, crises, and research.

4. Use the *Reader's Guide to Periodical Literature* to locate magazine and journal articles about energy.

5. Search through the index to *National Geographic* magazines to locate articles and photographs on natural and mineral resources.

6. Using the same list of key words you developed for searching the card catalog, check library reference books, including encyclopedias, for information. Look at the copyright (publication) date of the encyclopedias to see how recent their information is. If there are supplements to the encyclopedias, read the entries in them about your topic and take notes in your own words about the most important information.

7. Use the bibliographies in the books you find most helpful to locate additional information.

---

if we have students in the intermediate grades who are reading on a primary-grade level, we might choose Melvin Berger's *Energy from the Sun* (P) since it introduces the topic of solar energy at a very simple level. For instance, Berger suggests an experiment—fill a jar with cold water and put it in a sunny place—and explains that the heat from the sun warms the water. Later, he shows a diagram of a house with water being heated by the sun in tanks on the roof, tanks in the basement for storing the heated water, and pumps to circulate it. The simplicity of the explanation, however, which makes it appropriate for young children, is only simplistic to intermediate-grade students.

John Hoke's *Solar Energy* (I), written in an easily readable style, has a lucid text and clear illustrations to explain the basic methods of obtaining energy from the sun. Hoke's book, published in 1968, was revised in 1979, an index of the rapidity of development in the field. David C. Knight's *Har-*

nessing the Sun: The Story of Solar Energy (I-A), published in 1976, also reports some of the more recent developments. Knight also uses diagrams and photographs to explain the construction of photovoltaic cells, which convert sunlight directly to electricity, and solar heating in homes. Also included are photographs of various model homes with solar heating systems.

Florence Adams, in Catch a Sunbeam (I), presents basic information about solar study and outlines sixteen experiments students can do. Among other things, she shows how to separate salt water into fresh water and salt, how to use sun energy to ignite paper, and how to construct a solar furnace. The experiments are appropriate to the cognitive developmental level of the intermediate-grade reader, and the information is up-to-date.

To determine an author's qualifications in the subject of a book, examine the "flap copy" on the book jacket. In the case of authors of the books on solar energy just discussed, we find no information for either Melvin Berger or John Hoke, although the foreword for Hoke's book is written by Hubert Humphrey who supported solar research legislation while he was a Senator. According to the jacket of David C. Knight's book, he spent most of his working life as an editor, production man, and science editor for a publishing house and has written more than twenty-five books on scientific subjects. Florence Adams has a degree in mathematics and has worked with computers and data processing. One of her hobbies is conducting solar science experiments with her two sons (and perhaps we can assume that her own children tried out the experiments she details in the book). Her book is recommended by the National Science Teachers Association for 1978.

We must conclude on the basis of the information available that none of the authors works directly in solar energy research or development. This does not mean, however, that they do not have the credentials to write on the subject.

NUCLEAR ENERGY Some books that deal with the energy crisis contain sections on nuclear energy, but surprisingly few are devoted wholly to it. This may reflect the conviction that the subject is too complex for elementary-school students. Margaret O. Hyde and Bruce C. Hyde's Atoms Today and Tomorrow (I), first published in 1955, with the fourth edition in 1970, shows that we need not wait until an area is fully explored before we make what is known available to elementary students. The Hydes convey what is known about atoms and the progress made in using nuclear energy. They do not obscure the controversy and problems surrounding its use, and make clear distinctions between fact and theory. Their exposition of the subject is couched in tentative terms: "someday, electricity may be generated in full-scale reactors. . . . some statesmen feel that atomic energy is the key. . . . the future may bring such immense power requirements that only nuclear power can meet the needs".[10] This kind of distinction between what is known as fact and what is still in the realm of possibility shows respect for readers.

In Explorers of the Atom (I-A), Roy A. Gallant broaches a greater controversy—that is, are the problems of disposal of radioactive wastes, of leakage of radioactivity, and the potential for disaster in accidents so great that we should not use nuclear power at all? Many call for discontinuing operation of nuclear plants immediately. Gallant de-

One of the clear diagrams in Roy Gallant's account of the atom—from early discoveries to the present state of knowledge. He also discusses the use of nuclear energy and its dangers.
(Diagram by the Graphic Arts Dept. of the American Museum of Natural History, on p. 60 of Explorers of the Atom by Roy A. Gallant. Published in 1974 by Doubleday & Company, Inc. Reproduced by permission of the publisher.)

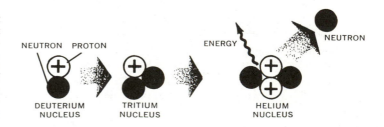

FIELD RESEARCH (I)   Field research combines curriculum areas with language and thinking skills. Science, social studies, and mathematics, speaking in interviews and presentations, and synthesizing information are all requisite for this activity.

Activity: Teacher to Student

SURVEYS AND STATISTICS (I)   After you have read several books on the world's resources, try some of the following:

1. Survey your community for firsthand information about energy. Look for sources of energy that do not pollute the environment. Environmentalists warn us about depleting the earth's limited resources and are responsible for proposing laws about protecting the environment. They are especially concerned about air and water pollution, fearful that we will ruin both for future generations. Photograph the places in your community that use energy, noting which pollute air or water and which do not. Watch for smoking chimneys, car exhausts, solar collectors, drainage into rivers, junkyards, wastepaper and aluminum collections for recycling, etc.

2. Find out where energy is generated or energy materials produced in your community. Photograph coal mines, strip mining, fuel depots, electrical generating plants. If there are none close enough to photograph, search for photographs or send for them.

3. Using a tape recorder, search your community for noise pollution, and record instances such as traffic sounds, emergency sirens, loud radios or televisions, factory sounds, and people noises.

4. Interview architects to find out what changes they are making in designing and constructing buildings to reduce energy costs. Get the plans for or design a solar-energy house, or build a model of one that shows how hot water, light, and heat can be provided by the sun. Draw a diagram of a solar energy collection system. Explain how it works. Make a working model and give a demonstration.

5. Write to your state, regional, and federal energy departments and ask them to send information about energy programs on which they are working. Ask how you can help support programs for new sources of energy. Write letters to the editor of your local newspaper expressing your concern about the energy supplies that might be depleted by the time you are an adult. Ask how are today's grown-ups planning or providing for an ecologically balanced world for tomorrow's children.

6. Interview candidates for political offices and ask them to give you a list of the things they plan to do to promote legislation and support for new energy sources.

7. Make a survey of the people in your community to find out:

if they believe the energy crisis is real
how they have been affected by shortages

(CONTINUED)

what they are doing to conserve energy
at what temperatures they keep their homes
how many miles per gallon their car goes
how fast they drive on open highways
their gasoline cost today and 10 years ago
if they would try solar energy
what problems they see in using solar energy
what problems they see in nuclear energy
what other types of energy they would use

Summarize the findings of your survey. Make a graph like the following to show the results of your survey.

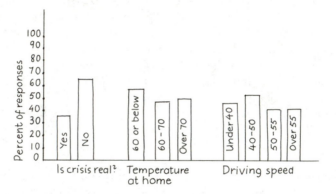

8. Predictions are that coal will be used up in fifty years and that oil will become more and more expensive to obtain. Make a chart, like the one below, showing the cost of oil and the amount produced from 1970 to 1980 and estimated through the year 2000.

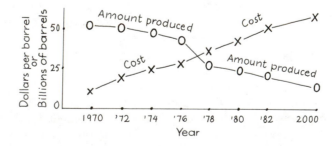

9. Interview officials at the local gas, oil, and coal companies to see if they agree with the predictions made in the last twenty years of the chart.

scribes the process by which a radioisotope enters the food chain and shows that once radioactive materials, with their potential for death and disease, enter ground water or air they are virtually uncontrollable. Although the nuclear industry cites a death rate lower than that in coal mining or oil drilling, much is unknown about suspected long-range effects, and doubts about the credibility of industry data are widespread. Students will want to read widely to research the topic; Gallant's book is a good start.

Isaac Asimov willingly apprises readers of the present state of knowledge in *How Did We Find Out About Nuclear Power?* (I). He traces the development of knowledge from the 1880s to the present day, focusing primarily upon the people who unraveled the scientific mysteries of the power wrapped up in the nucleus of the atom. Asimov asks rhetorical questions to show the present state of knowledge:

But can there be controlled nuclear fusion? Can hydrogen be heated up to hundreds of millions of degrees and made to fuse in very small quantities? Can it be made to give off energy without exploding? . . . Scientists in the United States and in other countries have been trying to bring this about for thirty years now and they haven't yet succeeded. Still, they are making progress.[11]

This is careful writing that indicates a healthy regard for the minds of young people.

GEOTHERMAL ENERGY Although geothermal energy, heat contained inside the earth, has been known and used for centuries, relatively little use was made of it until the new search for energy

Teaching Idea

COMPARING SOURCES (I)   Collect information on a current issue or event dealing with energy, paying special attention to reports found in the media, especially newspapers and magazines, and in government publications, scientific journals, first-person accounts in diaries, journals, or letters. File the articles and pictures by type of energy source, legislative action, conservation activity, etc.

Have your students examine the information in the file and then do the following:

1. List the events reported as facts. Identify contradictory facts reported and phrases that indicate personal opinion is being expressed—such as "in my view," "it seemed to me," "some people say."

2. List and compare the facts as given in the media, scientific journals, government documents, and personal reports. Determine which facts are verifiable, which are assumptions, and whether the assumptions follow logically from the facts.

3. Examine the perspective of each source and determine how that perspective might have influenced the presentation of the issue.

4. Determine what evidence is provided to support the statements and what documentation the author provides.

5. If information is given about the writer's authority in the area under discussion, evaluate it.

This kind of exercise gives students practice in the critical thinking skills of distinguishing between fact and opinion, verification, logic, identifying bias, and evaluating.

Activity: Teacher to Student

ANALYZE AND EVALUATE MEDIA REPORTS (I) When an energy issue is in the news, obtain newspapers from different parts of the country, or different newspapers from one city, or three magazines of the same date. This might be arranged through a newsstand or by phoning or writing to friends or relatives in different parts of the country. Then:

1. Note the number of energy issues that make headlines compared with other front-page news items.

2. Compare what issues are presented in the editorials of the different newspapers.

3. Look at ads about jobs, housing, building supplies, or fuel to see if issues about energy are reflected in them.

4. Identify any "slanting" in presenting the material. Distinguish between editorial, hidden persuasion, and objective reporting. Do articles that are supposedly objective reports contain editorializing or disguised persuasion?

---

sources began. Irene Kiefer's *Underground Furnaces: The Story of Geothermal Energy* (I) explains the subject through diagrams and text. Kiefer discusses the problems—particularly, that much of the heat is so scattered that tapping it does not seem feasible.

Although geothermal power is important, Kiefer's book appears to be one of the few on the subject for children.

WIND POWER Until very recently, little attention was given to the uses of wind other than for sailing and, in a few areas of the world, for pumping water, grinding corn, and draining wetlands. The one comprehensive book, written and illustrated in meticulous detail, is Peter Spier's *Of Dikes and Windmills* (I), which, rather than exploring the potential of windmills as a source of energy, deals principally with their role in the history of the Netherlands.

Harnessing the wind, itself a result of differential heating of air by solar radiation, is explained in several recent books that review historical and modern experimental windmills. Perhaps the best one, and the one that shows the author's enthusi-

asm for his subject most, is Landt Dennis's *Catch the Wind* (I), which conveys the ardor of those researchers and designers who see in the wind an environmentally sound source of energy. His book focuses on the people whose ideas animate the move toward wind power.

CONSERVATION AND POLLUTION Environmentalists believe that irresponsible practices in the search for energy can lead to an uninhabitable earth, which relates that search to issues of conservation and pollution and the preservation of endangered species.

J. J. McCoy, in *A Sea of Troubles* (I-A), delineates the many ways the sea is being polluted. He shows that what has happened to the oceans, with their delicate ecosystems and living resources, stems mainly from gross mismanagement of the sea. Dumping raw sewage, which could be used to generate methane; oil spills, which waste oil and kill birds and fish; and unlimited killing of fur seals, whales, and dolphins continue despite active work to stop such abuses. McCoy adds authenticity and a sense of urgency by inserting actual reports of ecological disasters and related

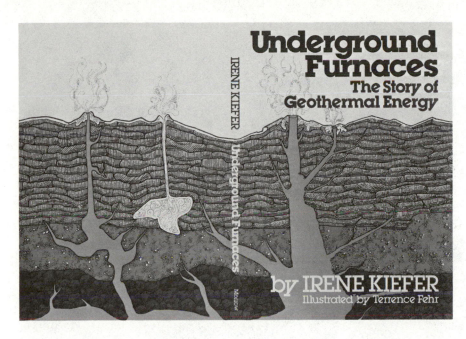

Terrence Fehr's graphic drawing for the cover of Irene Kiefer's book illustrates how ground water, heated in the depths of the earth, could be a source of energy.
(From *Underground Furnaces* by Irene Kiefer, 1976. Illustrated by Terrence Fehr. © 1976 by Terrence Fehr. Reprinted by permission of the publisher, William Morrow & Company, Inc.)

In sketching the role of windmills in the history of the Netherlands, Peter Spier shows hundreds of types that evolved over the centuries.
(Illustration from *Of Dikes and Windmills* by Peter Spier. Published in 1969 by Doubleday & Company, Inc. Reproduced by permission of the publisher.)

Student volunteers, concerned with the environment, help clean up after an oil spill. (Photograph by Mark Antman / STOCK, Boston, Mass.)

political events. McCoy's convincing tone and documentation earn the respect of his readers, as does his well organized bibliography, which is subdivided according to topic, such as ocean environment, polar bears, and porpoises. Students interested in wildlife conservation will recognize the author's earlier works, many of which received awards. The jacket flap lists many wildlife and conservation agencies McCoy works with; his involvement in the topics of his text suggests excellent qualifications for writing about it.

Lila Perl's topic in *The Global Food Shortage* (I) is broad: she examines the food shortage throughout the world, its connection with the energy crisis, and its effect on undeveloped and developed countries. Despite the breadth of the topic, Perl conveys a sense of urgency about food problems around the world, but because of the comprehensiveness, she is unable to provide a probing examination of the complex issue. For example, in an attempt to give some historical perspective to her topic, she states:

The Dark and Middle Ages appear to have been periods of slow population growth and relatively uncrowded conditions, but it is worth noting that the First Crusade, begun in 1095, and the others that followed, were composed largely of landless young men whose fathers' holdings had been inherited by firstborn sons. The opening up of the New World in the 1500s was the safety valve that was to spare Europe from some of Malthus's worst predictions. When conditions grew too crowded or people grew too hungry (usually the same thing), or political or religious persecution became unbearable, there was always somewhere else to go. The Irish migration to the United States, beginning in the 1840s, provides a dramatic example, for when the potato crop failed, the Irish faced starvation, even national extermination.[12]

Discussing the Dark and Middle Ages, the Crusades, the New World, Malthus's prediction, and the Irish potato famine in one paragraph suggests the shallowness of coverage. By narrowing her subject, the author might have given a more insightful analysis of food shortages. Some evidence of the author's qualifications to write on this subject can be obtained by looking at titles of her

PRESENTING WHAT YOU'VE LEARNED (I)   After your students have researched in the library and in the community various methods of conserving energy and reducing pollution, have them present their findings. Other students can take notes for a class discussion, for debating issues, or as a basis for papers advocating one or another energy source as the most feasible and advantageous. Committees for nuclear, solar, coal, wind, oil, manpower, and other matters may be formed. This will give students practice in oral presentation, listening, note taking, evaluation, and cooperative group work.

Plan an energy fair at which students will share the results of their research and other work during the energy study. Plan exhibits, demonstrations, debates, discussions, and presentations. Groups studying different aspects of the topic can decide the best way to share their findings with others. For example, those who study other ways to produce electricity can set up a demonstration booth to show how much electrical energy is required in an ordinary day. Attach a bicycle to a generator to see how much one must pedal to light a light bulb, to run a television set, a radio, or record player for a short time. Brainstorm with your students for other possible exhibits.

---

other work, which are listed in *Books in Print* or *Children's Books in Print*. There we find she has written several books of fiction and books about the geography of Africa and the Balkans, state and county fairs in America, and Colonial recipes. Notes in the global food shortage book cite several United Nations bodies and affiliated organizations as having supplied the materials and data for the author's research. Thoughtful readers will come away with many questions about the author's generalizations.

The Advanced-Grades Unit: Endangered Species

The contrast between the abundance of wildlife of the past and its present diminished state is startling. The dramatic situation engages students in several different ways. "Naturalists" will study species and habitats, politically inclined students will study laws and conservation programs, mystery readers will be intrigued with the search for clues about nesting places and the interrelationships

among creatures and plants in ecosystems, and animal lovers will rejoice when protective plans succeed and grieve when they fail. There is something for everyone in a study of endangered species, and it is a topic tomorrow's citizen must be concerned about today if we are not to be too late.

The unit of study on endangered species is organized to converge on specific critical reading skills. Only a few elements are developed to illustrate possibilities for this type of study; you will be able to create more with students especially interested in this area.

BIRDS   The story of birds as endangered species includes a discussion of the causes of extinction and possible plans for remediation of the conditions. It is used here to illustrate the approach one can take in the study of any species. Whereas informational books are used as the primary source of facts, no study of this topic could be complete without the use of several excellent magazines. Fine articles are found in *National Geographic, National Geo-*

B O O K S

PLANTS

Endangered Plants
Plants in Danger

FISH

Hunted Mammals of the Sea
Killer Whales
Thor: Last of the Sperm Whales
Killer Whale!
Whale Watch
Biography of a Killer Whale

BIRDS

Canada Geese
That Wonderful Pelican
Birds That Stopped Flying
A Vanishing Thunder
Falcon Flight
The Hunt for the Whooping Cranes
America's Endangered Birds

ANIMALS

Orangutan: Endangered Ape
Endangered Predators
The Gray Kangaroo at Home
Animal Rescue
The Controversial Coyote
In Defense of Animals
Coyotes: Last Animals on Earth?
Animals of Europe: The Ecology of the Wildlife
The Loggerhead Turtle

ENDANGERED SPECIES

GENERAL AND MAGAZINES

To the Brink of Extinction
Wild Orphan Babies
The Endangered Ones
Nature Sleuths
"National Geographic"
"National Wildlife"
"International Wildlife"
"Audubon Magazine"
"The Conservationist"
"National Geographic World"

ETHOLOGY: ANIMALS AND ENVIRONMENTS

The View from the Oak
Wild Animal Shelter
Lost Wild Worlds
Lost Wild America
Wild Refuge
Shadows Over the Land
The Island Ponies
Gadabouts and Stick-at-Homes

A C T I V I T I E S

Compare sources.
Analyze causes.
Generalize remedies.
Predict the future.
Spread the word on wildlife.

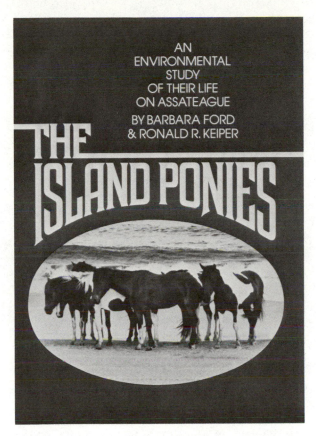

This informational book looks at the behavior, social organization, and ecological role of the ponies described in Marguerite Henry's fictional *Misty of Chincoteague*.
(From *The Island Ponies* by Ford & Keiper, 1979. Photos by Ronald R. Keiper. © 1979 by Ronald R. Keiper. Reprinted by permission of the publisher, William Morrow & Company, Inc.)

graphic World, National Wildlife, International Wildlife, and *The Conservationist.*

The tale of the passenger pigeon echoes the pathetic life story of other species that we will never again see on the face of the earth. Robert M. McClung states it forcibly in *Lost Wild America* (A):

In numbers they seemed as inexhaustible as drops of water in the ocean or as grains of sand on the shores. In vast flocks they swept through the skies, their bodies blotting out the sun, their roaring wings stirring up a mighty gale. Hour after hour they passed overhead, an awesome sight of wildlife abundance the likes of which

we will never again see. This was the passenger pigeon in its heyday.

Ornithologist Alexander Wilson viewed a Kentucky flight in 1810 that he figured to be at least a mile wide and 240 miles long. Considering the birds' speed of flight and the length of time it took for them to pass, Wilson calculated that there were more than two billion passenger pigeons in this flock alone. Judging from this and other accounts, they were probably the most abundant birds of one species in America at that time. Yet in the course of a century this seemingly inexhaustible population was completely wiped from the face of the earth.[13]

Gadabouts and Stick-at-Homes describes wild animals according to their predilections in homes: some restrict themselves to a carefully built place for a lifetime; others wander far, finding or adapting a space when the need arises. (Illustration by Sarah Landry from *Gadabouts and Stick-at-Homes* by Lorus and Margery Milne. Copyright © 1980 by Lorus and Margery Milne. Reprinted by permission of Charles Scribner's Sons.)

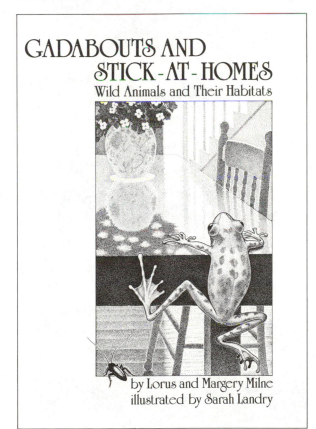

412 McClung relates other heartbreaking stories about the sea cow, the spectacled cormorant, the great auk, bison, sea mink, heath hen, and other species exterminated by humans. A few stories are more encouraging than that of the passenger pigeon, but many species still hang in the balance, profoundly vulnerable to human acts.

In another book, *America's Endangered Birds: Programs and People Working to Save Them* (I–A),

Robert McClung's *America's Endangered Birds* describes the continuing efforts to stem the slaughter of millions of endangered birds and the painstaking efforts to increase their populations.
(From *America's Endangered Birds* by R. M. McClung, 1979. Illustrated by George Founds. © 1979 by Robert M. McClung. Reprinted by permission of the publisher, William Morrow & Company, Inc.)

McClung states that in 1875 a hunter shot the last recorded Labrador duck. In 1914, the last passenger pigeon died in a cage at the Cincinnati Zoo, and the last Carolina parakeet in captivity died. In 1932, the last heath hen died on Martha's Vineyard. The grievous knowledge that we will never again see these species causes us to wonder how many more will go into oblivion in the near future.

McClung describes the programs and people working to help endangered wildlife. He traces the historical background of some endangered birds and attempts to explain how and why their numbers dwindled. The whooping crane, the bald eagle, the brown pelican, the California condor, Kirtland's warbler, and the ivory-billed woodpecker are among the threatened birds he studies. Maps showing the range and area of concentration of the disappearing species, the role of pesticides in their death, new developments in research, and programs to save them make this book a rare gem for students of conservation. The enormousness of the problem is presented without sensationalism.

The whooping crane, desperately close to extinction, was saved only by the devoted efforts of many people over a considerable number of years. J. J. McCoy tells the success story in *The Hunt for the Whooping Cranes* (A), which is truly a natural history detective story. In 1945, only twenty-seven whooping cranes—which wintered in the Aransas Wildlife Refuge on the Texas coast—were known to exist. Naturalists knew that unless the crane's summer nesting place, somewhere in Canada, could be located and protected, the beautiful majestic white birds might be lost to hunters or thoughtless destructionists. McCoy describes tracking the birds' migratory path along the Platte River in North Dakota, searching through Canadian wildernesses for nesting grounds, and mounting a poster campaign to solicit the help of hunters, school children, bird watchers, and others across America and Canada.

McCoy parallels the story of the search for the nesting place with another story, composed of beautifully written vignettes of a small whooping crane family blithely unaware that millions had joined to form a virtual army to protect them. Still, many of the birds were killed unthinkingly or unknowingly, and it seemed that the search to save them was hopeless.

The summer nesting grounds were finally discovered from the air in 1954, but that fall only twenty-one adult whoopers and not a single youngster returned to the Aransas Refuge. The hope for survival was very slim. In order to learn more about the bird's nesting habits, they had to be observed on the ground, which required a hazardous journey, for it was in the midst of Wood Buffalo National Park, a huge wilderness of lakes and streams, mountains, moraines, and ponds between Alberta and Mackenzie in the Canadian far north.

More than twenty five years have passed since the nesting place was found, but problems still exist for the whooping cranes. One group of conservationists, in an effort to raise some cranes in captivity, "stole" a few eggs from the nests each year. Another group, believing the chicks would have a better chance if they hatched in the wild, placed whooper eggs in sandhill cranes' nests in a reasonably successful experiment, reported by Roderick C. Drewien with Ernie Kuyt in "Teamwork Helps the Whooping Crane."[14] Sandhill cranes, more plentiful than whoopers, serve as satisfactory foster parents while the whoopers are young, but amazingly, the whoopers return to their own kind during adolescence. The whooping crane population is slightly increased, and because millions support the efforts to conserve them, the whooping crane has become a symbol for conservationists everywhere.

ETHOLOGY Ethology is concerned with the study of animals in their natural environment—how an animal experiences and perceives the world. Ethologists acknowledge that we cannot truly know what the world is like from the animal's point of view, but we can observe how the animal responds to its environment and from that draw inferences. Judith and Herbert Kohl present the ethologist's way of studying animal life in *The View from the Oak: The Private Worlds of Other Creatures* (I-A). They describe *umwelts*, the particular set of sensations and perceptions that make up each creature's world:

The world is neither the way an eagle sees it or a person or a mouse. The space felt by a mole is no more or less real than that sensed by a rattlesnake's third eye. Space is created by each animal and at the same time frames each animal's experience. It is a characteristic of the umwelt, not a common element of the experience of all creatures.[15]

The Kohls describe several experiments the reader can do to get some impression of the world as insects and animals experience it. They also intersperse excerpts from literature, such as Kafka's *Metamorphosis,* that portray life from the perspective of a non-human creature. Through the kind of study they recommend, we gain a new respect for other species and special insights into a unique realm of the earth.

BALANCE OF NATURE After years of trial and error, with traumatic consequences for many plants and animals, scientists now know that the balance of nature is delicate. Pesticides used to kill mosquitos, for example, have also killed birds, bees, ladybird beetles, and praying mantises. Ada and Frank Graham describe in *Bug Hunters* (I), those who destroy harmful insects through selective biological control. The often disastrous effects of the use of uncontrolled pesticides epitomizes the conflict between technology and the natural world.

J. J. McCoy also writes in a compelling style in *Shadows over the Land* (I). Statements like "Lake Erie is dying—does anybody care?" which rivet the reader's attention, are sweeping generalizations and could be called sensationalist were it not for the facts he provides to support them. He gives an account of the tons of raw sewage and chemicals dumped into the lake and the suffocation of fish and plants in its contaminated water. He also sketches the plight of areas beset with air pollution problems.

By reading about the potential and real dangers to plant and animal life, students learn not only that "no man is an island," but that anything we do in our environment affects all else that lives in it. This kind of understanding is basic to a study of endangered species.

One of the greatest advantages in using the unit study approach is that you can find material for students whatever their reading level. The wealth of beautiful books on a multitude of topics at many reading levels delights the intellect as well as the eye. For example, the series on endangered species by Jack Denton Scott with photographs by Ozzie Sweet presents, on large spacious pages, easily read photo essays that do not insult a student in the advanced grades who might be reading at a third- or fourth-grade level. In one of their books, *Canada Geese* (I-A), Scott discusses the latest theories about how the geese manage to return to the same breeding grounds year after year:

Some investigators believe that migrating birds are born with an inherited star map which is passed along in the genes from their parents. This means that the birds are born imprinted with a route which follows the stars. This theory of inheritance was tested by banding some wildfowl and releasing them long after the parent birds had left for the south. Until this experiment it was believed that the young merely followed the adults along the migratory trail. The theory was exploded when the banded young wildfowl turned up at the wintering grounds. Without guidance or experience, they had flown over unfamiliar territory straight to where their parents were. How? Was that route inherited through their genes? Did they really have a star map imprinted on them at birth?[16]

Students who cannot read the brief paragraphs learn from studying the excellent photographs on every page.

Some nonfiction has various shortcomings— inaccuracies, sensationalism, anthropomorphism. For example, in *Killer Whale* (I), by Joseph J. Cook and William L. Wisner, the animal is portrayed as a vicious, malicious, plundering mammal intent on destroying humans: "The killer whale is well designed for a career of destruction and mayhem. . . . These mighty jaws and their terrible teeth are a kind of animated chopping machine which can tear great chunks from a giant sea animal and bite a large fish in half."[17] "The list of the black beasts' victims includes sea lions, sea otters and even penguins. Penguins, able to waddle across the ice quite fast, usually are able to escape

Children who have read about wanton destruction of wildlife often become active in efforts to stop it.
(Photograph by Mike Mazzaschi / STOCK, Boston, Mass.)

the monsters".[18] In one chapter, the authors document their case against the whale with personal experiences, such as one reported by "Nick": "The killer whale was longer than the boat and his dorsal fin was higher than the skiff's rail! The mouth . . . looked to be at least four feet across, and he described the fearsome teeth as resembling large, white bananas. Worst of all were the evil eyes; each seemed almost as big as a saucer".[19] The sensationalist style seems a cross between *Moby Dick* and *Jaws,* not that of an informational book. Later the authors admit, "Actually we know very little about killer whales. Men who have studied them believe that they possess a rather remarkable intelligence in comparison to other members of the animal kingdom.''[20]

On the other hand, Ada and Frank Graham, in *Whale Watch* (I), say:

Perhaps the most feared members of the whale family are the killer whales. They are beautiful animals, dark with white patterns, a white oval face patch, and a tall fin on the back that reminds some people of a shark's fin. They have sharp teeth and powerful jaws. They travel in packs, hunting seals, walruses, penguins, and occasionally other whales. But killer whales are not the villains that people sometimes suppose them to be . [21]

Barbara Steiner's *Biography of a Killer Whale* (P-I) describes the birth of Karok, a fine calf whale, protected and nursed by his mother until he is nearly a year old:

For days Karok stayed in the shadow of his mother. Her swimming produced a current which carried Karok along. The current made it easier for him to keep up. His mother's skin felt soft and smooth. He liked to rub against her. She clicked and chattered to him. Often he swam under her and nuzzled her belly. She squirted milk into his mouth. Quickly he grew stronger and larger.[22]

Steiner goes on to report Karok's growth affectionately, often attributing human feelings to him. Later:

. . . the members of the pod split up into pairs. No one seemed interested in hunting or socializing. Even his mother and father snapped at him when he came near. . . . Karok felt a strange urge he'd not felt before. . . . Soon a female circled around him.
. . . The pair turned and twisted in the dim-lit water. Then they surfaced and spouted together. Karok leaped out of the water. He crashed back in a fountain of spray. The female swam closer. Her smooth body gently touched him. Over and over they rolled and tumbled.[23]

The story ends:

Within a few years they would have a calf . . . and . . . With no enemy except man, he could live for many years in the blue-green waters of his ocean home.[24]

The anthropomorphism in many of these passages—an attempt to make the information interesting to young children—diminishes the informational value of the book.

Teaching Ideas

ANALYZE THE PROBLEM OF ENDANGERED SPECIES (A) As part of the study of endangered species, have students take positions concerning which factors they see as most significant in bringing about extinction. Have them examine the source material cited in this chapter for evidence to support their views.

PREDICT THE FUTURE FOR ENDANGERED SPECIES (A) On the basis of their readings, have students hypothesize about the future of an endangered species. Ask them to predict how soon the species will become extinct if no action is taken and have them evaluate the effectiveness of present and proposed plans for protection.

GENERALIZE FROM FINDINGS (A) After students have completed individual studies and shared their information, the class can formulate principles based on the findings, generalizing across species and predicting possible results and solutions. One prediction that might arise is that man will become an endangered species. Whether or not students make that prediction, you might want to use it as a topic for a pro-or-con essay or a debate.

IDENTIFY THE MAJOR CAUSES OF EXTINCTION OF VARIOUS PLANTS AND ANIMALS (A)
Organize the causes of extinction into categories such as: humans killing for food, sport, and commercial reasons; environmental and pollution causes; other predators. With this end in mind do the following:

1. Analyze the process by which whooping cranes nearly became extinct and the steps taken to replenish and protect them.

2. Choose one endangered species, research its present status, analyze the major causes of extinction, and propose steps to ensure continuation and to reverse the downward trend in the species' population.

GATHER INFORMATION FOR GENERALIZATIONS (A) 1. Find out what has been done to preserve endangered species. (For example, in the case of the whooping cranes, nesting places were found and protected, eggs were placed with sandhill cranes for hatching and raising the young, wildlife preserves were established, and people were alerted to their scarcity.)

2. Learn as much as possible about the natural habitat, mating, and life patterns of one endangered species.

3. Generalize from the case of the whooping cranes to determine what needs to be done to protect the species you study. (For example, hunters must pass a bird-identification course and carry radios tuned to a station that warns of approaching whoopers.)

4. What might have been done to save the seal mink or the bison?

PREPARE A CLASSROOM NEWSPAPER OR NEWS RELEASE (A) Set up writing teams and choose one area for each to research and report. Some teams may choose to write about the poachers, looters, and unsportsmanlike hunters who rob us of natural wildlife beauty. Research some of the famous cases such as the "deer shiners" in North Dakota who blind deer at night with powerful spotlights to make bagging them easier; the alligator thieves in Florida and Georgia who use baited hooks to snare the alligators, then shoot them through the eyes; or the hawk and eagle killers in Pennsylvania who use long-range rifles with telescopic sights; and others who hunt down animals from helicopters. Along the Maine coast and in Long Island Sound, between New York and Connecticut, licensed lobstermen are allotted a limited catch of lobsters, but poachers set illegal traps and steal lobsters from the regulated ones.

Find out what measures are taken to control illegal killing and thefts in your area. Write your findings as a news story about an issue that causes local concern. You can distribute it as a flyer to fellow townspeople at the library or post office.

WRITE LETTERS TO AGENCIES THAT SUPPORT PROTECTION OF WILDLIFE (A) The National Wildlife Society, the International Wildlife Society, the Audubon Society, the Sierra Club, the Wilderness Society, and others provide guidelines and suggestions for projects you can carry out in your locale. Ask for materials to display and for things you can do to help with wildlife conservation.

Write letters to the editor of newspapers pleading the cause of wildlife conservation in your area. Describe cases in which people make changes in the natural environment that unintentionally become traps for birds, fish, and other animals.

Visit a game preserve, a bird sanctuary, or a wildlife refuge, and write an account of your visit for the school newspaper.

RESEARCH THE PRESENT STATUS OF SOME SPECIES (A) Find out how many whales, seals, or other endangered species now exist, how many have been killed in the last year, and the cause of their death. Describe the conditions needed for the species to remain alive, the current laws intended to protect them, and the legislation needed to assure survival.

Research the history of your area to find out what wildlife inhabited it fifty, one hundred, and two hundred years ago. Describe the changes in the environment that caused the wildlife to leave or reduced their number. Make predictions about the status of wildlife ten, fifty, and one hundred years from now if trends continue. Outline a list of steps that must be taken if your children are to see a living specimen of the wildlife.

DEVELOP A POSTER CAMPAIGN (A) Make posters calling attention to wildlife that needs protection. Much of the credit of the success of saving the whooping crane is attributed to the widespread poster campaign that alerted people along the migration path and around possible nesting grounds to be on the lookout for the diminishing species. (Several of those alerted by posters were partially responsible for the eventual tracking; there is no telling how many hunters' bullets the campaign averted from the rare birds.)

Select one from the following list of the world's rarest mammals or birds to be the subject of your poster campaign: red wolf (fewer than 100 in the U.S.), tamaraw (150 –200 in the Philippines), Calamian deer (fewer than 900 in the Philippines), Hawaiian monk seal (700–1,000 in the U.S.), Kauai o-o (fewer than 10 in the Hawaiian Islands), Puerto Rican parrot (26, including 10 in captivity), ivory-billed woodpecker (fewer than 30 in the U.S.), California condor (fewer than 40 in the U.S.), and whooping crane (115 in the U.S. and Canada).

Write slogans about saving the seals or boycotting sales of alligator bags, belts, and baby alligators. Post your slogans at local shops, the post office, and train stations, where many people will see them.

Design and construct a model billboard alerting your community to the need for action on a conservation issue, and see if a local billboard or sign company will erect it, or if wildlife societies will use it to support a campaign. You might try for permission to paint a mural of this design on an outside wall of a prominent building in town.

Robert M. McClung considers killer whales in *Hunted Mammals of the Sea* (I). He describes one that is killed as having the remains of thirteen porpoises and fourteen seals in its stomach. But he also states that the species has never been known to harm people. That one killer whale, accidentally caught in a net, proved docile and quick to learn, led to a rush to capture more of them for exhibition. By 1976 nearly 300 had been, but public disapproval was so strong that the last ones captured were eventually released.

According to Cook and Wisner, the killer whales are vicious; according to the Grahams, they are not the villains people think they are; and according to Steiner, they are almost lovable. Of all the books discussed here, McClung's deserves serious attention. His graduate studies in zoology at Cornell University seem to have taught him well to report objectively without sensationalizing or anthropomorphizing.

Helping students come to an appreciation of diverging perspectives is a goal for teachers who would want them to grow in critical reading and thinking. That there should be no single right answer, but instead many possible interpretations, characterizes thinking in a democratic society. Having varied sources in the classroom forces students to make informed judgments about the relative merits of each.

CRITERIA FOR SELECTING NONFICTION

Milton Meltzer, an outstanding biographer and historian, objects to the way most nonfiction is judged by reviewers. He decries the fact that critics look at how much information a book contains and how accurate or up-to-date it is, but rarely compare it with other books on the same subject. He also believes that critics must look at more than mere facts in a work of nonfiction and says:

I would want to ask how well it is organized. What principle of selection animated the writer; what is the writer's point of view; does the writer acknowledge other opinions of value? And then, beyond all this, what literary distinction, if any, does the book have? And here I do not mean the striking choice of word or image but the personal style revealed. I ask whether the writer's personal voice is heard in the book. In the writer who cares, there is a pressure of feeling which emerges in the rhythm of the sentences, in the choice of details, in the color of the language. Style in this sense is not a trick of rhetoric or a decorative daub; it is a quality of vision. It cannot be separated from the author's character because the tone of voice in which the book is written expresses how a human being thinks and feels. If the writer is indifferent, bored, stupid, or mechanical, it will show in the work.[25]

Criteria for evaluating nonfiction differ in some ways from those for evaluating fiction, and they also differ among subject areas. In craft books, for example, illustrations need to be clear, understandable, and near the passages they illustrate. In a book about government or law, however, illustrations may be totally irrelevant. In the final analysis, the usefulness of an informational book is dependent upon the needs of the child using it: the same book that answers one child's questions is totally inadequate to another's.

Criteria for science books have been explicated by professionals in the science field. A committee using these criteria and appointed by the National Science Teachers Association works in cooperation with the Children's Book Council to select the outstanding science trade books each year. The committee selects books that it considers accurate, readable, and pleasing in format. It also considers the following:

Does the book encourage independent work? If experiments are used, do they lead to some understanding of basic principles? Are they feasible and safe? Are facts and theories clearly distinguished? Are significant facts omitted? Are generalizations supported with facts? Are differing views presented on controversial subjects? Are animals and plants anthropomorphized? And, does the book violate our basic principles against racism, sexism and violence?[26]

As you select nonfiction for your students, ask yourself the following questions:

1. Are the concepts, level of language, format, and writing style likely to be understandable to the reader?

2. Does the author communicate enthusiasm for the subject?

3. Is the viewpoint objective?

4. Is sensational or overly dramatic presentation avoided? Is anthropomorphism generally avoided? (Where life is presented from the perspective of a non-human creature, is it done without attributing human characteristics to it?)

5. Is explanation simplistic—that is, simplified at the expense of accuracy? (Information need not be watered down or put in sugar-coated form. Excellent writers can make complex ideas accessible to children without such measures. It is often better to wait until the information can be apprehended in its complexity than to provide oversimplified explanations.)

6. Are theories distinguished from facts?

7. Are generalizations documented?

8. Is information up-to-date?

Notes

1. Kim Williams, "Requiem for a River," *The Living Wilderness,* 35 (Spring 1971), 8.
2. Mike Wilson and Robin Scagell, *Jet Journey* (New York: Viking, 1978), p. 22.
3. Joan Horvath, *What Girls Want to Know About Boys, What Boys Want to Know About Girls* (Nashville, Tenn.: Nelson, 1976), p. 26.
4. Ibid.
5. Ibid., p. 92.
6. Seymour Simon, *The Secret Clocks: Time Sense of Living Things,* illus. Jan Brett (New York: Viking, 1979), pp. 55–56.
7. Sidonie Matsner Gruenberg, *The Wonderful Story of How You Were Born,* illus. Symeon Shimin (New York: Doubleday, 1970), unpaged.
8. Paul Showers, *What Happens to a Hamburger?* illus. Anne Rockwell (New York: Crowell, 1970), p. 20.
9. Hanne Larsen, *Don't Forget Tom* (New York: Crowell, 1978), unpaged.
10. Margaret O. Hyde and Bruce G. Hyde, *Atoms Today and Tomorrow,* illus. Ed Molsberg (New York: McGraw-Hill, 1970), p. 127.
11. Isaac Asimov, *How Did We Find Out About Nuclear Power?* (New York: Walker, 1970), p. 60.
12. Lila Perl, *The Global Food Shortage: Food Scarcity on Our Planet and What We Can Do About It* (New York: Morrow, 1976), pp. 27–28.
13. Robert M. McClung, *Lost Wild America,* illus. Bob Hines (New York: Morrow, 1969), pp. 47–48.
14. Roderick C. Drewien with Ernie Kuyt, "Teamwork Helps the Whooping Crane," *National Geographic,* May 1979, pp. 680–692.
15. Judith Kohl and Herbert Kohl, *The View from the Oak: The Private Worlds of Other Creatures* (New York: Scribner's, 1977), p. 55.
16. Jack D. Scott, *Canada Geese,* illus. Ozzie Sweet (New York: Putnam's, 1976), p. 11.
17. Joseph J. Cook and William L. Wisner, *Killer Whale!* (New York: Dodd, Mead, 1963), p. 20.
18. Ibid., p. 26.
19. Ibid., p. 52.
20. Ibid., p. 60.

21. Ada Graham and Frank Graham, *Whale Watch*, illus. D. D. Tyler (New York: Delacorte, 1978), p. 46.
22. Barbara Steiner, *Biography of a Killer Whale*, illus. Bette J. Davis (New York: Putnam's, 1978), p. 16.
23. Ibid., pp. 60, 61.
24. Ibid., p. 62.
25. Milton Meltzer, "Where Do All the Prizes Go?: The Case for Nonfiction," *Horn Book Magazine*, 52, No. 1 (Feb. 1976), 21–22.
26. Glen O. Blough, ed., "Outstanding Science Trade Books for Children in 1978," *Science and Children*, 16, No. 6 (March 1979), 1.

Professional References

Blough, Glen O., ed. "Outstanding Science Trade Books for Children in 1978." Comp. Joint Committe of the Children's Book Council and the National Science Teachers Association. *Science and Children*, 17, No. 7 (March 1980), 33–36.

Brewton, John E., and Sara W. Brewton. *Index to Children's Poetry*. Annual. New York: H. W. Wilson.

Children's Books in Print. Annual. New York: Bowker.

Children's Catalog. Annual. New York: H. W. Wilson.

The Elementary School Library Collection. Annual. Williamsport, Pa.: Bro-Dart.

Meltzer, Milton. "Where Do All the Prizes Go? The Case for Nonfiction." *Horn Book Magazine*, 52, No. 1 (Feb. 1976), 17–23

Readers Guide to Periodical Literature. Annual. New York: H. W. Wilson.

Subject Guide to Children's Books in Print. Annual. New York, Bowker.

Children's Books Cited in Chapter

Adams, Florence. *Catch a Sunbeam: A Book of Solar Study and Experiments*. Illus. Kiyo Komoda. Harcourt Brace Jovanovich, 1978.

Aliki. *Green Grass and White Milk*. Crowell, 1974.

Alth, Max. *All About Mopeds*. Illus. Michael Horen. Watts, 1978.

Amon, Aline. *Orangutan: Endangered Ape*. Atheneum, 1976.

Anderson, Lucia. *The Smallest Life around Us*. Illus. Leigh Grant. Crowell, 1978.

Ardley, Neil. *Atoms and Energy*. Watts, 1976.

Asimov, Isaac. *How Did We Find Out About Nuclear Power?* Walker, 1976.

Austin, Elizabeth S. *Birds That Stopped Flying*. Random House, 1968.

Berger, Melvin. *Energy from the Sun*. Illus. Giulio Maestro. Crowell, 1976.

Black, Hallie. *Dirt Cheap: The Evolution of Renewable Resource Management*. Morrow, 1979.

Block, William A. *What Your Child Really Wants to Know About Sex*. Fawcett-World, 1974.

Branley, Franklyn M. *Solar Energy*, rev. ed. Illus. John Teppich. Crowell, 1975.

Brenner, Barbara. *Bodies*. Photographs by George Ancona. Dutton, 1973.

————. *Faces*. Photographs by George Ancona. Dutton, 1970.

Brenner, Erma. *A New Baby! A New Life!*. Illus. Symeon Shimin. McGraw-Hill, 1973.

Brown, Joseph E., and Anne Ensign Brown. *Harness the Wind: The Story of Windmills*. Dodd, Mead, 1977.

Burns, Marilyn. *The Book of Think: Or How to Solve a Problem Twice Your Size*. Illus. Martha Weston. Little, Brown, 1976.

————. *I Am Not a Short Adult: Getting Good at Being a Kid*. Little, Brown, 1977.

————. *The I Hate Mathematics Book*. Illus. Martha Hairston. Little, Brown, 1975.

Burton, Maurice. *Animals of Europe: The Ecology of the Wildlife*. Holt, Rinehart & Winston, 1973.

Carr, Rachel E. *Be a Frog, a Bird, or a Tree: Rachel Carr's Creative Yoga Exercises for Children*. Photographs by Edward Kimball, Jr. Illus. Don Hedin. Doubleday, 1973.

Cole, Joanna. *A Frog's Body*. Illus. Jerome Wexler. Morrow, 1980.

Cook, Joseph J., and William Wisner. *Killer Whale*. Dodd, Mead, 1963.

Cosner, Shaaron. *American Windmills: Harnessers of Energy*. McKay, 1977.

Cox, James A. *The Endangered Ones*. Crown, 1975.

Dennis, Landt. *Catch the Wind: A Book of Windmills and Windpower*. Four Winds-Scholastic, 1976.

De Paola, Tomie. *The Popcorn Book*. Holiday House, 1978.

Dickinson, Alice. *Carl Linnaeus: Pioneer of Modern Botany*. Watts, 1967.

Dobrin, Arnold. *Peter Rabbit's Natural Foods Cookbook*. Illus. Beatrix Potter. Warne, 1977.

Drewien, Roderick C. with Ernie Kuyt. "Teamwork Helps the

Whooping Crane.'' *National Geographic,* May 1979, pp. 680–93.

Fenten, Barbara, and D. X. Fenton. *Natural Foods.* Illus. Howard Berelson. Watts, 1974.

Ford, Barbara. *The Island Ponies: An Environmental Study of Their Life on Assateague.* Illus. Ronald Keiper. Morrow, 1979.

Fichter, George S. *The Future Sea.* Sterling, 1978.

Foster, John. *The Sea Miners.* Hastings, 1977.

Gallant, Roy. *Explorers of the Atom.* Doubleday, 1974.

Graham, Ada, and Frank Graham. *Bug Hunters.* Illus. D. D. Tyler. Delacorte, 1978.

————. *Falcon Flight.* Illus. D. D. Tyler. Delacorte, 1978.

————. *Whale Watch.* Illus. D. D. Tyler. Delacorte, 1978.

Gruenberg, Sidonie Matsner. *The Wonderful Story of How You Were Born.* Illus. Symeon Shimin. Doubleday, 1970.

Harris, John, and Aleta Pohl. *Endangered Predators.* Doubleday, 1976.

Harris, Robie H., and Elizabeth Levy. *Before You Were Three.* Photographs by Henry E. F. Gordillo. Delacorte, 1977.

Hogner, Dorothy Childs. *Endangered Plants.* Illus. Arabelle Wheatley. Crowell, 1977.

Hoke, John. *Solar Energy.* Watts, 1979.

Horvath, Joan. *What Girls Want to Know About Boys. What Boys Want to Know About Girls.* Nelson, 1976.

Hunt, Bernice. *Great Bread! The Easiest Possible Way to Make almost 100 Kinds.* Illus. Lauren Jarret. Viking, 1977.

Hyde, Margaret O. *For Pollution Fighters Only.* Illus. Don Lynch. McGraw-Hill, 1971.

Hyde, Margaret O., and Bruce G. Hyde. *Atoms Today and Tomorrow,* rev. ed. Illus. Ed Malsberg. McGraw-Hill, 1970.

Johnson, Eric W. *Love and Sex in Plain Language,* 3rd. ed. Lippincott, 1977.

————. *Sex: Telling It Straight.* Lippincott, 1970.

Jones, Hettie. *How to Eat Your ABC's: A Book About Vitamins.* Four Winds-Scholastic, 1976.

Kellner, Esther. *Wild Animal Shelter.* Scholastic, 1978.

Kiefer, Irene. *Underground Furnaces: The Story of Geothermal Energy.* Illus. Terrence Fehr. Morrow, 1976.

Knight, David C. *Harnessing the Sun: The Story of Solar Energy.* Morrow, 1976.

Kohl, Judith, and Herbert Kohl. *The View from the Oak: The Private Worlds of Other Creatures.* Illus. Roger Bayless. Scribner's, 1977.

Kohn, Bernice. *The Organic Living Book.* Illus. Betty Fraser. Viking, 1972.

Kraft, Betsy H. *Coal.* Watts, 1977.

Kraus, Robert. *Leo the Late Bloomer.* Illus. José Aruego. Windmill, 1971.

Krementz, Jill. *A Very Young Dancer.* Knopf, 1976.

————. *A Very Young Gymnast.* Knopf, 1978.

————. *A Very Young Rider.* Knopf, 1977.

Larsen, Hanne. *Don't Forget Tom.* Crowell, 1978.

Lauber, Patricia. *Tapping the Earth's Heat.* Illus. Edward Malsberg. Garrard, 1978.

Lefkowitz, R. J. *Save It! Keep It! Use It Again!: A Book About Conservation and Recycling.* Illus. John E. Johnson. Parents, 1977.

McClung, Robert M. *America's Endangered Birds.* Illus. George Founds. Morrow, 1979.

————. *Hunted Mammals of the Sea.* Illus. William Downey. Morrow, 1978.

————. *Lost Wild America: The Story of Our Extinct and Vanishing Wildlife.* Illus. Bob Hines. Morrow, 1969.

————. *Lost Wild Worlds: The Story of Extinct and Vanishing Wildlife of the Eastern Hemisphere.* Illus. Bob Hines. Morrow, 1976.

————. *Thor: Last of the Sperm Whales.* Illus. Bob Hines. Morrow, 1971.

McCoy, J. J. *The Hunt for the Whooping Crane.* Lothrop, Lee & Shepard, 1966.

————. *In Defense of Animals.* Seabury, 1978.

————. *Nature Sleuths: Protectors of Our Wildlife.* Lothrop, Lee & Shepard, 1969.

————. *A Sea of Troubles.* Illus. Richard Cuffari. Seabury, 1975.

————. *Shadows Over the Land.* Seabury, 1970.

Mack, Herb, et al. *What Was It Like? When Your Grandparents Were Your Age.* Pantheon, 1976.

Marshall, James. *Going, Going, Gone? The Waste of Our Energy Resources.* Coward, McCann & Geoghegan, 1976.

Milne, Lorus and Margery. *Gadabouts and Stick-at-Homes.* Scribner's, 1980.

Müller, Jorg. *The Changing City.* Atheneum, 1977.

————. *The Changing Countryside.* Atheneum, 1977.

Murray, Jerry. *Moped: The Wonder Vehicle.* Putnam's, 1976.

Perl, Lila. *The Global Food Shortage: Food Scarcity on Our Planet and What We Can Do About It.* Morrow, 1976.

Peterson, Jeanne W. *I Have a Sister. My Sister Is Deaf.* Illus. Deborah Ray. Harper & Row, 1977.

Pringle, Laurence. *The Controversial Coyote.* Harcourt Brace Jovanovich, 1977.

————. *Energy: Power for People.* Macmillan, 1975.

————. *Wild Foods: A Beginners Guide to Identifying, Harvesting and Cooking Safe and Tasty Plants from the Outdoors.* Four Winds-Scholastic, 1978.

Rau, Margaret. *The Gray Kangaroo at Home.* Illus. Eva Hulsmann. Knopf, 1978.

Ricciuti, Edward R. *Plants in Danger.* Illus. Ann Zwinger. Harper & Row, 1979.

————. *To the Brink of Extinction.* Harper & Row, 1974.

Rockwell, Anne. *Games (and How to Play Them).* Crowell, 1973.

Schneider, Tom. *Everybody's a Winner: A Kid's Guide to New Sports and Fitness.* Illus. Richard Wilson and Tom Schneider. Little, Brown, 1976.

Scott, Jack Denton. *Canada Geese.* Photographs by Ozzie Sweet. Putnam's, 1976.

————. *The Loggerhead Turtle: Survivor from the Sea,* Photographs by Ozzie Sweet. Putnam's, 1974.

_____. *That Wonderful Pelican*. Photographs by Ozzie Sweet. Putnam's, 1975.

Selsam, Millicent. *Eat the Fruit, Plant the Seed*. Photographs by Jerome Wexler. Morrow, 1980.

_____. *How Animals Live Together*. Morrow, 1979.

_____. *Popcorn*. Illus. Jerome Wexler. Morrow, 1976.

Sheffield, Margaret, and Sheila Bawley. *Where Do Babies Come From?* Knopf, 1973.

Showers, Paul. *The Moon Walker*. Illus. Susan Perl. Doubleday, 1975.

_____. *What Happens to a Hamburger?* Illus. Anne Rockwell. Crowell, 1970.

Simon, Seymour. *Killer Whales*. Lippincott, 1978.

_____. *The Long View into Space*. Crown, 1979.

_____. *Look to the Night Sky: An Introduction to Star Watching*. Viking, 1977.

_____. *The Paper Airplane Book*. Illus. Byron Barton. Viking, 1971.

_____. *Pets in a Jar: Collecting and Caring for Small Animals*. Illus. Betty Fraser. Viking, 1975.

_____. *The Secret Clocks: Time Sense of Living Things*. Illus. Jan Brett. Viking, 1979.

Spier, Peter. *Of Dikes and Windmills*. Doubleday, 1969.

Steiner, Barbara. *Biography of a Killer Whale*. Illus. Bette J. Davis. Putnam's, 1978.

Stoutenberg, Adrien. *A Vanishing Thunder: Extinct and Threatened American Birds*. Illus. John Schoenherr. Natural History Press, 1967.

Thomas, Harold E. *Coyotes: Last Animals on the Earth?* Lothrop, Lee & Shepard, 1975.

Vielvoye, Roger. *Oil*. Viking, 1975.

Weber, William J. *Wild Orphan Babies: Mammals and Birds: Caring for Them, Setting Them Free*. Holt, Rinehart & Winston, 1975.

Weitzman, David. *My Backyard History Book*. Illus. James Robertson. Little, Brown, 1975.

White, Paul. *Janet at School*. Illus. Jeremy Finlay. Crowell, 1978.

Wilson, Mike, and Robin Scagell. *Jet Journey*. Viking, 1978.

Wise, William. *Animal Rescue: Saving Our Endangered Wildlife*. Putnam's, 1978.

Wolfe, Louis. *Aquaculture: Farming in Water*. Putnam's, 1972.

Recommended Reading

Primary-Grades Unit

Several books explain reproduction and birth in terms that young children can understand, including Paul and Kay S. Showers's *Before You Were a Baby*, illustrated by Ingrid Fetz (P, Crowell, 1968), Russell Freedman's *Getting Born*, illustrated by Corbett Jones (P-I, Holiday House, 1978), and Julian May's *How We Are Born*, photographs by Don McCoy, illustrated by Michael Hampshire (P-I, Follett, 1969). Paul Showers's *A Baby Starts to Grow*, illustrated by Rosalind Fry (P, Crowell, 1969), covers the early stages of growth, while George Anacona's *It's a Baby* (P, Dutton, 1979) is a photographic study of a baby's first year of life.

Animal reproduction is the subject of several books, including those composing the excellent series by Joanna Cole and Jerome Wexler. *A Chick Hatches* (P-I, Morrow, 1976) and *My Puppy Is Born* (P-I, Morrow, 1973) contain clear, explicit photographs that explain the birth process.

Food is the subject of many poems, including those collected by Rose H. Agree in *How To Eat a Poem and Other Morsels: A Collection of Food Poems*, illustrated by Peggy Wilson (P-I, Pantheon, 1967), and Arnold Adoff's humorous verses in *Eats*, illustrated by Susan Russo (P-I, Lothrop, Lee & Shepard, 1979).

The Let's Read and Find Out books published by Crowell include many science books for young children that will be useful in a study of the human body. Exemplary are Paul Showers's *Sleep Is for Everyone*, illustrated by Wendy Watson (P, Crowell, 1974), and Aliki's *My Five Senses* (P, Crowell, 1972). John Burstein's presents an intriguing look at the body in his clever books *Slim Goodbody: The Inside Story*, illustrated by J. Paul Kirouac and Craigwood Phillips (P-I, McGraw-Hill, 1977), and *Slim Goodbody: What Can Go Wrong and How to Be Strong*, illustrated by J. Paul Kirouac and Craigwood Phillips (P-I, McGraw-Hill, 1978). Aaron E. Klein's *You and Your Body*, illustrated by John Lane (P-I, Doubleday, 1977), contains experiments that young readers can do to find out more about their own bodies, while Alvin and Virginia R. Silverstein's *Itch, Sniffle and Sneeze: All about Asthma, Hay Fever, and other Allergies*, illustrated by Roy Doty (P-I, Four Winds-Scholastic, 1978), explores ailments afflicting many children.

Harlow Rockwell wrote two very simple books that introduce young children to *My Doctor* (N-P, Macmillan, 1973) and *My Dentist* (N-P, Greenwillow, 1975), while Vicki Cobb tells *How the Doctor Knows You're Fine*, illustrated by Anthony Ravielli (P-I, Lippincott, 1973).

Intermediate-Grades Unit

The current emphasis on energy problems is responsible for many books on the subject. Among these are Franklyn M. Branley's *Energy for the Twenty-First Century*, illustrated by Henry Roth (I-A, Crowell, 1975), Isaac Asimov's *How Did We Find Out about Energy?* illustrated by David Wool (P-I, Walker, 1975), and Roy Doty and Len Maar's *Where Are You Going With That Energy?* (P-I, Doubleday, 1978).

Jane Werner Watson discusses *Alternate Energy Sources* (I, Watts, 1979), while Richard Cummings offers suggestions on how to *Make Your Own Alternative Energy* (I-A, McKay, 1979). Energy from the sun is discussed in Thomas H. Metos and Gary G. Bitter's *Exploring with Solar Energy* (I-A, Messner, 1978), while other energy sources are discussed in Dan Halacy's *Nuclear Energy* (I, Watts, 1978) and Laurence P. Pringle's *Nuclear Power: From Physics to Politics* (I-A, Macmillan, 1979).

Because the energy problems will be with us for a long time it will be necessary to search for new books on the subject continually. In addition, changes in our environment will produce new information. Irving Adler, a noted science authority, gives an overview of *The Environment,* illustrated by Peggy Adler (P-I, John Day, 1976). Beulah Tannenbaum and Myra Stillman wrote *Clean Air,* illustrated by Marta Cone (P-I, McGraw-Hill, 1974), several years ago, yet the information remains accurate. Reed Millard revised his *Clean Air-Clear Water for Tomorrow's World* (I-A, Messner, 1977) as others will undoubtedly do with similar books as new information and ideas are advanced.

Several books celebrate our environment by showing the beauty and majesty of nature. Hal Borland's *The Golden Circle: A Book of Months,* illustrated by Anne Ophelia Dowden (I-A, Crowell, 1977), contains lovely illustrations of seasonal wonders. Anne Ophelia Dowden illustrated her own *The Blossom on the Bough: A Book of Trees* (I-A, Crowell, 1975) and Phyllis S. Busch's *Wildflowers and the Stories Behind Their Names* (I-A, Scribner's, 1977) with delicate, painstaking botanical drawings that capture the glory of our natural world.

Advanced-Grades Unit
Margery Facklam's *Wild Animals, Gentle Women,* illustrated by Paul Facklam (I-A, Harcourt Brace Jovanovich, 1978), is an interesting look at several women who have dedicated their lives to working with animals. As is true of books about our energy and environment, there is a constantly growing supply of those that address themselves to the problems of endangered animals. Esther S. and Bernard L. Gordon's *Once There Was a Passenger Pigeon,* illustrated by Lawrence Di Fiori (P-I, Walck,

1976), discusses both the habits of these birds before their extinction as well as the mass slaughter that resulted in their disappearance.

Several publishers produce books that present information in a series format. The "Biography of . . . " books, one such series, is published by G. P. Putnam's. Among the well-written books that provide accurate information are Lorle Harris's *Biography of a Whooping Crane,* illustrated by Kazue Mizumura (P-I, Putnam's, 1977), and Alice L. Hopf's *Biography of a Snowy Owl,* illustrated by Fran Stiles (P-I, Putnam's, 1979).

Jean George wrote a series of books, "The Thirteen Moons," that describe the habits and behaviors of several animals; among them are *The Moon of the Mountain Lions,* illustrated by Winifred Lubell (I, Crowell, 1968), and *The Moon of the Wild Pigs,* illustrated by Peter Parnall, (I, Crowell, 1968). Laurence Pringle's *Animals and their Niches,* illustrated by Leslie Morrill (I, Morrow, 1977) is an accurate and respectful study of animals, with special emphasis on the special roles they play in the balance of nature.

Carl Sandburg's haunting poem, "Buffalo Dusk," in *The Sandburg Treasury: Prose and Poetry for Young People,* illustrated by Paul Bacon (I-A, Harcourt Brace Jovanovich, 1970), is a sorrowing tribute to the great beasts who once roamed the American prairies. Several poems in *Reflections On a Gift of Watermelon Pickle and Other Modern Verse,* edited by Stephen Dunning, et al. (I-A, Lothrop, Lee & Shepard, 1966), speak to nature and man's relationship with his environment; included are David McCord's "Crows," William Jay Smith's "Seal," Jerome Judson's "Deer Hunt," Ezra Pound's "Meditation," and William Beyer's "The Trap."

The Child and the Books

eleven

DENISE LEVERTOV   From *A SOLITUDE*

*"Here are the steps. And here we turn
to the right. More stairs now." We go
up into sunlight. He feels that,*

*the soft air. "A nice day,
isn't it?" says the blind man. Solitude
walks with me, walks*

*beside me, he is not with me, he continues
his thoughts alone. But his hand and mine
know one another. . . .*[1]

===

Literature and Children with Special Needs

Healthy, normal children require concern for their individual needs, and children with special needs require special consideration. Such children often find that, although not responsible for their problems, they are often treated as if they are. These children may face criticism, ridicule, and hostility far more than others, yet they are the ones who need encouragement, security, and acceptance the most. Children with special needs are portrayed in literature; through reading, other children can understand them and learn to treat them more humanely.

All children are special. We see how true this is when a child with severe learning disabilities finally reads at the age of thirteen and says, "Now I understand how people can read to themselves. They have to share it with their brains." Teachers, whose arduous task is not easily accomplished, share with their hearts. They know that people with impairments are real people whose lives have been shaped by genetic and environmental factors beyond their control, and that a distinction needs to be made between diversity and deviance.

In 1978, Public Law 94–142 mandated that all states provide educational services for the handicapped in the least restrictive educational setting commensurate with fulfillment of their individual educational development. Furthermore, a series of class action suits on behalf of the mentally retarded established the right to appropriately designed public education for all children, regardless of disability.

Encouraging signs of improvement in attitude toward children with disabilities are the increasing accommodations of their needs in the design of school plants, transportation, and curricula.

Children find out who they are and how they are valued as people from the way others regard them. It is as if children form a self-image from pieces of images others have of (and show) them. The most determining group, of course, is the immediate family—the significant others in a child's life. The group of significant others grows, however, as the child grows and reaches out into the community and the school. Disabled children who see fear or revulsion in another's face must neces-

428 sarily question their own worth. Fear and revulsion toward the disabled come from not knowing them or knowing about them.

Prejudice, discrimination, or paternalism from the able-bodied can be more destructive to the disabled than their own handicaps. A disability, such as deafness, need not handicap a person if society adjusts to the condition. On the other hand, if no adjustments are made, and the deaf person is forced to make all of the adjustments alone, the disability becomes a serious handicap indeed. Often, disabilities are handicaps only when situations and attitudes make them so. As Barbara H. Baskin and Karen H. Harris point out in *Notes from a Different Drummer:*

Technically, a disability is a reality, for example, the loss of vision. The restrictions and opportunities imposed by society determine whether or not the disability becomes a handicap. That is, "handicap" actually should be understood to be situational and attitude bound.[2]

When we are uninformed about people who differ from us, we tend to form stereotyped attitudes about them and to think them all alike. One important reason for mainstreaming disabled children is to allow others to know and become familiar with them. Books can serve this same end, helping inform children about their disabled peers. Handled thoughtfully, books help shape positive attitudes toward the disabled long before stereotypes are formed. Stories translate vague generalizations into specifics about individuals by focusing with the lens of fiction. And they inform the heart along with the mind as we learn.

While enjoying a good story, children are learning to understand others and to have compassion. In honest and objectively depicted stories, children see that, although disability circumscribes performance, this is a fact of existence and real differences are only a matter of degree. But literature about exceptional children extends the understanding of *both* groups, enabling the children with special needs to identify with someone in similar circumstances.

Sheila Garrigue traces a child's growth from ignorance to informed understanding in a perceptive novel about two girls in *Between Friends* (I). Twelve-year-old Jill has the conventional misinformation about the mentally retarded group she sees at the town pool. She wonders what the "retards" are doing there and stares in amazement at the group swimming. When she meets Dede, one of the retarded children, she begins to see her as a person rather than as a member of a strange group she knows nothing about.

As the friendship grows between Jill and Dede, Jill has to face her brother's intolerance: " 'So how come you're so friendly with a retard?' "[3] and the intolerance of friends:

"It's the retards' bus," Karen said. "Going to Pearson."

. . . Dede was waving in the back window. Jill waved back.

"Ugh!" Marla said. "How can you wave at them? I can't even look at them, they're so gross."[4]

From shared experiences with Dede, Jill's awareness deepens, but her other friends do not share her insights and she is pulled back and forth between friends. When one of them challenges her for spending time with Dede, Jill says, . . . " 'But she has feelings, that's for sure. . . . And she knows when someone's being mean to her.' "[5]

Ultimately, Jill and Dede become caring friends. Talking about why she is friends with Dede, Jill says:

. . . "Well, now I'm used to the way she is, she's sort of . . . comfortable to be with. She's quiet. She never wants anything. And she's never mean. I never heard her say one mean thing about anybody. And . . . well, I know it sounds funny . . . but she listens when I talk. But supposing I don't want to talk, say, just walk along . . . that's okay with her, too."[6]

And when Dede's mother moves with her to Arizona, Jill feels the loss of a true friend. Challenged again by Marla, who derides Dede, Jill defiantly retorts, " '. . . she knows more about being a friend than anyone else I know.' "[7] Jill's ability to know Dede as a true friend develops slowly and believably.

Disabled children learn firsthand that different does not mean deficient, and that there is more than one way to do almost anything. As one child says, "Being blind doesn't make life hopeless—only different." With mainstreaming comes an urgent responsibility for teachers to dispel the fear and ignorance most children have regarding the disabled. Able-bodied children need to be permitted to ask questions when they are curious about peers unlike themselves. They need to be told more than, "Don't stare! It's not nice"—because with new understanding comes acceptance.

Children who are disabled want to be treated in the same way as others. They do not need pity; they need acknowledgement of their accomplishments and frustrations and to feel good about themselves. They have the same desires for self-esteem, recognition, and security as others.

Disabled children face a hostile world: they are often taunted, jeered, ignored, and sometimes abused. Kin Platt mirrors such behavior in a tragic story, *Hey, Dummy* (I-A). During a football game Neil Comstock inadvertently tags brain-damaged Alan Harper with the enduring nickname "Dummy." Alan, watching from the sidelines, snatches and holds the ball when it comes his way, unaware that he should toss it back to the players. When Neil spends some time with Alan, he comes to understand Alan's differences. A friendship grows, and Neil becomes Alan's protector. When Neil unthinkingly gives a school report that causes the class to laugh about the brain-damaged boy, Neil's teacher scolds him:

"Congratulations, Comstock," he said. His eyes lifted to the others. "You are all to be congratulated—for your total lack of humanity and understanding." . . . "I was never before aware that there was the slightest thing funny about being retarded," he said. "Maybe I've been missing something." . . . "Is your subject brain-damaged?" . . . "It doesn't make too much difference, really. One such state is as helpless as the other. If you'll laugh at one, you'll find the other equally amusing."[8]

Neil, chagrined and chastened by Mr. Alvarado's scathing criticism, tries to befriend Alan in several ways. Mr. Alvarado's humanity, however, is hollow, for when Neil goes to him for help for Alan, he hypocritically refuses to become involved. More openly hostile, Neil's parents refuse to allow him to bring Alan into their home. His father is adamant:

"Forget it," he yelled, his face suddenly red and ugly, the big vein pulsing in his forehead. "They got places for misfits like that, and this house isn't one of them. Understand?"[9]

His mother takes the same view:

"Your father is absolutely right. We don't want any creepy morons in this house. Don't you understand? They're dangerous!"[10]

Kin Platt portrays the local community as a rock-throwing, jeering mob. In a devastating ending, when that mob comes to Alan's home, the one person who wants to help him is inadvertently responsible for the final cruel blow.

BOOKS ABOUT CHILDREN WITH SPECIAL NEEDS

Disabled characters appear with increasing frequency in children's books: the trend has been from nearly absolute neglect, to an occasional secondary character, to the present realistic distribution of disabled characters reflective of their incidence in our population. Changes in the overall field of children's literature brought about an opening of the floodgates to children's books concerned with problems—among them, every manner of disability. Once the early taboos were broken, during the 1960s, almost any subject was a suitable one for children's books; authors were not only freed to write about the full range of human concerns, but encouraged to focus on problem novels.

The movement toward greater flexibility in subject also led to variety in problem resolution. In today's novels, disabled characters do not always recover or improve, and sometimes they die. Attitudes toward the disabled of those around them do not always improve, often remaining narrow and cruel. For example, in Kin Platt's *Hey, Dummy* (I-A), mentioned above, Neil, the protagonist who

Though the jacket illustration of *Me Too* shows no differences between twins Lorna and Lydia, Lorna is severely retarded.
(From *Me Too* by Vera and Bill Cleaver. Lippincott, 1973.)

befriends Alan, the brain-damaged boy, responds to events by taking on a persona and functioning level like those of his disabled friend, and is ultimately institutionalized. Happy endings are no longer taken for granted in children's books.

Neither do devoted attempts to teach, train, or help a disabled character always result in progress as they would have two decades ago. For example, in Vera and Bill Cleaver's *Me Too* (I-A), Lydia works unflaggingly with her retarded twin, Lorna, to teach her to do simple tasks. Lydia hopes to make her twin acceptable to their father, who can not bear to stay in their home and face the

continual disappointment that Lorna represents. Despite Lydia's valiant efforts, her retarded sister does not respond, and Lydia must learn to accept the things she cannot change.

Early novels with disabled characters often contained episodes of miraculous cures, but the trend is toward gradual improvement and partial resolution of problems, or totally open-ended novels. A character's progress results from training programs, therapy, rehabilitation programs, or schools, rather than from the actions of some *deus ex machina*. Moral strength and personal determination, however, continue to be attributes of the characters who succeed.

Teachers will find several selection aids for books portraying the disabled. Barbara H. Baskin and Karen H. Harris, in *Notes from a Different Drummer,* provide excellent guidance for those seeking works on visual, intellectual, and orthopedic impairment, and emotional dysfunction. *The Bookfinder,* by Sharon Spredemann Dreyer, a comprehensive reference citing books with a variety of themes, is also a valuable resource for book selection about the disabled. An informational book, *What If You Couldn't . . .?* (I), by Janet Kamien, gives teachers valuable insights into special needs. The author asks readers to imagine that they are the disabled person in an attempt to foster acceptance and satisfy curiosity. Learning disabilities, emotional disturbances, auditory and visual impairments, and physical handicaps are covered.

Many books about handicaps directed to primary-age children do not qualify as purely fiction or nonfiction; they tell a simple story heavily laced with information. Some of these quasi-fictional stories are of poor quality insofar as the didactic intent far outweighs the slender story line. Like other new topics in children's books, handicaps are often treated self-consciously and sentimentally or in a highly technical vocabulary that is meaningless to the books' audience. As more books appear, the shallow ones disappear quickly.

Sarah Bonnett Stein avoids some of these problems by writing two books in one in *About Handicaps* (P). One story, for the primary-age group, is printed in bold type and illustrated with photographs. Joe has cerebral palsy, and the way he does many things frightens Matthew, who apes and mocks him. As Matthew learns about the things Joe can do—and about a man with an artificial arm—he loses some of his fear about handicaps. The parallel story, for adults, runs alongside the primary one. In this story, we find much more information about Joe's handicap and Matthew's fears of it.

Stories about the disabled child are sometimes told from the point of view of a sibling. Harriet Sobol has a younger sister tell the story in *My Brother Steven Is Retarded* (P); Jeanne Whitehouse Peterson has an older sister tell *I Have a Sister. My Sister Is Deaf* (P). In the first book, many of Beth's concerns about Steven revolve around her own feelings: embarrassment when others stare, happiness when Steven laughs. She worries about what he will do when he grows up and says longingly, "I hope he will be happy." Peterson's narrator emphasizes all the positive and joyous things her deaf

sister can do and subtly counterbalances them with the special considerations she requires. The positive tone makes the limitations seem minimal for a child who is spontaneous, active, and wholesome. It is evident that she is loved.

You will find many books about the disabled that lack redeeming qualities. Such books are hastily written in response to current social pressure and have little integrity. Called band-aid books (because they merely touch the surface of the wound), many sacrifice literary quality in their scramble to capitalize on a currently popular theme. Others contain inaccuracies and portray the disability inadequately. They give a superficial glimpse of complex issues and fail to stir the reader's interest or emotions.

Many offenses in inadequate books are committed in the name of informing the young about disabilities. Plastic characters move unfeelingly through illustrations and text, and some books are condescending (toward the disabled) and smack of

Matthew and Joe play happily when Matthew learns the facts about Joe's cerebral palsy and no longer fears it.
(From the book *About Handicaps* by Sarah Bonnet Stein. Published by Walker and Company, Inc., New York, NY © 1974 by Sarah Bonnet Stein.)

maudlin pity and sentimentality rather than sincere compassion. Furthermore, the illustrations of such books tend to be bland and undistinguished. Even the disability is glossed over or ignored, so that the central character remains anonymous.

Effective illustrations show the physical and psychological impact of the disability and mirror, in facial and bodily stance, the emotional life of the disabled character. Disabled people face despair, loneliness, and isolation, and their emotional distress should be evident. Similarly, their joy in success and achievement should also be visible. For example, in *Ben and Annie* (I), by Joan Tate, Annie's delight is evident when Ben gives her wheelchair rides down a hill. Her joy turns to despair when Ben's actions are misinterpreted and he is forbidden to see her. The illustrations convey Annie's unrepressed pleasure and later loneliness and dejection.

Illustrations that seek to make disabilities indiscernible by concealing them or inaccurately depicting what was truthfully detailed in the text contribute to the inauthenticity of a book and detract from its honesty. Most culpable are the designers of book jackets. For example, the cover of Vera and Bill Cleaver's *Me Too* (I) draws little physical distinction between mentally retarded Lorna and her twin sister Lydia, although the text suggests otherwise. On the other hand, Fran Ellen's emotional trauma and insecurities are clearly discernible on the cover and in the illustrations proper in Marilyn Sachs's *The Bears' House* (I). The contrast between the idyllic fantasy scene and Fran Ellen's pensive pose captures the essence of the story and parallels the word pictures the author paints. Similarly, Ted Lewin captures Joey's innocence and guilelessness in Gene Smith's *The Hayburners* (I). Lewin's charcoal sketches emphasize the humanity and selflessness of this trusting retarded adult.

As in other kinds of books, authentic illustrations complement and comment upon the text. They can be poignant revelations of the emotions of a disabled character.

Books about children with special needs are discussed below in groups according to the disability dealt with.

Deafness and Hearing Impairment

Deafness is an invisible handicap; there are no obvious signs of the disability, and, as a result, misunderstandings are frequent. Because the deaf look like everybody else they are expected to cope with the environment normally. When this does not happen, strange inferences are made—most often about their intellectual abilities.

The deaf and hearing-impaired communicate with the help of hearing aids, lip reading, and sign language. They express themselves through speech, writing, and sign language. Because speaking depends so heavily upon hearing, the age at which the hearing loss occurs correlates highly with the normalcy of the deaf person's speech: the earlier the age at which the loss occurred, the greater the divergence from normal speech.

The deaf person has language and knows what he wants to say; the difficulty arises in enunciation, for which he has had no models. It is a great accomplishment for the deaf to communicate with hearing people freely. Helen Keller once said that her most fervent wish was to be able to speak to another person without an interpreter; she accomplished this by working against multiple odds. Her autobiography describes the steps along the way and the role books played in her progress.

Books for children reflect the misunderstandings that vex the deaf and hearing-impaired. In Veronica Robinson's *David in Silence* (I), the neighborhood boys distrust David because they can neither understand his imperfect speech nor make him understand what they say. They tease and mock him, and one child suggests that David is only pretending to be deaf. One day David misinterprets their shouts of contempt as an invitation to play with them. The boys turn on him, and, frightened, he flees, loses his way, and when he is unable to make anyone understand him, panics. One child who had tried to befriend David finds him and helps him return home. Gradually, the other boys learn to respect David, and, in turn, he learns to respect himself.

In Barbara Corcoran's *A Dance to Still Music* (I-A), Margaret's sense of isolation imposed by her deafness is compounded when she moves from

Maine to Florida with her self-centered mother. Fearful of meeting new people, and yet resentful of the idea that she should attend a school for the deaf, fourteen-year-old Margaret starts to hitchhike back north to her former home. Along the way, when she finds an injured fawn and stops to care for it, she meets Josie, an older woman who persuades the girl to stay with her. Josie listens as Margaret haltingly expresses her fears of ridicule and convinces her that she can learn to overcome the social and emotional ramifications of her disability. They notify Magaret's mother who willingly turns over the responsibility for her to Josie. In the final scene Margaret joins a training program—a hopeful note that she has stopped running and is going to face her disability.

Bernard Wolf's *Anna's Silent World* (P-I) is a photo-documentary about a six-year-old deaf child. Anna leads a happy life as she plays with her friends and joins in many activities. Her deafness is explained, and lip reading and her hearing aid are described.

Jeanne Whitehouse Peterson drew on her own experiences with a younger sister to tell the story of *I Have a Sister. My Sister Is Deaf* (P). In a simple conversational style, she tells about the many things her sister can do and some that she cannot. The sisters talk to each other with their hands, their eyes, their faces, as well as with their mouths. She explains that although her sister's ears don't hurt, sometimes her feelings are hurt when people do not understand her or make fun of her. This loving report is a good introduction to deafness, one in which it is viewed not as a handicap but as a straightforward fact of life.

Visual Handicaps

Visually handicapped children range from those who are totally blind and read braille to those who are visually impaired and read large print or with the aid of special magnifying lenses or optical monoculars. A recent invention, the opticon, translates printed material into electrical patterns that can be read with the fingers. Tape recorded stories also allow blind children to experience the same literature as their sighted peers. Such tapes are available commercially and at libraries, but, of course, you can make your own. In one school, a talking-books project has students recording their favorite stories on cassette tapes and sending them to blind children at the local hospital. Other students become readers who keep a regular schedule visiting hospitalized people, including those who are blind.

Outstanding stories and poems are collected in an annual braille publication called *Expectations* that is provided without charge to blind children in grades 3 through 6 throughout the United States.[11]

The literature curriculum for blind and partially sighted children is the same as for children with

Braille books make the legacy of literature available to the blind child.
(Photograph by J. Berndt / STOCK, Boston, Mass.)

Jimmy's new guide dog, Leader, helps him adjust to his blindness, providing him with a feeling of independence and a renewed sense of his own worth.
(From *Follow My Leader* by James B. Garfield. Illustrated by Robert Greiner. Copyright © 1957 by James B. Garfield. Reprinted by permission of Viking Penguin Inc.)

normal vision; only the materials and techniques differ. As we all do, blind children need special role models, and although many accounts of Helen Keller's life are romanticized, children should certainly know her inspirational story. Several biographies of Helen Keller and of her teacher, Anne Sullivan Macy, tell the story well. *The Story of My Life* (I-A) is Helen Keller's own account and is supplemented, in some editions, with notes, letters, and documents by Anne Sullivan and others involved in her education.

Norman Richards's *Helen Keller* (I-A) is a photo-documentary portrait; her accomplishments are evident as she is seen with notable people from around the world. *The Helen Keller Story* (I), by Catherine Owens Peare, is a biography that shows children a warm, loving human being who happened to be deaf and blind. Helen Keller always

gave the greatest credit to her beloved teacher, Anne Sullivan, who, nearly blind herself, came to the rebellious and uncommunicative six-year-old Helen and, with tremendous dedication and determination, opened the doors of the world to her. Marion Brown and Ruth Crone tell Anne Sullivan's story in *The Silent Storm* (I-A); Anne overcame tremendous childhood suffering and grew to be the most influential person in Helen Keller's life.

Laura Bridgman was a mature resident at the Perkins Institute for the Blind when Anne Sullivan was a student there. Many of the methods developed to teach the blind and deaf Laura Bridgman were adapted by Anne Sullivan in her work with Helen Keller. Edith Hunter tells the story in *Child of the Silent Night: The Story of Laura Bridgman* (P-I).

Louis Braille, responsible for developing a system that makes reading possible for the blind, was blinded himself at the age of three. His longing to do something to help others like himself led to the Braille system, a landmark in the education of the blind. Anne E. Neimark's *Touch of Light: The Story of Louis Braille* (I), and Etta DeGering's *Seeing Fingers: The Story of Louis Braille* (I-A) introduce readers to him.

Fiction portraying the blind coping with their disability offers many fine stories. Children who read James Garfield's *Follow My Leader* (I) will not forget the baseball game that turns into tragedy for eleven-year-old Jimmy when one of his friends finds a firecracker. Despite warnings from the other boys to leave it alone, Mike hurls the firecracker, which explodes in Jimmy's face. Blinded by the accident, Jimmy refuses to speak to Mike; his bitterness grows until he hates himself, Mike, and the whole world. As he slowly adjusts to moving about with his new guide dog, Leader, he gradually accepts his blindness and, in a moving scene, comes to terms with Mike.

Jean Little's story, *From Anna* (I), is based on the life of the blind author. Anna is awkward and clumsy and the brunt of her family's scorn because she cannot do anything right. Her brothers and sisters tease her unmercifully and call her Awkward Anna when she stumbles and drops things. As

World War II becomes inevitable, the family leaves their native Germany to settle in Canada. There a doctor finally discovers that her problems are due to extremely poor vision and prescribes glasses and a special school for Anna. The family still considers her a problem, but Anna's self-image grows as she learns to cope with poor vision.

Jean Little continues Anna's story in *Listen for the Singing* (I). One of her brothers is blinded while fighting in the war; his depression and bitterness threaten to destroy him until Anna helps him face his disability, and, for the first time in her life, she becomes a valued human being to someone else.

Bernard Wolf's *Connie's New Eyes* (I), a photographic essay, opens when Alison begins raising a seeing eye dog as a part of a 4-H Club project. Her strong devotion to the dog is evident in the way she cares for and trains her, but she knows that at the end of a year the dog must be taken to Seeing Eye, Inc. for further training. A blind young teacher, Connie, then assumes ownership and learns to work with the dog, who will become her guide. Connie's story focuses on her independence, enhanced by the arrival of the dog, and her ability to succeed in a career.

In *Goldengrove* (A), by Jill Paton Walsh, young Madge Fielding reads regularly to a blind professor. One day, as she reads to him from Milton's *Paradise Lost,* the meaning of the verses overwhelms her, and she weeps at the words that describe the plight of her blind listener. Madge asks the professor how he can bear to hear words that echo his loss. His answer aptly portrays a role of literature in life:

. . . it puts things outside me. Makes them into objects external to the mind. . . . Another man's pain, against which to measure one's own. A scream to put against one's own silence. It helps me to grasp how much of what I am is blindness and how much is me.[12]

Literature provides a measuring stick for some; a portrait of another's life dominated by a disability for the rest. It enables all of us to share another's distress and celebrate the unconquerable joy in life.

Mental Retardation

Mentally retarded characters appear in children's books less often than blind or emotionally disturbed ones, or those with orthopedic problems, but more often than the deaf or speech impaired. Mental retardation was among the first special needs topics to appear in children's books when the prohibitions began to crumble in the late 1960s and early 1970s.

The Newbery Medal, given for Betsy Byars's *Summer of the Swans* (I-A), recognized the literary merit of a book that deals with retardation. Although his portrayal is a compassionate one, Charlie, the retarded child, appears essentially as a catalyst for his sister Sara's emotional growth. In the story, fourteen-year-old Sara finds Charlie to be

Mute Charlie wears the watch that is both a connection to and a shelter from the world around him.
(From *Summer of the Swans* by Betsy Byars. Illustrations by Ted CoConis. Copyright © 1970 by Betsy Byars. Reprinted by permission of Viking Penguin Inc.)

Profile

BETSY BYARS

Unlike many, Betsy Byars had no childhood aspirations of becoming an author. Although she has always been an avid reader, she says that she spent too much time enjoying herself ever to pursue anything seriously. It was not until she became a homemaker with time on her hands that she thought of writing. Her first efforts were humorous articles for popular magazines such as *Look, TV Guide,* and *Saturday Evening Post.* She turned to writing for children when her own four youngsters were growing up.

Besides being her most severe critics, her children provided endless material—from things that happened in school and with their friends. *The Midnight Fox* is her favorite among her books "because it is very personal. A great deal of my own children and their activities went into it, and a great deal of myself. It came closer to what I was trying to do than any of my other books" (Lee Bennett Hopkins, "Betsy Byars", in *More Books by More People* [Citation Press, 1974], p. 70). *Summer of the Swans* grew from an experience she had when she worked with mentally retarded children.

Betsy Byars describes herself as a wife and mother. She remembers that she had just thrown a load of laundry in the washing machine when she received the phone call telling her that she had won the Newbery Medal. It was "a startling experience" because "at that point in life I was not what you would think of as a professional-type writer. I knew very little about the publishing business; I had never been in an editor's office. I didn't even know any other writers." She still has no set rules for writing and, in fact, writes the way she does many other things—"fast, without patterns, and with great hope and determination" (Hopkins, "Betsy Byars," in *More Books,* pp. 71, 69).

Byars thoroughly enjoys life. She believes that the world is an exciting and lively place and that children are very bright and individualistic. In her stories, she explores the many challenges facing today's young people and tries to develop her characters so that they meet their world with humor, compassion, and understanding.

A native of North Carolina, Betsy Byars now lives in Morgantown, West Virginia. She does most of her writing in the winter; her summers are spent enjoying a cabin at a nearby lake and sharing her husband's hobby of gliding.

Jean Little is a person who has not allowed a disability to become a handicap. Born with very limited eyesight, she nonetheless developed an early love for language and books. Her earliest memories include being read to by her mother—in fact, one of her first spoken words was "book-a."

As she grew she made up her own stories and, at the age of ten, wrote her first book. When she was fifteen her father had a collection of her poems printed. Jean Little has always preferred stories about true-to-life people in a realistic context; even as a child she didn't "like fairy tales or legends much because the people weren't real enough" (Doris De Montreville and Elizabeth D. Crawford, eds., *Fourth Book of Junior Authors and Illustrators* [New York: Wilson, 1978], p. 228). Her stories are about real people, often children, who successfully cope with problems. Mental retardation, cerebral palsy, blindness, and even broken bones—all affect the lives of her characters but do not handicap them.

Although she wanted to be a writer, she thought authors "lived in garrets and starved" (De Montreville and Crawford, eds., *Fourth Book of Junior Authors and Illustrators,* p. 229), and so, to avoid that fate, became a teacher. It was only after she met Virginia Sorensen—who "looked well-nourished"—that she took the chance. The result of that first effort—winner of the 1961 Canadian Children's Book Award—was *Mine for Keeps,* a realistic story about a girl with cerebral palsy. She drew upon her own painful experiences when she wrote *From Anna,* a story about a young girl who suffers teasing and ostracism because of her poor eyesight.

A Canadian, she was born in Taiwan, where her parents were serving as medical missionaries. Her family returned to Canada when she was seven years old, and after one year in a special class, she attended regular school, though she was never able to see what was written on the blackboard. She received a Bachelor's degree in English language and literature from the University of Toronto. She likes to travel, but "what my life is really all about is writing. It's a terrible way to make a living but I wouldn't do anything else. I get to live so many extra lives this way" (De Montreville and Crawford, eds., *Fourth Book of Junior Authors and Illustrators,* p. 229).

JEAN LITTLE

just one more problem than she can handle during a summer of personal trauma. Concerned about her appearance, she cries in fits of self-pity about big feet and skinny legs. She loves Charlie but readily admits that he is a bother to her. Sara quickly forgets her self-preoccupation when Charlie disappears. Charlie, lost three blocks from home, is unable to ask for help. He is described as having huge blank spaces in his life that he can never fill. Her very real fright and subsequent relief on finding him cause her to reflect on the relative importance of people and events in her life. Sara is a volatile teen-ager who copes with more than the normal share of problems, but her wholesome acceptance and love for her retarded brother make her a memorable character. Sara's love and sense of responsibility for Charlie help her to clarify her personal values and sense of self.

Welcome Home, Jellybean (I-A), by Marlene Fanta Shyer, is told by twelve-year-old Neil. The return home of his one year older sister Geraldine, after years of living in institutions for the retarded, brings problems Neil and his parents can hardly bear. His father moves out, inviting Neil to go with him. The episode that precipitates his father's move is the discovery that the keys of his piano are sticky:

> "What from? What are they sticky from?" my father said.
> . . . I figured applesauce, but it didn't matter; we both knew that they were sticky from Gerri, that it was Gerri who had messed up the piano, that it was Gerri, again and again, who was fouling things up, snafuing everything.[13]

Gerri spoils more than the piano keys: she interrupts Neil's long-awaited chance to perform at school and is the cause for a petition to evict the family from their apartment. Finally, Neil, too, decides he has had enough and agrees to join his father. As he leaves the apartment Gerri calls out Neil's name, evidence of the slow but steady progress she is making. When Neil reaches his father's waiting car, he is torn and can go no farther:

> "Neil, what's the matter?" my father asked.
> I couldn't say it; it just jammed up in my throat like old rags, that not everybody can have perfect pitch, that even though Gerri would always be strange/different/funny/weird, she was the way she was, and she was my sister.[14]

Neil's story sensitively portrays, without sentimentality, a family's problems with a mentally retarded child. The honest confrontation of personal and familial torment that devastates the family shocks the reader, but the eternal strength of love and compassion inspire as well.

The strong characterization and understatement of Gene Smith's slender story *The Hayburners* (I) combine to create a subtle emotional wallop. Two events occur simultaneously in the life of overprivileged Will: he draws an unpromising young steer to raise for a 4-H Club project and his parents bring a mentally retarded adult, Joey, to work for them during the summer. Regarding the ungainly steer he is to raise, Will takes the view that there is no hope, and would totally ignore it. Joey, however, sees the animal as beautiful and cares for it lovingly. He feeds, waters, curries, massages, exercises, and talks to the steer. Astonishingly, it develops rapidly and ranks in the top ten at the end-of-summer judging. The undercurrent of the story—that we are quick to judge humans as we do animals and shunt the losers aside—builds slowly but has great impact in this finely crafted story.

Casey, the twelve-year-old girl in Sue Ellen Bridgers's *All Together Now* (I-A), spends the summer with her grandparents while her mother works two jobs and her father is overseas in the Korean War. Casey's name, too much like a boy's to suit her grandmother, works to her advantage in developing a friendship with Dwayne Pickens, a man in his thirties with the mind of a twelve-year-old. Casey hears Dwayne at play in a solitary baseball game before she meets him; he fills all positions and announces each play:

> "And here's the pitch. Robinson *bunts!* Holy cow!"
> Dwayne dashed to the plate, picked up the ball with

his bare hand, turned and made a throwing motion toward first base, although he still held the ball in his hand. He raced off toward first himself.

"Garagiola's off with the mask! He grabs the ball and fires it to first! Is it in time?"

At first base, Dwayne toed the bag and then snared the ball from its invisible flight with a flick of his gloved wrist.

"They've got him. Garagiola throws out Robinson on a beau-ti-ful play! And that's all for the Dodgers! In the top of the ninth, it's three up and three down!"[15]

Dwayne thinks Casey is a boy, and, so that he will let her play baseball with him, she tells him no different. Several subplots intricately undergird the story of the friendship between Casey and Dwayne, but the sympathetic portrayal of a retarded adult is paramount. Capitalizing upon a minor incident, Dwayne's brother attempts to institutionalize him, although he has always moved freely and with acceptance throughout their small village. Despite Dwayne's innocence, the villagers' unfounded fears and ignorance prevent them from resisting his brother's plan. Many stand silently by.

Books that portray mentally retarded characters are meant for readers who want a better understanding of the disability. Obviously, complexities of plot, theme, and language make most such books inaccessible to many mentally retarded children themselves. Retarded children, however, should not be denied the joys of fine books. If they are able to speak and to understand others, resourceful teachers can design literature programs that are realistic and effective in maximizing their responses. The child's mental age should be used as a guide for selecting books. Because mentally retarded children go through the same developmental stages as all children, although more slowly, the methods, techniques, and materials should correspond to that slower developmental rate and more limited cognitive capacity. All children grow through carefully sequenced experiences appropriately matched to their learning characteristics.

Dorothy Butler tells the story of the important part played by books in the early development of

Retarded Joey gazes at the ungainly young steer whose promise he can see but Will can not.
(Excerpted from *The Hayburners* by Gene Smith. Illustrated by Ted Lewin. Illustrations copyright © 1974 by Ted Lewin. Used by permission of Delacorte Press.)

her severely disabled granddaughter in *Cushla and Her Books* (adult). Although Cushla's problems were more physical than mental, her development was slow; the influence of books on her cognitive and language abilities was significant.

The teacher's role is crucial, for most literary experiences will need to be shared. Mentally retarded children delight in being read to, and colorful illustrations and film versions of stories intrigue them. Filmstrips or recordings of stories make it possible for all children to share in the bounties of literature. Once teachers sensitive to the unique needs of retarded children become aware of the many fine books suitable for the retarded, designing learning activities for them can become a joyful task.

Emotional Disturbance

Emotional disturbance is often poorly understood, misdiagnosed, and feared. This is understandable because it is such a complex syndrome, with bizarre and idiosyncratic manifestations. Some children who are emotionally disturbed cannot control their actions and require protection and a great deal of tolerance. Any situation may lead to hysteria or acting out of hostile impulses.

The lack of information about emotional disturbance leads to confusion in literature. For example, in Richard Parker's *He Is Your Brother* (I), au-

Deeply troubled Fran Ellen, with the doll house that plays a prominent part in her fantasy escapes from a painful life. (Illustration from *The Bear's House* by Marilyn Sachs. Illustrated by Louis Glanzman. Copyright © 1971 by Marilyn Sachs. Reproduced by permission of Doubleday & Company, Inc.)

tistic six-year-old Orry is unable to use a knife and fork, yet spontaneously and without instruction plays a very difficult musical piece on the piano. Despite the fact that some autistic children do possess unusual musical abilities, Orry's performance is difficult to believe.

In *Please Don't Say Hello* (I), Phyllis Gold uses children's questions about an autistic child, Eddie, who has moved into their neighborhood, to try to explain autism. Unfortunately, the platitudes and vague generalizations offered fail to inform the reader. In addition, the teasing injunction in the title will hardly explain to readers that autistic children cannot respond to the greeting.

John Neufeld is more successful in portraying erratic behavior (and the lack of understanding about it) in *Lisa, Bright and Dark* (A). In his novel, only Lisa's teen-age friends recognize that she is becoming more emotionally disturbed each day. Lisa herself thinks she is losing her mind and pleads with her parents to listen to her; they are too preoccupied to take her seriously. Lisa's friends try to persuade a number of adults to seek help for her, but find no one willing to take the necessary steps or to heed the warning signs. Some days are very bright for Lisa, but others are abysmally dark; the story ends on a very dark note.

Marilyn Sachs portrays an emotionally disturbed mother in *The Bears' House* (I), although the focus is the effect on her daughter, Fran Ellen, who is nearly ten years old, sucks her thumb, and smells bad. Fran Ellen's greatest joy is playing with a miniature dollhouse at school, where she moves the three bears about, puts Goldilocks to sleep in baby bear's bed, and endlessly replays the story. It is the only time she feels at ease:

. . . I'm me in the Bears' House.
The door is open, naturally, and I go up the stairs and stand by the bed. She opens her eyes.
"Move over!" I tell her, and she says, "Yes, ma'am."
"You sure are some pushy, good-for-nothing," I tell her.
"What kind of nerve you got, anyway, pushing yourself in here where you weren't invited and eating up a family's food and breaking their furniture and messing up their beds!"
"Yes, ma'am," says Goldilocks. She gets out of the

bed, and I get in. But I go on telling her what I think of her, and all she can say is, "Yes, ma'am," and suck her thumb.
"Thumb Sucker," I tell her.
Then we both suck our thumbs together for a while, and I get over being mad at her.[16]

Fran Ellen immerses herself in the fantasy play to escape the harshness of her real life. In the well-ordered, snug family of the bears, she finds all the things she wants—love, admiration, attention. In her own life, she faces unrelenting burdens with a wraithlike mother, no father, and four siblings who try to survive alone. The mother's devastating withdrawal is echoed in Fran Ellen's escape to a fantasy world.

Learning Disabilities

Specific learning disabilities suffer from lack of definition and clarification in schools as well as in children's books. "Neurological impairment," a frequent designation, seems to be an umbrella term for many different types of behavior; typically, children with reading problems, motor problems, visual problems, and others are called "learning disabled."

The lack of clarity of definition spills over into literature, and there are few books of literary quality that accurately portray a learning-disabled character. Errors in describing character behavior are particularly misleading for naive readers. Barbara H. Baskin and Karen H. Harris, in *Notes from a Different Drummer*, point out several such deficiencies in Glendon and Kathryn Swarthout's novel *Whales to See the* (I). In this case, the title itself is a gross misrepresentation, because, although learning disabled children do often reverse or substitute letters in words—*b* for *d*, *saw* for *was*, for example—they do not reorder syntax.

Doris Buchanan Smith gives the most adequate portrayal of a learning-disabled child in *Kelly's Creek* (I). Kelly knows that he is not like other nine-year-old children: he does not read, write, or draw circles the way they do. He is not successful in school, but he achieves great success in studying the marsh life at a nearby creek. Phillip, a college student in biology who is studying the marsh, be-

Disability need not always prevent participation. (Photograph by Anestis Diakopoulos / STOCK, Boston, Mass.)

friends Kelly. In fact, Phillip is Kelly's only friend; they share a common love for the marsh. When Kelly is at the creek, he is competent, agile, and relaxed, but in school he is tense and uncoordinated. After a bad report card from school, Kelly is forbidden to go to the marsh or to see Phillip, the only source of happiness he knows. Kelly's dejection and his joy are shown in hauntingly beautiful illustrations, especially those set in the marshlands. Kelly's parents typify well-intentioned adults whose decisions can deny a child the most meaningful part of his life.

Physical Disabilities

Physical impairments range from minimal muscular dysfunction to total paralysis, with as many causes as there are limitations on the disabled person's ability to move about. Orthopedic problems are central or peripheral elements in children's books more frequently than any other type of disability.

Joan Tate's *Ben and Annie* (I), discussed earlier, is a bittersweet story of the friendship between a boy and a young invalid girl who is restricted to a wheelchair. Ben relieves Annie's loneliness by wheeling her around the neighborhood and spending endless hours talking with the dying girl. Ben's friends join in, and the boys improvise activities that clearly delight Annie. Her squeals of joy gratify them when they carefully push her wheelchair down a gentle slope. A man, assuming that the boys are tormenting Annie, angrily intercedes, drags them off to Annie's house, and berates them before her mother. Ben is so crushed by the accusation that he is unable to explain what really happened, while Annie, devastated to think that her only pleasure has ended, remains silent. Annie's parents fear for her safety, yet in their desire to protect her, they take away the vestiges of happiness she found in Ben's companionship.

Physically disabled children have dreams and aspirations like any child's; overprotection and patronage, no matter how well intended, can destroy these. In *Let the Balloon Go* (I), Ivan Southall tells a story about John, who is twelve years old, has cerebral palsy, and wants more than anything to swim and climb and play like other boys. His anxious mother, though, constantly reminds him of what he cannot do: ride a bike, chop wood, get into fights; he is different with a capital *D*. On a rare day in which he is briefly left alone, John decides to build a tree house. His progress is slow and clumsy, but with the help of a ladder he drags to the tree, he persists until he reaches the topmost branches. He sits there exhilarated. He is strong, free, a boy like any other. But neighbors notice him, assume that he is stranded, and form a rescue party. The constable climbs the tree, but gets stuck before he reaches John. The boy defies orders to stay where he is and begins the dangerous descent unaided; he slips and struggles but reaches the constable, whom he frees, then continues with faltering and unsteady progress. He slips near the bottom and falls with a scream.

John awakens in his bed, and his mother confirms that he really climbed the tree—and got down unaided. His parents at last realize that John needs to take risks, needs to be free to try. He likens his release to a balloon, which is not really a balloon until someone cuts the string.

Bernard Wolf's *Don't Feel Sorry for Paul* (I) describes a heroic child's adjustment to the use of artificial limbs. Born with incomplete hands and feet, Paul wears prostheses—artificial body parts. Clear black-and-white photographs show Paul getting himself ready for and participating in many activities with his family and friends. He rides a horse, attends public school, helps his mother prepare dinner, wrestles with his sisters, and rides a

With fierce determination, John struggles against his cerebral palsy to climb to the top of a tree, where he will feel strong and free.
(From *Let the Balloon Go* by Ivan Southall. Illustrated by Ian Ribbons. 1968. Reprinted by permission of Methuen Children's Books Ltd., London.)

bike. Wolf gives factual information about Paul's regular visits to the Institute of Rehabilitation Medicine for examination and adjustment of the prosthetic devices. The honest, objective book is neither patronizing nor pallid.

Paraplegics are almost totally immobile, usually as the result of polio or injury. Robin Brancato relates the story of a boy injured in a high-school football game in *Winning* (A). Gary is unable to move from the neck down and faces the possibility of spending the rest of his life immobilized. He must deal not only with his feelings about himself, but also changes in his relationships with his peers,

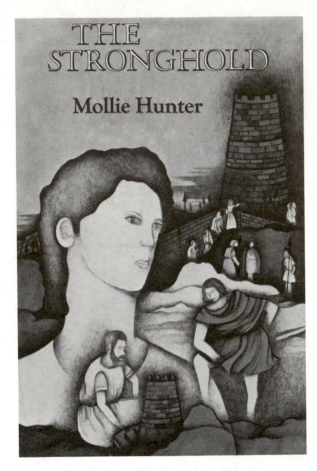

THE STRONGHOLD

Mollie Hunter

Young Coll, crippled when the Romans attack his people, envisions the fortress they will build against the invaders.
(From *The Stronghold* by Mollie Hunter. Harper & Row, 1974.)

especially his girl friend. Gary's English teacher, perceptive and insightful, acts as a go-between for the boy in his relations with the outside world. The author also chose to end the story on a hopeful note after sensitively showing the boy's progress from disbelief to anger to resignation and, finally, to acceptance of the disability.

Mollie Hunter's *The Stronghold* (A) is a historical novel about a young man whose vision far exceeds that of his contemporaries. The story takes place in the days when Roman slave raiders often descended on the Orkney Islands; a young man stands guard:

Reluctantly Coll turned his gaze from the settlement, and once more braced his sinewy frame to meet the cold sea wind whistling over the headland. The movement woke pain in his crippled leg, and he endured it with gritted teeth and a tightened grip on the long stem of the bronze warning trumpet in his right hand. The pain passed. His fingers relaxed, and his face regained its normal appearance of spare, bony strength.[17]

Coll understandably hates the Roman soldiers; one of them pulling him, as a baby, from his mother and throwing him against some rocks, had crushed his hipbone. Coll's strength and ingenuity pervade this story of a physically disabled young man in ancient times.

Gifted and Talented

Efforts aimed at broadening the literature curriculum for gifted and talented children—also a population with special needs—are sporadic. A high percentage of the gifted and talented come to school having already learned to read and with no need to plod through a lock-step basal reading program. Much more exciting for children and teacher is to guide them toward the wealth of glorious books available to them. Verbally gifted kindergarten children who know how to read can be started on a literature-based reading program that extends throughout their elementary and junior-high-school years.

Talented and gifted children exhibit consistently remarkable performance in a panoply of endeavors. Their gift may be intellectual or academic, the most frequently identified category, or they may be talented artistically, musically, mechanically, physically, or in other ways. Whatever the field, you can be sure there are books for them and about their interests to help you guide them.

Gifted children ascend the spiral of learning at a faster rate and characteristically acquire academic skills in a shorter time than usually allotted. Rather than lose such valuable students to boredom or neglect, we need to make provision for enriching their learning. Many of the "activities" described in this text meet the challenge directly.

We have said that when teachers take pleasure

in literature, their enthusiasm is contagious. This is especially significant for gifted students, who are prime candidates for becoming lifelong lovers of reading. The search for books to extend gifted students' interests becomes an engaging task for students and teachers alike.

Strategies to nourish divergent thinking give literature a high priority. For example, planning of literature programs—setting goals and selecting materials—in collaboration with students is essential. Providing many books on a variety of subjects enables application of the principles of self-selection and self-pacing so crucial to success.

Gifted children are often interested in books about others like themselves.
(Photograph by Cary Wolinsky / STOCK, Boston, Mass.)

You can begin by giving children a simple interest inventory that need not be more than a half dozen questions about what they like to do in their spare time, what they like to read, what they envision for their future, and what they would like to know. On the basis of their answers, you can give them literature to build upon their interests, which often run deep; literature serves to cultivate and to develop them.

Cooperatively planned literature programs will include opportunities for frequent teacher-guided discussion, which enables students to benefit from the insights of their peers and to validate their own positions. Collaboratively based insights are richer; students discover more about a book they have read as they talk about it with others. Establishing a dialogue is important for the growth of critical attitudes. The insatiable curiosity and wide range of interests of gifted and talented students can be taken into account in tasks requiring independent research, seminars, or meetings with authors and illustrators of children's books. Furthermore, such children need little encouragement to write their own books.

Modifying the curriculum to meet the needs of the gifted and talented requires that teachers and librarians be inventive and imaginative. This is no small task, yet nothing inspires us more than such experiences as the child who has read everything that Natalie Babbitt has ever written and asks for her address "so I can write to her and see what she's up to. Maybe I'll even send her an amaryllis bulb."

Books about gifted and talented characters are rare; of those, however, many offer characters who are extremely clever and a bit larger than life. Keith Robertson's *Henry Reed, Inc.* (I-A) is one such, and his ingenious enterprises will intrigue many. Sonia Levitin's *The Mark of Conte* (A) provides an alter ego for the student who considers skipping ahead by taking two school years in one. When the school computer prints out two programs for the same boy, one for Mark Conte and the other for Conte Mark, this clever young man decides to fulfill them both and thereby graduate a year early. The hilarity that ensues while he tries to

Profile

MOLLIE HUNTER

. . . the first light of literature on a young mind does more than illumine. A touch of glory descends, and that mind can never be truly dark again.

Talent Is Not Enough

Such is the belief of Mollie Hunter, who has brought touches of glory to innumerable young minds. Historical fact and legend mingle in her tales; her gift for bringing the spell of the past into modern stories is unmatched.

Mollie Hunter knows that things are not always what they seem, or may not be, and convinces readers to listen with an inner ear and to see, as the title has it, with *The Third Eye*. Her talent brings to the surface the secret hopes and emotions that nourish life and creative work:

I don't say that I am wedded to my craft, that I'm steeped in my craft, that I'm involved in it. I *am* my work (Janet Hickman, "Profile: The Person Behind the Book—Mollie Hunter," *Language Arts,* 56, No. 3 [March 1979], 302).

While facts have their place, Mollie Hunter has her fictions, which are far more convincing.

She grew up in the highlands of Scotland with an aura of myth and legend permeating her days. The visionary Coll in *The Stronghold,* who plans and builds an impregnable fortress for his people despite his physical handicap, could have been created by a Mollie Hunter imagination only. So, too, could it only have been a Mollie Hunter who described, in *The Walking Stones,* the relationship between Donald and the Bodach, believers in each generation who pass on the torch of legend to their heirs.

be in two places at the same time keeps the reader laughing and cheering.

Manus Pinkwater describes a character who is brighter than his parents, most of his teachers, and his counselor in *Alan Mendelsohn: The Boy from Mars* (A). The narrator, who artfully describes his own cunning as he tells about Alan Mendelsohn, thinks Alan is a master strategist. Both boys leave a wake of bewildered parents, teachers, and counselors behind them as they shrewdly manipulate them all. Gifted children will identify their counterparts in a hilarious book.

Teacher Portrayal

Teachers in books with disabled characters run the gamut of portrayal from saintly and well intentioned but ineffectual to malicious and destructive. The books discussed here can help us to see our role, learn from others' mistakes, and find worthy role models. Unfortunately, good models are found less frequently than bad. To start with the best, the English teacher in Robin Brancato's *Winning* (A) develops a close personal relationship with the injured boy and remains supportive through his difficult adjustment to immobility. The

Asked why many of her books are set in historical times, Mollie Hunter replied:

I'm interested in the past, and it just so happens that the past is all around me in the circumstances in which I live; there are reminders of it, for instance, in the form of old buildings. And, I've always been curious about what happened before I was born, and I've done a lot of research to find out. But I also have the sense of all the people who lived before me and I like to try to recreate their lives. . . . And I just like the sensation of wandering back into the past. It's like a country that I have come to know. I like walking through the past and coming back into my own time with a good story to tell (Jean Greenlaw, "An Interview with Mollie Hunter," in *From Writers to Students,* ed. M. Jerry Weiss [Newark, Del.: International Reading Association, 1979], p. 45).

Mollie Hunter's Scottish brogue and lilting laughter ring through her speech; chatting with her is like catching a sunbeam. Her powerful convictions about the goodness of people permeate her writing and life. Asked what her essential message is, she replied, ". . . if there is a message, it is that the most powerful force on earth is the capacity of human beings to reach out, to be warm, responsive to one another—to love" (Greenlaw, "An Interview with Mollie Hunter," in *From Writers to Students,* p. 46).

It is no wonder that Mollie Hunter's books are popular with young people; they evoke response in readers because of her ability to share love. Her peers have acclaimed her status as an exceptional writer by awarding her the Carnegie Medal (counterpart of the Newbery Medal) for *The Stronghold* and by inviting her to give the Arbuthnot Lecture in 1975. An outgrowth of the lecture series is a book of essays titled *Talent Is Not Enough,* which explores her strong beliefs about the craft and passion of writing.

teacher in the sight-saving class in Jean Little's *From Anna* (I), creates a supportive atmosphere and plans constructive activities for her students. Eleanor Clymer portrays an admirable teacher counselor in the orphan's home in *Luke Was There* (P-I). Luke listens, guides, and disciplines with love and understanding. He leaves his post when he is drafted but finds a way to return to the home when a crisis arises that only he can resolve.

More often teachers and counselors seem ineffectual as in John Neufeld's *Lisa, Bright and Dark* (A). In one episode, emotionally disturbed Lisa, found sticking pins into her arm, is referred to Mr. Bernstein, the school counselor:

After short conferences with all her teachers, Mr. Bernstein called Lisa's home and told her mother that Lisa was suffering from tension (ah-hah!) brought on by exams and by the fact that she and Brian were having some difficulty. He suggested that perhaps the Shillings should take Lisa out of school for a few weeks to rest, take her somewhere she could relax and think and pull herself together.

And that was that. No suggestion that anything was seriously wrong, or that poking yourself full of holes was anything rare in a sixteen-year-old girl who was supposed to have the world by the tail.[18]

Later attempts to turn to the counselor for help prove equally futile.

Neither perceptive and patient saints nor cruel, insensitive monsters, some teacher characters are torn between courses of action. For example, Mr. Alvarado, in Kin Platt's *Hey, Dummy* (I-A), discussed above, shows little courage in resolving a conflict between his beliefs in humane treatment for the disabled and possible repercussions (for the local Chicano community) of his sheltering a hunted child.

Some teacher characters passively ignore teasing and cruelties from the peers of a disabled child and thereby tacitly condone their behavior. For example, in Babbis Friis's story, *Kristy's Courage* (I), Kristy is subjected to cruel mockery at school, which her teacher tolerates out of cowardice.

Of several teachers in Kin Platt's *The Boy Who Could Make Himself Disappear* (I-A), some are unbelievably cruel and insensitive, but others are understanding and helpful. Mr. Rawling mocks Roger's lisp and ridicules his speech in front of the class. A former teacher, Miss Madison shows affection for Roger but explains, out of her ignorance, that he cannot pronounce the letter *r* because he has a "lazy tongue." Mr. Wilshire, the principal, issues edicts that no one dares question. But Miss Roberta Clemm, speech pathologist, stands out as a true professional and a caring teacher. Because Miss Clemm goes the extra mile, the story ends on a hopeful note. In one scene, Miss Clemm telephones Roger's totally self-centered mother:

"Mrs. Baxter? This is Roberta Clemm speaking. Dr. Clemm. Your son's therapist at school."

"Oh? Well—he isn't here." . . .

"I know, Mrs. Baxter. He's here with me—at the hospital."

"Oh?"

She didn't ask what hospital. Or where. Or why.

"Aren't you interested in how Roger is?"

"What's that?"

"Do you know where your boy has slept the past two nights?"

"Look honey," Mrs. Baxter said, "if I tried to keep track of everything that kid did, I'd have gray hairs."

. . . "Well, then"—her fury was mounting but she made her voice even and cool—" I don't suppose you'd mind if we kept Roger here with us for a few more days —"

"Can you make it a week?"

. . .

Miss Clemm couldn't believe all this was happening. She'd met them all, she thought, but this one—this one was really something.

"Don't worry," she said. "We'll see that your son is taken home properly. We'll have to run a few more tests but he seems to be responding to treatment."

"There, you see?" Mrs. Baxter said. "He always snaps out of it. You probably worry too much about it, I guess being a doctor and all."

"Mrs. Baxter, I guess being a doctor and all, as you put it, may have something to do with it. Don't you think we ought to have a talk sometime?"

"About what?"

Miss Clemm held the phone away from her face for a moment, "You know," she said finally, "there's a word for mothers like you."

And then she told it to her.[19]

Notes

1. Denise Levertov, "A Solitude," in *Beach Glass and Other Poems,* ed. Paul Molloy (New York: Four Winds-Scholastic, 1970), p. 37.
2. Barbara H. Baskin and Karen H. Harris, *Notes from a Different Drummer: A Guide to Juvenile Fiction Portraying the Handicapped* (New York: Bowker, 1977), p. x.
3. Sheila Garrigue, *Between Friends* (Scarsdale, N.Y.: Bradbury, 1978), p. 28.
4. Ibid., p. 55.
5. Ibid., p. 79.
6. Ibid., p. 51.
7. Ibid., p. 160.

8. Kin Platt, *Hey, Dummy* (New York: Chilton, 1971), p. 28.
9. Ibid., p. 77.
10. Ibid., p. 79.
11. Further information may be had from Betty Kalagian, Braille Institute Press, Braille Institute of America, Inc., 741 North Vermont Avenue, Los Angeles, California 90029.
12. Jill Paton Walsh, *Goldengrove* (Boston: G. K. Hall, 1973), p. 80.
13. Marlene Fanta Shyer, *Welcome Home, Jellybean* (New York: Scribner's, 1978), p. 111.
14. Ibid., p. 150.
15. Sue Ellen Bridgers, *All Together Now* (New York: Knopf, 1979), p. 16.
16. Marilyn Sachs, *The Bears' House* (New York: Doubleday, 1971), pp. 29–30.
17. Mollie Hunter, *The Stronghold* (New York: Harper & Row, 1974), p. 2.
18. John Neufeld, *Lisa, Bright and Dark* (New York: Phillip's, 1969), p. 28.
19. Kin Platt, *The Boy Who Could Make Himself Disappear* (New York: Chilton, 1968), pp. 233–35.

Professional References

Baskin, Barbara H., and Karen H. Harris. *Notes from a Different Drummer: A Guide to Juvenile Fiction Portraying the Handicapped.* Bowker, 1977.

Butler, Dorothy. *Cushla and Her Books.* Horn Book, Inc., 1980.

De Montreville, Doris, and Elizabeth D. Crawford, eds. *Fourth Book of Junior Authors and Illustrators.* H. W. Wilson, 1978.

Dreyer, Sharon Spredemann. *The Bookfinder.* American Guidance, 1977.

Hickman, Janet. "Profile: The Person Behind the Book—Mollie Hunter." *Language Arts,* 56, No. 3 (March 1979), 302–06.

Hunter, Mollie. *Talent Is Not Enough.* Harper & Row, 1976.

Weiss, M. Jerry, ed. *From Writers to Students.* International Reading Association, 1979.

Children's Books Cited in Chapter

Brancato, Robin. *Winning.* Knopf, 1977.

Bridgers, Sue Ellen. *All Together Now.* Knopf, 1979.

Brown, Marion, and Ruth Crone. *The Silent Storm.* Illus. Fritz Kredel. Abingdon, 1963.

Byars, Betsy. *Summer of the Swans.* Illus. Ted CoConis. Viking, 1970.

Cleaver, Vera, and Bill Cleaver. *Me Too.* Lippincott, 1973.

Clymer, Eleanor. *Luke Was There.* Illus. Diane de Groat. Holt, Rinehart & Winston, 1973.

Corcoran, Barbara. *A Dance to Still Music.* Atheneum, 1974.

DeGering, Etta. *Seeing Fingers: The Story of Louis Braille.* Illus. Emil Weiss. McKay, 1962.

Friis, Babbis. *Kristy's Courage.* Trans. Lise S. McKinnon. Illus. Charles Geer. Harcourt Brace Jovanovich, 1965.

Garfield, James B. *Follow My Leader.* Illus. Robert Greiner, Viking, 1957.

Garrigue, Sheila. *Between Friends.* Bradbury, 1978.

Gold, Phyllis. *Please Don't Say Hello.* Photographs by Carl Baker. Behavioral Publications, 1975.

Hunter, Edith F. *Child of the Silent Night.* Illus. Bea Holmes. Houghton Mifflin, 1963.

Hunter, Mollie. *The Stronghold.* Harper & Row, 1974.

_____. *The Third Eye.* Harper & Row, 1979.

_____. *The Walking Stones.* Harper & Row, 1970.

Kalagian, Betty. *Expectations.* Annual. Braille Institute Press.

Kamien, Janet. *What If You Couldn't . . .?: A Book About Special Needs.* Illus. Signe Henson. Scribner's, 1979.

Keller, Helen. *The Story of My Life.* Doubleday, 1954.

Levitin, Sonia. *The Mark of Conte.* Illus. Bill Negron. Atheneum, 1976.

Little, Jean. *From Anna.* Illus. Joan Sandin. Harper & Row, 1972.

_____. *Listen for the Singing.* Dutton, 1977.

Molloy, Paul, ed. *Beach Glass and Other Poems.* Four Winds-Scholastic, 1970.

Neimark, Anne E. *Touch of Light, The Story of Louis Braille.* Illus. Robert Parker. Harcourt Brace Jovanovich, 1970.

Neufeld, John. *Lisa, Bright and Dark.* Phillip's, 1969.

Parker, Richard. *He Is Your Brother.* Elsevier-Nelson, 1976.

Paton-Walsh, Jill. *Goldengrove.* Farrar, Straus & Giroux, 1972.

Peare, Catherine Owens. *The Helen Keller Story.* Crowell, 1957.

Peterson, Jeanne Whitehouse. *I Have a Sister. My Sister Is Deaf.* Illus. Deborah Ray. Harper & Row, 1977.

Pinkwater, Manus. *Alan Mendelsohn: The Boy from Mars.* Dutton, 1979.

Platt, Kin. *The Boy Who Could Make Himself Disappear.* Chilton, 1968.

_____. *Hey, Dummy.* Chilton, 1971.

Richards, Norman. *Helen Keller.* Childrens, 1968.

Robertson, Keith. *Henry Reed, Inc.* Illus. Robert McCloskey. Viking, 1958.

Robinson, Veronica. *David in Silence*. Illus. Victor Ambrus. Lippincott, 1966.

Sachs, Marilyn. *The Bears' House*. Doubleday, 1971.

Shyer, Marlene Fanta. *Welcome Home, Jellybean*. Scribner's, 1978.

Smith, Doris Buchanan. *Kelly's Creek*. Illus. Alan Tiegreen. Crowell, 1975.

Smith, Gene. *The Hayburners*. Illus. Ted Lewin. Delacorte, 1974.

Sobol, Harriet Langsam. *My Brother Steven Is Retarded*. Photographs by Patricia Agre. Macmillan, 1977.

Southall, Ivan. *Let the Balloon Go*. Illus. Ian Ribbons. St. Martin's, 1968.

Stein, Sarah Bonnett. *About Handicaps: An Open Family Book for Parents and Children Together*. Photographs by Dick Frank. Walker, 1974.

Swarthout, Glendon, and Kathryn Swarthout. *Whales to See the*. Illus. Paul Bacon. Doubleday, 1975.

Tate, Joan. *Ben and Annie*. Illus. Judith Gwyn Brown. Doubleday, 1974.

Wolf, Bernard. *Anna's Silent World*. Lippincott, 1977.

_____. *Connie's New Eyes*. Lippincott, 1976.

_____. *Don't Feel Sorry for Paul*. Lippincott, 1974.

Recommended Reading

Deafness and Hearing Impairment
E. L. Konigsburg's *Father's Arcane Daughter* (I-A, Atheneum, 1976) is an intricately woven story about a young girl whose deafness is only one of a myriad of severe disabilities that affect her life. Emily Hanlon's heroine in *The Swing* (I, Bradbury, 1979) struggles to achieve independence from her parents' anxious protection. Remy Charlip and Mary Beth Miller's *Handtalk: An ABC of Finger Spelling and Sign Language*, photographs by George Ancona (P-I, Parents, 1974) is a very useful guide for children wishing to learn sign language.

Visual Handicaps
Beverly Butler has written two stories about a young girl adjusting to blindness: *Light a Single Candle* (I-A, Dodd, Mead, 1962), which centers on the emotional impact of the disability, and *Gift of Gold* (I-A, Dodd, Mead, 1972), which continues with the acquisition of a guide dog and resumption of her active life. Theodore Taylor's *The Cay* (I, Doubleday, 1969) is a moving story of a young boy blinded during a World War II air attack and stranded on an island with an old man.

Mental Retardation
Several stories are told from the viewpoint of a brother or sister who must deal with a retarded sibling. In Colby Rodowsky's *What About Me?* (I-A, Watts, 1976) and Anne Norris Baldwin's *A Little Time* (I, Viking, 1978), young boys suffering from Down's syndrome cause conflicting feelings of resentment, guilt, anger, and love in their older sisters. In Jean Little's *Take Wing* (I, Little, Brown, 1968), a young girl assumes responsibilities beyond her years when her parents refuse to believe that there is anything wrong with their son. Other stories focussing on mental retardation include Gloria Goldreich's *Season of Discovery* (I-A, Elsevier-Nelson, 1976), Pamela Reynolds's *A Different Kind of Sister* (I-A, Lothrop, Lee & Shepard, 1968), Babbis Friis's *Don't Take Teddy*, translated by Lise McKinnon (I-A, Scribner's, 1967), and Patricia Wrightson's *A Racecourse for Andy*, illustrated by Margaret Horder (I, Harcourt Brace Jovanovich, 1968).

Emotional Disturbance
Autistic characters appear in several books, including Eleanor Spence's *The Devil Hole* (I-A, Lothrop, Lee & Shepard, 1977), which realistically portrays the shattering effects on a family as it struggles to deal with a troubled child.

Virginia Sorensen's *Miracles on Maple Hill*, illustrated by Beth and Joe Krush (I, Harcourt Brace Jovanovich, 1956), addresses the problems faced by the family of a former prisoner of war left unstable by his experiences. Severely disturbed teenagers appear in Roy Brown's *Find Debbie* (A, Seabury, 1976), about the search for a missing girl, and in Patricia McKillip's *The Night Gift*, illustrated by Kathy McKillip (I-A, Atheneum, 1976), in which a young girl tries to help a brother who has attempted suicide. *Tunnel Vision*, by Fran Arrick (A, Bradbury, 1980), explores the troubling problem of teen-age suicide.

Learning Disabilities
Among the relatively few books about children with learning problems are Stella Pevsner's *Keep Stompin' Till the Music Stops* (I, Seabury, 1977), which shows how Richard, who has been labeled dyslexic, gains new understanding and confidence as he fights his family to protect his aging grandfather. Mainstreaming is at the center of Louise Albert's story in which a learning-disabled girl faces public school for the first time, insisting *But I'm Ready to Go* (I-A, Bradbury, 1976).

Physical Disabilities
Serious diseases are not often the subject of children's books, but a few have appeared that deal successfully with such topics. The life and death of Brian Piccolo, a famous football player, was chronicled in William Blinn's *Brian's Song* (I-A, Bantam, 1972). Paige Dixon's *May I Cross Your Golden River?* (I-A, Atheneum, 1975) tells the story of a teen-age boy suffering from amyotrophic lateral sclerosis—the "Lou Gehrig" disease. The inevitability of his death forces his family to take a deeper look at the fragile threads of life. A young girl asks *Why Me?* (I, Harper & Row, 1973) in John Branfield's story about adjustments to diabetes.

Judy Blume's *Deenie* (I-A, Bradbury, 1973) suffers from scoliosis, a curvature of the spine that necessitates wearing a corrective brace. The effects of polio cannot be hidden, but a young boy learns to overcome the emotional handicap of his disease in Alberta Armer's *Screwball*, illustrated by W. T. Mars

(I, Tempo-Grosset & Dunlap, 1975). Jean Little has written parallel stories about the adjustments to be made when a family member suffers from cerebral palsy: *Mine for Keeps,* illustrated by Lewis Parker (I, Little, Brown, 1962), is Sally's story when she returns home after attending a special school, while her sister's viewpoint is presented in *Spring Begins in March,* illustrated by Lewis Parker (I, Little, Brown, 1966). Two books for younger children that show victims of cerebral palsy as they go through their school activities and therapy sessions are Nancy Mack's *Tracy,* photographs by Heinz Kluetmeier (P, Raintree Publishers, 1976), and Joan Fassler's *Howie Helps Himself,* illustrated by Joe Lasker, (P, Whitman, 1975), which convey to primary-grade children that not all of us are physically independent. Each of these children is shown successfully achieving limited, but very important, goals. Elizabeth Fanshawe's *Rachel,* illustrated by Michael Charlton (P, Bradbury, 1975), is in a wheelchair, although her specific disability is not named. Like the others, she is shown as a vital, functioning human being.

twelve

DAVID McCORD   From *BOOKS FALL OPEN*

Books fall open,
you fall in,
delighted where
you've never been;
hear voices not once
heard before,
reach world on world
through door on door;
find unexpected
keys to things
locked up beyond
imaginings.[1]

Using Books in the Classroom

John Cheetham, an adviser to the Lancashire Education Authority, in England, decries the limited use of books and poetry in the schools and would encourage more. He takes the position that:

. . . a well-chosen novel could stimulate many varied and interesting activities; it could be the mainspring of creative work in writing, art, drama and music. Such work could surely help the children to enjoy the book on many levels, increase their understanding and develop their imagination.[2]

Cheetham's position informs our approach to the subject of this chapter.

All the wonder, excitement, and joy of books can remain untapped if teachers do not create an environment in which books are essential. Children will eagerly read, learn, and create in an atmosphere in which books are valued and celebrated; they learn to love to read when they are around people who prize reading. The two most important factors in helping children become avid readers are time for reading books that they choose and listening to good books read aloud by enthusiastic readers.

Every classroom needs an inviting reading corner furnished with a soft rug, perhaps a rocking chair, pillows, or other comfortable places to sit, adequate light, and pleasing things to look at. It also should have, of course, a good and continually changing collection of books. In addition, children need freedom to explore many kinds of materials by themselves in the school library.

Research and practical experience show that most children who become involved in activities related to books read more than those who do not. The phenomenon is cyclical—reading leads to engagement and involvement, which lead to deeper understanding, more enjoyment, and, hence, more reading.

Extension activities allow children the time to savor and absorb books. Having just finished a good book, one doesn't want to begin another immediately; it is important to live with the book in one's life for a while. Students, too, need a chance to linger in the spell cast by a good book. This may mean *doing nothing* or it may mean using creative learning activities. Response and reflection are important ingredients of a child's complete learning experience; give time for both. In using literature-related activities, you will find that individual ones are often interrelated and, therefore, can enhance each other. The "Basic Skills Integration" chart, below, developed by Dorothy S. Strickland, illustrates how basic communication skills are interrelated in learning and instruction and how an integrated model makes teaching more efficient than a fragmented skill-drill approach, which divorces content from process. Learning is inherently easier and more interesting when the content of what is learned is based on important life experiences of the learner.

APPROACHES TO THE BOOK

Using and Misusing

There is a rhyme that goes "Mother said, 'Oh, stop a bit! / This is overdoing it!'"[4] This injunction can be applied to activities designed to extend the understanding and appreciation of literature—in particular to the urge to turn every book encounter into a concrete project. We should avoid overdoing a good thing, for in our zeal we may be engendering boredom instead of interest.

Children can be encouraged to respond to literature in many ways. They discover the intrinsic pleasure in extended activities when there are many to choose from. There is always the danger, however, that teachers may become so enthusiastic about activities that they spend time on them that might better be spent reading more books. The aesthetic nature of the reading experience requires personal involvement; the impact of the book determines the response one makes. Reading is a private affair that calls upon the emotions of the reader. Some books should be explored, others read, closed, and forever locked in the reader's soul. A sensitive teacher knows when a reader wants to make this choice.

Reading Aloud

Reading aloud is one of the most common and easiest means of sharing books—and a rich experience for all when done well. Select well-written stories to read aloud; don't settle for hamburger when you can have filet mignon. Books of quality abound, and it is a waste of precious time to use second-rate materials. Sometimes teachers read an inferior book "because the children love it," but students will love good books even more if they know about them. Your selections for reading aloud can influence and expand their literary tastes.

Find out which books are already familiar, ask children to list their favorites, and then build from there, selecting books that children will probably not discover on their own. By all means read them Roald Dahl's *James and the Giant Peach* (I), unless, of course, you know that most of them read this book on their own. Save reading-aloud time for the special books you want them to know. (A suggested list appears in Chapter 13.) Introduce children to all of an author's books by reading aloud from *one* of them. For example, read Beverly Cleary's *Ramona the Pest* (P-I), but let students discover Cleary's other characters on their own. Or read Keith Robertson's *Henry Reed, Inc.* (I), and point the way to the sequels, *Henry Reed's Journey* (I) and *Henry Reed's Babysitting Service* (I).

Reading from outstanding examples of all types of literature—contemporary realism, historical fiction, fantasy, folklore, and poetry—can help expand children's literary tastes, and you can extend their language by reading some books slightly above their reading abilities; they usually comprehend more than they can read. However, a good book can be spoiled for children by reading it to them before they can understand its subtleties. Most books can be understood on several levels, but it would be a waste to read E. B. White's *Charlotte's Web* (P-I) to first-grade children, who will only interpret it on a literal level as a funny story about a pig. It is far better to save it until children can appreciate the deeper meanings of friendship, sacrifice, and love in the story.

When reading aloud to children, know your material before you begin. Practice reading is important, especially in poetry, where the phrasing and cadence carry so much of the meaning. (The end of a line, for example, may not be the end of a

BASIC SKILLS INTEGRATION[3]

		LITERACY		ORACY		NUMERACY
		Reading	**Writing**	**Listening**	**Speaking**	**Problem Solving and Computation**
LITERACY	**Reading**		Reading serves as a model and stimulus for written composition. Children read each other's material and that of professional writers.	Reading and listening are receptive processes involving similar comprehension skills. Listening to literature read aloud for enjoyment or for specific purposes strengthens listening skills.	Reading provides material and models for oral composition: storytelling, reporting, plays, dramatic readings, poetry.	Reading provides access to information requiring mathematical solution or attention. Reading involves the interpretation of tables, charts, and graphs.
	Writing	Written composition produces charts, stories, books, reports for classroom use as reading materials.		Written composition read aloud or tape recorded for others to enjoy; gain information.	Writing and speaking are processes requiring ability to select significant ideas and organize them with clarity and sense of audience. Materials are read aloud with written notes used as basis for oral reports.	Written composition involves taking a set of circumstances and composing a problem in written form for solving. Information written in narrative is transformed to simple tables, charts, graphs.
ORACY	**Listening**	Listening to literature read aloud motivates reading by adding to one's store of information, enjoyment, and range of literary experiences.	Listening to stories and reports provides a base and stimulation for written composition.		Critical listening to spoken word strengthens ability to reason and respond orally. Listening provides models for oral composition.	Listening to a set of circumstances leads to determining how to proceed toward a solution involving mathematics.
	Speaking	Stories and poems are read aloud or dramatized. Oral reports, descriptions, and explanations are aided by written notes. Group discussion provides impetus for further reading.	Storytelling and reporting grow out of and stimulate written composition.	Reporting, sharing, and discussion provide material for various types of listening.		Oral description of set of facts or real life circumstances by children leads to a discussion of alternative approaches through mathematical problem solving.
NUMERACY	**Problem Solving and Computation**	Problems and examples are read for analysis and problem solving. Graphs, charts, math examples are analyzed and interpreted.	Story problems are written for others to solve. Problems are expressed in words and/or numerals and math signs.	Purposeful listening to solve a problem leads to mathematical solutions and the use of mathematical principles to make predictions, estimations.	Discussion of everyday situations translate into mathematical terms for problem solving. Problems are composed orally for others to solve.	

Adapted from "Basic Skills Integration Chart," copyright by Dorothy S. Strickland.

phrase.) Listening to poets reading their own work —mainly in recordings—can be useful; they know how it should sound. One such recording, "Poetry Parade" (Weston Woods), offers David McCord, Aileen Fisher, Karla Kuskin, and Harry Behn reading their poetry. There are other good reasons for practice sessions: Arlene Mosel's *Tikki Tikki Tembo* (P-I), contains a name that is repeated throughout the story—Tikki tikki tembo no sa rembo-chari bari ruchi-pip peri pembo; its rhythmic cadence and ear-tickling sounds carry the story and would be spoiled were the reader to stumble over it.

It is important to be thoroughly familiar with the content of the material read aloud. Some books contain words and incidents that might be offensive in some communities, or that are best kept as a private interchange between author and individual reader. For example, Judy Blume says that she thinks her book *Are You There God? It's Me, Margaret* (I), because it is an account of a personal experience, is best shared by just her and the individual reader, whereas *Blubber* (I), also by Judy Blume, begs to be read aloud because it deals with group behavior. You can avoid embarrassment in a group by being alert to sensitive issues. Jean George's *Julie of the Wolves* (I-A) contains a brief "rape" scene in which a young husband attempts to consummate a marriage that had been prearranged in childhood. The story holds together without this incident and is otherwise an excellent choice for reading aloud to fifth- and sixth-grade students. Some teachers prefer to omit the rape scene when reading aloud in order to avoid embarrassing preteens into defensive laughing and snickering, which would destroy the meaning of a serious episode. Not all books or all scenes are for group sharing.

When reading, use a natural voice, with inflections and modulations befitting the story. Avoid greatly exaggerated voice changes and overly dramatic gestures. Read slowly, enunciate clearly, project your voice directly, and maintain eye contact with your listeners as much as possible. Teachers who read aloud with their noses in the book soon lose their audience.

Reading a picture book to a group of children is an art easily mastered. Because the pictures are integral to the text, children need to see them while hearing the words. This can be effected by holding the book to one side as you read, so that the pages are clearly visible to you and your listeners. Group the children in front of you when you read to them. Sitting on a carpeted floor or cushions is best, but if chairs must be used, pull them together in a separate area of the room. Children should face away from distractions such as bright windows or busy doorways, so that their full attention can be on the story. If they must sit at their desks during story time, have them put away distracting material. Make story time a highlight of the day—a special treat that you share. Your enthusiasm and special preparations for the occasion set the tone; once you have begun, the magic of the story takes over.

Storytelling

Storytelling is a higher art than reading aloud and, as with most good things, requires more work and greater talent. Although storytelling is too individual a process for outright imitation to be useful, watching a gifted storyteller in action can provide clues to techniques that charm listeners.

Since your feelings about a story can become evident in the telling, tell a story you like. Block the story into parts. (Folk tales, which are frequently composed of three episodes, are easy to remember.) Try seeing the story in scenes and hearing the language in your mind. Memorize the major sequence of events but vary the story in your own style as you tell it. Word-for-word memory is seldom necessary, except for key phrases, for every storyteller adds a personal touch.

Put key phrases on cards ("prompt notes"), and refer to them to jog the memory during practice sessions. Because the magic of many stories lies in the language, there will usually be some phrases that should be preserved; for example, "I'm going to blow your house away" just will not substitute for "Then I'll huff and I'll puff and I'll blow your house down." Nor will "Little tree, give me new clothes" do for "Shiver and quiver, my little tree, silver and gold throw down on me."

Practice your story. Tell it in front of a mirror, record it (and listen critically), tell it to one person, and then tell it to a small group. Try to use your prompt notes less and less frequently until you no longer need them. The story may change as you continue to tell it, but that is a natural part of the process as you make the story your own. Tell your story as often as you can. Live audiences give you instant feedback, so you can know immediately where you need to heighten the drama, draw out or shorten the climax, add or expand a descriptive passage.

Children are brutally honest, but patient, critics who will help you perfect your skill. Occasionally, simple props or figures cut from felt can be used during a story, but the magic of the story itself is what holds listeners. For example, with a beginning such as: "One day a fox was digging behind a stump of an old tree and found a bumble bee. He put it in his bag, threw his bag over his shoulder, and traveled,"[5] you capture your audience, now eager to learn what happened to that bee and that fox. (This story, "Travels of a Fox," in Veronica Hutchinson's *Chimney Corner Stories,* is certain to intrigue children.)

Collections of stories selected by talented storytellers such as *Storytelling: Art and Technique,* by Augusta Baker and Ellin Greene, or *Handbook for Storytellers,* by Caroline Feller Bauer, provide excellent guidance. Eileen Colwell's three collections, *Tell Me a Story, Tell Me Another Story,* and *Time for a Story* also contain valuable materials and techniques.

Storytellers of a generation ago leave a valuable legacy of materials and techniques. Ruth Sawyer, in *The Way of the Storyteller,* discusses the history of folklore, the preparation of tales for telling, and includes the "fairy gold" of some of her favorite stories. Recordings of Ruth Sawyer reading Christmas stories from her book *Joy to the World* and Frances Clarke Sayers telling some of Carl Sandburg's *Rootabaga Stories* and some stories by Hans Christian Andersen are available (Weston Woods). Marie L. Shedlock's *The Art of the Storyteller* also contains essential material for beginning storytellers.

Book Talks

Book talks can be as simple or as elaborate as the occasion demands; they can be given by students, teachers, or others. Most often, in the classroom, a brief synopsis of the plot (without revealing the ending) and the reactions to it are all that are needed. (Consider the comments to be an advertisement or testimonial about the book that is intended to persuade others to read it.) A comprehensive book talk probes deeply content, style, and cumulative effect; it is aimed at helping an audience delve into the book as the reviewer has. If the story is a brief picture book, it should be read aloud straight through without interruption. If it is a longer novel, a brief summary to establish plot, character, setting, and theme should be given.

Here are some excerpts from a typical book talk—in this case, about Randall Jarrell's *Snow White and the Seven Dwarfs* (P-I), illustrated by Nancy Ekholm Burkert, and Paul Hein's *Snow White* (P-I), illustrated by Trina Schart Hyman:

When Nancy Ekholm Burkert's illustrations appeared, reviewers said she had freed Snow White from thirty-five years of enslavement to Walt Disney. Finally, Snow White looked like a real person instead of a hollow plastic shell. When Trina Schart Hyman's illustrations of Snow White came along, many people were intrigued with the deep psychological meanings she revealed about the story through her art.

Look at the illustrations to see how each artist depicts the characters. First, look at the two versions of Snow White's mother, the queen, pricking her finger. Burkert shows her from a distance through a casement castle window, slightly regal and remote. In contrast, Hyman shows her from inside the room as a dreaming, wistful young woman.

On the next page, Hyman shows the stepmother in the very same room, but she has made some changes: she has replaced the dead queen's devotional shrine with a magical mirror. She has also changed the atmosphere in the room from a homelike scene with tea and sewing to one filled with medicinal herbs, candles, and the mirror; the stepmother holds a tiny black kitten.

Hyman first shows the stepmother as a beautiful young woman, but as the story progresses and jealousy consumes her, the facial expressions and body are contorted. Notice especially that as her face shows in the mirror her emotions are reflected in the frame around it. The cunningly carved imps and furies in the frame be-

MORTON SCHINDEL

Profile

I'm a storyteller in today's media. Making films based on great books for children offers challenge and imposes responsibility. For in the age of telecommunications, filmed adaptations of outstanding stories, created with fidelity to the original, will inevitably find their way to larger and larger audiences among successive generations of children. (Letter received from Morton Schindel, 15 July 1980.)

Energetic teachers and librarians attending conventions in and around New York frequently visit Weston Woods Studios in Connecticut. The founder, Morton Schindel, makes those visits to the multimedia world of children's literature memorable. He and his wife Nancy regularly open their portals to kindred spirits—men and women who believe as Walter De La Mare that "Only the rarest kind of best is good enough for the very young. . . ."

Recipient of the 1979 Regina Medal, Schindel uses a variety of media to draw young readers to fine literature. Through sound filmstrips, cassettes, motion pictures, and recordings, he makes books sing and nourishes interest in reading. He feels that while none of these media duplicate the child's private pleasure in holding his own book, they *can* transmit with integrity what the author and illustrator have to say. He believes that the medium one chooses—reading a book aloud, showing a film or filmstrip, having children listen to records or tapes, or a combination of these—depends on the number of children you are trying to reach at any one time. As a consequence of his work, children beyond number have delighted in literature they might never have known.

We know that children eagerly seek books from libraries once they have seen filmed or televized versions. Schindel is reassuring about the positive role films—scrupulously faithful to the original book—can play in leading children back to books.

I've seen over and over again how book and film can become companions in motivating youngsters toward reading. Once the film has opened the book to a child, he will want to hold it in his hands and dwell to his

come increasingly demonic. The figure at the base is an ancient and ugly naked hag.

Burkert never shows the stepmother's face; her figure appears only twice, and then from behind, in settings filled with symbols of evil.

Children's book talks are not oral book reports but opportunities for the children to share their enthusiasm about something they have read. In a classroom where books are central, children give book talks spontaneously and often want to talk about a book the moment they finish reading it, if not before. Preplanned book talks are more fully developed, with props, a clever device, or the product of an art project.

USING BOOKS IN THE CLASSROOM

heart's content on the words and pictures that have some special meaning to him (Morton Schindel, "Making Reading Central to the Lives of All Children," *TAIR Newsletter,* Publication of the Texas Association for the Improvement of Reading, Jan. 1979, p. 6).

Teachers, parents, and librarians testify to the truth of his statement; his finely crafted films provide a channel which flows toward books rather than away from them.

Morton Schindel developed the iconographic technique for photographing picture stories. This type of filmmaking imparts an illusion of motion to still pictures through camera movement abetted by careful juxtaposition of sound elements. Looking at a book the way children might when they read, Schindel's cameras have made more than 200 outstanding picture books come to life. The Picture Book Parade Film Series has garnered many film festival awards and has been dubbed in many languages, winning an international following.

With his production of high-quality audio-visual materials, Morton Schindel extends and complements the lively art of picture books. He recognizes how critical certain early experiences are for learning how to read.

The words in a book (and even the pictures, we are beginning to realize) are symbols that require skills to decode and perceive. And yet, it is a time when youngsters' minds are most open and absorbent that they have the greatest reading limitations and are therefore least able to share the heritage that is preserved for them in books. It has been my task as a communicator in the audio-visual media to bridge this gap, to use with as much taste and integrity as I could muster the techniques that make it possible to open books to children before they are able to read by themselves (Morton Schindel, "Making Reading Central," *TAIR Newsletter,* Jan. 1979, p. 4).

Morton Schindel sees himself as a partner with both authors and illustrators, and with teachers, librarians, and parents in bringing to children the literary heritage trapped in the pages of good books.

Audio-Visual Presentations

Audio-visual materials used to present literature to children are not substitutes for books; they create a totally different literary experience. A group of nursery school children giggled as they watched *Rosie's Walk,* a film (Weston Woods) based on Pat Hutchins's picture book. They saw the fox sneak up behind Rosie the hen, jump to pounce upon her, land on a garden rake, and get smacked on the nose with the rake handle. The background country music enlivens Rosie's perky walk, the slyness of the crafty fox, and the trauma of each boomeranging blow. The children immediately ran for the book of the same title so they could relive the excitement of the film story, and they continued to reread it for weeks.

Some films illuminate books and leave room for the imaginative participation of the audience. Unfortunately, many do not. There are audio-visual adaptations of literature that insult the audience and sensationalize the work. Some of the most offensive are media presentations of folklore with cartoonlike illustrations, simplified plot retellings, and unadorned moralistic preachments. Full-length novels condensed into filmstrips often degenerate into a series of inconsequential pictures that rob children of the joy of creating their own mental images. Rather than inviting participation in creating images, some films spell out details unequivocally, undermining the subtle essence of characterization and expressive language, and diminishing the emotional power of the work. Evocative prose is reduced to a full-color slide show that requires a passive sponge instead of an active participant. The child's imagination, experience, and emotions are deadened and left to dull.

Some film makers, conscientious about the work they produce, take great pains. For example, because the film maker needs a great deal more art than appears in most picture books, the original art work is often painstakingly recreated in a style that suits the graphic requirements of the film medium, while embodying the styles of the original artist; in some cases it is the original artist who creates the drawings for the film productions. An informative film about the intricate and imaginative process of animation is *Gene Deitch: The Picture Book Animated* (Weston Woods).

Audio-visual presentations and media interpretations are an asset to a literature program as long as they complement the books and draw children back to literature. Evaluate audio-visual materials for use in a literature program first by considering the literary value of the work; a good film cannot improve a bad book. Also important is whether the treatment is appropriate to the literary work. Does it enrich and expand the book's original purpose without sensationalizing it into something beyond the author's intent? For example, were Robert McCloskey's *Time of Wonder* (P) presented with

blaring trumpets and flashing color, its sensitive tribute to nature would be totally destroyed.

A third point concerns appropriateness to the audience. Diluting a work of art to make it accessible to a younger audience changes the author's purpose and deceives children. A particularly conspicuous example of this is the Walt Disney Productions treatment of A. A. Milne's *Winnie the Pooh* (P-I). With Ernest Shepard's original winsome illustrations replaced with characterless cartoons, the stories now appear to be directed to the preschool set. More appalling is the distortion of Milne's poetic language. His subtle wit, strong characterization, and engaging themes are reduced to mechanical and stilted dialogue. And to Milne's already rich menagerie of characters has been added an insipid beaver that appears now and then to announce, "I'm not in the book!" Unfortunately, four- and five-year-old children having seen one film think they now know Winnie the Pooh, Eeyore, Tigger, Kanga, Piglet, and the others. Unless they are introduced to the original work at an appropriate age, such children have been robbed of the joy of really knowing these lovable characters.

Finally, in addition to maintaining the integrity of the original work, audio-visual materials should be technically excellent; clear sound and visual reproduction are vital. Child-proof records and filmstrips will probably never exist, but they should be durable enough to hold up to repeated use.

Selection, then, may be even more critical for audio-visual materials than for books.[6] The excellent films of poetry and color based on Mary O'Neill's *Hailstones and Halibut Bones* (P-I) (Sterling Educational Films), the animated drawings based on Leo Lionni's *Swimmy* (P) (Connecticut Films), and warmhearted stories such as Isaac Bashevis Singer's *Zlateh the Goat* (I) (Weston Woods) show that outstanding literary expriences are created in many excellent forms. The teacher's job is to select without compromise: the same standards for excellence apply to all presentations of literature.

The greatest advantage of audio-visual presentations is their flexibility: many more children can share a literary experience at the same time than with a book. (Especially in the case of small books, such as those of Beatrix Potter, which are simply not suitable for sharing with a large group of children.) And busy teachers do not have as much time to share books as they or the children would like. Filmstrip viewers, film loop projectors, and cassette tape players set up for individuals or small groups allow many children to use them at any time.

Media presentations do not, of course, replace oral reading by teachers. They can, however, supplement a strong read-aloud program. Children return to the media presentations of stories time and again for pleasure and reinforcement. Further, students with certain learning disabilities often learn best through audition; hearing and seeing the words at the same time provides important practice in fusing the printed letters and words into comprehensible language patterns.

Poetry

Integrated with activities and book sharing, poetry can enrich every experience. A personal collection of poetry is a vital tool for the teacher or librarian who plans to teach with poetry. Despite the abundance of poems on every topic, it is difficult to have the right poem ready at the right moment without a personal filing system. A card file has many advantages: poems on cards can be grouped or regrouped according to need and are readily available for use. Far better than searching desperately for a specific poem about snow, five minutes before reading Ezra Jack Keats's *The Snowy Day* (N-P) to a group of children, is to be able to turn to your collection and immediately find Dorothy Aldis's "Snow":

The fenceposts wear marshmallow hats
On a snowy day:
Bushes in their night gowns
Are kneeling down to pray—
And all the trees have silver skirts
And want to dance away.[7]

Poetry collections started as a beginning teacher grow and continue to be used throughout one's professional career. Categorize your poetry file by subjects useful to you. Topics such as seasons, animals, feelings, or others related to curriculum areas serve well.

A copy of a special poem that harmonizes with a story should be pasted inside the front cover of the book. For example, Dorothy Aldis's "Whistles," which begins

I want to learn to whistle.
I've always wanted to[8]

is a perfect complement to Ezra Jack Keats's *Whistle for Willie* (P-I), while Harry Behn's "Hallowe'en":

Tonight is the night
When dead leaves fly
Like witches on switches
Across the sky, . . .[9]

belongs with any number of Halloween stories.

There are poems that extend the enjoyment of books for older readers, too. Mary O'Neill's "My Friend, Leona," in her collection *People I'd Like to Keep* (I), includes these lines:

She says she has dresses
Too sweet to be seen
But the ones she wears
Are scrimped and mean. . . .[10]

which beg to be read with Eleanor Estes's *The Hundred Dresses* (I), one of the earliest books to deal realistically with prejudice. After reading Betsy Byars's *The TV Kid* (I), read Shel Silverstein's "Jimmy Jet and His TV Set" in *Where the Sidewalk Ends* (P-I), about a boy addicted to television, who

. . . watched all day, he watched all night
Till he grew pale and lean, . . .[11]

Children like to start their own poetry collections. These might take the same form as the teacher's, but more often poems are collected in a student-made book or journal that allows room for additions and for personal illustrations. Student collections often contain poems the students write as well as ones they find.

EXTENDING LITERATURE
THROUGH ACTIVITIES

Throughout this text we suggest activities to extend and enrich children's experiences with literature. We know that active involvement leads to greater understanding and deeper conceptualization of ideas.

Literature activities grow naturally from books and lead directly back to them. Children return to happy experiences and are curious, want to know. Activities rest on both tendencies, involving them in the pleasures of creating, exploring, and discovering. Once they have discovered the full range of joy that may derive from books, they invariably return for more.

Good activities are relevant activities. Making a bunny from a milk carton, pink paper, and cotton balls is *not* a valid extension of Adrienne Adams's lovely picture book *The Easter Egg Artists* (P); neither is giving children a pattern so that all of them can make identical cutout cats after they've heard Wanda Gág's *Millions of Cats* (P). Art projects need to show the creator's individuality. There is little pleasure in making carbon copies or exact replicas of what twenty others make. Children bring personal experience and understanding to a book; they should be able to draw upon these to create a unique interpretation with their own choice of methods. Through their activities, children clarify and organize thoughts and express themselves so that meanings and intentions are comprehensible. Children, no less than adults, need the space, the time, and the resources to enable their ideas to evolve into reality. Challenging activities provide for this.

Finally, activities need to be realistic and practical. Inability to attain a teacher's standards of perfection can only be frustrating for the child, who needs to have a feasible goal and know success. We know that red pencils need to be used more often than they are to point out excellence instead of error.

Art projects can be messy; it is important to have a place where spills won't cause permanent damage. Children need to be free to experiment without concern about spilling, slopping, or messing. This kind of freedom sets the tone in learning environments that foster and respect individual expression.

Drama

Children engage in imaginative play instinctively. They recreate what they see on television, in everyday life, and in their stories. "Let's pretend" games are children's natural way of expressing their thoughts and feelings in the guise of characters and roles. Informal dramatic play led by teachers and librarians uses children's natural desire to pretend and can be the forerunner of numerous drama experiences.

There are many forms of drama to be explored in the elementary classroom.[12] Pantomime, using body movements and expression but no words; interpreting, enacting or recreating a story or a scene; and improvising, extending and extrapolating beyond a story or a poem, are variations often called creative dramatics.

In pantomime a story or meaning is conveyed solely through facial expressions, shrugs, frowns, gestures, and other forms of body language. Situations, stories, or characters pantomimed should be ones that the children are familiar with or recognize easily. For example, after reading Beatrix Potter's *The Tale of Peter Rabbit* (N-P), pantomime the scene in which Peter, going about the garden nibbling the vegetables, is spotted and chased by Mr. McGregor.

Books that introduce children to the art of pantomime include two about the master of mime, Marcel Marceau. *The Story of Bip* (P-I) is an autobiographical account of the mimist, while *Marcel Marceau's Alphabet Book* (P), by George Mendoza, is a pictorial demonstration of this art. *Just Me* (P), by Marie Hall Ets, is a beautifully simple story of a child's pantomime of animals. Use all three to open the door to pantomime for your students.

A good time for acting out or creating a story can be immediately following a reading-aloud session. After reading aloud "The Three Billy Goats Gruff," for example, the teacher might ask, "Who wants to be the Troll? . . . the biggest billy goat? . . . the middle billy goat? . . . the littlest billy goat?" Useful then would be discussion with the children of how the troll sounds when he asks, "Who's that tripping across my bridge?" how he shows his anger, and how each of the billy goats sounds as he answers the troll. (Use a convenient chair, table, or desk as the bridge for the troll to hide under and let the story roll with dialogue and action.)

Interpretation can be introduced with a question from the teacher such as: "Who wants to read the parts of each character in the story we just read?" In Nonny Hogrogian's *One Fine Day* (N-P), for example, one child would read the part of the fox, while others read the parts of the old woman, the cow, the field, the stream, the fair maiden, and others met in the bargaining. This activity, sometimes called readers' theater (discussed later), builds enthusiasm for reading and develops oral reading skills.

Improvisation goes beyond acting out the basic story line. It could be initiated with the teacher saying, "Let's pretend that Goldilocks comes back to visit the three bears the next day." Goldilocks might bring her parents along, and a cake for the bears by way of apologizing for snooping around their house. A discussion with the group of what Goldilocks might say, how the bears might answer, and what might happen if they become friends can help move things along. Additional ideas may follow: suppose, for example, Goldilocks invites the bears to visit *her;* what might happen on this visit?

Improvisation can be developed further by exploring characterization. You might say, "Suppose Pippi Longstocking is coming to visit our class," or "What would Frances [in *A Bargain for Frances* (P), by Russell Hoban] say if you wanted to trade your old battered tea set for her new one with the blue willow design?" Well-developed characters, such as Homer Price, Madeline, Curious George, and Johnny Tremain, help lead to extensions into new situations.

Role-playing is a variation of drama, usually done with short vignettes or specific incidents from stories. For example, intermediate-grade students might role-play episodes from Jean George's *My Side of the Mountain* (I), such as the one in which Sam Gribley walks into the library to get maps from Miss Turner or runs into an old lady in the mountains, or the one in which the news reporter comes to interview the wild boy. Helpful would be discussion of the way Sam feels, the way he talks, and the reasons he wants to avoid telling his questioners too much about himself. Brief role-playing episodes often become scenes in more fully developed presentations.

In readers' theater, stories are presented in a quasi-play format such as that used in actors' auditions. It is not a formal play performance: lines are not memorized and there are virtually no sets, costumes, or staging. The "script" may be an adaptation of a story, a poem, an episode from a novel, or several stories with a single theme.

In "Readers' Theater: Handbook for Teachers of Grades Four through Six," Shirlee Sloyer suggests the following steps in producing a readers' theater performance—in this case, on the theme "fairy tales without fairies":

1. Select a story that fits the theme, such as *The Princess and the Pea,* by Hans Christian Andersen. The best stories have a taut plot and suggest strong images; they have an "and then"quality to pique your interest and make you want to know what will happen next.

2. Read the story aloud, round robin style, with a group of about five students.

3. Discuss the number of characters needed for the presentation. In addition to the prince, princess, king, queen, and narrator, you need someone to do sound effects. If you want to include more people, a chorus is always a possible addition.

4. Using the narrative as a guide, write the dialogue. Remember that you don't need to stay within the confines of the story's vocabulary. Enthusiasm builds if students are encouraged to incorporate contemporary expressions into traditional dialogue. For example, in one rendition of "The Princess and the Pea," the queen commented on the princess's delicate skin by saying, "Oh, my dear, it must be because you use Noxema." Such

comments make it fun for the listeners as well as the participants.

5. Once the dialogue is set it is time to stage your story. Generally costumes are not necessary, but for readers' theater, hats seem to add just the right touch. Since the princess arrives at the castle door in a downpour, a shiny yellow rain bonnet is all she needs.

6. Experience shows that the best staging is simple. Readers can stand statue-still in a straight line holding their scripts. (When not in a scene, readers turn around or keep their heads lowered. Turning or raising and lowering heads is very effective.) Sound effects, such as the clanging of a cymbal to signal the start of the show, used sparingly, add to the drama.

The following is a portion of an adaptation for readers' theatre of *Alexander and the Terrible, Horrible, No Good, Very Bad Day* (P), by Judith Viorst.[13]

ALEXANDER:	I went to sleep with gum in my mouth and now there's gum in my hair, and when I got out of bed this morning I tripped on the skateboard, and by mistake I dropped my sweater in the sink while the water was running, and I could tell it was going to be a terrible, horrible, no good, very bad day. At breakfast—
ANTHONY:	Hey, look, I got a Corvette Sting Ray car kit in my breakfast cereal box.
NICK:	I got a Junior Undercover Agent code ring in *my* breakfast cereal box.
ALEXANDER:	Hey, look I got—breakfast cereal in my breakfast cereal box. I think I'll move to Australia. (Directly) Then there was the car pool—
PHILLIP:	Oh boy, I got a seat by the window.
ALBERT:	Me, too.
PAUL:	Me, too.
ALEXANDER:	I'm being scrunched. I'm being smashed. If I don't get a seat by the window, I'm going to be carsick. (Directly) No one even answered. I could tell it was going to be a terrible, horrible, no good, very bad day. Then at school there was my teacher Mrs. Dickens—
MRS. DICKENS:	Alexander, I do think Paul's picture of the sailboat is much nicer than your

	picture of the invisible castle. At singing time, you sang too loud, and at counting time, you left out sixteen!
ALEXANDER:	Ah, who needs sixteen? (Directly) I could tell it was going to be a terrible, horrible, no good, very bad day. I could tell because Paul acted rotten.
PAUL:	Alexander, you aren't my best friend anymore. Phillip Parker is my best friend, and Albert Moyo is my next best friend. You are only my third best friend.
ALEXANDER:	I hope you sit on a tack. I hope the next time you get a double-decker strawberry ice cream cone, the ice cream part falls off the cone part and lands in Australia. (Directly) Things were even worse at lunchtime.
PHILLIP:	Look, I got two cupcakes for lunch.
ALBERT:	I got a Hershey bar with almonds for dessert.
PAUL:	Well, my mom gave me a piece of jelly roll with little coconut sprinkles on it.
ALEXANDER:	Guess whose mother forgot to put in dessert. Oh, this is a terrible, horrible, no good, very bad day. That's what it is. (Directly) After school my Mom took us all to the dentist and Dr. Fields found a cavity JUST IN ME.
DR. FIELDS:	Come back next week, and I'll fix it!
ALEXANDER:	Next week, I'm going to Australia.

Children who have seen a story presented in this way rush to read it. When a story is presented on television there are rarely enough copies of it on library shelves to satisfy the ensuing demand. Readers' theater, especially in view of the impact that a live performance can have, is capable of generating a similar enthusiasm.

Dramatization differs depending upon the purposes and goals of the experience—primarily according to whether it is done as a performance for others or for the joy of the participants themselves. A guiding rule in this area no less than in others is to hold the children's benefit as the highest value. This is not to say that performances for others should not be given; only that they not be given at the cost of exploiting children as performers. Plays for reading and presenting are discussed in Chapter 3.

A favorite story can set the creative impulse going.
(HBJ photo by Richard C. Polister.)

Art

Art activities can be as extensive as your creativity and energy permit. Resources expand when one has an art specialist; in any case, your classroom should house numerous supplies and examples of children's artistic work. Art projects related to books are used regularly, not saved for special occasions. A well-stocked art center leads to inventive projects in classrooms and libraries. Paper, fabric, yarn, buttons, socks, plastic bottles, paper bags, cardboard tubes, dowels, rods, wire, styrofoam balls, egg cartons, toothpicks, and pipe cleaners all have a potential in the hands of ingenious children and teachers. Needles and thread, glue and tape, and, of course, scissors, crayons, paints, and paint brushes are also needed. Items available free or for a nominal price can often be had from neighborhood shops. Found art materials are often available to teachers who search grocery, hardware, discount, and other stores for them. Pizza rounds (cardboard trays), five-gallon ice cream drums, boxes, and display materials, for example, often make good classroom art supplies.

COLLAGE To encourage a wider and more varied use of media, use two or more materials in additon to crayons for pictures. Simple collage techniques of cutting or tearing paper or fabric and arranging these with other materials make original composite scenes.

Books by Ezra Jack Keats, the master of collage, and stories set in the out-of-doors provide good subjects for collage pictures. Roger Duvoisin's *Petunia* (P), a barnyard goose whose adventures appear in several stories, inspires children to create collage pictures of farm scenes with dried grass, feathers, and twigs. Fairy tales can be interpreted with a variety of materials; surely Cinderella deserves a bit of lace on her fancy ballgown.

WALL HANGINGS Fabric provides a good alternative to creating pictures on paper. Burlap squares, a yard of plain muslin fabric, or a piece of terry cloth toweling provide the background for creative expression in stitchery or appliqué. Shapes of the characters or objects cut from other material are stitched or glued onto the fabric. A dowel or rod

The "flying-one" from Leo Lionni's *Pezzetino* (which means "small piece"), who finds that he is unique and does not need to be a part of something else.
(From *Pezzettino*, by Leo Lionni. Copyright © 1970 by Leo Lionni. Reprinted by permission of Pantheon Books, a Division of Random House, Inc.)

run through an upper hem makes the work hangable. E. B. White's *Charlotte's Web* (P-I) is the basis for a wall hanging that occupies a place of honor in one school library. You can make one, too, as an example for your children. The background is a medium brown burlap with lines, representing the corner of the barn, drawn in with black marker. Wilbur the pig is made of tan burlap that has Wilbur's image traced on it (made by enlarging an illustration from the book with an opaque projector). The spider web with "Some Pig" in it is embroidered with black string, while Charlotte, the spider herself, is made from fuzzy black fur with pipe cleaner legs. The pieces are glued to the background and dried grass or straw added to complete the wall hanging.

MOSAICS Mosaics can be made of small bits of colored paper arranged into designs or figures from books. Leo Lionni's *Pezzetino* (P) leads naturally into mosaics. The animals in Verna Aar-

A wrapping-paper mural by children recapitulates the bold forms and colors in Leo Leonni's stories.

dema's *Why Mosquitoes Buzz in People's Ears* (P), illustrated by Leo and Diane Dillon, walking with their hubbubbing and swishing sounds, were recreated in mosaics by a group of primary children. They enjoyed hearing the delicious-sounding words from the book several times and, since it was impossible to recreate the Dillon's majestic art, used another medium to portray the animals. Mosaics of the animals were attached to a mural of junglelike grass and trees.

FLANNEL BOARDS Several art projects not only extend children's literary experiences but also enable them to share stories with others and enliven storytelling. Flannel boards, one of these, can be used by teachers and students alike.

The best stories for use on the flannel board have a reasonable number of simple characters and objects that can be replicated and manipulated easily. Use stories with simple illustrations; detailed work is difficult to duplicate in cutouts.

Use an opaque projector for tracing the characters and objects on pieces of flannel, paper, or fabric. Heavy felt is the most durable but is also the most difficult to cut; however, once cut, pieces can be re-used endlessly. Construction paper or oak tag can be substituted for fabric, but a piece of flannel or sandpaper must be glued to the back of each piece if it is to stick to the flannel board.

Commercial flannel boards are available, but you can make your own by covering a large piece of fiberboard, soft wood, or heavy cardboard with flannel, felt, or any textured fabric. Cut and hinge the board in the middle so it can be folded for storage. Stretch the fabric across the board with the nappy side exposed, fold over the edges, and tack or staple on the back. Neutral colors are best for the cloth background because they do not detract from the color of the pieces used for the stories.

Traditional and literary folktales that have a sequential accumulation of characters and action are especially adaptable for flannel board retellings.

468 Other simple stories that can be used include the following:

> *Little Blue and Little Yellow* (P), by Leo Lionni   Cut the pieces from sheets of translucent colored acetate or cellophane so that the blue and yellow pieces form green where they overlap. The acetate sticks to the flannel, so there is no need to glue sandpaper or felt to the back.
>
> *Caps for Sale* (P), by Esphyr Slobodkina   Use felt to make hats of each color to stack on top of the man's head. The hats, the monkeys, the man, a tree, and a few houses are all that are necessary.
>
> *The Man Who Didn't Wash His Dishes* (P), by Phyllis Krasilovsky Many small pieces shaped like dishes, ashtrays, pots, and pans are needed to show the man's dilemma as he struggles to stack them.
>
> *Corduroy* (P), by Don Freeman   Tape a button to the back of the bear so that you can "sew" it on at the appropriate time.

ROLLER MOVIES   Roller movies allow children to present a continually changing visual accompaniment to their storytelling. To make one, cut an opening shaped like a television screen in a cardboard carton. For rollers, push two pieces of dowel, rod, or broomstick through the carton walls just inside and parallel to the opening—one just above and one below it. Draw the illustrations for a story on a long strip of shelf paper or window shade cut slightly wider than the box opening, or tape separate pieces together. Attach an end to each roller and roll up the strip onto the roller to which the last illustration was attached. Each scene will show through the screen as you turn the rollers. The long strip of paper is best prepared rolled out full length on the floor so the sequence of the story can be planned in the illustrations.

Stories easily adapted to the roller movie screen are those that move sequentially from one scene to the next, such as Crockett Johnson's *Harold and the Purple Crayon* (P). Other stories

Child's drawing inspired by a reading of *Where the Wild Things Are*, by Maurice Sendak.

easily adaptable to the roller movie include cumulative tales such as Nonny Hogrogian's *One Fine Day* (P) and Jack Kent's *The Fat Cat* (P), as well as Don Freeman's *The Chalk Box Story* (P) and Martha Alexander's *Blackboard Bear* (P).

FILMSTRIPS AND SLIDES   School closets and cupboards hold many hidden treasures you can recycle into exciting projects and activities. For example, damaged or out-of-date filmstrips and slides can be bleached and reused by students to create their own audio-visual presentations. You can also purchase clear acetate strips and use them for filmstrips or cut them apart to mount in slide frames.

Fine motor control is necessary to make pictures small enough for this medium. A mimeographed frame template laid under the clear strip will help guide the child artist. Fine-tipped felt marking pens or grease ("China-marking") pencils are used to make the drawings. Rather than attempting to letter a running commentary on the acetate, one can be recorded to be played along with the visual presentation.

SEWING Stitchery, needlepoint, and embroidery can be used to make book-related objects, often in the form of "soft sculpture," a term for any three-dimensional object made from fabric and stuffed with a loose filler. Grotesque faces with exaggerated features can be made by gathering, puckering, stitching, and stretching a five- or six-inch length of old hosiery stuffed with cotton. Adrienne Adams's *A Woggle of Witches* (P) leads to the creation in soft sculpture of fantastic witches, each one different and likely to enhance Halloween parties.

Pillows featuring book characters are favorite projects since they are immediately useful for softening a spot for story time. One group of upper-elementary students embroidered pictures of Mother Goose characters onto pillows and presented them to the kindergarten class. These pillows are durable and can be laundered. Oilcloth makes good pillows for outdoor use since it can be wiped clean easily.

Simple patterns for stuffed animals can be made or obtained from commercial sources. Marcia Newfield's *Six Rags Apiece* (P) includes patterns and instructions for making the stuffed cat and teddy bear in the story. Terry cloth or cotton coverings with washable filling extend the life of stuffed toys and make it possible to keep them clean. Parent volunteers with sewing machines can speed up the process and ease the stitching project for young children.

COOKING Children's books suggest projects for making food for conventional uses and for play. Making bread dolls would be appropriate after reading Tomie de Paola's *Watch Out for the Chicken Feet in Your Soup* (P); and making popcorn balls could reasonably follow a reading of de Paola's *The Popcorn Book* (P). (Shape snowmen, bunnies, and bears from the popcorn, too.)

Judy Delton's *Rabbit Finds a Way* (P) includes a recipe for carrot cake, and Dr. Seuss's *Green Eggs and Ham* (P) suggests some fun with food coloring. Carla Steven's *How to Make Possum's Honey Bread* (P) includes the list of ingredients, directions, and baking tips for honey bread. The com-

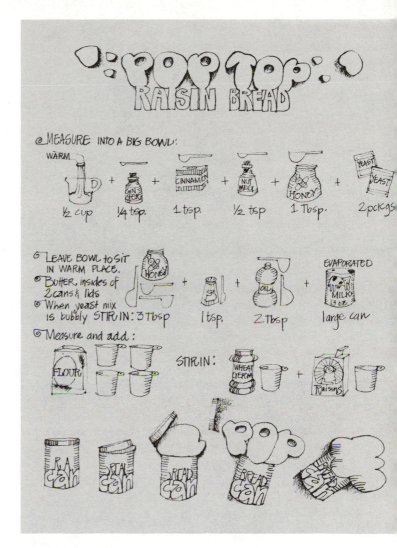

The recipe for "Pop Top Raisin Bread" from *Kids Are Natural Cooks*. Written in rebus form, the recipes are based on sound nutritional principles.
(From *Kids Are Natural Cooks* by Parents Nursery School, published by Houghton Mifflin Company. Copyright © 1972, 1974 by the Parents Nursery School, Inc. Reprinted by permission.)

plete recipe is repeated at the end of the story along with three variations.

Aileen Paul's *Kids Cooking Without a Stove: A Cookbook for Young Children* (P) gives thirty recipes that are easy to follow for dishes that can be prepared in the classroom. *Kids Are Natural Cooks*

470

Garth Williams's original illustrations from Laura Ingalls Wilder's "Little House" books grace the pages of the *Little House Cookbook*, which gives instructions for food preparation as it was done on the frontier. Here, Mary, Laura's sister, makes butter in an antique churn.
(Illustration by Garth Williams from *The Little House Cookbook: Frontier Foods from Laura Ingalls Wilder's Classic Stories*, compiled by Barbara M. Walker. Originally published in *The Little House in the Big Woods* by Laura Ingalls Wilder. Copyright, 1953, as to pictures, by Garth Williams. By permission of Harper & Row, Publishers, Inc.)

(P), by Parents Nursery School, stresses nutrition in its simple recipes. P. L. Travers put authentic English recipes in *Mary Poppins in the Kitchen: A Cookery Book with a Story* (I). The Banks children, left without their parents for a week, must cook for themselves with Mary Poppins's help. The daily menus and recipes they use are included.

Lorinda B. Cauley compiled *Pease Porridge Hot* (P-I), a collection of recipes suggested by Mother Goose verses. *The Pooh Cook Book* (P-I) and *The Pooh Party Book* (P-I), edited by Virginia Ellison, include Ernest Shepard's original illustrations. Winnie-the-Pooh fans enjoy the recipes, poems, and stories, which feature Pooh's favorite honey along with other bear-type foods. Carol MacGregor's *The Storybook Cookbook* (P-I) contains twenty-two recipes based on food mentioned

in books. The book is divided into sections on Breakfast, Lunch, Dinner, and Picnic foods, and includes "Uncle Ulysses' Doughnuts," from Robert McCloskey's *Homer Price* (I); "Heidi's Toasted Cheese Sandwich," from Johanna Spyri's *Heidi* (I); and "Ma's Pumpkin Pie," from Laura Ingalls Wilder's Little House books.

Other food and cooking ideas can be found in Arnold Dobrin's *Peter Rabbit's Natural Foods Cookbook* (P), described in Chapter 10, and Barbara M. Walker's *The Little House Cookbook: Frontier Foods from Laura Ingalls Wilder's Classic Stories* (I), discussed in Chapter 9.

DIORAMAS Three-dimensional scenes can help extend literary experiences. Cardboard cartons or shoe boxes, with the interior of the carton decorated to serve as background, make good dioramas. Place small figures in the scene to represent characters, furnishings, or other objects to reflect the period or setting of a story. A diorama of a log cabin, based on Ingri and Edgar Parin d'Aulaire's *Abraham Lincoln* (P-I), used a cardboard carton with the inside layer torn off to expose the corrugated layer, which was painted to mimic logs. The sides of the carton were cut, extended, and reinforced to give a wider view of the cabin interior. A furry bearskin on the wall, a fireplace made with pebbles glued to styrofoam, and primitive furniture carved from balsa wood completed the scene.

A diorama representing an interior can be divided into different levels with cardboard dividers to show two (or more) stories of a building. Appropriate wallpaper, contact paper, newspaper, or fabric glued onto the walls contribute to verisimilitude. Dividers (placed vertically) can also help show the sequence of events of a story. One diorama, made in the form of five wedges with a common center (like pie slices), permitted showing five scenes from a story in a carousel-like panorama.

A diorama of Sam Gribley's home in Jean George's *My Side of the Mountain* (I) was enclosed in a circle of tree bark. One for "The Doughnuts," a story in Robert McCloskey's *Homer Price* (I) used stacks of the prepared breakfast cereal Cheerios to represent miniature doughnuts.

Furniture made from balsa wood or clay adds to the authenticity of interior scenes from books. Twigs, crumpled newspaper, and pebbles can become trees, hills, and gravel driveways in realistic exterior scenes.

SCULPTURE Sculpture can enhance the sharing of book experiences. Wire, papier-mâché, stuffed paper bags, boxes, styrofoam, wood, spools, and other odds and ends can be used for sculpture and three-dimensional constructions. Other suitable materials, of a kind that is generally replenished steadily, are egg cartons (fearsome dragons), milk cartons (robots), bleach containers (hippopotamuses and pigs), egg-shaped hosiery containers (miniature peek-in scenes or monster eggs), cardboard tubes from paper towels and bathroom tissue, styrofoam scraps, fabric and linoleum remnants, yarn, rope, trimmings, and tape.

Harlow Rockwell provides many ideas in *I Did It* (P), an easy-to-read book that has directions for making paper bag masks, pictures out of dried peas and beans, a papier-mâché fish, and a paper airplane. Recipes for invisible ink and homemade bread add a touch of magic and a tasty surprise. Elyse Sommer, in *The Bread Dough Craft Book* (P-I), gives a recipe for a modeling material that can be used in place of clay for book characters, Christmas tree ornaments, and other items: crumble six slices of bread, add six teaspoons of white glue and one-half teaspoon of liquid detergent, and mix.

PUPPETRY Puppets are an indispensable resource in elementary-school classrooms and libraries. They can be used to introduce literature or to interpret it dramatically. (Behind the cover of a puppet stage, the shy child, reluctant to speak out in other

Diorama of a frontier cabin made of a cardboard carton and "Lincoln Logs."

Acting out "Goldilocks and the Three Bears" with the help of class-made puppets.
(HBJ photo by Richard C. Polister.)

activities, will often shine.) Children are enthusiastic about making puppets, putting on puppet shows, and serving as the audience for their classmates' productions. In this activity they learn to think on their feet, to ad lib, and to react to others.

Puppetry differs from dramatics in that it is partially a vicarious experience. In contrast to the case in dramatics, where children act out roles directly, the roles are an extension of the player through the persona of the puppet, which becomes something of an alter ego. The protective screen that this affords facilitates acting out stories that deal with personal emotional problems.

There are many types (some described below)—including paper plate, egg carton, stick, shadow, paper bag, milk carton, and sock puppets. There are also many fine commercially made puppets, but children take pride in making and manipulating their own. However, manufactured ones add a richness to the array, especially the two- and three-way puppet dolls that have Red Riding Hood, Grandma, and the Wolf all in one reversible doll.

Dramatizing stories with puppets is planned cooperatively; written scripts are unnecessary and may even inhibit children. Planning a story *before* using the puppets gives students a chance to identify with the characters and to concentrate on the sequence before they are distracted by actually manipulating the puppets.

Create a simple puppet stage by draping a blanket over a table, using a folding screen with an opening in the upper half, or using draped painting easels to hide the puppeteers. The action of the story is more important than elaborate settings or puppets, but there are times when you may want to add props and special effects such as lighting and sound. In *Child Drama,* Peter Slade states that puppetry arises organically from children's expressions with their fingers and hands. He recommends that we

. . . do not confine them to a stage; let them pop up over chairs, desks, or tables, anywhere. This introduces space, and puppets lead [children] to move about, so that space and journey are experienced just as and when needed. Drama is all about us. Actors and audience are one.[14]

You can use many different materials to make puppets, but imagination is the basic ingredient. Several kinds of puppets are described below.

PAPER PLATE PUPPETS

Paper plates can be used to make widemouthed frogs and toads (in addition to many other types of characters) by following these steps (shown in accompanying illustration):

1. Fold the paper plate in half.
2. Cut out paper eyes, tongue, and legs, and glue or staple them to the appropriate places. Add color with green and brown paint or with paper glued to the plate and used for eyes and legs.
3. Glue or staple a strip of paper across the paper plate to make a handle for manipulating the puppet.

Stories about frogs and toads are best to dramatize using these puppets. Use "The Widemouth Frog,"

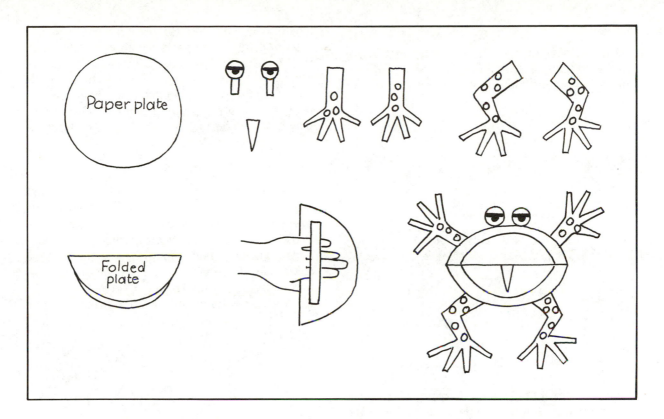

found in many collections of folk tales, or Arnold Lobel's *Frog and Toad Are Friends* (P).

EGG CARTON PUPPETS

Egg cartons can be used to make dragons, crocodiles, or other long-mouthed animals as follows (see figure):

1. Discard the top of the carton and cut the lower part in half lengthwise.
2. Use a mitten, or glue, tape, or staple a cuff of fabric to the small ends of the two carton parts to conceal the hand.
3. Decorate the head with nostrils, pointed scales, etc. to look like a dragon or crocodile; the humped sides of the egg carton should face each other on the inside to represent the teeth.

   Try dramatizing Ogden Nash's *Custard the Dragon* (P), with this puppet.

1.
Cut here →

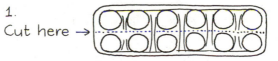

2.
TOP VIEW

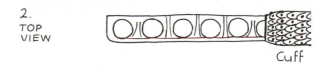

Cuff

3.
SIDE VIEW

Cuff

These puppets are made by stuffing small paper bags with tissue, painting faces on them, and adding yarn hair and fabric hats and costumes. Cos-

tumes for the puppet are attached with string, thread, or glue. A rod or heavy wire stuck into the puppet's head lets you manipulate it from below.

A variation (see accompanying figure) uses the flat bottom of the bag for the eyes and nose, and the fold for the mouth which can then open and close. With four fingers in the bottom of the bag and using the thumb as a lever, the puppet can be made to "talk".

The bunny rabbit paper bag puppet shown in the illustration can be used when you read Adrienne Adams's *The Easter Egg Artists* (P) and John Becker's *Seven Little Rabbits* (P). Use the donkey or burro (which is made from *two* bags, one for the neck, when you read William Steig's *Sylvester and the Magic Pebble* (P) or M. Jean Craig's *The Donkey Prince* (P).

Large grocery bags, decorated and worn as body masks transform children into human puppets. If not long enough, bags can be extended to the floor with added paper. With the bags over children's heads, mark the places for eyes, nose, mouth, and armholes and add the extra paper (for length) where needed. Children can then begin to draw or paint on faces and decorations. After reading Maurice Sendak's *Where the Wild Things Are* (P), they can create their own "Wild Things" body masks. Wearing the decorated bags, they can have their own wild rumpus, creating the action while playing the recording (Weston Woods) of the story.

MILK CARTON PUPPETS

Use a one-quart milk carton for this versatile puppet. First cut off the pointed top and cover the opening with a piece of construction paper. At the midsection of the carton cut through three sides and fold back along the fourth side so that half the carton lies above the other, as shown in the illustration. Insert four fingers in the top half of the carton and your thumb in the bottom half, so that

moving thumb and fingers opens and closes the resulting "mouth" (the space between the carton halves). Decorate with ears, eyes, nose, mouth, or other features to create the character you choose.

Use the lion milk carton puppet (see illustration) when reading James Daugherty's *Andy and the Lion* (P) and Louise Fatio's *The Happy Lion* (P) and *The Three Happy Lions* (P).

Other hand puppets can be made similarly from felt, mittens, socks or glove-type potholders. Frogs, snakes, ducks, cats, dogs, mice, bears, dinosaurs, donkeys, and various birds can be made in the form of hand puppets.

Books available for those who want to study puppetry further include several by Laura Ross, such as *Hand Puppets: How to Make and Use Them* (I). In this she gives the beginner step-by-step directions and diagrams for making simple paper bag, rod, and papier-mâché puppets. She also includes several play scripts so that children's puppets can be put into action quickly. Eleanor Boylan stresses the acting aspect of puppeteering in *How to Be a Puppeteer* (I). A beautiful puppet with nothing to do is not interesting, but a simple mitten or sock in the hands of a skilled puppeteer becomes an exciting character. Boylan gives a few simple instructions for making puppets, but stresses the puppet play—movement on stage and the voices given them. She also describes how to make a puppet theater and includes several plays and tips on special effects. Joyce Luckin, in *Easy-to-Make Puppets* (I), includes hand and glove puppets as well as marionettes with original stories to dramatize. For each she gives a list of the materials needed, detailed instructions, and a full-page pattern. There are numerous other resources for the teacher who wants to become involved with puppets.[15]

MOBILES AND STABILES Free-flowing forms of sculpture—mobiles—easily engage children's interest. They are usually created with a wire hanger and string, and are suspended to turn and drift in the breeze. Stabiles, on the other hand, start with a large, heavy piece of wood or clay as base. Wires or dowels projecting from it serve as appendages upon which to mount objects, character representations, or scenes.

One student created an intricate mobile based on Leo Lionni's *Swimmy* (P) by cutting out one black and many small red fish. She attached these to thread and arranged them from a wire so that all the parts—the entire mobile—composed one large fish, with Swimmy, the black one, serving as the eye. When the breeze played with it the large form shimmered and undulated like waves in the sea.

Another student created a stabile after reading Mary Norton's *The Borrowers Afield* (I). He began by forming a hemisphere of clay whose rounded surface served as a base from which shoots of wire, covered with green tape, were shaped to suggest cattails, tall grass, and weeds. Included were Arrietty in a miniature bird's nest, Homily resting against a toadstool, and Pod loading matches and string into his borrowing bag.

BULLETIN BOARDS Children do not need to be ad writers to create bulletin boards that draw attention to books; they create meaningful ones about books important to them. Boards devoted to one theme at a time are best, since doing too much in too small a space results in confusion and clutter. If the central purpose is immediately recognizable, the viewer is attracted to observe details.

Bulletin boards that feature changing displays of book jackets, information on authors, realia associated with books, and children's interpretations of books promote reading. Posters about books, maps, book marks, and other relevant materials are available, often free, from publishers. Lists of these are found regularly in "The Calendar", a publication of the Children's Book Council.

A group of young children used an eye-catching, moveable model of a pelican's bill against a brightly-colored corrugated background to "Fill the bill with books by Paul Galdone." On silhouettes of tiny fish they lettered the names of some of their favorites, such as *Henny Penny* (P), *The Frog Prince* (P), *The Little Red Hen* (P), *The Magic Porridge Pot* (P), and *Puss in Boots* (P).

An older group constructed logs from heavy wrapping paper and arranged these as a bonfire with leaping red foil flames. They called their display "Burning Issues in Books." Among the book jackets used were Terry Dunnahoo's *Who Cares about Espie Sanchez?* (A), Paula Danziger's *Can You Sue Your Parents for Malpractice?* (I-A), Judy Blume's *It's Not the End of the World* (I), Alice Childress's *A Hero Ain't Nothin' But a Sandwich* (A), and Paige Dixon's *May I Cross Your Golden River?* (I-A).

Vibrant color, texture, large size, and movement contribute to the effectiveness of bulletin boards. A balloon with passenger basket assures that books can take you anywhere, and an owl may ask "Who-o-o-?" or command "Be Wise! Read!" Keys may open doors to, and clocks may signal time for, varieties of experiences with literature, while cut-paper ships with white burlap sails can announce "Smooth Sailing," "Shipping Out," or "Launching" lively books.

Written Language

Books provide countless ways to stimulate written language. When they write simple captions on their drawings about stories and create their own books based on books they have read, children are refining their writing skills. Just as children learn to read by reading, so do they learn to write by writing. Furthermore, wide reading leads to better writing. Children who hear stories read aloud every day have a richer reading, speaking, listening, and writing vocabulary.

One day six-year-old Beth rushed up to her librarian shouting "I made a story. Let's put it in a book and make it real!" Indeed, a story in a book does seem more real: there is a certain dignity to written pages bound between covers. Beth's story was a simple one about a puppy. But when the librarian wrote, in a handmade book, the words Beth dictated, and the small girl added illustrations and signed her name to the title page—"because I'm the author"—the book in her eyes became worthy of the most esteemed literary prize.

CHILD-MADE BOOKS Blank books such as the one Beth used can be made beforehand and held ready for the youngsters who will make them into "real" books. Pages from wallpaper sample books (usually discarded by decorating stores), stapled or sewn over folded paper, make colorful book covers, which can be left in a convenient spot ready for young authors.

Keeping a journal develops and extends writing skills. Individual or group diaries can record events, thoughts, ideas, and plans.

One primary teacher has, as a permanent member of her class, a stuffed animal, Paddington. The bear's diary stays with him at all times so that his activities and feelings can be recorded. On weekends Paddington takes turns going home with a student, who is responsible for writing in the diary so that the rest of the class will know what they have done.

Children can create an alphabet book with unique interpretations for the letters. One variation is to use, as initial letters, only the letters of their names, listing words that tell something about them for each letter. One student teacher made her alphabet name this way:

B is for Brenda, black, beautiful, bright
R is for reading and running all right
E is for experience, extending my reach
N is for nursery school I want to teach

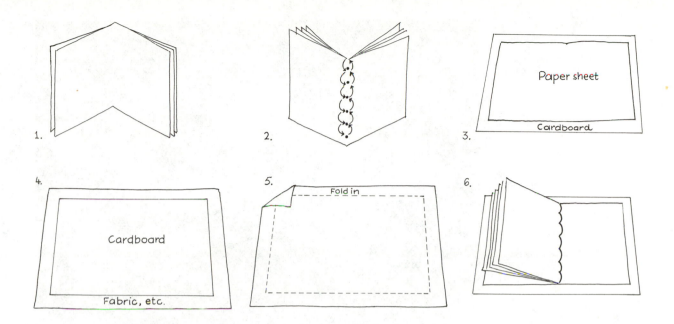

1.

2.

3. Paper sheet / Cardboard

4. Cardboard / Fabric, etc.

5. Fold in

6.

D is for dancing and digging each day
A is for ambitious, 'cause that's my way.

Children may want to use as a basis for an alphabet book animals, a make-believe word, a person's name, toys, or food items. Some may want to try to tell a story using just twenty-six words—one each beginning with each letter in the alphabet—or twenty-six sentences—each sentence featuring one letter in an alliterative story, in which all or many of the words in a phrase begin with the letter to be illustrated. For example: All apes are avid announcers, Bad books better be bumped, and Carol cooks crunchy cookies. Some can cut out letters and hang them in a mobile; others may want to draw, making the letters part of the pictures.

Sophisticated child-made books can be constructed of simple materials. Respect for children's work is shown when it is bound in a durable binding and placed on library shelves for others to enjoy. Steps in making a book are as follows:

1. Fold in half the sheets of paper that are to become the pages of the book. Nest the sheets together so that the folded edges become the spine of the book.

2. Stitch the pages (along the crease made by folding) on a sewing machine or by hand.

3. Cut a piece of oak tag or cardboard one half inch larger all around than the open pages.

4. Select fabric, contact paper, or heavy wallpaper for decorating the cover. (Illustrations and the title can be pasted onto the fabric and made more durable by putting them through a laminator.) Lay the cardboard book on the piece of covering material chosen. Cut the material at least one inch larger than the pages and cardboard all around.

5. Fold the covering material over the edges of the cardboard and glue it into place.

6. Paste the first and last sheets of paper to the covers to join the stitched pages to the cover.

Children who want to know more about how books are made can read Howard Greenfeld's *Books: From Writer to Reader* (I-A). He describes his research and writing and follows the process through agents, editors, illustrators, designers, printers, and book promoters to delivery for sale at a bookstore. After reading this, children may want to make a display for the class showing the progression of a book from the author's idea

A child-created book will often have as much interest for other children as those fashioned by adults.
(Photograph by Ginger Chih.)

through the completed book. Publishers will sometimes send sample press sheets, dummies, and folded and gathered pages of unbound books upon request.

THE LITERATURE NEWSLETTER A classroom newsletter devoted entirely to literature that children enjoy can provide an outlet for sharing books, book reviews, and other children's writing stimulated by their reading. It can also offer editorials, crossword puzzles, art work stimulated by books, an advice column directed to book characters, book-related cartoons, and feature articles on an author or illustrator of the month. The format can vary from a single sheet duplicated for all class members (or others in the school) to one with many pages covering a variety of topics. One school, which was being visited by an author, announced the event in its newsletter, enlarged and displayed on a huge bulletin board in the central hall, with headlines covering the entire entryway. In prepartion for the

visit, children read the author's books and so were able to discuss his work with him. A newsletter requires editors, reporters, feature writers, book reviewers, and art editors recruited from class members, whereas typing, printing, and duplicating may require help from parents or school aides, depending upon the age and skills of the group.

CREATIVE BOOK REPORTING Book reports are fun when they tap children's creative potential; they are valuable when they help a child to understand a book better by clarifying thoughts and feelings. Above all, as in all the activities described in this book, the prime goal is an intense experiencing of literature; everything else is secondary and aimed at achieving this. Being required to read a teacher-selected book and write a report about it has turned more children away from reading than perhaps any other activity. The traditional book reports we are force-fed—time consuming for the teacher who reads and grades them, boring for the children who must listen to them read aloud, and drudgery for the child who writes them—subvert our primary goal.

Book reports should take children back to the book and give them a chance to linger in the story just a little longer. Many ways of reporting about books are enjoyable and meaningful to the child and valuable to the teacher, who can discern from them what the child has gained from the book.

Presented below are some ideas that are certain to suggest others and that, put on index cards, could become the nucleus of a literature activity box of ideas for children's projects.

All aspects of the language arts are integrated in these ideas. Remember, however, that children need choices. Some may like to put themselves in imaginative situations as they discuss books read; others may prefer just to talk about a book, while some may choose to keep the reading experience personal. Be flexible. Encourage them to use these ideas as a springboard for others that may be more important to them. It is illuminating to put yourself in their place; if you ask yourself, concerning any of these ideas, "What is it good for?", you are on the right track. If it leads to thoughtful consideration of a book by the student or to further reading, then it has a place in your plans.

Devise a television or newspaper announcement to advertise a book. Include words and pictures.

Draw a map to show where events in a story took place.

Make puppet characters, write a play about a book, and put on a puppet show.

Choose a character in a book and write a new story about him or her.

Make a model of a creature or a building in a book. Use wood, clay, egg cartons, paper tubes, or other materials.

Write a story about what would happen if two characters from two different books met.

Give an account of what you would have done or how you would have acted had you been one of the characters in a book you read.

Point out parts in a book that show how a character has changed.

Tell or write about the author or illustrator of a book.

Write a summary of a book telling what you especially like or dislike about it.

Make bookmarks that illustrate a character or scene from a book.

Compare two books about the same subject.

Compare two books by the same author.

Draw a picture of your favorite character in a book.

Write a story about the funniest incident in a book.

Ideas of a more complex kind follow:

You have just completed a "time tunnel," which can transport one of the characters in a book you have read into another era. Select a period in the past or future and tell how the character would or would not adapt to that time.

List questions you would ask as a television interviewer of a main character in a book you have just read. For as many questions as possible, write what you think the character might answer.

You have been asked by one of the main characters in a book you have read to write a letter of recommendation for him or her for a job. Describe the character's good and bad points as honestly as possible.

A famous archaeologist wants to hire you for an expedition to a distant island. You may choose one character from a book you have read to go along. Since you will have to live there for about three months, you want someone who will be a good companion and a good explorer. Tell what traits made you select the character you did.[16]

Oral Language

Oral language is central to many book extension activities. These range from the spontaneous recommendations of a book by its reader to structured panel discussions about books by one author. Oral language activities need not take long; they can fit easily into those five spare minutes when the children put on their boots faster than you anticipated.

The Book Buddies system invites oral response to reading. In it, after a child completes reading a book, she selects a partner, and the two go off into a hall or corner where the reader gives a brief summary, discusses the parts that were good, and answers questions from the partner.

STORYTELLING BY CHILDREN Children's writing skills seldom match their oral language skills before the end of their elementary-school years. Storytelling activities contribute to their sense of story and provide opportunities for developing and expanding language. A strong read-aloud program is vital; children will use the literary language they hear in creating their own stories.

Wordless books are an excellent stimulus to storytelling. Because the story line depends entirely upon the illustrations, children become much more aware of the details in the pictures; they do not make a quick scan of them. These books provide a story structure—plot, characters, theme—as with any conventional books, and so provide the necessary framework on which to build their stories. Children can tell such stories to each other, to a group, to an older scribe, or into a recorder. Storytelling can be done with partners, in which case each takes the role of one or more of the characters as they interpret the story. In group storytelling, children pass a book along, each telling the story from one page. From the experience gained, children learn how the elements of the story interconnect and build on each other. When the stories are transcribed they become reading material for the child who provided the text, as well as for other children, who can then read several interpretations—given by their classmates—of the same story.

Tape recorders are indispensable for wordless book activities. When children record their stories, these become available for other children to listen to while looking at the book. Each storyteller's version of the book will be different, so that variety is thus added to the classroom collection. In addition to using tape recorders for recording stories based on books, children can use them in dictating original stories, making background sound tracks for stories read aloud, recording choral-speaking (discussed below), dialogue for puppet shows, and other dramatic activities.

CHORAL SPEAKING Choral speaking, that is, groups speaking in unison, can be adapted for any age level—for the youngest it may mean joining in as a refrain is read aloud; for older students it may involve blending tonal qualities of high, medium, and low voices in rehearsed poetry readings. Very young children unconsciously chime in when you read aloud passages that strike a sympathetic chord. For example, children quickly pick up and repeat the refrain when you read Maurice Sendak's *Chicken Soup with Rice* (N-P). Older students will work out intricate variations for presenting "The Charge of the Light Brigade," by Alfred Lord Tennyson. Rhythm and repetition in language, conducive to choral speaking, is found in abundance in literature for every age group.

Before introducing choral speaking, read aloud two or three times the story or poem being used, so that the rhythm of the language can be absorbed by your listeners. Encourage them to follow along with hand clapping until the beat is established, and then discuss the story or poem to determine which combination of voices will best underscore the meaning. Divide speakers into low, medium, and high as you divide the text for each group to speak. Favorite poems and refrains from stories, unconsciously committed to memory from repeated group speaking, stay in the mind as treasures to be savored for years. Stories with a repeatable refrain and euphonious language include Charlotte Pomerantz's *The Piggy in the Puddle* (P), Ruth Krauss's *The Carrot Seed* (N-P) and *A Very Special House* (N-P), Karla Kuskin's *Just Like Everyone Else* (P), Julian Scheer's *Rain Makes Applesauce* (P), Judith Viorst's *I'll Fix Anthony* (P), and Katy Hall's *Nothing But Soup* (P). A. A. Milne's poetry, including the phrase "James James Morrison Morrison Weatherby George Dupree," in the poem called "Disobedience,"[17] is favorite material for choral speaking. Older students enjoy more complex phrases, catch rhymes, ballads, and classic narrative poetry.

Plan for variety in choral speaking as the group gains experience. To add diversity and range, in addition to high and low voices, assign solos, and have small-group recitations or background rhythm groups. Leader-group response verses exploit the strong rhythm and melody of our language; the response is a phrase, chorus, or an action related to the story, as in this from Margaret Taylor Burroughs's *Did You Feed My Cow?*:

LEADER:	RESPONSE:
Did you feed my cow?	Yes, ma'am!
Will you tell me how?	Yes, ma'am!
Oh, what did you give her?	Corn and hay.
Oh, what did you give her?[18]	Corn and hay.

Many collections are specifically designed for use with choral-speaking groups, including Louise Abney's and Grace Rowe's *Choral Speaking Arrangements for the Lower Grades*. The arrangements, simple and complex, emphasize the rhythm, melody, and imagination of the verse. Bernice Wells Carlson collects stories and verse particularly suited to use in leader-group response; her *Listen! And Help Tell the Story* contains finger plays (wherein children speak a simple rhyme and simultaneously interpret it with finger and body movements) and action verses, as well as poems and stories with sound effects and refrains. Carlson points out:

We learn to listen in order to listen to learn. As a child learns to listen to increasingly difficult material, he learns to remember, to think, and to respond. Learning to listen should be a natural process, not a matter of forced drill. A child should listen because he wants to do so.[19]

DISCUSSION Books become a valued stimulus for discussion, but they can also lead to quiet contemplation; not every book needs to be examined. An important skill that teachers and librarians develop is the ability to recognize when discussion is appropriate and when it is not. No rules can be given for this; it is sensed by teachers and librarians who base decisions on knowledge of children in the group.

For discussion that *is* warranted, there are important guidelines. The purpose of the discussion determines the type of questions and children's responses are, in turn, largely determined by the types of questions, as the study *Critical Reading Ability of Elementary School Children*[20] has shown. Questions in which the aim is to clarify feelings are very different from those intended to expand understanding about literary techniques. Discussions to clarify information or to relate experiences from books to children's lives are equally valid.

Questioning is a primary tool for teachers; good questions elicit high-level thinking from children and poorly-framed ones invite surface thinking. The hierarchy of literal, interpretive, and critical levels of reading and thinking is paralleled in questioning. Literal questions seek to elicit recall of factual information explicitly stated in the printed material.

Literal questions based on the familiar "Goldilocks and the Three Bears" might be: Where did the three bears go? What did Goldilocks do in their house?

Interpretive questions seek information inferred from the text. They are best answered by reading between the lines and synthesizing information from two or more stated facts. Interpretive questions for the Goldilocks story could be: Why did Goldilocks go into the bears' house? Why did she fall asleep in Baby Bear's bed?

Critical questions intended to elicit evaluation of what is stated in the text invite judgments about the quality of writing and authenticity of information; they also encourage hypothesizing beyond the story—tasks requiring higher-level thinking. This level of question is not answered fully by personal opinion—the basis for the judgment is also given. Critical questions for Goldilocks (where two versions have been read) could include: Which version do you like best and why? What is another possible ending for the story? Which ending is most conclusive or satisfying? What did Goldilocks tell her parents when she got home? Why do you think she told them that? How does the repetition of three (three bowls of porridge, three chairs, three beds) fit the pattern of other folk tales? What other stories use the same pattern?

In the matter of questions, it is best to keep in mind that one gets what one asks for. A useful exercise, in respect to this, is to record the questions you typically ask and to tally them according to level. Most teachers ask only literal questions; try to vary yours.

Expanding Book Collections

Teachers are always concerned with finding ways to get more books into their classrooms and building a collection in a reading center to supplement those in the library. Among the means used to raise money for purchasing books are book sales, book fairs, and candy sales. Placing orders through paperback book clubs that offer bonus books is another productive means. Though this involves the tedium of tallying orders and collecting money, one ultimately reaps rewards in book dividends.

Another avenue is the popular and growing Reading is Fundamental (RIF) program sponsored by the U.S. Office of Education. On a more than even matching basis, RIF provides money for books purchased by local schools. Information on how to participate may be had by writing: RIF Program, 2500 L'Enfant Plaza, Washington, D.C. 20560. Books received through this program are given free to children on the assumption that ownership can be a factor in promoting a love of reading. The RIF newsletter, reflecting this view, offers ideas to help teachers build a meaningful program based on involvement; the program is not merely a book giveaway scheme.

Still another avenue for providing additional books for the library or classroom is the "Birthday Book Club." Instead of bringing soon forgotten and sugar-laden cupcakes to share with classmates, the child celebrates his special day by giving a book, which he selects, to his school. The child's name and birthdate are inscribed on a special bookplate and placed in the book so that he can share with pride the special book that commemorates his birthday.

Notes

1. David McCord, "Books Fall Open," in *One at a Time* (Boston: Little, Brown, 1977), p. 343.
2. John Cheetham, "Quarries in the Primary School," *Children's Literature in Education,* 16 (Spring 1975), 4.
3. Dorothy S. Strickland, "Basic Skills Integration Chart," in a manuscript in progress, Teachers College, Columbia Univ., 1980.
4. Harry Graham, as quoted in Reinbert Tabbert, "The Impact of Children's Books: Cases and Concepts, Part One," *Children's Literature in Education,* 10 No. 2 (Summer 1979), 99.
5. Veronica Hutchinson, "Travels of a Fox," in *Chimney Corner Stories,* illus. Lois Lenski (New York: Putnam's, 1905), p. 91.
6. Ellin Greene and Madalynne Schoenfeld, *A Multimedia Approach to Children's Literature,* 2nd ed. (Chicago: American Library Association, 1977).
7. Dorothy Aldis, "Snow," in *Time for Poetry,* 3rd ed., comp. May Hill Arbuthnot and Shelton Root (Chicago: Scott, Foresman, 1952), p. 168.
8. Dorothy Aldis, "Whistles," in *Time for Poetry,* p. 97.
9. Harry Behn, "Hallowe'en," in *Time for Poetry,* p. 164.
10. Mary O'Neill, "My Friend Leona", in *People I'd Like to Keep,* illus. Paul Galdone (New York: Doubleday, 1964), pp. 42–47.
11. Shel Silverstein, "Jimmy Jet and His TV Set," in *Where the Sidewalk Ends* (New York: Harper & Row, 1974), p. 28.

12. For a full discussion of each of these, see Charles Duke, *Creative Dramatics and English Teaching* (Urbana, Ill.: National Council of Teachers of English, 1973); Nellie McCaslin, *Creative Dramatics in the Classroom* (New York: David McKay, 1968); Winifred Ward, *Playmaking with Children,* 2nd ed. (New York: Appleton-Century-Crofts, 1957); and John Warren Stewig, *Exploring Language with Children* (Columbus, Ohio: Charles Merrill, 1974).

13. Adapted by Kathy Tolman, Doctoral candidate, School of Education, Health, Nursing, and Arts Professions, New York University, 1980.

14. Peter Slade, *Child Drama* (London: Verry, 1954), p. 318.

15. There are excellent resources for the teacher who wants to become involved with puppetry, including, Bill Baird, *The Art of the Puppet* (New York: Plays, Inc., 1966); David Currell, *Puppetry for School Children* (Watertown, Mass.: Branford, 1970); and Nancy Renfro, *A Puppet Corner in Every Library* (Austin, Tx.: Renfro Studios, 1978).

16. Adapted from Arlene Pillar, "Individualizing Book Reviews," *Elementary English,* 52, No. 4 (April 1975), 467–69.

17. A. A. Milne, "Disobedience," in *When We Were Very Young* (New York: Dutton, 1924), p. 32.

18. Margaret Taylor Burroughs, *Did You Feed My Cow?: Rhymes and Games from City Streets and Country Lanes,* illus. Joe E. De Velasco (Chicago: Follett, 1969), p. 2.

19. Bernice Wells Carlson, *Listen! And Help Tell the Story,* illus. Burmah Burris (New York: Abingdon, 1965), p. 9.

20. Willavene Wolf, Charlotte S. Huck, and Martha L. King, *Critical Reading Ability of Elementary School Children,* United States Office of Education Report, Project No. 5-1040, Contract No. OE-4-10-187 (Washington, D.C.: GPO, 1967).

Professional References

Abney, Louise, and Grace Rowe. *Choral Speaking Arrangements for the Lower Grades.* Expression, 1973.

Baird, Bill. *The Art of the Puppet.* Plays, 1966.

Baker, Augusta, and Ellin Greene. *Storytelling: Art and Technique.* Bowker, 1977.

Bauer, Caroline Feller. *Handbook for Storytellers.* American Library Association, 1977.

Cheetham, John. "Quarries in the Primary School." *Children's Literature in Education,* 16 (Spring 1975), 3–9.

Colwell, Eileen. *Tell Me a Story.* Penguin, 1962.

————. *Tell Me Another Story.* Penguin, 1964.

————. *Time For a Story.* Penguin, 1967.

Currell, David. *Puppetry for School Children.* Branford, 1970.

Duke, Charles. *Creative Dramatics and English Teaching.* National Council of Teachers of English, 1973.

Greene, Ellin, and Madalynne Schoenfeld, eds. *A Multimedia Approach to Children's Literature.* 2nd ed. American Library Association, 1977.

McCaslin, Nellie. *Creative Dramatics in the Classroom.* McKay, 1968.

Pillar, Arlene. "Individualizing Book Reviews." *Elementary English,* 52, No. 4 (April 1975), 467–69.

Renfro, Nancy. *A Puppet Corner in Every Library.* Renfro Studios, 1978.

Sawyer, Ruth. *The Way of the Storyteller.* Viking, 1962 (1942).

Shedlock, Marie L. *The Art of the Storyteller.* Dover, 1951.

Slade, Peter. *Child Drama.* Verry, 1954.

Sloyer, Shirlee. *Readers' Theater: Handbook for Teachers of Grades 4-6.* Diss. New York University 1979.

Stewig, John Warren. *Exploring Language with Children.* Merrill, 1974.

Strickland, Dorothy S. "Basic Skills Integration Chart." In a manuscript in progress. Teachers College, Columbia Univ.

Tabbert, Reinbert. "The Impact of Children's Books: Cases and Concepts." *Children's Literature in Education,* 10, No. 2 (Summer 1979), 92–102.

Ward, Winifred. *Playmaking with Children.* 2nd ed. Appleton, 1957.

Wolf, Willavene, Charlotte S. Huck, and Martha L. King. *Critical Reading Ability of Elementary School Children.* United States Office of Education Report. Project No. 5-1040, Contract No. OE-4-10-187. Washington, D.C.: GPO, 1967.

Children's Books Cited in Chapter

Aardema, Verna. *Why Mosquitoes Buzz in People's Ears: A West African Tale.* Illus. Leo and Diane Dillon. Dial, 1975.

Adams, Adrienne. *The Easter Egg Artists.* Scribner's, 1976.

484

_____. *A Woggle of Witches*. Scribner's, 1971.

Alexander, Martha. *Blackboard Bear*. Dial, 1969.

Andersen, Hans Christian. *The Princess and the Pea*. Illus. Paul Galdone. Seabury, 1978.

Arbuthnot, May Hill, and Shelton L. Root, Jr. *Time for Poetry*, 3rd ed. Scott, Foresman, 1967.

Becker, John. *Seven Little Rabbits*. Illus. Barbara Cooney. Walker, 1973.

Bemelmans, Ludwig. *Madeline*. Viking, 1939.

Blume, Judy. *Are You There, God? It's Me, Margaret*. Bradbury, 1970.

_____. *Blubber*. Bradbury, 1974.

_____. *It's Not the End of the World*. Bradbury, 1972.

Boylan, Eleanor. *How to Be a Puppeteer*. Illus. Tomie de Paola. McCall, 1970.

Burroughs, Margaret Taylor. *Did You Feed My Cow?: Rhymes and Games from City Streets and Country Lanes*. Illus. Joe E. De Velasco. Follett, 1969.

Byars, Betsy. *The TV Kid*. Illus. Richard Cuffari. Viking, 1976.

Carlson, Bernice Wells. *Listen! And Help Tell the Story*. Illus. Burmah Burris. Abingdon, 1965.

Cauley, Lorinda B. *Pease Porridge Hot: A Mother Goose Cookbook*. Putnam's, 1977.

Childress, Alice. *A Hero Ain't Nothin' But a Sandwich*. Coward, McCann & Geoghegan, 1973.

Cleary, Beverly. *Ramona the Pest*. Illus. Louis Darling. Morrow, 1968.

Craig, M. Jean. *The Donkey Prince*. Illus. Barbara Cooney. Doubleday, 1977.

Dahl, Roald. *James and the Giant Peach*. Illus. Nancy Ekholm Burkert. Knopf, 1961.

Danziger, Paula. *Can You Sue Your Parents for Malpractice?* Delacorte, 1979.

Daugherty, James. *Andy and the Lion*. Viking, 1938.

D'Aulaire, Ingri and Edgar Parin. *Abraham Lincoln*. Rev ed. Doubleday, 1957.

Delton, Judy. *Rabbit Finds a Way*. Illus. Joe Lasker. Crown, 1975.

De Paola, Tomie. *The Popcorn Book*. Holiday House, 1978.

_____. *Watch Out for the Chicken Feet in Your Soup*. Prentice-Hall, 1974.

Dixon, Paige. *May I Cross Your Golden River?* Atheneum, 1975.

Dobrin, Arnold. *Peter Rabbit's Natural Foods Cookbook*. Illus. Beatrix Potter. Warne, 1977.

Dunnahoo, Terry. *Who Cares About Espie Sanchez?* Dutton, 1975.

Duvoisin, Roger. *Petunia*. Knopf, 1950.

Ellison, Virginia H., and A. A. Milne. *The Pooh Cook Book*. Illus. Ernest H. Shepard. Dutton, 1969.

_____. *The Pooh Party Book*. Illus. Ernest H. Shepard. Dutton, 1973.

Estes, Eleanor. *The Hundred Dresses*. Illus. Louis Slobodkin. Harcourt Brace Jovanovich, 1944.

Ets, Marie Hall. *Just Me*. Viking, 1965.

Fatio, Louise. *The Happy Lion*. Illus. Roger Duvoisin. McGraw-Hill, 1964.

_____. *The Three Happy Lions*. Illus. Roger Duvoisin. McGraw-Hill, 1959.

Forbes, Esther. *Johnny Tremain*. Illus. Lynd Ward. Houghton Mifflin, 1946.

Freeman, Don. *The Chalk Box Story*. Lippincott, 1976.

_____. *Corduroy*. Viking, 1968.

Gág, Wanda. *Millions of Cats*. Coward, McCann & Geoghegan, 1928.

Galdone, Paul, illus. *The Frog Prince*. McGraw-Hill, 1974.

_____. *Henny Penny*. Seabury, 1968.

_____. *The Little Red Hen*. Seabury, 1973.

_____. *The Magic Porridge Pot*. Seabury, 1976.

_____. *Puss in Boots*. Seabury, 1976.

George, Jean Craighead. *Julie of the Wolves*. Illus. John Schoenherr. Harper & Row, 1972.

_____. *My Side of the Mountain*. Dutton, 1967.

Greenfeld, Howard. *Books: From Writer to Reader*. Crown, 1976.

Grimm Brothers. *Snow White*. Trans. Paul Heins. Illus. Trina Schart Hyman. Little, Brown, 1974.

_____. *Snow White and the Seven Dwarfs*. Trans. Randall Jarrell. Illus. Nancy Ekholm Burkert. Farrar, Straus & Giroux, 1972.

Hall, Katy. *Nothing But Soup*. Illus. Doug Taylor. Follett, 1976.

Hoban, Russell. *A Bargain for Frances*. Illus. Lillian Hoban. Harper & Row, 1970.

Hogrogian, Nonny. *One Fine Day*. Macmillan, 1968.

Hutchins, Pat. *Rosie's Walk*. Macmillan, 1968. (Film available from Weston Woods.)

Hutchinson, Virginia. *Chimney Corner Stories*. Illus. Lois Lenski. Putnam's, 1905.

Johnson, Crockett. *Harold and the Purple Crayon*. Vanguard, 1937.

Keats, Ezra Jack. *The Snowy Day*. Viking, 1962.

_____. *Whistle for Willie*. Viking, 1964.

Kent, Jack. *The Fat Cat: A Danish Folktale*. Parents, 1974.

Krasilovsky, Phyllis. *The Man Who Didn't Wash His Dishes*. Illus. Barbara Cooney. Doubleday, 1950.

Krauss, Ruth. *The Carrot Seed*. Illus. Crockett Johnson. Harper & Row, 1945.

_____. *A Very Special House*. Illus. Maurice Sendak. Harper & Row, 1953.

Kuskin, Karla. *Just Like Everyone Else*. Harper & Row, 1959.

Lindgren, Astrid. *Pippi Longstocking*. Trans. Florence Lamborn. Illus. Louis S. Glanzman. Viking, 1950.

Lionni, Leo. *Little Blue and Little Yellow*. Astor-Honor, 1959.

_____. *Pezzetino*. Pantheon, 1975.

_____. *Swimmy*. Pantheon, 1963. (Film available from Connecticut Films.)

Lobel, Arnold. *Frog and Toad Are Friends*. Harper & Row, 1970.

Luckin, Joyce. *Easy-to-Make Puppets*. Photo. Livia Rolandini. Plays, 1975.

McCloskey, Robert. *Homer Price*. Viking, 1949.

_____. *Time of Wonder*. Viking, 1957.

McCord, David. *One at a Time*. Illus. Henry B. Kane. Little, Brown, 1977.

MacGregor, Carol. *The Storybook Cookbook*. Illus. Ray Cruz. Doubleday, 1967.

Marceau, Marcel. *The Story of Bip*. Harper & Row, 1976.

Mendoza, George. *The Marcel Marceau Alphabet Book*. Photo. Milton Greene. Doubleday, 1970.

Milne, A. A. *When We Were Very Young*. Illus. Ernest H. Shepard. Dutton, 1924.

_____. *Winnie the Pooh*, Illus. Ernest H. Shepard. Dutton, 1926.

Mosel, Arlene. *Tikki Tikki Tembo*. Illus. Blair Lent. Holt, Rinehart & Winston, 1968.

Nash, Ogden. *Custard the Dragon*. Illus. Linell Nash. Little, Brown, 1961.

Newfield, Marcia. *Six Rags Apiece*. Illus. Nola Langner. Warne, 1976.

Norton, Mary. *The Borrowers Afield*. Illus. Beth and Joe Krush. Harcourt Brace Jovanovich, 1955.

O'Neill, Mary. *Hailstones and Halibut Bones*. Illus. Leonard Weisgard. Doubleday, 1961. (Film available from Sterling Educational Films.)

_____. *People I'd Like to Keep*. Illus. Paul Galdone. Doubleday, 1964.

Parents Nursery School. *Kids Are Natural Cooks*. Illus. Lady McCrady. Houghton Mifflin, 1964.

Paul, Aileen. *Kids Cooking Without a Stove: A Cookbook for Young Children*. Doubleday, 1975.

Pomerantz, Charlotte. *The Piggy in the Puddle*. Illus. James Marshall. Macmillan, 1974.

Potter, Beatrix. *The Tale of Peter Rabbit*. Warne, 1902.

Rey, Hans Augusto. *Curious George*. Houghton Mifflin, 1941.

Robertson, Keith. *Henry Reed, Inc.* Illus. Robert McCloskey. Viking, 1958.

_____. *Henry Reed's Babysitting Service*. Illus. Robert McCloskey. Viking, 1966.

_____. *Henry Reed's Journey*, Illus. Robert McCloskey. Viking, 1963.

Rockwell, Harlow. *I Did It*. Macmillan, 1974.

Ross, Laura. *Hand Puppets: How to Make and Use Them*. Lothrop, Lee & Shepard, 1969.

Sandburg, Carl. *Rootabaga Stories*. Illus. Maud and Miska Petersham. Harcourt Brace Jovanovich, 1922. (Record available from Caedmon Records.)

Sawyer, Ruth. *Joy to the World*. Illus. Trina Schart Hyman. Little, Brown, 1966. (Film available from Weston Woods.)

Scheer, Julian. *Rain Makes Applesauce*. Illus. Marvin Bileck. Holiday House, 1964.

Sendak, Maurice. *Chicken Soup with Rice*. Harper & Row, 1962.

_____. *Where the Wild Things Are*. Harper & Row, 1963. (Record available from Weston Woods.)

Seuss, Dr. *Green Eggs and Ham*. Random House, 1960.

Silverstein, Shel. *Where the Sidewalk Ends*. Harper & Row, 1974.

Singer, Isaac Bashevis. *Zlateh the Goat and Other Stories*. Illus. Maurice Sendak. Harper & Row, 1966.

Slobodkin, Esphyr. *Caps for Sale*. Addison Wesley, 1947.

Sommer, Elyse. *The Bread Dough Craft Book*. Illus. Guilio Maestro. Lothrop, Lee & Shepard, 1972.

Spyri, Johanna. *Heidi*. Illus. Greta Elgaard. Macmillan, 1962 (1884).

Steig, William. *Sylvester and the Magic Pebble*. Simon and Schuster, 1969.

Stevens, Carla. *How to Make Possum's Honey Bread*. Illus. Jack Kent. Seabury, 1976.

Travers, Pamela L., and Maurice Moore-Betty. *Mary Poppins in the Kitchen: A Cookery Book with a Story*. Illus. Mary Shepard. Harcourt Brace Jovanovich, 1975.

Viorst, Judith. *Alexander and the Terrible, Horrible, No Good, Very Bad Day*. Illus. Ray Cruz. Atheneum, 1972.

_____. *I'll Fix Anthony*. Illus. Arnold Lobel. Harper & Row, 1969.

Walker, Barbara M. *The Little House Cookbook: Frontier Foods from Laura Ingalls Wilder's Classic Stories*. Illus. Garth Williams. Harper & Row, 1979.

White, E. B. *Charlotte's Web*. Illus. Garth Williams. Harper & Row, 1952.

Williams, Barbara. *The Little House Cookbook*. Illus. Garth Williams. Harper & Row, 1979.

thirteen

JOHN MOFFITT   *TO LOOK AT ANY THING*

To look at any thing,
If you would know that thing,
You must look at it long:
To look at this green and say,
"I have seen spring in these
Woods," will not do —you must
Be the thing you see:
You must be the dark snakes of
Stems and ferny plumes of leaves,
You must enter in
To the small silences between
The leaves,
You must take your time
And touch the very peace
They issue from.[1]

_____

A Literature Curriculum

Many children read alone before they start school. Without formal instruction, these children learn to read in a natural, developmental way. While there are many differences among them—social, economic, intellectual, racial—there are some commonalities. One is that they are paper-and-pencil kids—ones who like to make marks on paper. They use the marks to express meaning, and invent their own spellings, often using one letter to represent whole words—as in such constructions as "U R Nis." They are also children who are read to and ones for whom someone answers questions. When they ask, "What is that?" or "What does that say?" someone tells them. In sum, their learning environment is supportive, nonthreatening, noncompetitive, and one in which symbols—marks on paper—serve a function. Further, reading is experienced as a joyful sharing of interesting things that come from books.

In many cases, these children have their special books—favorites that they want read to them repeatedly. As the father of one such child said, "If I have to read *Goodnight Moon* one more time, I think I'll die!" It is only the adult who tires of the repetition in Margaret Wise Brown's book, however; for the child, the repetition is a replay of a happy experience. Children possess their favorite books in more than one way: they carry them around, pore over them, say bits and pieces of the story until they come close to approximating the text, and gradually make the language in them their own. This reading-like behavior, in which children "read" and "reread" their version of a favorite book, is a critical step—called emergent reading—in the process of attaining literacy. Don Holdaway gives an example of one child's version of a text:

TEXT	REENACTMENT
and an ocean tumbled by with a private boat for Max and he sailed off through night and day	Max stepped into his private boat and sailed off one day and one night
and in and out of weeks and almost over a year to where the wild things are. And when he came to the	then when he came to where the wi——OO look at that thing—he's blowing smoke out of his

place where the wild things are they roared their terrible roars and gnashed their terrible teeth and rolled their terrible eyes and showed their terrible claws

nose and where the wild things are they lashed their terrible claws—*oh no!* they lashed their terrible teeth—Hrmm!—(Interviewer: 'What did they gnash?') They *lashed* their terrible claws!—showed their terrible claws and showed their terrible yellow eyes (but we've got blue eyes,)

called him the most wild thing of all

"BE STILL!" into all the yellow eyes without blinking once. And all the wild things said, "You wild thing!" (Note the elegant transformation into direct speech.)

till Max said "BE STILL!" and tamed them with a magic trick of staring into all their yellow eyes without blinking once and they were frightened and

till Max said, "BE STILL!" that's what he said. One of these ones have toes (turns the page to find the toed monster). Toes! (Laughs) until Max said

and made him king of all the wild things. "And now," cried Max, "let the wild rumpus start!"

And then Max said, "Let the wild rumpus start!"

No text.

That's got no words, has it?

(Picture of wild dance)

He'd better pull his tail out of the way.[2]

Max is pleased with his achievement in Rosemary Wells's durable board book with vivid illustrations and simple words. Such books are a good starting point for toddlers. (Excerpted from the book *Max's First Word* by Rosemary Wells. Copyright © 1979 by Rosemary Wells. Used by permission of The Dial Press.)

MAX'S ONE WORD WAS
BANG!

Holdaway notes that the child quoted above has just turned four, has had good experiences with books, and has had Maurice Sendak's *Where the Wild Things Are* read to her four times. The most salient features of what she does in this account is to display meaning from the text continuously and to approximate the text in a way similar to the way she (and most children) approximates speech.

The lesson we need to draw from this is that children will learn to read in the same way they learn to speak if we treat reading in a similar manner. The parallels between learning to talk and learning to read are striking, and children would be far more successful at learning to read were we to treat the process the way we do learning to speak. As they are learning to speak, we surround children with continual and voluminous stimulation through our speech. There is no sequence in the speech sounds we present, and children simply take from it what they will as they begin to form speech sounds. In learning to speak, most children's efforts are met with love and enthusiasm and immediate response. There *is* reinforcement: "Say it again, say it for Daddy, tell Mommy." This tremendous flood of response and affection is worth more than 10,000 jelly beans to a child. Meaning is also necessary, for children don't practice initial sounds apart from real words; they do say "ma ma ma" and "da da da," but they say them for totally meaningful reasons. The child,

Pre-readers can easily follow the pictorial narrative in Pat Hutchins's wordless text.
(Reprinted with permission of Macmillan Publishing Co., Inc., from *Changes, Changes* by Pat Hutchins. Copyright © 1971 by Pat Hutchins.)

then, selects from all he hears and practices what is meaningful. His oral language is self-regulated, meaning-centered, and develops naturally in a supportive environment.

So, too, will reading develop naturally if it is nurtured by a supportive environment. If a child regularly sits on a loving adult's lap or snuggles safe and warm in bed as he is read to, he associates feelings of love and joy with reading; his schema of reading includes happy associations, shared pleasures, and feelings of security. The child who has had the experience repeatedly has powerful, positive emotional underpinnings supporting his mental posture toward reading. Further, by seeing those he loves and respects enjoying the act of reading, he comes to view that act as something good to do for its own sake.

Similarly, negative feelings, especially those derived from punishment, militate *against* productive learning. A child embarrassed by the teacher for making a mistake in oral reading will avoid that type of mistake to the extent he can tell what it was. But, since he was trying to do the right thing anyway, the punishment is likely to make him avoid oral reading altogether, because *any* response may seem to him unsafe in that it can invite punishment. The greater possibility, however, is that his avoidance will spread to reading in general, to the person who embarrasses him, and to the context of the reading lesson itself. His aversion may influence him deeply, especially if the punishment is repeated often and he searches for ways to protect himself, finding defenses and developing blocks to reading.

It is abundantly clear that intellect and emotion cannot be separated in any learning task, try as we might to pretend that the cognitive and affective domains are distinct. Don Holdaway states it emphatically :

It is our way in educational matters to value the cognitive and devalue the emotional. The emotional accompaniments—or should we say, the emotional heart—of any

Memorable moments are enhanced by experiencing literature in a pleasant, supportive setting. (Photograph by Susie Fitzhugh.)

human activity refuses to be ignored. No matter how meticulous we are about getting things intellectually right, unless things are *emotionally* right, human activity is tragically deformed.[3]

The lesson, again, is that the introduction to literacy should be developmentally appropriate, pleasurable, and meaning-centered.

The emotional context in which anything is learned colors the learning. Each of us can recall trying to learn something new when the emotional context—anxiety, perhaps—made it impossible. Our job as teachers and parents is to accentuate the positive and make learning about literature the joyous experience it can be. It cannot be denied that seeds planted early take deep root, and as we plant the seeds of literacy, we want to plant them in soil made fertile by imagination, joy, and meaning. Literature can make that job easier.

The function of imagination should not be underestimated; it is an absolute necessity for learning. Children who have not been encouraged to imagine will have difficulty creating images when reading. This latter ability is critical in reading,

since stories deal with inner feelings, intentions, and purposes—elusive abstractions for which there are few literal referents and that can be grasped only when the child evokes in his imagination some corresponding experience. Unless we can see in the mind's eye, create mental images, envision meanings, imagine possibilities, we are less than able to do our part in filling in the gaps and making meaning when interacting with a text.

RESPONSE-ORIENTED APPROACH

A response-oriented approach to the literature curriculum is one that values equally the diversity and uniqueness of whatever it is a child has to say about a book. It encourages versatility of perceptions by the child and assumes that each reader—child and adult—creates his own meaning in interaction with a text. Teachers who insist upon one preconceived right response stand the chance of clipping children's wings before they fly, of eliciting only responses children think we want to hear. The response-oriented view advocates using informed judgment first to determine where a child is, then to open the doorway that will take him to greater literary experiences.

Two conceptual constructs central to the response-oriented approach are reader response theory and developmental psychology. Reader response theory grows from the early work of Louise Rosenblatt and was first advanced in *Literature as Exploration* and, more recently, in *The Reader, the Text, the Poem*. Before Rosenblatt's work, it was believed that the reader's task was solely to absorb and interpret meaning from a text, that a writer embeds meaning in a text and a reader works at extracting it, that the correct meaning waits to be discovered by the clever reader. A major proponent of this view was I. A. Richards, who, in his *Practical Criticism,* pursued the idea by carefully analyzing reader responses to various poems and pointing out the many "misinterpretations." Richards lamented the fact that a reader's predisposition and experience could lead him away from the "one right meaning" of a poem.

Rosenblatt, on the other hand, casts the reader into a much more important and active role. She sees the literary work existing in the "live circuit set up between reader and text: the reader infuses intellectual and emotional meanings into what he reads."[4] It is a circular process in which the reader responds to the words on the page and at the same time draws upon his own experiences in order to create a personal meaning. For Rosenblatt, the validity of each personal response is established by verification with the text. (Thus a response is invalid if contradicted by the text.) Such a flexible position leaves room for a wide range of responses —all valid. Furthermore, in the classroom it leads to lively discussions as children share with each other their unique perceptions of a piece of literature enjoyed in common.

The work of Wolfgang Iser (Chapter 1), compatible with Rosenblatt's, describes the relation between reader and author. Insofar as a writer uses particular narrative techniques, he circumscribes the impression a reader takes from his work. If he paints a totally explicit picture, according to Iser, the text is dull because there are no gaps to activate the readers' imaginations, to allow them to make inferences and individually realize the intentions of a text. (If the author sketches too briefly, the reader is required to fill in too many gaps and may tire of the effort.) This implies that a single work will have many (more or less complete) realizations, as many as there are readers filling in the gaps.

What does this mean for the literature curriculum? Initially, it means that we need to create an environment in which readers can take risks in expressing their responses, and that this can best be achieved if we entertain a variety of possibilities and do not impose our own interpretations as the "one right answer" or by moralizing about the issues involved. For example, children discussing Katherine Paterson's *The Great Gilly Hopkins* (I) have strong feelings about the ending of the story. Some insist that Gilly should have stayed in the secure world provided by Maime Trotter. Others are equally vehement that Gilly rightfully belongs with her grandmother or that Courtney, her natural mother, really wants her and will return to claim her. The sensitive discussion leader will draw out such readers' responses and their underlying reasoning, sometimes asking, for example, "What is it in the book that makes you feel that way?"

Further, small-group discussions should be encouraged. Although consensual validation of one's peers is important during some developmental stages, when children hear interpretations different from their own they gradually learn that others may have valid positions and may come to entertain these alternate possibilities, with consequent expansion of their own perceptions and responses. Teachers, responsible for directing the course of discussion, can help engender respect for divergent views and encourage students to think about things in ways they had not.

A developmental perspective allied with reader response theory provides further insights for the literature teacher. James Squire and Alan Purves were among the first to study response to literature; they concluded that responses could be categorized and coded along generalized descriptive

Tana Hoban uses her camera to capture scenes for children who are at a stage of active conceptual development. (Illustration from *Dig, Drill, Dump, Fill* by Tana Hoban. Copyright © 1975. Reproduced by permission of Greenwillow Books, A Division of William Morrow & Company, Inc.)

lines. Hundreds of studies followed, categorizing responses according to Squire and Purves's schemas. Recognizing a need for a kind of inquiry to more adequately describe responses, researchers began to view response from a developmental perspective. For example, Arthur Applebee began to look at children's responses to literature from a developmental perspective, tracing the concept of story as it changed with the child's age. He found that their use of conventions, attitudes toward story, and organizational patterns reflected general cognitive developmental trends. (See Chapter 1 for discussion of stages of cognitive development.) Preoperational children, for example, cannot analyze themes or author's motives and, rather than summarizing a story in broad, generalized terms, will retell it in great detail, embellishing the original with their unique poetic version.

On the other hand, children at the stage of formal operations are able to analyze and generalize from stories, concentrating on how the work interacts with their view of the world.

Anthony Petrosky also studied reader's response from a developmental perspective. His case studies of four fourteen- and fifteen-year-olds corroborated Applebee's findings that stage-specific capacities influence response markedly. Petrosky also demonstrated the usefulness of group discussions in helping readers clarify and validate their responses. Discussing a story with significant others, he found, influences responses to it, and, as Norman Holland and G. Mills had contended, discussion helps filter out responses inappropriate to the text and may also expand responses since readers take in statements about the work as they take in the work itself. These findings suggest that discussion after reading is one good way to help children clarify their responses. As one child said, "I never thought about it that way, but now it makes a lot of sense."

James Britton argues against piecemeal analysis of stories children write as well as ones they read, taking the position that it interferes with apprehension of a work as an integrated whole, which he advocates. Reading something with the aim of remembering each tiny detail, we lose the overarching meaning; the same thing happens if we discuss the story bit by bit. Teachers' questions about stories, then, need to be broad, open-ended ones rather than the narrow detail-seeking kind.

S. Lee Galda explored uniqueness in patterns of response and the effect of group discussion or individual response in a study of eleven-year-old girls. She found that each child had a characteristic way of responding and that some were more open to the possibilities in stories than others. She also found that they sometimes used labels to express literary concepts that were ill-formed, whereas at other times they struggled to express intuitively known concepts for which they had no labels. From studies of this kind we know how children's responses to literature can serve as guides to teachers; their responses tell us what literary concepts need to be taught and what basic experiences with literature need to be provided. No hierarchical list of literary concepts to be taught in a predetermined order exists, but concepts and labels needed to discuss literature should be provided when there is a need to know them. Galda gives the example of two children who talked about the way Katherine Paterson "broke moods" when she moved from direct dialogue to a third-person narrator in *Bridge to Terabithia* (I). It was apparent that these children were dealing with the effect of point of view on narration, but they did not have the words to discuss it. Children's responses, then, can inform teachers about what to teach and when to teach it.

What else does this say to the literature teacher? Most important, the methods teachers use need to be informed by a knowledge of cognitive developmental stages. This not only directs their choice of books for specific age groups but also tells them what expectations are reasonable with respect to kinds of response and levels of response.

Each child's response depends upon the level of cognitive and emotional development attained, his or her construct of the world, and the conviction with which each holds those constructs. Because young children see literature as a representation of the real world, they are more likely to accept it as true. Applebee points out:

For very young children the world of stories is part of the world in which they live; its events are as important and meaningful to them as anything else that happens. The separation of these worlds when they are finally confronted with the distinction between fact and fantasy is often relatively distressing; for a while, at least, a story is accepted only if the child thinks it is true. Slightly older children, once they have reconciled themselves to the distinction between fact and fantasy, continue to view stories from a single perspective: the events in a story remain made-up correlatives of events in the world.[5]

Eventually, children begin to view a story as a representation of one of many possible worlds and are able to construe it as one alternative of many. Therefore, the stages of response differ developmentally and individually—variables that any literature curriculum must consider.

One specific aspect of development that affects response to literature is moral development. Jean Piaget's pioneering work in the psychology of development provides a scaffolding upon which researchers such as Lawrence Kohlberg and his associates have built a theory about children's reasoning concerning right and wrong, good and bad. Their conceptualization of children's comprehension of morality views growth as movement through a series of invariant stages. The developmentally early stage, called a morality of constraint, is oriented toward obedience to adult rules and attention to external physical consequences.

A developmentally later stage, called a morality of cooperation, is characterized by increases in the use of reciprocity as a basis for judgment, in the notions of relativism of value, and in the questioning of adult authority. Children at this stage are able to take another's perspective, can consider possible diversity in views of right and wrong, and place great importance on peer relationships. For example, a child at this level thinks that a lie told to a peer is worse than one told to an adult because it breaches mutual trust, opening the possibility for a reciprocal breach—a possibility they find intolerable.

Literature is replete with moral dilemmas that can elicit discussions of values. James Miller, Jr. says:

Literature properly presented should confront the student (like life itself) with a multiplicity of ethical systems and moral perspectives. This expansion and deepening of the student's moral awareness constitutes the education of his moral imagination. It is one important (but not the sole) aim of literary study.[6]

Probing children's reasoning behind a moral position and their resulting defense of it can help them to develop the strength of their own convictions as well as to examine the values they hold. Teachers aware of their own values (which may or may not be similar to their students') help students probe the multiple ethical systems and moral perspectives by withholding personal judgments and providing an atmosphere where divergent views are respected. This is an area in which teachers help students learn *how* to think; they do not tell them *what* to think. This stance, along with questions that tap and expand the structure of children's reasoning, can facilitate a fuller response to literature.

PERSPECTIVES

Experiencing literature and studying literature are *not* the same, yet both have a place in elementary school. Even before coming to school or learning to read independently, children can have had rich literary experiences. For the youngest child, literature attracts for the pure pleasure it brings, and teachers will rarely have any agenda for modifying attitudes or achieving behavioral objectives. Even while listening for pure pleasure, however, children unconsciously internalize a sense of the total form of a literary work.

The *study* of literature does not begin until *after* the literature is experienced: someone tells, reads, or dramatizes a story, and a fortunate child just enjoys it. When the time comes for children to look at literature analytically and to make abstrac-

Sal picks blueberries in McCloskey's classic story, sometimes called the perfect picture book for its deft blend of text and illustration.
(From *Blueberries for Sal* by Robert McCloskey. Copyright 1948, © renewed 1976 by Robert McCloskey. Reprinted by permission of Viking Penguin Inc.)

tions about its forms, structures, archetypes, and patterns, such children have joyful experiences upon which to draw.

With older children, enjoyment is still uppermost, and the study of literature is sensitively introduced only as it adds to their appreciation and insight. The study of literature does *not* replace the original literary experience; neither does study always need to follow the experience. There is a time and a place for both.

Children can come to recognize similarities between the sisters in "Cap O'Rushes" and the stepsisters in "Cinderella." Later, this recognition can contribute insights concerning the behavior of the daughters in *King Lear*. They see the same rags-to-riches theme in "Cinderella" and in the Horatio Alger stories, and, although they may not be able to verbalize it, they recognize the theme as an expression of wish fulfillment. They see the underdog fighting against great odds in "Jack and the Beanstalk," "Jack the Giant Killer," and "David and Goliath," and add to their expectations of what stories are all about.

Simultaneously, children meet ever richer language in their books as they move from "'Not I,' said the cat, 'Not I,' said the dog," through "They roared their terrible roars and gnashed their terrible teeth and rolled their terrible eyes," and then on to watching a "mermaid morning" and searching for "shadows that haunt one's soul." Concomitantly, they meet increasingly complex forms in their experience with simple narratives—from cumulative repetition of "The Gingerbread Boy," to the parallel plots in McCloskey's *Blueberries for Sal* (N-P), to slightly more complex plots of detective stories such as Sobol's *Encyclopedia Brown* (P-I), to the alternating narrators in Zindel's *The Pigman* (A), to the story within a story in Chambers's *Breaktime* (A). Appreciating increasingly complex literature can occur only so long as the cognitive capacity of the developing child increases.

Responses are the only way a teacher can know what a child has made of a literary experience. Response takes many forms: it becomes the material from which sensitive teachers derive insights about their students.

Children's books are discussed from many different perspectives; certain perspectives appear time after time in literary criticism, classroom practice, and research methodologies. Outlined below are some of the most prevalent of the many possible ways to view literature. Teachers who know many ways to approach literature are able to provide a wealth of choices for their students, choices based on both the students' abilities and interests and the nature of the literary texts.

Aesthetic Experience

Literature as an aesthetic experience is a perspective with one primary dimension—basic, elemental, no-strings-attached, pure, totally engaging enjoyment. Since the time of Aristotle, in the West, the aesthetic experience has been held to be primal in the search for goodness, truth, and beauty. Today, the aesthetic experience still carries great meaning for our lives. At the elementary school level, for example, poetry is best experienced in this way. Building a love for poetry rests upon the pleasure children first experience with verse, *not* upon analysis of meter or rhyme scheme, or upon memorization.

Young children discovering ladybugs, for example, will probably take pleasure in David McCord's poem ''I Want You to Meet . . .'':

> . . . Ladybug,
> her little sister Sadiebug,
> her mother, Mrs. Gradybug,
> her aunt, that nice oldmaidybug,
> and Baby—she's a fraidybug.[7]

After they've built a snowman, they will look at it —or any everyday phenomenon—differently if they've heard David McCord's ''Snowman'':

> My little snowman has a mouth,
> So he is always smiling south.
> My little snowman has a nose;
> I couldn't seem to give him toes,
> I couldn't seem to make his ears.
> He shed a lot of frozen tears
> Before I gave him any eyes—
> But they are big ones for his size.[8]

Whatever enterprise you are engaged in with your students, literature shared aesthetically infuses

This intricate fantasy has complex parallel plots that develop a theme concerning society's treatment of divergent groups. (Illustration by Zena Bernstein from *Mrs. Frisby and the Rats of NIMH* by Robert C. O'Brien. Copyright © by Robert C. O'Brien. Reprinted by permission of Atheneum Publishers.)

greater meaning and imparts a sense of joy in the process. An aesthetic perspective keeps the emotional as an equal partner to the intellectual, and holds that learning is more effective when the emotions are involved positively.

Structure

A structural perspective focuses on the components of literature, such as the plot, theme, characterization, point of view, setting, and language style. Factors in the work itself (as opposed to factors external to it, such as the period in which it was written or the life of the author) engage the structuralist critic.

Children, notorious plot readers, want to find out what *happens,* and will discard a book that has

ABEL'S ISLAND ○ *William Steig*

FARRAR / STRAUS / GIROUX

Abel contemplates his fate in William Steig's vivid characterization of a genteel Victorian mouse who is transformed into a rugged individualist.
(Illustration reproduced by permission of Farrar, Straus & Giroux, Inc., from *Abel's Island* by William Steig. Copyright © 1976 by William Steig.)

little or no action. Plot action, carried forward through incident and dialogue, is generally more lively in children's books than in adult novels, with their introspection and reminiscence. Plot sequence may be presented through a straightforward chronology, flashbacks, or multiple concurrent scenes. As children develop their concept of story, they choose to read stories with more complex plots.

A theme, the underlying meaning of a work, unifies plot, character, setting, language, and point of view. Universal truths, moral dilemmas, and human concerns provide themes for books for young children and adolescents. Sensing theme in a story is one of the subtle and elusive capacities that cannot be hurried in a child's literary education. Recognizing underlying meaning comes long before children can verbalize it; it takes even longer for them to label it a theme. Although theme is the main idea of a story, that it can be explicated in many ways and interpreted differently by each reader is a realization to which children can be led gradually through discussion.

In the structuralist approach, characterization refers to the techniques—description, dialogue, incident, introspection, or revelation of thoughts—authors use to make a character memorable. What most sharply defines a character is what the author tells us about him. Among the other things that contribute to the portrait an author paints of a protagonist are what he has him think, say, and do, and what others have to say to and about him. In the very first chapter of *Call It Courage* (I-A), Armstrong Sperry uses all these ways to establish character. Well-developed characters seem real to children and often become part of their fantasy life. Many children know Madeline, Charlotte, and Henry Huggins as real people and true friends.

The point of view from which a story is told affects all other components of the story. In many books, a central character tells the story in the first person—as an observer or as a participant in events. A third-person, omniscient narrator reports events, describes scenes, and reveals thoughts of characters as an all-seeing eye. Sometimes different chapters are told from the point of view of different characters. Young children, in an egocentric stage of development, imagine themselves into the roles of characters; older children can maintain multiple points of view and comprehend the complexity brought about by conflict in points of view.

A setting may represent the real world with verisimilitude, it may portray a totally fanciful world of the author's invention, or it may create a sense that the story could have occurred at any place and time. Setting reveals character: describing a person's home partially describes the person.

As is true for other components, setting is woven into the fabric of the story.

Some stories could take place in almost any setting. Others are possible only because the characters are in a particular place at a particular time. For example, Robert McCloskey's *Time of Wonder* (P-I) could take place only on an island at the end of summer. Historical novels, too, depend heavily upon setting, as in the story of *Boris* (I), by Jaap ter Haar, dramatically shaped by events of the siege of Leningrad during World War II. Theme, plot, and character, all woven into the physical and social fabric of time and place, interact with setting.

The style of language used to tell a story affects and is affected by all else in it. The order of words, the sounds of words, and the meanings of words artfully shaped by an author make life radiate from literature. Visual images created in the mind as sounds fall felicitously on the ear distinguish great art from the mundane.

The literary concepts that a structuralist approach emphasizes can and should be taught to children, but only when they are ready to learn them—when they have a need to know and an experiential base upon which to anchor the concepts. Labels without concepts are detrimental to children's growth in the study of literature and often obscure the areas of study that need to be emphasized. Teachers aware of literary concepts *and* the levels of children's development can provide information and support when it is appropriate.

Language Expansion

The most fully developed and beautiful forms of language are found in literature. Literature *is* language and children's language grows through experience with literature. Children learn language naturally in an environment that is filled with language in use; the language children learn is the language they hear, or read. It follows that the richer the language environment, the more fully developed a child's language will be. Books extend the language environment and provide myriad opportunities to talk about life, as well as language itself.

In L'Engle's intricate blend of fantasy and historical legend, the setting of Charles Wallace's perilous journey shifts through time.
(Cover art by Leo and Diane Dillon from *A Swiftly Tilting Planet* by Madeleine L'Engle. 1978. Farrar, Straus & Giroux, Inc.)

All of us know a child who wants a favorite story read and reread, and who eventually takes the book and proceeds to "read" his inimitable version of that story. The way a child tells it is the way it makes sense to him; he focuses on the features of the text that are most salient for him. Gradually he achieves closer approximations of the book's language and soon, after repeated experience of the book, adopts its language as his own.

Children often mimic words and phrases they meet in books, and since language in literature is modeled by writers who use it well, it becomes an excellent means for expanding vocabulary. For example, Jack Prelutsky's *The Mean Old Mean Hyena* (P) utters ear-tickling threats to the other animals as he connives to get them to make him laugh. In much the same way as Brer Rabbit finagles Brer Fox to throw him into the briar patch, the laughing hyena deviously leads the animals to make him do what he was born to do. His own self-description—"lazy and lanky, sneaky and slinky and lean, clever and crafty and cranky, oh! he was ever so mean"—is quickly mimicked by young children who delight in the tongue-tangling verses.

Older children grow to appreciate the way language can be used to express their own feelings. In *Julia and the Hand of God* (I), by Eleanor Cameron, the tousled young heroine envies her immaculate friend Maisie, who "slipped sideways through the days instead of flying head-on the way Julia did." Words such as these help children form their thoughts into meaningful descriptive phrases. Rich literary experiences give children the words they need to express elusive feelings—and having the words to label experience means having a powerful tool for communicating.

Children gradually grow beyond mere fascination with interesting language into the double-edged pleasure of appreciating language interacting with form. As twelve-year-old Russell exclaimed after discovering the intricate word play in Ellen Raskin's *The Westing Game* (I), "How did she *do* that! The whole book tricks you with one verse of a song!" His admiration was based not only upon the clever use of words, but upon the centrality of the word play as a plot device. When teachers share literature with children, they are giving them a gift of words. It is easy to overlook this subtle reward that comes from memorable book experiences.

Mutual joy in delicious words, acknowledged by a teacher's knowing smile, encourages children to make language their toy when they are young and spurs them, as they mature, to become word collectors who value the nuances in beautiful word images. It is not mere coincidence that people with large vocabularies read a lot; there is a direct connection between the two.

Literature parallels every level of language competence from labeling (participation books) to subtle and sophisticated novelistic imagery and complex poetic symbols. (Books that reflect the stages of children's language development are discussed in Chapter 3.) Clear correspondences are found between the language used in literature and the language learned by the developing child exposed to that literature.

The language contained in literature can also serve as a pattern for children's *written* language production. Rather than learning styles of writing through drill exercises, children can imitate the styles of the authors they read. This is not to say that children should write to a prescribed pattern: they will intuitively use those patterns they have found pleasing, and the style in which they write will become more complex as they grow older and read more widely.

Archetypes

Archetypes are those fundamental themes, motifs, and patterns that appear repeatedly throughout the literature of humankind and that are most evident in folklore. Identification of these fundamental elements and comparisons across literary works are basic to an archetypal approach. Certain themes, characters, images, incidents, and conventions in story form are among the archetypes identified by literary critics. A theme of the struggle between light and dark, a character such as the lost child or a superhuman, an image of eternal spring, an incident such as the transformation of a frog into a prince, or the convention of repetitive cycles in story patterns are archetypal elements recurring throughout literature.

Teachers can plan for and encourage children's discovery of archetypes by using a rich array of traditional literature. As suggested in Chapter 5, when comparing several variants of one story, or identifying one theme across several stories, children unearth archetypes for themselves. As in the case of any learning, the basic concepts and the process are far more important than knowing labels. Does it serve any useful educational end to know that three and seven are symbolic numbers without remembering the joy of the three wishes, the magic of the three charms, the mystic aura of the seven ravens? Certainly in the elementary school, children discover archetypes intuitively by reading stories in which they continually reappear. Teachers, of course, can plant the seeds of interest by showing their own enthusiasm for folklore and by planning discussions about pertinent stories. These comparisons and discussions will also lead to more abstract and theoretical literary discussions as the children grow more capable of that kind of thinking.

Values

Among other things, literature imitates life and, in doing so, reflects the social concerns of human beings. Numerous studies show that children's books, like any others, reflect a country's social and political philosophy. Therefore, literature can be viewed from a socio-moral perspective, which requires focussing on the values expressed.

Children's literature is often seen as propagating the values society prizes and instilling precepts as to how life should be lived. Traditional families, alternate life styles, and relationships with peers are the backdrops against which contemporary values are played. In the past, problems were most often resolved by having virtue rewarded, justice triumphant, and evil overcome by good. In today's books, dilemmas are left open-ended or the central character accepts a less-than-perfect world. Whether for good or for ill, there appears to be a hiatus in the happy-ending syndrome.

Contemporary books discuss such issues as divorce, abortion, sexual exploration, drug abuse, discrimination, violence, and sex role stereotyping. On the one hand, these can present a problem for the classroom teacher, but on the other — where any of these problems may have touched the life of a child — they can be the reason for high enthusiasm for reading. Contemporary books are dilemma-laden, and children will look to teachers for a chance to discuss and resolve conflicts in values. In such situations, teachers dare not be di-

dactic or moralistic; the best course is to serve as a sounding board, encouraging children to use literature to explore their own reasoning. We can show them how to look, but not what they should see.

AN INTEGRATED APPROACH WITH TWO BOOKS

A literature curriculum is built upon wide exposure to excellent books that are developmentally appropriate to the children in your group. The curriculum is enriched if you have an array of approaches and are flexible in their use. The following classroom examples illustrate an integrated approach to literature.

First, from a stance that integrates several perspectives, let us look at Robert Kraus's picture storybook for young children, *Leo the Late Bloomer* (N-P), about a young tiger, Leo, who can't do anything right:

He couldn't read. He couldn't write. He couldn't draw. He was a sloppy eater. And, he never said a word.[9]

Leo's mother assures his concerned father that Leo is just a late bloomer. Leo's father watches for signs of blooming, but, although the seasons come and go, it seems Leo will not bloom. In his own good time, however, he does — reading, writing, drawing, and eating neatly; and he also spoke:

And it wasn't just a word. It was a whole sentence. And that sentence was . . . "I made it!"[10]

From a language development perspective, *Leo the Late Bloomer* has much to offer. One nursery school teacher presented the book to four- and five-year-old children and then discussed the concept of blooming with them.[11] Children talked about what they had bloomed at and what they were still working toward. "I bloomed at climbing the jungle gym," one would say, "but I haven't bloomed at reading." Or, "I bloomed at writing my name, but I'm still blooming at tying my shoes." The group discussed blooming and growing as a normal developmental process, using the

500 word in numerous ways that led children to assimilate the concept. Another group that heard the book read aloud used the word bloom to mean experiencing happiness, as in "I bloom when I see my Dad on Sundays."

A serendipitous result of discussing blooming was the compassion evident among the children, who responded affectively as well as cognitively, saying such things as, "Don't worry, Nancy, I didn't bloom at that either but now I do . . . and you will, too," as they responded to the theme that children will develop in their own way and in their own good time.

From an aesthetic point of view, *Leo the Late Bloomer* can be examined in terms of Jose Aruego's illustrations, which convey and extend the meaning of the text, translating "blooming" into a fantasia of blossoms and riotous colors. Leo's dissatisfaction with himself is conveyed through his expressions and his placement on the page. Before Leo succeeds, he is at the bottom of the page, scrunched and woebegone, crumpled and beaten down by failure, surrounded by flowers that are still tightly closed buds. When he masters his tasks, he is placed at the top of the page, physically on top of blooming flowers, filling entire pages with his glorious accomplishments.

An appropriate perspective is determined by the nature of the book and the characteristics of the children. It is clear that *Leo the Late Bloomer*, intended for a young audience, does not lend itself to an archetypal approach. The language development and aesthetic perspectives, on the other hand, would be consonant with both child and text. For older groups and other purposes, a structuralist perspective would highlight the foreshadowing, strong characterization, explicit theme, and repetitive language. In whatever perspective taken, it is the teacher's task to enable children to discover, in the least directive way, the riches that lie within the book.

Older students are drawn to Katherine Paterson's *Bridge to Terabithia* (I), a well-crafted novel, because it is both gripping and memorable, its images evocative. The story concerns a friendship between two children who create an imaginary kingdom, Terabithia, and the tragic death of one of them when she tries to go to Terabithia alone. It celebrates the vision of imagination and touches children's hearts. The wealth of emotions and insights in the book hold potential for rich response from a number of perspectives.

The fact that children pass the book gently along to their best friends, and that its pages are dog-eared, testifies to the strong aesthetic response it elicits. Katherine Paterson enables readers to validate the depths of friendship, comparing her story with what they know. Where the match is true, some of Jesse's and Leslie's courage and strength pass into the reader's own fiber. Further, just as Leslie's move to rural Virginia enabled her to see how others lived, so do readers expand their understandings of life and friendship by reading about this special relationship.

Likewise, Jesse's growth, in daring to be different, and his coming to terms with grief at Leslie's death serve readers as virtual experience or rehearsal for life.

Some teachers may want to help children probe *Bridge to Terabithia* from a structuralist perspective—focusing on the well-developed characters for example. Leslie's intelligence and imagination raise Jesse's consciousness and inspire him to move toward maturity:

For hadn't Leslie, even in Terabithia, tried to push back the walls of his mind and make him see beyond to the shining world—huge and terrible and beautiful and very fragile? . . . Now it was time for him to move out. She wasn't there, so he must go for both of them. It was up to him to pay back to the world in beauty and caring what Leslie had loaned him in vision and strength.[12]

Just as Jesse finds in Leslie a model to emulate, so, too, can readers find a mirror of their own development or a window through which they view the lives of others.

Discussion of characterization is appropriate to this text once students respond to Jesse and Leslie as believable characters. They can then proceed to an examination of minor characters, including a consideration of the role they play in shaping the story. A discussion of the way the respective families interact with their children—how differently

Jesse and Leslie were reared—can lead to penetrating insights for children about how this story relates to their own lives.

It could also be fruitful to discuss the effect of other elements in the story, such as point of view and setting. Or, the story as a whole may be compared with other works of contemporary realistic fiction dealing with the death of a child, such as Smith's *A Taste of Blackberries* (I), Greene's *Beat the Turtle Drum* (I), and Lowry's *A Summer to Die* (I-A).

Katherine Paterson marks her story with another important element—language, and the role it plays in both circumscribing Jesse's life and then freeing him. Paterson vividly contrasts the language of the Aarons family with that of the Burkes, and highlights Jesse's growth with changes in his language. Initially he speaks a restricted Appalachian dialect and turns to Leslie to make the magic in Terabithia. As the story draws to a close, he is making the magic himself. Upon his return to Terabithia after Leslie's death, Jesse says:

"Father, into Thy hands I commend her spirit." He knew Leslie would have liked those words. They had the ring of the sacred grove in them.[13]

The process of language growth itself develops into a theme about the way in which language can either delimit or enlarge one's world.

From the perspective of theme, the story centers on the importance of life continuing after tragedy. Rather than being destroyed by his friend's death, Jesse builds on the legacy Leslie leaves him and continues Terabithia, passing it on to his younger sister, May Belle. In the final scene, he puts flowers in May Belle's hair and leads her across the newly constructed bridge, his belief in the promise of life shining in his words as he says to her:

"Can't you see 'um?" he whispered. "All the Terabithians standing on tiptoe to see you."

"Me?"

"Shhh, yes. There's a rumor going around that the beautiful girl arriving today might be the queen they've been waiting for."[14]

Jesse's act of love honors Leslie's life.

If looked at from an archetypal perspective, Jesse's journey toward maturity can be viewed as a variation of the quest. Leslie's death is analogous to the trials that must traditionally be endured before the goal, in this case maturity, is attained. Jesse is aware of being put to the test; Paterson writes:

As for the terrors ahead—for he did not fool himself that they were all behind him—well, you just have to stand up to your fear and not let it squeeze you white. Right, Leslie? Right.[15]

Children draw conclusions from discussions of larger meanings, making comparisons with other stories embodying similar quests. They will evaluate this story in terms of other literature they have experienced and use it as a base for evaluating texts read in the future.

Terabithia, in its metaphoric sense, stands for the world of possibilities sometimes reached through the painful process of maturation. There, Leslie helps Jesse to recognize his potential. Probing of the text is enhanced by recognizing how this pervasive metaphor shapes the story. Since the capacity to understand metaphor is developmentally linked, the depth of analysis of this sort necessarily depends upon the developmental level of the children involved.

That the preceding discussion illustrates many different approaches to books does not imply that teachers must use them all. One needs to be selective, using a butterfly's touch and avoiding the heavy hand.

BASIC BOOKS FOR A LITERATURE PROGRAM

Presented below is a list of books organized according to the age group for whom they hold greatest interest. The books listed have an energy that makes them seem timeless and fresh as they are read and reread, and are ones it would be a loss not to have experienced.

One basis for selection is that the books have lasting value. Undoubtedly, among the two thou-

502 sand books published annually there are additional outstanding ones, but the ones cited here contain special experiences basic to a literary education.

We believe that, as children read books from this list, they begin to build a strong foundation for a lifelong love of reading. The choices reflect our personal and professional taste and belief that these books have the potential for becoming children's favorites for all times. It is informed by our work with children and our knowledge of their literature. While some good books must certainly have been overlooked, we are certain that the ones ultimately selected represent the finest writing for children today. Although not all those listed are of equal merit, all possess marks of quality that distinguish them from the mass of unenduring books and make them worthy of literary study.

Designation according to age of reader is, of course, flexible; all of us have seen how children will read well beyond their normal level when a book strikes to the center of their interest. Most of the books can be read aloud—and most students comprehend at a higher listening level than reading level. Finally, these books stand a good chance of becoming champion repeaters among readers because, although they may demand more, they also pay a richer dividend in joy.

NURSERY (N)

Brown, Margaret Wise. *Goodnight Moon*. Illustrated by Clement Hurd. Harper & Row, 1947.
Crews, Donald. *Trucks*. Greenwillow, 1980.
Grimm Brothers. *Little Red Riding Hood*. Illustrated by Paul Galdone. McGraw-Hill, 1974.
Jeffers, Susan, adaptor and illustrator. *Three Jovial Huntsmen*. Bradbury, 1973.
Lobel, Arnold, selector and illustrator. *Gregory Griggs and Other Nursery Rhyme People*. Greenwillow, 1978.
Watson, Clyde. *Father Fox's Pennyrhymes*. Illustrated by Wendy Watson. Crowell, 1971.
Wildsmith, Brian. *Brian Wildsmith's Mother Goose*. Watts, 1964.

NURSERY-PRIMARY (N-P)

Asbjørnsen, Peter Christian, and Jorgen E. Moe. *The Three Billy Goats Gruff*. Illustrated by Paul Galdone. Seabury, 1973.
Burningham, John. *Mr. Gumpy's Outing*. Holt, Rinehart & Winston, 1971.
Carle, Eric. *The Very Hungry Caterpillar*. World, 1970.
De Angeli, Marguerite. *Marguerite de Angeli's Book of Nursery and Mother Goose Rhymes*. Doubleday, 1954.
Emberley, Barbara. *Drummer Hoff*. Illustrated by Ed Emberley. Prentice-Hall, 1967.
Freeman, Don. *Corduroy*. Viking, 1968.
Gág, Wanda. *Millions of Cats*. Coward, McCann & Geoghegan, 1928.
Hoban, Tana. *Dig, Drill, Dump, Fill*. Greenwillow, 1975.
Hutchins, Pat. *Changes, Changes*. Macmillan, 1971.
Keats, Ezra Jack. *Peter's Chair*. Harper & Row, 1967.
Kraus, Robert. *Leo the Late Bloomer*. Illustrated by José Aruego. Dutton, 1973.
McCloskey, Robert. *Blueberries for Sal*. Viking, 1948.
Potter, Beatrix. *The Tale of Peter Rabbit*. Warne, 1902.
Seuss, Dr. *Horton Hatches the Egg*. Random House, 1940.
Slobodkina, Esphyr. *Caps for Sale*. Childrens, 1947.
Tripp, Wallace. *A Great Big Ugly Man Came Up and Tied His Horse to Me*. Little, Brown, 1973.
Zemach, Margot, illustrator. *Hush, Little Baby*. Dutton, 1976.

Bemelmans, Ludwig. *Madeline*. Viking, 1939.

De Paola, Tomie. *Strega Nona*. Prentice-Hall, 1975.

Feelings, Muriel. *Jambo Means Hello: Swahili Alphabet Book*. Illustrated by Tom Feelings. Dial, 1974.

Grimm Brothers. *Hansel and Gretel*. Translated by Charles Scribner, Jr. Illustrated by Adrienne Adams. Scribner's, 1975.

Hall, Donald. *Ox-Cart Man*. Illustrated by Barbara Cooney. Viking, 1979.

Hoban, Russell. *Bread and Jam for Frances*. Illustrated by Lillian Hoban. Harper & Row, 1964.

Hoberman, Mary Ann. *A House Is a House for Me*. Illustrated by Betty Fraser. Viking, 1978.

Hogrogian, Nonny. *One Fine Day*. Macmillan, 1971.

Lionni, Leo. *Swimmy*. Pantheon, 1963.

Lobel, Arnold. *Days With Frog and Toad*. Harper & Row, 1979.

McCloskey, Robert. *Make Way for Ducklings*. Viking, 1941.

Milne, A. A. *When We Were Very Young*. Illustrated by Ernest H. Shepard. Dutton, 1924.

Minarik, Else. *Little Bear*. Illustrated by Maurice Sendak. Harper & Row, 1957.

Ness, Evaline. *Sam, Bangs and Moonshine*. Holt, Rinehart & Winston, 1966.

Rockwell, Anne, reteller and illustrator. *The Old Woman and Her Pig and Ten Other Stories*. Crowell, 1979.

Sendak, Maurice. *Where the Wild Things Are*. Harper & Row, 1963.

Spier, Peter. *Noah's Ark*. Doubleday, 1977.

Steptoe, John. *Stevie*. Harper & Row, 1969.

Zolotow, Charlotte. *William's Doll*. Illustrated by William Pène du Bois. Harper & Row, 1972.

PRIMARY-INTERMEDIATE (P-I)

Aardema, Verna. *Why Mosquitoes Buzz in People's Ears*. Illustrated by Leo and Diane Dillon. Dial, 1975.

Andersen, Hans Christian. *Thumbelina*. Retold by Amy Erhlich. Illustrated by Susan Jeffers. Dial, 1979.

Cleary, Beverly. *Ramona and Her Father*. Illustrated by Alan Tiegreen. Morrow, 1977.

Fisher, Aileen. *Out in the Dark and Daylight*. Illustrated by Gail Owens. Harper & Row, 1980.

Frost, Robert. *Stopping by Woods on a Snowy Evening*. Illustrated by Susan Jeffers. Dutton, 1978.

Goble, Paul. *The Girl Who Loved Wild Horses*. Bradbury, 1978.

Grimm Brothers. *The Sleeping Beauty*. Retold and illustrated by Trina Schart Hyman. Little, Brown, 1977.

_____. *Snow White and the Seven Dwarfs*. Translated by Randall Jarrell. Illustrated by Nancy Ekholm Burkert. Farrar, Straus & Giroux, 1972.

Kuskin, Karla. *Near the Window Tree*. Harper & Row, 1975.

McCord, David. *One at a Time*. Illustrated by Harry B. Kane. Little, Brown, 1977.

Prelutsky, Jack. *Nightmares: Poems to Trouble Your Sleep*. Illustrated by Arnold Lobel. Greenwillow, 1976.

Silverstein, Shel. *Where the Sidewalk Ends*. Harper & Row, 1974.

White, E. B. *Charlotte's Web*. Illustrated by Garth Williams. Harper & Row, 1952.

Wilder, Laura Ingalls. *Little House in the Big Woods*. Illustrated by Garth Williams. Harper & Row, 1953.

Babbitt, Natalie. *Tuck Everlasting*. Farrar, Straus & Giroux, 1975.

Byars, Betsy. *The Pinballs*. Harper & Row, 1977.

Cameron, Eleanor. *Julia and the Hand of God*. Illustrated by Gail Owens. Dutton, 1977.

Grimm Brothers. *The Juniper Tree and Other Tales from Grimm*. Translated by Lore Segal and Randall Jarrell. Illustrated by Maurice Sendak. Farrar, Straus & Giroux, 1973.

Hunter, Mollie. *A Stranger Came Ashore*. Harper & Row, 1975.

L'Engle, Madeleine. *A Wrinkle in Time*. Farrar, Straus & Giroux, 1962.

Lewis, C. S. *The Lion, the Witch, and the Wardrobe*. Illustrated by Pauline Baynes. Macmillan, 1951.

Lindgren, Astrid. *Pippi Longstocking*. Translated by Florence Lamborn. Illustrated by Louis S. Glanzman. Viking, 1950.

Livingston, Myra Cohn. *O Sliver of Liver and Other Poems*. Illustrated by Iris Van Rynbach. Atheneum, 1979.

Merriam, Eve. *It Doesn't Always Have to Rhyme*. Illustrated by Malcolm Spooner. Atheneum, 1964.

Milne, A. A. *Winnie the Pooh*. Illustrated by Ernest H. Shepard. Dutton, 1926.

Norton, Mary. *The Borrowers*. Illustrated by Beth and Joe Krush. Harcourt Brace Jovanovich, 1953.

Paterson, Katherine. *Bridge to Terabithia*. Illustrated by Donna Diamond. Crowell, 1977.

Raskin, Ellen. *The Westing Game*. Dutton, 1978.

Singer, Isaac Bashevis. *Zlateh the Goat and Other Stories*. Illustrated by Maurice Sendak. Harper & Row, 1966.

Steig, William. *Abel's Island*. Farrar, Straus & Giroux, 1976.

INTERMEDIATE-ADVANCED (I-A)

Alexander, Lloyd. *Taran Wanderer*. Holt, Rinehart & Winston, 1967.

Cleaver, Vera and Bill. *Where the Lilies Bloom*. Illustrated by James Spanfeller. Lippincott, 1969.

Collier, James Lincoln, and Christopher Collier. *My Brother Sam Is Dead*. Four Winds-Scholastic, 1974.

Cooper, Susan. *The Dark Is Rising*. Illustrated by Alan Cober. Atheneum, 1973.

Dunning, Stephen, et al, eds. *Reflections on a Gift of Watermelon Pickle . . . and Other Modern Verse*. Lothrop, Lee & Shepard, 1967.

George, Jean. *Julie of the Wolves*. Illustrated by John Schoenherr. Harper & Row, 1972.

Hamilton, Virginia. *M.C. Higgins, the Great*. Macmillan, 1974.

Hunter, Mollie. *The Third Eye*. Harper & Row, 1979.

Le Guin, Ursula. *A Wizard of Earthsea*. Illustrated by Ruth Robbins. Parnassus, 1968.

McCaffrey, Anne. *Dragondrums*. Atheneum, 1979.

McKinley, Robin. *Beauty: A Retelling of the Story of Beauty and the Beast*. Harper & Row, 1978.

O'Brien, Robert. *Z for Zachariah*. Atheneum, 1975.

O'Dell, Scott. *Island of the Blue Dolphins*. Houghton Mifflin, 1960.

Rawls, Wilson. *Where the Red Fern Grows*. Doubleday, 1961.

Reiss, Johanna. *The Upstairs Room*. Crowell, 1972.

Sandburg, Carl. *Early Moon*. Illustrated by James Daugherty. Harcourt Brace Jovanovich, 1930.

Taylor, Mildred. *Roll of Thunder, Hear My Cry*. Illustrated by Jerry Pinkney. Dial, 1976.

Tolkien, J. R. R. *The Hobbit*. Houghton Mifflin, 1938.

Adams, Richard. *Watership Down*. Macmillan, 1972.

Cormier, Robert. *The Chocolate War*. Pantheon, 1974.

Engdahl, Sylvia. *Enchantress from the Stars*. Illustrated by Rodney Shackell. Atheneum, 1970.

Highwater, Jamake. *Anpao: An American Indian Odyssey*. Illustrated by Fritz Scholder. Lippincott, 1977.

Hoover, Helen. *The Delikon*. Viking, 1977.

Myers, Walter Dean. *The Young Landlords*. Viking, 1979.

Patton-Walsh, Jill. *Unleaving*. Farrar, Straus & Giroux, 1976.

Peck, Richard. *Father Figure*. Viking, 1978.

Zindel, Paul. *The Pigman*. Harper & Row, 1968.

The following twenty books are important works for classroom teachers and librarians who want to pursue the study of children's literature:

Butler, Dorothy. *Cushla and Her Books*. Horn Book, Inc., 1980.

Cameron, Eleanor. *The Green and Burning Tree: On the Writing and Enjoyment of Children's Books*. Atlantic-Little, Brown, 1969.

Carlsen, G. Robert. *Books and the Teenage Reader: A Guide for Teachers, Librarians and Parents*. 2nd rev. ed. Harper & Row, 1980.

Chambers, Aidan. *Introducing Books to Children*. Heinemann Educational Books, 1973.

Cianciolo, Patricia. *Picture Books for Children*. American Library Association, 1973.

Cullinan, Bernice E., and Carolyn Carmichael, editors. *Literature and Young Children*. National Council of Teachers of English, 1977.

Donelson, Kenneth, and Aileen Nilsen. *Literature for Today's Young Adults*. Scott, Foresman, 1980.

Egoff, Sheila, G. T. Stubbs, and L. F. Ashley. *Only Connect: Readings in Children's Literature*. 2nd ed. Oxford Univ. Press, 1980.

Glazer, Joan I., and Gurney Williams, III. *Introduction to Children's Literature*. McGraw-Hill, 1979.

Haviland, Virginia, editor. *Children and Literature: Views and Reviews*. Scott, Foresman, 1973.

Hazard, Paul. *Books, Children and Men*. Translated by Marguerite Mitchell. Horn Book, Inc., 1960.

Heins, Paul, editor. *Crosscurrents of Criticism: Hornbook Essays 1968–1977*. Horn Book, Inc., 1977.

Hopkins, Lee Bennett. *The Best of Book Bonanza*. Holt, Rinehart & Winston, 1980.

Huck, Charlotte S. *Children's Literature in the Elementary School*. 3rd ed. rev. Holt, Rinehart & Winston, 1979.

Hunter, Mollie. *Talent Is Not Enough: Mollie Hunter on Writing for Children*. Harper & Row, 1976.

Larrick, Nancy. *A Parent's Guide to Children's Reading*. Doubleday, 1975.

Meek, Margaret, Aidan Warlow, and Griselda Barton. *The Cool Web: The Pattern of Children's Reading*. Atheneum, 1978.

Smith, Lillian. *The Unreluctant Years: A Critical Approach to Children's Literature*. American Library Association, 1953.

Sutherland, Zena, and May Hill Arbuthnot. *Children and Books*. 4th ed. Scott, Foresman, 1976.

Townsend, John Rowe. *Written for Children: An Outline of English Language Children's Literature*. Horn Book, Inc., 1974.

1. John Moffitt, "To Look at Any Thing," *To Look at Any Thing,* ed. Lee Bennett Hopkins, photographs by John Earl (New York: Harcourt Brace Jovanovich, 1978), p. 13.
2. Don Holdaway, *The Foundations of Literacy* (New York: Ashton-Scholastic, 1979), p. 41.
3. Ibid., p. 97.
4. Louise Rosenblatt, *Literature as Exploration,* 3rd ed. (New York: Noble and Noble, 1976), p. 25.
5. Arthur Applebee, *The Child's Concept of Story* (Chicago: Univ. of Chicago Press, 1978), p. 132.
6. James Miller, Jr., "Literature and the Moral Imagination," *Response to Literature,* ed. James R. Squire (Urbana, Ill.: National Council of Teachers of English, 1968), p. 30.
7. David McCord, "I Want You to Meet," in *One at a Time,* illus. Harry B. Kane (Boston: Little, Brown, 1977), p. 141.
8. McCord, "Snowman," in *One at a Time,* p. 140.
9. Robert Kraus, *Leo the Late Bloomer,* illus. José Aruego (New York: Windmill-Dutton, 1971), unpaged.
10. Ibid.
11. Amy Waldhorn, Bank Street School for Children, New York, New York.
12. Katherine Paterson, *Bridge to Terabithia,* illus. Donna Diamond (New York: Crowell, 1977), p. 126.
13. Ibid., p. 120.
14. Ibid., p. 128.
15. Ibid., p. 126.

Professional References

Applebee, Arthur N. *The Child's Concept of Story.* Univ. of Chicago Press, 1978.

————. "The Spectator Role: Theoretical and Developmental Studies of Ideas about and Response to Literature, with Special Reference to Four Age Levels." Diss. University of London 1973. ERIC Document Reproduction Service No. 114 840.

Britton, James. "Composition in Context." Lecture presented at the 1979 Summer Institute, sponsored by the English Education Program in the Department of Communication Arts and Sciences, School of Education, Health, Nursing, and the Arts Professions (SEHNAP), New York University. 24 July 1979.

Galda, S. Lee. "Three Children Reading Stories: A Developmental Approach to Response to Literature In Preadolescents." Diss. New York University 1980.

Holdaway, Don. *The Foundations of Literacy.* Ashton-Scholastic, 1979.

Holland, Norman N. *Five Readers Reading.* Yale Univ. Press, 1975.

Iser, Wolfgang. *The Act of Reading: A Theory of Aesthetic Response.* Johns Hopkins Univ. Press, 1978.

————. *The Implied Reader: Patterns of Communication in Prose Fiction From Bunyan to Beckett.* Johns Hopkins Univ. Press, 1974.

Kohlberg, Lawrence, et al. *Assessing Moral Stages: A Manual.* Harvard University Center for Moral Education, 1976.

Mills, G. *Hamlet's Castle: The Study of Literature as a Social Experience.* Univ. of Texas Press, 1976.

Petrosky, Anthony R. "Genetic Epistemology and Psychoanalytic Ego Psychology: Clinical Support for the Study of Response to Literature." *Research in The Teaching of English.* Vol. 11 (Spring 1977), 28–38.

Purves, Alan C., and Richard Beach. *Literature and the Reader: Research in Response to Literature, Reading Interests, and the Teaching of Literature.* National Council of Teachers of English, 1972.

Purves, Alan C., with Victoria Rippere. *Elements of Writing about a Literary Work: A Study of Response to Literature.* National Council of Teachers of English, 1968.

Richards, Ivor A. *Practical Criticism: A Study of Literary Judgment.* Harcourt Brace Jovanovich, 1956.

Rosenblatt, Louise. *Literature as Exploration*. 3rd ed. Noble and Noble, 1976.

_____. *The Reader, the Text, the Poem*. Southern Illinois Univ. Press, 1978.

Squire, James R., ed. *Response to Literature*. National Council of Teachers of English, 1968.

_____. *The Responses of Adolescents While Reading Four Short Stories*. Research Report No. 2. National Council of Teachers of English, 1964.

Children's Books Cited in Chapter

Brown, Margaret Wise. *Goodnight Moon*. Illus. Clement Hurd. Harper & Row, 1947.

Cameron, Eleanor. *Julia and the Hand of God*. Illus. Gail Owens. Dutton, 1977.

Chambers, Aidan. *Breaktime*. Harper & Row, 1979.

Galdone, Paul, illus. *The Gingerbread Boy*. Seabury, 1975.

Greene, Constance C. *Beat the Turtle Drum*. Illus. Donna Diamond. Viking, 1976.

Haar, Jaap ter. *Boris*. Delacorte, 1970.

Hoban, Tana. *Dig, Drill, Dump, Fill*. Greenwillow, 1975.

Hopkins, Lee Bennett, ed. *To Look at Any Thing*. Photographs by John Earl. Harcourt Brace Jovanovich, 1978.

Hutchins, Pat. *Changes, Changes*. Macmillan, 1973.

Kraus, Robert. *Leo the Late Bloomer*. Illus. José Aruego. Dutton, 1973.

L'Engle, Madeleine. *A Swiftly Tilting Planet*. Farrar, Straus & Giroux, 1978.

Lowry, Lois. *A Summer to Die*. Illus. Jenni Oliver. Houghton Mifflin, 1977.

McCloskey, Robert. *Blueberries for Sal*. Viking, 1948.

_____. *Time of Wonder*. Viking, 1957.

McCord, David. *One at a Time*. Illus. Harry B. Kane. Little, Brown, 1977.

O'Brien, Robert. *Mrs. Frisby and the Rats of NIMH*. Atheneum, 1971.

Paterson, Katherine. *Bridge to Terabithia*. Illus. Donna Diamond. Crowell, 1977.

_____. *The Great Gilly Hopkins*. Crowell, 1978.

Prelutsky, Jack. *The Mean Old Mean Hyena*. Illus. Arnold Lobel. Greenwillow, 1978.

Raskin, Ellen. *The Westing Game*. Dutton, 1978.

Sendak, Maurice. *Where the Wild Things Are*. Harper & Row, 1963.

Smith, Doris Buchanan. *A Taste of Blackberries*. Illus. Charles Robinson. Crowell, 1973.

Sobol, Donald. *Encyclopedia Brown, Boy Detective*. Nelson, 1963.

Sperry, Armstrong. *Call It Courage*. Macmillan, 1940.

Steig, William. *Abel's Island*. Farrar, Straus & Giroux, 1976.

Wells, Rosemary. *Max's First Word*. Dial, 1979.

Zindel, Paul. *The Pigman*. Harper & Row, 1968.

fourteen

CARL SANDBURG   *PRIMER LESSON*

Look out how you use proud words.
When you let proud words go, it is
*   not easy to call them back.*
They wear long boots, hard boots; they
*   walk off proud; they can't hear you*
*   calling—*
Look out how you use proud words.[1]

Issues in the World of Children's Books

Because people care, are concerned about what is good for children, it is clear that what a society values will be reflected in the books it gives its children. Today's books mirror current social values no less than the "teach and preach" books of Colonial days mirrored the Puritan ethic. Controversial issues prevalent in a society will also be manifest in children's books; in respect to current issues, however, since we do not have the perspective conferred by time, we may not see as clearly the relation between them and their representation in children's books. They are there, nonetheless, perhaps more obviously than in the past because of the greater resources of communication of our times. Today, every swing in the mood of the nation will sooner or later show up in some children's books, and in people's reactions to them.

The field of children's literature is growing and changing, and there are many who have a passionate involvement in it. With so much yeast in the brew controversy is inevitable. Students of children's literature need to know about the issues; in this chapter we present some aspects of them. We do not lay claim to any "right" answers nor can we know the situation in every community. Some issues have many defensible positions; these are topics to think about and explore.

THE ISMS

During the past decade, a barrage of criticism concerning a number of "isms" hit the field of children's literature with all the shouting and action and reaction that attend any controversy. It was clear beyond question that children's books contained derogatory and false images of many groups and that topics once forbidden now appear in them. Controversy still rages.

Racism

Beyond a shadow of a doubt, children's books of the distant and recent past either omitted blacks or portrayed them in narrowly stereotyped ways. Authors knew very little about black life styles, aspirations, or culture, though they wrote as if they did. In the rare case that blacks appeared, their status

Sounder, from William Armstrong's book of the same name. Controversy—over whether a white could tell a black's story —erupted when the Newbery Medal was awarded to this retelling of a story told the author by an elderly black man. (Illustration by James Barkley from *Sounder* by William H. Armstrong. Illustrations copyright © 1969 by James Barkley. By permission of Harper & Row, Publishers, Inc.)

was generally menial, their language an exaggerated plantation dialect, and their roles in the stories insignificant.

Sounder (I-A), by William Armstrong, and *The Slave Dancer* (I-A), by Paula Fox (both authors are white) brought smouldering criticism to a head. Both books, which received the Newbery Medal (1970 and 1974, respectively), deal with painful issues in history. *Sounder* is the story of a devastatingly poor black sharecropper family during the Depression. The father is sentenced to serve time on a chain gang for stealing food for his starving family, and, in a central event in the story, the boy sees his father beaten brutally and his dog seriously wounded. The family endures degradation and suffering with tremendous courage and quiet dignity. In spite of the strength of character portrayed, there was strong criticism of the book.

The mere fact that a white author would try to interpret the black experience was unacceptable to many. In addition, the pathetic circumstances of life in the story and the characters' seemingly unresisting acceptance of them angered others. Finally, the fact that the author chose not to give his characters names provoked further criticism. The author explained this last as a deliberate effort to cast his characters in a mythic mode in order to suggest their universality.

Paula Fox's *The Slave Dancer* (discussed in Chapter 9) is set in the pre-Civil War period. Thirteen-year-old Jessie is kidnapped and taken aboard a slave ship to play his fife when the slaves are brought up from the hold for exercise. Conditions aboard the slave ship, described in unrelieved horror, show that all those connected with slavery are corrupted by it. The Council on Interracial Books for Children severely criticized the book; Sharon Bell Mathis, a black writer and librarian, condemned the practice of whites telling the blacks' story, and decried parading sordid aspects of the past before black children today. The book was documented as historically faithful to the period of its setting. Paula Fox responded to the criticism in her Newbery Medal acceptance speech:

There are others who feel that black people can be only humiliated by being reminded that once they were brought to this country as slaves. But it is not the victim who is shamed. It is the persecutor who has refused the shame of what he has done and, as the last turn of the screw, would burden the victims with the ultimate responsibility of the crime itself.[2]

Since these books were published, many competent black writers have written vivid stories from their perspective. At the time of the controversy, Augusta Baker, noted librarian and storyteller (who is black), declared:

Some people have criticized *Sounder* and *The Slave Dancer* particularly for a lack of militancy on the part of the black characters. Courage is shown in many ways and by many different reactions under stress. Will we deny children books about the past, books about the ugliness, the humiliation, the cruelty, and the destruction of human dignity that existed during slavery days and during the days when the Ku Klux Klan rode openly and often? I hope not—for all children, black and white, deserve the truth.[3]

In the same article, she quotes Jeanne Noble's speech at the American Library Association: "We are uncommonly common. This might bring us to that ultimate moment of truth when we all—black and white, rich and poor—might say together, 'I am you, and you are me; what have we done to each other?'"[4]

The social and political consciousness of a time affect the way books are viewed. Some books once widely accepted have been re-evaluated in terms of today's awareness. For example, Helen Bannerman's *Little Black Sambo* (P), published in 1923, was considered a nursery classic until social consciousness caused us to recognize that the images portrayed are outright stereotypes. The book has been taken off library shelves. On the other hand, the controversy that surrounded Garth Williams's *The Rabbit's Wedding* (P)—in which a black and a white rabbit marry—has died among all but the most fanatical, and the book is enjoyed for its celebration of love and joy.

Sexism

Year after year, when asked what they want to be when they grow up, young girls have said: mommy, nurse, teacher, actress; and young boys: astronaut, president, doctor, lawyer. Is there some unwritten script that dictates what each sex aspires to? More reasoned explanations suggest that children select role models from the live, print, and visual images in their environment. Books, part of that environment, play a part in portraying to children what is possible.

The women's movement brought a new consciousness, which caused us to look carefully at the role models contained in children's books. Research of the late 1960s and early 1970s showed consistently that, in books, boys appeared more often as central characters than girls, that boys engaged in more creative, outgoing, daring activities than girls, that boys were portrayed as doing, achieving, excelling, whereas girls were portrayed as standing aside watching, holding their hands behind their backs, or playing house.

The publishing world responded to the criticism quickly: many instituted guidelines to replace sexist language, others sought books with strong female characters, and some produced books in which boys showed emotions not conventionally theirs, or equally unusual behavior such as playing with dolls. Charlotte Zolotow's *William's Doll* (P) is hailed as the first story in which that revolutionary event occurred, though some complain even yet that an apology is implicit in the story's explanation that William is practicing to become a good father by doing so.

Marjorie R. Hendler examined all picture books published by nearly seventy publishers during 1973, 1974, and 1975 for evidence of sexism. Although she predicted that the women's movement had not effectively changed the image of females in the first half of the 1970s, her results showed otherwise. In fact, from 1973 on, the trend was toward equality, with boys and girls portrayed equally in the 1975 books. The only category still underrepresented in children's picture books of the early 1970s was the adult female; women were still seldom shown, and when they did appear, were most often in the role of mother, nurse, or teacher.

Controversy still exists in relation to sexism. Some critics will not consider things equal until women appear in a variety of occupational roles, the stereotyped apron is missing from mothers, and girls appear in leadership roles as often as boys.

Activists in the women's movement know that even though publishers are presently aware of sex-

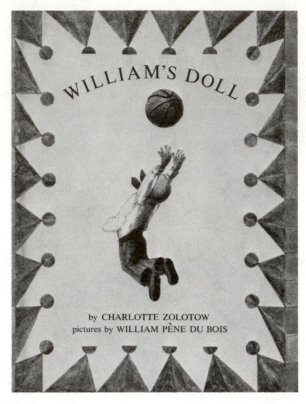

WILLIAM'S DOLL

by CHARLOTTE ZOLOTOW
pictures by WILLIAM PÈNE DU BOIS

Cover of *William's Doll* by Charlotte Zolotow, a landmark by virtue of its depiction of a boy who plays with dolls.
(From *William's Doll* by Charlotte Zolotow, illustrated by William Pène du Bois. Harper & Row, 1972.)

ist language and stereotypes, thousands of books on library shelves are sexist. The new consciousness caused us to look again at books long accepted as part of the standard collection. For example, Carol Ryrie Brink's *Caddie Woodlawn* (I), acclaimed for its literary merit since 1936, suddenly received negative criticism for its portrayal of a tomboy who belatedly but happily accepts the traditional role for women. Modern readers believe that it was totally out of character for Caddie to do so.

Feminists also find fault with Irene Hunt's *Up a Road Slowly* (I-A) because of this advice, "Accept the fact that this is a man's world and learn how to play the game gracefully, my sweet," or the further

statement that "a woman is never completely developed until she has loved a man. . . . You might say that she knows completeness."[5] They object to the passive roles girls are assigned in *I'm Glad I'm a Boy! I'm Glad I'm a Girl!* (P), by Whitney Darrow Jr., and in *A Letter to Amy* (P), by Ezra Jack Keats.

Realism

The world of children's books is filled with contradictions that derive, perhaps, from the fact that publishers are reluctant to do anything that will hamper the sale of books. In order to survive, they must serve the public by publishing what sells, sometimes following a sensationalist trend, nowhere more evident than in contemporary realism, where quality often becomes the sacrificial lamb.

The endless stream of realistic titles covers the gamut of human experience, so that topics heretofore considered outside the realm of children's reading are now commonplace. Since literature reflects life, and life is lived so openly in our times, it is a natural setting for discussions of such topics of concern as drugs, divorce, the many facets of sexuality, and mental illness.

The problem arises when books are written on such socially relevant themes mainly as a means of capitalizing on a trend. Certainly little fault can be found with books on realistic themes that are not unrelievedly grim and that promote an awareness of the richness of life's possibilities or that help children test and question currently held values. Unrelieved melancholy, disaster, and sordidness can be just as unrealistic as unceasing sweetness and light.

Few people who know children and books would want to return to the antiseptic stories found in basal readers, which Diana Goldsborough describes so aptly:

Dick and Jane's world must be one of perfect harmony, without any of the threats from without, or splits from within, that menaced the Victorian fictional child. Home is an antiseptic sunny suburbia, their dog never befouls the footpath, they never see a poverty pocket, or a car crash, or a rumble, and . . . mother is . . . saintly. . . .[6]

Charlotte Zolotow, a courageous author and editor, broke traditional role stereotypes when, in *William's Doll,* she portrayed a boy who had and cherished a doll.

William's grandmother smiled. "He needs it," she said, "to hug and to cradle and to take to the park so that when he's a father like you, he'll know how to take care of his baby and feed him and love him and bring him the things he wants, like a doll, so that he can practice being a father" (Charlotte Zolotow, *William's Doll,* illus. William Pène du Bois [New York: Harper & Row, 1972], unpaged).

An innovative author of more than sixty books and an editor of hundreds more, Charlotte Zolotow knows how to remind children of the beauty and love in simple things. Just as William's doll helps him learn how to be a loving father, Charlotte Zolotow's sensitive portrayals invite children to explore their immediate world and look again at the people in it. She says:

A good picture book must be unpretentious and direct. There should be some universal truth or feeling in it, and what Margaret Wise Brown called the "unexpected inevitable." I love children's books because they are part of the freshness and originality of children, qualities that open to infinite variety in theme and treatment. My children and their friends often remind me of feelings from my childhood which become the theme of a book. It is a kind of double exposure—the adult awareness of a phenomenon and the memory of what it seemed as a child (*Harper & Row promotional material*).

CHARLOTTE ZOLOTOW

What Charlotte Zolotow demands as an editor she fulfills as an author. In *The Storm Book, The Summer Night,* and *When the Wind Stops,* she contrasts the frightening external world with the security and comfort found in the relationship between a child and an adult. She paints a panorama of human emotions with the language of childhood and fills her stories with lightheartedness and charm.

Zolotow encourages the careers of young writers and artists and can count many distinguished names among her list of discoveries as an editor. A native of Norfolk, Virginia, she lives in New York City and is a Vice President of Harper & Row, Publishers, Inc.

Most people would opt for straightforward consideration of themes that are important to maturing young adults. Realistic books may have outgrown the they-lived-happily-ever-after endings that present life as a series of joyful occasions, but the cynicism, disenchantment, and harsh realities of the daily newspapers do not always constitute the better—or more realistic—direction.

Children see the evening news and read the daily headlines. If they are to know the stark facts, should they not also see them portrayed sensitively in their literature? Do we do children a disservice in only reporting the number of overdose cases without conveying an understanding of the heart-ache that surrounds each one? News accounts can not do what literature can—portray the human dimension. Literature may paint a realistically bleak canvas, true to some lives, but it does so with a sense of the suffering that touches common chords of feeling. Further, to catalogue contemporary realism exclusively by content is to do injustice to the truly creative authors sensitive to today's children and their needs. The issue is not so much a matter of *what* is portrayed as *how* it is. There *are* books of quality from which to choose: many flowers among the weeds.

The issue of how much and what kind of realism is surely a problematic one. In pondering this issue, it is important to keep in mind that books help children try on roles and answer the question: Where do I fit in?

Accusations and Answers

While the children's book world was being soundly criticized for racism, it became evident that it was guilty of sexism as well. Some parents of handicapped children then declared that disabled children and adults were either omitted or stereotyped in children's books. Defenders of senior citizens quickly pointed out that the aging person is shown in inferior and negative ways, and the word "ageism" was coined. In the heat of the battle, the Council on Interracial Books for Children (CIBC) issued a statement called *Human (and Anti-Human) Values in Children's Books,* in which they declared:

> . . . examination of thousands of children's books [shows that] . . . the value-system that dominates in them is very white, very contemptuous of females except in traditional roles, and very oriented to the needs of the upper classes. It is very geared to individual achievement rather than community well-being. It is a value-system that can serve only to keep people of color, poor people, women and other dominated groups "in their place," because directly or indirectly it makes children—our future adults—think that this is the way things should be. So powerful is that system that authors can write *totally unaware* of its influence upon them. More often than not, they are unconscious tools of that system.[7]

As a means of calling attention to destructive, culturally conditioned behavior, council members analyzed and rated over 250 books on the basis of a checklist for sexist, racist, materialist, individualist, ageist, conformist, and escapist references, in addition to literary and artistic quality. They proposed guidelines for writing, publishing, and evaluating children's books, with some group to determine the values to be promoted.

Lillian Gerhardt, editor of *School Library Journal,* opposed the position taken by CIBC, saying that such an approach, whether from the Left or the Right, constituted censorship. In order to show the folly of CIBC's checklist, as a means of evaluating children's books, Lillian Gerhardt applied it to Beatrix Potter's *The Tale of Peter Rabbit:*

> Peter is shown as actively naughty and his sisters as placidly obedient. (On CIBC's checklist, tick off "sexist.") Mr. McGregor is old, crotchety, and violent (tick off "ageist"). The picture and story show a fussy concern over clothes and food (tick off "materialist"). Peter's disobedience gets him a dose of medicine and his good sisters a lovely supper (tick off "conformism"). Consider the fact that Mr. McGregor fails to catch Peter and Peter is thus allowed to evade the reality of being eaten (tick off "escapist"). Refuse to consider any of Potter's well-documented intentions in writing and illustrating the story. What did she know? She might have included a positive note about race and she didn't (tick off "racist by omission").[8]

Though avoidance of stereotypes is certainly important, there are other elements that bear upon the use of books with diverse cultural groups. One of these—the attitude of the teacher or librarian—is of primary importance, for through lack of awareness of our own prejudice, we can make children uncomfortably self-conscious and can contribute to poor self-concepts.

Augusta Baker has described her discovery of her own unwitting prejudice: When invited to tell a story to a group of American Indian children, she protested that she did not know any "Indian" stories. Urged simply to tell a story, she again protested, saying that the only story she had at her fingertips was a Carribean folktale about a crab and that she was certain the children would not understand a story about an animal they had never seen.

On further urging she told the children the story about the crab. And, she reported, "Of course they understood the story—and I became aware of my own biases in the process."

Augusta Baker also quotes Ann Nolan Clark's statement (in *Journey to the People*) to the effect that children are children and, being so, are interested in all manner of stories. With personal experience she underscores the point that black children need more than books about black characters and American Indian children need books in addition to those about American Indians. While she defends the right of every child to see others like himself in books, she would not single out a child of any group by pointing him toward a book simply because it had in it a character with his ethnic and social background. To do so would be to draw subtle attention to the fact of the similarity, and with it the fact of the child's *dis*similarity from the others in his group—something that would make children uncomfortable at best. In actual practice in the classroom, and with the best intentions, we might show a child the picture of his counterpart just a little longer or speak more directly to him and, in the process, make him hate the book, for the child must then visibly reject it to establish his much desired membership in his classroom peer group.

WHO DECIDES WHAT CHILDREN READ

Before a child gets to make a choice to read or not to read a book, several adults—gatekeepers between the books and the child—must make decisions about whether it will come into being and what it will contain if it does.

The Author

An author makes the first decision; books start in people's minds. In *Books: From Writer to Reader* (I), Howard Greenfeld states:

. . . authors usually begin with a character or set of characters. Very often the writer will have no plot when he begins to write—merely a set of characters who espe-

cially interest him or her, and by placing these diverse characters in certain situations, a plot may evolve.[9]

Before or during the writing process, authors must answer several questions for themselves: What kind of book will it be? Who is its audience? What is its theme? What research needs to be done? After all of these have been answered, and the author has spent many hours or years writing, there is a manuscript to submit for publication.

Getting a book into final form also takes hard work. Judy Blume, popular writer for the nine-to-eleven-year-olds, says she rewrites a book five, six, or seven times. Richard Peck, a favorite of adolescent readers, says he rewrites each book at least six times, with specific tasks in mind for each rewrite. S. E. Hinton rewrote *Rumble Fish* (A) several times and then finally decided it needed to be told from a different character's point of view; therefore, she began all over to tell the story as this character would have seen it.

The Agent

A literary agent is usually the next person to make decisions. These are concerned with whether the manuscript is saleable, which publisher would be most likely to be interested in it, whether changes are needed before it is submitted, and which editor will be interested in it. When these decisions are made, the agent submits the manuscript to one editor at one publishing house, for multiple submission (submitting the same manuscript to more than one publisher at a time) is not accepted practice in the publishing world. When an editor receives the manuscript, the decision process continues.

The Publisher

Finding a publisher to accept a manuscript is not an easy task. Some noted authors received many rejection slips before their work was accepted. Madeleine L'Engle says that *Meet the Austins* (I) was turned down by several publishers because the story opens with a death and, at that time, death was not discussed in children's books. Scott O'Dell's *Island of the Blue Dolphins* (I-A) was re-

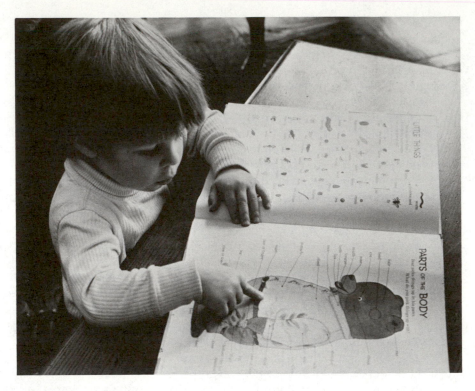

Children can spend many happy hours exploring the endless detail of a book that critics might fault for its absence of story. (Photograph by Suzanne Szasz.)

jected several times because editors thought Karana, the central female character, should be male since she was a strong character and, hence, not believable as a female at that time.

Before a manuscript is accepted, questions about the economic feasibility of publishing the book need to be answered: How many people will be interested in this book? What will it cost to publish? What must its price be to cover that cost? How many copies should be printed for sale in the first year? How many copies can be expected to sell beyond that? Are color illustrations—mainly a part of the cost question—required?

The Editor

The next gatekeeper in the decision process is an editor. Editors stay abreast of literary and educational developments and often seek an author to write a book for which they see a need. Regardless of origin—author-initiated or editor-initiated—the manuscript goes through an editing process.

Editors serve as professional critics for a writer; they are the first persons to look at the work objectively and to note its strengths and weaknesses. They work closely with the author, suggesting improvements in the manuscript.

Many books die at this point if an author does not persevere—or if a conflict between an editor's convictions and an author's cannot be resolved. If all these problems are solved, the book may see the light of day, but whether a child gets a chance to read it still depends upon a further complicated network of gatekeepers.

The Promotion Staff

In each publishing house, a promotion staff is responsible for bringing a new book to the public's attention. The promotion staff announces a new book with a press release—a brief statement about the book—sent to reviewers (with a review copy) and to the publishing industry's weekly magazine, *Publisher's Weekly*. Galley proofs (first stage in which text is set in type) are sometimes sent to reviewers so that the reviews can appear at the time of publication of the book.

The Reviewer

Reviewers can play a pivotal gate-keeping role in determining whether a book gets to library or bookstore shelves. Because librarians and others who purchase them cannot possibly read all of the 2,000 books, on the average, published for children each year, they often depend upon the recommendations of reviewers. Some large school and library systems have their own review panels, but most librarians depend upon the reviews in *School Library Journal, Kirkus Reviews, ALA Booklist, Horn Book Magazine,* and the *Bulletin of the Center for Children's Books.*

Reviewers must decide their major responsibility—whether it is to the author, librarian, publisher, or the children for whom the books are written. Many tend to make their decisions with a number of these interested groups in mind. Many valuable reviewers, however, base their judgments primarily upon the literary quality of a book. From this viewpoint, a book's appeal to children—its popularity—is not relevant to a judgment of its literary merit. Others review books in terms of their appeal to and useability with children. Both types of reviews are necessary in order to maintain high standards in the field and to help buyers make wise selections.

The librarian and teacher who read reviews must also ask some questions: What are the reviewer's qualifications? Does he or she work with children, know their needs and tastes, have frequent contact with them, and follow their reading patterns? Reviewers for *School Library Journal,* for example, are practicing librarians and teachers who know children firsthand. This does not guarantee unbiased and quality reviewing, of course, but it gives the review reader confidence that the judgments are based upon an understanding of children's interests and needs. These reviewers often focus on the usefulness of a book.

The most unhelpful review says something along the lines of: "This is a book about a boy and his dog who gets into trouble." A brief plot synopsis is usually available on the book jacket, and such a review suggests that the reviewer has read the synopsis but not the book. You learn not to trust such reviewers. One author complained that most of the reviews he reads of his books are merely restatements of the jacket copy, and, since he often writes these himself, he is, in effect, writing his own reviews. He and other serious authors welcome worthwhile criticism and feel they profit from thoughtful analyses of their work.

The most useful reviews consider both the literary merit and the audience of the book. Further, they discuss the book in relation to others of its genre, point out what is unique, suggest possible uses, and recommend age and types of children to whom the book might appeal.

An issue in reviewing children's books is the advisability of including warnings that a book contains subject matter or vocabulary that may be offensive to some. One group maintains that value judgments and personal sensitivities have no place in objective reviewing. Others believe that reviewers are obligated to point out explicit language and incidents so that the purchaser can decide if the book will be acceptable in the community.

The Last Gate: Selecting the Book

Librarians usually have the primary responsibility for selecting books for the school library. Teachers, too, read reviews and suggest books that enrich the curriculum for their students. Many fine publications, which inform their judgment, are described in Book Selection Aids in the Appendix.

It is important to recognize that reviewers may disagree about a book. For this reason and others, you cannot depend solely upon another's judgment; you know your students and your community best and you must make the ultimate choice. You also know your students' enthusiasm for a particular author or topic and may choose to rely more upon these factors than upon a published review for selection purposes.

A typical process in deciding whether to buy a book might take the following course. You have a chance to buy William Steig's *Tiffky Doofky* (P).

Tiffky Doofky dreams of the fulfillment of a wish. Reviewers of this unconventional book differed markedly in their views of it. (Illustration reproduced by permission of Farrar, Straus & Giroux, Inc., from *Tiffky Doofky* by William Steig. Copyright © 1978 William Steig.)

You know that your students adore his *Sylvester and the Magic Pebble* (P) and *Amos and Boris* (P). You also know that Steig has earned a reputation as a distinguished storyteller and is a Caldecott medalist. Several reviews of *Tiffky Doofky* have appeared, and you read the following three:

Steig, William. *Tiffky Doofky;* written and illus. by William Steig. Farrar, 1978. 78–19657. 28 p. $7.95.

Tiffky Doofky, a canine garbage collector, goes to a fortune teller and is informed that he will, that very day, meet the one he will love and marry. An old hen shoots a "magic arrow" and tells him to follow its path to find his true love. His first sight of a graceful figure is followed by disappointment: it's a scarecrow. After other misadventures, he ends a nap to find himself in the coils of a boa constrictor, but it proves to be a pet snake, and its owner appears in the sunset light. A charming French poodle! Instant love, reciprocal variety. Steig's pictures have their usual raffish ebullience, but the story is—despite the al-

lure of comic mishaps—perhaps less likely, as a love story, to appeal to the read aloud audience than earlier Steig books. (The book is rated: Additional book of acceptable quality for collections needing more material in the area. It is called appropriate for K-2).[10]

Steig, William. *Tiffky Doofky* color illus. by author. unpaged. Farrar. Nov. 1978. CSm $7.95. ISBN 0-374-37542-9, LC 78-19657.

Gr. 2 Up—*Tiffky Doofky* is a garbage dog whose life, one fine day, takes on added brilliance when, on a whim, he visits Madame Tarsal, a duck of a fortune teller. "Before the sun goes down," she quacks, "you will fall in love . . ." and "nothing . . . can keep it from happening." As if to prove the point, Tiffky finds an emerald necklace in the middle of some dumped sauerkraut. Fastening it around his neck, he goes off in his truck to the Oil & Vinegar Club picnic—eyes peeled for the lucky lady. But wait! A malevolent biddy sends him on a wild goose (hen?) chase and gets him thoroughly lost. A mandolin playing cat, from whom he asks directions, sends him over a cliff into a cow pasture, whereupon a lunatic with a butterfly net shows him back to his truck. Depressed by the gloomy end of such a promising day, Tiffky dreams by the side of the road of the caresses of his true love—almost erotic, but not quite. Suddenly the dream embrace changes into a crushing real one. A boa constrictor has wound itself around him. Tiffky is sure his end has come. But wait! The boa constrictor is owned by a gorgeous poodle, a snake trainer named Estrella. "That's my necklace you're wearing" says she, as she calls off her snake, and then love blooms when Estrella tells Tiffky her father was a garbage dog too. The warm afterglow of that strange and glorious day bathes them both. You know what the pictures are like: Steig's personified charmers. But the deep, gentle humanity that audiences have learned to expect from his exemplary animal tales is missing here. It is the text that is at fault. Causes snatched from nowhere have effects snatched from someplace else; what might have been silly and funny turns out to be silly and unfunny.[11]

William Steig, Author-Illustrator. *Tiffky Doofky*. 32 pp. 8½" X 12" Farrar, 1978 ISBN 0-374-37542-9 $7.95

Garbage collector for the town of Popville, Tiffky Doofky, an affable pooch blessed with pride in his calling and an optimistic outlook, decides one fine spring day to have his fortune told, for he senses that "something out of the ordinary was bound to happen, and he had to know what it was going to be." His premonition is reinforced by the local fortune-telling duck, who quacks out the prediction that he will meet his true love before sunset. At the dump, however, his penchant for sorting treasures from trash leads to his finding an emerald necklace lying on a bed of sauerkraut—a necklace that leads him to fall under the spell of a malevolent witch. After a series of adventures in an unfamiliar land, he notes that the sun has nearly set without his having located the promised love. His rescue from a final trial and the beginnings of his romance conclude a droll tale which parodies the structure of a sentimental novel—including a last view of the canine couple in the afterglow of the setting sun. The descriptive, witty text is finely honed to complement the extraordinarily articulate line with which the characters are limned. The illustrations further extend the parody in the contrast between the beauty of the watercolors and the absurdity of the concept. The picture storybook will probably be most appreciated by an audience slightly older than that which enjoys *Sylvester and the Magic Pebble* (Windmill/Dutton) or *Amos and Boris* (Farrar).[12]

After you have read the book, critically evaluate the reviews. (This may mean returning to a review here and there.)

As you read the reviews, you may sometimes feel that their authors were not discussing the same book. You consider whether they focus more on the text or illustrations, or the way they work together. And you look for bias. The decision is now yours; you are the final gatekeeper between the child and the book.

Books can be ordered on approval, which means that you can return those you find unsuitable. Where you feel indecisive about a book it is sometimes useful to have some children read it and to get their reactions to it. If you feel uncomfortable about the language or story, ask other teachers to read it, and discuss it with them. Controversy and book discussions are healthful and stimulating.

THE ROLES OF AWARDS AND CRITICISM

Children are not born with good taste in respect to the books they choose to read. Children may read widely and yet never read an important book. A statement made nearly forty years ago still holds much truth:

Children read comparatively few books. It has been pointed out that if one estimates one book a fortnight from seven to fourteen years . . . the number read during the period is 416. These four hundred books often influence a child far more powerfully than parents realize, and the attitudes and conduct of the authors' heroes may be temporarily adopted by the reader. A steady diet of second-rate reading can be as deleterious to the mind as poor food to the body. There is more than one form of malnutrition.[13]

Dorothy White and many others argue that we should make certain that many excellent books are among the four hundred children read during childhood. Others are vehement that children should be left to their own devices in choosing books they read. They believe that *what* children read is not as important as *that* they do read. Indeed they defend the child's right to read "rubbish."

Peter Dickinson defends children's right to read rubbish, which he defines as "all forms of

520

reading matter which contain to the adult eye no visible value, either aesthetic or educational.''[14] He cites the importance to children of discovering on their own the art of comparing and making critical judgments about books, for how can you know what is good if you haven't tasted the bad? Or, conversely, how can you know what is bad if you haven't tasted the good?

Part of the controversy about selecting books lies in the differences between children's choices and critics choices. Children's book awards, conferred by adults, have ''literary quality'' as their basis; book awards by children reflect popularity. And popularity and literary quality are not synonymous.

The most prestigious awards for children's books are the annual Newbery Medal and the Caldecott Medal—given for books selected by a nationally recognized panel of children's literature experts under the auspices of the American Library Association.[15] The Newbery Medal, established in 1922 and given for the most distinguished contribution to literature for children in America, honors John Newbery, the eighteenth-century English bookseller who was the first to publish books for children. The Caldecott Medal, established in 1938, honors Randolph Caldecott, a nineteenth-century illustrator of children's books, and is presented to the illustrator of the most distinguished picture book for children in America.

The Newbery and Caldecott awards reflect the best that an informed group of professionals finds in the books published each year. The awards draw national attention to children's books and encourage serious criticism of them.

In the past, one could rightfully say that children seldom read the award-winning books, particularly the Newbery Award winners. There are changes, however, and reports show that more children are choosing to read many of these books. Is it that children's tastes are improving? Have literary critics become more sensitive to children's tastes? Are authors improving, not only in the craft of writing for children, but in their understanding of what children like? Are editors and publishers more in tune with what children want, as well as

with standards of excellence, so that they demand a combination of quality and appeal? Perhaps all of these things are true to some extent. Wherever the truth lies, children and those of us who work with them and their books are the winners.

DEALING WITH REWRITTEN CLASSICS

From time to time a child will bring a book to class and ask that you read it. As you skim it you will realize that it is not the book you know: the language choppy, written down, supposedly to make it comprehensible to younger children. Here is an example from such a version of Hansel and Gretel:

Every morning the old witch hobbled out to the cage and stuck her hand inside. ''Boy'' she cried, ''let me feel your arm. I want to know if you are fat enough to eat yet.'' But Hansel knew that the witch did not see very well. So he held out a stick for her to feel. The witch thought the stick was Hansel's arm. ''Why, you're not any fatter than you were yesterday,'' she cried. ''I want a little meat on those bones before I eat you.[16]

The language in the versions edited by Andrew Lang or of the more direct translations of the Brothers Grimm (such as the one illustrated by Adrienne Adams) flows from the tongue, while these short, stodgy, declarative sentences simply plod.

Sometimes classics are rewritten in verse, again, supposedly to appeal to younger children; most often the sing-song doggerel induces boredom. Here is a specimen of such verse; again the story is Hansel and Gretel:

So, every day she gave a pinch
To see if Hansel grew an inch.
But Hansel fooled the blind old crone
And held out an old chicken bone.
She said, ''How little you must weigh,
We'll fatten you just one more day.''[17]

Especially with folklore, a tale is all in the telling, the language part of the enchantment. Watered-down versions deny the child the good, hearty meat of the original stories and should be avoided. In folklore, reasonably faithful versions will usually carry the name of the translator or reteller on the title page.

The rewriting of children's classics is rampant. Rumer Godden gave a clever account of such activity in "An Imaginary Correspondence"—an exchange between the ghost of Miss Beatrix Potter and "Mr. V. Andal, editor of the DeBase Publishing Company." The exchange begins with a letter from Mr. V. Andal to Miss Potter announcing that he is developing a series for beginning readers called "Masterpieces for Mini-Minds." The masterpieces were to be produced whole and entire but there were to be certain modifications in the texts. In order to show her what he meant, he included a copy of Hans Christian Andersen's "Ti-ny Thum-my," originally issued as "Thumbelina." When Miss Potter asks for clarification, Mr. V. Andal explains that modern philologists will replace her old fashioned words with simpler ones that a modern child can understand, as in these examples from her classic *The Tale of Peter Rabbit:*

"Mother" must read "Momma" throughout.

p. 45. ". . . some friendly sparrows . . . flew to him in great excitement, and implored him to exert himself." Not all children will be able to identify sparrows; suggest the more general "bird-ies"; last five words especially difficult; suggest "to try again" or "try harder."

p. 52. "Kertyschoo" for sneezing. Unfamiliar. "Tishoo" is more usual.

p. 58. "Lippity lippity." Not in the dictionary.

p. 69. "Scr-r-ritch." Might confuse. Onomatopoeia, though allowable, should not distort a word.

Same page. "Scuttered." Unfamiliar again. Suggest "ran away and hid," which has the advantage that three out of the four words have only three letters.

p. 80. "Camomile tea." Not in use now. Suggest "tranquilizer" or "sedative."

. . .

Illustrations are also to be modernized:

We now have a report from our art panel, and though these illustrations have charm we believe fresh ones should be used. The rabbits' furniture and clothing are out of date; i.e., the red cloaks used by Flopsy, Mopsy and Cottontail; the length of Mrs. Rabbit's skirts; the suspended pan and open cooking fire on p. 81. We therefore propose to commission a young Mexican artist who specializes in vivid outline drawing. (Less expensive to reproduce.)[18]

The imaginary correspondence continues, with the bastardization becoming more flagrant and Miss Potter disagreeing more violently. Finally Mr. V. Andal tells her that, in his expert opinion, parents, teachers, and children will neither buy, nor understand, nor like *Peter Rabbit* in its present form. Miss Potter's ghost replies: "Seven million have. I rest in peace."

Comic books offer similar travesties of literature. A great Greek myth, for example, is adapted into comic strip format with dialogue in balloons and characters who look like Wonder Woman and Spiderman. Since the plots of the Greek myths are not copyrighted and, in fact, flow through much literature, there is little to be done except ignore these versions of them and guide children to the real thing. Children can judge the difference when they have both an authentic version and an imitation before them.

SELECTION AND CENSORSHIP

During the past decade the number of censorship disputes concerning books has increased dramatically, with reports abounding of textbooks "on trial" or books withdrawn from school library shelves. Major complaints center around a movement in the schools called "secular humanism" or "scientific humanism," which many believe will destroy belief in God, undermine parental authority, and call into question (and thus erode) moral and ethical values.

Thoughtful examination of the process that gives rise to censorship cases ultimately involves the book selection process. Someone must select a book before another censors it, but when we try to separate the two steps we find the distinction between selection and censorship to be a fine one: what may seem to one a selection decision is to another censorship; censorship is a relative matter. As Robert F. Hogan, Executive Secretary of the National Council of Teachers of English, put it:

Children in a sculpture park in Oslo, Norway, display their curiosity about the body.
(Photograph by Fredrik D. Bodin / STOCK, Boston, Mass.)

When I look at my choices, I concentrate on the ones I mean to include in the library; when I look at the other person's stack, I focus on the books he or she wants to keep out of the library. I select; they censor. Our criteria blend: the books I reject are ones I don't think the children are ready for; the ones they censor are books they don't think their children are ready for.[19]

In the final analysis, says Hogan

The uncomfortable truth is that we are all censors. The difference is that when . . . teachers practice censorship, we call it "book selection."[20]

Perhaps, though, some distinctions can be made: selection is usually a personal, individual act based, at least in part, on literary (writing) quality as often as it is on some relativistic moral judgment. Censorship, on the other hand, is more often a group action and, in children's books, one that is frequently based on a fear of corruption of the reader. Most often at issue is whether given language or descriptions are "obscene." For example, most of the objections to J. D. Salinger's *Catcher in the Rye* (A), the subject of more censorship cases and litigation than any other book, are based on the language and behavior of Holden Caulfield, the principal character. *Go Ask Alice* (A), written anonymously and subsequently attributed to Beatrice Sparks, runs a close second with its explicit sex descriptions and language, as well as its focus on drugs.

Although only certain persons have the *power* to suppress, remove, stop circulation, or limit availability that is censorship, many would-be censors, bringing pressure to bear on those who have this power, multiply their own impact exponentially. Censorship—if one defines it broadly enough to include selection—emanates generally from three main groups. One group includes school personnel—teachers, administrators, librarians—who, when they decide not to put a particular book on the shelf or to remove one from circulation, act in their role of people professionally responsible for making decisions in the best interests of children. An example of this would be the decision by one librarian, after reading Willo Davis Roberts's *Don't Hurt Laurie* (I-A) and reviews of the book, that it was not suitable for her elementary school collection because of its vivid description of child abuse. Another example is the case of Barbara Cooney's illustrations for Delmore Schwartz's poem "I Am Cherry Alive," the *Little Girl Sang*. (P-I), in which frontal nudity of a little girl is shown. Some teachers and librarians who liked the poetry and the magnificent illustrations said they would not be able to use the book because of parents' objections and because, with groups of children, the nude pictures would elicit self-conscious giggling, which would detract from the very beautiful message of the book.

A second group includes parents, school board

members, or other members of the community. Members of this group might lodge an objection to a book with a school board member or a teacher, librarian, or principal. An example is the parent who objected to her fifth-grade daughter reading Norma Klein's *Mom, the Wolf Man and Me* (I-A) because "The mother in that book is living in sin." This mother, although she is exerting her parental rights, differs from the parent who wants the book removed from the library shelves in that the latter, in effect, is attempting to deny access to the book to all children who use the library in question. Individual parental objections to books for their own children can hardly be construed as censorship.

A third source of group pressure for censorship is the formal or informal body that sees its role as watchdog of children's reading. The group may be a local one of concerned parents or a nationally organized network with newsletters and pamphlets devoted to the dissemination and promotion of their ideals. William Golding's *Lord of the Flies* (A) was banned by one such group as a "socialistic" statement.

What is viewed with disfavor tends to vary with the mood of the nation. A conservative swing may produce a back-to-basics movement and a yearning for reading materials that enhance so-called American values. In such times a child protagonist who outwits or is more clever than adults may provoke disapproval, and books that do not depict worthy adult models or that take a negative posture regarding fictional parents will be seen as denigrating the family and, thereby, striking at the fiber of society.

Other back-to-basics proponents object to stories with ungrammatical dialogue, and standard English is favored over dialect. Even those who recognize the validity of nonstandard dialects as an oral form object to its use in print, since this confers legitimacy on it.

According to James E. Davis, most censorship cases have one or more of the following objections as their basis: that the book in question ridicules faith, calls biblical stories fables or myths, uses obscene language, implies moral relativism, invades privacy, treats God as human, tends to subvert family relationships, treats of sex, is anti-American, uses nonstandard English, is disrespectful of authority, shows cruelty or violence, has an unhappy or pervasive sadness, is overconcerned with minority, racial, and ethnic groups.[21]

The lines between selection and censorship blur as librarians make decisions about controversial books. Barbara Cooney's sensual illustrations for Delmore Schwartz's poem "I Am Cherry Alive" sometimes had the effect of limiting its use. (Illustration by Barbara Cooney from *"I Am Cherry Alive," the Little Girl Sang.* by Delmore Schwartz. Illustrations copyright © 1979 by Barbara Cooney. By permission of Harper & Row, Publishers, Inc.)

Dealing with Attempts at Censorship

Being prepared to deal with attempts at censorship requires first, of course, that you know the books you recommend to children. It is impossible to defend a book you are unfamiliar with; thus, if someone complains about—or recommends—a book you haven't read, the first step is to read it and to decide for yourself why you want (or don't want) it in your classroom. Discuss the book with your colleagues at school and in your professional organizations. Concomitantly, books should be selected from reliable sources. If you are not so fortunate as to have a school librarian who stays abreast of new books, reads numerous reviews, and guides the selection process, you need to read many reviews, go to review centers to examine the books, and turn to lists, such as the following, recommended by informed subject-area specialists: "Outstanding Science Trade Books," "Notable Children's Trade Books in the Field of Social Studies," and "Children's Choices"—cosponsored by professional organizations and the Children's Book Council.

You should have a clearly defined, systematic procedure for dealing with complaints. This may include an impartial but informed review panel of professional staff and parents (who read books being challenged and make a judgment) as well as a prepared review form such as the one below,[22] which was developed by a committee of the National Council of Teachers of English.

Citizen's Request for Reconsideration of a Work

Hardcover_____

Author_____

Paperback_____

Title_____

Publisher (if known)_____

Request initiated by_____

Telephone_____ Address_____

City_____ Zip Code_____

Complainant represents

_____himself

_____(name of organization)_____

_____(identify other group)_____

To what in the work do you object? Please be specific;

cite pages_____

In the event, then, that use of a book is challenged, read the book and professional reviews of it. Decide if it is worth defending. Discuss the issue with informed professionals, including advisers in your professional organizations.

Should a simple explanation not satisfy the challenger of the book, then the form described above should be filled out and the review procedure by the panel instituted.

Finally, decisions about which books to defend (and select) should be made on the basis of literary quality and redeeming social value. Some books appear to be written to shock and to show that yet another taboo is being broken. These seldom hold the interest of the reader after the initial surprise. As John Rowe Townsend says, "you can't turn a bad novel into a good one by filling it with pregnancy, pot, and the pill."[23]

The question of "suitability" of a book (particularly with respect to the age of a child) is one central to many issues of censorship. Through education, we attempt to improve the quality of choices children make about what they read. By making choices, children gradually develop taste and standards concerning what they read; standards and taste cannot be imposed. But the right to make these choices—in effect, the right to read—is beset with controversy. One confusion central to the controversy is the belief that approval of a book, as a literary work, is tantamount to approval of the behavior of characters in the book—something even the author is not likely to do. On the other hand, a judgment that a book is unsuitable for a particular age group can be taken to be censorship—even where those who make the judgment might staunchly defend older readers' right to read it. An example of such a book is Judy Blume's *Forever* (A), which deals with premarital sex and, for that reason, is considered by many to be inappropriate for elementary-school children. With regard to the latter issue, one may ask: At what point *is* a child old enough to read about sex, drugs, rape, and any number of similar matters that many believe beyond the realm of childhood. The issue may be not so much chronological age as emotional age. More important is the fact that it is doubtful that a child will be permanently scarred by first encountering four-letter words or a violent incident in a book and that such books probably carry very little meaning for a reader who is too young. Years of observation show that children skip parts in books they do not understand or that do not fit their view of the world. For example, when reading Judy Blume's *Deenie* (I-A), which includes a brief incident of masturbation, children too young to comprehend it skipped over it and went on to a much more important question about Deenie's choices in her life.

Librarians in libraries that serve a wide age range refuse, for good reason, to separate books by age levels: children read far beyond their supposed reading level when they find a topic of great interest. Some elementary-school librarians keep a special shelf of books for mature readers, recognizing that some books will be appreciated more if children wait to read them.

There are always parents who do not want their children to read books of certain content, and others who request that any and all books be made available to their children. You must know the general mood of your community, talk with parents to learn their feelings, and base your decisions on both your professional knowledge and your understanding of the community.

The Council of the American Library Association, mindful of the many selection/censorship issues, has drawn up a "Library Bill of Rights," which sets out the following policy that it feels "should govern the services of all libraries":

I. As a responsibility of library service, books and other library materials should be chosen for values of interest, information and enlightenment of all people of the community. In no case should library materials be excluded because of the race or nationality or the social, political, or religious views of the authors.

II. Libraries should provide books and other materials presenting all points of view concerning the problems and issues of our times; no library materials should be proscribed or removed from libraries because of partisan or doctrinal disapproval.

III. Censorship should be challenged by libraries in the maintenance of their responsibility to provide public information and enlightenment.

Which books will be used in the schools can provoke issues taken very seriously by school boards and community groups. (Photograph by George Bellerose / STOCK, Boston, Mass.)

IV. Libraries should cooperate with all persons and groups concerned with resisting abridgment of free expression and free access to ideas.

V. The rights of an individual to the use of a library should not be denied or abridged because of his age, race, religion, national origins, or social or political views.

VI. As an institution of education for democratic living, the library should welcome the use of its meeting rooms for socially useful and cultural activities and discussion of current public questions. Such meeting places should be available on equal terms to all groups in the community regardless of the beliefs and affiliations of their members, provided that the meetings be open to the public.

TELEVISION AND READING

Television is a mixed blessing, and, since it is not going to go away, most of us try to improve the quality of the offerings and to guide children's viewing. Several psychologists see negative effects in televiewing; the title of a recent article expresses some of their concern: "Is Human Imagination Going Down the Tube?"[24]

Marie Winn, in *The Plug-In Drug*, contrasts television viewing and reading:

The great difference between . . . "reading images" and the images we take in when viewing television is this: we *create* our own images when reading, based upon our own life experiences and reflecting our own individual needs, while we must accept what we receive when watching television images. This aspect of reading, which might be called "creative" in the narrow sense of the word, is present during all reading experiences, regardless of *what* is being read. The reader "creates" his own images as he reads, almost as if he were creating his own, small, inner television program. The result is a nourishing experience for the imagination. As Bruno Bettelheim notes, "Television captures the imagination but does not liberate it. A good book at once stimulates and frees the mind."[25]

Other critics point out that it is not only the imagination that suffers, but also language skills. Although children watching television hear many words, they are not using them in conversations. Watching television is a passive experience, and so does not invite the meaningful interchange and active involvement upon which language learning depends. While it is true that young children mimic the words they hear on television, there is little evidence that they know what the words mean. (Take, for example, the case reported by one mother of her television-watching child's first word: "Clairol.") Studies have produced further evidence that words picked up from television carry only surface meaning (because they are not based upon firsthand experience). Research shows that young children who watch television have larger vocabularies than those who do not watch it. Yet research also shows that a decline in reading comprehension scores, which occurs during the middle or intermediate-school years, is attributable to inadequate knowledge of vocabulary. Children, then, can decode words without knowing what they mean; the television-related early gains in vocabulary may be like fool's gold—more apparent than actual, with children who can say more words because they have heard them on television, but have little understanding of them.

Teachers' reports about children's television viewing identify a "tired-child" syndrome. In addition to falling asleep in school, such children are passive in their play, want to be entertained, and have short attention spans.

Children consistently choose television over reading for their leisure hours. The arguments about the effects of television on children's imagination, language development, and attention spans are difficult to prove. We do know, however, that studies over the past twenty-five years show a steady decline in time children spend reading, and an increase in time spent watching television. The latter is now three times that of the former. Numerous studies show that, on the average, young children spend over 60 percent of their waking time watching television; before they enter first grade they will have logged 5,000 hours in front of the television screen. Comparison of time in school and time watching television shows school running a poor second. By high-school graduation, most students have spent 11,000 hours in school and 22,000 hours watching television. The content of what they view raises other questions:

By the age of fourteen a child has seen 18,000 human beings killed on television.[26]

Teachers can mobilize some of children's televiewing to increase reading. There is evidence that children do read television material published in print form. Studies of the relationship between the televiewing and reading interests of seventh-grade pupils show that television tie-ins (most often a book adapted from a television series, but sometimes a television play based on a book) are preferred over general fiction not tied into television. Further, television scripts can be used effectively to build enthusiasm for reading as well as to guide children in critical viewing of television. One children's group meets after every television episode of "Little House on the Prairie" to discuss what was right and what wrong according to their expert knowledge of the books.

Children's literature is used as the base for many television adaptations, often tastefully, the best retaining the integrity of the original story. Thousands of children rush to read the book after seeing it on television. For example, the "Little House on the Prairie" series brought renewed interest to Laura Ingalls Wilder's excellent books. Similarly, many single productions of children's novels remain authentic retellings of the stories.

On the other hand, television can sink to the banal: Saturday morning cartoons contain vivid examples of vapid distortions of children's literature. Frances Clarke Sayers, in "Walt Disney Accused," indicts the vulgarizing of classics:

Disney takes a great masterpiece and telescopes it. He reduces it to ridiculous lengths, and in order to do this he has to make everything very obvious. It all happens very quickly and is expressed in very ordinary language. There is nothing to make a child think or feel or imagine.[27]

The compressed time sequence, the cartoon images, and the stiff language turn a fanciful tale into a travesty of itself.

Isaac Asimov, prolific author of science fiction and informational books, describes a device of the future that could be an answer to questions raised in the foregoing:

528 What we need is something that consumes no energy, is mobile, can be used in complete privacy, does not distract anyone else, and can be controlled by an act of will.[28]

This device, Asimov concludes, "we already have —a book."

MEASURING GROWTH IN LITERATURE

At a time when parents and school boards call for objective evidence of performance in the basic skills, the literature program may be shunted aside for tasks some consider more basic. Some people are not convinced that reading literature has anything to do with reading per se. They presume that filling in blanks on worksheets and answering simple questions about shallow comments is what reading is all about.

We know that what is measured in such tests is what is taught, making a self-fulfilling circuit of testing what we teach and teaching for the test. Thus, tests come to determine the curriculum. Even those who condone testing in literature acknowledge that literature tests are not easy to draw up. Current tests consist of questions that deal with what students have read in years past: Who wrote *Charlotte's Web*?, for example, or In what series do Ma, Pa, and Laura appear? Tests such as these are biased, for even children who read widely may not have read the particular books dealt with in the test. The only solution to this problem would be to identify the books children are expected to read and no one would countenance such a nationally approved reading list. (Establishing such a list would be tantamount to saying that only the assigned books were worthy of careful reading.)

Some literature tests contain passages to read and react to, as with basic reading comprehension tests, but restricted to literary selections. These tests are deficient in that generally they deal only with literal questions and low-level inferences. A further problem is the fact that there is rarely, if ever, only one "correct" response to a piece of literature.

What, then, is the answer to demands for evidence of performance in the face of inadequate measures for obtaining it? Obviously, it is not to ignore literature! Neither is it to submit to inappropriate tests that count up irrelevant things. Nor is it to say, "We can't test in literature, but trust me, they're learning."

Complex issues don't usually have simple answers and we are a long way from having all of them. We do know that children who read avidly perform better on standard reading tests, and that there *is* transfer of skill from reading literature to reading other types of material. Furthermore, attempts to develop more appropriate reading and literature tests continue, as do the efforts of The National Assessment of Educational Progress to develop new ways of measuring growth. Finally, The National Council of Teachers of English has published (and continues to update) a series of experimental works called *Measures for Research and Evaluation in the English Language Arts,* which may lead to more adequate instruments for evaluation.

Notes

1. Carl Sandburg, "Primer Lesson," in *Complete Poems* (New York: Harcourt Brace Jovanovich, 1950), p. 306.
2. Paula Fox, Newbery Medal Acceptance Speech, in *Newbery and Caldecott Medal Books: 1966–1975,* ed. Lee Kingman (Boston: Horn Book, Inc., 1975), p. 120.
3. Augusta Baker, "The Changing Image of the Black in Children's Literature," *Horn Book Magazine,* 51, No. 1 (Feb. 1975), 85.
4. Ibid., 88.
5. Irene Hunt, *Up a Road Slowly* (Chicago: Follett, 1966), pp. 31, 105.
6. Diana Goldsborough, "Goodbye Humphrey, Hello Dick and Jane," in *Only Connect,*

ed. Sheila Egoff, G. T. Stubbs, and L. F. Ashley (New York: Oxford Univ. Press, 1969), p. 105.

7. Council on Interracial Books for Children, *Guidelines for Selecting Bias-Free Textbooks and Storybooks* (New York: Council on Interracial Books for Children, 1980), p. 7.

8. Lillian N. Gerhardt, "The Would-be Censors of the Left," Editorial, *School Library Journal,* 23, No. 3 (Nov. 1976), 7.

9. Howard Greenfeld, *Books: From Writer to Reader* (New York: Crown, 1976), p. 6.

10. Rev. of *Tiffky Doofky,* by William Steig, *Bulletin of the Center for Children's Books,* 32, No. 8 (April 1979), 144–45.

11. Marjorie Lewis, rev. of *Tiffky Doofky,* by William Steig, *School Library Journal,* 25, No. 5 (Jan. 1979), 48.

12. Mary M. Burns, rev. of *Tiffky Doofky,* by William Steig, *Horn Book Magazine,* 55, No. 1 (Feb. 1979), 54–55.

13. Dorothy White, *About Books for Children* (New York: Oxford Univ. Press, 1946), p. 11.

14. Peter Dickinson, "A Defense of Rubbish," in *Children and Literature: Views and Reviews,* ed. Virginia Haviland (Chicago: Scott, Foresman, 1973), p. 101.

15. A list of the Newbery and Caldecott Medal books appears in the Appendix.

16. Linda Hayward, reteller, *Hansel and Gretel,* illus. Sheilah Beckett (New York: Random House, 1974), unpaged.

17. Susan Horowitz, adapter, *Hansel and Gretel with Benjy and Bubbles,* illus. Jim Razzi, ed. Ruth Lerner Perle (New York: Holt, Rinehart & Winston, 1978), unpaged.

18. Rumer Godden, "An Imaginary Correspondence," in *Children and Literature: Views and Reviews,* p. 138.

19. Robert F. Hogan, "Some Thoughts on Censorship in the Schools," in *Dealing with Censorship,* ed. James E. Davis. (Urbana, Ill.: National Council of Teachers of English, 1979), p. 89.

20. Ibid, p. 88.

21. James E. Davis, ed., *Dealing with Censorship,* pp. x–xi.

22. "Citizen's Request for Reconsideration of a Work," in *The Students Right to Read,* ed. Kenneth L. Donelson (Urbana, Ill.: National Council of Teachers of English, 1972), p. 18.

23. John Rowe Townsend, "It Takes More Than Pot and the Pill," *The New York Times Book Review,* 9 Nov. 1969, p. 2.

24. Dorothy G. Singer and Jerome L. Singer, "Is Human Imagination Going Down the Tube?" in *The Chronicle of Higher Education,* 23 April, 1979, p. 56.

25. Marie Winn, *The Plug-In Drug* (New York: Viking, 1977), p. 50.

26. Nancy Larrick, *A Parent's Guide to Children's Reading* (New York: Doubleday, 1975), p. 9.

27. Frances Clarke Sayers, "Walt Disney Accused," in *Children and Literature: Views and Reviews,* pp. 118–19.

28. "An Interview with Isaac Asimov," writ. Bernice E. Cullinan, *Teaching Critical Reading and Thinking to Children and Adolescents,* taught by Bernice E. Cullinan, dir. Roy Allen, New York University's Sunrise Semester, CBS, 3 May 1978.

Professional References

Baker, Augusta. "The Changing Image of the Black in Children's Literature." *Horn Book Magazine,* 51, No. 1 (Feb. 1975), 79–88.

Burns, Mary M. Rev. of *Tiffky Doofky,* by William Steig. *Horn Book Magazine,* 55, No. 1 (Feb. 1979), 54–55.

Clark, Ann Nolan. *Journey to the People.* Viking, 1969.

Council on Interracial Books for Children. *Guidelines for Selecting Bias-Free Textbooks and Storybooks.* Council on Interracial Books for Children, 1980.

Davis, James E., ed. *Dealing with Censorship.* National Council of Teachers of English, 1979.

Donelson, Kenneth L., ed. *The Students' Right to Read.* National Council of Teachers of English, 1972.

530

Egoff, Sheila, G. T. Stubbs, and L. F. Ashley, eds. *Only Connect: Readings on Children's Literature*. Oxford Univ. Press, 1969.

Fagan, William T., Charles R. Cooper, and Julie M. Jensen, eds. *Measures for Research and Evaluation in the English Language Arts*. National Council of Teachers of English, 1975.

Gerhardt, Lillian. "The Would-be Censors of the Left." Editorial. *School Library Journal*, 23, No. 3 (Nov. 1976), 7.

Haviland, Virginia, ed. *Children's Literature: Views and Reviews*. Scott, Foresman, 1973.

Hendler, Marjorie R. "An Analysis of Sex Role Attributes, Behaviors, and Occupations in Contemporary Children's Picture Books." Diss. New York University 1976.

Issues in Children's Book Selection: A School Library Journal/Library Journal Anthology. Bowker, 1973.

"An Interview with Isaac Asimov." Writ. Bernice E. Cullinan. *Teaching Critical Reading and Thinking to Children and Adolescents*. Taught by Bernice E. Cullinan. Dir. Roy Allen. New York University's Sunrise Semester, CBS, 3 May 1978.

Kingman, Lee, ed. *Newbery and Caldecott Medal Books: 1966–1975*. Horn Book, Inc., 1975.

Larrick, Nancy. *A Parent's Guide to Children's Reading*. Doubleday, 1975.

Lewis, Marjorie. Rev. of *Tiffky Doofky*, by William Steig. *School Library Journal*, 25, No. 5 (Jan. 1979), 48.

Rev. of *Tiffky Doofky*, by William Steig. *Bulletin of the Center for Children's Books*, 32, No. 8 (April 1979), 144–45.

Singer, Dorothy, and Jerome Singer. "Is Imagination Going Down the Tube?" *The Chronicle of Higher Education*, 23 April 1979, p. 56.

Townsend, John Rowe. "It Takes More than Pot and the Pill." *The New York Times Book Review*. 9 Nov. 1979, p. 2.

White, Dorothy. *About Books for Children*. Oxford Univ. Press, 1946.

Winn, Marie. *The Plug-In Drug*. Viking, 1977.

Children's Books Cited in Chapter

Armstrong, William H. *Sounder*. Harper & Row, 1969.

Bannerman, Helen. *Little Black Sambo*. Lippincott, 1923.

Blume, Judy. *Deenie*. Bradbury, 1973.

————. *Forever*. Bradbury, 1975.

Brink, Carol Ryrie. *Caddie Woodlawn*. Illus. Trina Schart Hyman. Macmillan, 1973 (1936).

Darrow, Whitney, Jr. *I'm Glad I'm a Boy! I'm Glad I'm a Girl!* Simon and Schuster, 1970.

Fox, Paula. *The Slave Dancer*. Bradbury, 1973.

Golding, William. *Lord of the Flies*. Coward, McCann & Geoghegan, 1962.

Greenfeld, Howard. *Books: From Writer to Reader*. Crown, 1978.

Grimm Brothers. *Hansel and Gretel*. Illus. Adrienne Adams. Scribner's, 1975.

Hayward, Linda, adaptor. *Hansel and Gretel*. Illus. Sheilah Beckett. Random House, 1974.

Hinton, S. E. *Rumble Fish*. Delacorte, 1975.

Horowitz, Susan, adaptor. *Hansel and Gretel with Benjy and Bubbles*. Illus. Jim Razzi. Ed. Ruth Lerner Perle. Holt, Rinehart & Winston, 1978.

Hunt, Irene. *Up a Road Slowly*. Follett, 1966.

Keats, Ezra Jack. *A Letter to Amy*. Harper & Row, 1968.

Klein, Norma. *Mom, the Wolfman and Me*. Pantheon, 1972.

L'Engle, Madeleine. *Meet the Austins*. Vanguard, 1960.

O'Dell, Scott. *Island of the Blue Dolphins*. Houghton Mifflin, 1960.

Potter, Beatrix. *The Tale of Peter Rabbit*. Warne, 1902.

Roberts, Willo Davis. *Don't Hurt Laurie*. Illus. Ruth Sanderson. Atheneum, 1977.

Salinger, J. D. *Catcher in the Rye*. Little, Brown, 1951.

Schwartz, Delmore. *"I Am Cherry Alive," the Little Girl Sang*. Illus. Barbara Cooney. Harper & Row, 1979.

Sparks, Beatrice. *Go Ask Alice*. Prentice-Hall, 1971.

Steig, William. *Amos and Boris*. Farrar, Straus & Giroux, 1971.

————. *Sylvester and the Magic Pebble*. Simon and Schuster, 1969.

————. *Tiffky Doofky*. Farrar, Straus & Giroux, 1978.

White, E. B. *Charlotte's Web*. Illus. Garth Williams. Harper & Row, 1952.

Williams, Garth. *The Rabbits' Wedding*. Harper & Row, 1958.

Zolotow, Charlotte. *The Storm Book*. Illus. Margaret Bloy Graham. Harper & Row, 1952.

————. *The Summer Night*. Illus. Ben Shecter. Harper & Row, 1974.

————. *When the Wind Stops*. Illus. Howard Knotts. Harper & Row, 1975.

————. *William's Doll*. Illus. William Pène du Bois. Harper & Row, 1972.

Appendixes

Acknowledgments

Indexes

appendixes

Children's Book Awards

THE JOHN NEWBERY MEDAL

The John Newbery Medal, named for an eighteenth-century British publisher and bookseller, the first to publish books for children, is given annually for the most distinguished contribution to literature for children published in the United States in the year preceding the award.

Selection of the award winner is made by a committee of the Association for Library Services for Children of the American Library Association.

The list below gives the title, author, and publisher of winners and of runners-up (honor books) since inception of the award in 1922.

1922 *The Story of Mankind* by Hendrik Willem van Loon, Liveright
Honor Books: *The Great Quest* by Charles Hawes, Little; *Cedric the Forester* by Bernard Marshall, Appleton; *The Old Tobacco Shop* by William Bowen, Macmillan; *The Golden Fleece and the Heroes Who Lived before Achilles* by Padraic Colum, Macmillan; *Windy Hill* by Cornelia Meigs, Macmillan
1923 *The Voyages of Doctor Dolittle* by Hugh Lofting, Lippincott
Honor Books: No record
1924 *The Dark Frigate* by Charles Hawes, Atlantic/Little
Honor Books: No record

1925 *Tales from Silver Lands* by Charles Finger, Doubleday
Honor Books: *Nicholas* by Anne Carroll Moore, Putnam; *Dream Coach* by Anne Parrish, Macmillan
1926 *Shen of the Sea* by Arthur Bowie Chrisman, Dutton
Honor Book: *Voyagers* by Padraic Colum, Macmillan
1927 *Smoky, the Cowhorse* by Will James, Scribner's
Honor Books: No record
1928 *Gayneck, The Story of a Pigeon* by Dhan Gopal Mukerji, Dutton
Honor Books: *The Wonder Smith and His Son* by Ella Young, Longmans; *Downright Dencey* by Caroline Snedeker, Doubleday
1929 *The Trumpeter of Krakow* by Eric P. Kelly, Macmillan
Honor Books: *Pigtail of Ah Lee Ben Loo* by John Bennett, Longmans; *Millions of Cats* by Wanda Gág, Coward; *The Boy Who Was* by Grace Hallock, Dutton; *Clearing Weather* by Cornelia Meigs, Little; *Runaway Papoose* by Grace Moon, Doubleday; *Tod of the Fens* by Elinor Whitney, Macmillan
1930 *Hitty, Her First Hundred Years* by Rachel Field, Macmillan
Honor Books: *Daughter of the Seine* by Jeanette Eaton, Harper; *Pran of Albania* by Elizabeth Miller, Doubleday; *Jumping-Off Place* by Marian Hurd McNeely, Longmans; *Tangle-Coated Horse and Other Tales* by Ella Young, Longmans; *Vaino* by Julia

Davis Adams, Dutton; *Little Blacknose* by Hildegarde Swift, Harcourt Brace Jovanovich

1931 *The Cat Who Went to Heaven* by Elizabeth Coatsworth, Macmillan
Honor Books: *Floating Island* by Anne Parrish, Harper; *The Dark Star of Itza* by Alida Malkus, Harcourt Brace Jovanovich; *Queer Person* by Ralph Hubbard, Doubleday; *Mountains Are Free* by Julia Davis Adams, Dutton; *Spice and the Devil's Cave* by Agnes Hewes, Knopf; *Meggy Macintosh* by Elizabeth Janet Gray, Doubleday; *Garram the Hunter* by Herbert Best, Doubleday; *Ood-Le-Uk the Wanderer* by Alice Lide and Margaret Johansen, Little

1932 *Waterless Mountain* by Laura Adams Armer, Longmans
Honor Books: *The Fairy Circus* by Dorothy P. Lathrop, Macmillan; *Calico Bush* by Rachel Field, Macmillan; *Boy of the South Seas* by Eunice Tietjens, Coward; *Out of the Flame* by Eloise Lownsbery, Longmans; *Jane's Island* by Marjorie Allee, Houghton; *Truce of the Wolf and Other Tales of Old Italy* by Mary Gould Davis, Harcourt Brace Jovanovich

1933 *Young Fu of the Upper Yangtze* by Elizabeth Foreman Lewis, Winston
Honor Books: *Swift Rivers* by Cornelia Meigs, Little; *The Railroad to Freedom* by Hildegarde Swift, Harcourt Brace Jovanovich; *Children of the Soil* by Nora Burglon, Doubleday

1934 *Invincible Louisa* by Cornelia Meigs, Little
Honor Books: *The Forgotten Daughter* by Caroline Snedeker, Doubleday; *Swords of Steel* by Elsie Singmaster, Houghton; *ABC Bunny* by Wanda Gág, Coward; *Winged Girl of Knossos* by Erik Berry, Appleton; *New Land* by Sarah Schmidt, McBride; *Big Tree of Bunlahy* by Padraic Colum, Macmillan; *Glory of the Seas* by Agnes Hewes, Knopf; *Apprentice of Florence* by Ann Kyle, Houghton

1935 *Dobry* by Monica Shannon, Viking
Honor Books: *Pageant of Chinese History* by Elizabeth Seeger, Longmans; *Davy Crockett* by Constance Rourke, Harcourt Brace Jovanovich; *Day on Skates* by Hilda Van Stockum, Harper

1936 *Caddie Woodlawn* by Carol Ryrie Brink, Macmillan
Honor Books: *Honk, the Moose* by Phil Stong, Dodd; *The Good Master* by Kate Seredy, Viking; *Young Walter Scott* by Elizabeth Janet Gray, Viking; *All Sail Set* by Armstrong Sperry, Winston

1937 *Roller Skates* by Ruth Sawyer, Viking
Honor Books: *Phoebe Fairchild: Her Book* by Lois Lenski, Stokes; *Whistler's Van* by Idwal Jones, Viking;

Golden Basket by Ludwig Bemelmans, Viking; *Winterbound* by Margery Bianco, Viking; *Audubon* by Constance Rourke, Harcourt Brace Jovanovich; *The Codfish Musket* by Agnes Hewes, Doubleday

1938 *The White Stag* by Kate Seredy, Viking
Honor Books: *Pecos Bill* by James Cloyd Bowman, Little; *Bright Island* by Mabel Robinson, Random; *On the Banks of Plum Creek* by Laura Ingalls Wilder, Harper

1939 *Thimble Summer* by Elizabeth Enright, Rinehart
Honor Books: *Nino* by Valenti Angelo, Viking; *Mr. Popper's Penguins* by Richard and Florence Atwater, Little; *"Hello the Boat!"* by Phyllis Crawford, Holt; *Leader by Destiny: George Washington, Man and Patriot* by Jeanette Eaton, Harcourt Brace Jovanovich; *Penn* by Elizabeth Janet Gray, Viking

1940 *Daniel Boone* by James Daugherty, Viking
Honor Books: *The Singing Tree* by Kate Seredy, Viking; *Runner of the Mountain Tops* by Mabel Robinson, Random; *By the Shores of Silver Lake* by Laura Ingalls Wilder, Harper; *Boy with a Pack* by Stephen W. Meader, Harcourt Brace Jovanovich

1941 *Call It Courage* by Armstrong Sperry, Macmillan
Honor Books: *Blue Willow* by Doris Gates, Viking; *Young Mac of Fort Vancouver* by Mary Jane Carr, Crowell; *The Long Winter* by Laura Ingalls Wilder, Harper; *Nansen* by Anna Gertrude Hall, Viking

1942 *The Matchlock Gun* by Walter D. Edmonds, Dodd
Honor Books: *Little Town on the Prairie* by Laura Ingalls Wilder, Harper; *George Washington's World* by Genevieve Foster, Scribner's; *Indian Captive: The Story of Mary Jemison* by Lois Lenski, Lippincott; *Down Ryton Water* by Eva Roe Gaggin, Viking

1943 *Adam of the Road* by Elizabeth Janet Gray, Viking
Honor Books: *The Middle Moffat* by Eleanor Estes, Harcourt Brace Jovanovich; *Have You Seen Tom Thumb?* by Mabel Leigh Hunt, Lippincott

1944 *Johnny Tremain* by Esther Forbes, Houghton
Honor Books: *These Happy Golden Years* by Laura Ingalls Wilder, Harper; *Fog Magic* by Julia Sauer, Viking; *Rufus M.* by Eleanor Estes, Harcourt Brace Jovanovich; *Mountain Born* by Elizabeth Yates, Coward

1945 *Rabbit Hill* by Robert Lawson, Viking
Honor Books: *The Hundred Dresses* by Eleanor Estes, Harcourt Brace Jovanovich; *The Silver Pencil* by Alice Dalgliesh, Scribner's; *Abraham Lincoln's World* by Genevieve Foster, Scribner's; *Lone Journey: The Life of Roger Williams* by Jeanette Eaton, Harcourt Brace Jovanovich

1946 *Strawberry Girl* by Lois Lenski, Lippincott

Honor Books: *Justin Morgan Had a Horse* by Marguerite Henry, Rand; *The Moved-Outers* by Florence Crannell Means, Houghton; *Bhimsa, the Dancing Bear* by Christine Weston, Scribner's; *New Found World* by Katherine Shippen, Viking

1947 *Miss Hickory* by Carolyn Sherwin Bailey, Viking
Honor Books: *Wonderful Year* by Nancy Barnes, Messner; *Big Tree* by Mary and Conrad Buff, Viking; *The Heavenly Tenants* by William Maxwell, Harper; *The Avion My Uncle Flew* by Cyrus Fisher, Appleton; *The Hidden Treasure of Glaston* by Eleanore Jewett, Viking

1948 *The Twenty-One Balloons* by William Pène du Bois, Viking
Honor Books: *Pancakes-Paris* by Claire Huchet Bishop, Viking; *Li Lun, Lad of Courage* by Carolyn Treffinger, Abingdon; *The Quaint and Curious Quest of Johnny Longfoot* by Catherine Besterman, Bobbs; *The Cow-Tail Switch, and Other West African Stories* by Harold Courlander, Holt; *Misty of Chincoteague* by Marguerite Henry, Rand

1949 *King of the Wind* by Marguerite Henry, Rand
Honor Books: *Seabird* by Holling C. Holling, Houghton; *Daughter of the Mountains* by Louise Rankin, Viking; *My Father's Dragon* by Ruth S. Gannett, Random; *Story of the Negro* by Arna Bontemps, Knopf

1950 *The Door in the Wall* by Marguerite de Angeli, Doubleday
Honor Books: *Tree of Freedom* by Rebecca Caudill, Viking; *The Blue Cat of Castle Town* by Catherine Coblentz, Longmans; *Kildee House* by Rutherford Montgomery, Doubleday; *George Washington* by Genevieve Foster, Scribner's; *Song of the Pines* by Walter and Marion Havighurst, Winston

1951 *Amos Fortune, Free Man* by Elizabeth Yates, Aladdin
Honor Books: *Better Known as Johnny Appleseed* by Mabel Leigh Hunt, Lippincott; *Gandhi, Fighter Without a Sword* by Jeanette Eaton, Morrow; *Abraham Lincoln, Friend of the People* by Clara Ingram Judson, Follett; *The Story of Appleby Capple* by Anne Parrish, Harper

1952 *Ginger Pye* by Eleanor Estes, Harcourt Brace Jovanovich
Honor Books: *Americans Before Columbus* by Elizabeth Baity, Viking; *Minn of the Mississippi* by Holling C. Holling, Houghton; *The Defender* by Nicholas Kalashnikoff, Scribner's; *The Light at Tern Rock* by Julia Sauer, Viking; *The Apple and the Arrow* by Mary and Conrad Buff, Houghton

1953 *Secret of the Andes* by Ann Nolan Clark, Viking

Honor Books: *Charlotte's Web* by E. B. White, Harper; *Moccasin Trail* by Eloise McGraw, Coward; *Red Sails to Capri* by Ann Weil, Viking; *The Bears on Hemlock Mountain* by Alice Dalgliesh, Scribner's; *Birthdays of Freedom*, Vol. 1, by Genevieve Foster, Scribner's

1954 *. . . and now Miguel* by Joseph Krumgold, Crowell
Honor Books: *All Alone* by Claire Huchet Bishop, Viking; *Shadrach* by Meindert DeJong, Harper; *Hurry Home Candy* by Meindert DeJong, Harper; *Theodore Roosevelt, Fighting Patriot* by Clara Ingram Judson, Follett; *Magic Maize* by Mary and Conrad Buff, Houghton

1955 *The Wheel on the School* by Meindert DeJong, Harper
Honor Books: *The Courage of Sarah Noble* by Alice Dalgliesh, Scribner's; *Banner in the Sky* by James Ullman, Lippincott

1956 *Carry on, Mr. Bowditch* by Jean Lee Latham, Houghton
Honor Books: *The Secret River* by Marjorie Kinnan Rawlings, Scribner's; *The Golden Name Day* by Jennie Linquist, Harper; *Men, Microscopes, and Living Things* by Katherine Shippen, Viking

1957 *Miracles on Maple Hill* by Virginia Sorensen, Harcourt Brace Jovanovich
Honor Books: *Old Yeller* by Fred Gipson, Harper; *The House of Sixty Fathers* by Meindert DeJong, Harper; *Mr. Justice Holmes* by Clara Ingram Judson, Follett; *The Corn Grows Ripe* by Dorothy Rhoads, Viking; *Black Fox of Lorne* by Marguerite de Angeli, Doubleday

1958 *Rifles for Watie* by Harold Keith, Crowell
Honor Books: *The Horsecatcher* by Mari Sandoz, Westminster; *Gone-Away Lake* by Elizabeth Enright, Harcourt Brace Jovanovich; *The Great Wheel* by Robert Lawson, Viking; *Tom Paine, Freedom's Apostle* by Leo Gurko, Crowell

1959 *The Witch of Blackbird Pond* by Elizabeth George Speare, Houghton
Honor Books: *The Family Under the Bridge* by Natalie Savage Carlson, Harper; *Along Came a Dog* by Meindert DeJong, Harper; *Chucaro: Wild Pony of the Pampa* by Francis Kalnay, Harcourt Brace Jovanovich; *The Perilous Road* by William O. Steele, Harcourt Brace Jovanovich

1960 *Onion John* by Joseph Krumgold, Crowell
Honor Books: *My Side of the Mountain* by Jean George, Dutton; *America Is Born* by Gerald W. Johnson, Morrow; *The Gammage Cup* by Carol Kendall, Harcourt Brace Jovanovich

1961 *Island of the Blue Dolphins* by Scott O'Dell, Houghton
Honor Books: *America Moves Forward* by Gerald W. Johnson, Morrow; *Old Ramon* by Jack Schaefer, Houghton; *The Cricket in Times Square* by George Selden, Farrar

1962 *The Bronze Bow* by Elizabeth George Speare, Houghton
Honor Books: *Frontier Living* by Edwin Tunis, World; *The Golden Goblet* by Eloise McGraw, Coward; *Belling the Tiger* by Mary Stolz, Harper

1963 *A Wrinkle in Time* by Madeleine L'Engle, Farrar
Honor Books: *Thistle and Thyme* by Sorche Nic Leodhas, Holt; *Men of Athens* by Olivia Coolidge, Houghton

1964 *It's Like This, Cat* by Emily Cheney Neville, Harper
Honor Books: *Rascal* by Sterling North, Dutton; *The Loner* by Ester Wier, McKay

1965 *Shadow of a Bull* by Maia Wojciechowska, Atheneum
Honor Books: *Across Five Aprils* by Irene Hunt, Follett

1966 *I, Juan de Pareja* by Elizabeth Borden de Treviño, Farrar
Honor Books: *The Black Cauldron* by Lloyd Alexander, Holt; *The Animal Family* by Randall Jarrell, Pantheon; *The Noonday Friends* by Mary Stolz, Harper

1967 *Up a Road Slowly* by Irene Hunt, Follet
Honor Books: *The King's Fifth* by Scott O'Dell, Houghton; *Zlateh the Goat and Other Stories* by Isaac Bashevis Singer, Harper; *The Jazz Man* by Mary H. Weik, Atheneum

1968 *From the Mixed-Up Files of Mrs. Basil E. Frankweiler* by E. L. Konigsburg, Atheneum
Honor Books: *Jennifer, Hecate, Macbeth, William McKinley, and Me, Elizabeth* by E. L. Konigsburg, Atheneum; *The Black Pearl* by Scott O'Dell, Houghton; *The Fearsome Inn* by Isaac Bashevis Singer, Scribner's; *The Egypt Game* by Zilpha Keatley Snyder, Atheneum

1969 *The High King* by Lloyd Alexander, Holt
Honor Books: *To Be a Slave* by Julius Lester, Dial; *When Shlemiel Went to Warsaw and Other Stories* by Isaac Bashevis Singer, Farrar

1970 *Sounder* by William H. Armstrong, Harper
Honor Books: *Our Eddie* by Sulamith Ish-Kishor, Pantheon; *The Many Ways of Seeing: An Introduction to the Pleasures of Art* by Janet Gaylord Moore, World; *Journey Outside* by Mary Q. Steele, Viking

1971 *Summer of the Swans* by Betsy Byars, Viking
Honor Books: *Kneeknock Rise* by Natalie Babbitt, Farrar; *Enchantress from the Stars* by Sylvia Louise Engdahl, Atheneum; *Sing Down the Moon* by Scott O'Dell, Houghton

1972 *Mrs. Frisby and the Rats of NIMH* by Robert C. O'Brien, Atheneum
Honor Books: *Incident at Hawk's Hill* by Allan W. Eckert, Little; *The Planet of Junior Brown* by Virginia Hamilton, Macmillan; *The Tombs of Atuan* by Ursula K. Le Guin, Atheneum; *Annie and the Old One* by Miska Miles, Atlantic-Little; *The Headless Cupid* by Zilpha Keatley Snyder, Atheneum

1973 *Julie of the Wolves* by Jean Craighead George, Harper
Honor Books: *Frog and Toad Together* by Arnold Lobel, Harper; *The Upstairs Room* by Johanna Reiss, Crowell; *The Witches of Worm* by Zilpha Keatley Snyder, Atheneum

1974 *The Slave Dancer* by Paula Fox, Bradbury
Honor Book: *The Dark Is Rising* by Susan Cooper, Atheneum-McElderry

1975 *M.C. Higgins, the Great* by Virginia Hamilton, Macmillan
Honor Books: *Figgs & Phantoms* by Ellen Raskin, Dutton; *My Brother Sam Is Dead* by James Lincoln Collier & Christopher Collier, Four Winds; *The Perilous Gard* by Elizabeth Marie Pope, Houghton; *Philip Hall Likes Me. I Reckon Maybe* by Bette Greene, Dial

1976 *The Grey King* by Susan Cooper, Atheneum-McElderry
Honor Books: *The Hundred Penny Box* by Sharon Bell Mathis, Viking; *Dragonwings* by Lawrence Yep, Harper

1977 *Roll of Thunder, Hear My Cry* by Mildred D. Taylor, Dial
Honor Books: *Abel's Island* by William Steig, Farrar; *A String in the Harp* by Nancy Bond, McElderry-Atheneum

1978 *Bridge to Terabithia* by Katherine Paterson, Crowell
Honor Books: *Ramona and Her Father* by Beverly Cleary, Morrow; *Anpao: An American Indian Odyssey* by Jamake Highwater, Lippincott

1979 *The Westing Game* by Ellen Raskin, Dutton
Honor Book: *The Great Gilly Hopkins* by Katherine Paterson, Crowell

1980 *A Gathering of Days: A New England Girl's Journal, 1830–32* by Joan Blos, Scribner's
Honor Book: *The Road from Home: The Story of an Armenian Girl* by David Kherdian, Greenwillow

1981 *Jacob Have I Loved* by Katherine Paterson, Crowell

Honor Books: *The Fledgling* by Jane Langton, Harper; *A Ring of Endless Light* by Madeleine L'Engle, Farrar

THE RANDOLPH CALDECOTT MEDAL

The Randolph Caldecott Medal, named for a nineteenth-century British illustrator of books for children, is given annually for the most distinguished picture book for children published in the United States in the year preceding the award.

Selection of the award winner is made by a committee of the Association for Library Services for Children of the American Library Association.

The list below gives the title, author, illustrator, and publisher of winners and runners-up (honor books) since inception of the award in 1938. Where only one name is given, the book was written and illustrated by the same person.

1938 *Animals of the Bible* by Helen Dean Fish, ill. by Dorothy P. Lathrop, Lippincott

Honor Books: *Seven Simeons* by Boris Artzybasheff, Viking; *Four and Twenty Blackbirds* by Helen Dean Fish, ill. by Robert Lawson, Lippincott

1939 *Mei Li* by Thomas Handforth, Doubleday

Honor Books: *The Forest Pool* by Laura Adams Armer, Longmans; *Wee Gillis* by Munro Leaf, Ill. by Robert Lawson, Viking; *Snow White and the Seven Dwarfs* by Wanda Gág, Coward; *Barkis* by Clare Newberry, Harper; *Andy and the Lion* by James Daugherty, Viking

1940 *Abraham Lincoln* by Ingri and Edgar Parin d'Aulaire, Doubleday

Honor Books: *Cock-a-Doodle Doo . . .* by Berta and Elmer Hader, Macmillan; *Madeline* by Ludwig Bemelmans, Viking; *The Ageless Story,* by Lauren Ford, Dodd.

1941 *They Were Strong and Good* by Robert Lawson, Viking

Honor Book: *April's Kittens* by Clare Newberry, Harper

1942 *Make Way for Ducklings* by Robert McCloskey, Viking

Honor Books: *An American ABC* by Maud and Miska Petersham, Macmillan; *In My Mother's House* by Ann Nolan Clark, ill. by Velino Herrera, Viking; *Paddle-to-the-Sea* by Holling C. Holling, Houghton; *Nothing at All* by Wanda Gág, Coward

1943 *The Little House* by Virginia Lee Burton, Houghton

Honor Books: *Dash and Dart* by Mary and Conrad Buff, Viking; *Marshmallow* by Clare Newberry, Harper

1944 *Many Moons* by James Thurber, ill. by Louis Slobodkin, Harcourt Brace Jovanovich

Honor Books: *Small Rain: Verses from the Bible* selected by Jessie Orton Jones, ill. by Elizabeth Orton Jones, Viking; *Pierre Pigeon* by Lee Kingman, ill. by Arnold E. Bare, Houghton; *The Mighty Hunter* by Berta and Elmer Hader, Macmillan; *A Child's Good Night Book* by Margaret Wise Brown, ill. by Jean Charlot, Scott; *Good Luck Horse* by Chin-Yi Chan, ill. by Plao Chan, Whittlesey

1945 *Prayer for a Child* by Rachel Field, ill. by Elizabeth Orton Jones, Macmillan

Honor Books: *Mother Goose* ill. by Tasha Tudor, Walck; *In the Forest* by Marie Hall Ets, Viking; *Yonie Wondernose* by Marguerite de Angeli, Doubleday; *The Christmas Anna Angel* by Ruth Sawyer, ill. by Kate Seredy, Viking

1946 *The Rooster Crows . . .* (traditional Mother Goose) ill. by Maud and Miska Petersham, Macmillan

Honor Books: *Little Lost Lamb* by Golden MacDonald, ill. by Leonard Weisgard, Doubleday; *Sing Mother Goose* by Opal Wheeler, ill. by Marjorie Torrey, Dutton; *My Mother Is the Most Beautiful Woman in the World* by Becky Reyher, ill. by Ruth Gannett, Lothrop; *You Can Write Chinese* by Kurt Wiese, Viking

1947 *The Little Island* by Golden MacDonald, ill. by Leonard Weisgard, Doubleday

Honor Books: *Rain Drop Splash* by Alvin Tresselt, ill. by Leonard Weisgard, Lothrop; *Boats on the River* by Marjorie Flack, ill. by Jay Hyde Barnum, Viking; *Timothy Turtle* by Al Graham, ill. by Tony Palazzo, Viking; *Pedro, the Angel of Olvera Street* by Leo Politi, Scribner's; *Sing in Praise: A Collection of the Best Loved Hymns* by Opal Wheeler, ill. by Marjorie Torrey, Dutton

1948 *White Snow, Bright Snow* by Alvin Tresselt, ill. by Roger Duvoisin, Lothrop

Honor Books: *Stone Soup* by Marcia Brown, Scribner's; *McElligot's Pool* by Dr. Seuss, Random; *Bambino the Clown* by George Schreiber, Viking; *Roger and the Fox* by Lavinia Davis, ill. by Hildegard Woodward, Doubleday; *Song of Robin Hood* ed. by Anne Malcolmson, ill. by Virginia Lee Burton, Houghton

1949 *The Big Snow* by Berta and Elmer Hader, Macmillan

Honor Books: *Blueberries for Sal* by Robert McCloskey, Viking; *All Around the Town* by Phyllis McGinley, ill. by Helen Stone, Lippincott; *Juanita* by Leo Politi, Scribner's; *Fish in the Air* by Kurt Wiese, Viking

1950 *Song of the Swallows* by Leo Politi, Scribner's
Honor Books: *America's Ethan Allen* by Stewart Holbrook, ill. by Lynd Ward, Houghton; *The Wild Birthday Cake* by Lavinia Davis, ill. by Hildegard Woodward, Doubleday; *The Happy Day* by Ruth Krauss, ill. by Marc Simont, Harper; *Bartholomew and the Oobleck* by Dr. Seuss, Random; *Henry Fisherman* by Marcia Brown, Scribner's

1951 *The Egg Tree* by Katherine Milhous, Scribner's
Honor Books: *Dick Whittington and His Cat* by Marcia Brown, Scribner's; *The Two Reds* by William Lipkind, ill. by Nicholas Mordvinoff, Harcourt Brace Jovanovich; *If I Ran the Zoo* by Dr. Seuss, Random; *The Most Wonderful Doll in the World* by Phyllis McGinley, ill. by Helen Stone, Lippincott; *T-Bone, the Baby Sitter* by Clare Newberry, Harper

1952 *Finders Keepers* by William Lipkind, ill. by Nicholas Mordvinoff, Harcourt Brace Jovanovich
Honor Books: *Mr. T. W. Anthony Woo* by Marie Hall Ets, Viking; *Skipper John's Cook* by Marcia Brown, Scribner's; *All Falling Down* by Gene Zion, ill. by Margaret Bloy Graham, Harper; *Bear Party* by William Pène du Bois, Viking; *Feather Mountain* by Elizabeth Olds, Houghton

1953 *The Biggest Bear* by Lynd Ward, Houghton
Honor Books: *Puss in Boots* by Charles Perrault, ill. and tr. by Marcia Brown, Scribner's; *One Morning in Maine* by Robert McCloskey, Viking; *Ape in a Cape* by Fritz Eichenberg, Harcourt Brace Jovanovich; *The Storm Book* by Charlotte Zolotow, ill. by Margaret Bloy Graham, Harper; *Five Little Monkeys* by Juliet Kepes, Houghton

1954 *Madeline's Rescue* by Ludwig Bemelmans, Viking
Honor Books: *Journey Cake, Ho!* by Ruth Sawyer, Ill. by Robert McCloskey, Viking; *When Will the World Be Mine?* by Miriam Schlein, ill. by Jean Charlot, Scott; *The Steadfast Tin Soldier* by Hans Christian Andersen, ill. by Marcia Brown, Scribner's; *A Very Special House* by Ruth Krauss, ill. by Maurice Sendak, Harper; *Green Eyes* by A. Birnbaum, Capitol

1955 *Cinderella, or the Little Glass Slipper* by Charles Perrault, tr. and ill. by Marcia Brown, Scribner's
Honor Books: *Book of Nursery and Mother Goose Rhymes*, ill. by Marguerite de Angeli, Doubleday; *Wheel on the Chimney* by Margaret Wise Brown, ill. by Tibor Gergely, Lippincott; *The Thanksgiving Story* by Alice Dalgliesh, ill. by Helen Sewell, Scribner's

1956 *Frog Went A-Courtin'* ed. by John Langstaff, ill. by Feodor Rojankovsky, Harcourt Brace Jovanovich
Honor Books: *Play with Me* by Marie Hall Ets, Viking; *Crow Boy* by Taro Yashima, Viking

1957 *A Tree Is Nice* by Janice May Udry, ill. by Marc Simont, Harper
Honor Books: *Mr. Penny's Race Horse* by Marie Hall Ets, Viking; *1 Is One* by Tasha Tudor, Walck; *Anatole* by Eve Titus, ill. by Paul Galdone, McGraw; *Gillespie and the Guards* by Benjamin Elkin, ill. by James Daugherty, Viking; *Lion* by William Pène du Bois, Viking

1958 *Time of Wonder* by Robert McCloskey, Viking
Honor Books: *Fly High, Fly Low* by Don Freeman, Viking; *Anatole and the Cat* by Eve Titus, ill. by Paul Galdone, McGraw

1959 *Chanticleer and the Fox* adapted from Chaucer and ill. by Barbara Cooney, Crowell
Honor Books: *The House That Jack Built* by Antonio Frasconi, Harcourt Brace Jovanovich; *What Do You Say, Dear?* by Sesyle Joslin, ill. by Maurice Sendak, Scott; *Umbrella* by Taro Yashima, Viking

1960 *Nine Days to Christmas* by Marie Hall Ets and Aurora Labastida, ill. by Marie Hall Ets, Viking
Honor Books: *Houses from the Sea* by Alice E. Goudey, ill. by Adrienne Adams, Scribner's; *The Moon Jumpers* by Janice May Udry, ill. by Maurice Sendak, Harper

1961 *Baboushka and the Three Kings* by Ruth Robbins, ill. by Nicolas Sidjakov, Parnassus
Honor Book; *Inch by Inch* by Leo Lionni, Obolensky

1962 *Once a Mouse . . .* by Marcia Brown, Scribner's
Honor Books: *Fox Went Out on a Chilly Night* by Peter Spier, Doubleday; *Little Bear's Visit* by Else Holmelund Minarik, ill. by Maurice Sendak, Harper; *The Day We Saw the Sun Come Up* by Alice E. Goudey, ill. by Adrienne Adams, Scribner's

1963 *The Snowy Day* by Ezra Jack Keats, Viking
Honor Books: *The Sun Is a Golden Earring* by Natalia M. Belting, ill. by Bernarda Bryson, Holt; *Mr. Rabbit and the Lovely Present* by Charlotte Zolotow, ill. by Maurice Sendak, Harper

1964 *Where the Wild Things Are* by Maurice Sendak, Harper
Honor Books: *Swimmy* by Leo Lionni, Pantheon; *All in the Morning Early* by Sorche Nic Leodhas, ill. by Evaline Ness, Holt; *Mother Goose and Nursery Rhymes* ill. by Philip Reed, Atheneum

1965 *May I Bring a Friend?* by Beatrice Schenk De Regniers, ill. by Beni Montresor, Atheneum
Honor Books: *Rain Makes Applesauce* by Julian

Scheer, ill. by Marvin Bileck, Holiday; *The Wave* by Margaret Hodges, ill. by Blair Lent, Houghton; *A Pocketful of Cricket* by Rebecca Caudill, ill. by Evaline Ness, Holt

1966 *Always Room for One More* by Sorche Nic Leodhas, ill. by Nonny Hogrogian, Holt
Honor Books: *Hide and Seek Fog* by Alvin Tresselt, ill. by Roger Duvoisin, Lothrop; *Just Me* by Marie Hall Ets. Viking; *Tom Tit Tot* by Evaline Ness, Scribner's

1967 *Sam, Bangs and Moonshine* by Evaline Ness, Holt
Honor Book: *One Wide River to Cross* by Barbara Emberley, ill. by Ed Emberley, Prentice

1968 *Drummer Hoff* by Barbara Emberley, ill. by Ed Emberley, Prentice
Honor Books: *Frederick* by Leo Lionni, Pantheon; *Seashore Story* by Taro Yashima, Viking; *The Emperor and the Kite* by Jane Yolen, ill. by Ed Young, World

1969 *The Fool of the World and the Flying Ship* by Arthur Ransome, ill. by Uri Shulevitz, Farrar
Honor Book: *Why the Sun and the Moon Live in the Sky* by Elphinston Dayrell, ill. by Blair Lent, Houghton

1970 *Sylvester and the Magic Pebble* by William Steig, Windmill
Honor Books: *Goggles!* by Ezra Jack Keats, Macmillan; *Alexander and the Wind-Up Mouse* by Leo Lionni, Pantheon; *Pop Corn and Ma Goodness* by Edna Mitchell Preston, ill. by Robert Andrew Parker, Viking; *Thy Friend, Obadiah* by Brinton Turkle, Viking; *The Judge* by Harve Zemach, ill. by Margot Zemach, Farrar

1971 *A Story—A Story* by Gail E. Haley, Atheneum
Honor Books: *The Angry Moon* by William Sleator, ill. by Blair Lent, Atlantic-Little; *Frog and Toad Are Friends* by Arnold Lobel, Harper; *In the Night Kitchen* by Maurice Sendak, Harper

1972 *One Fine Day* by Nonny Hogrogian, Macmillan
Honor Books: *If All the Seas Were One Sea,* by Janina Domanska, Macmillan; *Moja Means One: Swahili Counting Book* by Muriel Feelings, ill. by Tom Feelings, Dial; *Hildilid's Night* by Cheli Durán Ryan, ill. by Arnold Lobel, Macmillan

1973 *The Funny Little Woman* retold by Arlene Mosel, ill. by Blair Lent, Dutton
Honor Books: *Anansi the Spider* adapted and ill. by Gerald McDermott, Holt; *Hosie's Alphabet* by Hosie, Tobias and Lisa Baskin, ill. by Leonard Baskin, Viking; *Snow White and the Seven Dwarfs* translated by Randall Jarrell, ill. by Nancy Ekholm Burkert, Farrar;

When Clay Sings by Byrd Baylor, ill. by Tom Bahti, Scribner's

1974 *Duffy and the Devil* by Harve Zemach, ill. by Margot Zemach, Farrar
Honor Books: *Three Jovial Huntsmen* by Susan Jeffers, Bradbury; *Cathedral: The Story of Its Construction* by David Macaulay, Houghton

1975 *Arrow to the Sun* adapted and ill. by Gerald McDermott, Viking
Honor Book: *Jambo Means Hello* by Muriel Feelings, ill. by Tom Feelings, Dial

1976 *Why Mosquitoes Buzz in People's Ears* retold by Verna Aardema, ill. by Leo and Diane Dillon, Dial
Honor Books: *The Desert Is Theirs* by Byrd Baylor, ill. by Peter Parnall, Scribner's; *Strega Nona* retold and ill. by Tomie de Paola, Prentice

1977 *Ashanti to Zulu: African Traditions* by Margaret Musgrove, ill. by Leo and Diane Dillon, Dial
Honor Books: *The Amazing Bone* by William Steig, Farrar; *The Contest* retold and ill. by Nonny Hogrogian, Greenwillow; *Fish for Supper* by M. B. Goffstein, Dial; *The Golem* by Beverly Brodsky McDermott, Lippincott; *Hawk, I'm Your Brother* by Byrd Baylor, ill. by Peter Parnall, Scribner's

1978 *Noah's Ark* by Peter Spier, Doubleday
Honor Books: *Castle* by David Macaulay, Houghton; *It Could Always Be Worse* by Margot Zemach, Farrar

1979 *The Girl Who Loved Wild Horses* by Paul Goble, Bradbury
Honor Books: *Freight Train* by Donald Crews, Greenwillow; *The Way to Start a Day* by Byrd Baylor, ill. by Peter Parnall, Scribner's

1980 *Ox-Cart Man* by Donald Hall, ill. by Barbara Cooney, Viking
Honor Books: *Ben's Trumpet* by Rachel Isadora, Greenwillow; *The Treasure* by Uri Shulevitz, Farrar; *The Garden of Abdul Gasazi* by Chris Van Allsburg, Houghton

1981 *Fables* by Arnold Lobel, Harper
Honor Books: *The Bremen-Town Musicians* by Ilse Plume, Doubleday; *The Grey Lady and the Strawberry Snatcher* by Molly Bang, Four Winds; *Mice Twice* by Joseph Low, Atheneum-McElderry; *Truck* by Donald Crews, Greenwillow

THE LAURA INGALLS WILDER AWARD

The Laura Ingalls Wilder Award, named for its first winner, the author of the "Little House" books, is given every five years to an author or illustrator whose books, published in the United States, have made a substantial and lasting contribution to literature for children. Selection of the award winner is made by the Association for Library Services for Children of the American Library Association. Winners since inception of the award in 1954 are:

1954	Laura Ingalls Wilder
1960	Clara Ingram Judson
1965	Ruth Sawyer
1970	E. B. White
1975	Beverly Cleary
1980	Dr. Seuss

THE NATIONAL COUNCIL OF TEACHERS OF ENGLISH AWARD FOR EXCELLENCE IN POETRY FOR CHILDREN

This award, first presented in 1977, is given annually to a living American poet in recognition of his or her entire body of work. Winners are as follows:

1977	David McCord
1978	Aileen Fisher
1979	Karla Kuskin
1980	Myra Cohn Livingston

THE HANS CHRISTIAN ANDERSEN AWARD

The Hans Christian Andersen Award is given biennially by the International Board on Books for Young People to one living author and (since 1965) one illustrator for his or her entire body of work. The winner is selected by a committee of five persons, each from a different country.

1956	Eleanor Farjeon (Great Britain)
1958	Astrid Lindgren (Sweden)
1960	Erich Kästner (Germany)
1962	Meindert DeJong (U.S.A.)
1964	René Guillot (France)

1966	Author: Tove Jansson (Finland)
	Illustrator: Alois Carigiet (Switzerland)
1968	Authors: James Krüss (Germany)
	Jose Maria Sanchez-Silva (Spain)
	Illustrator: Jiri Trnka (Czechoslovakia)
1970	Author: Gianni Rodari (Italy)
	Illustrator: Maurice Sendak (U.S.A.)
1972	Author: Scott O'Dell (U.S.A.)
	Illustrator: Ib Spang Olsen (Denmark)
1974	Author: Maria Gripe (Sweden)
	Illustrator: Farshid Mesghali (Iran)
1976	Author: Cecil Bodker (Denmark)
	Illustrator: Tatjana Mawrina (U.S.S.R.)
1978	Author: Paula Fox (U.S.A.)
	Illustrator: Svend Otto (Denmark)
1980	Author: Bohumil Riha (Czechoslovakia)
	Illustrator: Suekichi Akaba (Japan)

INTERNATIONAL READING ASSOCIATION (IRA) CHILDREN'S BOOK AWARD

The IRA award, sponsored by the Institute for Reading Research and administered by the IRA, is presented annually for a children's book (published in the year preceding the award) by an author who shows unusual promise. Books originating in any country are eligible. For a book written in a language other than English, the IRA first determines if the book warrants an English translation and, if so, then extends to it an additional year of eligibility.

The list below gives title, author, and publisher of winners since inception of the award in 1975.

1975	*Transport 7-41-R* by T. Degens (Viking)
1976	*Dragonwings* by Lawrence Yep (Harper)
1977	*A String in the Harp* by Nancy Bond (Atheneum)
1978	*A Summer to Die* by Lois Lowry (Houghton)
1979	*Reserved for Mark Anthony Crowder* by Alison Smith (Dutton)
1980	*Words by Heart* by Ouida Sebestyen (Little)
1981	*My Own Private Sky* by Delores Beckman (Dutton)

Book Selection Aids

BOOKS

AAAS Science Book List for Children comp. by Hilary J. Deason, American Association for the Advancement of Science, 1972.

Adventuring with Books: A Booklist for Pre-K-Grade 8 ed. by Mary Lou White, National Council of Teachers of English, 1981.

The Best in Children's Books: The University of Chicago Guide to Children's Literature 1966-1972 ed. by Zena Sutherland, The University of Chicago Press, 1973.

The Black Experience in Children's Books selected by Barbara Rollock, New York Public Library, 1974.

The Bookfinder: A Guide to Children's Literature about the Needs and Problems of Youth Aged 2-15 by Sharon Spredemann Dryer, American Guidance Service, 1977.

Canadian Books for Children (Livres Canadiens pour Enfants) comp. by Irma McDonough, University of Toronto Press, 1976.

Children's Books: Awards and Prizes comp. by the Children's Book Council, Children's Book Council (Biennial).

Children's Book Showcase comp. by the Children's Book Council, Children's Book Council, 1977.

Children's Books in Print, Bowker (Annual).

Children's Books of International Interest, 2d ed., ed. by Virginia Haviland, American Library Association, 1978.

Children's Catalog, 13th ed., Wilson (Annual).

Children's Literature: A Guide to Reference Sources comp. by Virginia Haviland et al., Government Printing Office, 1966 (Supplement, 1972).

The Elementary School Library Collection, 13th ed., ed. by Louis Winkler, Bro-Dart Foundation, 1982.

Growing Up with Books, Bowker, 1977.

Growing Up with Paperbacks, Bowker, 1977.

Index to Poetry for Children and Young People: 1964–1969, comp. by John E. Brewton, Sara W. Brewton, and G. Meredith Blackburn III, Wilson, 1972.

Juniorplots: A Book Talk Manual for Teachers and Librarians by John T. Gillespie and Diana L. Lembo, Bowker, 1967.

Matters of Fact: Aspects of Non-Fiction for Children by Margery Fisher, Crowell, 1972.

More Juniorplots by John T. Gillespie, Bowker, 1977.

A Multimedia Approach to Children's Literature, 2d. ed., by Ellin Greene and Madalynne Schoenfeld, American Library Association, 1977.

New Books for Young Readers comp. and ed. by Norine Odland, College of Education, University of Minnesota (Annual).

Notable Children's Books comp. by Association for Library Service to Children, American Library Association, 1977 (Annual).

Notes from a Different Drummer: A Guide to Juvenile Fiction Portraying the Handicapped comp. by Barbara H. Baskin and Karen H. Harris, Bowker, 1977.

Paperback Books for Children comp. by the Committee on Paperback Lists for Elementary School of the American Library Association, Citation, 1972.

Paperback Books for Young People: An Annotated Guide to Publishers and Distributors, 2nd ed., ed. by John T. Gillespie, American Library Association, 1977.

Paperback Books in Print, Bowker (Annual).

A Parent's Guide to Children's Reading by Nancy Larrick, Doubleday, 1975.

Periodicals for School Media Programs ed. by Selma K. Richardson, American Library Association, 1978.

Picture Books for Children ed. by Patricia Cianciolo, American Library Association, 1973.

Reading Ladders for Human Relations, 6th ed., ed. by Eileen Tway, National Council of Teachers of English, 1981.

The School Library Media Center: A Force for Educational Excellence ed. by Ruth Ann Davis, Bowker, 1974.

Selecting Materials for Children and Young Adults: A Bibliography of Bibliographies and Review Sources. American Library Association, 1980.

Subject Guide to Children's Books in Print, Bowker (Annual).

Subject Index to Poetry for Children and Young People 1957–1975 comp. by Dorothy B. Frissell Smith and Eva L. Andrews, American Library Association, 1977.

Your Reading: A Booklist for Junior High Students, 5th ed., ed. by Jerry L. Walker et al., National Council of Teachers of English, 1975.

JOURNALS

Book Review Digest, Wilson.

Bookbird, ed. by Richard Bamberger, International Board on Books for Young People, Package Library of Foreign Children's Books.

The Booklist, American Library Association.

The Bulletin, Council on Interracial Books for Children, Inc.

The Bulletin of the Center for Children's Books, Graduate Library School, Univ. of Chicago Press.

The Calendar, Children's Book Council.

Children's Literature in Education, APS Publications, Inc.

Horn Book Magazine, Horn Book, Inc.

Instructor, Instructor Publications, Inc.

Language Arts, National Council of Teachers of English.

Media and Methods, North American Publishing.

The New York Times Book Review, New York Times.

Phaedrus: An International Journal of Children's Literature Research, Phaedrus, Inc., K. G. Saur Publishing.

Previews, Bowker.

Publisher's Weekly, Spring and Fall specials, Bowker.

School Library Journal, Bowker.

School Media Quarterly, American Association of School Librarians, American Library Association.

Science and Children, National Science Teachers Association.

Teacher, Macmillan Professional Magazines, Inc.

Top of the News, Association for Library Services to Children and Young Adult Services Division, American Library Association.

The Web, Center for Language, Literature, and Reading, Ohio State University.

Wilson Library Bulletin, Wilson.

Books About Authors and Illustrators

The Art of Nancy Ekholm Burkert ed. by David Larkin, Harper, 1977.

Authors and Illustrators of Children's Books: Writings on their Lives And Works ed. by Miriam Hoffman and Eva Samuels, Bowker, 1972.

Books Are by People: Interviews with 104 Authors and Illustrators of Books for Young Children by Lee Bennett Hopkins, Citation, 1969. (Companion volume: *More Books by More People.* Citation, 1974.)

From Writers to Students: The Pleasures and Pains of Writing ed. by M. Jerry Weiss, International Reading Association, 1979.

Hans Christian Andersen by Elias Bredsdorff, Scribner's, 1975.

Illustrators of Children's Books 1967–1976 comp. by Lee Kingman, Grace Allen Hogarth, and Harriet Quimby, Horn Book, 1978. (Companion volumes available for the years 1744–1945, 1946–1956, and 1957–1966.)

The Junior Book of Authors ed. by Stanley Kunitz and Howard Haycraft, Wilson, 1951. (Companion volumes: *More Junior Authors, Third Book of Junior Authors,* and *Fourth Book of Junior Authors.*)

The Kate Greenaway Book: A Collection of Illustration, Verse and Text ed. by Bryan Holme, Viking, 1976.

The Kate Greenaway Treasury ed. by Edward Ernest, World, 1967.

Newbery and Caldecott Medal Books, 1966–1975 ed. by Lee Kingman, Horn Book, 1975. (Companion volumes: *Newbery Medal Books, 1922–1955; Caldecott Medal Books, 1938–1957;* and *Newbery and Caldecott Medal Books, 1956–1965.*)

The Pied Pipers by Justin Wintle and Emma Fisher, Two Continents, 1975.

Perverse and Foolish: A Memoir of Childhood and Youth by L. M. Boston, Atheneum, 1979.

Randolph Caldecott, "Lord of the Nursery." by Rodney K. Engen, Two Continents, 1976.

A Sense of Story: Essays on Contemporary Writers for Children by John Rowe Townsend, Lippincott, 1971.

Something About the Author (A continuing series) ed. by Anne Commire, Gale, 1971 to present.

A Sounding of Storytellers: Essays on Contemporary Writers for Children by John Rowe Townsend, Lippincott, 1979.

The Tale of Beatrix Potter: A Biography by Margaret Lane, Warne, 1946.

Who's Who in Children's Books: A Treasury of the Familiar Characters of Childhood by Margery Fisher, Holt, 1975.

The Who's Who of Children's Literature comp. and ed. by Brian Doyle, Schocken, 1968.

Yesterday's Authors of Books for Children ed. by Anne Commire, Gale, 1977.

Publishers of Children's Books

Abelard-Schuman
 257 Park Avenue
 New York, NY 10010
Abingdon Press
 201 Eighth Avenue South
 Nashville, TN 37202
Addison-Wesley Publishing Co., Inc.
 Jacob Way
 Reading, MA 01867
Ariel (Farrar)
 19 Union Square
 New York, NY 10003
Astor Honor
 48 East 43d St.
 New York, NY 10017
Atheneum Publishers
 597 Fifth Avenue
 New York, NY 10017
The Atlantic Monthly Press
 8 Arlington St.
 Boston, MA 02116
Avon Books
 959 Eighth Avenue
 New York, NY 10019
Bantam Books
 666 Fifth Avenue
 New York, NY 10019

Bobbs-Merrill
 4300 West 62d St.
 Indianapolis, IN 46206
Bowmar
 Box 3623
 Glendale, CA 91201
Bradbury Press, Inc.
 2 Overhill Road
 Scarsdale, NY 10583
Carolrhoda Books
 241 First Avenue North
 Minneapolis, MN 55401
Childrens Press
 1224 West Van Buren St.
 Chicago, IL 60607
William Collins Publishers, Inc.
 200 Madison Avenue
 New York, NY 10016
Coward, McCann & Geoghegan, Inc.
 200 Madison Avenue
 New York, NY 10016
Crowell Junior Books
(Harper Junior Books Group)
 10 East 53rd St.
 New York, NY 10022
Creative Education
 123 South Broad St.
 Mankato, MN 56001

Crown Publishers, Inc.
 One Park Avenue
 New York, NY 10016
Delacorte Press
 1 Dag Hammarskjold Plaza
 245 East 47th St.
 New York, NY 10017
Dell Publishing Co., Inc.
 1 Dag Hammarskjold Plaza
 245 East 47th St.
 New York, NY 10017
The Dial Press
 1 Dag Hammarskjold Plaza
 245 East 47th St.
 New York, NY 10017
Dodd, Mead & Co., Inc.
 79 Madison Avenue
 New York, NY 10016
Doubleday & Co., Inc.
 245 Park Avenue
 New York, NY 10017
Dover Publications, Inc.
 180 Varick St.
 New York, NY 10014
E. P. Dutton
 2 Park Avenue
 New York, NY 10016

Elsevier/Nelson Books
2 Park Avenue
New York, NY 10016

M. Evans & Co., Inc.
216 East 49th St.
New York, NY 10017

Farrar, Straus & Giroux, Inc.
19 Union Square West
New York, NY 10003

Follett Publishing Co.
1010 West Washington Boulevard
Chicago, IL 60607

Four Winds Press
50 West 44th St.
New York, NY 10036

Garrard Publishing
1607 North Market St.
Champaign, IL 61820

Golden Gate Junior Books
1247½ North Vista St.
Los Angeles, CA 90046

Golden Press (Western Publishing)
Mound Ave.
Racine, WI 53404

Greenwillow Books
(A Division of William Morrow & Co.)
105 Madison Avenue
New York, NY 10016

Grosset & Dunlap, Inc.
51 Madison Avenue
New York, NY 10010

Harcourt Brace Jovanovich, Inc.
757 Third Avenue
New York, NY 10017

Harper & Row, Publishers, Inc.
10 East 53rd St.
New York, NY 10022

Harvey House, Publishers
20 Waterside Plaza
New York, NY 10010

Hastings House Publishers, Inc.
10 East 40th St.
New York, NY 10016

Holiday House
18 East 53rd St.
New York, NY 10022

Holt, Rinehart & Winston
383 Madison Avenue
New York, NY 10017

Houghton Mifflin Co.
2 Park Street
Boston, MA 02107

Houghton Mifflin/Clarion Books
52 Vanderbilt Avenue
New York, NY 10017

Alfred A. Knopf, Inc.
201 East 50th St.
New York, NY 10022

Larousse & Co., Inc.
572 Fifth Avenue
New York, NY 10036

Lerner Publications
241 First Ave. N.
Minneapolis, MN 55401

Lippincott Junior Books
(Harper Junior Books Group)
10 East 53rd St.
New York, NY 10022

Little, Brown & Co.
34 Beacon Street
Boston, MA 02106

Lothrop, Lee & Shepard Co.
105 Madison Avenue
New York, NY 10016

Margaret K. McElderry Books
(A Division of Atheneum Publishers)
597 Fifth Avenue
New York, NY 10017

McGraw-Hill Book Co.
1221 Avenue of the Americas
New York, NY 10020

David McKay
750 Third Avenue
New York, NY 10017

Macmillan Publishing Co., Inc.
866 Third Avenue
New York, NY 10022

Julian Messner
(A Simon & Schuster Division of
Gulf & Western Corporation)
1230 Avenue of the Americas
New York, NY 10020

Methuen, Inc.
733 Third Avenue
New York, NY 10017

William Morrow & Co., Inc.
105 Madison Avenue
New York, NY 10016

The New American Library, Inc.
1301 Avenue of the Americas
New York, NY 10019

Oxford University Press
200 Madison Avenue
New York, NY 10016

Pantheon Books
201 East 50th St.
New York, NY 10022

Parents Magazine Press
(A Division of Parents Magazine
Enterprises)
685 Third Avenue
New York, NY 10017

Platt & Munk
1055 Bronx River Avenue
Bronx, NY 10472

Plays, Inc.
8 Arlington St.
Boston, MA 02116

Pocket Books
1230 Avenue of the Americas
New York, NY 10020

Prentice-Hall, Inc.
Englewood Cliffs, NJ 07632

G. P. Putnam's Sons
200 Madison Avenue
New York, NY 10016

Harlin Quist Books
192 East 75 St.
New York, NY 10021

Rand McNally & Co.
P. O. Box 7600
Chicago, IL 60680

Random House
201 East 50th Street
New York, NY 10022

Schocken Books, Inc.
200 Madison Avenue
New York, NY 10016

Scholastic Book Services
50 West 44th St.
New York, NY 10036

Scott, Foresman and Co.
1900 East Lake Avenue
Glenview, IL 60025

Charles Scribner's Sons
597 Fifth Avenue
New York, NY 10017

Sierra Club Books
  53 Bush St.
  San Francisco, CA 94108
Tundra Books of Northern New York
  51 Clinton St.
  P. O. Box 1030
  Plattsburgh, NY 12901
Unicorn Books
(An Imprint of E. P. Dutton)
  306 Dartmouth St.
  Boston, MA 02116

Viking Penguin, Inc.
  625 Madison Avenue
  New York, NY 10022
Walker & Co.
  720 Fifth Avenue
  New York, NY 10019
Wanderer Books
  Simon & Schuster Building
  1230 Avenue of the Americas
  New York, NY 10020
Frederick Warne & Co., Inc.
  2 Park Avenue
  New York, NY 10016
Franklin Watts, Inc.
  730 Fifth Avenue
  New York, NY 10019

Western Publishing Co.
  850 Third Avenue
  New York, NY 10022
The Westminster Press
  925 Chestnut St.
  Philadelphia, PA 19107
Windmill Books
  Simon & Schuster Bldg.
  1230 Avenue of the Americas
  New York, NY 10020

A Year of Holiday Books

GENERAL

Alexander, Sue. *Small Plays for Special Days*. Ill. by Tom Huffman. Seabury, 1977.

Cole, Ann, et al. *A Pumpkin in a Pear Tree: Creative Ideas for Twelve Months of Holiday Fun*. Ill. by Debby Young. Little, 1976.

Fisher, Aileen, comp. *Holiday Programs for Boys and Girls*. Plays, Inc., 1970.

Larrick, Nancy, comp. *More Poetry for Holidays*. Ill. by Harold Berson. Garrard, 1973.

_____. *Poetry for Holidays*. Ill. by Kelly Oechsli. Garrard, 1966.

Livingston, Myra Cohn, ed. *O Frabjous Day! Poetry for Holidays and Special Occasions*. Atheneum, 1977.

Manning-Sanders, Ruth, comp. *Festivals*. Ill. by Raymond Briggs. Dutton, 1972.

Purdy, Susan. *Festivals for You to Celebrate*. Lippincott, 1969.

Quackenbush, Robert, selector and illustrator. *The Holiday Song Book*. Lothrop, 1977.

Sechrist, Elizabeth Hough. *Poems for Red Letter Days*. Ill. by Guy Fry. Macrae Smith, 1951.

_____. *Red Letter Days: A Book of Holiday Customs*. Ill. by Elsie Jane McCorkell. Macrae Smith, 1965.

Tudor, Tasha. *A Time to Keep: The Tasha Tudor Book of Holidays*. Rand, 1977.

HALLOWEEN

Adams, Adrienne. *A Woggle of Witches*. Scribner's, 1971.

Alexander, Sue. *Witch, Goblin and Sometimes Ghost*. Ill. by Jeanette Winter. Pantheon, 1976.

Anderson, Lonzo. *The Halloween Party*. Ill. by Adrienne Adams. Scribner's, 1974.

Balian, Lorna. *Humbug Witch!* Abingdon, 1965.

Bang, Molly. *The Goblins Giggle and Other Stories*. Scribner's, 1973.

Barth, Edna. *Jack-O'-Lantern*. Ill. by Paul Galdone. Seabury, 1974.

Bright, Robert. *Georgie's Halloween*. Doubleday, 1971.

Coombs, Patricia. *Dorrie and the Halloween Plot*. Lothrop, 1976.

Dobrin, Arnold. *Make a Witch, Make a Goblin: A Book of Halloween Crafts*. Four Winds, 1977.

Gibbons, Gail. *Things to Make and Do for Halloween*. Watts, 1976.

Godden, Rumer. *Mr. McFadden's Halloween*. Viking, 1975.

Harper, Wilhelmina, comp. *Ghosts and Goblins: Stories for Halloween and Other Times*. Ill. by William Wiesner. Dutton, 1965.

Hopkins, Lee Bennett, ed. *Hey-How for Halloween*. Ill. by Janet McCaffrey. Harcourt Brace Jovanovich, 1974.

548 _____. *Monsters, Ghoulies and Creepy Creatures*. Ill. by Vera Rosenberry. Whitman, 1977.

Hurd, Edith. *The So-So Cat*. Ill. by Clement Hurd. Harper, 1964.

McGovern, Ann. *Squeals and Squiggles and Ghostly Giggles*. Ill. by Jeffrey Higginbottom. Four Winds, 1973.

Massey, Jeanne. *The Littlest Witch*. Ill. by Adrienne Adams. Knopf, 1959.

Miller, Edna. *Mousekin's Golden House*. Prentice-Hall, 1964.

Moore, Lilian. *See My Lovely Poison Ivy: And Other Verses about Witches, Ghosts and Things*. Ill. by Diane Dawson. Atheneum, 1975.

Prelutsky, Jack. *It's Halloween*. Ill. by Marylin Hafner. Greenwillow, 1977.

_____. *Nightmares: Poems to Trouble Your Sleep*. Ill. by Arnold Lobel. Greenwillow, 1976.

Riley, James Whitcomb. *The Gobble-uns'll Git You Ef You Don't Watch Out!* Ill. by Joel Schick, Lippincott, 1975.

Schulman, Janet. *Jack the Bum and the Halloween Handout*. Ill. by James Stevenson. Greenwillow, 1977.

Seuling, Barbara, reteller and illustrator. *The Teeny Tiny Woman: An Old English Ghost Tale*. Viking, 1976.

Thayer, Jane. *Gus Was a Gorgeous Ghost*. Ill. by Seymour Fleishman. Morrow, 1978.

Zolotow, Charlotte. *A Tiger Called Thomas*. Ill. by Kurt Werth. Lothrop, 1963.

THANKSGIVING

Alcott, Louisa May. *An Old Fashioned Thanksgiving*. Ill. by Holly Johnson. Lippincott, 1974.

Balian, Lorna. *Sometimes It's Turkey, Sometimes It's Feathers*. Abingdon, 1973.

Child, Lydia Maria. *Over the River and Through the Wood*. Ill. by Brinton Turkle. Coward, 1974.

Dalgliesh, Alice. *The Thanksgiving Story*. Ill. by Helen Sewell. Scribner's, 1954.

Devlin, Wende, and Harry Devlin. *Cranberry Thanksgiving*. Parents, 1971.

Harper, Wilhelmina, comp. *Harvest Feast: Stories of Thanksgiving Yesterday and Today*. Ill. by W. T. Mars. Dutton, 1967.

Hays, Wilma Pitchford. *Pilgrim Thanksgiving*. Ill. by Leonard Weisgard. Coward, 1955.

Hopkins, Lee Bennett, ed. *Merrily Comes Our Harvest In: Poems for Thanksgiving*. Ill. by Ben Shecter. Harcourt Brace Jovanovich, 1978.

Ipcar, Dahlov. *Hard Scrabble Harvest*. Doubleday, 1976.

Janice. *Little Bear's Thanksgiving*. Ill. by Mariana. Lothrop, 1967.

Luckhardt, Mildred Corell, comp. *Thanksgiving: Feast and Festival*. Ill. by Ralph McDonald. Abingdon, 1966.

Rock, Gail. *The Thanksgiving Treasure*. Ill. by Charles C. Gehm. Knopf, 1974.

Weisgard, Leonard. *The Plymouth Thanksgiving*. Doubleday, 1967.

CHANUKAH

Aleichem, Sholem. *Hanukkah Money*. Tran. and adap. by Uri Shulevitz and Elizabeth Shub. Ill. by Uri Shulevitz. Greenwillow, 1978.

Becker, Joyce. *Hanukkah Crafts*. Bonim, 1978.

Greenfeld, Howard. *Chanukah*. Designed by Bea Feitler. Holt, 1976.

Hirsh, Marilyn. *The Hanukkah Story*. Bonim, 1977.

_____. *Potato Pancakes All Around: A Hanukkah Tale*. Bonim, 1978.

CHRISTMAS

Adams, Adrienne. *The Christmas Party*. Scribner's, 1978.

Adshead, Gladys. *Brownies — It's Christmas*. Walck, 1955.

Aichinger, Helga. *The Shepherd*. Crowell, 1966.

Alden, Raymond MacDonald. *Why the Chimes Rang*. Ill. by Rafaello Busoni. Hale, 1963 (1906).

Andersen, Hans Christian. *The Fir Tree*. Ill. by Nancy Ekholm Burkert. Harper, 1970.

_____. *The Little Match Girl*. Ill. by Blair Lent. Houghton, 1968.

Baker, Laura Nelson. *The Friendly Beasts*. Ill. by Nicolas Sidjakov. Parnassus, 1957.

Balian, Lorna. *Bah! Humbug?* Abingdon, 1977.

Belting, Natalia. *Christmas Folk*. Ill. by Barbara Cooney. Holt, 1969.

Bonsall, Crosby. *Twelve Bells for Santa*. Harper, 1977.

Brewton, Sara, and John E. Brewton, comps. *Christmas Bells Are Ringing: A Treasury of Christmas Poetry*. Ill. by Decie Merwin. Macmillan, 1951.

Brown, Margaret Wise. *Christmas in the Barn*. Ill. by Barbara Cooney. Crowell, 1952.

_____. *The Steamroller*. Ill. by Evaline Ness. Walker, 1974.

Bruna, Dick. *The Christmas Book*. Methuen, 1976.

Carrick, Carol. *Paul's Christmas Birthday*. Ill. by Donald Carrick. Greenwillow, 1978.

Caudill, Rebecca. *A Certain Small Shepherd*. Ill. by William Pène du Bois. Holt, 1965.

Chalmers, Mary. *Merry Christmas, Harry*. Harper, 1977.

Clifton, Lucille. *Everett Anderson's Christmas Coming*. Ill. by Evaline Ness. Holt, 1971.

Coskey, Evelyn. *Christmas Crafts for Everyone*. Ill. by Roy Wallace. Abingdon, 1976.

Dalgliesh, Alice. *Christmas: A Book of Stories Old and New*. Ill. by Hildegard Woodward. Scribner's, 1950.

De Angeli, Marguerite. *The Lion in the Box*. Doubleday, 1975.

_____. *Turkey for Christmas*. Westminster, 1965.

De Paola, Tomie, reteller. *The Clown of God*. Harcourt Brace Jovanovich, 1978.

Domanska, Janina. *Din Dan Don: It's Christmas*. Greenwillow, 1975.

Duvoisin, Roger. *Petunia's Christmas*. Knopf, 1952.

Erickson, Russell E. *Warton's Christmas Eve Adventure*. Ill. by Lawrence Di Fiori. Lothrop, 1977.

Ets, Marie Hall. *Nine Days to Christmas*. Viking, 1959.

Fisher, Aileen. *Christmas Plays and Programs*. Plays, Inc., 1970.

Frost, Frances Mary. *Christmas in the Woods*. Ill. by Aldren A. Watson. Harper, 1976.

Goodall, John S. *An Edwardian Christmas*. Atheneum, 1978.

Graham, Lorenz. *Every Man Heart Lay Down*. Ill. by Colleen Browning. Crowell, 1970.

Harper, Wilhelmina. *Merry Christmas to You*. Ill. by Fermin Rocker. Dutton, 1965.

Hays, Wilma Pitchford. *Christmas on the Mayflower*. Ill. by Roger Duvoisin. Coward, 1956.

Hoban, Lillian. *Arthur's Christmas Cookies*. Harper, 1972.

Hoban, Russell. *Emmet Otter's Jug-Band Christmas*. Ill. by Lillian Hoban. Parents, 1971.

_____. *The Mole Family's Christmas*. Ill. by Lillian Hoban. Parents, 1969.

Hoffmann, Felix, illus. *The Story of Christmas*. Atheneum, 1975.

Hopkins, Lee Bennett, ed. *Sing Hey for Christmas Day*. Ill. by Laura Jean Allen. Harcourt Brace Jovanovich, 1975.

Hurd, Edith Thatcher. *Christmas Eve*. Ill. by Clement Hurd. Harper, 1962.

Hutchins, Pat. *The Silver Christmas Tree*. Macmillan, 1974.

Irion, Ruth Hershey. *The Christmas Cookie Tree*. Westminster, 1976.

Janice. *Little Bear's Christmas*. Ill. by Mariana. Lothrop, 1964.

Johnson, Lois S., ed. *Christmas Stories 'Round the World*. Ill. by D. K. Stone. Rand, 1970.

Jones, E. Willis. *The Santa Claus Book*. Walker, 1976.

Kahl, Virginia. *Gunhilde's Christmas Book*. Scribner's, 1972.

Keats, Ezra Jack, illus. *The Little Drummer Boy*. Words and music by Katherine Davis, Henry Onorati, and Harry Simeone. Macmillan, 1968.

Krahn, Fernando. *The Biggest Christmas Tree on Earth*. Little, 1978.

Kroll, Steven. *Santa's Crash-Bang Christmas*. Ill. by Tomie de Paola. Holiday, 1977.

Kurelek, William. *A Northern Nativity: Christmas Dreams of a Prairie Boy*. Scribner's, 1976.

Langstaff, John, comp. *On Christmas Day in the Morning*. Ill. by Antony Groves-Raines. Harcourt Brace Jovanovich, 1959.

_____. *Saint George and the Dragon: A Mummer's Play*. Ill. by David Gentleman. Atheneum, 1973.

_____. *The Season for Singing: American Christmas Songs and Carols*. Musical setting by Seymour Barab. Doubleday, 1974.

Lenski, Lois. *Lois Lenski's Christmas Stories*. Lippincott, 1968.

Lindgren, Astrid, and Ilon Wikland. *Christmas in Noisy Village*. Tran. by Florence Lamborn. Viking, 1964.

_____. *Christmas in the Stable*. Ill. by Harald Wiberg. Coward, 1962.

Luckhardt, Mildred Corell, ed. *Christmas Comes Once More: Stories and Poems for the Holiday Season*. Ill. by Grisha Dotzenko. Abingdon, 1962.

McGinley, Phyllis. *A Wreath of Christmas Legends*. Ill. by Leonard Weisgard. Macmillan, 1967.

_____. *The Year Without a Santa Claus*. Ill. by Kurt Werth. Lippincott, 1957.

Manifold, Laurie Fraser. *The Christmas Window*. Houghton, 1971.

Menotti, Gian Carolo. *Amahl and the Night Visitors*. Adap. by Frances Frost. Ill. by Roger Duvoisin. McGraw, 1952.

Moeri, Louise. *Star Mother's Youngest Child*. Houghton, 1975.

Moore, Clement Clarke. *The Night Before Christmas*. Ill. by Elisa Trimby. Doubleday, 1977.

_____. *The Night Before Christmas*. Ill. by Tasha Tudor. Rand, 1976.

Northrop, Marguerite, ed. *The Christmas Story: From the Gospels of Matthew and Luke*. Metropolitan Museum of Art, 1966.

Parish, Peggy. *December Decorations: A Holiday How-To Book*. Ill. by Barbara Wolff. Macmillan, 1975.

Pettit, Florence Harvey. *Christmas All Around the House: Traditional Decorations You Can Make*. Ill. by Wendy Watson. Crowell, 1976.

Potter, Beatrix. *The Tailor of Gloucester*. Warne, 1904.

Purdy, Susan Gold. *Christmas Cookbook*. Watts, 1976.

Raskin, Ellen. *Twenty-Two, Twenty-Three*. Atheneum, 1976.

Reeves, James, comp. *The Christmas Book*. Ill. by Raymond Briggs. Dutton, 1970.

Robbins, Ruth. *Baboushka and the Three Kings*. Ill. by Nicolas Sidjakov. Parnassus, 1960.

Robinson, Barbara. *The Best Christmas Pageant Ever*. Ill. by Judith Gwyn Brown. Harper, 1972.

Rock, Gail. *The House Without a Christmas Tree*. Knopf, 1974.

Rockwell, Ann. *Befana: A Christmas Story*. Atheneum, 1974.

Sawyer, Ruth. *Joy to the World: Christmas Legends*. Ill. by Trina Schart Hyman. Little, 1966.

Sechrist, Elizabeth Hough, comp. *Christmas Everywhere: A Book of Christmas Customs of Many Lands*. Ill. by Elsie Jane McCorkell. Macrae-Smith, 1962.

Seuss, Dr. *How the Grinch Stole Christmas*. Random, 1957.

Tolkien, J. R. R. *The Father Christmas Letters*. Ed. Baillie Tolkien. Houghton, 1976.

Tudor, Tasha. *Becky's Christmas*. Viking, 1961.

_____. *Take Joy! The Tasha Tudor Christmas Book*. Collins-World, 1966.

Van Leeuwen, Jean. *The Great Christmas Kidnaping Caper*. Ill. by Steven Kellogg. Dial, 1975.

Von Juchen, Aurel. *The Holy Night: The Story of the First Christmas*. Ill. by Celestino Piatti. Atheneum, 1968.

Wells, Rosemary. *Morris's Disappearing Bag: A Christmas Story*. Dial, 1975.

Wenning, Elisabeth. *The Christmas Mouse*. Illustrated by Barbara Remington. Holt, 1959.

Wiberg, Harald. *Christmas at the Tomten's Farm*. Coward, 1968.

Wildsmith, Brian. *Brian Wildsmith's The Twelve Days of Christmas*. Watts, 1972.

VALENTINE'S DAY

Barth, Edna. *Cupid and Psyche: A Love Story*. Ill. by Ati Forberg. Seabury, 1976.

Cohen, Miriam. *"Bee My Valentine!"* Ill. by Lillian Hoban. Greenwillow, 1978.

De Paola, Tomie. *Things to Make and Do for Valentine's Day*. Watts, 1976.

Hays, Wilma Pitchford. *The Story of Valentine*. Ill. by Leonard Weisgard. Coward, 1956.

Hopkins, Lee Bennett, ed. *Good Morning to You, Valentine*. Ill. by Tomie de Paola. Harcourt Brace Jovanovich, 1976.

Krahn, Fernando. *Little Love Story*. Lippincott, 1976.

Mariana. *Miss Flora McFlimsey's Valentine*. Lothrop, 1961.

Milhous, Katherine. *Appolonia's Valentine*. Scribner's, 1954.

Quinn, Gardner. *Valentine Crafts and Cookbook*. Ill. by Madeline Crossman. Harvey, 1977.

Schweninger, Ann. *The Hunt for Rabbit's Galosh*. Ill. by Kay Chorao. Doubleday, 1976.

Yaroslava, ed. *I Like You and Other Poems for Valentine's Day*. Scribner's, 1976.

EASTER

Adams, Adrienne. *The Easter Egg Artists*. Scribner's, 1976.

Balian, Lorna. *Humbug Rabbit*. Abingdon, 1974.

Brown, Margaret Wise. *The Golden Egg Book*. Ill. by Leonard Weisgard. Golden, 1947.

Coskey, Evelyn. *Easter Eggs for Everyone*. Ill. by Giorgetta Bell. Abingdon, 1973.

Harper, Wilhelmina, comp. *Easter Chimes: Stories for Easter and the Spring Season*. Ill. by Hoot von Zitzewitz. Dutton, 1967.

Heyward, Du Bose. *The Country Bunny and the Little Gold Shoes*. Ill. by Marjorie Flack. Houghton, 1939.

Hoban, Lillian. *The Sugar Snow Spring*. Harper, 1973.

Hoban, Tana. *Where Is It?* Macmillan, 1974.

Keats, Ezra Jack. *Jennie's Hat*. Harper, 1966.

Kraus, Robert. *Daddy Long Ears*. Simon & Schuster, 1970.

Milhous, Katherine. *The Egg Tree*. Scribner's, 1950.

Tresselt, Alvin. *The World in the Candy Egg*. Ill. by Roger Duvoisin. Lothrop, 1967.

Tudor, Tasha. *A Tale for Easter*. Walck, 1941.

Weil, Lisl. *The Candy Egg Bunny*. Holiday, 1975.

Birthdays of Selected Authors and Illustrators

JANUARY

2   Isaac Asimov, Crosby Bonsall, Jean Little
3   Carolyn Haywood, J. R. R. Tolkien
4   Jakob Grimm
6   Carl Sandburg, Vera Cleaver
7   Kay Chorao
9   Clyde Robert Bulla
10   Remy Charlip
11   Robert O'Brien
12   Charles Perrault, Jack London
13   Michael Bond
14   Hugh Lofting
18   A. A. Milne, Raymond Briggs
19   Edgar Allen Poe
22   Blair Lent, Brian Wildsmith
25   James Flora
26   Mary Mapes Dodge
27   Lewis Carroll, Jean Merrill
29   Bill Peet
30   Lloyd Alexander

FEBRUARY

1   Langston Hughes
2   Rebecca Caudill
4   Russell Hoban
5   Patricia Lauber
7   Laura Ingalls Wilder
8   Jules Verne
9   Hilda Van Stockum
10   Elaine Konigsburg, Charles Lamb
11   Jane Yolen
12   Judy Blume
15   Norman Bridwell, Doris Orgel
16   Nancy Ekholm Burkert
19   Louis Slobodkin
24   Wilhelm Grimm
25   Frank Bonham
27   Henry Wadsworth Longfellow, Uri Shulevitz
28   Sir John Tenniel

MARCH

2 Dr. Seuss, Leo Dillon
4 Meindert DeJong
5 Errol Le Cain
8 Kenneth Grahame
11 Wanda Gág, Ezra Jack Keats
12 Virginia Hamilton
13 Ellen Raskin, Dorothy Aldis, Diane Dillon
14 Marguerite de Angeli
16 Sid Fleischman
17 Kate Greenaway
20 Ellen Conford, Mitsumasa Anno
22 Randolph Caldecott
23 Eleanor Cameron
24 Mary Stolz, Bill Cleaver
26 Robert Frost

APRIL

2 Hans Christian Andersen
3 Washington Irving
8 Trina Schart Hyman
9 Joseph Krumgold, Leonard Wibberley
12 Beverly Cleary, Hardie Gramatky
13 Marguerite Henry, Genevieve Foster, Lee Bennett Hopkins
19 Jean Lee Latham
23 William Shakespeare
24 Evaline Ness
25 Walter De La Mare
27 Ludwig Bemelmans, John Burningham
29 Jill Paton Walsh

MAY

6 Leo Lionni
7 Nonny Hogrogian
8 Milton Meltzer
9 Eleanor Estes, Sir James Barrie, William Pène du Bois, Keith Robertson
10 John Rowe Townsend
11 Zilpha Keatley Snyder
12 Edward Lear
14 George Selden
18 Lillian Hoban, Irene Hunt
21 Virginia Haviland
22 Arnold Lobel
23 Scott O'Dell, Susan Cooper
25 Martha Alexander
30 Millicent Selsam
31 Jay Williams, Elizabeth Coatsworth

JUNE

1 James Daugherty
2 Norton Juster, Paul Galdone, Helen Oxenbury
3 Anita Lobel
5 Franklyn M. Branley
6 Peter Spier
7 Gwendolyn Brooks, John Goodall
10 Maurice Sendak
14 Penelope Farmer
18 Pat Hutchins
24 John Ciardi, Leonard Everett Fisher
25 Eric Carle
26 Pearl Buck, Charlotte Zolotow, Lynd Ward, Robert Burch, Wallace Tripp
30 Mollie Hunter

JULY

2 Jean Craighead George
4 Nathaniel Hawthorne
6 Beatrix Potter
11 E. B. White, Helen Cresswell
12 Johanna Spyri, Herbert S. Zim
13 Marcia Brown
14 Isaac Bashevis Singer, Peggy Parish
15 Walter Edmonds
16 Arnold Adoff
17 Karla Kuskin
19 Eve Merriam, John Newbery
23 Robert Quackenbush
27 Scott Corbett
28 Natalie Babbitt

AUGUST

6 Matt Christopher, Barbara Cooney
7 Betsy Byars
8 Jan Pienkowski
9 José Aruego
10 Margot Tomes
11 Don Freeman
15 Walter Crane, Brinton Turkle
17 Myra Cohn Livingston, Ariane Dewey
19 Ogden Nash
26 Patricia Beatty
28 Phyllis Krasilovsky, Roger Duvoisin, Tasha Tudor
30 Virginia Lee Burton

SEPTEMBER

2 Eugene Field
3 Aliki
4 Syd Hoff, Joan Aiken
7 C. B. Colby
9 Aileen Fisher
11 Alfred Slote
13 Roald Dahl, Else Minarik
14 William Armstrong
15 James Fenimore Cooper, Robert McCloskey
16 H. A. Rey
19 Arthur Rackham, Rachel Field
24 Harry Behn, Leslie Brooke, Jane Curry
27 Bernard Waber, Paul Goble
28 Kate Douglas Wiggin
30 Alvin Tresselt

OCTOBER

3 Natalie Savage Carlson, Molly Cone
4 Julia Cunningham, Robert Lawson, Munro Leaf, Donald Sobol
5 Louise Fitzhugh
6 Steven Kellogg
7 James Whitcomb Riley, Alice Dalgliesh, Susan Jeffers
10 James Marshall
13 Arna Bontemps
14 Lois Lenski
19 Ed Emberley
21 Ursula Le Guin
23 Marjorie Flack
24 Bruno Munari
27 Constance Greene
29 Philip Ressner

NOVEMBER

1 Symeon Shimin
7 Armstrong Sperry
12 Marjorie Weinman Sharmat
13 Nathaniel Benchley, Robert Louis Stevenson
14 Astrid Lindgren, William Steig
15 David McCord, Manus Pinkwater
16 Jean Fritz
20 William Cole
21 Elizabeth George Speare, Leo Politi
24 C. Collodi, Sylvia Engdahl
26 Doris Gates
28 Tomi Ungerer
29 Louisa May Alcott, Madeleine L'Engle, C. S. Lewis
30 Mark Twain, Margot Zemach

DECEMBER

2 David Macaulay
5 Christina Rossetti, Harve Zemach
6 Elizabeth Yates
8 Padraic Colum, Edwin Tunis
9 Joel Chandler Harris
10 Emily Dickinson, Rumer Godden, Ernest Shepard
12 Barbara Emberley
13 Leonard Weisgard
16 Marie Hall Ets, Arthur C. Clarke
18 Marilyn Sachs
22 William O. Steele
24 Feodor Rojankovsky
28 Carol Ryrie Brink
30 Rudyard Kipling, Mercer Mayer

National Children's Book Week

National Children's Book Week, established in 1919, is celebrated annually in the third week in November. The Book Week Committee, composed of editors, designers, and school-library promotion personnel, selects a different theme each year and invites professionals in the field to expand on the theme in a variety of ways, including posters, plays and stories, literary rebuses, bookmarks, story playing cards, and mobiles. The Children's Book Council oversees production and distribution of posters, mobiles, and bookmarks to schools, libraries, and homes across the country. The first Book Week poster, in 1919, was by Jessie Willcox Smith and used the theme "More Books in the Home." Used again in 1979, sixty years later, it was just as meaningful.

Further information about National Children's Book Week may be obtained from The Children's Book Council, Inc., 67 Irving Place, New York, NY. 10003.

(First poster for National Children's Book Week [1919] by Jessie Willcox Smith. Reproduced courtesy of The Children's Book Council, Inc., New York, N.Y., sponsor of National Children's Book Week.)

acknowledgments

Chapter 1

p. 2   N. M. Bodecker, ''Hello Book,'' from a bookmark for Children's Book Week (Children's Book Council, 1978). Used by permission of author.

p. 8   From *The Educated Imagination* by Northrop Frye. © 1964. Used by permission of Indiana University Press.

pp. 23 and 24   From *A Wizard of Earthsea* by Ursula K. Le Guin. Published by Houghton Mifflin Company / Parnassus Press. Copyright © 1968 by Ursula K. Le Guin. Reprinted by permission.

p. 28   ''The Little Turtle,'' from *Collected Poems* of Vachel Lindsay. Copyright © 1920 by Macmillan Publishing Co., Inc., renewed 1948 by Elizabeth C. Lindsay. Used by permission.

p. 28   ''Motor Cars,'' from *Songs from Around a Toadstool Table* by Rowena Bastin Bennett. Copyright © 1967 by Rowena Bastin Bennett. Used by permission of Follett Publishing Company.

p. 28   ''Hold Fast Your Dreams'' by Louise Driscoll. © 1916 by The New York Times Company. Reprinted by permission.

Chapter 2

p. 34   ''Time, You Old Gipsy Man,'' from *Collected Poems* by Ralph Hodgson. Reprinted by permission of Mrs. Ralph Hodgson and Macmillan Publishing Co., London and Basingstoke.

p. 58   From *Piping Down the Valleys Wild* by William Blake. Used with permission of Oxford University Press.

Chapter 3

p. 71   ''Books,'' from *One at a Time*. Copyright © 1939, 1952 by David McCord; copyright © 1961, 1962 by David McCord. By permission of Little, Brown and Company.

p. 72   From *Ramona the Pest* by Beverly Clearly. Reprinted by permission of William C. Morrow Company.

pp. 83−84   From *Toad of Toad Hall* by A. A. Milne. Reprinted by permission of Charles Scribner's Sons.

p. 88   Text excerpt from *Frog and Toad Together,* written and illustrated by Arnold Lobel. Copyright © 1971, 1972 by Arnold Lobel. By permission of Harper & Row, Publishers, Inc.

p. 88   From ''Arnold Lobel and Friends: An Interview'' by David W. McCullough. © 1979 by The New York Times Company. Reprinted by permission.

p. 89   Text excerpt from *And I Mean It, Stanley,* written and illustrated by Crosby Bonsall. Copyright © 1974 by Crosby Bonsall. By permission of Harper & Row, Publishers, Inc.

p. 97   ''The Mion and the Louse'' used by permission of Mr. Norton Mockridge.

p. 98   ''Some speeches are like the horns of a steer . . .'' from *Pun Fun* by Ennis Rees. © Copyright 1965 by Ennis Rees. An Abelard-Schuman Book. By permissin of Thomas Y. Crowell, Publishers.

p. 103   Reprinted by permission of Farrar, Straus and Giroux, Inc. Selection from *Eyes of the Amaryllis* by Natalie Babbitt. Copyright © 1977 by Natalie Babbitt.

pp. 103−104   Text excerpts from *Bridge to Terabithia* by Katherine Paterson. Copyright © 1977 by Katherine Paterson. By permission of Thomas Y. Crowell, Publishers.

Chapter 4

p. 114   ''Red Wheelbarrow,'' from *Collected Earlier Poems by William Carlos Williams.* Copyright © 1938 by New Directions Publishing Corporation. Reprinted by permission of the publisher.

p. 117 From "Caldecott Award Acceptance" by Ed Emberley, in *Newbery and Caldecott Medal Books: 1966–1975,* ed. Lee Kingman, The Horn Book, Inc. 1975.

p. 118–19 From *The Horn Book Magazine* (August 1976, August 1977). © by The Horn Book, Inc.

p. 120 "Leave Me Alone," from *At the Top of My Voice and Other Poems* by Felice Holman. Text copyright © 1970 by Felice Holman. Reprinted by permission of Charles Scribner's Sons.

p. 122 "The End," from *Now We Are Six* by A. A. Milne. Copyright © 1927 by E. P. Dutton and Co., Inc. Reprinted by permission of the publisher, E. P. Dutton.

pp. 124–25 "Us Two," from *Now We Are Six* by A. A. Milne. Copyright © 1927 by E. P. Dutton and Co., Inc. Reprinted by permission of the publisher, E. P. Dutton.

p. 127 "Binker," from *Now We Are Six* by A. A. Milne. Copyright © 1927 by E. P. Dutton and Co., Inc. Reprinted by permission of the publisher, E. P. Dutton.

p. 128 Text excerpt from *Where the Wild Things Are* by Maurice Sendak. Copyright © 1963 by Maurice Sendak. By permission of Harper & Row, Publishers, Inc.

p. 133 From *Amifika* by Lucille Clifton. Copyright © 1977 by E. P. Dutton and Co., Inc. Reprinted by permission of the publisher, E. P. Dutton.

p. 135 "Little" reprinted by permission of G. P. Putnam's Sons from *All Together* by Dorothy Aldis. Copyright © 1925; renewed 1953 by Dorothy Aldis.

p. 136 Text of "For Sale," from *Where the Sidewalk Ends: The Poems and Drawings of Shel Silverstein.* Copyright © 1974 by Shel Silverstein. By permission of Harper & Row, Publishers, Inc.

p. 137 Text excerpt from *Daddy* by Jeannette Caines. Text copyright © 1977 by Jeannette Franklin Caines. By permission of Harper & Row, Publishers, Inc.

p. 137 "Afternoon with Grandmother," in *Favorite Poems Old and New,* ed. Helen Ferris, Doubleday, 1957. Reprinted by permission of the author, Barbara Huff.

pp. 138–39 Text excerpt from *My Grandson Lew* by Charlotte Zolotow. Text copyright © 1974 by Charlotte Zolotow. By permission of Harper & Row, Publishers, Inc.

pp. 142 and 144 "Mud" by Polly Boyden. Reprinted by permission of Barbara Boyden Jordan.

p. 144 Text excerpt from *Listen, Rabbit* by Aileen Fisher. Text copyright © 1964 by Aileen Fisher. By permission of Thomas Y. Crowell, Publishers.

p. 150 Text excerpt from *The Moon Jumpers* by Janice May Udry. Text copyright © 1959 by Janice May Udry. By permission of Harper & Row, Publishers, Inc.

p. 152 From *Madeline* by Ludwig Bemelmans. Copyright © 1939 by Ludwig Bemelmans, © renewed 1967 by Madeleine Bemelmans and Barbara Bemelmans Marciano. Reprinted by permission of Viking Penguin Inc.

Chapter 5

p. 160 Text of "Invitation," from *Where the Sidewalk Ends: The Poems and Drawings of Shel Silverstein.* Copyright ©

1974 by Shel Silverstein. By permission of Harper & Row, Publishers, Inc.

p. 167 "After Ever Happily" by Ian Serraillier. Copyright © 1963 by Ian Serraillier. By permission of Oxford University Press.

p. 182 "Terrible Troll's Tollbridge," from *The Phantom Ice Cream Man: More Nonsense Verse* by X. J. Kennedy (A Margaret McElderry Book). Copyright © 1979 by X. J. Kennedy. Used by permission of Atheneum Publishers.

p. 188 "Sonnet" by Paul Heins. Reprinted from *The Horn Book Magazine* (Feb. 1979). © by The Horn Book, Inc.

p. 188 Ursula Le Guin, "The Child and the Shadow," in *Quarterly Journal of Library of Congress.* Permission granted by Library of Congress Publishing Office.

p. 190 *Persephone and the Springtime.* Copyright © 1973 by Margaret Hodges. By permission of Little, Brown and Company.

p. 190 Penelope Farmer, *The Story of Persephone.* Reprinted by permission of William C. Morrow.

p. 190 Excerpt from *Demeter and Persephone* translated and adapted by Penelope Proddow. Translation copyright © 1972 by Mary Parkinson Proddow. Reprinted by permission of Doubleday & Company, Inc.

Chapter 6

p. 208 "who knows if the moon's" is reprinted from *Tulips & Chimneys* by e. e. cummings by permission of Liveright Publishing Corporation. Copyright © 1923, 1925 and renewed 1951, 1953 by e. e. cummings. Copyright © 1973, 1976 by Nancy T. Andrews. Copyright © 1973, 1976 by George James Firmage.

p. 211 Edward Eager, *Half Magic.* Harcourt Brace Jovanovich, Inc., 1954. Reprinted by permission of publisher.

pp. 212–13 Reprinted by permission of Coward, McCann & Geoghegan, Inc., from *The Return of the Twelves* by Pauline Clark. Copyright © 1962 by Pauline Clark.

p. 216 Excerpt from *The Velveteen Rabbit* by Margery Williams. Reprinted by permission of Doubleday & Company, Inc.

p. 217 Kenneth Grahame, *Wind in the Willows.* Used by permission of Charles Scribner's Sons.

pp. 217–18 Text excerpts from *Charlotte's Web* by E. B. White. Courtesy of Harper & Row, Publishers, Inc.

p. 220 Permission granted by Lillian Brightly, King's Road School, Madison, N.J.

pp. 219–20 Reprinted by permission of Farrar, Straus and Giroux, Inc. Selection from *Farmer Palmer's Wagon Ride* by William Steig. Copyright © 1974 by William Steig.

p. 219 William Steig, "Caldecott Acceptance Speech." Used by permission of The Horn Book, Inc. Lee Kingman, ed. *Newbery and Caldecott Medal Books: 1966–1975.* Published by The Horn Book, Inc., 1975.

p. 221 From "Burnt Norton," in *Collected Poems 1909–1962* by T. S. Eliot. Copyright © 1963 by T. S. Eliot. Used by permission of Harcourt Brace Jovanovich, Inc.

p. 221 Reprinted by permission of Farrar, Straus and Giroux,

558 Inc. Selections from *A Wrinkle in Time* by Madeleine L'Engle. Copyright © 1962 by Madeleine L'Engle.

pp. 222 and 227   *The Lion, the Witch and the Wardrobe* by C. S. Lewis. Copyright © 1950 by Macmillan Publishing Co., Inc., renewed 1978 by Arthur Owen Barfield. *The Magician's Nephew* by C. S. Lewis. Copyright © 1955 by C. S. Lewis.

p. 223   Permission granted by Margaret Anzul. Madison Elementary School, Madison, N.J.

p. 223   Text excerpt from *To Nowhere and Back* by Margaret Anderson. Courtesy of Alfred A. Knopf, Inc.

p. 229   Excerpt from *A Stranger Came Ashore: A Story of Suspense* by Mollie Hunter. Courtesy of Harper & Row, Publishers, Inc.

p. 231   Text excerpt from *Zlateh the Goat and Other Stories* by Isaac Bashevis Singer. Courtesy of Harper & Row, Publishers, Inc.

p. 232   Excerpt from *Beauty: A Retelling of the Story of Beauty and the Beast* by Robin McKinley. Courtesy of Harper & Row, Publishers, Inc.

p. 234   Robert Heinlein, *Farmer in the Sky*. 1950. Used by permission of Charles Scribner's Sons.

p. 236   Text excerpt from *Dolphin Island* by Arthur C. Clarke. Copyright © 1963 by Arthur C. Clarke. Reprinted by permission of Holt, Rinehart and Winston, Inc.

Chapter 7

p. 246   "Eating Poetry" by Mark Strand. From *Reasons for Moving* by Mark Strand. Copyright © 1966 by Mark Strand. Reprinted by permission of Antheneum Publishers.

p. 248   Text of "The Witches' Ride," from *The Rose on My Cake* by Karla Kuskin. By permission of Harper & Row, Publishers, Inc.

p. 248   "Sea Spirit" by Patricia Hubbell. From *The Apple Vendor's Fair*. Copyright © 1963 by Patricia Hubbell.

p. 249   From *Bequest of Wings* by Annis Duff. Copyright 1944, © renewed 1972 by Annis Duff. Reprinted by permission of Viking Penguin Inc.

p. 249   From "Stopping by Woods on a Snowy Evening," from *The Poetry of Robert Frost,* ed. Edward Connery Lathem. Copyright 1923, © 1969 by Holt, Rinehart and Winston. Copyright © 1951 by Robert Frost. Reprinted by permission of Holt, Rinehart and Winston, Publishers.

p. 250   Copyright © by Jack Prelutsky. Reprinted by permission of Jack Prelutsky.

p. 250   Excerpt of poem from *Alexander Soames: His Poems*. Copyright © 1962 by Karla Kuskin. Reprinted by permission of the author.

p. 250   From *A House Is a House for Me* by Mary Ann Hoberman. Copyright © 1978 by Mary Ann Hoberman. Reprinted by permission of Viking Penguin Inc.

p. 251   Excerpt from "Galoshes" by Rhoda Bacmeister from *Stories to Begin On*. Copyright © 1940 by E. P. Dutton & Co., Inc. Copyright renewal 1968 by Rhoda Bacmeister. Reprinted by permission of E. P. Dutton.

p. 252   Text for "The Fourth," from *Where the Sidewalk Ends: The Poems and Drawings of Shel Silverstein*. Copyright © × 1974 by Shel Silverstein. By permission of Harper & Row, Publishers, Inc.

p. 252   From *Garbage Delight* by Dennis Lee. Published by Houghton Mifflin Company. Copyright © Dennis Lee. 1977. Reprinted by permission.

p. 252   Text of "Tree House," from *Where the Sidewalk Ends: The Poems and Drawings of Shel Silverstein*. Copyright © 1974 by Shel Silverstein. By permission of Harper & Row, Publishers, Inc.

p. 252   "Runover Rhyme" by David McCord. Copyright © 1939, 1952 by David McCord; Copyright © 1961, 1962 by David McCord. By permission of Little, Brown and Company.

p. 254   Excerpt from "Inside a Poem," from *It Doesn't Always Have to Rhyme* by Eve Merriam. Copyright © 1964 by Eve Merriam. Published by Atheneum. Reprinted by permission of the author.

p. 254   Reprinted with permission of Macmillan Publishing Co., Inc. from *Circus* by Jack Prelutsky. Copyright © 1974 by Jack Prelutsky.

p. 255   "Bananas and Cream" by David McCord. Copyright © 1939, 1952 by David McCord. Copyright © 1961, 1962 by David McCord. By permission of Little, Brown and Company.

p. 255   Robert Louis Stevenson. "From a Railway Carriage," in *A Child's Garden of Verses*. Used by permission of Charles Scribner's Sons.

p. 255   Robert Louis Stevenson. "Where Go the Boats?" in *A Child's Garden of Verses*. Used by permission of Charles Scribner's Sons.

p. 256   "Serpent," from *Outloud* by Eve Merriam. Copyright © 1973 by Eve Merriam. Published by Atheneum. Reprinted by permission of the author.

p. 256   "Windshield Wiper," from *Outloud* by Eve Merriam. Copyright © 1973 by Eve Merriam. Published by Atheneum. Reprinted by permission of the author.

p. 256   "The Truth Is Quite Messy" by William Harris. From *Nine Black Poets*, ed. R. Baird Shuman. Moore Publishing Co., Durham, N.C. Used by permission of the publisher.

p. 259   "Tiger Lily" by David McCord. Copyright 1939, 1952 by David McCord. Copyright © 1961, 1962 by David McCord. By permission of Little, Brown and Company.

p. 259   "Watermelons" by Charles Simic. Reprinted by permission of George Braziller, Inc.

p. 259   "Metaphor," from *It Doesn't Always Have to Rhyme* by Eve Merriam. Copyright © 1964 by Eve Merriam. Published by Atheneum. Reprinted by permission of the author.

p. 259   "Dandelion," from *Poems by a Little Girl* by Hilda Conkling. Copyright © 1920 by J. B. Lippincott Co., 1949 by Hilda Conkling. Reprinted by permission of the author.

p. 259   "April Rain Song" by Langston Hughes. From *The Dream Keeper* by Langston Hughes. Published by Alfred A. Knopf, 1932. Reprinted by permission of the publisher.

p. 259 "Chairs," from *Small Poems* by Valerie Worth. Copyright © 1972 by Valerie Worth. Reprinted by permission of Farrar, Straus and Giroux, Inc.

p. 260 "Dust of Snow," from *New Hampshire* by Robert Frost. Copyright © 1936 by Robert Frost. Reprinted by permission of Holt, Rinehart and Winston, Inc.

p. 260 From *Moon Whales* by Ted Hughes. Copyright © 1968, 1973, 1975 by Ted Hughes. Reprinted by permission of Viking Penguin Inc.

p. 260 "Names" by Dorothy Aldis. Reprinted by permission of Dorothy Aldis and the Association for Childhood Education International. 3615 Wisconsin Avenue, N.W., Washington, D.C. Copyright © 1935 by the Association.

p. 261 "Reflections on a Gift of Watermelon Pickle Received from a Friend Called Felicity" by John Tobias, from *New Mexico Quarterly* (Spring 1961). © 1961 by the University of New Mexico Press. Reprinted by permission of the author.

p. 261 Excerpt from "How to Eat a Poem," from *It Doesn't Always Have to Rhyme* by Eve Merriam. Copyright © 1964 by Eve Merriam. Published by Atheneum. Reprinted by permission of the author.

p. 263 Excerpt from "Bad Sir Brian Botany," from *When We Were Very Young* by A. A. Milne. Copyright © 1924 by E. P. Dutton & Co., Inc. Copyright renewal, 1952 by A. A. Milne. Reprinted by permission of the publisher, E. P. Dutton.

p. 263 Text excerpts from *Sing, Little Mouse* by Aileen Fisher. Copyright © 1969 by Aileen Fisher. By permission of Thomas Y. Crowell, Publishers.

p. 264 Excerpt from *The Pied Piper of Hamelin* by Robert Browning. Reprinted by permission of Coward, McCann & Geoghegan, 1971.

p. 265 Excerpt from *The Rime of the Ancient Mariner* by Samuel Taylor Coleridge. Reprinted by permission of Coward, McCann & Geoghegan, 1971.

p. 265 From "The Highwayman," from *Collected Poems* by Alfred Noyes. Copyright © 1906, renewed 1934 by Alfred Noyes. Reprinted by permission of Harper & Row, Publishers, Inc.

p. 266 Text of "Sarah Cynthia Sylvia Stout Would Not Take the Garbage Out," from *Where the Sidewalk Ends: The Poems and Drawings of Shel Silverstein*. Copyright © 1974 Shel Silverstein. By permission of Harper & Row, Publishers, Inc.

p. 266 "A Big Deal for the Tooth Fairy," from *The Phantom Ice Cream Man: More Nonsense Verse* by X. J. Kennedy (A Margaret McElderry Book). Copyright © 1979 by X. J. Kennedy. Used by permission of Atheneum Publishers.

p. 267 "There Was an Old Lady Whose Folly," from *The Complete Nonsense Book* by Edward Lear. Dodd Mead, 1958. Used by permission of publisher.

p. 267 "A Flea and a Fly in a Flue," anonymous, from *Golden Treasury* compiled by Louis Untermeyer. Used by permission of Western Publishing Co., Inc.

p. 269 Text of "Poem Written on the Neck of a Giraffe," from *Where the Sidewalk Ends: The Poems and Drawings of Shel Silverstein*. Copyright © 1974 Shel Silverstein. By permission of Harper & Row, Publishers, Inc.

p. 269 "Winter Tree," from *O Sliver of Liver and Other Poems* by Myra Cohn Livingston, drawings by Iris Van Rynbach (A Margaret K. McElderry Book). Copyright © 1979 by Myra Cohn Livingston. Reprinted by permission of Atheneum Publishers.

p. 270 Giose Rimanelli and Paul Pimsleur. "Zero," from *Poems Make Pictures*. Pantheon, 1972. Used by permission of the publisher.

p. 271 "Cello" by Richard Lester. Used by permission of Richard Lester. Copyright © Richard Lester.

p. 272 "Mothers" by Nikki Giovanni, from *Celebrations: A New Anthology of Black American Poetry*, ed. Arnold Adoff. Copyright © 1977. Used by permission of Follett Publishing Company, a division of Follett Corporation.

p. 275 *Just the Way You Are*, words and music by Billy Joel. © 1977, 1978 Impulsive Music and April Music Inc. Administered by April Music Inc., 1350 Avenue of the Americas, New York, N.Y. 10019. International Copyright Secured. Made in U.S.A. All Rights Reserved. Used by permission.

p. 276 From *A Short Walk from the Station* by Phyllis McGinley. Copyright © 1947 by Phyllis McGinley. Reprinted by permission of Viking Penguin Inc.

p. 277 "Goose, Moose, Spruce" by David McCord. Copyright 1939, 1952 by David McCord. Copyright © 1961, 1962 by David McCord. By permission of Little, Brown and Company.

p. 277 A text excerpt from "Mummy Slept Late and Daddy Fixed Breakfast," from *You Read to Me, I'll Read to You* by John Ciardi. Copyright © 1962 by John Ciardi. By permission of J. B. Lippincott, Publishers.

p. 278 Excerpt from interview with David McCord from *Books Are by People* by Lee Bennett Hopkins. Copyright © 1969 by Scholastic Magazines, Inc. Used by permission of the publisher.

Chapter 8

p. 288 Reprinted by permission of Farrar, Straus and Giroux, Inc. Lines from "Children Selecting Books in a Library," from *The Complete Poems of Randall Jarrell*. New Republic Republic © 1941. Copyright renewed © 1969 by Mrs. Randall Jarrell.

p. 290 Text excerpts from *Blubber* by Judy Blume. Reprinted with permission of Bradbury Press, Inc., Scarsdale, N.Y. 10583.

pp. 292–93 Reprinted by permission of the American Library Association. From "Of Life, Love, Death, Kids, and Inhalation Therapy" by Audrey Eaglen. *Top of the News* (Winter 1978) Vol. 34, No. 2, pp. 178–85. Copyright © 1978 by The American Library Association.

p. 292 Text excerpt from *The Effect of Gamma Rays on Man-in-the-Moon Marigolds: A Drama in Two Acts* by Paul

560

Zindel. Copyright © 1971 by Paul Zindel. By permission of Harper & Row, Publishers, Inc.

pp. 293–94   Text excerpts from *Philip Hall Likes Me. I Reckon Maybe* by Bette Green. Copyright © 1974 by Bette Green. Reprinted by permission of The Dial Press.

pp. 295–96   Text excerpts from *Harriet the Spy* by Louise Fitzhugh. Copyright © 1964 by Louise Fitzhugh. By permission of Harper & Row, Publishers, Inc.

p. 297   Text excerpts from *M.C. Higgins, the Great* by Virginia Hamilton. Copyright © 1974 by Virginia Hamilton. Reprinted with permission of Macmillan Publishing Co., Inc.

p. 297   Text excerpts from *A Summer's Lease* by Marilyn Sachs. Used by permission of Elsevier-Dutton Publishing Co., Inc.

pp. 297–98   From *The Young Landlords* by Walter Dean Myers. Copyright © 1979 by Walter Dean Myers. Reprinted by permission of Viking Penguin Inc.

pp. 299–300   From *Representing Super Doll* by Richard Peck. Copyright © 1974 by Richard Peck. Reprinted by permission of Viking Penguin Inc.

pp. 299–301   Permission granted by Susan L. Marinoff, Walt Whitman Junior High School, Brooklyn, N.Y.

p. 304   Text excerpts from *Roll of Thunder, Hear My Cry* by Mildred Taylor. Copyright © 1976 by Mildred Taylor. Used by permission of The Dial Press.

p. 306   Text excerpts from *Words by Heart* by Ouida Sebestyen. By permission of Atlantic-Little, Brown.

p. 306   Text excerpts from *Bitter Herbs and Honey* by Barbara Cohen. Reprinted by permission of Lothrop, Lee & Shepard.

p. 309   Excerpt from *The Third Eye* by Mollie Hunter. Courtesy of Harper & Row, Publishers, Inc.

p. 309   Excerpt from *Where the Lilies Bloom* by Vera and Bill Cleaver. Courtesy of J. B. Lippincott, Publishers.

p. 310   Text excerpt from *Julie of the Wolves* by Jean Craighead George. Courtesy of Harper & Row, Publishers, Inc.

p. 312   Selection from *Unleaving* by Jill Paton Walsh. Copyright © 1976 by Jill Paton Walsh. Reprinted by permission of Farrar, Straus and Giroux, Inc.

p. 316   Excerpt from *The Great Gilly Hopkins* by Katherine Paterson. Courtesy of Thomas Y. Crowell, Publishers.

p. 317   Text excerpts from *Bridge to Terabithia* by Katherine Paterson. Copyright © 1977 by Katherine Paterson. By permission of Thomas Y. Crowell, Publishers.

Chapter 9

p. 328   "Ancient History," from *Gaily the Troubadour* by Arthur Guiterman. Copyright © 1936. Reprinted by permission of Louise H. Sclove.

p. 331   Text excerpt from *Fire Hunter* by Jim Kjelgaard. Courtesy of Holiday House, 1951.

p. 337   Text excerpt from *Gods, Graves and Scholars* by C. W. Ceram. Courtesy of Alfred A. Knopf.

p. 337   From *White Stag* by Kate Seredy. Copyright 1937 ©

renewed 1965 by Kate Seredy. Reprinted by permission of Viking Penguin Inc.

p. 338   Text excerpt from *The Lantern Bearers* by Rosemary Sutcliff. Copyright © 1979. Reprinted by permission of Oxford University Press.

p. 340   From *American History Revisited* by Frances FitzGerald. Little, Brown and Company, 1979.

p. 351   From *Lexington and Concord 1775: What Really Happened.* Copyright © 1975 by Jean Poindexter Colby. Permission by Hastings House Publishers, Inc.

p. 352   Text excerpts from *Anpao: An American Indian Odyssey* by Jamake Highwater. Courtesy of J. B. Lippincott, Publishers.

p. 355   Permission granted by Sally H. Hollaman, Saxe Junior High School, New Canaan, Conn. 06820.

p. 355   Permission granted by Diane R. Confer, Kane Public Schools, Kane, Pa.

p. 361   Text excerpt from *Little House in the Big Woods* by Laura Ingalls Wilder. Copyright © 1932, as to text, by Laura Ingalls Wilder. Renewed 1959 by Roger L. MacBride. By permission of Harper & Row, Publishers, Inc.

p. 363   Text excerpt from *Strawberry Girl* by Lois Lenski. Copyright 1945 by Lois Lenski. Renewed 1973 by Lois Lenski (Covey). By permission of J. B. Lippincott, Publishers.

p. 366   Excerpt from *Never to Forget: The Jews of the Holocaust,* written by Milton Meltzer. Courtesy of Harper & Row, Publishers, Inc.

p. 366   Text excerpt from *Boris* by Jaap ter Haar. Copyright © 1969 by Blackie and Son, Ltd. Used by permission of Delacorte Press / Seymour Lawrence. Delacorte, 1966.

p. 370   Text excerpt from *The Life and Death of Martin Luther King, Jr.,* by James Haskins. Reprinted by permission of Lothrop, Lee & Shepard, 1977.

p. 371   Rosemary Sutcliff, "History Is People." Reprinted by permission of the author.

Chapter 10

p. 382   "Requiem for a River" by Kim Williams. Permission granted by The Wilderness Society.

p. 386   Text excerpt from *Jet Journey* by Mike Wilson and Robin Scagell. Used by permission of Marshall Cavendish Books Ltd.

p. 388   Reprinted from *The Long View into Space* by Seymour Simon. © 1979 by Seymour Simon. By permission of Crown Publishers Inc.

pp. 388–89   Text excerpt from *What Boys Want to Know About Girls. What Girls Want to Know About Boys* by Joan Horvath. Copyright 1976 by Joan Horvath. Reprinted by permission of Elsevier-Nelson Books.

p. 389   From *The Secret Clocks* by Seymour Simon. Copyright © 1979 by Seymour Simon. Reprinted by permission of Viking Penguin Inc.

p. 390   Excerpt from *The Wonderful Story of How You Were*

Born by Sidonie Matsner Gruenberg. Copyright © 1952, 1953, 1959, 1970 by Doubleday & Company, Inc.

pp. 392–93   Text excerpt from *What Happens to a Hamburger* by Paul Showers. Copyright © 1970 by Paul Showers. A Let's-Read-and-Find-Out Book. By permission of Thomas Y. Crowell, Publishers.

p. 395   Text excerpt from *Don't Forget Tom* by Hanne Larsen, translated from the Danish by Peggy Blakely. © 1974 (English text), A&C Black Ltd. First published in 1972 by Borgens Forlag, Denmark. A John Day Book. By permission of Thomas Y. Crowell, Publishers.

p. 405   From the book *How Did We Find Out About Nuclear Power* by Isaac Asimov. Text copyright © 1976 by Isaac Asimov. Used with permission of the publisher, Walker and Company, New York.

p. 408   From *The Global Food Shortage* by Lila Perl. Reprinted by permission of William C. Morrow.

p. 411   From *Lost Wild America* by Robert C. McClung. Reprinted by permission of William C. Morrow.

p. 414   From *Canada Geese* by Jack Denton Scott. Reprinted by permission of G. P. Putnam's Sons from *Canada Geese* by Jack Denton Scott. Copyright © 1976 by Jack Denton Scott.

p. 414   From *Killer Whale!* by Joseph J. Cook and William L. Wisner. Used by permission of Dodd, Mead & Co.

p. 415   Text excerpt from *Whale Watch* by Ada and Frank Graham, Jr. Copyright © 1978 by Ada and Frank Graham, Jr. Reprinted by permission of Delacorte Press.

p. 415   Reprinted by permission of G. P. Putnam's Sons from *Biography of a Killer Whale* by Barbara Steiner. Copyright © 1978 by Barbara Steiner.

p. 418   "Where Do All the Prizes Go?" by Milton Meltzer. Reprinted from *The Horn Book Magazine* (Feb. 1976). © 1976 by The Horn Book, Inc.

p. 418   Reprinted with permission of *Science and Children* (March 1980). Copyright © 1980 by the National Science Teachers Association, 1742 Connecticut Avenue, N.W., Washington, D.C. 20009.

Chapter 11

p. 426   "A Solitude," from *Jacob's Ladder* by Denise Levertov. Copyright © 1958 by Denise Levertov Goodman. Reprinted by permission of New Directions Publishing Corporation.

p. 428   Copyright © 1978 from the book *Between Friends* by Sheila Garrigue. Reprinted with permissin of Bradbury Press, Inc., Scarsdale, N.Y. 10583.

p. 429   From *Hey Dummy!* by Kin Platt. Copyright © 1971 by Kin Platt.

p. 435   Selection from *Goldengrove* by Jill Paton Walsh. Copyright © 1972 by Jill Paton Walsh. Reprinted by permission of Farrar, Straus and Giroux, Inc.

p. 438   Text excerpt from *Welcome Home, Jellybean* by Marlene Fanta Shyer. Reprinted by permission of Charles Scribner's Sons.

pp. 438–39   Text excerpt from *All Together Now* by Sue Ellen Bridgers. Reprinted by permission of Alfred A. Knopf.

p. 441   Excerpt from *The Bears House* by Marilyn Sachs. Copyright © 1971 by Marilyn Sachs. Reprinted by permission of Doubleday & Company, Inc.

p. 444   Excerpt from *The Stronghold* by Mollie Hunter. Courtesy of Harper & Row, Publishers, Inc.

p. 448   From *The Boy Who Could Make Himself Disappear* by Kin Platt. Copyright © 1968 by Kin Platt.

Chapter 12

p. 452   "Books Fall Open," from *One at a Time* by David McCord. Copyright 1939, 1952 by David McCord. Copyright 1961, 1962 by David McCord.

p. 455   Basic Skills Integration Chart. Permission granted by Dorothy S. Strickland, Teachers College, Columbia University.

p. 461   "Snow" reprinted by permission of G. P. Putnam's Sons from *Everything and Anything* by Dorothy Aldis. Copyright 1925. Renewed © 1953 by Dorothy Aldis.

p. 461   "Whistles" reprinted by permission of G. P. Putnam's Sons from *Here, There and Everywhere* by Dorothy Aldis. Copyright 1927, 1928. Renewed © 1955, 1956 by Dorothy Aldis.

p. 461   From "Hallowe'en," in *The Little Hill*. Copyright 1949 by Harry Behn. Renewed 1977 by Alice L. Behn. Reprinted by permission of Harcourt Brace Jovanovich, Inc.

p. 461   Verses from "My Friend Leona," which appeared in *People I'd Like to Keep* by Mary O'Neill. Copyright © 1964 by Mary O'Neill. Reprinted by permission of Doubleday & Company, Inc.

p. 461   Text excerpt from "Jimmy Jet and His TV Set," from *Where the Sidewalk Ends: The Poems and Drawings of Shel Silverstein*. Copyright © 1974 by Shel Silverstein. By permission of Harper & Row, Publishers, Inc.

p. 464   Adaptation of *Alexander and the Terrible, Horrible, No Good Very Bad Day* by Judith Viorst, by Kathy Tolman. Used by permission of Kathy Tolman. New York University.

p. 481   "Did You Feed My Cow" by Margaret Taylor Burroughs. Permission granted by Margaret Taylor Burroughs.

Chapter 13

p. 486   "To Look at Any Thing" by John Moffitt. © 1961 by John Moffitt. Reprinted from his volume *The Living Seed* by permission of Harcourt Brace Jovanovich, Inc.

pp. 487–89   Don Holdaway, *Foundations of Literacy*. Copyright © 1979 by Don Holdaway. Permission granted by Ashton Scholastic, 1979.

p. 495   "I Want You to Meet," from *One at a Time* by David McCord. Copyright © 1961, 1962 by David McCord. By permission of Little, Brown and Company.

p. 495   "Snowman," from *One at a Time* by David McCord. Copyright © 1961, 1962 by David McCord. By permission of Little, Brown and Company.

562 p. 499 Text excerpts from *Leo the Late Bloomer* by Robert Kraus. Text copyright © 1971 by Robert Kraus. A Windmill Book. By permission of Thomas Y. Crowell, Publishers.

p. 499 Discussion of *Leo the Late Bloomer* and art from children. Permission granted by Amy Waldhorn, Bank Street School for Children, New York, N.Y.

pp. 500–501 Text excerpts from *Bridge to Terabithia* by Katherine Paterson. Copyright © 1977 by Katherine Paterson. By permission of Thomas Y. Crowell, Publishers.

Chapter 14

p. 508 "Primer Lesson" by Carl Sandburg. Copyright 1920 by Harcourt Brace Jovanovich, Inc., copyright © 1948 by Carl Sandburg. Reprinted from his volume *The Sandburg Treasury* by permission of the publisher.

p. 510 Paula Fox, "Newbery Medal Acceptance Speech." Used by permission of the author.

p. 511 "The Changing Image of the Black in Children's Literature" by Augusta Baker. Reprinted from *The Horn Book Magazine* (Feb. 1975). © 1975 by The Horn Book, Inc.

p. 513 Text excerpt from *William's Doll* by Charlotte Zolotow. Text copyright © 1972 by Charlotte Zolotow. By permission of Harper & Row, Publishers, Inc.

p. 514 Used by permission of The Council on Interracial Books for Children, Inc., from *1980 Guidelines for Selecting Bias-Free Textbooks and Storybooks*. Council on Interracial Books, Inc., 1980.

p. 514 "The Would-Be Censors of the Left," editorial reprinted from *School Library Journal* (Nov. 1976). With permission from R. R. Bowker, Co., A Xerox publication.

p. 518 Review of Tiffky Doofky. Reprinted from *Bulletin of the Center for Children's Books* by permission of the University of Chicago Press.

pp. 518–19 Review by Marjorie Lewis of *Tiffky Doofky*. Reprinted from *School Library Journal* (Jan. 1979). With permission from R. R. Bowker Co., A Xerox publication.

p. 519 Review by Mary Burns of *Tiffky Doofky*. Reprinted from *The Horn Book Magazine* (Feb. 1979). © by The Horn Book, Inc.

p. 520 *Hansel and Gretel* retold by Linda Hayward. Copyright © 1974 by Random House. Used by permission of the publisher.

p. 520 *Hansel and Gretel with Benjy and Bubbles,* adapted by Susan Horowitz. Copyright © 1978 by Ruth Lerner Perle. Reprinted by permission of Holt, Rinehart and Winston, Inc.

p. 521 "Imaginary Correspondence" by Rumer Godden. Reprinted by permission of Curtis Brown, Ltd. Copyright © 1963 by Rumer Godden.

p. 526 From *The Plug-In Drug* by Marie Winn. Copyright © 1977 by Marie Winn Miller. Reprinted by permission of Viking Penguin Inc.

subject index

author/title index

C
D 4
E 5
F 6
G 7
H 8
I 9
J 0